Street by Street

G000038404

WEST KENT

PLUS BIGGIN HILL, ORPINGTON, OXTED, TILBURY

Enlarged Areas Chatham, Gillingham, Maidstone, Rochester, Royal Tunbridge Wells, Sevenoaks

Ist edition May 2001

© Automobile Association Developments Limited 2001

This product includes map data licensed from Ordnance Survey® with the permission of the Controller of Her Majesty's Stationery Office. © Crown copyright 2000. All rights reserved. Licence No: 399221.

All rights reserved. No part of this publication may be reproduced, stored in a retrieval system, or transmitted in any form or by any means– electronic, mechanical, photocopying, recording or otherwise – unless the permission of the publisher has been given beforehand.

Published by AA Publishing (a trading name of Automobile Association Developments Limited, whose registered office is Norfolk House, Priestley Road, Basingstoke, Hampshire, RG24 9NY. Registered number 1878835).

Mapping produced by the Cartographic Department of The Automobile Association.

A CIP Catalogue record for this book is available from the British Library.

Printed by in Italy by Printer Trento srl

The contents of this atlas are believed to be correct at the time of the latest revision. However, the publishers cannot be held responsible for loss occasioned to any person acting or refraining from action as a result of any material in this atlas, nor for any errors, omissions or changes in such material. The publishers would welcome information to correct any errors or omissions and to keep this atlas up to date. Please write to Publishing, The Automobile Association, Fanum House, Basing View, Basingstoke, Hampshire, RG21 4EA.

Ref: MD101

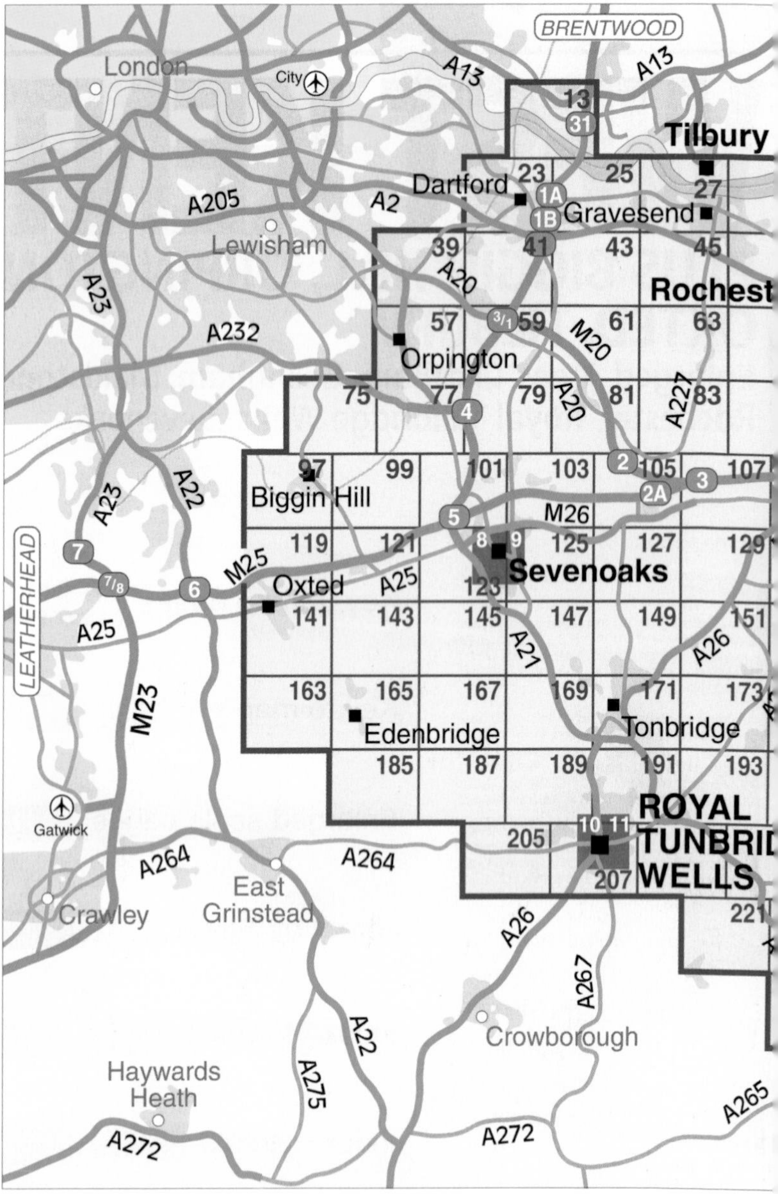
BRENTWOOD
London
City
A13
A13
13
31
Tilbury
23
25
27
Dartford
1A
1B
Gravesend
A205
A2
Lewisham
39
41
43
45
A20
Rochest
A23
57
3/1
59
61
63
M20
A232
Orpington
75
77
4
79
A20
81
A227
83
97
99
101
103
2
105
3
107
Biggin Hill
2A
M26
5
A22
A23
119
121
8
9
125
127
129
7
M25
Sevenoaks
LEATHERHEAD
7/8
6
Oxted
A25
123
141
143
145
147
149
151
A25
A21
A26
163
165
167
169
171
173
M23
Edenbridge
Tonbridge
185
187
189
191
193
Gatwick
ROYAL
TUNBRID
WELLS
10
11
205
207
A264
A264
East
Grinstead
Crawley
221
A26
A267
Crowborough
A22
A275
Haywards
Heath
A272
A272
A265

Enlarged scale pages 1:17,500

3.6 inches to 1 mile

0 — 1/2 — miles — 1

0 — 1/2 — 1 — kilometres — 1 1/2

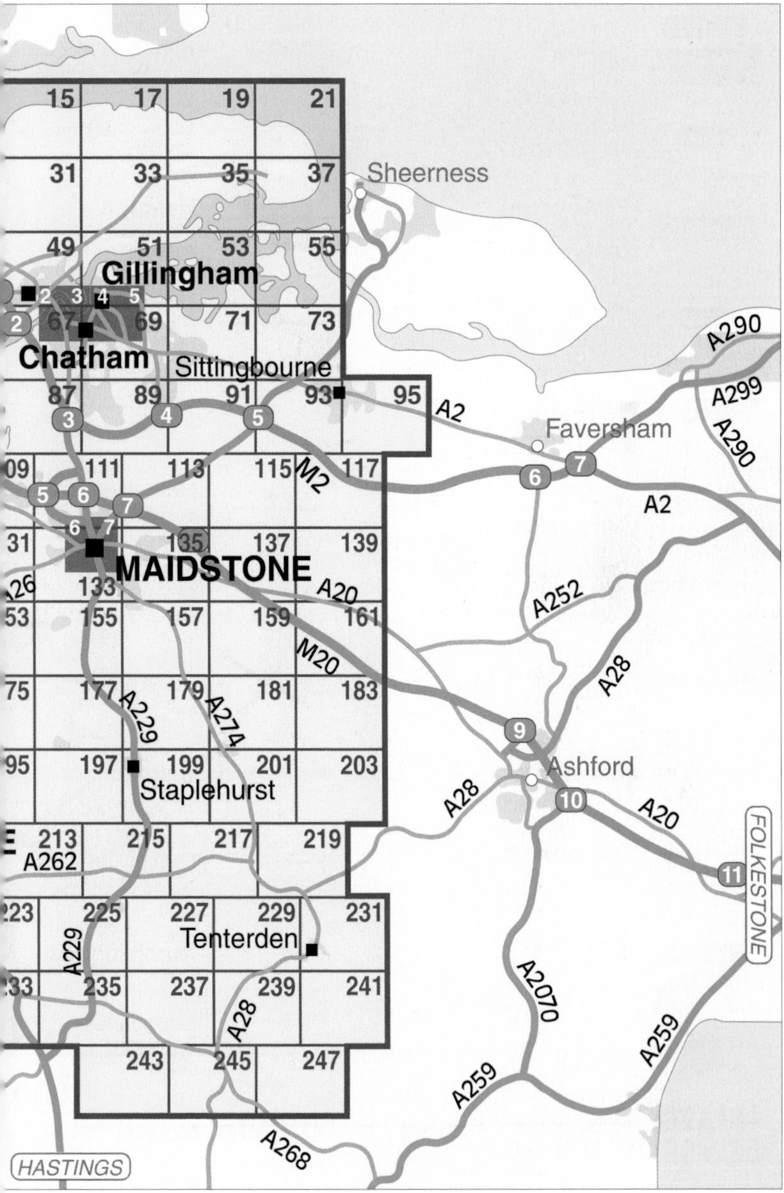

2.5 inches to 1 mile

Scale of main map pages 1:25,000

0 1/2 miles 1 1 1/2

0 1/2 1 kilometres 1 1/2 2

Symbol	Meaning
Junction 9	Motorway & junction
Services	Motorway service area
	Primary road single/dual carriageway
Services	Primary road service area
	A road single/dual carriageway
	B road single/dual carriageway
	Other road single/dual carriageway
	Restricted road
	Private road
	One way street
	Pedestrian street
	Track/ footpath
	Road under construction
	Road tunnel
P	Parking
P+	Park & Ride
	Bus/coach station
	Railway & main railway station
	Railway & minor railway station
	Underground station
	Light railway & station
	Preserved private railway
LC	Level crossing
	Tramway
	Ferry route
	Airport runway
	Boundaries- borough/ district
	Mounds
93	Page continuation 1:25,000
7	Page continuation to enlarged scale 1:17,500

Map Symbols I

Symbol	Meaning
	River/canal lake, pier
	Aqueduct lock, weir
465 ▲ Winter Hill	Peak (with height in metres)
	Beach
	Coniferous woodland
	Broadleaved woodland
	Mixed woodland
	Park
	Cemetery
	Built-up area
	Featured building
	City wall
A&E	Accident & Emergency hospital
	Toilet
	Toilet with disabled facilities
	Petrol station
PH	Public house
PO	Post Office
	Public library
i	Tourist Information Centre
	Castle
	Historic house/ building
Wakehurst Place NT	National Trust property
M	Museum/ art gallery
	Church/chapel
	Country park
	Theatre/ performing arts
	Cinema

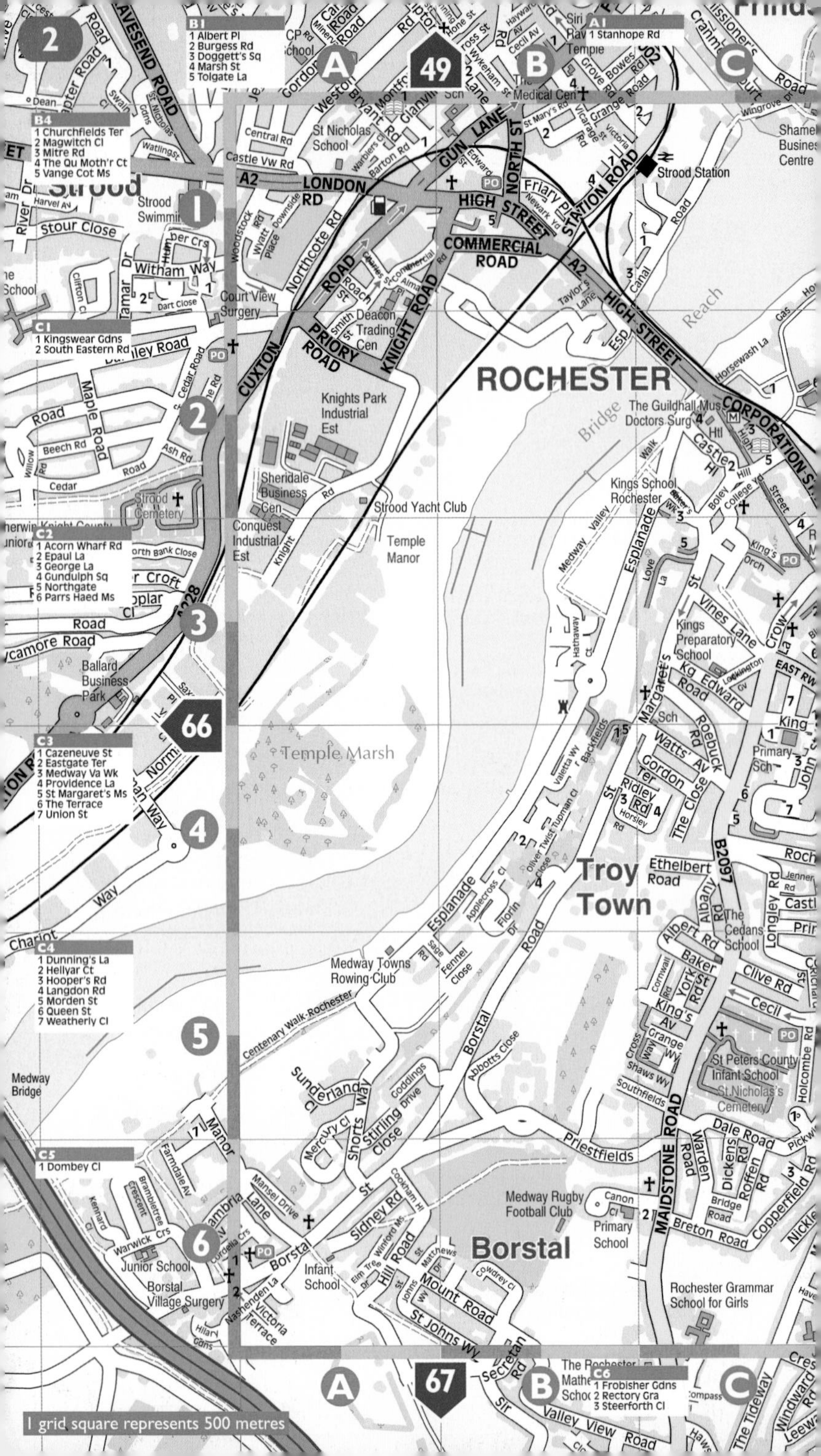
2
B1
1 Albert Pl
2 Burgess Rd
3 Doggett's Sq
4 Marsh St
5 Tolgate La
A1
1 Stanhope Rd
B4
1 Churchfields Ter
2 Magwitch Cl
3 Mitre Rd
4 The Qu Moth'r Ct
5 Vange Cot Ms
C1
1 Kingswear Gdns
2 South Eastern Rd
C2
1 Acorn Wharf Rd
2 Epaul La
3 George La
4 Gundulph Sq
5 Northgate
6 Parrs Haed Ms
C3
1 Cazeneuve St
2 Eastgate Ter
3 Medway Va Wk
4 Providence La
5 St Margaret's Ms
6 The Terrace
7 Union St
C4
1 Dunning's La
2 Hellyar Ct
3 Hooper's Rd
4 Langdon Rd
5 Morden St
6 Queen St
7 Weatherly Cl
C5
1 Dombey Cl
C6
1 Frobisher Gdns
2 Rectory Gra
3 Steerforth Cl
A
B
C
49
66
67
1
2
3
4
5
6
Strood
Strood Station
ROCHESTER
Troy Town
Borstal
Temple Marsh
Knights Park Industrial Est
Sheridale Business Cen
Conquest Industrial Est
Strood Yacht Club
Temple Manor
The Guildhall Mus
Doctors Surg
Kings School Rochester
Kings Preparatory School
Medway Towns Rowing Club
Medway Rugby Football Club
Rochester Grammar School for Girls
St Peters County Infant School
St Nicholas's Cemetery
The Cedars School
Canon Cl Primary School
Borstal Village Surgery
Junior School
Infant School
Ballard Business Park
Strood Cemetery
Court View Surgery
Deacon Trading Cen
St Nicholas School
Medway Bridge
LONDON RD
HIGH STREET
COMMERCIAL ROAD
NORTH ST
STATION ROAD
GUN LANE
CUXTON ROAD
PRIORY ROAD
KNIGHT ROAD
CORPORATION ST
MAIDSTONE ROAD
B2097
A2
A228
Esplanade
Borstal Road
St Margaret's St
Priestfields
Centenary Walk-Rochester
Medway Valley Walk
Ethelbert Road
Vines Lane
Kg Edward Road
Dale Road
Breton Road
Mount Road
St Johns Wy
Valley View Road
Stour Close
Witham Way
Maple Road
Beech Rd
Sycamore Road
Chariot Way
1 grid square represents 500 metres

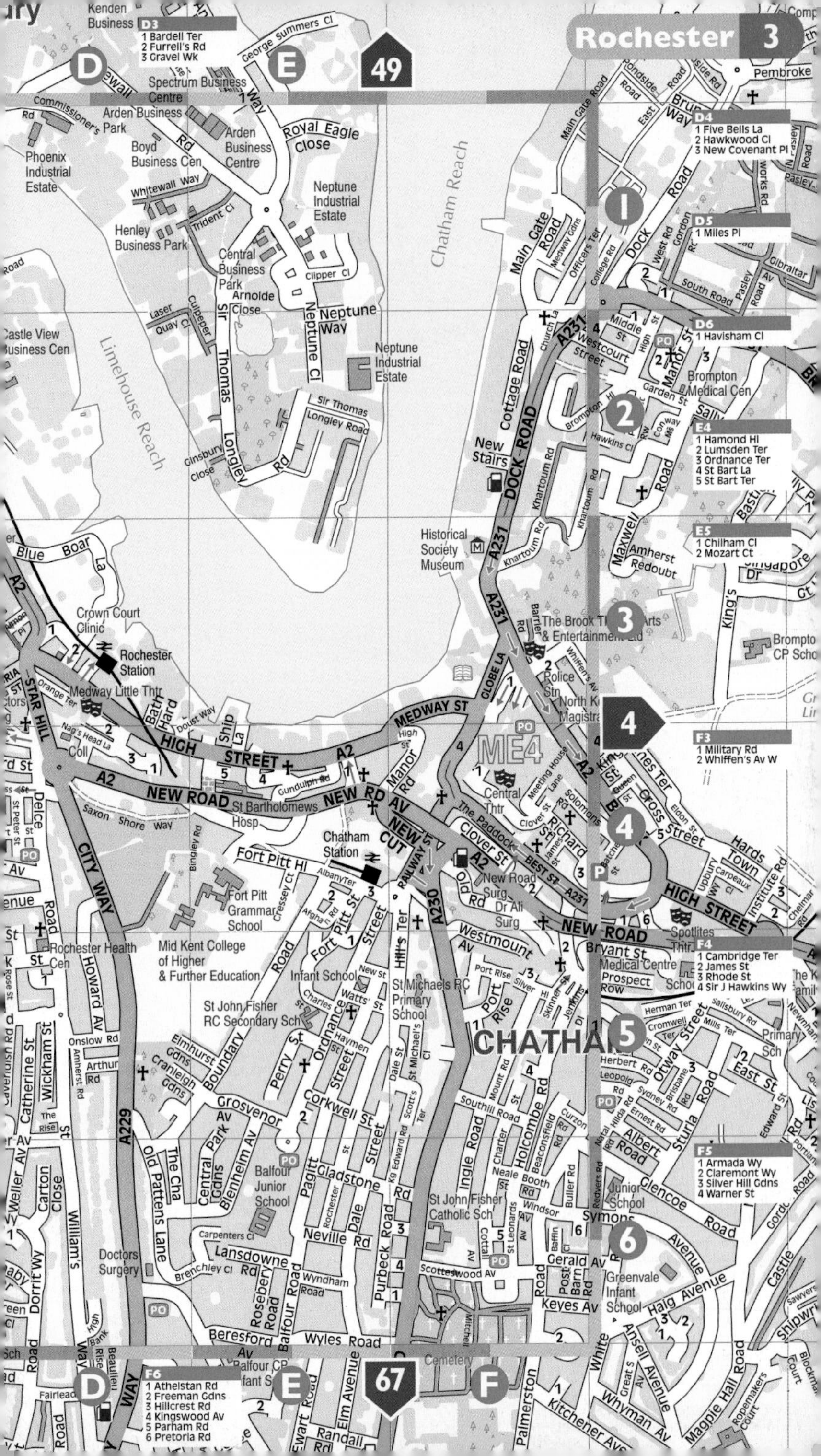
49
67
D3
1 Bardell Ter
2 Furrell's Rd
3 Gravel Wk
D4
1 Five Bells La
2 Hawkwood Cl
3 New Covenant Pl
D5
1 Miles Pl
D6
1 Havisham Cl
E4
1 Hamond Hl
2 Lumsden Ter
3 Ordnance Ter
4 St Bart La
5 St Bart Ter
E5
1 Chilham Cl
2 Mozart Ct
F3
1 Military Rd
2 Whiffen's Av W
F4
1 Cambridge Ter
2 James St
3 Rhode St
4 Sir J Hawkins Wy
F5
1 Armada Wy
2 Claremont Wy
3 Silver Hill Gdns
4 Warner St
F6
1 Athelstan Rd
2 Freeman Gdns
3 Hillcrest Rd
4 Kingswood Av
5 Parham Rd
6 Pretoria Rd
Kenden Business
Spectrum Business Centre
Arden Business Park
Boyd Business Cen
Arden Business Centre
Royal Eagle Close
George Summers Cl
Phoenix Industrial Estate
Neptune Industrial Estate
Whitewall Way
Trident Cl
Henley Business Park
Central Business Park
Clipper Cl
Arnolde Close
Neptune Way
Neptune Cl
Laser Quay Cl
Culpeper
Castle View Business Cen
Limehouse Reach
Chatham Reach
Sir Thomas Longley Rd
Sir Thomas Longley Road
Ginsbury Close
Main Gate Road
Medway Gdns
Officers Ter
College Rd
Dock Road
West Rd
Gordon
South Road
Gibraltar
Pasley
Pembroke
Brunswick Way
Cottage Road
Dock Road
New Stairs
Westcourt Street
Middle St
High St
Manor St
Garden St
Brompton Hl
Brompton Medical Cen
Hawkins Cl
Khartoum Rd
Maxwell Road
Amherst Redoubt
Singapore Dr
King's
Brompton CP Sch
Historical Society Museum
A231
Barrier Rd
The Brook Theatre Arts & Entertainment Ltd
Police Stn
North Kent Magistrates
Whiffen's Av
Globe La
Medway St
Blue Boar La
Crown Court Clinic
Rochester Station
Medway Little Thtr
Orange Ter
Star Hill
Nag's Head La
Bath Hard
Doust Way
Ship La
High Street
A2
New Road
Gundulph Rd
St Bartholomews Hosp
Saxon Shore Way
New Rd Av
New Cut
Manor Rd
High St
ME4
Central Thtr
Meeting House Lane
Solomons Rd
Clover St
Richard St
The Paddock
Best St
James St
Batchelor St
Cross Street
Elden St
Hards Town
Institute Rd
Upbury Way
Carpeaux Cl
High Street
Chelmar
Chatham Station
Fort Pitt Hl
Albany Ter
Railway St
A230
Old Rd
New Road Surg
Dr Ali Surg
Westmount Av
New Road
Spotlites Thtr
Bryant St
Medical Centre
Prospect Row
Fort Pitt Grammar School
Mid Kent College of Higher & Further Education
Cressey Ct
Afghan Rd
Fort Pitt St
Street
Hill's Ter
Infant School
New St
Watts' St
St Michaels RC Primary School
Port Rise
Silver Hl
Skinner St
Jenkins Dl
CHATHAM
Herman Ter
Cromwell Ter
Mills Ter
Salisbury Rd
Primary Sch
Herbert Rd
Leopold Rd
Otway Street
Sydney Rd
Brisbane Rd
Sturla Road
East St
Edward St
Ernest Rd
Hilda Rd
Albert Road
Natal Rd
Rochester Health Cen
Howard Av
Delce
St Peter St
City Way
St John Fisher RC Secondary Sch
Charles St
Ordnance Street
Haymen St
Perry St
Boundary Road
Elmhurst Gdns
Cranleigh Gdns
Onslow Rd
Arthur Rd
Amherst Rd
Catherine St
Wickham St
The Rise
A229
Grosvenor Av
Corkwell St
Dale St
St Michael's Cl
Scott's Ter
Southill Road
Mount Rd
Holcombe Rd
Ingle Road
Charter St
Beaconsfield
Curzon Rd
Neale St
Booth Rd
Buller Rd
Redvers Rd
Junior School
Glencoe Road
Symons
Old Pattens Lane
The Cha
Central Park Gdns
Blenheim Av
Balfour Junior School
Pagitt St
Gladstone Rd
Rochester St
Kg Edward Rd
St John Fisher Catholic Sch
Windsor Av
St Leonards Av
Cottall Av
Baffin Cl
Gerald Av
Post Barn Rd
Greenvale Infant School
Avenue
Haig Avenue
Castle
Carpenters Cl
Lansdowne Rd
Neville Rd
Purbeck Road
Wyndham Road
Brenchley Cl
Doctors Surgery
Rosebery Road
Balfour Road
Scotteswood Av
Mitchell Av
Keyes Av
Cemetery
Beresford Av
Wyles Road
Balfour CP Infant Sch
Elm Avenue
Randall
Palmerston
Kitchener Av
White
Ansell Avenue
Great S Av
Whyman Av
Magpie Hall Road
Ropemakers Court
Sawyers
Shipwright
Blockmakers Court
Carton Close
William's
Dorrit Wy
Weller Av
High Bank
High Rise
Beaulieu Rise
Fairlead
City Way
Commissioner's Rd
D
E
F
1
2
3
4
5
6

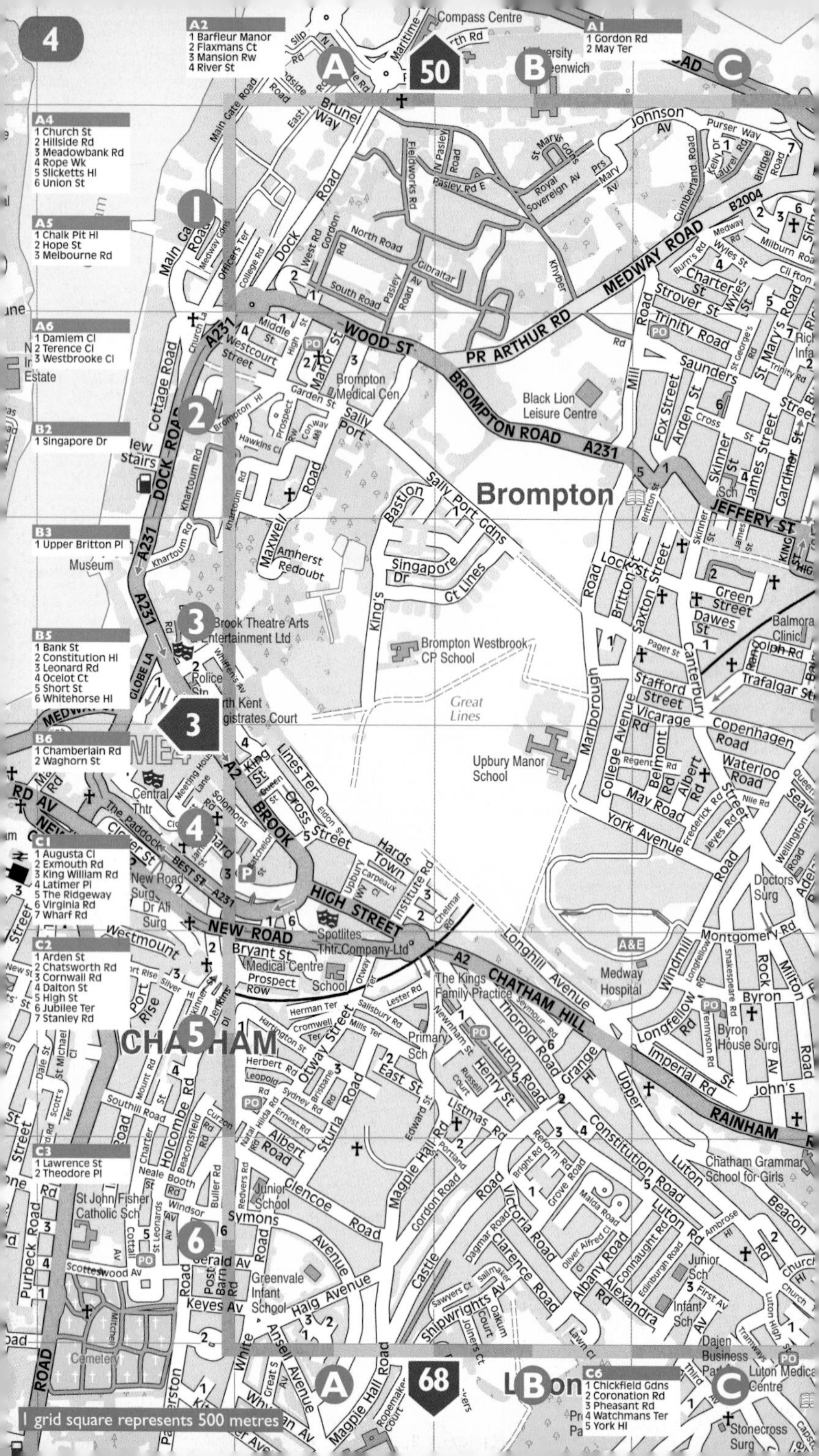
4
A2
1 Barfleur Manor
2 Flaxmans Ct
3 Mansion Rw
4 River St
A1
1 Gordon Rd
2 May Ter
A4
1 Church St
2 Hillside Rd
3 Meadowbank Rd
4 Rope Wk
5 Slicketts Hl
6 Union St
A5
1 Chalk Pit Hl
2 Hope St
3 Melbourne Rd
A6
1 Damiem Cl
2 Terence Cl
3 Westbrooke Cl
B2
1 Singapore Dr
B3
1 Upper Britton Pl
B5
1 Bank St
2 Constitution Hl
3 Leonard Rd
4 Ocelot Ct
5 Short St
6 Whitehorse Hl
B6
1 Chamberlain Rd
2 Waghorn St
C1
1 Augusta Cl
2 Exmouth Rd
3 King William Rd
4 Latimer Pl
5 The Ridgeway
6 Virginia Rd
7 Wharf Rd
C2
1 Arden St
2 Chatsworth Rd
3 Cornwall Rd
4 Dalton St
5 High St
6 Jubilee Ter
7 Stanley Rd
C3
1 Lawrence St
2 Theodore Pl
C6
1 Chickfield Gdns
2 Coronation Rd
3 Pheasant Rd
4 Watchmans Ter
5 York Hl
50
68
3
Compass Centre
Brompton
CHATHAM
Black Lion Leisure Centre
Brompton Medical Cen
Amherst Redoubt
Brompton Westbrook CP School
Great Lines
Upbury Manor School
Medway Hospital
Chatham Grammar School for Girls
Museum
Brook Theatre Arts Entertainment Ltd
Central Thtr
Spotlites Thtr Company Ltd
The Kings Family Practice
St John Fisher Catholic Sch
Greenvale Infant School
Cemetery
MEDWAY ROAD
PR ARTHUR RD
WOOD ST
BROMPTON ROAD
DOCK ROAD
HIGH STREET
NEW ROAD
CHATHAM HILL
RAINHAM
JEFFERY ST
1 grid square represents 500 metres

D1
1 Camden Rd
2 Devonshire Rd
3 Lincon Rd
D
E
51
D2
1 Brooklyn Pad
2 Cleveland Rd
3 Crown St
4 Macdonald Rd
D3
1 Avondale Rd
2 Balmoral Rd
3 Buckingham Rd
4 Connaught Rd
5 Edinburgh Rd
6 Glanville Rd
7 Osborne Rd
D4
1 Marathon Pad
E2
1 Firethorn Cl
2 Lobelia Cl
E6
1 Austin Cl
1
2
3
4
5
6
PIER ROAD
A289
Pier Approach
The Strand
Saxon Shore Way
Strand Ap Rd
Leslie Road
Shottenden Rd
St Andrew Rd
Selbourne Rd
Hamilton Rd
Baden Rd
Milner Rd
Corporation Road
Knight Avenue
Davenport Av
St Albans Cl
Baron Cl
Christmas St
Leet Cl
Layfield Road
Court Ldg Rd
Kg Edward Rd
Eastern Road
Dial Cl
Dial Rd
Waterside Lane
Arden Junior School
County
Rosebery Rd
Garfield Rd
Parr Avenue
Forge La
Sch
Margate Cl
Church St
Holly Close
Shore Way
Saxon
Gillingham Green
Church Pth
Oak
Victoria St
East St
Kingswood Rd
Hillyfields Junior Sch
Railway Street Industrial Est
Infant Sch
Greenfield Road
Springfield Road
Ingram Road
Elm Rd
Oak Av
Portland Rd
Cavendish Avenue
Maple Avenue
Grange Road
Castlemaine Avenue
Carrington Close
Bluebell Cl
The Vineries
Poppy Cl
Speedwell Cl
Freesia Close
Cypress Close
Hewitt Cl
Lwr Woodlands Rd
West St
Jeffery St
Railway St
LC
Granville Rd
Gillingham Stn
Windsor Road
Balmoral Road
DUNCAN ROAD
Sikh Temple
Franklin Road
Doctors Surgery
Ferndale Rd
Linden Rd
Priestfield Road
Gordon Road
Redfern Av
Sunnymead Avenue
Gillingham Football Club
Chicago Av
Livingstone Road
Woodlands Road
Buttermere
Tangmere Cl
Gillingham
Beresford Road
Coulman St
Beaconsfield Av
Barnsole CP Infant Sch
Harold Av
Canadian Av
Toronto Road
Woodlands Road Cemetery
69
Cornwallis Avenue
Napier Road Junior Sch
Road
Albany Road
Junior Sch
School Av
Haig Av
Sturdee Av
Valley Road
Acorn Rd
Avenue
Woodlands CP School
The Gillingham College
Secondary School
Louisville Av
Barnsole Rd
Carlton Avenue
Alexandra Av
Fourth Av
Gillingham Medical Centre
Beatty Avenue
A231
Borough Rd
Napier Rd
Junction Road
Larkfield Av
Brasenose Rd
Third Avenue
Doctors Surgery
Pretoria
St Barnaba Cl
Oxford Road
The Robert Napier School
Byron CP School
NELSON ROAD
Cowper Rd
Chada Avenue
Seaton Rd
Second Avenue
Tennis Club
Glebe Rd
Park Avenue
Cleave Road
Malvern Road
Holmside
CANTERBURY ST
Eva Rd
Stuart Rd
Crosley Rd
Chester Rd
Jezreels Rd
GILLINGHAM
First
WILL ADAMS WAY
A289
WATLING STREET
Doctors Surgery
Watling Av
Star Mill Lane
Maynard Pl
Corral Cl
Beechwood Av
Montrose Av
Osprey Avenue
SOVEREIGN BOULEVARD
Gillingham Golf Club Ltd
Woodlands Road
Zetland Av
Derby Road
Ash Tree Lane
Hunters Wy West
Kingsway
Rowland Cl
Rowland Av
Darland
Leyton Av
Allison Av
Preston
Hunters Way
Queens Rd
King's Rd
F
Will Adams Wy
Yeoman Dr
Grosvenor Rd
A2 SOVEREIGN BOULEVARD
Hotel Rd
Bailey Drive
Ambley Rd
Priory Rd
Abbey Rd
Hanway
The Chase
Chalkenden Av
Geneva Av
Cecil Av
Locarno Av
Broadway
Doctors Surgery
Eastcourt
Elmfield
Sanctuary Rd
Chilham Road
Featherby Junior School
Featherby CP School
Allington Rd
Teynham Gn
Broadway
Beechings Way
Beechings Industrial Ce
Bredgar Rd
FEATHERBY ROAD
Featherby
A289
Hazlemere Drive
Coniston Cl
Grange Road
Plantation Road
Danes Hill
Owens Wy
PIER ROAD
Gillingham Road
Sher Cl

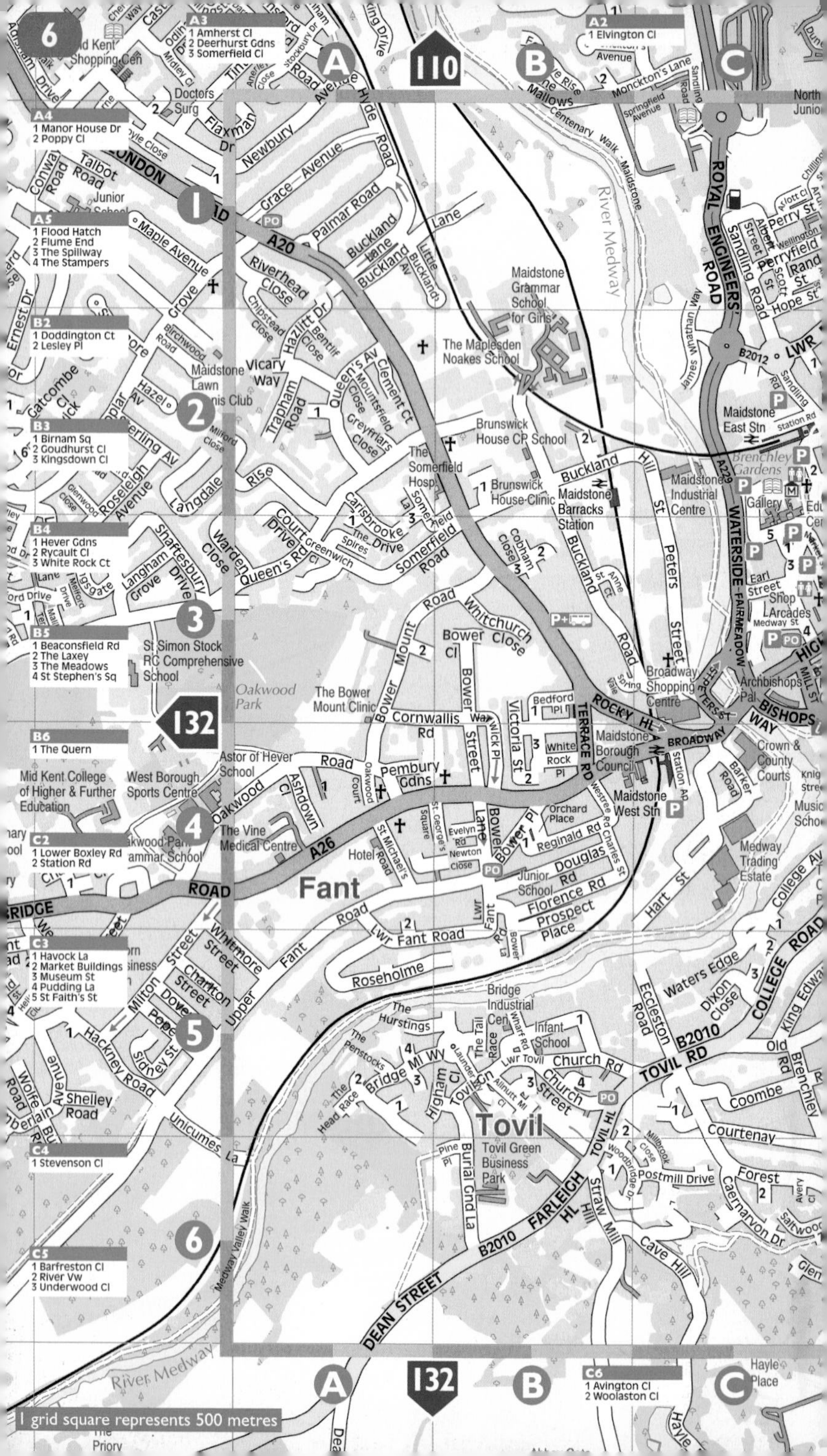
110
A
B
C
A3
1 Amherst Cl
2 Deerhurst Gdns
3 Somerfield Cl
A2
1 Elvington Cl
A4
1 Manor House Dr
2 Poppy Cl
A5
1 Flood Hatch
2 Flume End
3 The Spillway
4 The Stampers
B2
1 Doddington Ct
2 Lesley Pl
B3
1 Birnam Sq
2 Goudhurst Cl
3 Kingsdown Cl
B4
1 Hever Gdns
2 Rycault Cl
3 White Rock Ct
B5
1 Beaconsfield Rd
2 The Laxey
3 The Meadows
4 St Stephen's Sq
B6
1 The Quern
C2
1 Lower Boxley Rd
2 Station Rd
C3
1 Havock La
2 Market Buildings
3 Museum St
4 Pudding La
5 St Faith's St
C4
1 Stevenson Cl
C5
1 Barfreston Cl
2 River Vw
3 Underwood Cl
C6
1 Avington Cl
2 Woolaston Cl
1
2
3
4
5
6
132
Mid Kent Shopping Cen
Doctors Surg
Flaxman Dr
Newbury Avenue
Grace Avenue
Hyde Road
Palmar Road
Buckland Lane
Buckland Av
Little Buckland Av
Mallows
Monckton's Lane
Centenary Walk - Maidstone
River Medway
Springfield Avenue
Sandling Road
ROYAL ENGINEERS' ROAD
North Junction
LONDON ROAD
A20
Maple Avenue
Riverhead Close
Chipstead Close
Hazlitt Dr
Bentlif Close
Maidstone Grammar School for Girls
The Maplesden Noakes School
Maidstone Lawn Tennis Club
Vicary Way
Trapham Road
Queen's Av
Mountsfield Close
Clement Ct
Greyfriars Close
James Whatman Way
Perry St
Albert Street
Wellington
Perryfield St
Scott St
Rand St
Hope St
B2012
LWR
Maidstone East Stn
Station Rd
A229
Brenchley Gardens
Gallery
Maidstone Industrial Centre
WATERSIDE-FAIRMEADOW
Brunswick House CP School
Brunswick House Clinic
The Somerfield Hosp
Buckland Hill
Maidstone Barracks Station
St Peters Street
Milford Close
Langdale Rise
Roseleigh Avenue
Glenwood Close
Court Drive
Queen's Rd
Greenwich Cl
Carisbrooke Drive
The Spires
Somerfield La
Somerfield Road
Cobham Close
Buckland Road
St Anne Ct
Earl Street
Shop Arcades
Medway St
Warden Close
Shaftesbury Drive
Langham Grove
Melrose Drive
Road
Mount Road
Whitchurch Close
Bower Cl
Bower Street
Bower Mount Road
St Simon Stock RC Comprehensive School
Oakwood Park
The Bower Mount Clinic
Cornwallis Rd
Warwick Pl
Victoria St
Bedford Pl
White Rock Pl
ROCKY HL
TERRACE RD
Spring Vale
Broadway Shopping Centre
ST PETERS ST
BROADWAY
Archbishops Pal
BISHOPS WAY
Maidstone Borough Council
Station Ap
Maidstone West Stn
Crown & County Courts
Barker Road
Music School
Astor of Hever School
Mid Kent College of Higher & Further Education
West Borough Sports Centre
Oakwood Road
Ashdown Cl
Oakwood Court
Pembury Gdns
A26
The Vine Medical Centre
Oakwood Park Grammar School
Hotel
St Michael's Road
St George's Square
Evelyn Rd
Newton Close
Bower Lane
Bower Pl
Orchard Place
Reginald Rd
Westree Rd
Charles St
Douglas Rd
Junior School
Florence Rd
Prospect Place
Medway Trading Estate
Hart St
College Avenue
Fant
ROAD
TONBRIDGE
Whitmore Street
Charlton Street
Milton Street
Dover St
Pope St
Sidney St
Upper Fant Road
Lwr Fant Road
Lwr Fant Rd
Roseholme
Eccleston Road
Waters Edge
Dixon Close
COLLEGE ROAD
B2010
TOVIL RD
Old Tovil Rd
Brenchley
Coombe
Courtenay
Hackney Road
Wolfe Road
Shelley Road
Unicumes La
Bridge Industrial Cen
The Hurstings
The Penstocks
Bridge Ml Wy
The Head Race
Higham Cl
Launder Wy
Tovil Gn
The Tail Race
Wharf Rd
Infant School
Lwr Tovil
Church Rd
Church Street
Allnutt Ml Cl
Tovil
Tovil Green Business Park
Pine Pl
Burial Gnd La
TOVIL HL
Millbrook Close
Woodbridge Dr
Postmill Drive
Forest
Caernarvon Dr
Saltwood
Avery
FARLEIGH HL
Straw Mill Hill
Cave Hill
Medway Valley Walk
B2010
DEAN STREET
Glen
Hayle Place
River Medway
The Priory
132
1 grid square represents 500 metres

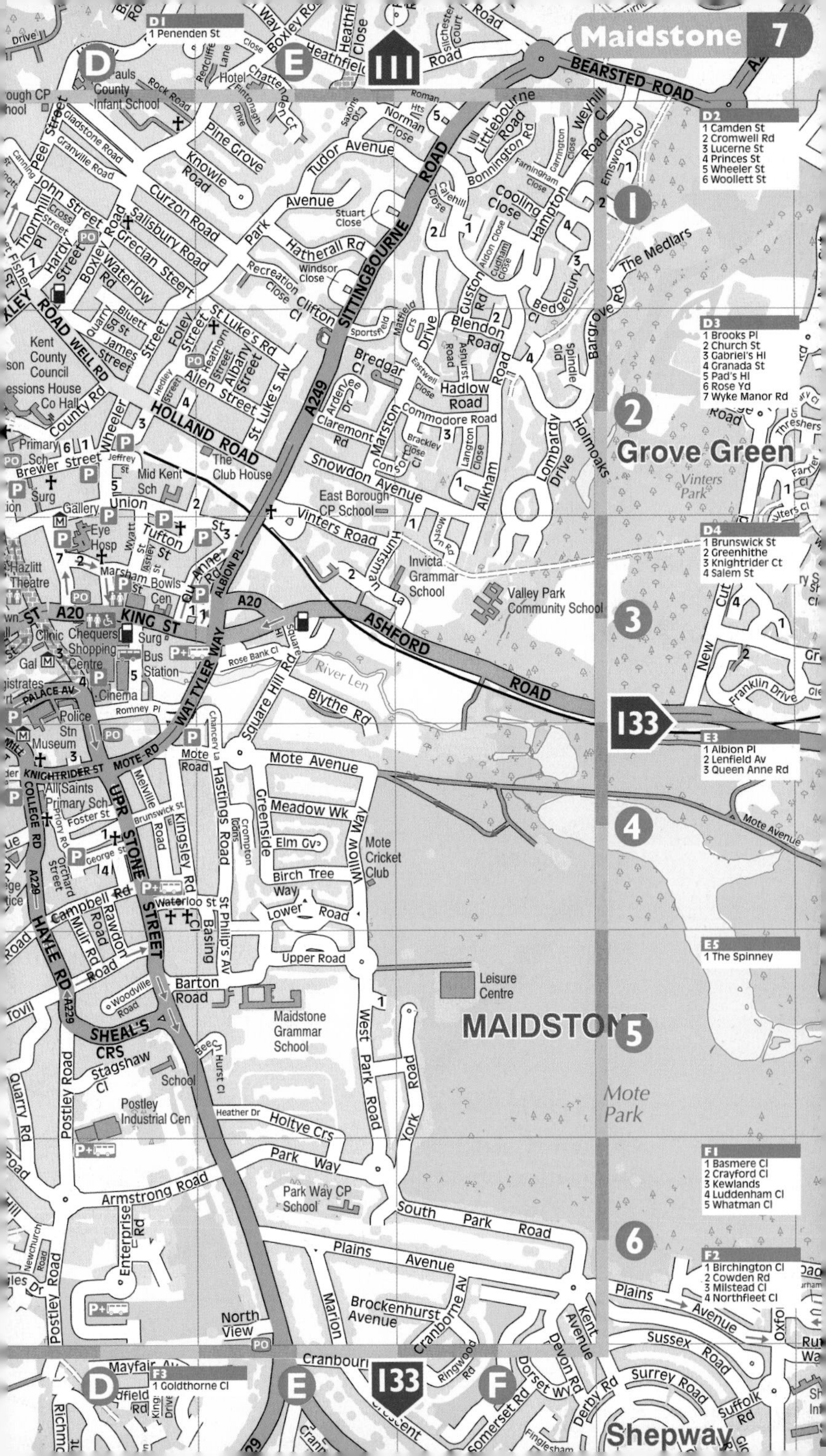
D1
1 Penenden St
D2
1 Camden St
2 Cromwell Rd
3 Lucerne St
4 Princes St
5 Wheeler St
6 Woollett St
D3
1 Brooks Pl
2 Church St
3 Gabriel's Hl
4 Granada St
5 Pad's Hl
6 Rose Yd
7 Wyke Manor Rd
D4
1 Brunswick St
2 Greenhithe
3 Knightrider Ct
4 Salem St
E3
1 Albion Pl
2 Lenfield Av
3 Queen Anne Rd
E5
1 The Spinney
F1
1 Basmere Cl
2 Crayford Cl
3 Kewlands
4 Luddenham Cl
5 Whatman Cl
F2
1 Birchington Cl
2 Cowden Rd
3 Milstead Cl
4 Northfleet Cl
F3
1 Goldthorne Cl
D
E
F
1
2
3
4
5
6
133
BEARSTED ROAD
SITTINGBOURNE ROAD
A249
HOLLAND ROAD
ASHFORD ROAD
A20
KING ST
WAT TYLER WAY
UPR STONE STREET
HAYLE RD
SHEAL'S CRS
A229
Grove Green
MAIDSTONE
Mote Park
Shepway
Vinters Park
Valley Park Community School
Invicta Grammar School
East Borough CP School
Maidstone Grammar School
Mote Cricket Club
Leisure Centre
Postley Industrial Cen
Park Way CP School
Kent County Council
Sessions House
Co Hall
Mid Kent Sch
The Club House
Chequers Shopping Centre
Bus Station
Cinema
Museum
Hazlitt Theatre
All Saints Primary Sch
River Len

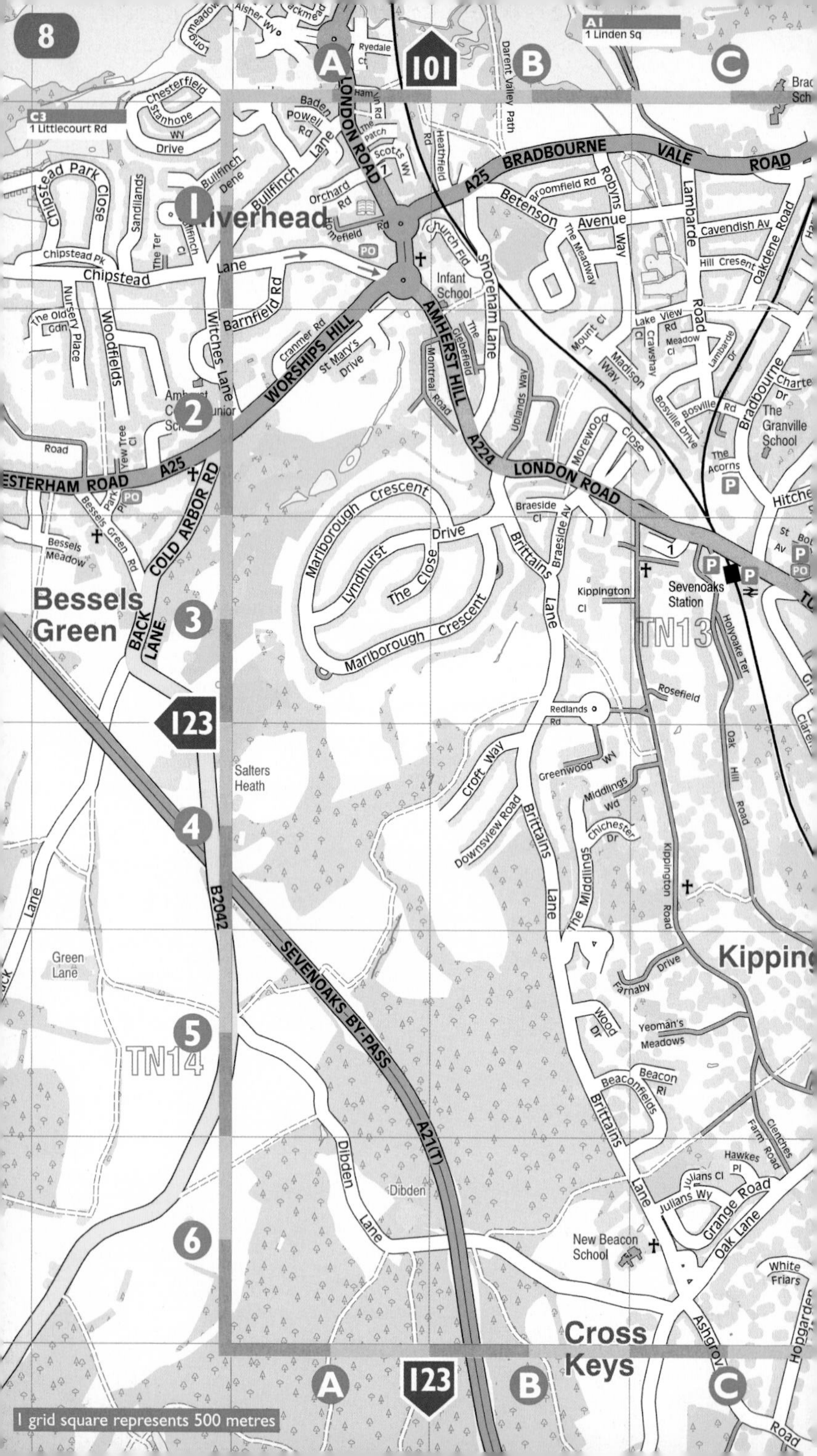
A
B
C
101
A1
1 Linden Sq
C3
1 Littlecourt Rd
Longmeadow
Alsher Wy
Ryedale Ct
Chesterfield
Stanhope Wy
Drive
Baden Powell Rd
LONDON ROAD
Hamlin Rd
The Patch
Scotts Wy
Orchard Rd
Homefield Rd
Bullfinch Lane
Bullfinch Dene
Bullfinch Cl
Darent Valley Path
Heathfield Rd
A25
BRADBOURNE VALE ROAD
Chipstead Park Close
Chipstead Pk
Chipstead Lane
Sandilands
The Ter
Riverhead
PO
Church Fld
Infant School
Shoreham Lane
Betenson Avenue
Broomfield Rd
The Meadway
Robyns Way
Lambarde Road
Cavendish Av
Hill Crescent
Oakdene Road
The Old Gdn
Nursery Place
Woodfields
Witches Lane
Barnfield Rd
Cranmer Rd
WORSHIPS HILL
St Mary's Drive
AMHERST HILL
The Glebefield
Montreal Road
Uplands Way
Mount Cl
Madison Way
Lake View Rd
Crawshay Cl
Meadow Cl
Lambarde Dr
Bosville Drive
Bosville Rd
Bradbourne
Charter Dr
The Granville School
Amherst C Junior Sch
Yew Tree Cl
Road
ESTERHAM ROAD
COLD ARBOR RD
Park Pl
Bessels Green Rd
Bessels Meadow
A224
LONDON ROAD
Morewood Close
The Acorns
P
Hitchen
Marlborough Crescent
Lyndhurst
The Close
Drive
Braeside Cl
Braeside Av
Brittains Lane
1
Sevenoaks Station
Kippington Cl
TN13
Holyoake Ter
Bessels Green
BACK LANE
123
Rosefield
Redlands Rd
Salters Heath
Croft Way
Greenwood Wy
Middlings Wd
Chichester Dr
Oak Hill Road
Downsview Road
The Middlings
Kippington Road
B2042
SEVENOAKS-BY-PASS
Lane
Green Lane
Kipping
Drive
Farnaby
Wood Dr
Yeoman's Meadows
TN14
Beacon Ri
Beaconfields
A21(T)
Dibden Lane
Dibden
Farm Road
Clenches
Hawkes Pl
Julians Cl
Julians Wy
Grange Road
Oak Lane
New Beacon School
White Friars
Cross Keys
Ashgrove
Hopgarden
1 grid square represents 500 metres

E3
1 Holly Bush La
D
E
102
SEAL
Pinewood
Wildernesse School
Wilderness
Dorton Coll
Further Edu
Sevenoaks Hosp
Hillingdon Rise
Avenue
The Cresent
Mill Pond
Little Wd
James's Road
Sevenoaks Town Council
John's
St George's Road
Davis Cl
Golding Rd
Westfield
Swaffield Rd
Wickenden Road
St Johns Hill Surgery
Garden Rd
The Green
Wildernesse Mt
Wildernesse Avenue
Camden Rd
Bradbourne Road
Sevenoaks CP School
St Hilarys School
Amherst Rd
Morel Ct
Nursery Cl
Allotment La
Lansdowne Rd
Quaker's Hall Lane
Kennedy Gdns
Linden Chase
Pineneedle La
Lyle Pk
PO
Prospect Rd
Cobden Rd
Bethel Road
Sandy La
Cedar Ter Rd
Hartsland Road
Bayham Road
Serpentine Road
Hillside Rd
Quarry Hill
ROAD
Woodland
Birch Cl
Blair Dr
Harry Rd
Pendennis Rd
Hunsdon Dr
DARTFORD ROAD A225
ST JOHN'S HILL
Knole Rd
Quaker Cl
Blackhall Lane
Carrick Dr
Woodside Rd
Hatch Lane
White Lodge Cl
Court Rd
HOLLOW
Chestnut La
Ashley Close
Ashley Rd
Avenue Rd
Vine Avenue
Hollybush Cl
Pound La
Park La
Holly Bush Lane
SEAL
ST BOTOLPH'S ROAD
THE VINE
A224 LONDON ROAD
The Drive
Chartway
Plymouth Pk
Blackhall
SEVENOAKS
124
Eardley Rd
Zobel College
Plymouth Drive
Warren Court
Council Offices
Gordon Road
Pembroke Rd
Suffolk Wy
Knole Way
Lady Boswell C of E School
Argyle Rd
Bligh's Rd
Pegasus Gallery
Sevenoaks Swimming Centre
Walk
Beech Rd
Lime Tree Wk
HIGH ST A225
Surg
Buckhurst Lane
Duchess'
South Pk
Town Medical Cen
Chantry Medical Practice
Crownfields
The Bank Street Gallery
Stag Theatre
Valley Dr
The Dene
Rectory La
Knole Lane
Cemetery
Oak La
Hotel Oakfields
Sevenoaks School
Knole (NT)
Glebe La
Knole Park
Lane
Grassy Lane
Wellmeade Dr
Lawn Pk
Soleoak Dr
Solefield School House
Fiennes Wy
Solefields School
Burntwood Gv
Burntwood Road
Oak Av
Road
Lea Rd
Hurst Wy
Stafford Wy
Clare Wy
Shenden Close
TONBRIDGE
Heath
Solefields
F

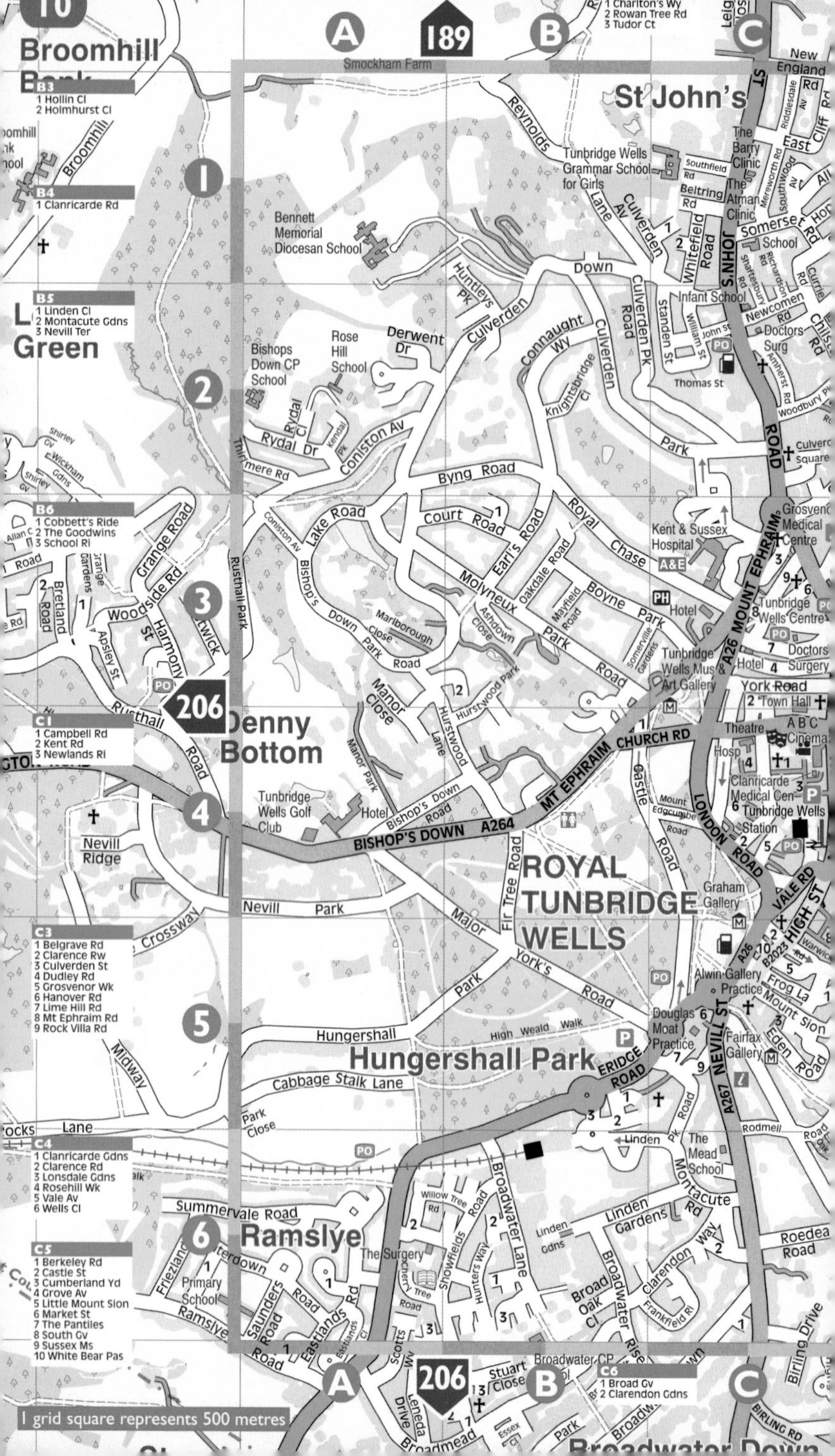
Broomhill Bank
B3
1 Hollin Cl
2 Holmhurst Cl
B4
1 Clanricarde Rd
B5
1 Linden Cl
2 Montacute Gdns
3 Nevill Ter
Green
B6
1 Cobbett's Ride
2 The Goodwins
3 School Ri
C1
1 Campbell Rd
2 Kent Rd
3 Newlands Ri
C3
1 Belgrave Rd
2 Clarence Rw
3 Culverden St
4 Dudley Rd
5 Grosvenor Wk
6 Hanover Rd
7 Lime Hill Rd
8 Mt Ephraim Rd
9 Rock Villa Rd
C4
1 Clanricarde Gdns
2 Clarence Rd
3 Lonsdale Gdns
4 Rosehill Wk
5 Vale Av
6 Wells Cl
C5
1 Berkeley Rd
2 Castle St
3 Cumberland Yd
4 Grove Av
5 Little Mount Sion
6 Market St
7 The Pantiles
8 South Gv
9 Sussex Ms
10 White Bear Pas
A6
1 Charlton's Wy
2 Rowan Tree Rd
3 Tudor Ct
C6
1 Broad Gv
2 Clarendon Gdns
A
B
C
189
206
1
2
3
4
5
6
Smockham Farm
St John's
Tunbridge Wells Grammar School for Girls
Bennett Memorial Diocesan School
Bishops Down CP School
Rose Hill School
Denny Bottom
Tunbridge Wells Golf Club
Hotel
BISHOP'S DOWN A264
MT EPHRAIM
CHURCH RD
A26 MOUNT EPHRAIM
LONDON ROAD
ROYAL TUNBRIDGE WELLS
Kent & Sussex Hospital
A&E
Tunbridge Wells Mus & Art Gallery
Tunbridge Wells Centre
Tunbridge Wells Station
Grosvenor Medical Centre
The Barry Clinic
The Atman Clinic
Infant School
Doctors Surg
Clanricarde Medical Cen
Graham Gallery
Alwin Gallery
Fairfax Gallery
Douglas Moat Practice
Hungershall Park
High Weald Walk
ERIDGE ROAD
A267 NEVILL ST
HIGH ST
VALE RD
The Mead School
Ramslye
The Surgery
Primary School
Broadwater CP Sch
Nevill Ridge
Nevill Park
Rusthall Park
Rusthall Road
Reynolds Lane
Culverden Down
Byng Road
Lake Road
Molyneux Park Road
Royal Chase
Boyne Park
York Road
Major York's Road
Fir Tree Road
Hungershall
Cabbage Stalk Lane
Summervale Road
Broadwater Lane
Broadwater Rise
Linden Gardens
Montacute Rd
Roedean Road
Birling Drive
BIRLING RD
Broadwater Down
1 grid square represents 500 metres

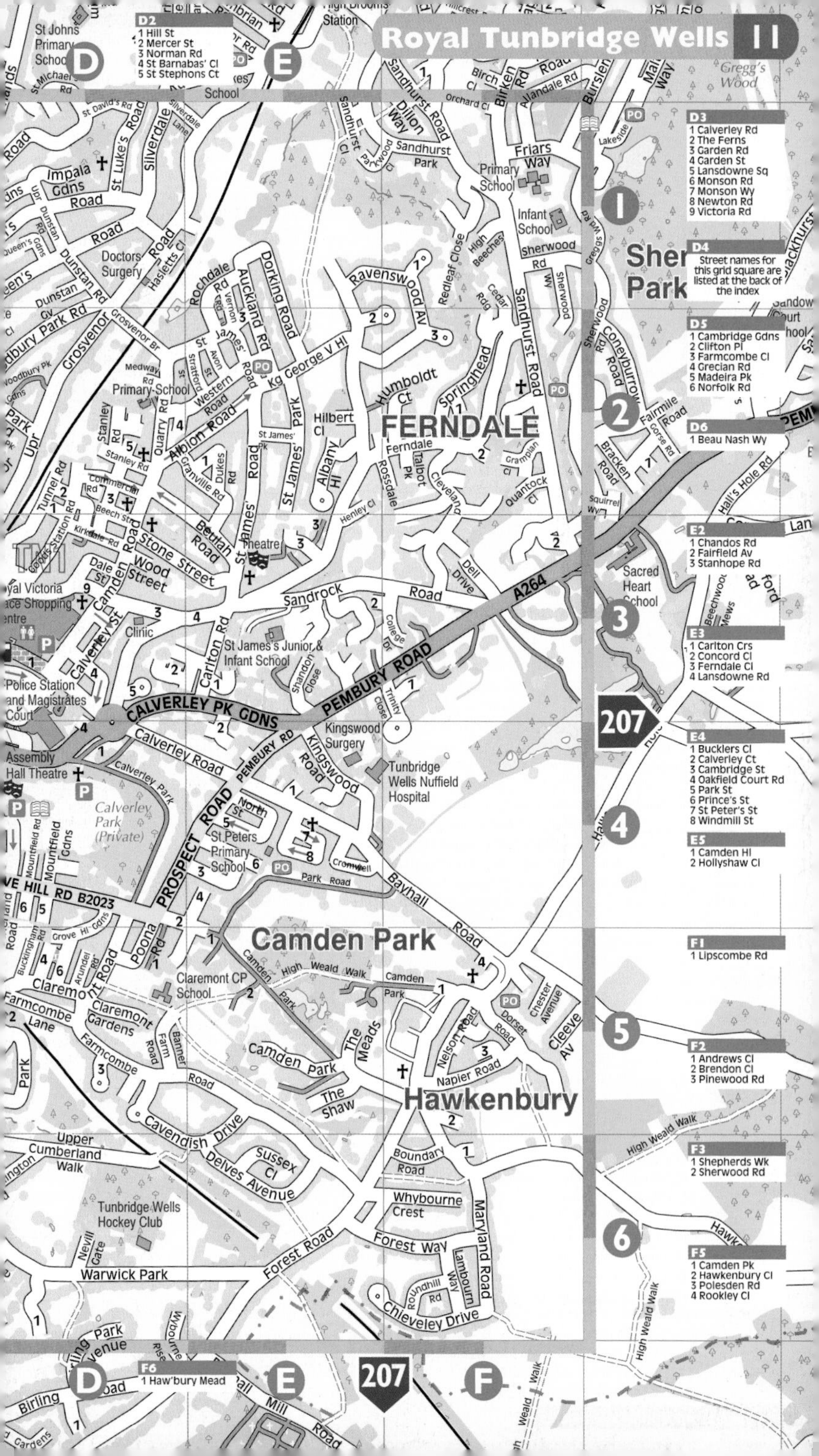
D2
1 Hill St
2 Mercer St
3 Norman Rd
4 St Barnabas' Cl
5 St Stephons Ct
D3
1 Calverley Rd
2 The Ferns
3 Garden Rd
4 Garden St
5 Lansdowne Sq
6 Monson Rd
7 Monson Wy
8 Newton Rd
9 Victoria Rd
D4
Street names for this grid square are listed at the back of the index
D5
1 Cambridge Gdns
2 Clifton Pl
3 Farmcombe Cl
4 Grecian Rd
5 Madeira Pk
6 Norfolk Rd
D6
1 Beau Nash Wy
E2
1 Chandos Rd
2 Fairfield Av
3 Stanhope Rd
E3
1 Carlton Crs
2 Concord Cl
3 Ferndale Cl
4 Lansdowne Rd
E4
1 Bucklers Cl
2 Calverley Ct
3 Cambridge St
4 Oakfield Court Rd
5 Park St
6 Prince's St
7 St Peter's St
8 Windmill St
E5
1 Camden Hl
2 Hollyshaw Cl
F1
1 Lipscombe Rd
F2
1 Andrews Cl
2 Brendon Cl
3 Pinewood Rd
F3
1 Shepherds Wk
2 Sherwood Rd
F5
1 Camden Pk
2 Hawkenbury Cl
3 Polesden Rd
4 Rookley Cl
F6
1 Haw'bury Mead
FERNDALE
Camden Park
Hawkenbury
Sherwood Park
Gregg's Wood
St Johns Primary School
High Brooms Station
Friars Way Primary School
Infant School
Doctors Surgery
Medway Primary School
Sacred Heart School
St James's Junior & Infant School
Kingswood Surgery
Tunbridge Wells Nuffield Hospital
Police Station and Magistrates Court
Assembly Hall Theatre
Calverley Park (Private)
St Peters Primary School
Claremont CP School
Tunbridge Wells Hockey Club
Clinic
Theatre
Royal Victoria Place Shopping Centre
TN1
PEMBURY ROAD
A264
CALVERLEY PK GDNS
PROSPECT ROAD
GROVE HILL RD B2023
Sandhurst Road
Ravenswood Av
Dorking Road
Auckland Rd
Rochdale Rd
Albion Road
Western Road
St James' Road
St James' Park
Kg George V Hl
Humboldt Ct
Springhead
Sandrock Road
Carlton Rd
Calverley Road
Calverley Park
Camden Road
Stone Street
Wood Street
Beulah Road
Bayhall Road
Park Road
Camden Park
The Meads
Nelson Road
Napier Road
Dorset Road
Chester Avenue
Cleeve Av
Claremont Road
Claremont Gardens
Farmcombe Lane
Farmcombe Road
Cavendish Drive
Delves Avenue
Sussex Cl
Upper Cumberland Walk
Warwick Park
Forest Road
Forest Way
Whybourne Crest
Boundary Road
Maryland Road
Lambourn Way
Roundhill Rd
Chieveley Drive
High Weald Walk
Dell Drive
Coneyburrow Road
Fairmile Road
Bracken Road
Halls Hole Rd
Silverdale Road
St Luke's Road
Impala Gdns
Dunstan Road
Grosvenor Br
Quarry Rd
Stanley Rd
Commercial Rd
Tunnel Rd
Goods Station Rd
Kingswood Road
Hilbert Cl
Albany Hl
Rossdale
Ferndale
Talbot Pk
Cleveland
Quantock Cl
Grampian Cl
Sherwood Rd
Cedar Rdg
Redleaf Close
High Beeches
Poona Rd
Banner Farm Road
Birling Road
Mill Road
207

ROAD B1335
Wennington Gn
Wennington
E5
1 Church Hollow
E4
1 St Clements Ct
A
B
C
D
E
SANDY
Sandy Lane Farm
NEW ROAD
A13(T)
Wennington Marshes
Havering
Thurrock
Kerry Avenue
Juliette Way
A13(T)
LONDON ROAD
Aveley Marshes
Fanns F
LC
Milehams Industrial Estate
Water Surg
Marlow Av
Fanns Rise
Thamley
Thurrock Council
Marine Court
Centurion Way
Crusader Close
Chieftan Drive
Mulberry Drive
ROAD
TANK HILL
A1090
Comet
Purfleet Primary School
Church Lane
The Lines
Harrisons Wharf
Purfleet
1
2
3
4
5
6
7
8
Erith Rands
River
Thames
Crayford Ness
Landau Way
Dayton Drive
Maypole Crescent
Burnett Road
Ness Road
Manford Industrial Estate
Ray Lamb Way
Canada Road
Snipe Cl
Durlun Way
Longreach Rd
Jenningtree Rd
Beacon Rd
Sheppey Cl
Hilden Dr
Brompton Dr
Hollywood Wy
Rodeo Cl
Haze Dr
Wallhouse Road
Darent Valley Path
Joyce Green Lane
Dartford Marshes
Crayford Marshes
Slade Green Football Club
Lane
lade
reen
23
Kent County
Bexley
Joyce Green Hospital
Street
Marsh

1 grid square represents 500 metres

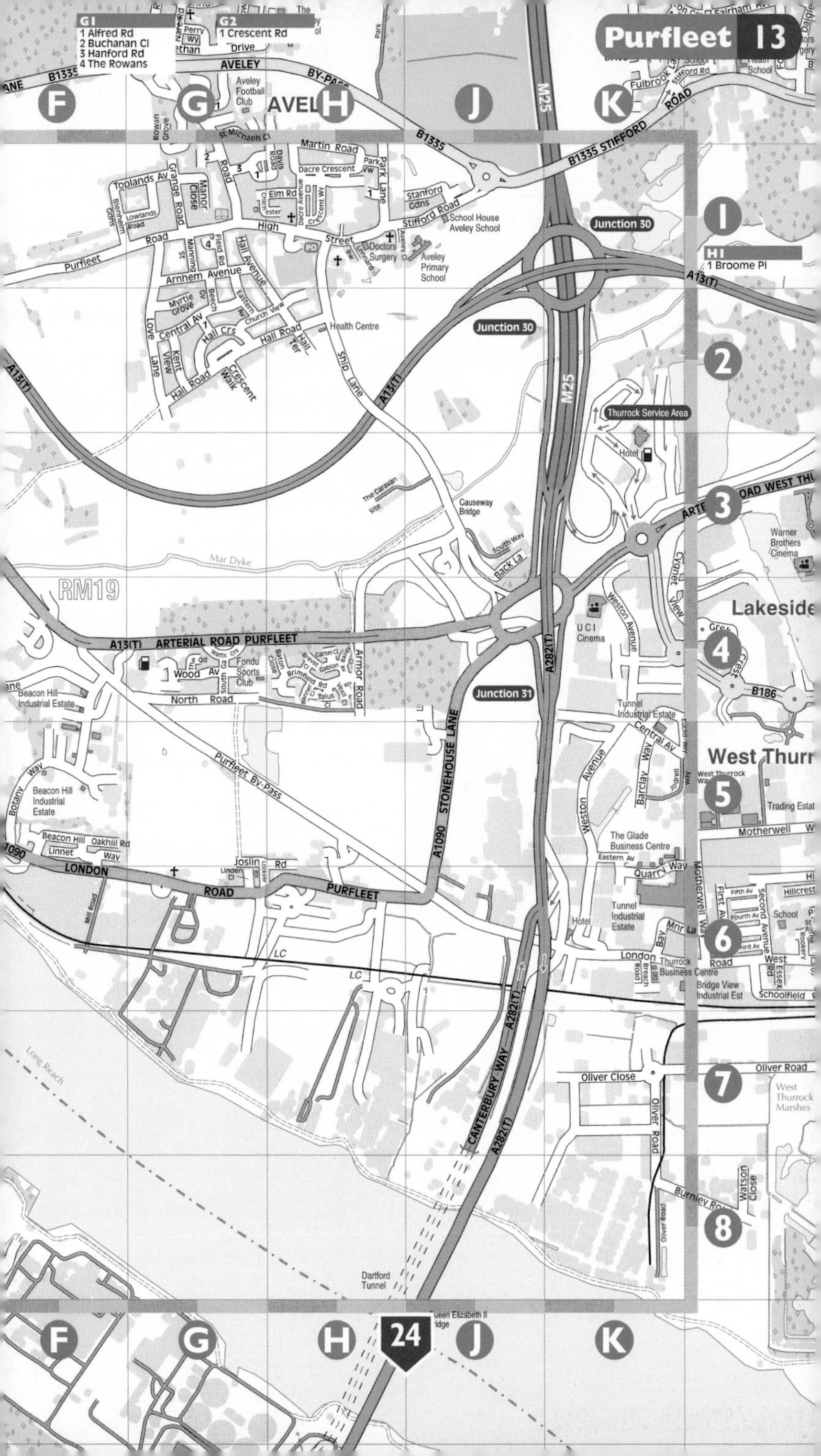
G1
1 Alfred Rd
2 Buchanan Cl
3 Hanford Rd
4 The Rowans
G2
1 Crescent Rd
H1
1 Broome Pl
AVELEY
AVELEY BY-PASS
B1335
B1335 STIFFORD ROAD
Aveley Football Club
M25
Junction 30
Junction 31
Martin Road
Dacre Crescent
Park Lane
Toplands Av
Grange Road
Manor Close
Stanford Gdns
Stifford Road
School House
Aveley School
High Street
Purfleet Road
Doctors Surgery
Aveley Primary School
Arnhem Avenue
Hall Avenue
Myrtle Grove
Central Av
Church View
Hall Road
Hall Crs
Crescent Walk
Love Lane
Health Centre
Ship Lane
A13(T)
Thurrock Service Area
Hotel
The Caravan Site
Causeway Bridge
South Way
Back La
Mar Dyke
RM19
A13(T) ARTERIAL ROAD PURFLEET
ARTERIAL ROAD WEST THURROCK
Warner Brothers Cinema
Lakeside
UCI Cinema
Weston Avenue
Cygnet View
B186
Wood Av
North Road
Fondu Sports Club
Armor Road
Beacon Hill Industrial Estate
Purfleet By-Pass
A1090 STONEHOUSE LANE
A282(T)
Tunnel Industrial Estate
Central Av
Barclay Way
West Thurrock
Trading Estate
Motherwell Way
The Glade Business Centre
Quarry Way
Botany Way
Beacon Hill
Oakhill Rd
Linnet Way
Joslin Rd
A1090 LONDON ROAD PURFLEET
Mill Road
LC
London Road
Thurrock Business Centre
Bridge View Industrial Est
West Road
Schoolfield Rd
Hillcrest
School
Second Avenue
First Av
Long Reach
CANTERBURY WAY
Oliver Close
Oliver Road
West Thurrock Marshes
Burnley Road
Watson Close
Dartford Tunnel
Queen Elizabeth II Bridge
24
F
G
H
J
K
1
2
3
4
5
6
7
8

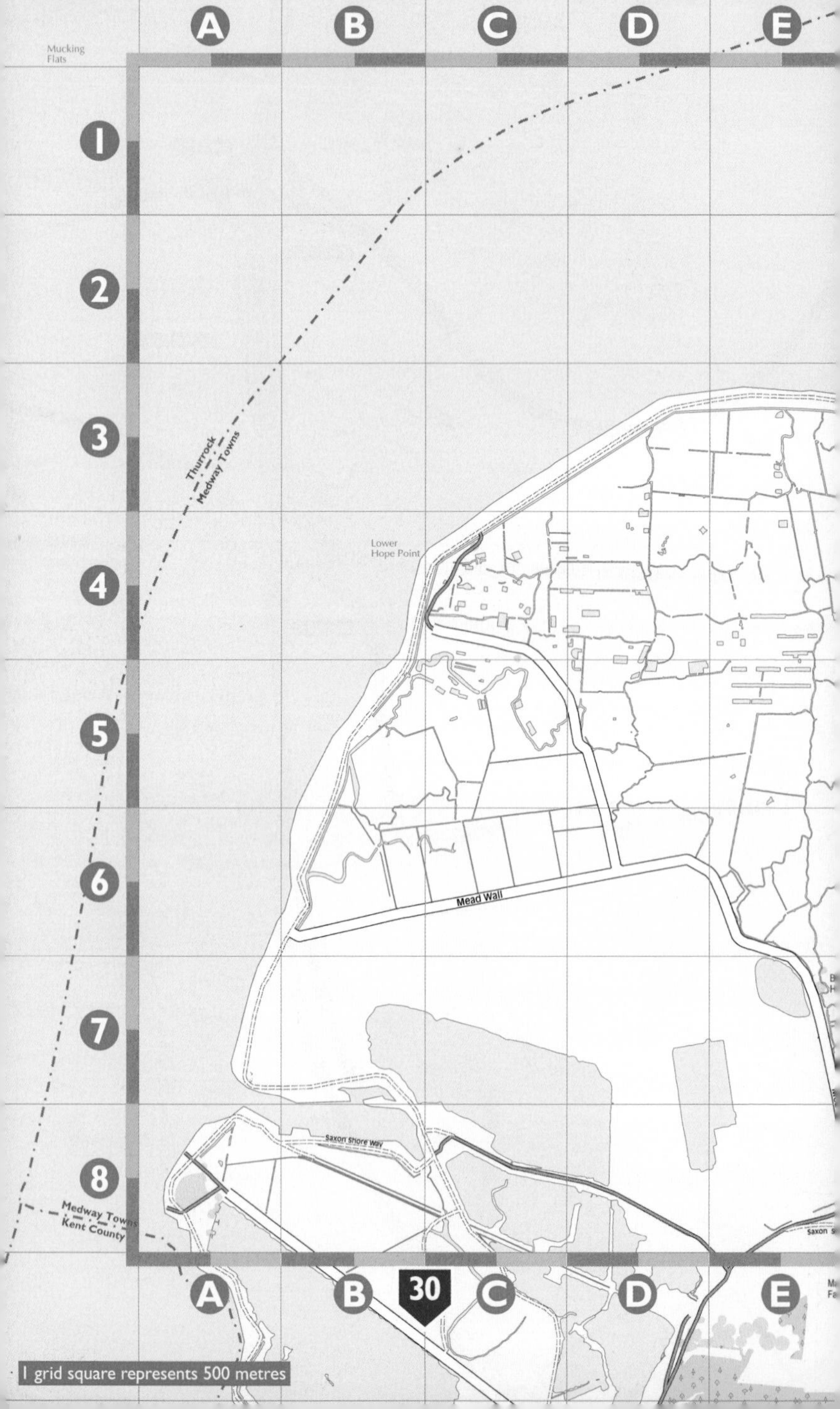
A
B
C
D
E
1
2
3
4
5
6
7
8
Mucking Flats
Thurrock
Medway Towns
Lower Hope Point
Mead Wall
Saxon Shore Way
Medway Towns
Kent County
30
1 grid square represents 500 metres

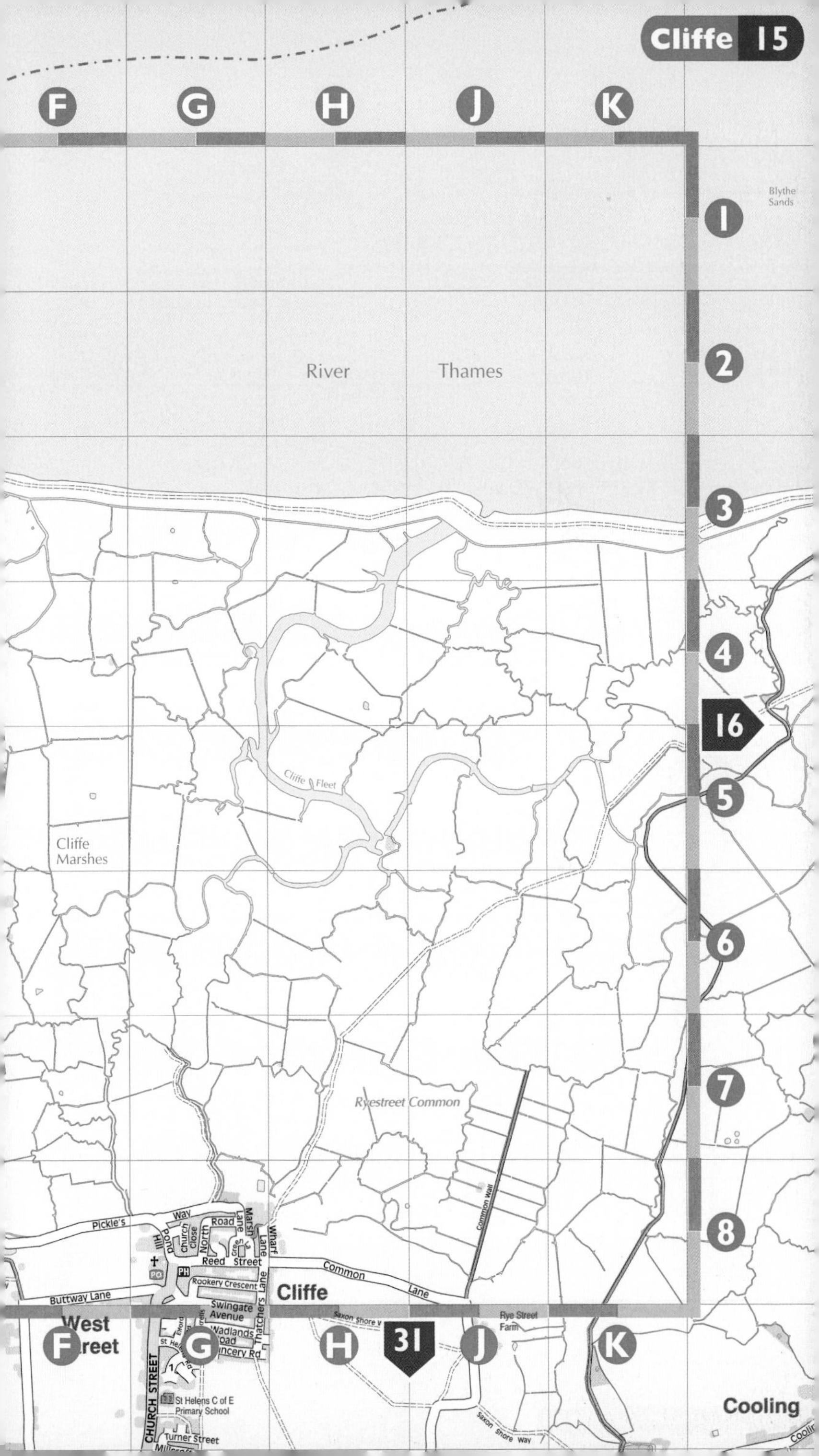
F
G
H
J
K
1
2
3
4
5
6
7
8
Blythe Sands
River Thames
Cliffe Fleet
Cliffe Marshes
Ryestreet Common
16
Pickle's Way
Hill
Pond
Church Close
North Road
Marsh Lane
Wharf Lane
Reed Street
Common Lane
Rookery Crescent
Thatchers Lane
Cliffe
Buttway Lane
Swingate Avenue
Wadlands Road
West Street
Common Wall
Saxon Shore Way
Rye Street Farm
31
St Helens C of E Primary School
CHURCH STREET
Turner Street
Cooling

A
B
C
D
E
1
2
3
4
5
6
7
8
15
32
Blythe Sands
Salt Fleet
Hope Fleet
Halstow Marshes
Cooling Marshes
Decoy Fleet
Buckland Fleet
Whalebone Marshes
Saxon Shore Way
Farm
Cooling
1 grid square represents 500 metres

F
G
H
J
K
1
2
3
4
5
6
7
8
West Point
18
Swigshole
Decoy
Farm
Decoy
Hill
Road
St Mary's
Hoo
Moat Farm
Hall
Road
33
Newlands
Farm
Clinchstreet
Farm

A
B
C
D
E
1
2
3
4
5
6
7
8
17
34
St Mary's Marshes
Dagnam Farm
Homewards
Ratcliffe Highway
Shakespeare Farm Road
Brick House Farm
Coombe Farm Lane
Moat Farm
Moat Farm Road
St Mary's Ho
Hall
Road
Newhall Farm
New Hall
Hoopers Lane
Cuckold's Green
Cuckolds Green
1 grid square represents 500 metres

G6
1 Avery Cl
2 St Matthew's Wy

F
G
H
J
K
1
2
3
4
5
6
7
8
20
35
River Thames
Allhallows-on-Sea
The Brimp
Avery Way
Avery Close
Queensway
The Elms Medical Practice
St Luke's Way
St David's Rd
Binney Road
Allhallows
Jurland Close
Binney Farm
Allhallows Marshes
Yantlet Creek
Stoke Road
Lane
Marshland View
Button Drive
Allhallows Road
Stoke Marshes
Lower Stoke

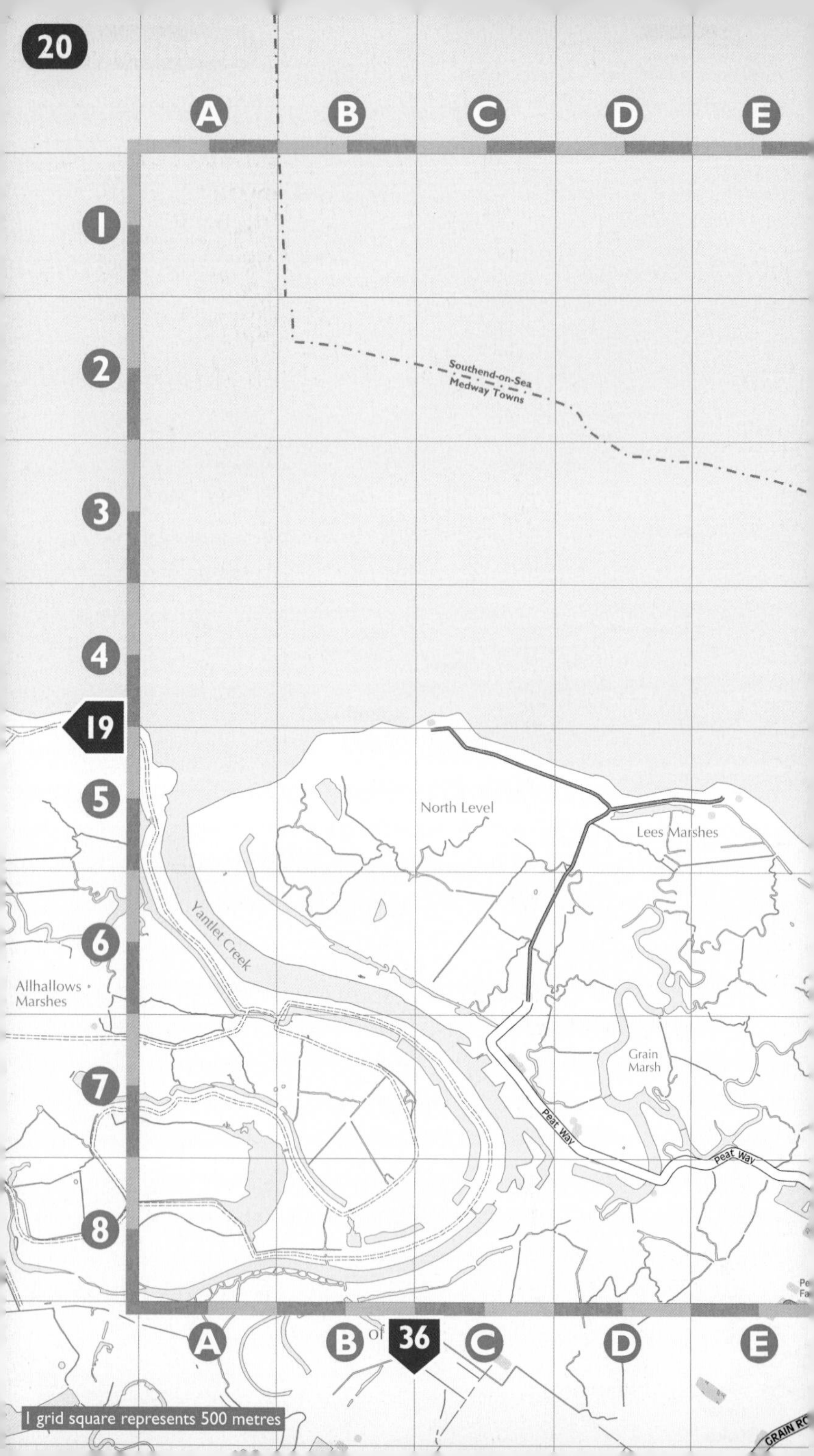
A
B
C
D
E
1
2
3
4
5
6
7
8
19
Southend-on-Sea
Medway Towns
North Level
Lees Marshes
Yantlet Creek
Allhallows
Marshes
Grain
Marsh
Peat Way
Peat Way
of
36
GRAIN RO
1 grid square represents 500 metres

F8	G8
1 Fry Cl	1 Doggetts Rw 2 Levett Cl 3 Pintail Cl

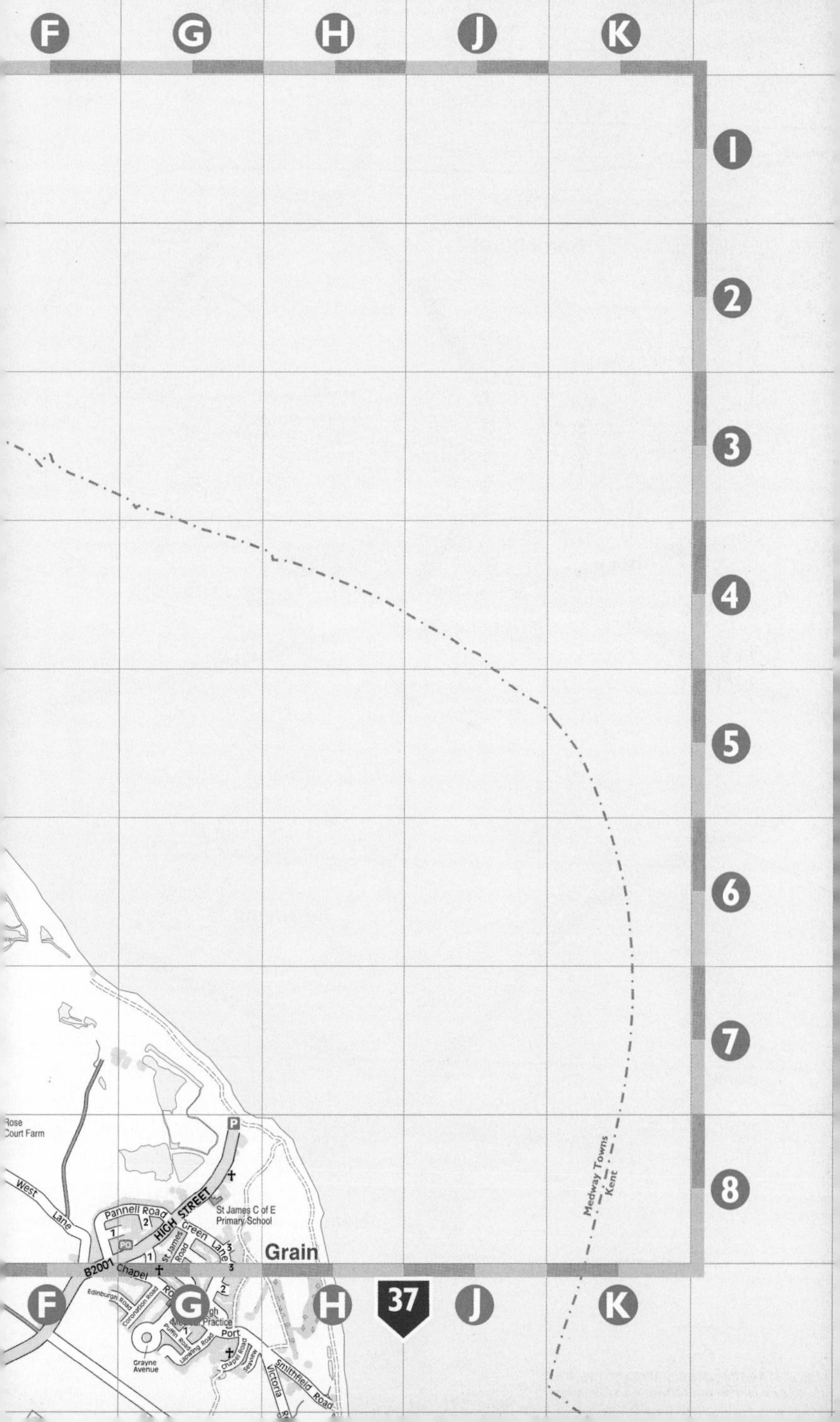
F
G
H
J
K
1
2
3
4
5
6
7
8
Rose Court Farm
West Lane
Pannell Road
HIGH STREET
St James C of E Primary School
Green Lane
St James Road
Grain
B2001 Chapel Rd
Edinburgh Road
Coronation Road
Puffin Road
Lapwing Road
Port
Chapel Road
Seaview
Smithfield Road
Victoria Rd
Grayne Avenue
Medway Towns
Kent
37

1 grid square represents 500 metres

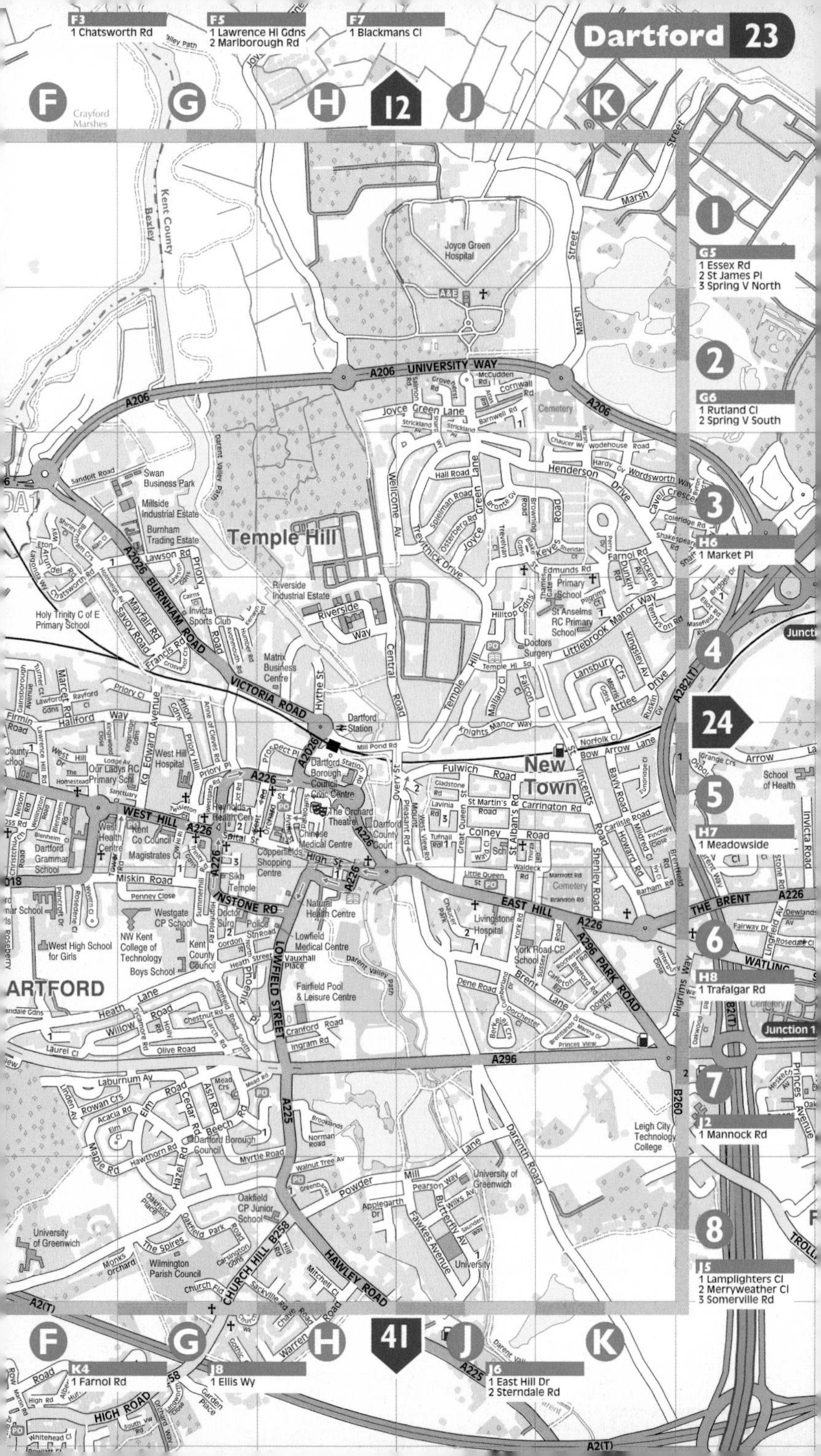
F3
1 Chatsworth Rd
F5
1 Lawrence Hl Gdns
2 Marlborough Rd
F7
1 Blackmans Cl
G5
1 Essex Rd
2 St James Pl
3 Spring V North
G6
1 Rutland Cl
2 Spring V South
H6
1 Market Pl
H7
1 Meadowside
H8
1 Trafalgar Rd
J2
1 Mannock Rd
J5
1 Lamplighters Cl
2 Merryweather Cl
3 Somerville Rd
K4
1 Farnol Rd
J8
1 Ellis Wy
J6
1 East Hill Dr
2 Sterndale Rd
F
G
H
J
K
12
24
41
1
2
3
4
5
6
7
8
Crayford Marshes
Kent County
Bexley
Joyce Green Hospital
A&E
A206 UNIVERSITY WAY
A206
Temple Hill
Swan Business Park
Millside Industrial Estate
Burnham Trading Estate
Riverside Industrial Estate
Holy Trinity C of E Primary School
Invicta Sports Club
Matrix Business Centre
A2026 BURNHAM ROAD
VICTORIA ROAD
Dartford Station
West Hill Hospital
Our Ladys RC Primary Sch
Reynolds Health Cen
Dartford Borough Council Civic Centre
The Orchard Theatre
Dartford County Court
Chinese Medical Centre
Kent Co Council
Magistrates Ct
Coppercfields Shopping Centre
Sikh Temple
Dartford Grammar School
West High School for Girls
NW Kent College of Technology
Boys School
Westgate CP School
Kent County Council
Police Stn
Natural Health Centre
Lowfield Medical Centre
Fairfield Pool & Leisure Centre
DARTFORD
WEST HILL
A226
LOWFIELD STREET
A225
A296
EAST HILL
A296 PARK ROAD
THE BRENT
WATLING
New Town
Livingstone Hospital
York Road CP School
Primary School
St Anselms RC Primary School
Doctors Surgery
Cemetery
School of Health
Leigh City Technology College
University of Greenwich
University
Oakfield CP Junior School
Wilmington Parish Council
Dartford Borough Council
CHURCH HILL B258
HAWLEY ROAD
HIGH ROAD
A2(T)
A282(T)
B260
Junction 1
Pilgrims Way
Darent Valley Path
Marsh Street
Joyce Green Lane
Henderson Drive
Littlebrook Manor Way
Temple Hill
Central Road
Fulwich Road
Powder Mill Lane
Dartford Road
Princes Avenue

1 grid square represents 500 metres

F3
1 Crest Vw
F4
1 Borland Cl
2 Cutty Sark Ct
3 Riverview Rd
4 Wheatley Cl
G4
1 Admirals Wk
2 Skippers Cl
G5
1 Starboard Av
H5
1 Austen Cl
2 Bevans Cl
3 Johnsons Wy
J4
1 Craylands Sq
K5
1 Madden Cl
2 Mayfield
3 Wallace Gdns
F
G
H
J
K
1
2
3
4
5
6
7
8
26
43
Watson Close
Stone Ness
Thurrock
Kent County
HIGH STREET
Sara Crs
Kestner Industrial Est
STATION RD
Eagles Road
Manor Way
Pilgrims' Road
Lower's Lane
LONDON ROAD
A226
GALLEY HILL ROAD
Kraft Industrial Estate
Swanscombe Business Centre
Galley Hill Industrial Estate
Craylands Lane
Greenhithe for Bluewater Stn
Park Terrace
Knockhall
Greenhithe Health Clinic
Ivy Bower Surgery
Greenhithe
Knockhall Road
Eynsford Rd
Abbey Rd
Broomfield Rd
DA10
Milton
Lewis Rd
Swanscombe
Ames
Moore Rd
Broad Rd
Park Road
Cemetery
Doctors Surgery
Mounts Road
Bean Road
Port Av
Spring Vale
Alkerden Lane
Milton St
Manor Rd
Gunn Road
Manor Rd
Leonard Avenue
Durrant Way
New Swan Valley Community School
Stone Castle
Lime Tree Av
B255
A206
ROMAN ROAD
A296
A2(T)
Bean Lane
Stonewood
Bean
HIGH STREET
Beacon Drive
School Lane
Claywood Lane

C5
1 Kingston Ct
C4
1 Fishermen's Hl
2 Ford Rd
3 Hamerton Rd
D5
1 Vicarage Dr
E6
1 Buckingham Rd
2 Hartfield Pl
3 Salem Pl
Broadness
Northfleet Hope
Tilbury Ness
Manor Way
Kent Kraft Industrial Estate
Northfleet Industrial Estate
Lower Rd
Pilgrims' Road
LONDON ROAD
A226
GALLEY HILL ROAD
Swanscombe Business Centre
All Saints Cl
Swanscombe Station
B259 HIGH STREET
STANHOPE RD
Taunton Road
Grove Road
Park Wallis
College Road
The Creek
The Shore
STONEBRIDGE ROAD
Northfleet Station
Station Road
Rose St
Railway St
HIGH STREET
Northfleet
Lawn CP School
Gravesend & Northfleet Football Club
Factory Rd
Hive La
Lawn Rd
Granby Road
Portland Road
THE HILL
The Surgery
Huntley Avenue
Bankside
West Kent Avenue
Church Pth
A226 LOND
Laburnum
Lime Ave
Robinia Av
B261
B2175
SPRINGHEAD RD
York Rd
Shepherd St
Tooley St
St Josephs RC School
DOVE
Vale Rd
DA11
A2260
THAMES
Gravesham Borough Council
Cemetery
Haldane Gardens
Camden Cl
Meadow Road
Waterdales
Mitchell Avenue
Colyer
SPRINGHEAD ROAD
A2260
Gwynn Road
Broomfield Rd
Craylands La
Lewis Rd
Milton St
Moore Rd
Trebble Road
Broad Rd
Park Road
Gunn Road
Manor Rd
Durrant Way
Leonard
Gasson Rd
Stanley Rd
Church Road
Hope Rd
Harmer Rd
Albert Rd
Herbert Rd
Doctors Surgery
Castle Rd
Vernon Road
Sun Road
Eglinton Rd
B259
Swanscombe Street
St Paul's Cl
St Peter's Cl
Keary Road
Milford Dr
New Swan Valley Community School
Sweyne CP Junior School
Cemetery
The Grove
SOUTHFLEET ROAD
B259
Spring Head
A2(T)
PARK CORNER ROAD
Park Cnr Road
WATLING STREET
Fleet Road
Viking Rd
Pepper Hl
Roman Road
Saxon Cl
Painters Ash Lane
Masefield Rd
Primary School
Chaucer
Pepys Cl
Pickwick Gdns
Hog La
Tenny
25
44
1 grid square represents 500 metres

F6
1 Collington Cl
F7
1 Falcon Ms
2 St Thomas Rd
F8
1 Harrowby Gdns
2 Sunninghill
G1
1 Alexandra Rd
2 Broadway
3 Ellerman Rd
4 Rossell Rd
G5
1 Chestnut Cl
G6, H7, J5
Street names for these grid squares are listed at the back of the index
G7
1 Lansdown Rd
2 Southfleet Rd
G8
1 Greenhill Rd
H1
1 Canberra Sq
H5
1 Barrack Rw
2 Darnley Rd
3 New Rd
4 St James's St
J1
1 Bown Cl
2 Edinburgh Ms
3 Elizabeth Cl
J6
1 North St
2 St Andrew's Rd
3 Woodville Pl
4 Zion Pl
J7
1 Spire Cl
K1
1 Austen Cl
2 Bronte Cl
3 Wordsworth Cl
K5
1 Gordon Pl
2 Milton Rd
K8
1 Canterbury Rd
K7
1 Belvedere Cl
K6
1 Albert Murray Cl
2 Blenheim Gv
3 Christ Church Rd
4 Cumberland Av
5 Waterloo St
28
45
Tilbury Town Station
St Andrew's Road
A1089
Ferry Road
A126
Tilbury Fort
Fort Road
River
Gravesend Reach
Thurrock
Kent County
Rosherville
Perry Street
New House
Parrock Farm
Overcliffe
Thames Way
Dover Rd
Old Road West
Old Rd East
Milton Road
Wrotham Road
Imperial Retail Park
Gravesend & North Kent Hospital
Gravesham Borough Council
Gravesend Grammar School for Girls
Cemetery

A8
1 Evesham Rd
A6
1 Copper Beech Cl
2 Sycamore Cl
A5
1 Brunswick Wk
B8
1 Lindisfarne Cl
C7
1 Barham Cl
2 Farriers Cl
3 Kingsdown Cl
4 Maypole Rd
C8
1 Oxford Cl
2 Terence Cl
E8
1 Beckley Cl
2 Manor Cl
3 Shirley Cl
4 Sutherland Cl
A
B
C
D
E
1
2
3
4
5
6
7
8
27
46
West Tilbury Marshes
Tilbury Fort
River Thames
GRAVESEND
Gravesend Yacht Club
Canal Basin
Milton
Wharf Road
Canal Ind Park
Norfolk Road
Milton Road Business Park
MILTON ROAD
E MILTON ROAD
ROCHESTER ROAD
Waterton Av
Alexandra Rd
Havengore Av
Denton
Gravesend Grammar School for Boys
St Johns RC Primary School
St Johns RC Comprehensive School
Primary School
North West Kent College
Chalk
Lower Higham Road
Copperfield Cl
Nickleby Rd
Havisham Rd
Castle Lane
Saxon Shore Way
OLD ROAD EAST B261
Bellman Av
Abbey Road
Milton Hall Road
Pine Avenue
St Josephs Preparatory School
Westcourt County Primary School
West Court
Doctors Surgery
Barr Road
Bourne Road
A226 ROCHESTER ROAD
Thong Lane
Parrock Farm
Kings Farm
Raynehurst CP School
Thamesview School
Fleetway Sports Club
Trinity Rd
The Clinic
1 grid square represents 500 metres

East Tilbury Marshes
F
G
H
J
K
Coalhouse Point
1
2
Saxon Shore Way
3
4
30
Shorne Marshes
5
Canal Road
6
Queen's Farm
Road
Queen's Farm
7
Lower Higham Road
King's Farm
East Court Manor
Lane
Lower Road
Lower Road
8
Church
Green
Church La
Green Farm
47
Farm
Lane
Hill Farm

1 grid square represents 500 metres

G1
1 Chesterton Rd
G6
1 Mallingdene Cl
2 Masefield Dr
3 Newbury Cl
Pickle's Way
Pond Hill
Church Close
Wharf Lane
Common Wall
15
Cliffe
Buttway Lane
West Street
Swingate Avenue
Wadlands Road
Chancery Rd
Thatchers Lane
Saxon Shore Way
Rye Street Farm
St Helens Rd
CHURCH STREET
St Helens C of E Primary School
Turner Street
Millcroft Road
Cooling
G7
1 Dorchester Cl
Norwood Close
New Rd
Higham Road
Cooling Road
Symonds Road
Berry Court Farm
Well Penn Road
B2000
STATION ROAD
Gattons Farm
Cooling Court Farm
Rectory Road
South Bank
Buckland Road
New Barn Farm
32
Cooling Street
Spendiff Farm
Perry Hill Farm
Perry Hill
Merry Boys Road
Cooling Common
Wentworth Drive
View Road
Cliffe Woods Surgery
Cliffe Woods C P School
Milton Avenue
Mortimers Avenue
Cardens Rd
Ladyclose Avenue
Parkside
Shaw Cl
Cliffe Woods
Tennyson Avenue
Goodwin Road
Brewer Road
Great Chattenden Wood
Lodge Hill Lane
Archery Close
Sedley Close
Ashwood Close
Brookmead Road
Lochat Road
Englefield Crs
Hilton Rd
Graveney Close
North Terrace
Central Ter
Ham River Hill
TOWN ROAD
Common Road
Lee Green
Hill La
Swinton Av
Chattenden
49
Kirby Road
Chillwack Road
Chattenden Lane
Mockbeggar
Bunters Hill
Haven Street
F
G
H
J
K
1
2
3
4
5
6
7
8

Whalebone Marshes
16
Saxon Shore Way
Bromhey Farm
Cooling
Cooling Road
Lipwell Hill
Buckhole Farm
Buckhole Farm Road
Dalham Farm
High Prima
Cooling Road
LC
Wybournes Lane
Wybournes Farm
Cooling Court Farm
New Barn Farm
31
Spendiff Farm
Ducks Court
Deangate
Dux Court Road
Lodge Hill Lane
Lochat Road
North Terrace
Central Ter
Chattenden Farm
A228
Blackman Close
Wall Cl
Fourwents Road
Bell's La
Rochester Crescent
Kingshill Dr
Webb Close
Pankhurst Road
Linton Dann Close
Morrement Rd
Marley Rd
Vidgeon Av
Knights
Robson Drive
Aveling Close
Wylie Rd
Stonebridge
RATCLIFFE HIGHWAY
Hoo St Werburgh
Hl La
Lodge Road
Elmwood Road
Swinton Av
Chattenden
Kirby
Chilliwack Rd
Lane
50
St Werburgh CP Junior School
The Hundred of Hoo School
Hoo St Werburgh C P School
Herdsdown
Gordon Road
Werburgh Crescent
Main Road
1 grid square represents 500 metres

Hoo
F
G
H
17
J
K
Decoy Hill Road
Hall Road
Moat Farm Rd
Newlands Farm
Saxon Shore Way
Clinchstreet Farm
Clinch Street
Newlands Farm Road
Ratcliffe Highway
Marsh Crescent
Northwood Avenue
Thames Av
Longfield Avenue
Medway Avenue
Walnut Tree Farm
ME3
Harrison Drive
Eden Rd
Willowbank Drive
Leaman Close
Street
Goodwood Cl
Drayton Close
Holmes Ct
Valentine Drive
A228
Bellwood Court
Turkey Hall Farm
MALMAYNES
The Street
High Halstow
Fenn Street
RATCLIFFE HIGHWAY
Christmas Lane
Solomons Farm
Sharnal Street
Cold Arbour
Tunbric
Hill
Roper's Green Lane
Stoke Road
LC
Roper's Lane
Beluncle Farm
Tile Barn Farm
Jetty Road
Gamma Road
Alpha Close
Main Road
Jacob's Lane
Eshcol Road
Grandsire Gardens
Walters Road
Wylie Rd
St Werburgh Medical Centre
Bell's Lane
Saxon Shore Way
Kingsnorth
Peal Cl
Knights Road
Coombe Road
Flack Gdns
Abbot's Court
Brookside
Church
Court
1
2
3
4
34
5
6
7
8
F
G
H
51
J
K

Mary's Hoo
Moat Farm
Moat Farm Road
Hall
Road
Coombe Farm Lane
Newhall Farm
New
Hoopers Lane
Cuckold's Green
Cuckolds Green
Ratcliffe Highway
Malmaynes Hall Farm
Mackay Court F
Mallard
Bellwood Court
Turkey Hall Farm
MALMAYNES HALL ROAD
A228
GRAIN
Stoke
Vicarage Close
Dickensian Cl
Tudor Farm
North Street
Cold Arbour
Stoke Road
Tunbridge Hill
LC
Alpha Close
Beta Rd
Jetty Road
Gamma Road
Main Road
East Hoo Creek
Damhead Creek
Eshcol Road
Kingsnorth
Oakham Ness Jetty
Slede Ooze
A B C D E
1 2 3 4 5 6 7 8
18
33
52
1 grid square represents 500 metres

F2
1 Denison Ms
2 Grebe Cl
3 High St
4 Little Oakham Ct

F3
1 Anchorage Cl

20
35
54
A
B
C
D
E
1
2
3
4
5
6
7
8
Isle of Grain
A228
Kent Oil Refinery
B2001
GRAIN ROAD
LC
Colemouth Creek
Elphinstone Point
Medway Towns
Kent
River Medway
Saltpan Reach
Sharp Ness
Burntwick Island
Stangate Spit
Stangate Cr
1 grid square represents 500 metres

Rose Court Farm
G1
1 Puffin Rd
2 Shelldrake Cl
3 Teal Cl
West
Pannell Road
St James C of E Primary School
21
Grain
B2001
Chapel Road
St James Road
Lane
Edinburgh Road
Coronation Road
St Werburgh Medical Practice
Grayne Avenue
Puffin Road
Lapwing Road
Chapel Road
Seaview
Port Victoria Road
Smithfield Road
Victoria Road
Medway Towns
Kent
Garrison Point
River Medway
West Minster
Cromwell Road
B2007
WHITEWAY ROAD
Queenborough Spit
Deadmans Island
West Swale
Jubilee Crescent
Coronation
High Street
South Street
West Street
Queenborough Yacht Club
West Point
55
F
G
H
J
K
1
2
3
4
5
6
7
8

B2
1 Black Horse Rd
2 Nelson Rd
A7
1 Petersham Gdns
A1
1 Rangeworth Pl
2 Studland Cl
B5
1 Ockham Dr
2 Ticehurst Cl
B6
1 Blackberry Fld
2 Flint Down Cl
3 Little Wood Cl
B8
1 Barcombe Cl
2 Clarendon Cl
C2
1 Cross Rd
2 The Lawns
C5
1 Dorchester Cl
2 Lullingstone Cl
D1
1 Rosewood Cl
D2
1 Sedcombe Cl
D8
1 Bannister Gdns
2 Stonegate Cl
3 Whitefield Cl
E8
1 Andrews Cl
Chislehurst & Sidcup Grammar School
School House Grammar School
Sidcup Station
Longlands Road
HURST
Birkbeck Primary School
Sidcup
HIGH STREET
ELM ROAD
STATION ROAD
THE GREEN
SIDCUP HILL
Queen Marys Hospital
A&E
Frognal Corner
Middlesex Hospital Sports Ground
DA14
Foots Cray
FOOTS CRAY HIGH ST
MAIDSTONE ROAD
CRAY ROAD
SIDCUP BY-PASS ROAD
EDGINGTON WAY
Ruxley Corner Industrial Estate
Scadbury Park
Midfield Primary School
Grays Farm Primary School
St Paul's Wood Hill
St Paul's Cray
SEVENOAKS WAY
Crayfield Industrial Park
Rectory Paddock School
Golf Centre
Ski Slope
Murray Business Centre
Sevenoaks Way Industrial Estate
St Pauls Cray C of E Primary School
Leesons Infant School
Orpington Retail Park
Poverest
56
1 grid square represents 500 metres

F3 1 Chantrey Cl
F4 1 Calvert Cl
Coldblow
F
G
H
J
K
Mount Mascal Farm
Betterton Dr
Riverside Road
Burnham Road
Water Lane
A223
Goldsmiths College Sports Ground
Royal Park Primary School
North Cray
NORTH CRAY ROAD
Bunkers Hill
Leafield La
Cocksure Lane
Tile Kiln Lane
Wickstead Cl
Briar Rd
Bexley
Kent County
K7 1 Nursery Cl
Eden Road
Summerhouse
Joyden's Wood
Woodlands
Park
Norfield Road
Squires Way
Chalet Cl
Summerhouse
Greenfield
Gattons Wy
Cemetery
Parsonage Lane
The Grove
The Spinney
James Way
Manor Farm
High Beeches
Bedensfield Clinic
Burdett Close
Cornell Close
Honeyden Road
N. Cray Rd
Barton Rd
North Cray Primary School
Ruxley
Whitney Walk
Chalk Wood
Golf Course
Stonehill Green
40
Bexley
Bromley
MAIDSTONE ROAD
Old Maidstone Road
B2173
A20(T)
Birchwood Road
Upper Hockenden
Cookham Road
Harst Way
Selah Drive
Leyton Cross
Birchwood County Primary School
Conifer Way
Russett Way
Wisteria Gdns
Alder Way
LONDON ROAD
Walnut Way
Elm Dr
Crescent Gdns
Lawn Cl
Heathwood Gdns
Cedar Close
Woodview Rd
Ash Cl
Hibbs Close
Almond Drive
Lesley Close
Kent County
Bromley
Chapman's Lane
Hockenden Lane
Lane
Hockenden
The Croft
Dale Road
Sermon Drive
Farm Avenue
Laburnum Av
Brook Road
Hart Dyke Road
Oliver Road
Reeves Cresent
Lime Road
Lavender Hill
Lilac Gdns
Star Lane
Lynden Way
Cherry Avenue
Moreillo Close
Hewett Place
Swanley Station
Sheepcote La
Sheepcote Farm
57
Ladds Way
Furness Swanley

A7
1 Greenside
2 The Orchard
3 Pear Tree Cl
4 St Lukes Cl
A6
1 Aspen Cl
A2
1 Joyden's Wd Rd
A8
1 Westharold
B7
1 Heath Cl
2 Maple Cl
3 Strawberry Flds
4 Whitecroft
B8
1 London Rd
2 Pemberton Gdns
3 Ruxton Ct
C7
1 Woodgers Gv
2 Woodlands Cl
3 Woodlands Ri
C8
1 Downsview Cl
2 The Grove
3 Old Farm Gdns
D6
1 Millbro
22
39
58
A
B
C
D
E
1
2
3
4
5
6
7
8
Coldblow
Leyton Cross
Dartford Golf Club
Bexley Hospital
Wilmington Grange Grammar School for Girls
Grammar School for Boys
High School
Primary School
Hook Green
Joyden's Wood
Joydens Wood CP School
Puddledock
Stonehill Green
Stanhill Farm
Hextable
Hextable CP School
Furness School
Hotel
Hextable Comprehensive School
Highlands Farm
Swanley Village
White Oak
Birchwood County Primary School
Swanley White Oak County Primary School
St Bartholomews Hospital
Primary School
Police Station
Swanley School
Doctors Surgery
Swanley Town Council
Park Road Industrial Estate
SWANLEY
Downsview Junior School
St Paul's C of E School
Parkwood Hall School
St Marys C of E Primary School
Swanley Station
High Firs CP School
Moreton Industrial Estate
Tile Kiln Lane
Dykewood Close
Summerhouse Drive
Birchwood Road
Hook Green Lane
Broad Lane
Common Lane
Leyton Cross Road
Rowhill Road
Puddledock Lane
TOP DARTFORD ROAD
Lower Road
St David's Road
Claremont Road
College Road
Egerton Avenue
Leydenhatch Lane
New Barn Road
MAIN ROAD B258
Highlands Hill
LONDON ROAD B2173
BARTHOLOMEW WAY
SWANLEY LANE
HIGH ST
Lullingstone Avenue
Beechenlea Lane
GOLDSEL ROAD
A20(T)
1 grid square represents 500 metres

K6
1 Smythe Rd
University of Greenwich
Oakfield CP Junior School
Powder Mill
Pearson Way
University of Greenwich
Applegarth Dr
Butterfly Av
Wilks Av
Saunders Way
Fawkes Avenue
Greenbanks
Oakfield Park Road
Carsington Gdns
The Spires
Monks Orchard
Wilmington Parish
Church Fld
CHURCH HILL B258
Hill Rd
Sackville Rd
Chave Road
Warren Road
Church Wk
Gothic Cl
A2(T)
A225
Darent Valley Path
River Darent
Road
Albert Rd
Huntfield
The Close
High Rd
Martin Rd
HIGH ROAD B258
Langworth Close
Garden Place
Orchard Way
South Vw Rd
Barn End Dr
PO
Whitehead Cl
Rowlatt Cl
Gerdview Dr
Rowhill School
Stock Lane
Brewers Field
Meadow Wk
Capel Pl
Kent County Council
B258
Burnt House Lane
Saxon Rd
Ethelbert Rd
Alfred Road
Harold Road
Ash Road
May Rd
Bott Rd
Cross Rd
Mill Road
Shirehall Road
Shirehall Road
Hawley
DA2
Royal Road
Junction
Darenth Road South
BARN END LANE
M25
Sutton Place
Parsonage Lane
Keith Av
Broadoak Cl
Goss Hill
Clement Street
Clement Street
Arnolds Lane
Cemetery
Church Road
Hone & Hawley
C of E Primary School
Hotham Cl
Sutton at Hone
Gildenhill Road
Balmoral Rd
Dairy Cl
Gravel Rd
Dartford FC
Barton Road
Barfield
Russell Place
Long Marsh Vw
Mead
Darent
Devon
Cedar Drive
Church Road
Ship Lane
Wood Street
Ship Lane
Road
Park Lane
Farningham Road Station
Homefield Farm
M25
A225
ROAD
Button Street
DARTFORD
Darent Valley Path
F G H J K
1 2 3 4 5 6 7 8
23
42
59

B7
1 Axtane Cl
2 Mill Stone Cl
B6
1 Mallys Pl
A6
1 Pembroke Pl
Fleet Downs
Darenth Park Av
Darenth Wood
Reading Cl
Foord Cl
TROLLING DOWN HILL B260
24
A
B
C
D
E
1
2
3
4
5
6
7
8
A2(T)
Darenth Wood
Junction 2
DA2
GREEN STREET GREEN ROAD
Coombfield Drive
Sinclair Way
Bennett Way
Moss Way
The Surgery
Lordswood Cl
Collier Crs
Langlands Dr
Hill Rise
Hillside
Court Rd
Stevens Cl
Riggeway
St Lukes Cl
Ladywood Road
Lane End
B260
Darenth Road South
Darenth Hill
Darenth
Darent Valley Path
Sutton Place
Parsonage Lane
Keith Av
Broadoak Cl
Arnolds Lane
Darenth CP School
St Margaret's Road
Cemetery
Church
41
MAIN ROAD
A225
Sutton at Hone & Hawley Parish Council
Tallents Cl
School
Hotham Cl
Sutton at Hone
Balmoral Rd
Dairy Cl
Gravel Rd
PO
Roman Villa Road
St Margaret's
Dartford FC
Barton Road
Barfield
Longmarsh Vw
Holmesdale Hill
Holmesdale Road
South Darenth
Gill's Road
Gill's Farm
Paddock Close
The Grange
Towers Wood
Coopers Close
Montgomery Road
Shrubbery Road
Mead
Darent
Devon Road
Cedar Drive
Mill Way
Millstone Mews
Water
Horton Kirby Trading Estate
East Hill
New Road
Farningham Road Station
Station Road
Gorringe Avenue
Victoria Dr
Pr Charles Avenue
Rabbits Farm
Rabbits Road
Wilson
Horton Kirby & South Darenth Parish Council
Skinney Lane
Horton Road
Horton Kirby C of E Primary School
ROAD A225
Glebe Pl
Forge Lane
The Street
Stack Road
60
Darent Valley Path
Lombard Street
Rashleigh Way
1 grid square represents 500 metres

K8
1 Park Dr
ROMAN ROAD
A296
F
G
H
25
J
K
Bean Lane
Stonewood
B255
Turner Rd
Fallowfield
Foxwood Rd
Drudgeon Way
Bramble Av
The Surgery
Beacon Drive
Stonewood
The Thrift
Page Cl
School Lane
Sandy Lane
Claywood Lane
Bean
HIGH STREET
PO
Bean Primary School
SOUTHFLEET ROAD
Sandy Lane
Park Corner Road
Northend
I
2
Lords Wood
B262
Bets
Craybourne
Mates Farm
Shellbank Lane
B255
BETSHAM ROAD B262
Westwood Road
3
SANDBANKS HILL
4
B262
Green Street Green
HIGHCROSS ROAD
44
Banbury Villas
Westwood
B255
B260
5
WHITEHILL RD
Grubb Street
GREEN STREET
B255
WHITEHILL ROAD
6
GREEN RD
MAIN ROAD B260
Pinden
West Shaw
Northdown Road
7
MAIN ROAD
Essex Road
Rowans Close
Kent Road
Station Road
Hartley Road
Langafel Close
PO
MAIN ROAD
Longfield Station
Oakwood
Cavendish Square
Dene Wk
Rl
St Marys Wy
B260
Dean Bottom
Bramblefield Close
The Crs
Bramblefield Close
Copse Side
8
Longfiel
Hottsfield
Ash Road
Quakers Close
Northfield
Culcroft
Merton Av
Pitfield
F
G
H
61
J
K
Hawthorns
Brambledown
Caxton
Well Field
Hoselands View
Larkwell Lane
Larks Field
Fawkham Rd
Downs Valley
Gresham Avenue

D8
1 Deerhurst Cl
2 Fawkham Av
C8
1 Firecrest Cl
2 The Maples
C7
1 The Close
E1
1 Ashmore Gdns
E7
1 Penshurst Cl
26
43
62
A2(T)
B259
A2260
Spring Head
WATLING STREET
HALL RD
PARK CORNER RD
Park Corner Road
STATION ROAD
B262
Northend
Sandy
Betsham
Crayburne
Mates Farm
Westwood Road
Dale Road
Sedleys C of E Primary School
Church St
Warren Road
Sedley
Southfleet
Monks Wk
Rectory Meadow
Red Street
Gloxinia Road
Brakefield Road
Hook Green
Banbury Villas
Hook Green Road
New Barn Road
Northfleet Green
Hazells
Broad Ditch Road
Fleet Road
Viking Rd
Pepper Hill
Pepper Hl
Painters Ash Lane
Roman Road
Masefield Rd
Primary School
Pickwick Gdns
Hog La
Ridgewood
New Barn
Southfleet Avenue
Hart Shaw
Studley Crescent
Birch Close
Foxwood Way
Longfield Avenue
Orchard Close
Dene Drive
Turnstone
Nuthatch
Starling Close
Shearwater
Lapwings
Bentley Cl
The Gables
Woodlea
Deerhurst Cl
Festival Avenue
Greenways
Fawkham Avenue
North Riding
Nurstead Avenue
Pescot Avenue
The Drive
The Hollies
Weird Wood
Oval
The Laurels
Fairlight Cross
The Yews
Pincroft Wood
Ferndene
MAIN ROAD
B260
Axton Chase School
Longfield
Dartford Hospital School
Langafel C of E Primary School
Gorse Wood Road
Longfield Station
Station Road
Hartley Road
Langafel Close
Oakwood
St Mary's Wy
Northdown Road
Hottsfield
Quakers Close
Culcroft
Ash Road
Merton Av
Pitfield
Porchester Close
Banckside
Well Field
Larks Field
Hartley Wood
Nurstead Lane
Nurstead Farm
Longfield Hill
Ryecroft
1 grid square represents 500 metres

F1
1 Everest Cl
2 Tensing Av
F2
1 Brightlands
2 Campion Cl
3 Mallow Cl
4 Nightingale Cl
5 Sorrell Wy
6 Wrens Cft
27
New House
St Georges C of E School
The Fairway
Dennis Road
Ascot Road
Smarts Road
Kings Farm
F5
1 Hadlow Wy
G1
1 Garden Rw
2 St Clements Cl
G2
1 Grangeways Cl
Singlewell
46
G5
1 Bramley Cl
G6
1 Bracondale Av
H3
1 Appleshaw Cl
2 Wentworth Cl
WATLING STREET
Watling Street
Mid Kent Golf Course
Shears Green CP School
Kings Farm Junior School
Kings Farm Infant School
Southfields School
Ifield School
Singlewell CP School
Istead Rise
Istead Rise
Istead Rise CP School
Arcadia Road
WROTHAM ROAD
A227
Nash Street
Nash Bank
Nash St
Walnut Hill Road
Church Road
Wealdway
Round Street
F
G
H
J
K
63
K2
1 Mcmillan Cl
J3
1 Broadwood
Nurstead
White Post Lane
Round Street

B3 1 Ryecroft 2 Salcote Rd
B2 1 Sara Pk
A3 1 Codrington Gdns
A226 ROCHESTER ROAD
28
C2 1 Mermerus Gdns
C8 1 Sarsens Cl
Parrock Farm
Kings Farm
Westcourt County Primary School
Raynehurst CP School
Thamesview School
Cascades Leisure Centre
Riverview Park
Riverview Primary School
Riverview Park Surgery
Riverview Clinic
Kings Farm Infant School
Ifield School
Southfields School
DA12
Singlewell
Singlewell CP School
Thong
Claylane Wood
45
WATLING STREET
A2(T)
Thong Lane
Shorne Ifield Road
Scotland Lane
Halfpence Lane
Henhurst
Henhurst Road
Jeskyns Farm
Jeskyns Road
Owletts (NT)
Battle Street
Church Road
Round Street
Cobham
Cobham CP School
The Street
Lodge Lane
Sole Street
64
1 grid square represents 500 metres

East Co H3
Manor 1 Crown Gn
F
G
H
29
J
K
Lower Road
Church
Church La
Green
Farm
Lane
Green Farm
Hill Farm
Burdett Av
Coutts Avenue
GRAVESEND ROAD
A226
Crown
Lane
Lane
Forge
Cob Drive
Shorne C of E Primary School
Hollands Cl
The Surgery
Shorne
Mill Hill Lane
The Street
PO
Manor Fld
Swiller's La
Warren View
Lodge Cl
Tanyard
Hill
Upper Ifield
Walmers Avenue
Briar Dale
Carton Road
Evergreen Close
Hollytree Drive
Chilton Drive
Darby Gardens
Norah Lane
Oak Drive
Villa
Brice Road
Peggoty Cl
Irvine
Court Wood
Lane
Peartree
Crutches Lane
48
Shorne Ridgeway
Randall Wood
Racefield Cl
Lane
Woodlands
The Ridgeway
Pondfield Lane
Bowesden Lane
Bowesden Lane
Great Crabbles Wood
Shorne Wood Country Park
Brewers Road
A2(T) WATLING STREET
A289
Pale Park
Old Watling Street
Colewood Drive
Crutches Lane
Junction 1
Squires Cl
Sharnfleet Dr
Golf Course
Knights Place
Cobham Park
Kent County
Medway Towns
Great Wood
1
2
3
4
5
6
7
8
Lode
F
G
H
65
J
K

B7
1 Cormorant Cl
2 Shearwater Cl
B3
1 The Larches
B2
1 Highwoods Cl
B8
1 Guildford Gdns
C8
1 Coventry Cl
2 Norwich Cl
3 Penguin Cl
4 Uplands Cl
D5
1 Conway Cl
D6
1 Burleigh Cl
2 Deacon Cl
E5
1 Hillyfield Cl
2 Hyperion Dr
3 Orchard Av
4 Sandycroft Rd
E6
1 Roan Ct
2 Westergate Rd
E7
1 The Mews
2 Tintagel Gdns
30
47
66
A
B
C
D
E
1
2
3
4
5
6
7
8
Higham
Gadshill
Strood
Chalk Road
Lower Rochester Road
Lake Drive
Higham Hall
Steadman Close
Station
School Lane
Way
Two Gates Farm
Higham CP School
White House Farm
Land
Hill Farm
Taylors Lane
The Knowle
High View
St John's Rd
Mountbatten Av
Hermitage Road
Hillyfield
Avenue
Norah Lane
Briar Dale
Carton Road
Evergreen Close
Hollytree Drive
Chilton Drive
Darby Gardens
Oak Drive
Beech Grove
Ash Crs
Marshlands Medical Practice
Elm Close
Telegraph Hill
The Braes
Hayes Cl
Forge Lane
Dombey Close
Brice Rd
Villa Road
Peggoty Cl
Irvine Rd
A226
GRAVESEND ROAD
Gads Hill House School
Charles Dickens Avenue
Copperfield Crescent
Crutches Lane
A289
Kent County
Medway Towns
Dillywood Lane
Little Hermitage
Great Crabbles Wood
BROMPTON
Hanlech Close
B2108
Woodview Rise
Hill Farm
Westergate
Gorse Road
Broom Hill Road
Fountain Rd
Carisbrooke Rd
Beaufort
Abbey Court Special Sch
REDE COURT ROAD
Romsey Close
Clinton Av
Cobb Cl
Russet
Crispin
Bramley Rise
Worcester Close
Allington Drive
Abbey Road
Leybourne Road
Chapter Road
Linwood Av
Cadnam Cl
Dean Rd
Swain
Chapter Farm
Colewood Drive
Old Watling Street
WATLING STREET
A2
Squires Cl
The Shades
Millfordhope Rd
Stangate Rd
Parkfields
Chetney Cl
Swale Road
Copperhouse Rd
Yantlet Drive
Chapter School
Carnation Road
Thurston Drive
Columbine Close
Daffodil
Lancelot Avenue
Elaine Avenue
River Dr
Cobham Cl
Harvel Av
Stour Close
Strood Swimming Pool
Witham Way
Bligh Way CP Sch
Scholars Rise
Elaine CP School
Clifton Cl
Tamar Dr
Dart Close
Orchid Close
Pelican Close
Albatross Av
Bligh Way
Tern Crs
Curlew Crs
Seagull Road
Hyacinth Road
Columbine Road
Galahad Av
Darnley Road
Maple Road
Cedar Road
Hawthorn Road
Beech Rd
Ash Rd
Widgeon
Southwell
St Albans
Portsmouth Cl
Fulmar Road
Southwark Rd
Child Health Cen
Hawthorn Rd
Oak
Willow
Holly Road
Chelmsford
Chester
Lilac Crs
Lilac Road
Strood Cemetery
Sherwin Knight County Junior & Infant School
Winston Rd
Laburnam
Road
Poplar
Sycamore Road
Ballard Business Park
M2
Great Wood
Rushdean Rd
A228
1 grid square represents 500 metres

F5
1 Goldsworth Dr
2 Rosemount Ct
3 Sherbourne Dr
F6
1 Morgan Rd
F7
1 Stanhope Rd
G5
1 Smetham Gdns
G6
1 Florence St
2 Martin Rd
3 Millpond Cl
4 St Michaels Ct
G7
1 Albert Pl
2 Burgess Rd
3 Doggett's Sq
4 Marsh St
5 Tolgate La
H5
1 Mayfair
2 Thirlmere Cl
H6
1 Murray Rd
2 Peckham Cl
3 Watermill Cl
H7
1 Kingswear Gdns
2 South Eastern Rd
H8
1 Acorn Wharf Rd
2 Epaul La
3 George La
4 Gundulph Sq
5 Northgate
6 Parrs Haed Ms
K6
1 Chaucer Cl
J4
1 Jarrett Av
J3
1 Greenfields Cl
31
50
67
Mockbeggar
Chattenden
Noke Street
Wainscott
Frindsbury
Upper Upnor
Lower Upnor
ROCHESTER
Bunters Hill Road
Common Road
Haven Street
Lochat Road
Dillywood Lane
LOWER ROCHESTER ROAD
B2000
Higham Road
Islingham Road
Woodfield Way
Upchat Road
FOUR ELMS HILL
HOO ROAD
HOLLYWOOD LANE
A289
B2108
BROMPTON FARM ROAD
FRINDSBURY HILL A228
ANTHONYS WAY A289
FRINDSBURY ROAD
Upnor Road
Stonehorse Lane
Stone House Farm
Temple School
Hilltop Primary School
Wainscott CP School
Doctors Surgery
Loaland Business Centre
Sheldon Business Cen
Kenden Business Park
Spectrum Business Centre
Arden Business Park
Boyd Business Cen
Arden Business Centre
Shamel Business Centre
Phoenix Industrial Estate
Neptune Industrial Estate
Henley Business Park
Central Business Park
Castle View Business Cen
Knights Park Industrial Est
Strood Station
Strood Yacht Club
Temple Manor
Rochester Station
Medway Little Thtr
Crown Clinic
Kings School Rochester
The Guildhall Mus
Doctors Surg
St Nicholas School
Sikh Temple
Siri Guru Ravidass Temple
The Medical Cen
Deacon Trading Cen
LONDON RD
HIGH STREET
COMMERCIAL ROAD
STATION ROAD
NORTH ST
GUN LANE
KNIGHT ROAD
PRIORY ROAD
CORPORATION STREET
A2 HIGH STREET
Limehouse Reach
Saxon Shore Way
Royal Eagle Close
Neptune Way
Sir Thomas Longley Rd
Commissioner's Road
Cranmere Court
Whitewall Road
Parsonage Lane
Church Green
Cooling Road
Cliffe Road
Mill Rd
Goddington Rd
Kitchener Road
Brompton Rd
Cambridge Road
Gordon Road
Weston Road
Northcote Rd
MEDWAY ST
GLOBE LA
Cottage Road

B7
1 Gordon Rd
2 May Ter
A5
1 Admiralty Rd
2 Admiralty Ter
3 Richmond Cl
A2
1 Old School Ct
32
A
B
C
D
E
Hoo St Werburgh
Chattenden
Swinton Av
Kirby Road
Chilliwack Road
Chattenden Lane
Lochat Road
RATCLIFFE HIGHWAY
Pankhurst Road
Robson Drive
St Werburgh CP Junior School
The Hundred of Hoo School
Hoo St Werburgh C P School
Pottery Road
Main Road
B8
1 Barfleur Manor
2 Flaxmans Ct
3 Mansion Rw
4 River St
Kitchener Road
MAIN ROAD
A228
Broadwood Rd
Elm Avenue
Broad Street
Saxon Shore Way
Hoo Lodge
C4
1 M'dowsweet Vw
FOUR ELMS HILL
Upchat Road
Medway Yacht Club
Lower Upnor
Upnor Road
C5
1 Partridge Dr
2 The Whimbrels
River Medway
St Mary's Island
The Kings Family Practice
Redshank Road
Woodlark Road
Island Way East
Primary School
The Crescent
Maritime Way
Upnor Castle
High St
49
Upper Upnor
C8
1 Singapore Dr
A289
Quayside
Compass Centre
North Rd
Pembroke
University of Greenwich
BARRACK ROAD
Pier Approach Rd
PIER RD
D7
1 Augusta Cl
2 Exmouth Rd
3 King William Rd
4 Latimer Pl
5 The Ridgeway
6 Virginia Rd
7 Wharf Rd
3
4
Chatham Reach
Main Gate Road
Dock Road
MEDWAY ROAD
B2004
Cumberland Road
Sidney Rd
St Andrew Rd
Selbourne Rd
Hamilton Rd
D8
1 Arden St
2 Chatsworth Rd
3 Cornwall Rd
4 Dalton St
5 High St
6 Jubilee Ter
7 Stanley Rd
Neptune Industrial Estate
WOOD ST
PR ARTHUR RD
Trinity Road
Richmond County Infants Sch
Arden Junior School
A231
BROMPTON ROAD
Brompton Medical Cen
Black Lion Leisure Centre
Cottage Road
DOCK ROAD
New Stairs
Brompton
JEFFERY ST
Railway Street Industrial Est
Historical Society Museum
The Brook Theatre Arts & Entertainment Ltd
68
Brompton Westbrook CP School
E7
1 Camden Rd
2 Devonshire Rd
3 Lincon Rd
E8
1 Brooklyn Paddock
2 Cleveland Rd
3 Crown St
4 Macdonald Rd
Sikh Temple
Franklin Road
1 grid square represents 500 metres
Great Lines

F1
1 Nursery Gdns
F2
1 Whitehouse Cl
F3
Street names for this grid square are listed at the back of the index
33
F
G
H
J
K
Jacob's
Lane
Eshcol
Kingsnorth
Grandsire Gardens
Werburgh Medical Centre
Bell's Lane
Peal Cl
Peal Cl
Stoke Road
Coombe Road
Flack Gdns
Butt Haw Close
Brookside
PO
Church St
Everest Dr
Everest Ms
Vicarage
Lane
Church Farm
Abbots
Court
Road
Abbot's Court
Saxon Shore Way
Vicarage La
Saxon Shore Way
Poplar Close
Cedar Road
Birch Rd
Copse
Hoo Flats
1
2
3
4
5
6
7
8
F8
1 Firethorn Cl
2 Lobelia Cl
J8
1 Copperhouse La
Darnet Fort
52
Pinup Reach
RSPB Site
Gillingham Reach
5
The Strand
Strand Ap Rd
A289
Saxon Shore Way
St Albans Cl
Baron Cl
Christmas
Layfield Road
Waterside Lane
Margate Cl
Church St
Holly Close
Leet Cl
Shore Way
Court Ldg Rd
Kg Edward Rd
Eastern
Dial Cl
Dial Rd
PIER ROAD
Lower Wy
Gillingham Green
Saxon
Grange
Road
Church
Castlemaine Avenue
Carrington Close
Hewitt Cl
Lwr Woodlands Rd
Cypress Close
Grove Road
Danes Hill
Lwr Rainham Rd
Plantation Road
Grange
LOWER RAINHAM ROAD
B2004
Saxon Shore Way
Saxon Shore Way
East Court Farm
Portland Rd
Cavendish Avenue
Elm Rd
Oak Av
Maple Avenue
The Vineries
Bluebell
Freesia Close
Ingram Road
Granville Rd
Coniston
Grange Road
Road
Woodlands Road
Hazlemere Drive
Thirlmere Cl
Tangmere Cl
69
Featherby Road
ROAD
Road
Eastcourt Lane
Lower Twydall
LOWER RAINHAM ROAD
Sharps Green
Riverside Country Park
Sunnymead Avenue
Redfern Av
Gillingham Football Club
Chicago Av
Road
Woodlands Road Cemetery
Grange Road
Lane

A
B
34
C
D
E
1
2
3
4
5
6
7
8
51
70
Slede Ooze
Long Reach
River Medway
Darnet Fort
South Yantlet Creek
Pinup Reach
RSPB Site
Nor Marsh
Bartlett Creek
Saxon Shore Way
East Court Farm
Sharps Green
LOWER RAINHAM ROAD
Riverside Country Park
Rainham Creek
Motney Hill
Eastcourt Lane
Lower Twydall
Road
1 grid square represents 500 metres

F
G
H
35
J
K
Burntwick Island
Oakham Ness
Keitholé Reach
Bishop Spit
Sharfleet
Medway Towns
Kent
Ham Ooze
Bishop Ooze
54
Half Acre
Bayford
Shoregate Lane
Poot Lane
Saxon Shore Way
Ham Green
71
Wetham Green
Otterham Creek
Horsham Marsh
1
2
3
4
5
6
7
8

Sharp Ness
...ntwick ...and
Stangate Spit
36
A
B
C
D
E
1
2
3
4
5
6
7
8
53
72
Stangate Creek
Sharfleet Creek
Greenborough Marshes
Slayhills Marsh
Slaughterhouse Point
Millfordhope Marsh
Twinney Creek
Halstow Creek
Barksore Marshes
Saxon Shore Way
Funton
1 grid square represents 500 metres

Queenborough Spit
Deadmans Island
37
F
G
H
J
K
WHITEWAY ROAD
Jubilee Crescent
Coronation Crescent
High Street
South Street
West Street
Queenborough Yacht Club
West Point
Klondyke Industrial Estate
Long Reach
Rushenden Road
Alsager Avenue
First Avenue
Second Avenue
Well Road
Swale Avenue
River View
Ferry View
Hillside Avenue
Rushenden
Manor
Rushenden
Chetney Marshes
Saxon Shore Way
Ferry Marshes
Chetney Cotts
Old Ferry Road
Bedlams Bottom
Raspberry Hill Lane
73
1
2
3
4
5
6
7
8

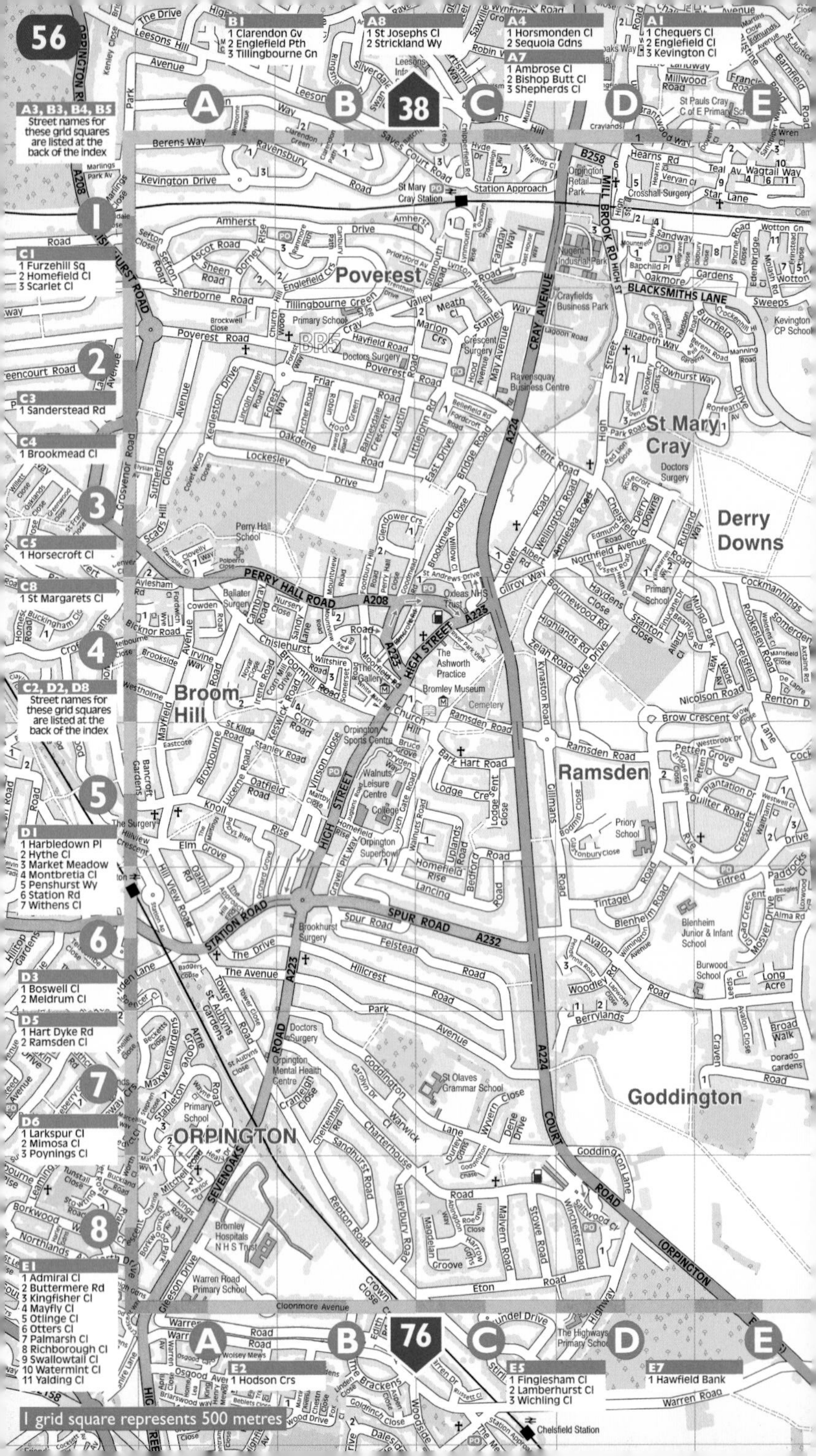
B1
1 Clarendon Gv
2 Englefield Pth
3 Tillingbourne Gn
A8
1 St Josephs Cl
2 Strickland Wy
A4
1 Horsmonden Cl
2 Sequoia Gdns
A7
1 Ambrose Cl
2 Bishop Butt Cl
3 Shepherds Cl
A1
1 Chequers Cl
2 Englefield Cl
3 Kevington Cl
38
A3, B3, B4, B5
Street names for these grid squares are listed at the back of the index
C1
1 Furzehill Sq
2 Homefield Cl
3 Scarlet Cl
C3
1 Sanderstead Rd
C4
1 Brookmead Cl
C5
1 Horsecroft Cl
C8
1 St Margarets Cl
C2, D2, D8
Street names for these grid squares are listed at the back of the index
D1
1 Harbledown Pl
2 Hythe Cl
3 Market Meadow
4 Montbretia Cl
5 Penshurst Wy
6 Station Rd
7 Withens Cl
D3
1 Boswell Cl
2 Meldrum Cl
D5
1 Hart Dyke Rd
2 Ramsden Cl
D6
1 Larkspur Cl
2 Mimosa Cl
3 Poynings Cl
E1
1 Admiral Cl
2 Buttermere Rd
3 Kingfisher Cl
4 Mayfly Cl
5 Otlinge Cl
6 Otters Cl
7 Palmarsh Cl
8 Richborough Cl
9 Swallowtail Cl
10 Watermint Cl
11 Yalding Cl
E2
1 Hodson Crs
E5
1 Finglesham Cl
2 Lamberhurst Cl
3 Wichling Cl
E7
1 Hawfield Bank
76
Poverest
St Mary Cray
Derry Downs
Broom Hill
Ramsden
ORPINGTON
Goddington
BR5
St Mary Cray Station
Chelsfield Station
PERRY HALL ROAD
HIGH STREET
CRAY AVENUE
SPUR ROAD
STATION ROAD
SEVENOAKS ROAD
COURT ROAD
MILL BROOK RD
BLACKSMITHS LANE
1 grid square represents 500 metres

K1
1 Wood End
K3
1 Sounds Lodge
Hockenden
K4
1 Barnfield Cl
39
58
77
F
G
H
J
K
1
2
3
4
5
6
7
8
Star Lane
Sheepcote Lane
Bourne Wood
Sheepcote Farm
Furness Swanley Football Club
Swanley Station
Lynden Way
Laburnum Avenue
Rowan Road
Cherry Avenue
Lilac Gdns
Hewett Place
Lime Road
Stones Cross Road
Green Court Road
Shawcroft School
Kevingtown
ROAD
B258
Crouch Farm
Crockenhill CP School
Cemetery
Bransell Close
CRAY ROAD B258
MAIN RD
Church Road
Tylers Green Road
Old Chapel Road
Tudor Court
Crockenhi
Darns Hill
Harvest Way
Waldens Road
East Hall Road
Lane
Lone Barn
Daltons Road
Gorse Road
Crown Wood
Skeet Hill Lane
Skibbs Lane
Bromley
Kent County
Parkgate Road
Well Hill
Park House
Chelsfield Park Hospital
Cannock House School
Chelsfield Primary School
Bucks Cross Road
Hawstead Lane
Woodlands
Chelsfield
Well
Firmingers Road

A3
1 West View Rd
A2
1 Heather End
A1
1 Apple Orch
2 Edwards Gdns
3 Ellis Waterton Cl
4 Leewood Pl
5 Southern Pl
B1
1 Greenacre Cl
2 Lila Pl
3 Station Rd
B2
1 Hazel End
2 Leyhill Cl
3 Overmead
C1
1 Bevan Pl
2 Pine Cl
3 St Georges Rd
4 Springfield Av
D1
1 Bremner Cl
2 Rogers Ct
3 Southview Cl
D2
1 Mead Cl
40
57
78
SWANLEY
BR8
Swanley Station
St Marys C of E Primary School
Swanley Town Council
Swanley School
High Firs CP School
Furness Swanley Football Club
Moreton Industrial Estate
Pedham Place Industrial Estate
Junction 3/1
Petham Court
Gosenhill Farm
Crockenhill
Crockenhill CP
Cemetery
Wested
Hulberry
Highcroft
Woodmount
Park Gate House
Lullingstone Park Farm
Darent Valley Path
Beechen Wood
M25
A20(T)
B258
B2173
Eynsford Road
Crockenhill Lane
Wested Lane
Green Court Road
Church Road
Newports
Parkgate Road
Goldsel Road
London Road
Beechenlea Lane
Cranleigh Drive
Pinks Hill
Glendale
Salisbury Avenue
Montague Close
Azalea Drive
Station Approach
Ladds Way
Phillip Avenue
1 grid square represents 500 metres

G8
1 Station Rd
F
G
H
41
J
K
Button Street
Farningham Woods
(Nature Reserve)
Calfstock Lane
DARTFORD
ROAD
A225
1
Darent Valley Path
2
Franks
Lane
Darent Valley Path
The Folly
Hill Farm
Farningham Hill Rd
ardrop
strial Park
Old Dartford Road
LONDON ROAD
A20
MAIN ROAD
M20
3
Eglantine
PO
Dartford Road
High Street
River Darent
The Mill House
Horton Way
Hillside
Farningham
4
Sparepenny Lane
Oliver Crescent
South Hall Cl
Till Av
White Post Hill
Tilmans Mead
Braeside Surgery
60
EYNSFORD ROAD
Alban Crescent
Beesfield Lane
DA4
5
MAIN
A225
Old Mill Cl
Mill Lane
Priory Lane
Priory Fields
Beesfield Farm
Anthony Roper
County Primary
School
Eynsford Castle
HIGH STREET
Tower Croft
Donkey
Lan
6
Eynsford Cricket Club
EYNSFORD
Darent Valley Path
Riverside
Lane
Home Farm
PO
PH
Bower Lane
Maplescombe Lane
Lullingstone
STATION ROAD
Saddler's Park
Pollyhaugh
7
Pollyhaugh Farm
St. Martins Drive
Birch Close
Eynsford Rise
8
Eynsford Station
Chalkhurst
F
G
H
79
J
K
Park House
Maplescomb
Road
Austin

Horton Road
Skinney
Horton Primary
42
A
B
C
D
E
Stack Road
Horton Kirby
The Street
Glebe Pl
Forge Lane
Churchill Road
Lombard Street
Rashleigh Way
Darent Valley Path
Rays Hill
Reynolds Place
Franks Lane
Saxon Pl
Eglantine Lane
Eglantine Farm
Mussenden Farm
Mussenden Lane
School Lane
DARTFORD ROAD
A225
1
2
3
4
5
6
7
8
M20
Farningham
Charton
Horton Wood
White Post Hill
Braeside Surgery
59
Beesfield Lane
Beesfield Farm
MAIN ROAD
GORSE HILL
A20
Donkey Lane
Maplescombe Lane
Gabrielspring Rd
Gabriel Spring Road (East)
Speed Gate
Scratchers Lane
Colin Chapman Way
Brands Hatch Motor Racing Circuit
80
Maplescombe
Symonds Close
Road
Gillies Road
Viking Way
1 grid square represents 500 metres

K6
1 Ayelands
2 Coltstead
Dean Bottom
F
G
H
43
J
K
Chase School
Longfiel
Hottsfield
Quakers Close
Copse Side
The Crs
Ash Road
Merton Av
Culcroft
Pitfield
Brambledown
Caxton
Bankside
Hoselands View
Larkwell Lane
Larks Field
Downs Valley
Fawkham Road
Gresham Avenue
Woodland Avenue
Beeches Farm
Castle Hill
Old Downs
Dickens Close
Green Way
Stack Lane
Church Road
Hartley Green
Broomfields
Culvey Cl
Carmelite Way
School
Hartley
Cherry Trees
Canada Farm Road
Hartley CP School
Round Ash Wy
Conifer Av
Oast Way
The Warrens
St John's Lane
Hill Shaw
Corinthian Sports Club
Fairby Lane
Billings
Scudders Hill
Chantry Avenue
Tates Orchard
1
2
3
4
5
6
7
8
Court Lodge
DA3
Manor Lane
Three Gates Road
Grove Farm
62
Fawkham Primary School
Valley Road
Milestone
Fawkham Manor
Calinn Croft
Farm Holt
Fawkham Manor Hospital
Chapel Wood Road
Chapel Wood
Penenden
Church Road
Bazes Shaw
Speedgate Hill
Ayelands
Millfield La
Millfield
Butchers Lane
New Ash Green County Primary School
Michaels Lane
The Surgery
Sun Hill
Turner's Oak Shaw
The Mo
Centre Rd
Over Minnis
Minnis
Lambarde
North
PH
PO
Small Grains
Fawkham Green
Coltstead
West Yoke
Brands Hatch Road
Fawkham Green Road
Beechcroft Farm Industrial Estate
Punch Croft
Mnr Forstal
Knights Cft
Redhill Road
Hotel
Rogers Wood Lane
Billet Hill
Ash Road
Road
81
Crowhurst Lane
The Street
A

Longfield
Hartley
Hartley Green
New Ash Green
Longfield Hill
Ash
New Street
DA3
44
61
82
A
B
C
D
E
1
2
3
4
5
6
7
8
A2
1 Wickhams Wy
A1
1 Everglade Cl
2 Merryfields Cl
3 Perran Cl
4 Silverdale
MAIN ROAD
B260
Pescot Avenue
The Drive
Fawkham Avenue
Fairlight Cross
The Hollies
The Oval
The Laurels
Ferndene
North Riding
Pincroft
Old
Axton Chase School
Hottsfield
Quakers Close
Culcroft
Merton Av
Pitfield
Bramblecown
Caxton Cl
Porchester Close
Well Field
Larks Field
Gresham Avenue
Woodland Avenue
Downs Valley
Old Downs
Ash Road
Dickens Close
Green Way
Church Road
Stack Lane
Carmelite Way
Cherry Trees
School
Culvey Cl
Hartley CP School
Round Ash Wy
Conifer Av
Oast Way
Fairby Lane
The Warrens
St John's Lane
Billings
Hill Shaw
Grange Way
Tates Orchard
Gorse Wood Road
Gorse Way
Beechlands Close
Springcroft
Manor Drive
Manor Lane
Hartley Wood
Nurstead Lane
Nurstead Farm
Ryecroft
Manor Road
Manor Farm
Middleton Farm
Grange Lane
Hartley Bottom Road
Milestone School
Caling Croft
Farm Holt
Bazes Shaw
Chapel Wood Road
Chapel Wood
Millfield
Ayelands Lane
Penenden
New Ash Green County Primary School
The Surgery
Turner's Oak Shaw
Coltstead
Centre Rd
Over Minnis
Lambardes
North Ash Road
Spring Cross
Punch Croft
Knights Cft
Redhill Road
Bowes Wood
Redhill Wood
Hartley Hill
Idleigh Court
Idleigh Court Road
New Street Road
Rectory Road
The Street
Langafield C of E Primary School
Elbo Woo
1 grid square represents 500 metres

H3
1 Cedar Cl
2 The Medlars
H4
1 Lances Cl
2 School Cl
F
G
H
45
J
K
Round Street
Round Street
Wealdway
Copt Hall Road
Park Hill
Nurstead Church Lane
White Post Lane
1
H6
1 Meadfield Rd
2 Oakmead
Meopham Station
Station Road
Birtrick Dr
John's Road
Orchard Drive
New Road
Edmund Cl
Ediva Rd
Nursery Road
Fairview Gardens
Meopham Station
Sole Street
Sallows Shaw
Manor Road
Green Lands
2
J4
1 Dormers Dr
Sole Street Station
LONGFIELD ROAD
Chesnunt Close
Pine Rise
A227
WROTHAM ROAD
Norwood Lane
Rowan Close
Walnut Tree Way
Melliker Lane
Melliker
Hook Green
The Russets
The Pippins
Wrotham Rd
Denesway
Walk
Poplar
Tradescant Dr
Mulberry Close
Lilac Place
3
Camer Road
Camer Street
J6
1 Blenheim Cl
Camer
Camer Park Country Park
Strand Cl
Evenden Road
Huntingfield Road
Green Lane
B260
DA13
Camer Park Road
4
Helen Alison School
Meopham CP School
64
5
Shipley Hills
Shipley Hills Road
Foxendown Lane
The Street
MEOPHAM
Foxendown
Brimstone Hill
Meopham School
Arnold Av
Hadley Close
Cheyne Walk
Warwick Gdns
Meopham Medical Centre
Lomer Farm
WROTHAM ROAD
Millers Walk
Grenville Close
Whitehill Road
6
Brimstone Wood
Cricketers Drive
Pitfield Drive
Meopham Green
7
Dean Lane
Meopham Parish Council
Windmill Business Centre
SOUTH STREET
Steele's Lane
Bowes Industrial Centre
Field Road
Steele's Lane
8
Horn's Oak Road
Chandler's Hill
Leylands
Priestwood
Road
F
G
H
83
J
K
Street
Chandler's Road
Plug Lane
Priestwood Green

Round Street
Cobham
The Street
Cobham CP School
Lodge Lane
Lawrence Dr
Owletts (NT)
46
Battle Street
Sole Street
Sallows Shaw
The Beeches
Manor Road
Manor Ct
Scratton Fields
Green Lands
Gold Street
Sole Street Station
Batt's Road
Cobhambury Road
Cobhambury Wood
Camer
Camer Street
Camer Park Country Park
DA13
Henley Street
63
Park Road
Pigsdean Rd
Buckland Road
Luddesdown Road
Cutter Ridge Road
Oakenden
Oakenden Road
Luddesdown
Lane
Foxendown
Brimstone Hill
Brimstone Wood
Wealdway
Dene Manor
Dean Lane
Coomb Hill
Chandler's Hill
Chandler's Road
84
Plug Lane
Lockyers Hill
Wrangling Lane
Green
1 grid square represents 500 metres

F
G
H
47
J
K
Kent County
Medway Towns
Great Wood
Lodge Farm
1
2
3
4
5
6
7
8
Warren Road
Lower Bush
Bush Road
North Downs Way
Nine Acres Rd
Poplicans Road
Charles
Ladywood Rd
Court Lodge
Upper Bush Road
Upper Bush
Red Wood
Bush Road
Cuxton County
Woodhurst Cl
66
Kent County
Medway Towns
Dean Farm
North Wood
Rochester Road
North Downs Way
North Halling
A228
Formby Rd
Wingate Wood
Pilgrims Road
New Town
Stake
Kent Rd
F
G
H
85
J
K
Halling Station
Marsh Road
Halling
Upper Halling
Primrose Road
Grove Road
Bradley Rd
The Street
Vicarage Cl
A228
High Street
Low Meadow
Cem

1 grid square represents 500 metres

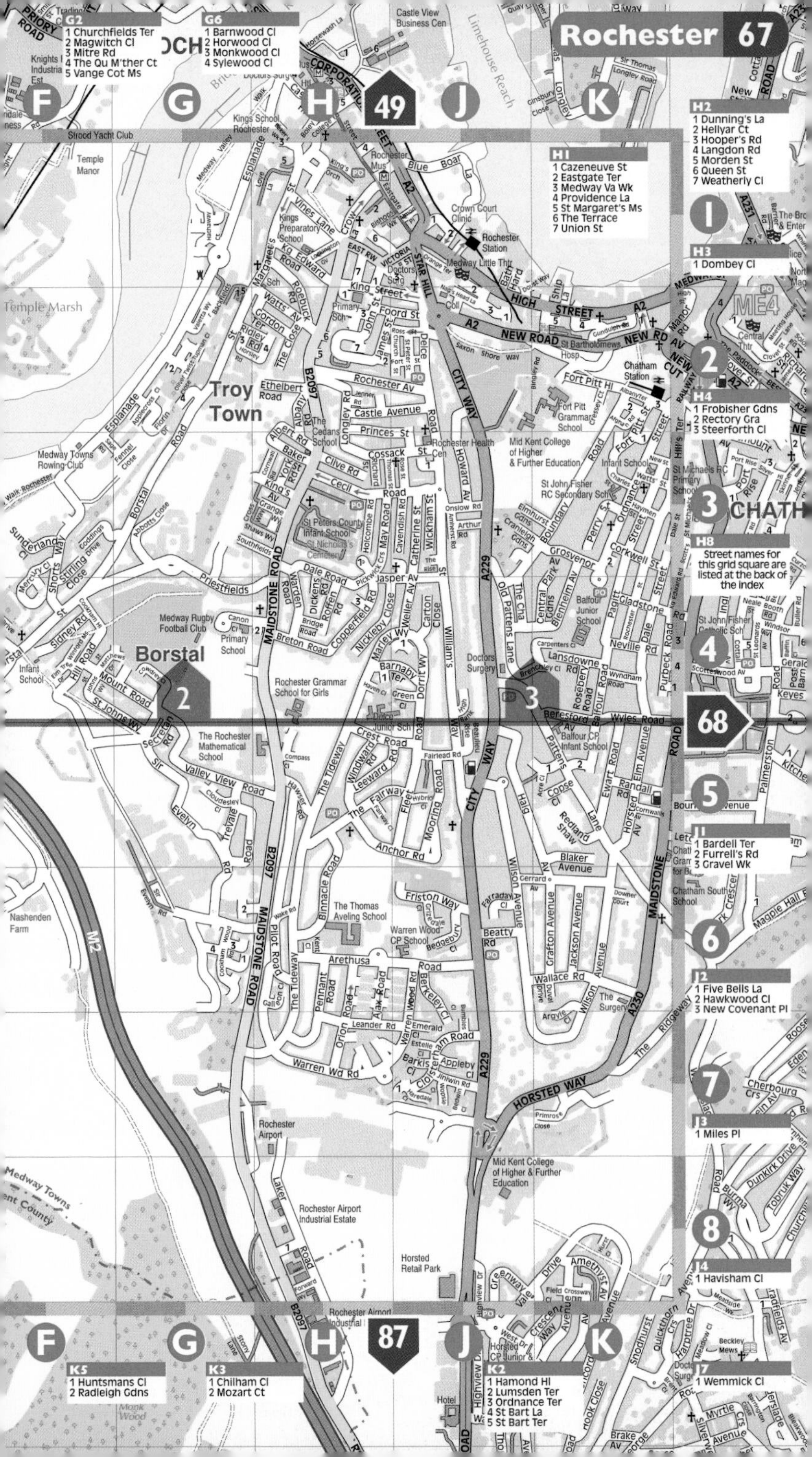
G2
1 Churchfields Ter
2 Magwitch Cl
3 Mitre Rd
4 The Qu M'ther Ct
5 Vange Cot Ms
G6
1 Barnwood Cl
2 Horwood Cl
3 Monkwood Cl
4 Sylewood Cl
H1
1 Cazeneuve St
2 Eastgate Ter
3 Medway Va Wk
4 Providence La
5 St Margaret's Ms
6 The Terrace
7 Union St
H2
1 Dunning's La
2 Hellyar Ct
3 Hooper's Rd
4 Langdon Rd
5 Morden St
6 Queen St
7 Weatherly Cl
H3
1 Dombey Cl
H4
1 Frobisher Gdns
2 Rectory Gra
3 Steerforth Cl
H8
Street names for this grid square are listed at the back of the index
J1
1 Bardell Ter
2 Furrell's Rd
3 Gravel Wk
J2
1 Five Bells La
2 Hawkwood Cl
3 New Covenant Pl
J3
1 Miles Pl
J4
1 Havisham Cl
J7
1 Wemmick Cl
K2
1 Hamond Hl
2 Lumsden Ter
3 Ordnance Ter
4 St Bart La
5 St Bart Ter
K3
1 Chilham Cl
2 Mozart Ct
K5
1 Huntsmans Cl
2 Radleigh Gdns
49
68
87
F
G
H
J
K
1
2
3
4
5
6
7
8
Troy Town
Borstal
Temple Marsh
Temple Manor
Strood Yacht Club
Castle View Business Cen
Limehouse Reach
Kings School Rochester
Rochester Mus
Crown Court Clinic
Rochester Station
Medway Little Thtr
Chatham Station
Fort Pitt Grammar School
Mid Kent College of Higher & Further Education
St John Fisher RC Secondary Sch
Kings Preparatory School
The Cedars School
Rochester Health Cen
St Peters County Infant School
St Nicholas's Cemetery
Medway Towns Rowing Club
Medway Rugby Football Club
Rochester Grammar School for Girls
The Rochester Mathematical School
The Thomas Aveling School
Warren Wood CP School
Balfour Junior School
Balfour CP Infant School
Chatham South School
Rochester Airport
Rochester Airport Industrial Estate
Horsted Retail Park
Nashenden Farm
ME4
Central Thtr
CHATHAM
CORPORATION STREET
HIGH STREET
NEW ROAD
CITY WAY
MAIDSTONE ROAD
HORSTED WAY
Esplanade
Borstal Road
Priestfields
Ethelbert Road
Rochester Av
Castle Avenue
Princes St
Cossack St
Cecil Road
Dale Road
Jasper Av
Crest Road
Valley View Road
Arethusa Road
Anchor Rd
Friston Way
Warren Wd Rd
Wilson Avenue
Grafton Avenue
Jackson Avenue
Blaker Avenue
Wyles Road
Beresford Av
Lansdowne Rd
Gladstone Rd
Corkwell St
Grosvenor Av
The Ridgeway
M2
A2
A229
A230
A231
B2097

B7, C4, C7, D1
Street names for these grid squares are listed at the back of the index
A6
1 Thorndike Cl
A8
1 Walderslade Rd
A5
1 Underdown Av
A3
1 Armada Wy
2 Claremont Wy
3 Silver Hill Gdns
4 Warner St
A1, A2, A4, B3
Street names for these grid squares are listed at the back of the index
B2
1 Church St
2 Hillside Rd
3 Meadowbank Rd
4 Rope Wk
5 Slicketts Hl
6 Union St
B4
1 Damiem Cl
2 Terence Cl
3 Westbrooke Cl
B8
1 Timberbank
C1
1 Upper Britton Pl
C3
1 Bank St
2 Constitution Hl
3 Leonard Rd
4 Ocelot Ct
5 Short St
6 Whitehorse Hl
C6
1 Cameron Cl
2 Greenbank
C8
1 Defoe Cl
2 Shackleton Cl
3 Wren Wy
D4
1 Chickfield Gdns
2 Coronation Rd
3 Pheasant Rd
4 Watchmans Ter
5 York Hl
D6
1 Maunders Cl
D7
1 Hampshire Cl
D5, D7, D8
Street names for these grid squares are listed at the back of the index
E1, E2
Street names for these grid squares are listed at the back of the index
1 grid square represents 500 metres
50
67
88
Brompton
CHATHAM
Luton
Wayfield
HALE
Great Lines
Historical Society Museum
The Brook Theatre Arts & Entertainment Ltd
North Kent Magistrates Court
Brompton Westbrook CP School
Upbury Manor School
Medway Hospital
Chatham Grammar School for Girls
Medway Community College
Fort Luton Museum
Chatham Grammar School for Boys
Chatham South School
Wayfield CP School
Kingfisher CP School
Bradfields School
Capstone Park Country Park
Walderslade Medical Cen
Princes Park Medical Cen
Churchill Clinic
Premier Business Park
Luton Medical Centre
Stonecross Surg
Byron CP School
Napier Road Junior Sch
Secondary School
Greenvale Infant School
St John Fisher Catholic Sch
St Michaels RC Primary School
St John Fisher RC Secondary Sch
Balfour CP Infant School
Cemetery
HIGH STREET
NEW ROAD
CHATHAM HILL
RAINHAM ROAD
MAIDSTONE ROAD
NELSON ROAD
DUNCAN ROAD
BROMPTON ROAD
JEFFERY ST
MEDWAY ST
Magpie Hall Road
Walderslade Road
Princes Avenue
North Dane Way
Shawstead Road
Capstone Road
Luton Road
Constitution Road
Beacon Road
Longhill Avenue
Magpie Hall Rd
Churchill Avenue
Heron Way
Wayfield Road
Roosevelt Avenue
The Ridgeway
Letchworth Av
Bournville Avenue
Kitchener Avenue
Haig Avenue
Glencoe Road
Sturla Road
Castle Road
Victoria Road
Canterbury Street

F4
1 Austin Cl
G5
1 Embassy Cl
2 Highridge
H3
1 Mereworth Cl
J2
1 Headcorn Rd
J7
1 Hoath Wy
J8
1 Elder Ct
K3
1 Cranbrook Cl
2 Frinsted Cl
3 Minster Rd
4 Sandhurst Cl
K4
1 Newnham Cl
K5
1 Elizabeth Ct
Grange
51
70
89
Lower Twydall
Twydall
GILLINGHAM
Hempstead
Darland
Spekes Bottom
Ambley Wood
ME7
LOWER RAINHAM ROAD
Riverside Country Park
East Court Farm
FEATHERBY ROAD
A289
WILL ADAMS WAY
SOVEREIGN BOULEVARD
A2 SOVEREIGN BOULEVARD
A2 LONDON ROAD
HOATH WAY
A278
Woodlands Road Cemetery
Woodlands CP School
The Gillingham College
Gillingham Medical Centre
Gillingham Football Club
Barnsole CP Infant Sch
The Robert Napier School
Tennis Club
Gillingham Golf Club Ltd
Danecourt School
Beechings Industrial Cen
Featherby CP School
Featherby Junior School
Doctors Surgery
Twydall Hlth & Welfare Clinic
Infant School
Junior School
Primary School
Rainham Mark Grammar School
Thames View CP School
Howard School
Rainham School for Girls
Bryony School
Hempstead Infant School
Fairview Schools
Doctors Surg
Sunnymead Avenue
Chicago Av
Canadian Av
Cornwallis Avenue
Beatty Avenue
Pear Tree Lane
Star Lane
Hempstead Road
Maidstone Road
Edwin Road
Marshall Road
Courteney Road
Ambley Road
Grosvenor Rd
Bailey Drive
Academy Drive
Hamelin Road
Durham Road
Cambridge Road
Asquith Road
Woodside
Kenilworth Drive
Capstone Road
Fairview

A8
1 Cowbeck Cl
2 Kyetop Wk
3 Napwood Cl
4 Sunningdale Cl
A7
1 Balmer Cl
2 Highfield Cl
A6
1 Ringwood Cl
A3
1 Ripon Cl
B4
1 Chestfield Cl
2 Pembury Wy
B7
1 Tavistock Cl
2 Wentworth Dr
B8
1 Honey Bee Gld
C4
1 Hartpiece Cl
C5
1 Caversham Cl
2 Gresham Cl
3 Maplins Cl
4 Streetfield Rd
C6
1 Cherry Amber Cl
2 Pudding Rd
3 Stratford La
C7
1 Nightingale Cl
D4
1 Cobdown Gv
2 Twyford Cl
D5
1 Pearman Cl
2 Warlingham Cl
E4
1 Caldecote Cl
2 Littiefield Rd
D6, E5, E6
Street names for these grid squares are listed at the back of the index
52
69
90
RSPB Site
Motney Hill
Lower Twydall
Riverside Country Park
Rainham Creek
Saxon Shore Way
LOWER RAINHAM ROAD
B2004
Bloors Wharf
Pump Farm
Lower Rainham
Bloors Place
Macklands
Rainham Mark Grammar School
Thames View CP School
Rainham Station
Meredale CP Infant School
Wakeley CP School
LONDON ROAD
A2
HIGH STREET
MOOR STREET
STATION ROAD
Howard School
Rainham School for Girls
Doctors Surgery
Anchorians All Weather Sports Club
Oasthouse Theatre
Thames County Primary Infant School
St Margarets C of E Junior School
ME8
RAINHAM
The Surgery
Mierscourt Primary School
Siloam Farm
Hills Surgery
Junior School
Parkwood Infant School
Meresborough
Maidstone Road
Berengrave Lane
Bloors Lane
Pump Lane
Mierscourt Road
Meresborough Road
Otterham Quay Lane
Motney Hill Road
Broadview Avenue
Lonsdale Drive
Kenilworth Drive
Cambridge Road
Springvale
Woodside
1 grid square represents 500 metres

F
G
H
53
J
K
Wetham Green
Horsham Marsh
Otterham Creek
Saxon Shore Way
The Poles
The Street
Upchurch
Woodruff Close
Otterham House
Horsham Lane
Primary School
Crosier Court
Forge Lane
Church Farm Road
Windmill Hill
Oak Lane
Bradshaw Close
Quay Lane
Wallbridge Lane
Bishop La
Chaffe's Close
Marstan Cl
Drakes Close
Holywell
Otterham Quay
Gore Farm
Holywell Lane
Breach Lane
Canterbury Lane
Oak Lane
Boxted
Boxted Lane
Seymour Road
Breach
Farriers Court
Gore House
LONDON ROAD
HARTLIP HILL
A2
Hartlip Hill
Mill Lane
Newington Industrial Estate
Spade Lane
Lower Hartlip Road
Munn's Lane
Dane Close
Hartlip
The Street
Hollow Lane
Auger Close
Hartlip Place
Place
Orchard Dr
Playstool Road
London Rd
Bull Lane
1
2
3
4
72
5
6
7
8
Lapwing Drive
Landrail Road
Burntwick Drive
School
Lower Halstow CP School
Cemetery
Newington C of E Primary School
Denham Road
Newington Station
Station Rd
Church
HIGH
Willows
Brookes Place
Newington Manor
91

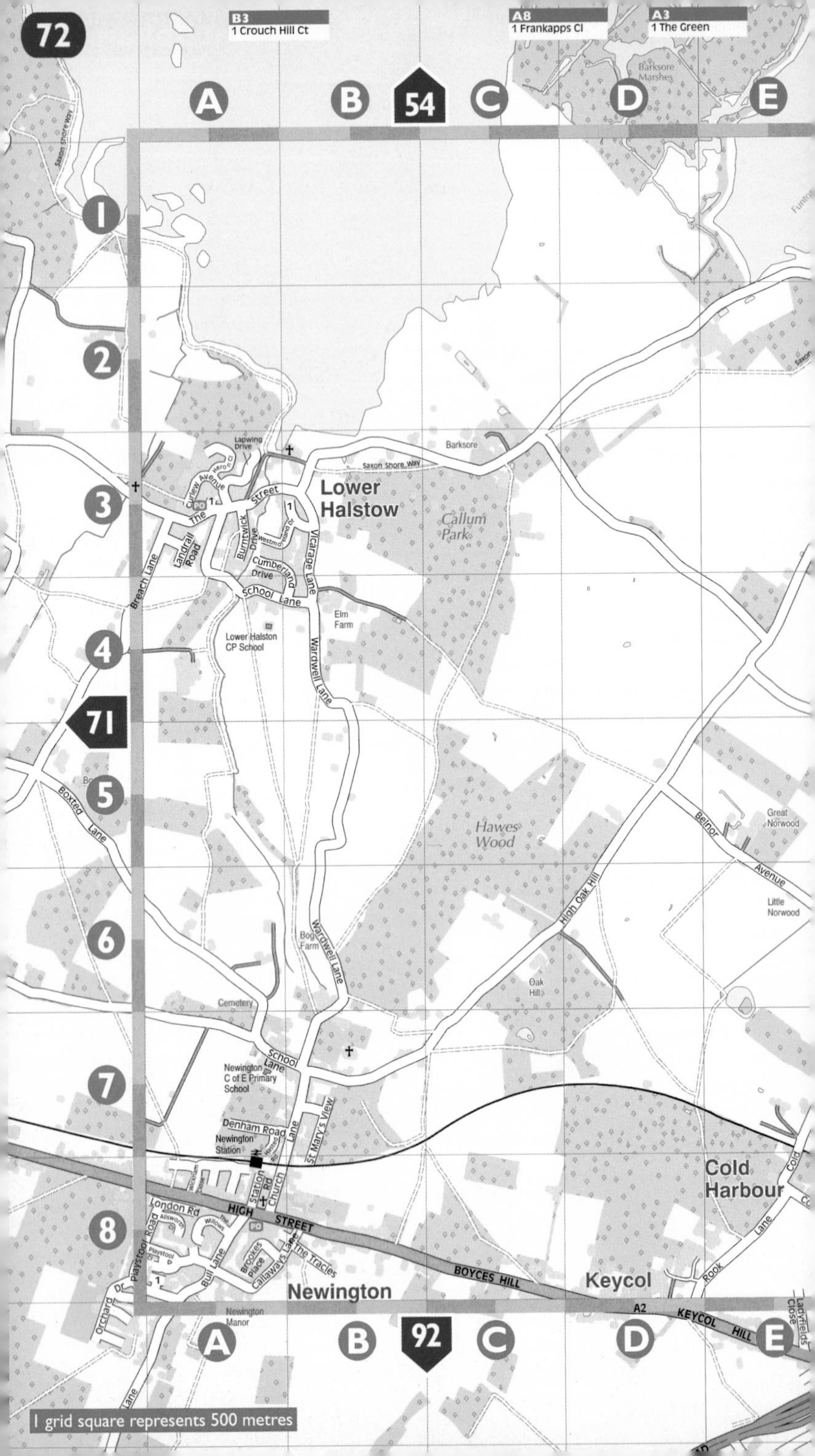
B3
1 Crouch Hill Ct
A8
1 Frankapps Cl
A3
1 The Green
Barksore Marshes
A
B
54
C
D
E
1
2
3
4
5
6
7
8
71
Saxon Shore Way
Lapwing Drive
Heron Cl
Curlew Avenue
The Street
Lower Halstow
Burntwick Drive
Westmoreland Dr
Landrail Road
Breach Lane
Cumberland Drive
Vicarage Lane
School Lane
Elm Farm
Lower Halstow CP School
Wardwell Lane
Barksore
Saxon Shore Way
Callum Park
Boxted Lane
Hawes Wood
High Oak Hill
Belnor Avenue
Great Norwood
Little Norwood
Bogg Farm
Wardwell Lane
Oak Hill
Cemetery
School Lane
Newington C of E Primary School
Denham Road
Newington Station
St Mary's View
Church Lane
Station Rd
Wickham Close
London Rd
Playstool Road
Bull Lane
Brookes Place
Callaways Lane
The Tracies
HIGH STREET
BOYCES HILL
Newington
Keycol
Cold Harbour
Rook Lane
Orchard Dr
Newington Manor
A2
KEYCOL HILL
Ladyfields Close
92
1 grid square represents 500 metres

J2
1 Meadow Cl
J8
1 Pippin Cl
Bedlams Bottom
Chetney Cotts
Old Ferry Road
Lane
F
G
H
55
J
K
Sheppey Way
1
K6
1 Pastime Cl
2
K7
1 Alexandra Cl
3
K8
1 Cortland Cl
2 Cortland Ms
3 Cross La
4 Dyngley Cl
5 Frobisher Cl
6 Oyster Cl
4
5
6
7
8
Saxon Shore Way
The Street
Iwade CP School
Evergreen Close
Fans Lane
Linkway
Iwade
Springvale
Meadow Rise
Sheerstone
Ferry Road
Helen Thompson Close
Kingfisher Close
Grovehurst Road
Funton
Orchard Farm
School Lane
Coleshall
Sheppey Way
Culnells
Featherbed La
A249(T)
B2005
Danes Md
Godwin Cl
Stickfast Lane
Cambray Farm
Pheasant Farm
Menin Rd
Mons Ct
Flanders
Hurst La
Bramblefield Lane
John Goodhew Medical Centre
Grovehurst Surgery
Kemsley Station
GROVEHURST ROAD
Coldharbo
Castle Rough
Pavilion Dr
Grovehurst Avenue
Kems
Howt Green
Parsonage
Lane
Nether Toes
Upper Toes
Celt Close
Eclipse Drive
Meteor Cl
Eleanor Drive
Attlee Way
Burnham
Phillipa
Foxgrove Ct
Walk
Hambrook Walk
Satis Av
Volante Drive
Jessica Mews
Richmond Dr
Challenger Close
Cardine Cl
Genesta Close
Donemowe Dr
Newman
Vaughan Dr
GROVEHURST ROAD
SAFFRON WAY
Porch Close
Trinity Road
Regis Crs
Langley Road
St Bartholomews Sch
Quinton Road
Bobbing
Bobbing CP School
The Meads Avenue
Knightsfield Road
Vicarage Rd
Laxton Way
Roberts
Middletune Av
Denbigh Cl
Grove
Milburne Grove
Newbridge Avenue
Primary School
Attlee Way
North Court Rd
Hawkins Cl
Sprotshill Close
Dobbie Close
Infants School
Forge Rd
Brewery Rd
High Street
Tribune Drive
Trinity Trading Est.
Musgrave
Cooks Lane
Hall Close
Lammas Drive
Beechwood Av
Dean Rd
Larkfield Av
Chappell Wy
Stable Cl
Worcester Drive
Cherry Close
Windmill Road
Derby Cl
Howard Avenue
Crown Road
B2005 MILL WAY
ME10
Saxon Shore
Gas Rd
King St
B2006
ROAD
STAPLEHURST RD
Bobbing Court
SHEPPEY WAY
MAIDSTONE
Hill
Grove Dairy Farm Business Centre
Grove Park CP School
Hilton Dr
Key Street
Milton Regis
93
Gore Court Cricket Club
Gibbons Rd
Sandford Road
Chatsworth Dr
Gadby Road
Kenilworth Ct
Sittingbourne Industrial Park
Staplehurst
Cavell Way
Springfield Rd
Waterloo Rd
WELL ROAD
Hythe Rd
Wood Road
Watson's Hill
Charlotte Street
Periwinkle Close
Jubilee St
The Wall
B2006
MILL WAY
Sittingbourne Industrial Park
KEY STREET
Cherry Flds
Grove Pk Av
Brier
A2
LONDON
Bourne
Well Winch Rd
Warwick Crs
Prentis Cl

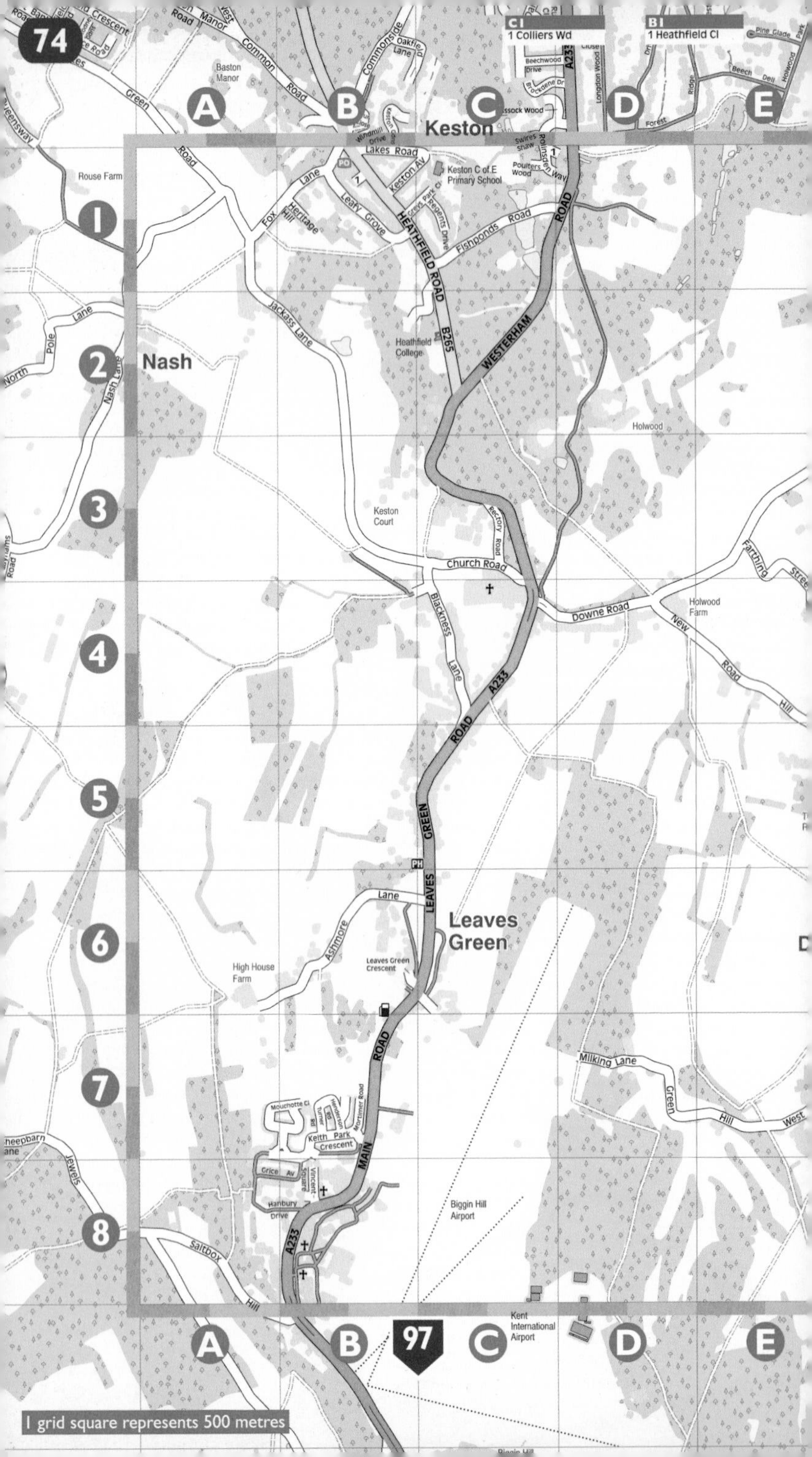
C1
1 Colliers Wd
B1
1 Heathfield Cl
Baston Manor
Manor Road
Common Road
Commonside
Oakfield Lane
Keston
Rouse Farm
Lakes Road
Keston Av
Keston C of E Primary School
Fox Lane
Heritage Hill
Leafy Grove
HEATHFIELD ROAD
Fishponds Road
Beechwood Drive
Longdon Wood
Swires Shaw
Rollinsden Way
Poulters Wood
Pine Glade
Beech Dell
Holwood Park
Forest Ridge
Jackass Lane
B265
Heathfield College
WESTERHAM ROAD
A233
Nash
Pole Lane
North Pole Lane
Nash Lane
Holwood
Keston Court
Rectory Road
Church Road
Blackness Lane
Downe Road
Holwood Farm
Farthing Street
New Road Hill
LEAVES GREEN ROAD
PH
Ashmore Lane
Leaves Green
Leaves Green Crescent
High House Farm
MAIN ROAD
Milking Lane
Green Hill
West
Mouchotte Cl
Henderson Rd
Turner Rd
Mortimer Road
Keith Park Crescent
Grice Av
Vincent Square
Hanbury Drive
Sheepbarn Lane
Jewels
Saltbox Hill
Biggin Hill Airport
Kent International Airport
A B C D E
1 2 3 4 5 6 7 8
97
1 grid square represents 500 metres

HI
1 Crabbs Croft Cl
2 Ladycroft Gdns
3 Starts Hill Av
JI
1 Saphora Cl
KI
1 Downsway
2 Wentworth Cl
F
G
H
J
K
I
2
3
4
76
5
6
7
8
98
Farnborough
Green Street Green
Hazelwood
FARNBOROUGH COMMON
FARNBOROUGH WAY A21
FARNBOROUGH HILL
HIGH STREET
B2158
A21
A223
Bromley Hospitals NHS Trust
Warren Road Primary School
Farnborough Primary School
Friends of Orpington Hospital
Doctors Surgery
Green St Primary School
Downe Primary School
Cemetery
Butchers Yard
Pleasant View
The Larches
Hook
North End Farm
High Elms Country Park
High Elms Golf Course
Cuckoo Wood
Gorringes
Hazel Wood
Mace Farm
Hostye Farm
New Years Wood
Church Road
Tye Lane
Shire Lane
Old Hill
Cudham Lane North
North End Lane
High Elms Road
Court Lane
Mill Lane
Standard Road
Belle Vue Road
High Street
Cudham Road
Luxted Road
Hang Grove Hill
Downe Road
Cudham Park Road
Spinney Way
Downe Avenue
Hazelwood Road
Snag Lane
Mace Lane
Kent Close
Beechwood Avenue
Cleave Av
Cockmannings
Winnipeg Drive
Lezayre
Vine Road
Kingsley Road
Glentrammon Avenue
Pinchbeck Road
Warren Road
Gleeson Drive
Woodlands
Borkwood Way
Borkwood Park
North Drive
Oakleigh Gdns
Southlands Avenue
South Drive
Pinewood
Shire Lane
Tubbenden Close
Curzon Close
Ashbourne Rise
Leamington
Beechcroft Road
St Leonards Rise
Cherrycot Rise
Isabella Dr
Hilda Vale Rd
Winton Road
Broadwater Gdns
Starts Hill Rd
Ladycroft Way
Peel Road
Gladstone Rd
Dane Cl
Hilborough Way
Oleander Cl
Durrant Way
Darwin Cl
Contessa
Woolsey Mews
Amberley Close
Briarswood

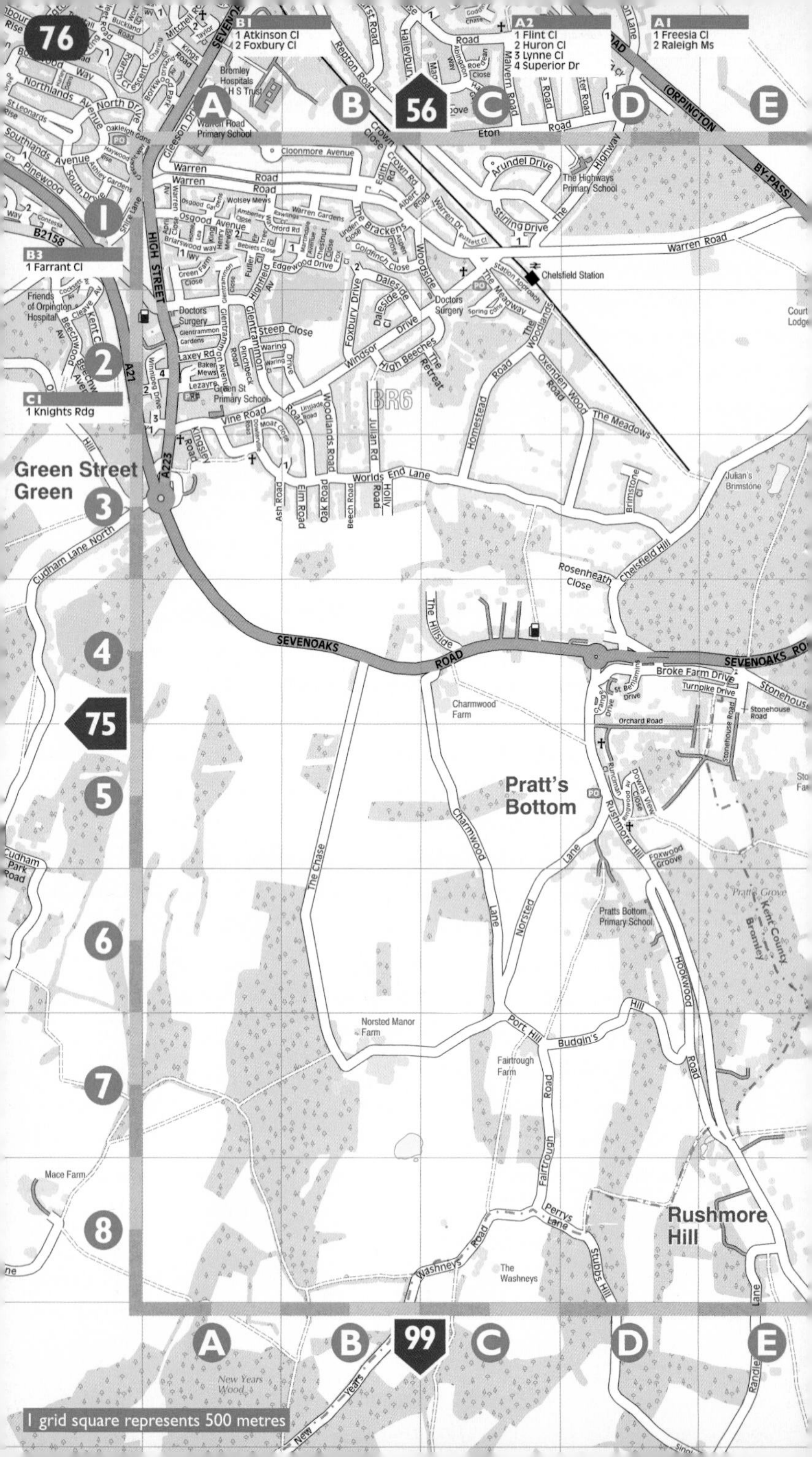
B1
1 Atkinson Cl
2 Foxbury Cl
A2
1 Flint Cl
2 Huron Cl
3 Lynne Cl
4 Superior Dr
A1
1 Freesia Cl
2 Raleigh Ms
B3
1 Farrant Cl
C1
1 Knights Rdg
56
75
99
A
B
C
D
E
1
2
3
4
5
6
7
8
Bromley Hospitals N H S Trust
Warren Road Primary School
Eton
Cloonmore Avenue
Warren Road
Osgood Avenue
Wolsey Mews
Warren Gardens
The Brackens
Goldfinch Close
Edgewood Drive
Crown Close
Crown Rd
Arundel Drive
The Highways Primary School
Stirling Drive
Warren Road
Chelsfield Station
Station Approach
The Meadway
Doctors Surgery
Spring Gdns
Woodside
Daleside
Foxbury Drive
Windsor Drive
High Beeches
The Retreat
The Woodlands
Oxenden Wood Road
The Meadows
Homestead Road
Steep Close
Waring Drive
Glentrammon Road
Glentrammon Avenue
Glentrammon Gardens
Pinchbeck Road
Laxey Rd
Baker Mews
Lezayre
Green St Primary School
Vine Road
Moat Close
Kingsley Road
Woodlands Road
Julian Rd
Worlds End Lane
Ash Road
Elm Road
Oak Road
Beech Road
Holly Road
BR6
HIGH STREET
A21
A223
B2158
Green Street Green
Friends of Orpington Hospital
Beechwood Av
Kent Cl
Northlands Avenue
North Drive
Southlands Avenue
Pinewood
South Drive
Shire Lane
Cudham Lane North
Cudham Park Road
Julian's Brimstone
Brimstone Cl
Rosenheath Close
Chelsfield Hill
The Hillside
SEVENOAKS ROAD
Broke Farm Drive
Turnpike Drive
St Benjamins Drive
Orchard Road
Stonehouse Road
Charmwood Farm
Pratt's Bottom
Charmwood Lane
The Chase
Norsted Lane
Rushmore Hill
Downs View Close
Foxwood Groove
Pratts Bottom Primary School
Pratts Grove
Kent County
Bromley
Hookwood Road
Norsted Manor Farm
Port Hill
Budgin's Hill
Fairtrough Farm
Fairtrough Road
Perrys Lane
Stubbs Hill
Washneys Road
The Washneys
Rushmore Hill
Mace Farm
Court Lodge
New Years Wood
New Years Lane
Randle Lane
(ORPINGTON BY-PASS)
1 grid square represents 500 metres

F1
1 Orlestone Gdns
H5
1 Sandersons Av
F
G
H
57
J
K
Parkgate Road
Park Gate House
I
J6
1 Crest Cl
Chelsfield Primary School
Chelsfield Park Hospital
Cannock House School
Woodlands
Bucks Cross Road
Hawstead Lane
Chelsfield
Well Hill
Firmingers Road
Maypole Road
Jubilee Road
Hollybush Lane
Rock Hill
Well Hill
Well Hill Lane
2
Great Cockerhurst
Maypole
Shoreham Lane
Road
Hewitts
Hewitts
M25
A224
3
Golf Course
Chelsfield Lane
A21
M25
Knockholt Station
Junction 4
Wheatsheaf Hill
London Road
A224
Hollows Wood
4
Chelsfield
Orpington
Badgers Mount
78
Golf Course
Johnsons Avenue
Badgers Road
Badgers Road
Old
Badgers Rise
PO
Milton Avenue
5
Cadlocks Hill
Watercroft Road
Christies Av
By-Pass
London Road
Highland Road
Charles Road
Shacklands Road
6
Station Road
Beldam Haw
Colgates
Halstead Place School
Stonehouse Lane
Clarks Lane
Shoreham Lane
A224
M25
7
Halstead Primary School
Halstead
Southdene
PO
The Meadows
Otford Lane
Road
Parkside
Meadway
London Road
A224
8
Lane
Park Farm
Kilnwood
Knockholt
F
G
H
100
J
K
Hunters Walk
Curry Farm

C6
1 Palmers Orch
Lullingstone Park Farm
Parkgate Road
Park Gate House
A
B
58
C
D
E
Lullingstone Park
Lullingstone Castle
Darent Valley Path
1
Beechen Wood
Armingers Road
2
Great Cockerhurst
Ridge Farm
Redmans Lane
Castle Farm
M25
3
Dalhanna
Road
Junction 4
Cockerhurst Road
Castle Farm
Darent Valley Path
4
Chelsfield Lane
Preston Farm
77
Darenthdale
Shacklands Road
Badgers Road
5
High
Timberden Bottom
Mill Lane
Crown Road
Street
Shoreham
PO
Forge Way
Dunstall Priory
Shacklands Road
6
Boakes Meadow
Darenth Way
Mildmay Place
Church Street
Bowers Road
Shoreham County Primary School
Mesne Way
Station Road
Shoreham Station
A225
Shoreham Place
Darent Valley Path
7
M25
Water Lane
Filston Hall
LONDON ROAD
A224
8
Filston Lane
Filston Farm
A
B
101
C
D
E
Darent Valley Path
A225
1 grid square represents 500 metres
Sepham Farm

Eynsford Rise
Eynsford Station
F
G
H
59
J
K
Upper Austin Lodge Road
Chalkhurst
Park House
Lower Austin Lodge
Bower Park Farm
Bower Lane
The Birches
Hog Wood
Upper Austin Lodge
Golf Course
80
East Hill
Romney Street
Dunstall Farm
Magpie Bottom
Eastdown
Fackenden Lane
Highfield
East Hill Road
Goodbury Road
Clarkes Green Road
Fernbank Farm
Greenhill Wood
102
1
2
3
4
5
6
7
8

E4
1 Ash Tree Cl
2 Birchway
3 Blackthorn Cl
4 Meadow Bank Cl
5 Pound Bank Cl
D3
1 Bakers Av
2 Kingsingfield Cl
3 Wood View Cl
D2
1 Howells Cl
2 Lovelace Cl
3 Penshurst Cl
4 Stacklands Cl
5 Whitegates Av
A
B
60
C
D
E
Brands Hatch Motor Racing
A20
Kingsdown Farm
Maplescombe
Bower Park Farm
Bower Lane
Symonds Close
Gillies Road
Viking Way
Phelps Cl
Neal Road
Oaklands Cl
Brakes Place
Avenue
Regency Close
Sherbourne Close
Millfield Road
Botsom Lane
Hever Road
Multon Rd
PO
Hever Rd
Astor Rd
Hever Wood Road
The Briars
Mitchem Cl
Clearways Industrial Estate
Church Road
Chancel Close
Rushetts Road
Southfields Road
Ash Tree Drive
West Kingsdown Industrial Estate
West Kingsdown Medical Centre
The Grange
Kingsingfield Road
WEST KINGSDOWN
Hog Wood
High Castle Wood
Knatts Valley Road
Ashen Grove Road
Cherry Tree Grove
East Hill
79
Knatts Valley
The Grove
School Lane
Knatts Lane
St Clere Hill
Knockmill
East Hill Road
Hills Lane
Goodbury Road
Fackenden Lane
Golf Course
Tinker Pot Lane
Woodlands
Tinkerpot Rise
Clarkes Green Road
Fernbank Farm
103
Drane Farm
1
2
3
4
5
6
7
8
1 grid square represents 500 metres

K5
1 Parsons La
2 Wise's La
Hotel
Rogers Wood Lane
Road
Billet
F
G
H
61
J
K
Ash
Road
The Street
Ash
Crownhurst Lane
1
Pease Hill
Berr
Map
South Ash Road
2
Kingsdown House
Wise's Lane
3
Crowhurst
The Old Malt House
Ash Lane
Wise's Lane
4
Hazelden Close
82
Forge Lane
Stans
Prim
5
Road
Hatham Green Lane
2
1
Green Road
Stansted Lane
LONDON ROAD
Wrotham Parish Council
Pells Farm
Plaxdale
Stanstead
A20
Road
6
Turn Road
Ash Lane
ollywood
anor
Pells Lane
Bennets Avenue
Plaxdale Green Farm
Green
7
Road
Plaxdale
Lodge
8
Terry's Lodge Farm
Wrotham Hill Ro
Knock
A20
Labour-in-Vain Road
M20
Terry's
F
Mill
G
H
104
J
Tower Industrial Estate
Labour-in-Vain Road
K
Lane
Junction 2
Exedown Road
A20
Old

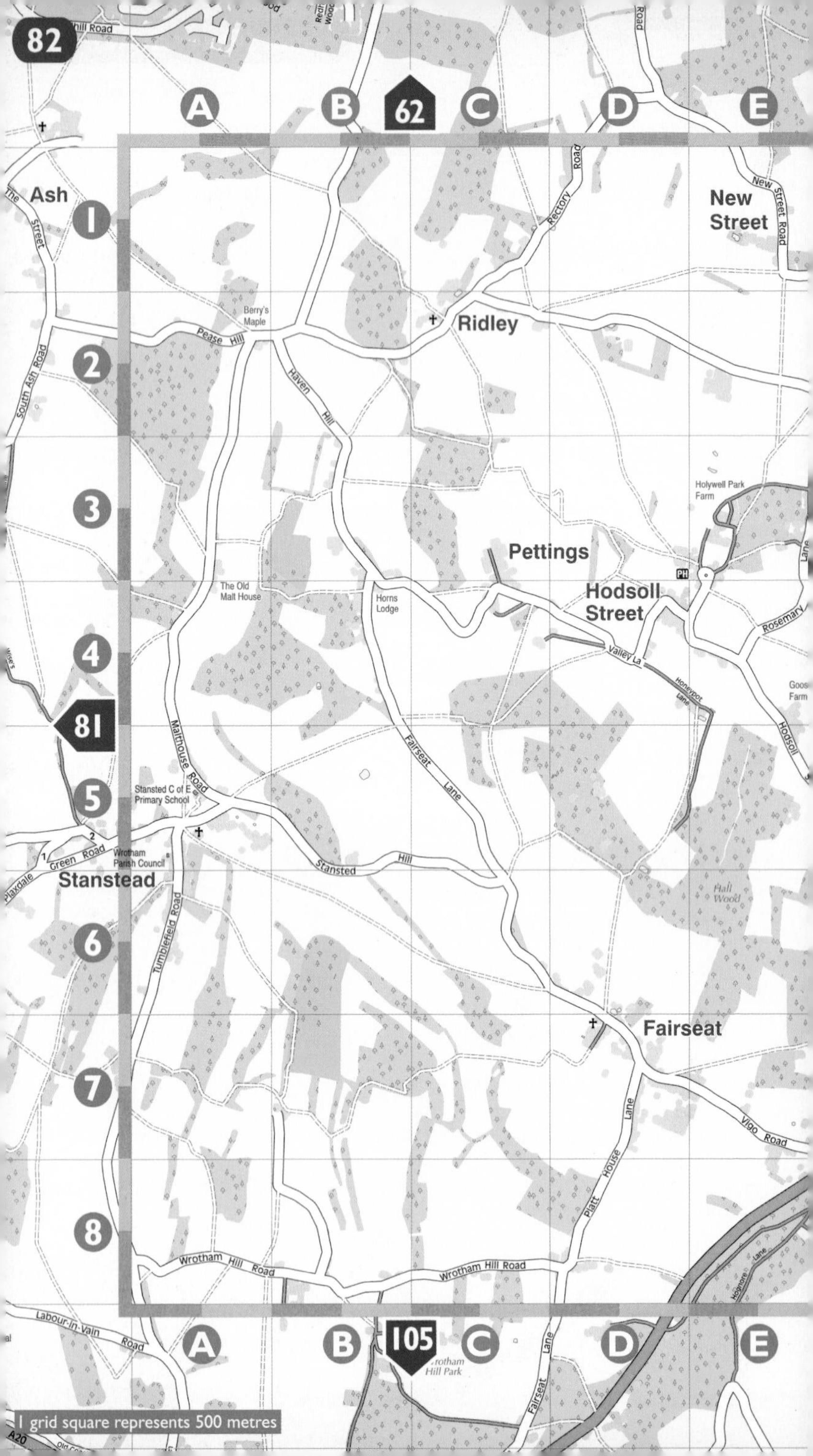
62
A
B
C
D
E
1
2
3
4
5
6
7
8
81
105
Ash
The Street
South Ash Road
New Street
New Street Road
Rectory Road
Berry's Maple
Pease Hill
Ridley
Haven Hill
Holywell Park Farm
Pettings
PH
Hodsoll Street
The Old Malt House
Horns Lodge
Rosemary
Valley La
Honeypot Lane
Goos Farm
Hodsoll
Fairseat Lane
Malthouse Road
Stansted C of E Primary School
Green Road
Wrotham Parish Council
Plaxdale
Stanstead
Stansted Hill
Hall Wood
Tumblefield Road
Fairseat
Vigo Road
Platt House Lane
Hognore Lane
Wrotham Hill Road
Labour-in-Vain Road
Wrotham Hill Park
Fairseat Lane
A20
1 grid square represents 500 metres

F7
1 The Coach Dr
G7
1 Bramble Bank
Steele's Lane
F
G
H
63
J
K
Leylands
Horn's Oak Road
Chandler's Hill
Road
Chandler's
Priestwood
David Street
1
H6
1 Croftside
2 Stonecroft
Road
Priestwood Green
Priestwood
A227
South Street
Chapman's
Hill
Heron Hill Lane
2
J6
1 Admers Wy
Wilsons Way
Leafy Lane
Harvel
St Francis Rd
Ridge Lane
3
Harvel Street
Culverstone GM Primary School
Willow Walk
Willow Wood Road
Willow
Rhododendron
Harvel Lane
PO
lverstone
reen
Carter's Hill Lane
School Lane
Ridge Lane
Ridge Wood
Valley Lane
4
Mountfield Close
Whitepost
WROTHAM ROAD
Lane
Conifer Drive
Avenue
84
Beechwood Drive
Valley La
Silver Birch Av
The Shieling
Ashleigh Close
Meadow Lane
Beech Wood Gardens
White Horse Ro
Newlands
Lane
Southfield Shaw
Harvel Lane
Harvel Road
5
Vigo Rugby Club
Oak Farm Lane
Whitepost Lane
Beechwood Drive
Highview
Whitehorse Wood
GRAVESEND ROAD
Vigo Village
Fern Down
The Coppice
Highview
Commority Road
Ash Keys
6
Harvel Road
Vigo CP School
Bank
PO
Road
Timber
2
Churchside
Churchside
Kent County Council
1
Erskine
Hornbeams
Chestnut La
Downs Wood
Woodside
1
The Gallops
Waterlow Road
Trosley Country Park
Harvel Road
The Paddock
7
7
North Downs Way
The Covert
7
Pilgrims Way
Wealdway
Pinesfield
8
Taylors
Lane
Downsview
Coldrum
Lane
F
G
Green Lane
H
106
J
K
Trottiscliffe
Church
Ryarsh Wood
The Street
School Lane
Trottiscliffe C of E Primary School

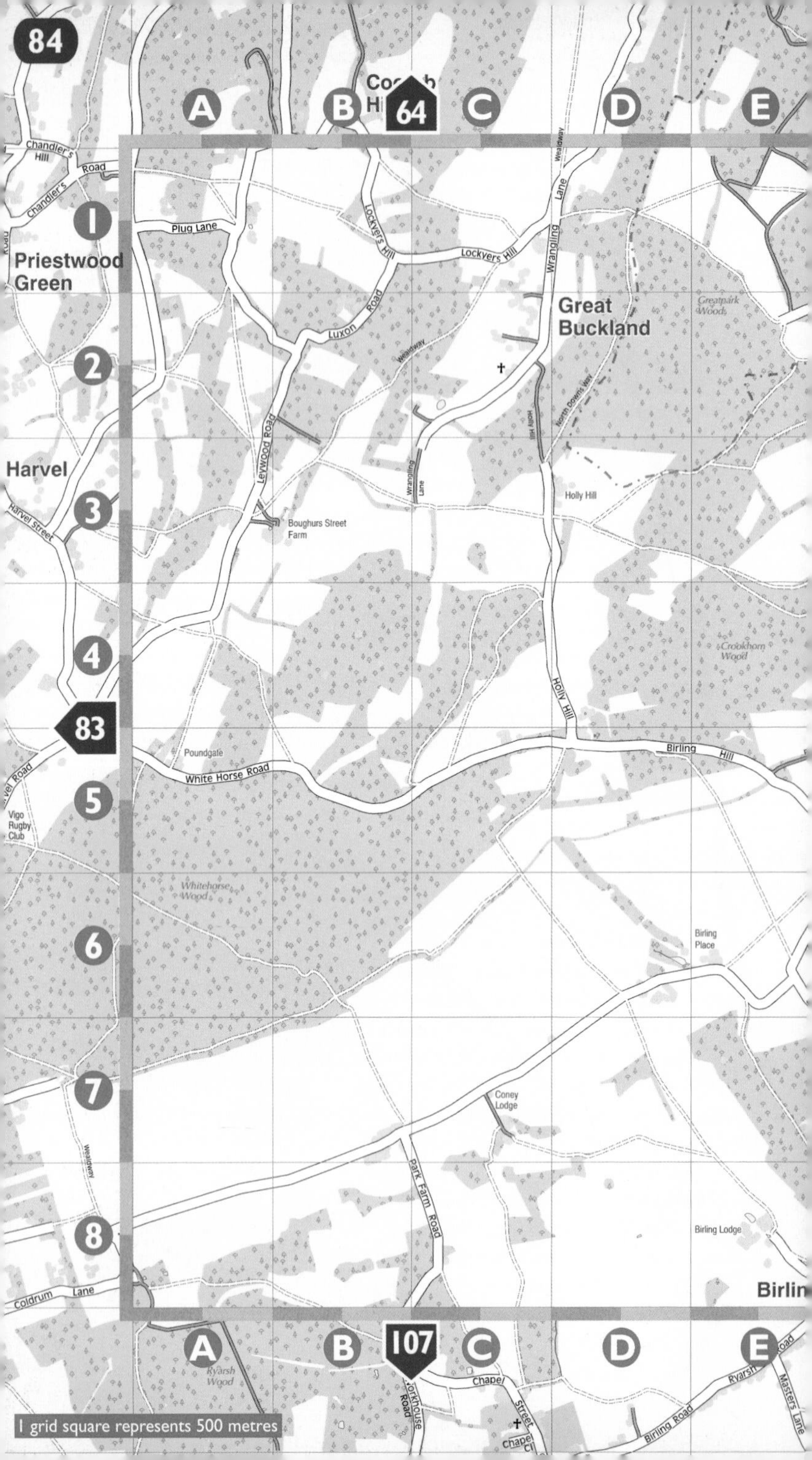
A
B
C
D
E
64
1
2
3
4
5
6
7
8
83
107
Chandler's Hill
Chandler's Road
Priestwood Green
Plug Lane
Lockyers Hill
Luxon Road
Wealdway
Leywood Road
Wrangling Lane
Great Buckland
Greatpark Wood
North Downs Way
Holly Hill
Harvel
Harvel Street
Boughurs Street Farm
Crookhorn Wood
Poundgate
White Horse Road
Birling Hill
Vigo Rugby Club
Whitehorse Wood
Birling Place
Coney Lodge
Park Farm Road
Birling Lodge
Birlin
Coldrum Lane
Ryarsh Wood
Workhouse Road
Chapel Street
Chapel Cl
Birling Road
Ryarsh Road
Masters Lane
1 grid square represents 500 metres

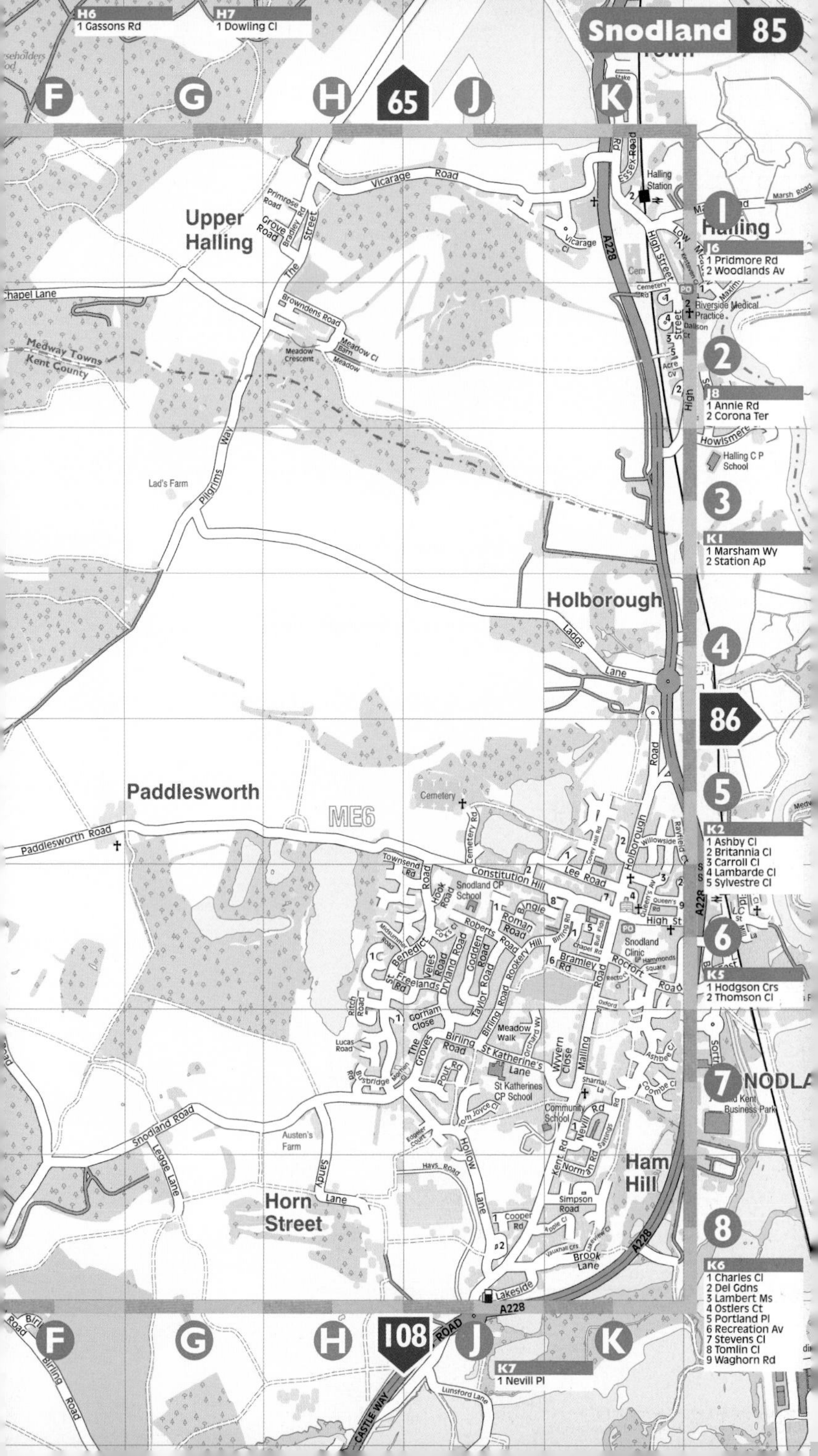
H6
1 Gassons Rd
H7
1 Dowling Cl
F
G
H
65
J
K
Upper Halling
Vicarage Road
Primrose Road
Bradley Rd
Grove Road
The Street
Chapel Lane
Browndens Road
Meadow Cl
Barn Meadow
Meadow Crescent
Medway Towns
Kent County
Essex Road
Halling Station
Vicarage Cl
A228
High Street
Low
Cem
Cemetery Rd
Riverside Medical Practice
Dalison Ct
Acre Gv
High
Halling
J6
1 Pridmore Rd
2 Woodlands Av
Marsh Road
J8
1 Annie Rd
2 Corona Ter
Howlsmere
Halling C P School
K1
1 Marsham Wy
2 Station Ap
Lad's Farm
Pilgrims Way
Holborough
Ladds Lane
86
Holborough Road
K2
1 Ashby Cl
2 Britannia Cl
3 Carroll Cl
4 Lambarde Cl
5 Sylvestre Cl
Paddlesworth
Paddlesworth Road
ME6
Cemetery
Cemetery Rd
Townsend Rd
Constitution Hill
Covey Hall Rd
Lee Road
Willowside
Rayfield Ct
Queen's Av
Queen's Rd
High St
Snodland CP School
Hook Road
Angle
Roberts Road
Roman Road
Rookery Hill
Birling Rd
Chapel Rd
Bull Flds
Snodland Clinic
Hammonds Square
Rocfort Road
Rectory Cl
Bramley Rd
Oxford St
Coxs Cl
Midsummer Road
St Benedict Road
Veles Road
Dryland Road
Godden Road
Taylor Road
Freelands Rd
Ritch Road
Gorham Close
Birling Road
Meadow Walk
Orchard Wy
Wyvern Close
Malling Road
Ashbee Cl
Lucas Road
Busbridge Rd
The Groves
Pout Rd
St Katherine's Lane
St Katherines CP School
Sharnal La
Coombe Cl
Community School
Nevill Rd
Saltings Rd
Tom Joyce Cl
Edgeler Court
Hollow Lane
Hays Road
Kent Rd
Norman Rd
Ham Hill
Snodland Road
Legge Lane
Austen's Farm
Sandy Lane
Horn Street
Simpson Road
Cooper Rd
Apple Cl
Vauxhall Crs
Lakeview Cl
Brook Lane
Lakeside
A228
K5
1 Hodgson Crs
2 Thomson Cl
NODLA
Business Park
K6
1 Charles Cl
2 Del Gdns
3 Lambert Ms
4 Ostlers Ct
5 Portland Pl
6 Recreation Av
7 Stevens Cl
8 Tomlin Cl
9 Waghorn Rd
108
Birling Road
Castle Way
Road
Lunsford Lane
K7
1 Nevill Pl
1
2
3
4
5
6
7
8

86
New Town
B1
1 Walter Burke Av
A2
1 Benedict Cl
2 Ferry Rd
A1
1 Wendover Cl
66
A B C D E
Ringshill Place
School Farm
School Lane
Pilgrims Way
Hill Road
Halling Station
Marsh Road
Halling
Wouldham
B2
1 Castle St
Trafalgar Rd
Nelson Rd
High Street
Ferry La
Portland Rd
Riverside Medical Practice
Dallison Ct
Cornwall Crs
Knowle Road
E8
1 Alma Rd
2 Hayman Wk
3 St Marks Ct
Scholey Cl
Howlsmere Cl
Halling C P School
Hall Road
Rochester Road
Scarborough
olborough
Ladds Lane
85
Scarborough Lane
Margetts Lane
Burham Court
River Medway
Medway Valley Walk
Downs Vw
Court Road
Old Church Road
Church St
Baker St
Rochester Rd
New Rd
Snodland Station
Church Fld
Hendy Rd
Holborough Rd
Lee Road
A228
High St
Bramley Rd
Rocfort Road
May St
East St
Brook St
Mid Kent Business Park
Sortmill Rd
SNODLAND
Malling Rd
Ham Hill
Simpson Road
Brook Lane
Aylesford St Marks C of E Primary Sch
Eccles Row
Cork Street
109
Rowe Place Farm
New Hythe Business Park
1 grid square represents 500 metres

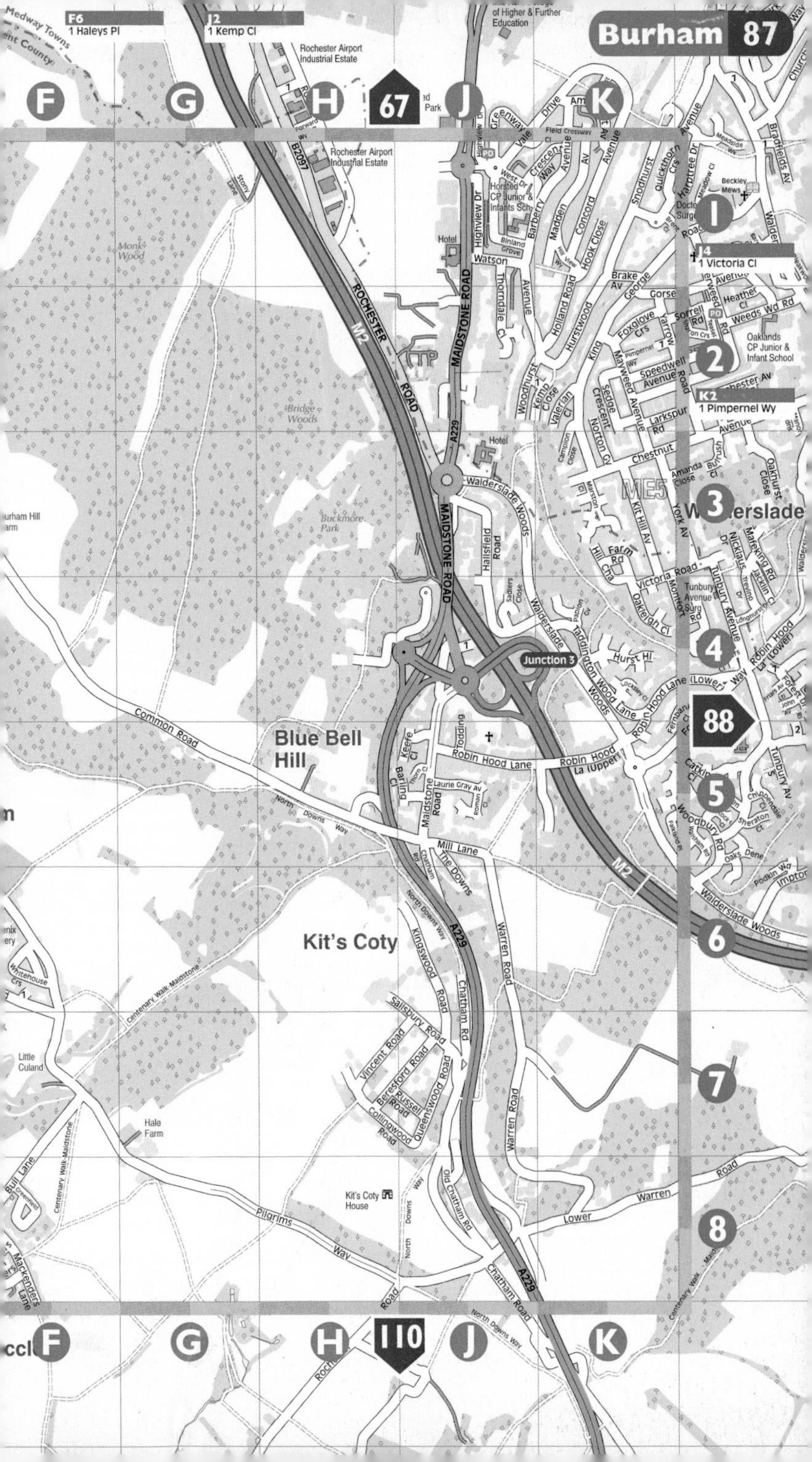
F6
1 Haleys Pl
J2
1 Kemp Cl
J4
1 Victoria Cl
K2
1 Pimpernel Wy
67
88
110
Medway Towns
Kent County
Rochester Airport Industrial Estate
of Higher & Further Education
Monk Wood
Bridge Woods
Buckmore Park
Blue Bell Hill
Kit's Coty
Kit's Coty House
Little Culand
Hale Farm
Walderslade
ME5
Junction 3
M2
A229
B2097
ROCHESTER ROAD
MAIDSTONE ROAD
Common Road
North Downs Way
Mill Lane
The Downs
Chatham Rd
Kingswood Road
Salisbury Road
Vincent Road
Beresford Road
Russell Road
Queenswood Road
Collingwood Road
Warren Road
Lower Warren Road
Old Chatham Rd
Pilgrims Way
Chatham Road
Centenary Walk-Maidstone
Bull Lane
Mackenders Lane
Whitehouse Crs
Robin Hood Lane
Robin Hood La (Upper)
Robin Hood Lane (Lower)
Taddington Wood Lane
Walderslade Woods
Hallsfield Road
Sadlers Close
Keere Cl
Barling Cl
Thorn Cl
Maidstone Road
Laurie Gray Av
Roman Cl
Todding
Highview Dr
Horsted CP Junior & Infants Sch
Watson Avenue
Thorndale Cl
Binland Grove
Barberry Avenue
Madden Avenue
Concord Avenue
Hook Close
Holland Road
Hurstwood
Woodhurst
Kemp Close
Valerian Cl
Campion Close
Norton Gv
Sedge Crescent
Mayweed Avenue
Larkspur Rd
Chestnut Avenue
Speedwell Avenue
Pimpernel Wy
Yarrow Rd
Foxglove Crs
George Avenue
Gorse Avenue
Brake Av
King
Snodhurst
Quickthorn Crs
Harptree Dr
Brent Road
Doctor Surgery
Beckley Mews
Meadow Cl
Meadside Wk
Bradfields Av
Heather Cl
Weeds Wd Rd
Sorrell Rd
Oaklands CP Junior & Infant School
Amanda Close
Burrush Cl
Oakhurst Close
Kit Hill Av
York Av
Marston
Hill Cha
Farm Rd
Victoria Road
Montfort Rd
Oakleigh Cl
Nicklaus Dr
Mafeking Rd
Jacklin Cl
Tunbury Avenue
Tunbury Av
Tunbury Avenue Surg
Hurst Hl
Locksley Cl
Papion Gv
Fernbank
Catkin Cl
Woodbury Rd
Sheraton Ct
Chippendale Cl
Oaks Dene
Podkin Wd
Robin Hood La (Lower)
Friars Av
Greenway
Vale Drive
Field Crossway Cl
West Dr
Crescent Way
Hotel
Forward Wy
Stony Lane
Greenfield
Burham Hill Farm
Hotel
PO
F
G
H
J
K
1
2
3
4
5
6
7
8

B3
1 Mossbank
B4
1 Beechmore Dr
2 Buckland Cl
3 Leybourne Cl
B2
1 The Beeches
2 Southbourne Gv
A5
1 Feldspar Cl
2 Frensham Wk
3 Hawthorns
A1
1 Bradfields Av West
A4
1 Olliffe Cl
68
B5
1 Cinnabar Cl
2 Galena Cl
3 Goldstone Wk
4 Micawber Cl
C1
1 Lydd Rd
2 Tenterden Rd
3 Woodchurch Cl
C3
1 Beeching Rd
2 Huckleberry Cl
3 Octavia Ct
4 Port Cl
5 Spindlewood Cl
C5
1 The Covert
2 The Spinney
D1
1 Redbridge Cl
2 Stable Cl
87
D2
1 Shepperton Cl
D4
1 Japonica Cl
2 Mincers Cl
3 Newton Cl
D5
1 Huntersfield Cl
D6
1 Sandstone Ri
B1, B6, C2, C4
Street names for these grid squares are listed at the back of the index
Walderslade
Lords Wood
Westfield Sole
Cossington Fields
M2
Walderslade Woods
Bell Lane
Harp Farm Road
Lower Warren Road
Sharsted Farm
Shawstead Road
Lordswood Leisure Centre
Gibraltar Farm
North Dane Way
Princes Avenue
Lords Wood Lane
Boxley Road
Dargets Road
Walderslade Road
Tunbury Avenue
Robin Hood La (Lower)
Robin Hood La (Upper)
Tunbury CP School
Oaklands CP Junior & Infant School
Walderslade CP School
St Thomas More RC Primary School
Maundene CP School
St Benedicts School
Swingate County Infant School
Lordswood Health Cen
Lordswood Industrial Est
Alexandra Hospital
The Family Medical Cen
Doctors Surgery
Bradfields School
111
E4
1 Bentley Cl
2 Compton Cl
3 Ladyfields
4 Pirbright Cl
E5
1 Dogwood Cl
1 grid square represents 500 metres

G2
1 Honeysuckle Cl
H1
1 Green Bank Cl
F
G
H
69
J
K
Hempstead
Doctors Surg
Hempstead Infant School
Hempstead Junior School
Capstone Road
Hempstead Road
Meadow Drive
Lamplighters Close
Gilbert Close
Pine Gv
Cedar Grove
Birch Grove
Hempstead Valley Drive
Wildwood Gld
Kingsdown Cl
Medlar Gv
Plumtree Gv
Almond Gv
Chapel La
Barncroft Dr
The Old Carriageway
HOATH WAY
HOATH WAY A278
Swain Rd
Zillah Gdns
Woodside
Tanglewood Close
Lakewood Dr
Edwards Close
Carvoran Way
St Margarets Drive
Maidstone Road
Woodpecker
Deanwood
Hills Surgery
Chamberlain Ct
The Hazels
Wigmore Rd
Fairview Avenue
Drewery Drive
Fairview Schools
Fairview Av
Norman Close
Wigmore Road
Primrose Av
Foulds Cl
Bredhurst Road
Wigmore
Prinys Drive
Georgian Way
Rutland Place
Grain Road
Harty Av
Park Wood
Lime Court
Fowler Close
Chart Place
Sedley Cl
Hawbeck Rd
Rowbrocke Cl
Harding Close
Dixwell Close
Capel Close
Queendown Av
Hallwood Cl
Lineacre Close
Holtwood Close
Campleshon Rd
H2
1 Thistledown Cl
Beke Road
Doctors Surgery
Chipstead
H3
1 Martin Ct
Deanwood Dr
Walsingham Close
J2
1 Black Rock Gdns
2 Coppice Ct
3 Stalham Ct
I
1
2
3
4
5
6
7
8
90
Blowers Gv
Houghton Av
Lullingstone
Lambsfrith Gv
Hadleigh Ct
Sharsted Way
The Landor Ct
Rise
Marquis Dr
Coppergenny Dr
Lambtrith Gv
Hempstead Va
Maidstone Rd
Junction 4
Ham Lane
Medway Towns
Kent County
Lidsing Rd
Chapel Lane
Forge Lane
Blind Lane
M2
The Street
Kemsley Street
Kemsley Street Road
White Hill
Bredhurst C of E School
Fir Tree Gv
Hurstwood Road
Bredhurst
Lidsing
Lidsing Road
Sole Rd
Dunn Street Road
Dunn Street
Bredhurst Hurst
Hurstwood Road
Scragged Oak Road
Scragged Oak
Lower Cox Street
Little Halstead Farm
Monkdown Wood
Newlands Wood
Scragged Oak Rd
F
G
H
112
J
K
Pollyfield
Lane
Cox Street
Grange Farm

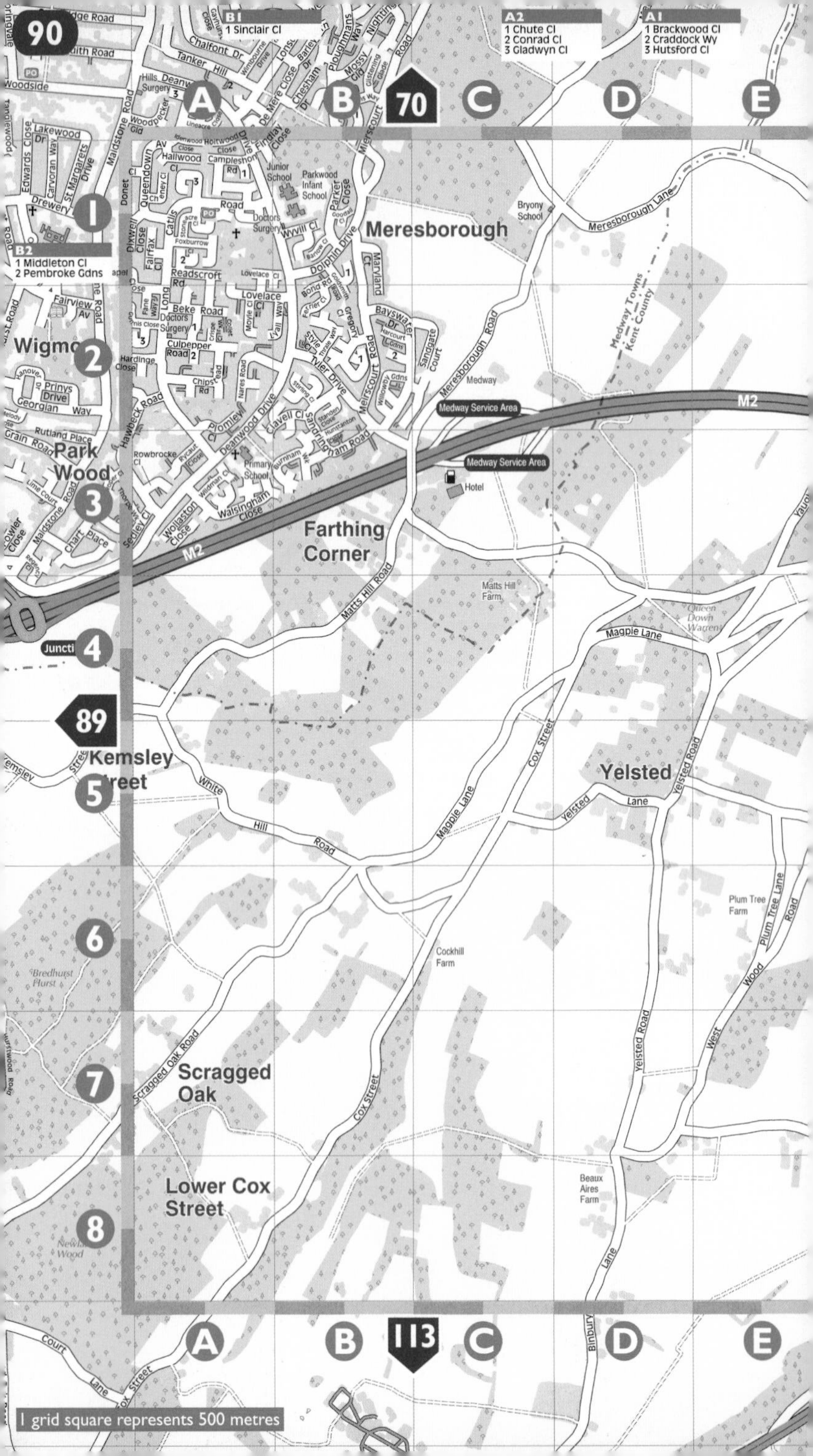
B1
1 Sinclair Cl
A2
1 Chute Cl
2 Conrad Cl
3 Gladwyn Cl
A1
1 Brackwood Cl
2 Craddock Wy
3 Hutsford Cl
B2
1 Middleton Cl
2 Pembroke Gdns
70
89
113
A
B
C
D
E
1
2
3
4
5
6
7
8
Meresborough
Wigmo
Park Wood
Farthing Corner
Kemsley Street
Yelsted
Scragged Oak
Lower Cox Street
Chalfont Dr
Tanker Hill
Woodside
Hills Surgery
Maidstone Road
Lakewood Dr
Edwards Close
Carvoran Way
St Margarets Drive
Drewery
Donet Cl
Queendown Av
Hallwood Cl
Holtwood Close
Campleshon Rd
Findlay Close
Junior School
Parkwood Infant School
Parker Close
Mierscourt Road
Doctors Surgery
Wyvill Cl
Dolphin Drive
Maryland Ct
Bryony School
Meresborough Lane
Meresborough Road
Medway Towns
Kent County
Dixwell Close
Fairfax Cl
Catlis
Foxburrow
Readscroft Rd
Lovelace Cl
Long
Beke Road
Doctors Surgery
Culpepper Road
Chipstead Rd
Hardinge Close
Bayswater Dr
Harcourt Gdns
Sandgate Court
Gregory Cl
Tyler Drive
Hawbeck Road
Deanwood Drive
Clavell Cl
Sandringham Road
Medway Service Area
Medway
M2
Hotel
Fairview Av
Prinys Drive
Georgian Way
Rutland Place
Grain Road
Rowbrocke Cl
Wollaston Close
Walsingham Close
Primary School
Sedley Cl
Chart Place
Maidstone Road
Lime Court
Fowler Close
Matts Hill Road
Matts Hill Farm
Queen Down Warren
Magpie Lane
Juncti
White Hill Road
Magpie Lane
Cox Street
Yelsted Lane
Yelsted Road
Plum Tree Farm
Plum Tree Lane
Road
Cockhill Farm
West Wood
Bredhurst Hurst
Scragged Oak Road
Yelsted Road
Beaux Aires Farm
Lane
Newland Wood
Binbury
Court Lane
Cox Street
1 grid square represents 500 metres

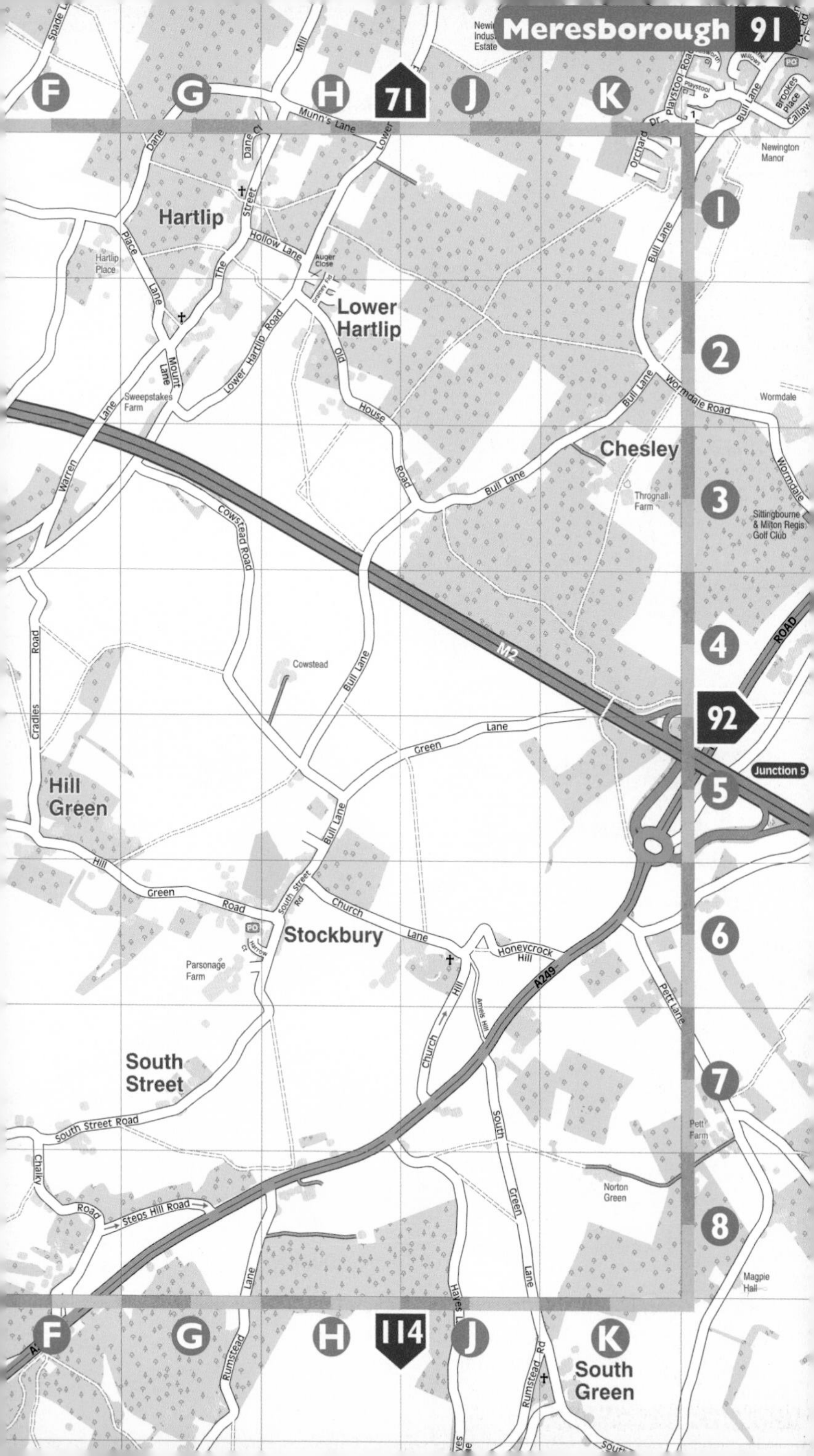

F
G
H
71
J
K
Spade
Mill
Munn's Lane
Lower
Dane
Dane Ct
Street
Hartlip
Hollow Lane
Hartlip Place
Place
The
Lane
Auger Close
Lower Hartlip
Old
House
Road
Lower Hartlip Road
Mount Lane
Sweepstakes Farm
Lane
Warren
Orchard Dr
Bull Lane
Newington Manor
Wormdale Road
Wormdale
Chesley
Thrognall Farm
Sittingbourne & Milton Regis Golf Club
Cowstead Road
Cowstead
M2
ROAD
92
Junction 5
Green
Lane
Cradles
Road
Hill Green
Hill
Green
Road
Church
Lane
Stockbury
South Street Rd
Harrow Ct
Parsonage Farm
Honeycrock Hill
A249
Pett Lane
Church
Hill
Amels Hill
South Street
South Street Road
Chalky
Road
Steps Hill Road
South
Green
Lane
Pett Farm
Norton Green
Magpie Hall
Hayes
Rumstead
Rumstead Rd
114
South Green
1
2
3
4
5
6
7
8

72
Newington
Newington Manor
High Street
London Rd
Station Rd
Church
Playstool Road
Brookes Place
Callaways Lane
The Tracies
Boyces Hill
Keycol
A2
Keycol Hill
Cold Harbour
Rook Lane
Ladyfields Close
Bull Lane
Orchard Dr
Wormdale Road
Wormdale
Wormdale Hill
Chesley
Sittingbourne & Milton Regis Golf Club
Maidstone Road
A249(T)
Maidstone Road
Chestnut Street
Chestnut Street
Chestnut Wd La
Borden Primary
Sunnyhill
Munsgore Lane
Munsgore Farm
Danaway
Woodgate Lane
Eyehorn Hatch Farm
91
Junction 5
Oad Street
Pond
M2
Pett Lane
Pett Farm
Frid Wood
Stiff Street
Manns Place
Wrens Road
Norton Green
Little Pett Farm
Magpie Hall
Deans Hill
Silver Street
Cemetery
Gore
Dean Bottom
115
Bicknor Lane
Deans Hill Road
Silver
South Green
1 grid square represents 500 metres
A
B
C
D
E
1
2
3
4
5
6
7
8

G1
1 Gainsborough Cl
H1
1 Ashington Cl
2 Wentworth Dr
73
Key Street
Milton Regis
Chalkwell
Borden
Harman's Corner
Hearts Delight
Tunstall
Grove End
Woodstock
Highsted
Broadoak
ME10
I
Sittingbourne Industrial Park
H2
1 Perth Gdns
Sittingbourne Station
EUROLINK WAY
2
H3
1 Chartwell Gv
2 Oakfields
3
J2
1 Walnut Tree Dr
Sittingbourne Memorial Hospital
Highsted School for Girls
Fulston Manor School
4
94
5
K1
1 Kings Mill Cl
2 Prentis Quay
3 St Paul's St
6
K2
1 Arthur St
2 Church St
3 Dover St
4 Fountain St
5 Laburnum Pl
6 Pembury St
7
8
F
G
H
J
K
116
KEY STREET
A2
LONDON ROAD
WEST STREET
CHALKWELL ROAD
SHEPPEY WAY
MAIDSTONE ROAD
A249(T)
B2005 MILL WAY
B2006
ST PAUL'S ST
Westlands Secondary School
Gore Court Cricket Club
Sittingbourne Industrial Park
Barrow Grove CP School
St Peters RC Primary School
Minterne CP School
Oaks County Infant School
Tunstall C of E Primary School
Wrens Farm
Oakwood Farm
Borden Lane
Cryalls Lane
Riddles Road
Starveacre Lane
Minterne Avenue
Homewood Avenue
Park Avenue
Cromer Road
Hearts Delight Road
Tunstall Road
Broadoak Road
Ruins Barn Road
Wrens Road
Wises Lane
The Street
Bexon Lane

C2
1 Homeview
2 Smeed Cl
3 Tonge Rd
A3
1 The Burrs
A2
1 Crown Quay La
C3
1 George St
2 Temple Gdns
3 Woodlands Rd
C4
1 Cedar Cl
2 Step Style
3 Warren Cl
D2
1 Gordon Cl
ME10
B2005 MILL WAY
Trinity Trading Est.
Anchor Business Park
Brickmakers Industrial Estate
D2 Trading Estate
Castle Road Industrial Park
Church Road Business Centre
Mere Court
Saxon Shore Way
Symmonds Drive
Dolphin Yard Sailing Barge Museum
Sittingbourne Industrial Park
Eurolink Industrial Estate
Eurolink Industrial Centre
West Lane Trading Estate
Murston CP Junior School
Murston CP Infant School
East Hall
Oak Road
Broom Rd
Gorse Road
Portland Av
Meeres Court Lane
East Hall La
Swale Heritage Trail
Murston
Tonge Road
All Saints Rd
Lomas
Sittingbourne Station
EUROLINK WAY
Eurolink Way
A2
ST MICHAEL'S ROAD
WEST STREET
High Street
East Street
Shortlands Road
Bell Shopping Centre
Avenue Theatre
Sittingbourne Sports Centre
EAST STREET
CANTERBURY ROAD
A2
FOX HILL
Snipeshill
Lansdowne CP School
Bapchild & Tonge C of E Primary School
Borden Grammar School
Avenue Of Remembrance
Chilton Avenue
Milfield
South Avenue County Infant School
Canterbury Road CP School
Stanhope Av
Osprey Court
Caldew Grove
Cemetery
Sittingbourne Memorial Hospital
Highsted School for Girls
Fulston Manor School
St Thomas School
Swanstree Avenue
Penn Close
Fairleas
SITTINGBOURNE
The Meadows
Gerrards Drive
Clarendon Close
Crossways
Cromer Road
Highsted Road
Morris Ct
Church Street
Rodmersh
Rodmersham Green
Stockers Hill
Browings Orchards
Rodmersham CP School
Green Lane
Highsted
Woodstock
Rodmersham Squash Club
Bottles Lane
Upper Rodmersham
Bargains Hill
Broadoak
Pitstock Farm
Cheney Hill
ST PAUL'S ST
Crown Road
Lammas Drive
Park Aven
Blandford Gardens
Woodstock Road
Barn Road
Ruins
93
117
1 grid square represents 500 metres

K4
1 Morello Cl
Blacketts
Cheke's Court
Church Road
Blacketts Road
Saxon Shore W
F
G
H
J
K
1
2
3
4
5
6
7
8
Binny Cotts
Bax
LC
Scraps Hill
Lower Road
Hempstead Lane
pchild
STREET
A2
LONDON ROAD
Radfield
Teynham
Barrow Green
Station
Orchard Vw
Harrys Rd
Baker Cl
Roper Road
The Crescent
Honeyball Wk
Broadacre
Roundel Close
Rivers Road
Teynham Parochial C of E (Controlled) Primary School
Belle Friday Cl
Station Road
Frognal Lane
Frognal Close
Frognal Gdns
Donald Moor Av
New Gardens Rd
Cherry Gdns
Nobel Close
Teynham Medical Centre
Nutberry Close
Avenue
PO
Doctors Surgery
Panteny Lane
Dully Road
Haywood
Little Dully
Claxfield Road
Cellarhill
Lynsted Lane
Batteries Close
Cellar Hill
Nouds Road
Nouds
Dully House
Wood Street
Batteries Farm
Bogle Road
Nouds Farm
Tenacre
Nouds Lane
Lynsted CP School
The Street
Tickham
Tickham Lane
The Vallance
Aymers
Lynsted
Park Fa
Mill Lane
Ludgate
Loyterton

A
B
C
D
E
1
2
3
4
5
6
7
8
Fickleshole
Featherbed Lane
Road
Blackman's Lane
Park
Skid Hill Lane
Skid Hill Farm
Fairchildes Road
Farleigh Ct Rd
Scotshall Lane
Holt Wood
Church Lane
Ledgers Farm
Hesiers Road
Hesiers Hill
Chelsham Court Road
Washpond Lane
Chelsham Court Farm
Beddlestead Lane
Ledgers Road
Worms Heath
Broom Bank
Beech Farm Road
Vanguard Way
Barnard Road
B269
Beech Farm
Beddlestead Farm
Cheverells Farm
CROYDON ROAD
118
1 grid square represents 500 metres

F6
1 Richmond Cl
G5
1 Bankside Cl
2 Kembleside Rd
F
G
H
74
J
K
A233
Kent
International
Airport
Lusted
1
G8
1 Wedgwoods
Bird House
Biggin Hill
Business
Park
Churchill Wy
Wireless Rd
Airport
Industrial
Estate
Surex
Swimming
Pools
Nightingale
Close
Crossley Close
Hawthorne
Avenue
Costains
Farm
Charles
Darwin
School
2
J3
1 Blackthorn Rd
Oaklands
Lane
Victoria Gardens
Sunningvale
Christy Road
Arthur Road
Avenue
Sunningvale
Close
Camelot
Close
Lambert
Close
Lunar Close
Magnolia
Drive
Jail Lane
Acer Road
Spruce
Road
Sopwith
Close
A233 MAIN ROAD
Oaklands
Junior School
Oakland
Primary School
Doctors
Surgery
Lane
Melrose
Road
Old Tye
Avenue
Cudham
School
3
Berr
Gree
Norheads
Farm
Norheads
Latham
Close
View
Close
Chalcock Close
Grand View
Av
Eastern View
Highfield
Road
Kingsmead
Hillcrest
Road
Forgefield
Biggin Hill
Junior School
K5
1 Rosecroft Cl
BIGGIN
HILL
Stock
Hill
Church
Road
Aperfield
Road
Juniper
Close
Doctors
Surgery
Police
Station
Mount
Pleasant
Walk
Rusndene
Nelson
Close
Village Green Avenue
Malan
Close
Allenby
Road
Haig
Road
Aperfield
4
Beech Road
Kings Road
Sunningvale Avenue
Dawell
Drive
Rosehill
Road
Steeple Hts Dr
Lebanon
Gdns
Falcons Close
Sutherland
Village Green
Way
98
Hillingdale
Spring
Gdns
Road
Timbertop
Road
Churchside
Close
Treebourne
Rd
Charlton Drive
Everglade
Mewsend
Lillie
Road
Valley View
Foley
Road
St Mary's Grove
St Mary's Green
Upper Drive
Eagles Drive
The Grove
Avenue
Edward Road
Moselle Road
St Winifred's Road
Lotus
Rd
Foxearth
Close
Belvedere Road
Clarence Road
5
Melody
Scarborough
Close
Swievelands
Road
Springholm
Close
Wood
Road
Wakely Close
Greenoak
Rise
Ricketts
Hill
Road
Paynesfield Road
Woodbury
Close
East
Hill
Alexandra Road
Flamborough
Close
Whitby
Close
Bridlington
Close
York Road
Bromley
Surrey County
Kemsley
Road
Beech
Avenue
Hillside
Road
Cudham
Road
6
South
Street
MAIN
ROAD
Lusted Hall Lane
Lusted Hall
Farm
Goatsfield Road
Shaw
Road
Greenway
Westmore
Road
Tatsfield
John's
Road
Paynesfield
Road
John's Road
George's
Road
Manor
Road
Avenue
Road
7
Crossways
Crossways
Whitewood
Cottages
Grove
Road
Westmore Road
The Square
Maesmaur Road
Barnfield
Road
Old Lane
Redhouse Road
PO
Ninehams Road
Tatsfield
Lane
Rag Hill Road
Parkwood Road
8
Ship
Field
Close
Edgar Road
Maesmaur Road
Borough
Road
Ship Hill
Old Lane
New
Surgery
Tatsfield
Primary
School
F
G
H
119
J
K
Chestnut
Betsom's
Hill
The Avenue
Chestnut Avenue
Church
Hill
Clarks Lane
Farm
Approa

Luxted
Luxted Road
Hang Grove Hill
75
Mace Farm
Hostye Farm
Mace Lane
Downe Road
Cudham Lane North
Bird House Lane
Luxted Road
Single Street
Berry's Hill
Church Hill
Cemetery
Angas Home
Cudham
Cudham Lane South
Cacket's Farm
Cacket's Lane
Charles Darwin School
Cudham School
Berry's Green
Berry's Green Road
Newbarn Lane
Aperfield
97
New Barn Farm
St Winifred's Road
Belvedere
Lotus Rd
Woodbury Close
South Street
A233 MAIN ROAD
Cudham Frith
Southwood
Bombers Lane
Bombers Farm
Cudham Grange
Bucknurst Road
Grays Road
Silversted Lane
Tatsfield Lane
Grays Farm
Hawley's Corner
Palace Road
Avenue
Bromley
Kent County
A233
120
Chestnut
Betsom's Hill
TN16
1 grid square represents 500 metres

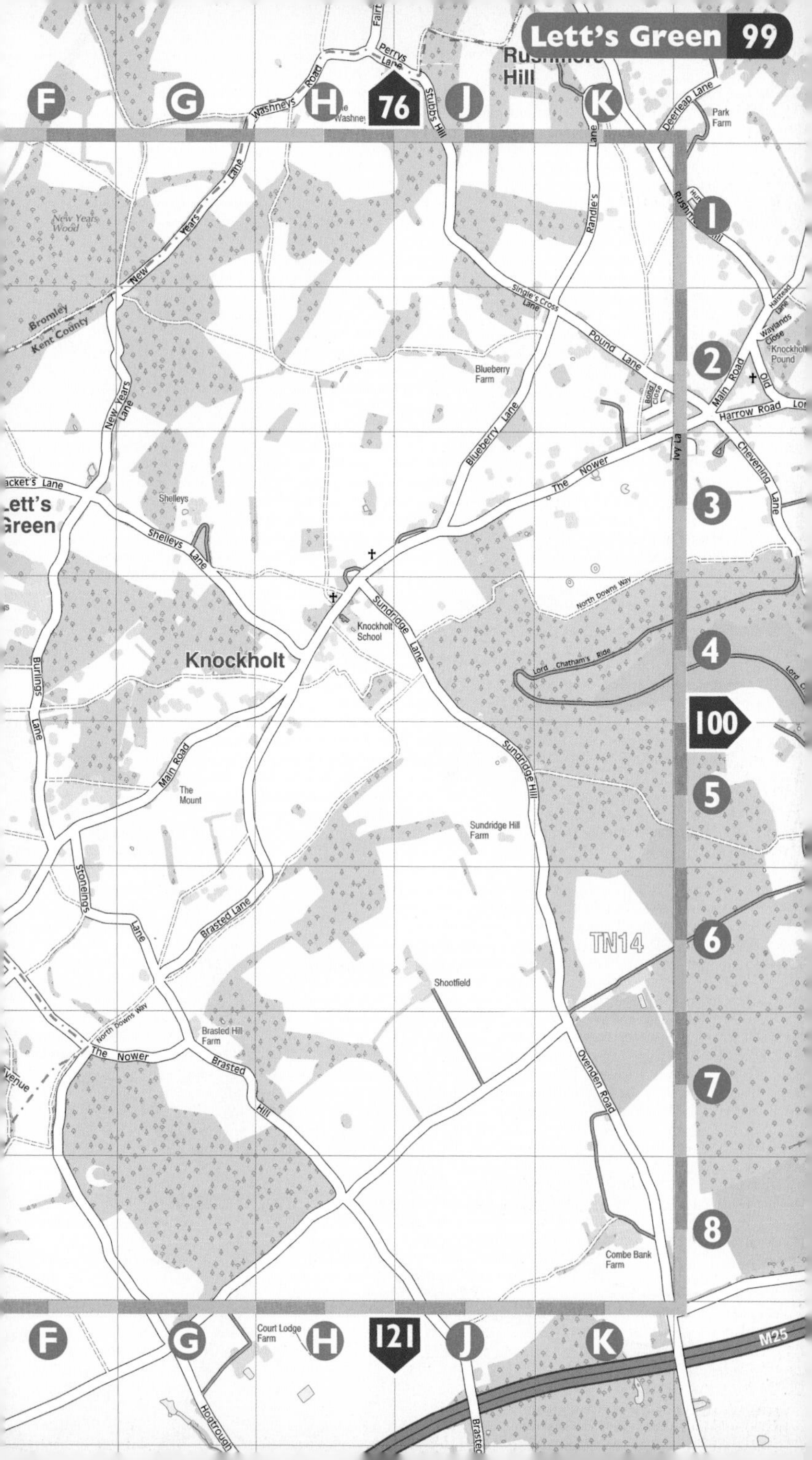
F
G
H
76
J
K
Rushmore Hill
Washneys Road
Perrys Lane
Stubbs Hill
Deerleap Lane
Park Farm
New Years Wood
New Years Lane
Bromley
Kent County
Randle's Lane
Rushmore Hill
Single's Cross Lane
Pound Lane
Halstead Lane
Waylands Close
Knockholt Pound
Main Road
Old
Bond Close
Harrow Road
Blueberry Farm
Blueberry Lane
Ivy La
Chevening Lane
The Nower
Lett's Green
Shelleys
Shelleys Lane
North Downs Way
Sundridge Lane
Knockholt School
Knockholt
Lord Chatham's Ride
Burlings Lane
100
Main Road
The Mount
Sundridge Hill
Sundridge Hill Farm
Stoneings Lane
Brasted Lane
TN14
Shootfield
North Downs Way
The Nower
Brasted Hill Farm
Brasted Hill
Ovenden Road
Combe Bank Farm
1
2
3
4
5
6
7
8
Court Lodge Farm
121
M25
Hogtrough

A
B
77
C
D
E
1
2
3
4
99
5
TN 6
7
8
A
B
122
C
D
E
Deerleap Lane
Park Farm
Knockholt Road
Parkside
The Meadows
Kilnwood
Otford Lane
London Road
Randle's Lane
Rushmore Hill
Hunters Walk
Curry Farm
Halstead Lane
Waylands Close
Knockholt Pound
Cross
Pound
Bond Close
Main Road
Old
Harrow Road
London Road
Birchwood Lane
Ivy La
The Nower
Chevening Lane
Star Hill Road
Beckman Cl
Crow Drive
Fort Rd
Armstrong Close
Crow Dr
North Downs Business Park
North Downs Way
Lord Chatham's Ride
Star House
Lime Pit Lane
Star Hill Rd
Sundridge Rd
Morants Court Farm
Morants Court
M25
Turvins Farm
Chevening
Chevening Park
Chevening Road
Ovenden Road
Sundridge Road
M26
Chevening Cross
B2211 Ovenden Road
Junction 5
Combe Bank Farm
Chevening Primary School
Willow Farm
Darent
Valley Path
Darent Cl
High Street
Martin's Shaw
1 grid square represents 500 metres

G7
1 Carey's Fld
G8
1 Anthony Cl
2 The Orchard
K3
1 Colets Orch
Filston Hall
Filston Farm
Sepham Farm
Lower Barn
Twitton
Wickham Field
OTFORD
Otford Medical Practice
Otford County Primary School
Otford Station
Broughton House
Hotel
Dunton Green
Dunton Green Station
Dunton Green County Primary School
Longford
Riverside Retail Park
Vestry Industrial Estate
Connections Business Park
Sevenoaks Business Cen
Bat & Ball Station
Sevenoaks Hosp
Bradbourne School
Riverhead
St Johns
St Johns Hill Surgery
Sevenoaks CP School
St Hilarys School
Infant School
M25
M26
A224
A225
A25
LONDON ROAD
SEVENOAKS ROAD
OTFORD ROAD
STATION ROAD
SHOREHAM ROAD
High Street
Pilgrims Way West
Greenhill Road
Hillydeal
Coombe Rd
Tudor Drive
Evelyn Road
Sidney Gdns
Well Road
Bubblestone Rd
The Butts
The Old Walk
Warham Rd
Leonard Av
Twitton Lane
Twitton Meadows
Great Till
Orchard Rd
Knighton Rd
Telston Lane
Willow Park
Darnets Fld
Hale Lane
Dane Road
Saxon Cl
Flowerfield
Ryecroft Rd
Rye Lane
The Charne
Filston Lane
Ivy House Lane
London Road
North Downs Way
Darent Valley Path
River Darent
Old Otford Road
Vestry Road
Crampton's Road
The Moor Rd
Coombe Av
Berwick Wy
Otford Rd
Watercress Drive
Queen's Drive
Orchard La
Farm Rd
Weavers Lane
Greatness Rd
Grove Rd
North Vw
Hillingdon
Barretts Rd
Glyn Davies Cl
Lennard Road
Hillfield Road
London Rd
Station Cotts
Cottages Road
Kingswood Rd
Mill Rd
Killick Rd
Bankside
Milton Rd
Pounsley Road
Darenth Lane
The Pinnacle
Packhorse
Alsher Wy
Longmeadow
Ryedale Ct
Ham Rd
Chesterfield Drive
Stanhope Wy
Baden Powell Rd
Patch
Scotts Wy
Heathfield Rd
Park Close
Sandilan
Bullfinch Dene
Bullfinch
Chipstead Lane
Orchard Rd
Homefield Rd
Church Fld
Shoreham
Broomfield Rd
Betenson Avenue
The Meadway
Lambarde
Cavendish Av
Hill Cresent
Oakdene Road
Harrison Way
Park Road
Sackville
Sevenoaks Council
George's Road
Camden Rd
Bradbourne Road
Amherst Rd
Linden
St John's Road
St John's Hill
James's Road
Golding Rd
Davis Cl
Westfield
Swaffield Rd
Wickenden
Nursery Cl
Allotment
Quaker's Hall
F
G
H
J
K
78
102
123
1
2
3
4
5
6
7
8

79
A
B
C
D
E
Eastdown
Fackenden Lane
Clarke
1
2
3
4
5
6
7
8
A225
Greenhill Wood
Greenhill Road
Hillydeal Road
SHOREHAM ROAD
North Downs Way
Birchin Cross Road
Shorehill Lane
Otford Court
Otford Mount
Rowdow Lane
Coombe Rd
Pilgrims Way East
St Michaels Drive
Otford Medical Practice
Leonard Av
Street
STATION ROAD
Station Rd
Otford Station
County School
Warham Rd
PO
Bubblestone Rd
The Butts
The Old Walk
Well Road
Sidney Gdns
Evelyn Road
Tudor Drive
Tudor Crs
SEVENOAKS ROAD
Chalkways
Pilgrims Way
The Chase
Highfield Road
Beechy Lees Rd
Hill Road
Park
Northdown Rd
Barnfield Crs
Hillside Rd
Collet Road
Copperfields Wk
Copperfields
Dippers Close
Orchard Way
The Landway
Treetops
Kemsing CP Sch
Dynes Road
Knave Wood Rd
Norman Close
Nightingale Road
Edgar Rd
Oxenhill Road
Brookfield
Castle Road
Cleves Road
Boleyn Rd
Montfort Rd
Greystones
Drive
West End
Spring Head Rd
Old Barn Close
KEMSING
101
M26
Childsbridge La
Rushymead
Park Lane
Falcon
Old Otford Road
ROAD
Childsbridge Lane
Childsbridge
Noah Arks
Riverside Retail Park
Road
Vestry Industrial Estate
Vestry
Connections Business Park
Bentley's Meadow
Mills Crs
Copse Bank
Penfo
The Shellings
Childsbridge Way
Crampton's Road
The Moor Rd
Swanzy Rd
Watercress Drive
Farm Rd
OTFORD ROAD
Zambra Way
Meadowlands
Wilmar Way
Ragge Way
Landway
Church
Greatness
Coombe Av
Sevenoaks Business Cen
Berwick Wy
Otford Rd
Queen's Drive
Orchard Cl
Farm Rd
Cemetry
Greatness Park Cemetry
Mill Lane
Weavers Lane
Grove Rd
Mill Lane
Old Mill Cl
Flimer Lane
Pinehurst
Highlands Pk
Ash Platt Rd
Jubilee Ri
School La
Church Rd
Seal
Bat & Ball Station
Chatham Hill
Greatness La
Greatness Rd
SEAL
A25
ROAD
HIGH STREET
Pinewood Av
Mill Pond Cl
B2019
Wilderness Sports Centre
Wildernesse School
Seal Drive
Avenue
North Vw Rd
Hillingdon
Avenue
The Cresent
Sevenoaks Hosp
Hospital Rd
Wildernesse
Dorton College of Further Education
Wildernesse Avenue
Dorton House
Grove Road
James's
Sevenoaks Town Council
Sackville
St John's
George's Road
Davis
Golding
Swaffield Rd
Little Wd
Hillingdon
The Green
124
John's
Road
Camden Rd
St Johns Hill Surgery
Wickenden Road
Sevenoaks CP School
Bradbo
Linden
ST JOHN'S HILL
Nursery Cl
Quaker's Hall
Garden Rd
Wildernesse
Lansdowne
Dorton Dr
Woodland Rise
Wildernesse Golf Club
Wilderness Avenue
1 grid square represents 500 metres

Golf Course
Tinker Pot La
Tinker Pot Lane
Woodlands
80
F
G
H
J
K
Knock Mill
Road
Tinkerpot Rise
Fernbank Farm
Drane Farm
1
Cotman's Ash Lane
North Downs Way
2
Old Terry's Lodge Road
Kester
Orford Manor
Pilgrims Way
3
St Clere
Heaverham Road
Church Lane
Street
Crowdleham
Heaverham
4
Lower St Clere
Broughton
104
5
M26
Ark
Chaucer Business Park
6
Honeypot Lane
Kemsing Station
Watery Lane
7
Tanners Cross
Stonepitts
Manor Farm
Fullers Hill
Broomsleigh
8
Styants Bottom
MAIDSTONE ROAD
A25
Saxbys Road
125
Pillar Box
Bottom
The Grove

81
103
126
A
B
C
D
E
1
2
3
4
5
6
7
8
Terry's Lodge
Mill Lane
Terry's Lodge Road
Old Terry's Lodge Road
M20
Vain Road
Labour-in-Vain
Cooper's Wood
Tower Industrial Estate
Junction 2
A20
Old Coach Rd
LONDON
North Downs Way
Exedown Road
Exedown Road
Kemsing Road
New House Farm
Yaldham Manor
Lower St Clere
M26
TN15
Fen Meadow
Fen Pond Road
Ightham Court
SEVENOAKS ROAD
A25
IGHTHAM BY-PASS
Rushmere Ct
BOROUGH GREEN ROAD
A227 BOROUGH GREEN ROAD
Manor Farm
Oldbury
Styants Bottom
PH
THE ST
Trycewell Lane
Busty La
Chapel Rd
Cob Ct
Oldbury Lane
Ightham County Primary School
Jubilee Crs
BATES HILL A2
Mill Lane
Spring Lane
Upr Spring Lane
Styants
Lane
Prestons
Ightham
ROAD
1 grid square represents 500 metres

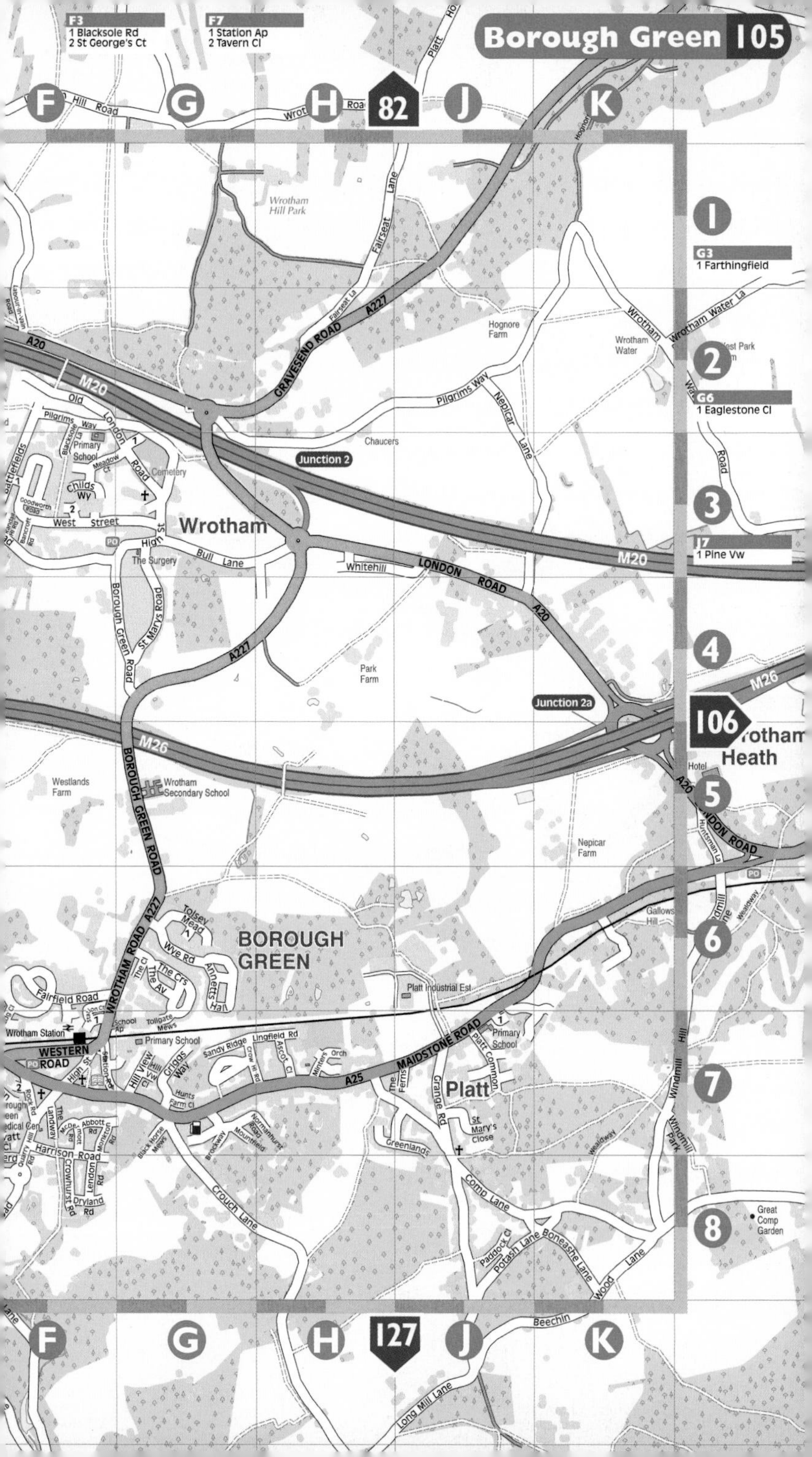
F3
1 Blacksole Rd
2 St George's Ct
F7
1 Station Ap
2 Tavern Cl
G3
1 Farthingfield
G6
1 Eaglestone Cl
J7
1 Pine Vw
82
106
127
Wrotham Hill Park
Fairseat Lane
Gravesend Road
A227
A20
M20
M26
Junction 2
Junction 2a
Hognore Farm
Wrotham Water
Pilgrims Way
Nepicar Lane
Chaucers
Wrotham
Whitehill
London Road
Bull Lane
The Surgery
Borough Green Road
St Marys Road
Park Farm
Westlands Farm
Wrotham Secondary School
Wrotham Heath
Hotel
Nepicar Farm
Gallows Hill
Borough Green
Tolsey Mead
Wye Rd
Annetts Hall
Fairfield Road
Wrotham Road
Wrotham Station
Western Road
Primary School
Platt Industrial Est
Maidstone Road
A25
Platt
Platt Common
Grange Rd
Greenlands
St Mary's Close
Comp Lane
Crouch Lane
Potash Lane
Boneashe Lane
Wood Lane
Windmill Hill
Great Comp Garden
Long Mill Lane
Harrison Road
Crowhurst Rd
Dryland Rd
Sandy Ridge
Lingfield Rd
Ascot Cl
Griggs Way
Hunts Farm Cl
Hill View
West Street
High St
Childs Wy
Cemetery
Old London Road

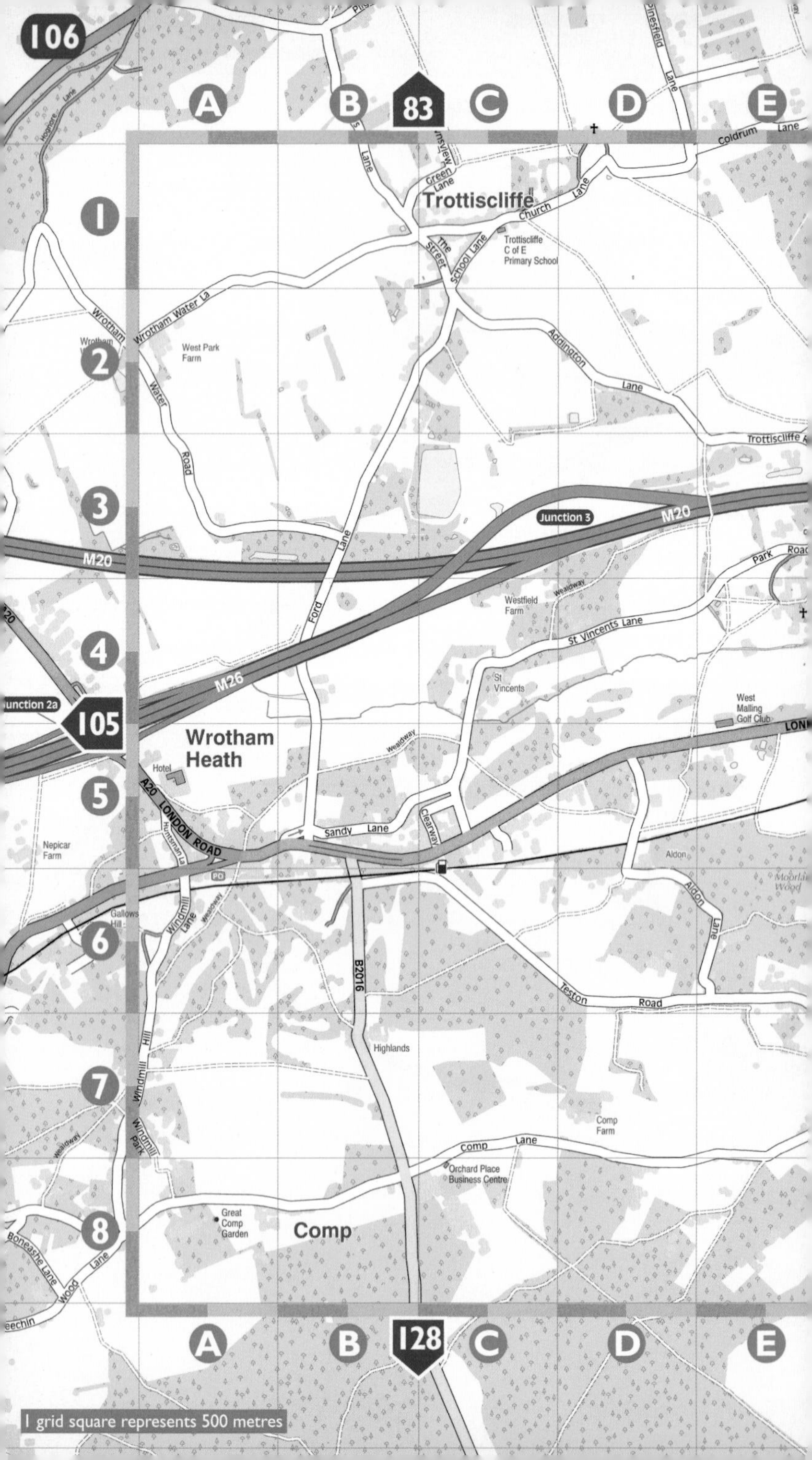

106
83
105
128
A
B
C
D
E
1
2
3
4
5
6
7
8
Trottiscliffe
Trottiscliffe C of E Primary School
Church Lane
The Street
School Lane
Green Lane
Coldrum Lane
Addington Lane
Trottiscliffe Road
Wrotham Water La
Wrotham Water Road
West Park Farm
Ford Lane
Junction 3
M20
M26
Junction 2a
Park Road
Westfield Farm
Wealdway
St Vincents Lane
St Vincents
West Malling Golf Club
Wrotham Heath
Hotel
A20 LONDON ROAD
Huntsman La
Sandy Lane
Clearway
PO
Nepicar Farm
Gallows Hill
Windmill Lane
Aldon
Aldon Lane
Teston Road
B2016
Highlands
Windmill Hill
Windmill Park
Comp Farm
Comp Lane
Orchard Place Business Centre
Great Comp Garden
Comp
Boneashe Lane
Wood Lane
Hognore Lane
1 grid square represents 500 metres

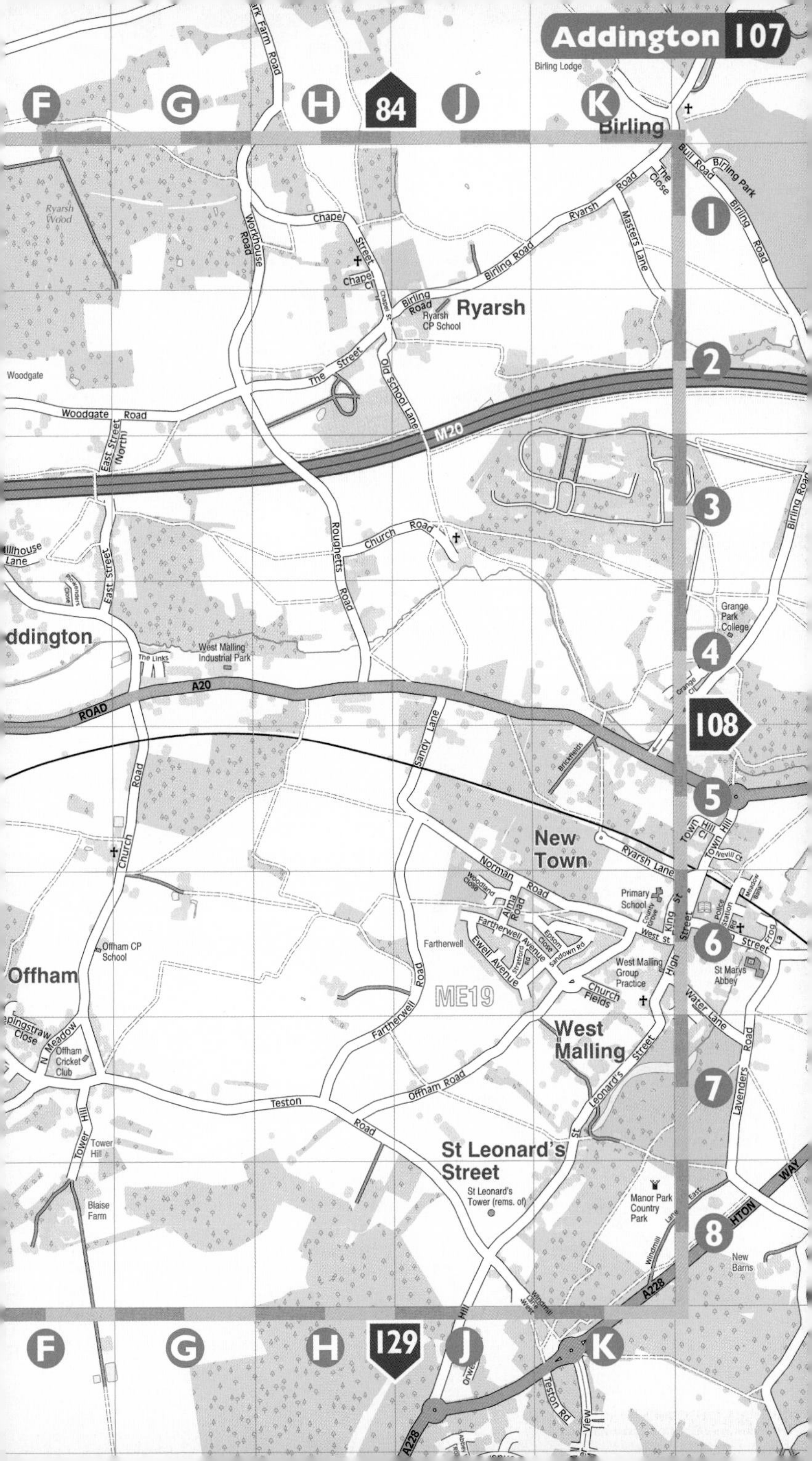
F
G
H
84
J
K
Birling Lodge
Birling
Bull Road
Birling Park
Birling Road
The Close
Ryarsh Road
Masters Lane
Ryarsh Wood
Workhouse Road
Chapel Street
Chapel Cl
Chapel St
Birling Road
Ryarsh
Ryarsh CP School
The Street
Old School Lane
Woodgate
Woodgate Road
East Street (North)
M20
Roughetts Road
Church Road
Millhouse Lane
Pownders Close
East Street
Addington
The Links
West Malling Industrial Park
A20
ROAD
Grange Park College
Grange Cl
108
Sandy Lane
Brickfields
Church Road
New Town
Ryarsh Lane
Town Hill Cl
Town Hill
Nevill Ct
Norman Road
Woodland Close
Alma Road
Primary School
Country Grove
King St
Police Station
Meadow Bank
Fartherwell Close
Fartherwell Avenue
Epsom Close
Sandown Rd
West St
High Street
Swan Street
Frog La
Ewell Avenue
Stratford Rd
Fartherwell
West Malling Group Practice
St Marys Abbey
Offham CP School
Offham
ME19
Church Fields
Fartherwell Road
Water Lane
West Malling
Lavenders Road
Leonard's Street
St Leonard's Street
St Leonard's Tower (rems. of)
Pepingstraw Close
N Meadow
Offham Cricket Club
Teston Road
Offham Road
Tower Hill
Blaise Farm
Manor Park Country Park
Windmill Lane East
Windmill Lane West
New Barns
A228
1
2
3
4
5
6
7
8
F
G
H
129
J
K
Teston Rd
A228

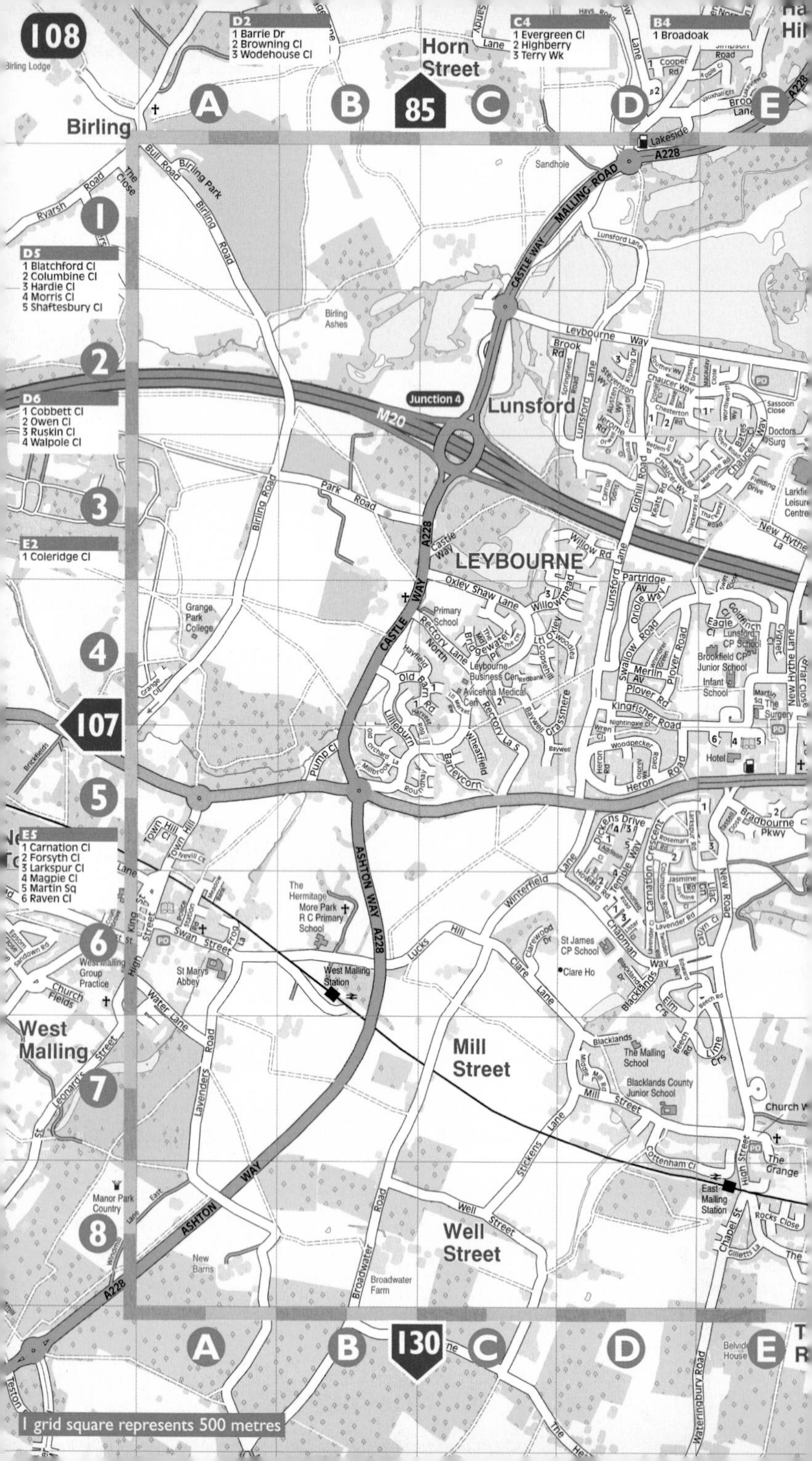

1 grid square represents 500 metres

F5
1 Ditton Court Cl
G2
1 Westmead
H4
1 Trewin Cl
J4
1 The Lindens
2 Teapot La
J5
1 Rowan Cl
86
110
131
Eccles
AYLESFORD
Millhall
DITTON
Holt Hill
Royal British Legion Village
ME20
M20
A20 LONDON ROAD
A20
LONDON ROAD
HERMITAGE LANE
B2246
HERMITAGE
Larkfield Trading Estate
New Hythe Business Park
Larkfield Trading Est
New Hythe Lane
New Hythe Station
Central Road
West Mill Road
Mill Hall Road
College Road
Bellingham Way
Perimeter Road
Medway Valley Walk
Rowe Place Farm
Bull Lane
High Street
Cork Street
Skinners Cl
Mackenders Cl
Mackenders Lane
Forstal Road
Bush Row
Yew Tree Industrial Est
Aylesford Station
Station Road
Heathcote Close
Sedley Close
Aylesford Cem
Robson Drive
Priory Grove
Aylesford Secondary School
Aylesford CP School
Teapot Lane
Premier Pl
The Avenue
The Hawthorns
Elm Walk
The Oaks
Firs Close
Ash Close
The Coppice
Hall Road
Homefarm Estate
Greenacres Dental Health Cen
Orchard Avenue
The Bounds
Sycamore Drive
Clark Mews
Admiral Moore Drive
Preston Hall Hospital
East Park Road
Coldharbour Lane
Cobdown Close
Orchard Grove
Bell Lane
Fernleigh Rise
The Ferns
Downderry Wy
Ditton Pl
Streamside
Bradbourne Lane
St Peters Cl
The Stream
St Peters Road
Wilton Drive
Kingsdown Industrial Estate
New Road
Medina Rd
Woodlands Rd
Ditton C of E Junior School
Ditton Infant School
Linkway
Nursery Rd
Pear Tree Avenue
Scott Close
Kiln Barn Road
Cherry Orchard
Cedar Close
Primrose Drive
Birch Crs
Holt Wood Avenue
Brassey Dr
Acorn Grove
Corse Crescent
Finch Close
Russett Close
South Aylesford Retail Park
Mills Road
Lake Road
Wood Close
Burntash Road
Brittania Business Park
Quarry Wood Industrial Estate
Ragstone Court
Barming Station
Easterfield
Hermitage Court
Hermitage Farm
Millhall
Aylesford Primary School
Blackthorn Drive
Juncti

C8
1 Bramshott Cl
2 Eversley Cl
C7
1 Cranleigh Gdns
2 Hextable Cl
A3
1 Unwin Cl
87
Pilgrims
Lower
Eccles
Eccles Rw
Cork Street
Skinners Cl
Mackenders Cl
Mackenders Lane
Bull Lane
Centenary Way
Chatham Rd
Chatham Road
A229
North Downs Way
Rochester Road
A
B
C
D
E
Rowe Place Farm
D6
1 Charlock Cl
2 Thirlemere Cl
1
2
Lane
D7
1 Lacy Cl
2 Lockswood
3 Rayleigh Cl
3
Medway Valley Walk
Pratling Street
Pratling Street
Tollgate Way
Chatham Road
AYLESFORD
E2
1 Higham Vw
High Street
Primary School
Mount Pleasant
Rochester Road
Powell Cl
Bush Row
Old Mill Lane
St Michaels Close
Beddow Way
Forstal Road
Deacon Industrial Estate
Cottage Industrial Estate
Motorway Industrial Estate
Forstal
4
Station Close
Aylesford
Junction 6
Forstal Road
River Medway
109
M20
Homefarm Estate
Coldharbour Lane
Little Preston
5
Clark Mews
E3
1 Pilgrims Vw
Junction 5
East Park Road
Kent County Council
Lock Lane
Forstal Road
Medway Valley Walk
Allington
Castle Road
Liphook Way
Laverstoke Road
St Leonards Road
Twenty Twenty Industrial Est
Orchard Business Cen
A20
6
LONDON ROAD
Royal British Legion Village
E7
1 Fawley Cl
2 Monckton's Dr
St Laurence Avenue
Ringlestone
HERMITAGE LANE
B2246
7
Blackmanstone Way
Fordwich Close
Eastry Close
Chillham Road
Hildenborough Crescent
The Computer Surg
School
Mid Kent Shopping Cen
Castle Rd
Lullingstone Road
Eynsford Road
Beckenham Drive
Braunstone Drive
Larking Drive
Egerton Road
Dickens Road
Foxglove Rise
The Mallows
Beaver Road
Trenton Close
Juniper Close
Aylesham Drive
Nursery Avenue
Tintern Road
Odiham Drive
Stansted Close
Doctors Surg
Flaxman Dr
Hildenborough
Newbury Avenue
Hale Road
Barming Station
8
Headingley Road
Allington Way
Conway Road
Talbot Road
Junior School
Maple Avenue
Grace Avenue
Palmar Road
Buckland Lane
Buckland Av
Little Buckland
Lane
Maidstone Grammar School for Girls
Ash Grove
Maxwell Drive
Leonard Close
Howard Drive
Grove
Riverhead Close
Hazlitt Dr
Chilham Close
The Maplesden Noakes School
132
Vicary Way
Maidstone Lawn Tennis Club
Trapham Road
Clement Ct
Greyfriars Close
Brunswick House CP School
Keswick Dr
Poplar Gr
Sterling Av
Kenward Road
Roseleigh Avenue
Langdale Rise
The Somerfield Hosp
Brunswick House Clinic
Maidstone Barracks
Hermitage Court
Hermitage
1 grid square represents 500 metres

F6
1 Ringlestone Crs
G6
1 Becksbourne Cl
2 Downs Cl
F
G
H
88
J
K
1
G7
1 The Hedges
2
G8
1 Penenden St
3
H6
1 Ashburnham Rd
2 Clewson Ri
3 Harbourland Cl
4 Staplers Ct
4
112
5
H7
1 Woodlands Cl
6
J8
1 Basmere Cl
2 Crayford Cl
3 Kewlands
4 Luddenham Cl
5 Whatman Cl
7
Junction 7
K8
1 Netley Cl
2 Newenden Cl
8
Harp Farm Road
Lidsing Road
Centenary Walk Maidstone
Harp Farm
Lidsing
Road
Pilgrims
Way
Pilgrims Way
Boarley Farm
Boarley Lane
Boxley House
The Street
Forge Lane
Abbey Gate
Tyland
Lane
Boxley
Park House
Boxley Road
Grange Lane
Sandling
Harbourland
Sandy Lane
Burleigh Dr
Sandling Lane
Sandling CP School
Woodcut
Erith Cl
Downs View Rd
Raymer Road
Neville Close
Downs Road
Boxley Cl
M20
Park Wood
Chatham Road
Command Road
Park Lane
Grapple Road
The Hedges
Bannister Road
Woodland Way
Byron Road
Wordsworth
North Way
Penenden Heath
Penenden Heath Road
Heathfield Av
Faraday Road
Heathfield Close
Heathfield
Sittingbourne Road
BEARSTED ROAD
A249
Hillary Road
St Pauls County Infant School
North Borough CP Junior School
Pine Grove
7
Tudor Avenue
Knowle Road
Curzon Road
Salisbury Road
Grecian Street
Waterlow Rd
Boxley Road
John Street
Peel Street
Perry St
Sandling Road
Randall St
Hope St
ROYAL ENGINEERS' ROAD
Park Avenue
Hatherall Rd
Recreation Close
Clifton Cl
SITTINGBOURNE ROAD
Littlebourne Road
Bonnington Rd
Cooling Close
Hampton Road
Bedgebury Cl
The Medlars
Blendon Rd
Boxgrove Rd
Bearsted
New Cut Rd
Henley Fields
Grovewood Drive
LWR BOXLEY ROAD
Prison
Kent County Council
Sessions House
Maidstone East Stn
Brenchley Gardens
HOLLAND ROAD
The Club House
Mid Kent Sch
Union
Brewer Street
Snowdon Avenue
East Borough CP School
Hadlow Road
Commodore Road
Lombardy Drive
Grove Green
Lodge Road
Vinters Park
Medical Centre
133
F
G
H
J
K

1 grid square represents 500 metres

Lower Cox Street
Beaux Aires Farm
F
G
H
90
J
K
1
2
3
4
5
6
7
8
114
135
Binbury
Binbury Lane
A249
Longton Wood
Squirrel Wood
Little Budds Farm
Rumstead Lane
Friningham
Coldblow Lane
Coldharbour Lane
Castle Hill
North Downs Way
Coldblow
Coldharbour
Scragged Oak Road
Aldington Lane
Pilgrims Way
Thurnham Keep Farm
Cobham Manor Farm
Whitehall
Whitehall Road
Water Lane
Broad Street
Lane

1 grid square represents 500 metres

92

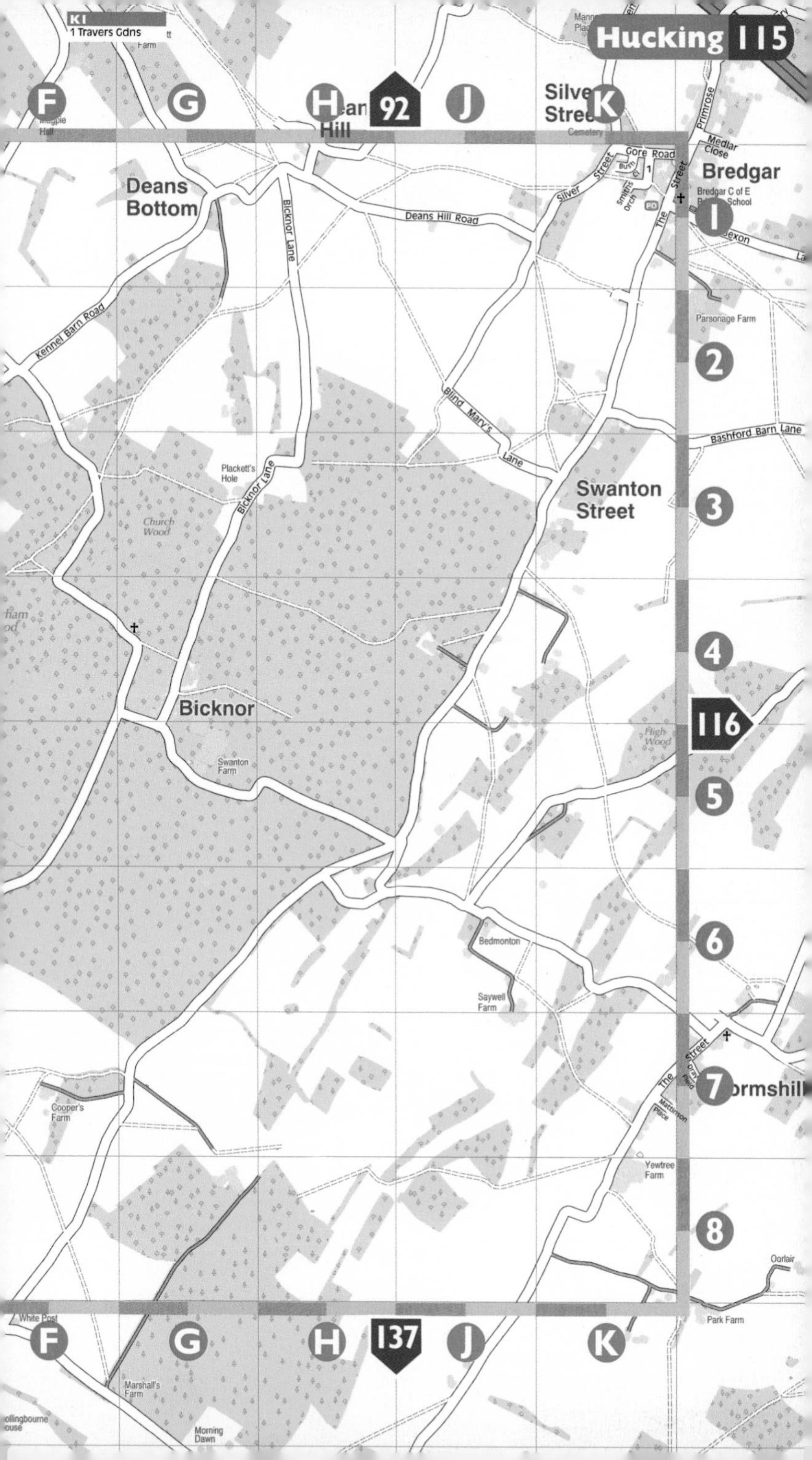
K1
1 Travers Gdns
F
G
H
J
K
Deans Bottom
Kennel Barn Road
Bicknor Lane
Deans Hill Road
Silver Street
Gore Road
Bush
Smiths Orch
The Street
Cemetery
Primrose
Medlar Close
Bredgar
Bredgar C of E
1
2
3
4
5
6
7
8
Parsonage Farm
Bashford Barn Lane
Blind Mary's Lane
Swanton Street
Plackett's Hole
Church Wood
Bicknor
Swanton Farm
High Wood
Bedmonton
Saywell Farm
The Street
Mattinson Place
Cooper's Farm
Yewtree Farm
Oorlair
Park Farm
White Post
Marshall's Farm
Morning Dawn

116

137

116
Silver Street
Cemetery
Wren
Lane
Primrose
Rookery Cl
Woodstock
Oakwood Farm
93
A
B
C
D
E
Medlar Close
Core Road
Bush Cl
Smiths Cl
Silver Street
The Street
Bredgar
Bredgar C of E Primary School
M2
Bexon Lane
Parsonage Farm
Ruins Barn Road
ME9
Bexon
Bexon Lane
Bottom
Bashford Barn Lane
Swanton Street
Bottom Pond Road
Horn Hill
Bottom Pond
Trundle Wood
115
Frinsted Road
Bottom Pond Road
Norwood
Stock Wood
Milstead Manor Farm
Milstead & F C of E Prima
Frinsted
The Street
Gray's Field
Wormshill
Copes
The Mattinson Place
Kippen
Yewtree Farm
Oorlair
Park Farm
Yoke's Court
138
Madam's Court
Lord's Hill
1 grid square represents 500 metres
1
2
3
4
5
6
7
8

Rodmersham Squash Club
Bottles
Hill
Upper Rodmersham
Bargain Hill
94
F
G
H
J
K
Cheney
Bottles Lane
Dully Road
1
Pitstock Farm
Cheney H
Road
Penfield House
Lane
Road
Penfield
Rawling Street
Slough
Pitstock
Dully Road
Kingsdown
2
Ludgate
Road
Kingsdown Road
Dungate
3
M2
Mintching Wood Lane
Sawpit Road
M2
Mintching Wood
Kingsdown Wood
4
ad
5
Manor Road
Bluetown
Hollybushes
Great Higham
Down Court Road
6
Down Court
Torry Hill
West End
Little Higham
Doddington
PO
7
The Street
8
Timbold Hill
Coalpit Lane
139
F
G
H
J
K
Old Lenham Road
Solomons Temple
Syndale Bottom
Wichling
Temple Farm

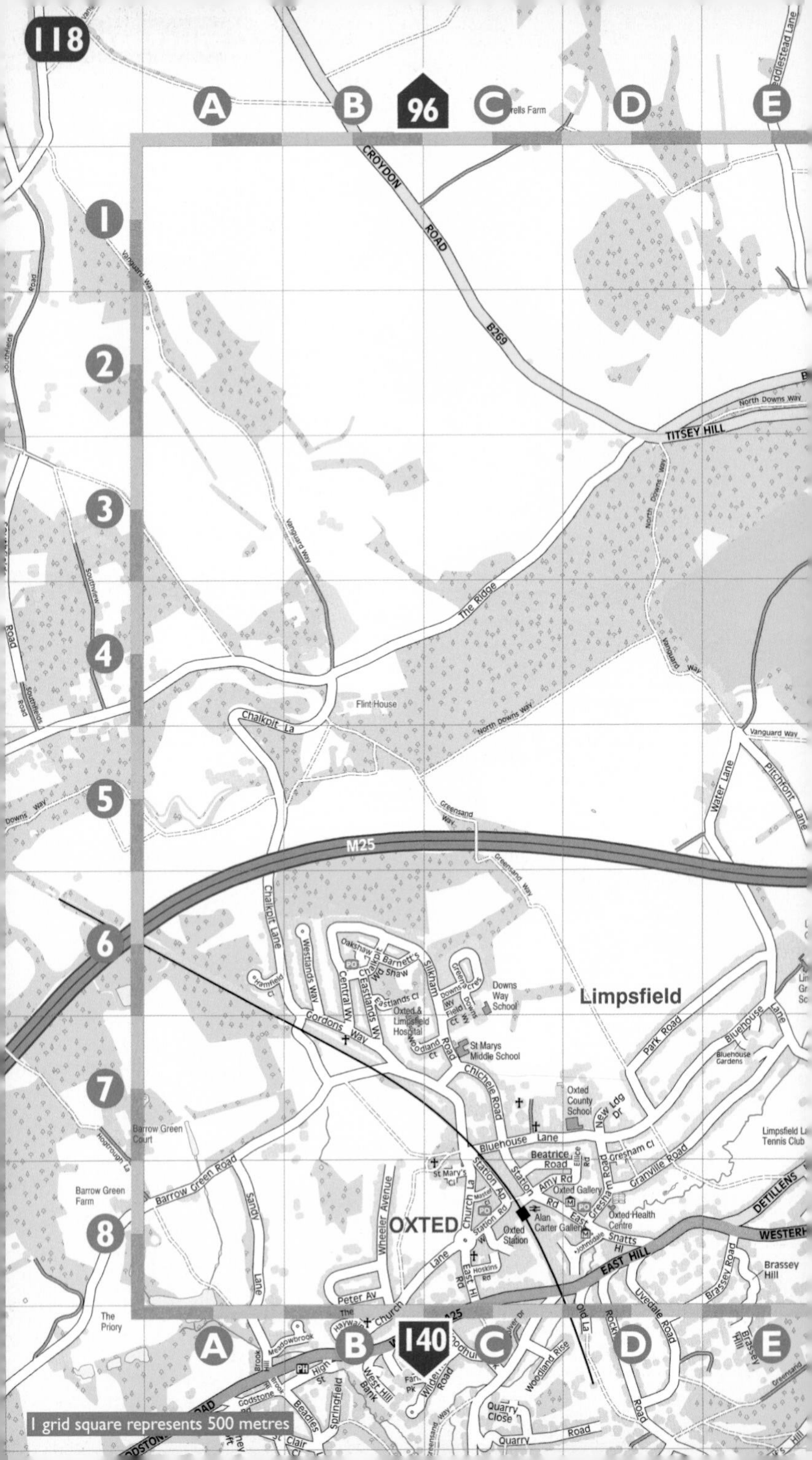

96
140
A
B
C
D
E
1
2
3
4
5
6
7
8
rells Farm
Beddlestead Lane
CROYDON ROAD
B269
Vanguard Way
Southfields Road
Southview
Road
North Downs Way
TITSEY HILL
The Ridge
Flint House
Chalkpit La
Chalkpit Lane
Greensand Way
Vanguard Way
Water Lane
Pitchfront Lane
Downs Way
M25
Limpsfield
Hamfield Cl
Westlands Way
Oakshaw
Chalkpit Wd
Barnett's Shaw
Silkham
Greenacre
Central Wy
Eastlands Wy
Eastlands Cl
Downs Way School
Oxted & Limpsfield Hospital
Gordons Way
Woodland Ct
Road
St Marys Middle School
Chichele Road
Park Road
Bluehouse Lane
Bluehouse Gardens
Oxted County School
New Ldg Dr
Limpsfield Lawn Tennis Club
Barrow Green Court
Barrow Green Farm
Hooptrough La
Barrow Green Road
Sandy Lane
Bluehouse Lane
Beatrice Road
Ellice Rd
Gresham Cl
Granville Road
Gresham Road
St Mary's Cl
Station App
Station Rd
Amy Rd
Oxted Gallery
Oxted Health Centre
Church La
Wheeler Avenue
OXTED
Station Rd W
Oxted Station
Alan Carter Gallery
East Snatts Hl
Johnsdale
EAST HILL
DETILLENS
WESTERHAM
Brassey Road
Brassey Hill
East Hl Rd
Hoskins Rd
Peter Av
Lane
The Priory
The Haywain
Church
A25
Old La
Rockfield Road
Uvedale Road
Meadowbrook
Brook Hill
High St
West Hill Bank
Wilderness Road
Woodland Rise
Quarry Close
Quarry Road
Godstone Road
Beadles
Springfield
Greensand Way
1 grid square represents 500 metres

F
G
H
97
J
K
1
2
3
4
5
6
7
8
120
141
Ninehams Road
Maesmaur Road
Edgar Road
Ship Field Close
Ship
Old Lane
Hill Road
Parkwood Road
Palace Road
Avenue
School
Chestnut
Betsom's Hill
The Avenue
Chestnut Avenue
Church Hill
Clarks Lane Farm
Approach Road
LARKS LANE
North Downs Way
White Lane
Tatsfield Court Farm
Rectory Lane
Gaysham Farm
B269
Pilgrims Farm
Clacket Lane
Pilgrims Lane
Titsey
Clacket Lane Service Area
Park Farm
Clacket Lane Service Area
Titsey Wood
Vanguard Way
M25
ROAD
Broomlands Farm
Westwood Farm
Clacket Lane
Broomlands Lane
Sandy Lane
Moorhouse Bank
Hookwood
Hookwood Corner
B269
Limpsfield C of E School
Ballards Lane
Limpsfield Chart Golf Club
A25
Grub Street
Wolf's Road
Road
Limpsfield Common
Stoneswood Road
Brick Kiln Lane
KENT HATCH ROAD
Ridlands Grove
Ridlands Lane
Ridlands
Stoneleigh Road
Chapel Road
The High Chart

D5
1 Darenth Gdns
2 Grange Cl
3 Hollingworth Wy
4 Market Wy
C6
1 Lodge La
2 Squerryes Mede
3 Stratton Ter
C5
1 Bartlett Rd
Grays Road
Tatsfield Lane
Palace Road
Avenue
Chestnut
Betsom's Hill
The Avenue
A233
WESTERHAM HILL
North Downs Way
Pilgrim House
TN16
The Avenue
Hill School
Hill Park
Betsoms Farm
A233
LONDON ROAD
Force Green Lane
Force Green
Gaysham Farm
Westerham Wood
M25
BEGGARS LANE
Ash Road
Elm Road
Hartley Road
Oak Road
London Road
Sandy Lane
Oak Lodge Lane
Madan Road
Court Lodge
Churchill School
Roselare Close
Hortons Way
The Flyers Way
The White House Gallery
Churchill Business Park
CROYDON ROAD
B2024
Buckham Thorns Road
The Slip
The Paddock
Rysted Lane
South Bank
Croft Road
Marwell
Farleycroft
Granville Road
Westways
Delagarde Road
Grange Close
St Mary's Court
The Green
Quebec Avenue
Costells Meadow
Westbury Terrace
Trotts Lane
Farley Nursery
New Street
MARKET SQUARE
VICARAGE HILL A25
Mill Street
Winterton Surgery
Churchill Gallery
Greensand Way
Westwood Farm
Clacket Lane
Covers Farmhouse
Farley Lane
Wellers Close
Black Eagle Close
HIGH STREET
Mill Lane
WESTERHAM
HOSEY HILL
B2026
Moorhouse Bank
Moorhouse
Greensand Way
Hosey Hill
HOSEY COMMON ROAD
Goodley Stock Road
Moorhouse Road
Kent County
Surrey County
B2026
Goodley Stock
A
B
98
C
D
E
1
2
3
4
119
5
6
7
8
142
1 grid square represents 500 metres

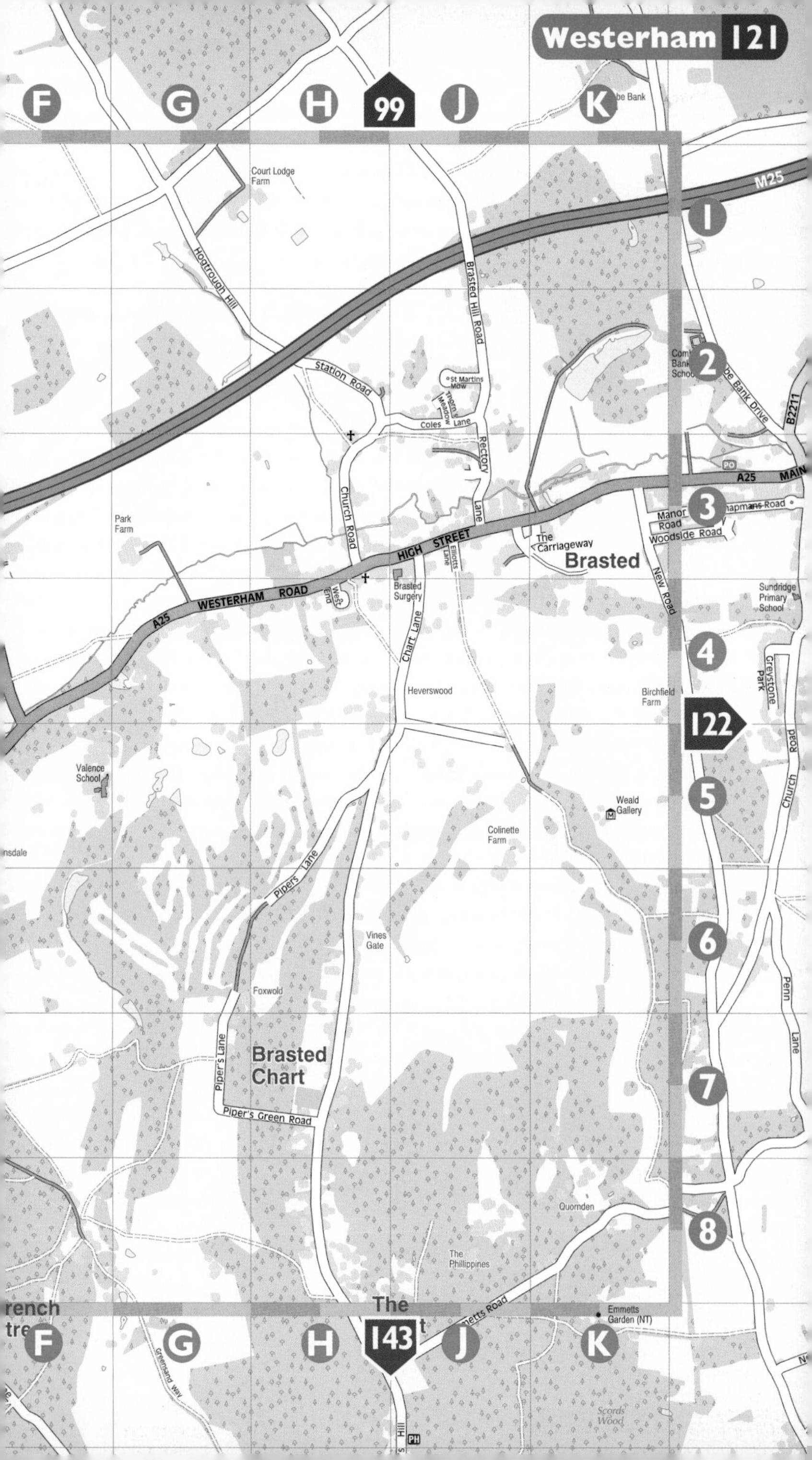
F
G
H
99
J
K
I
2
3
4
122
5
6
7
8
143
M25
Court Lodge Farm
Hogtrough Hill
Brasted Hill Road
Station Road
St Martins Mdw
Thorn's Meadow
Coles Lane
Rectory Lane
Church Road
Park Farm
HIGH STREET
A25 WESTERHAM ROAD
West End
Brasted Surgery
Elliotts Lane
The Carriageway
Brasted
Manor Road
Chapmans Road
Woodside Road
New Road
A25 MAIN
PO
Combe Bank School
Combe Bank Drive
B2211
Sundridge Primary School
Greystone Park
Chart Lane
Heverswood
Birchfield Farm
Church Road
Valence School
Weald Gallery
Colinette Farm
Pipers Lane
Vines Gate
Foxwold
Penn Lane
Brasted Chart
Piper's Lane
Piper's Green Road
Quornden
The Phillippines
Emmetts Road
Emmetts Garden (NT)
The
Greensand Way
Scords Wood
PH

1 grid square represents 500 metres

G1
1 Linden Sq
J3
1 Littlecourt Rd
F
G
H
101
J
K
8
9
Riverhead
St John's
Bradbourne School
BRADBOURNE VALE ROAD
A25
A224
LONDON ROAD
AMHERST HILL
WORSHIPS HILL
Chipstead Lane
Amherst County Junior School
Infant School
Shoreham Lane
Sevenoaks Station
TN13
TN14
ST BOTOLPH'S ROAD
B2020
TUBS HILL
HIGH ST
A225
DARTFORD ROAD
ST JOHN'S HILL
Sevenoaks CP School
St Hilarys School
The Granville School
Zobel College
Council Offices
Pegasus Gallery
Town Medical Cen
Chantry Medical Practice
Stag Theatre
124
Kippington
Kippington Road
Brittains Lane
Marlborough Crescent
Salters Heath
SEVENOAKS BY-PASS
A21(T)
B2042
COLD ARBOR RD
BACK LANE
Dibden Lane
Dibden
New Beacon School
Cross Keys
Ashgrove Road
Oak Lane
Solefield School
Sevenoaks School
Sevenoaks Swimming Centre
TONBRIDGE
Mill Bank Wood
West Heath School
Sevenoaks Common
Gracious Lane
Letter Box Lane
Windmill Road
Hubbard's Hill
White House Road
145
Weald Place
1
2
3
4
5
6
7
8

Seal
A3 1 Holly Bush La
Bat & Ball Station
Greatness Park Cemetery
Pinehurst
Highlands Pk
Ash Platt
SEAL A25 ROAD
HIGH STREET
Wilderness Sports
Wilderness School
102
Sevenoaks Hosp
Hillingdon
North Vw Rd
Avenue
Wildernesse
Dorton College of Further Education
Dorton House
Seal Drive
Grove Rd
St John's
Sevenoaks Town Council
9
Hillingdon Rise
The Green
Wickenden
Swaffield Rd
Westfield
St Johns Hill Surgery
Sevenoaks CP School
St Hilarys School
Bradbourne
Linden Chase
ST JOHN'S HILL
Quaker's Hall Lane
Kennedy Gdns
Lansdowne Rd
Wildernesse Mt
ROAD
Prospect Rd
Cobden Rd
Bethel Road
Hartsland Road
Bayham Road
Serpentine
Hillside Rd
Knole Rd
Quaker Cl
Quarry Hill
HOLLOW
Woodland Rise
Wilderness Golf Club
Dorton Dr
Park Lane
Parkfield
Blackhall Lane
Pineneedle La
Mount
Woodside Rd
Hatch Lane
Hunsdon Dr
DARTFORD ROAD A225
Court Rd
Avenue Rd
Hollybush Cl
Chestnut La
Ashley Close
Avenue
Vine
2020 ST BOTOLPH'S ROAD
THE VINE
SEAL
Blackhall
SEVENOAKS
HILL A224 LONDON ROAD
The Drive
Eardley Rd
Zobel College
Council Offices
Gordon Road
Pembroke Rd
Chartway
Plymouth Pk
Plymouth Drive
Warren Court
Knole Way
Lady Boswell C of E School
Sevenoaks Swimming Centre
HIGH ST A225
Suffolk Wy
Pegasus Gallery
Buckhurst Lane
The Bank Street Gallery
South Pk
Town Medical Centre
Chantry Medical Practice
123
Back Lane
Duchess Walk
Stake Farm
Rectory La
Knole Lane
Cemetery
Oak La
Hotel
Oakfields
Glebe Rd
Sevenoaks School
Knole (NT)
Knole Park
Grassy Lane
Lane
Solefields School House
Fiennes Wy
Solefields School
Burntwood Rd
Burntwood Road
Oak Av
Stafford Wy
Hurst Wy
Shenden Close
TONBRIDGE ROAD
Turners Gdns
Solefields Road
West Heath
Ashgrove Rd
Weald
Road
Garth Road
Cade La
Wood
The Rise
Shenden Wy
White Hart Cl
Broad Walk
Chestnut Walk
West Heath School
Brattle Wood
Hart Wood
White
Letter Box Lane
Parkland Cl
Fernside La
A225
Windmill Road
Beechmont Rd
Gracious Lane
St Julian's
146
River Hill
Hubbard's Hill
Hill
Lane
1 grid square represents 500 metres
Riverhill House
Und
A B C D E
1 2 3 4 5 6 7 8

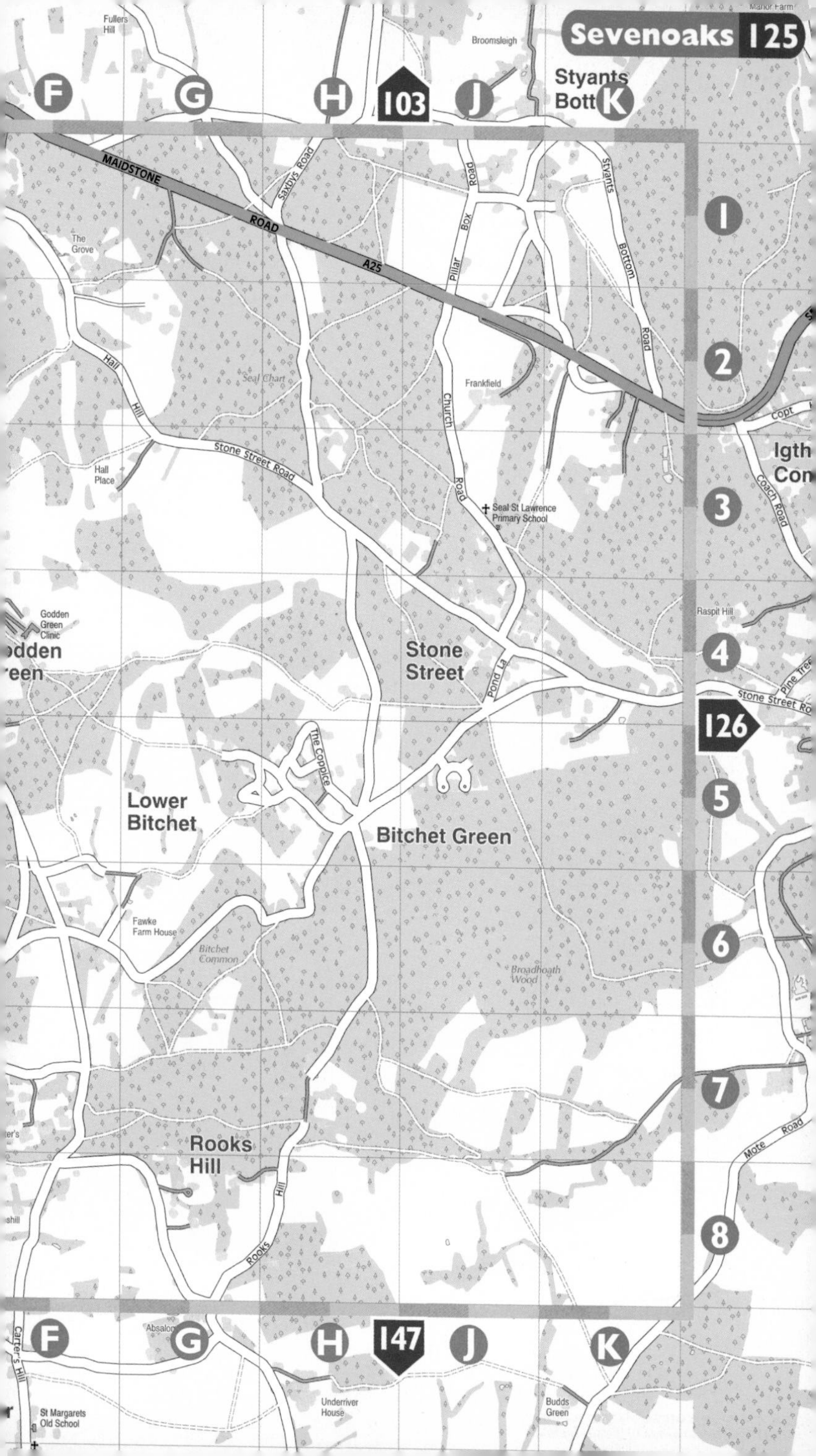
Fullers Hill
Broomsleigh
Manor Farm
Styants Bott
F
G
H
103
J
K
MAIDSTONE ROAD
A25
Saxbys Road
Pillar Box Road
Styants Bottom Road
The Grove
Hall Hill
Seal Chart
Frankfield
Church Road
Copt
Igth Con
Coach Road
Stone Street Road
Hall Place
Seal St Lawrence Primary School
Raspit Hill
Godden Green Clinic
odden reen
Stone Street
Pond La
Pine Tree
126
The Coppice
Lower Bitchet
Bitchet Green
Fawke Farm House
Bitchet Common
Broadhoath Wood
Rooks Hill
Mote Road
1
2
3
4
5
6
7
8
Absalom
147
Carter's Hill
Underriver House
Budds Green
St Margarets Old School

Styants Bottom
Manor Farm
Oldbury
104
A
B
C
D
E
Ightham County Primary School
A227 BOROUGH GR
THE ST
Busty La
Trycewell Lane
Mill Lane
Rectory Lane
BATES HILL A2
Oldbury
Spring Lane
Upr Spring Lane
SEVENOAKS ROAD A25
Prestons
Ightham
Ightham Warren
Old Lane
Redwell
Nutfields
Common Road
Copt Hall Road
Crowhurst Lane
Crowhurst Farm
Igtham Common
Coach Road
Sandy Lane
Tebbs Way
Back Lane
TONBRIDGE ROAD
Bewley Farm
Winfield
Raspit Hill
Ismays Road
Bewley Lane
Pine Tree La
Stone Street Road
Ivy Hatch
125
PH
A227
Sheet Hill
High Cross Road
Yopps Green
Plaxtol Lane
Tree Lane
Church Hill
Ightham Mote (NT)
Fairlawne
Plaxtol CP School
Mote Road
Greensand Way
Shipbourne
148
Fairlawne Home Farm
Upper Green Road
Reeds Lane
Budds Green
Shipbourne
1
2
3
4
5
6
7
8
1 grid square represents 500 metres

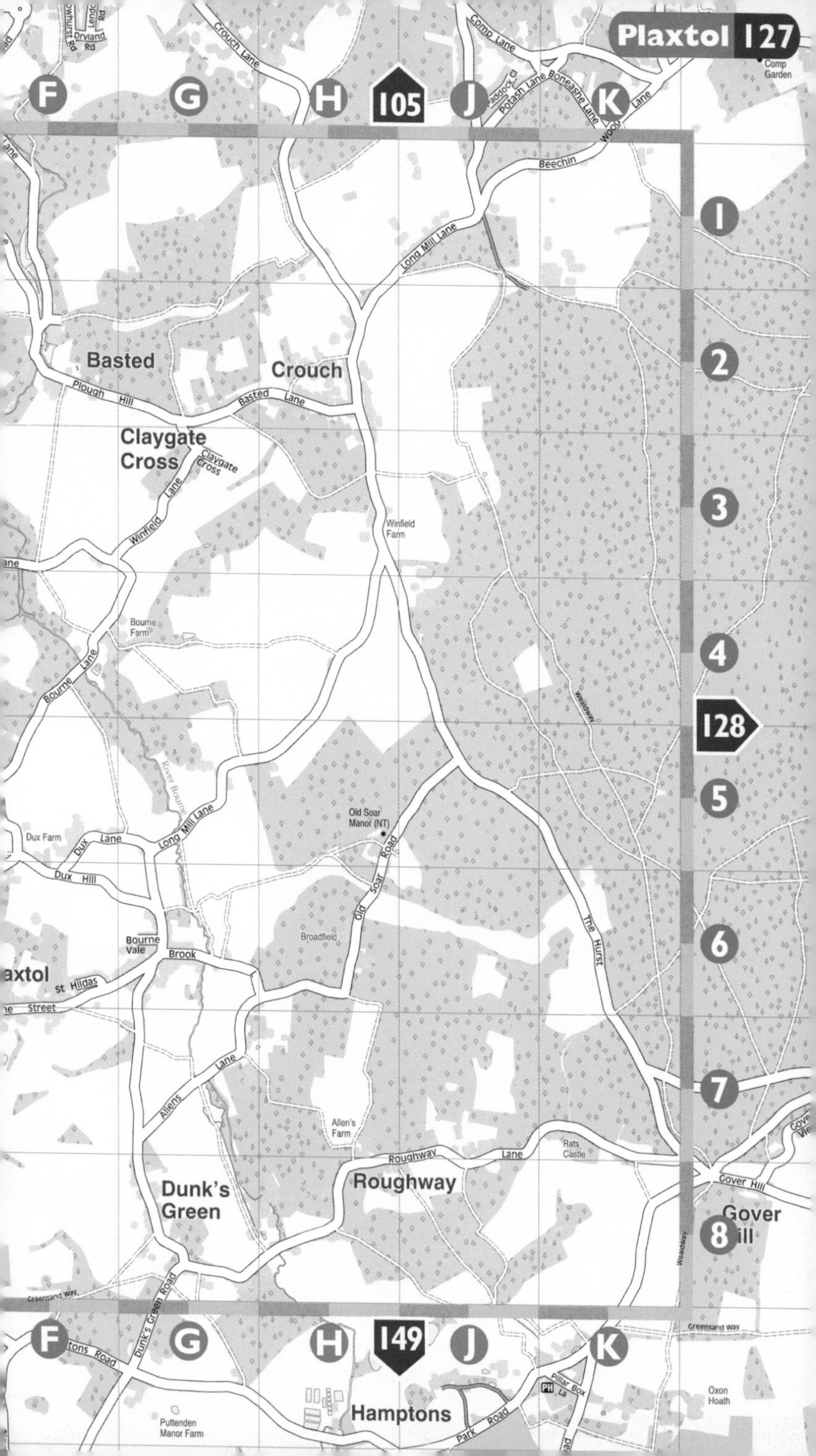
Crouch Lane
Comp Lane
Comp Garden
Dryland Rd
Paddock Cl
Potash Lane
Boneashe Lane
Wood Lane
F
G
H
105
J
K
Beechin
Long Mill Lane
1
2
3
4
128
5
6
7
8
Basted
Crouch
Plough Hill
Basted Lane
Claygate Cross
Claygate Cross
Winfield Lane
Winfield Farm
Bourne Farm
Bourne Lane
River Bourne
Wealdway
Long Mill Lane
Old Soar Manor (NT)
Old Soar Road
Dux Farm
Dux Lane
Dux Hill
Broadfield
The Hurst
Bourne Vale
Brook
St Hildas
Street
axtol
Allens Lane
Allen's Farm
Rats Castle
Roughway Lane
Roughway
Dunk's Green
Gover Hill
Gover Hill
Greensand Way
Dunk's Green Road
149
Pillar Box La
PH
Oxon Hoath
Puttenden Manor Farm
Hamptons
Park Road

1 grid square represents 500 metres

H3
1 Mustang Rd
J4
1 Mercers Pl
Street
St Leonard's Tower (rems. of)
Farm
F
G
H
107
J
K
A228
New Barns
Windmill Lane West
King Hill
Orwell Spike
Testson Rd
Tower View
Abbey Rd
Avenue
Kings Hill
KING HILL A228
1
2
3
4
5
6
7
8
Gibson Drive
Spitfire Road
Hurricane Road
Lysander Rd
Beaufighter Rd
Javelin
Mosquito Road
Lancaster Way
Tempest Rd
Forest Way
Churchill Square
Crispin Way
Typhoon Road
Meteor Road
Stirling Rd
Blenheim Rd
University of Greenwich
Kings Hill Primary School
Anson Av
Discovery Drive
Mitchell Rd
Lambourne Dr
Chestnut Cl
Worcester Av
Kings Hill Golf Club
Crabtree Cl
Russet Way
Garden Way
Bramley Way
Kent Street
Herne Pound
Beech Road
Kent Street
Lapins La
Saxon Cl
Lapins Lane
Pippin Way
Strumer Ct
Peregrine Road
Montfort Dr
Victoria Dr
Admiral Way
Great Canon Court
130
Canon Lane
MALLING ROAD
A228
Danns Lane
Wents
Moorcocks
Butcher's Lane
Torrington Close
Church Close
Tonbridge Road
orth
The Street
A26
Bull Farm
Pavilion Lane
TONBRIDGE ROAD
A26
Cemetery
Old Road
Pizien Well
Pizien Well Road
Mereworth Castle
The Alders
Nettlestead Lane
Nettles
Rock Farm
Forge Farm
151
Gibbs Hill
Old Church Road
Park Road
Roydon
MAIDSTONE ROAD

Manor Park Country Park
Windmill Lane
East
ASHTON WAY
A228
Teston Rd
Tower View
Broadwater Road
Broad Farm
108
Well Street
Well Street
East Malling Station
Chapel St
Rocks Close
Gilletts La
Pikey Lane
Belvidere House
Waterinbury Road
Lavenders Road
The Heath
Sweets
East Malling Heath
Waterinbury Road
Teston Road
Barming Road
Ketridge Lane
Cattering Wood
Great Canon Court
Hoath Wood
Livesey Street
Malling Road
Livesey Street
129
Little Canon
Canon Lane
Red Hill
Red Hill
Waterinbury
Doctors Surgery
The Orchines
Nestor Court
A26
Cemetery
Mill Lane
Upper Mill
Lodge Close
Love Lane
Red House Gardens
Old Road
Pizien Well
Fields Lane
Cobbs Cl
The Brucks
BOW ROAD
Warden Mill Close
Rivers Rd
Phoenix Dr
Teston
B2015
Waterside Mews
Wateringbury Station
Medway Valley Walk
Nettlestead
LC
Rock Farm
Bryant Close
Bishops Cl
Gibbs Hill
MAIDSTONE ROAD
152
Hill
Hunt Street
A B C D E
1 2 3 4 5 6 7 8
1 grid square represents 500 metres

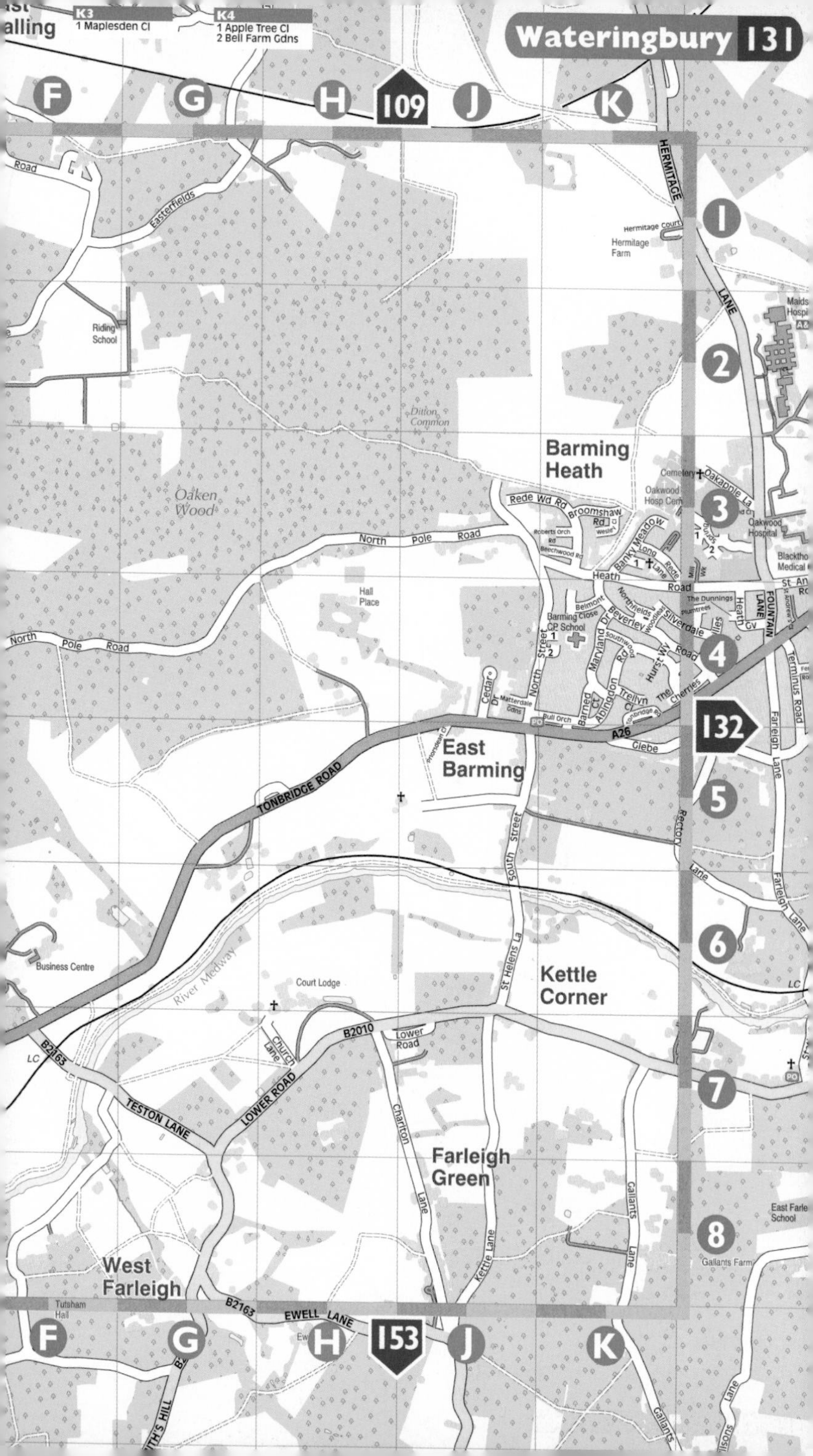
alling
K3
1 Maplesden Cl
K4
1 Apple Tree Cl
2 Bell Farm Gdns
F
G
H
109
J
K
Road
Easterfields
HERMITAGE
LANE
Hermitage Court
Hermitage Farm
Riding School
Ditton Common
Barming Heath
Cemetery
Oakapple La
Oakwood Hosp Cem
Oakwood Hospital
Blackthorn Medical
Rede Wd Rd
Broomshaw Rd
Westers
Roberts Orch Rd
Beechwood Rd
Banky Meadow
Long Rede Lane
Mill Wk
Heath Road
St Andrews
Oaken Wood
North Pole Road
Hall Place
The Dunnings
Plumtrees
Heath Gv
FOUNTAIN LANE
Belmont
Barming Close
Barming C.P. School
Northfields
Beverley
Woodleas
Silverdale
Maryland Dr
Southwood Rd
Hurst Wy
Road
North Street
Cedar Dr
Matterdale Gdns
Barned Ct
Abingdon
Trellyn Cl
The Cherries
Tonbridge Rd
Bull Orch
PO
A26
Glebe
Priorsdean Cl
Terminus Road
Farleigh Lane
132
East Barming
TONBRIDGE ROAD
South Street
Rectory Lane
Business Centre
River Medway
St Helens La
Kettle Corner
LC
Court Lodge
B2010
Lower Road
Church Lane
B2163
TESTON LANE
LOWER ROAD
Charlton Lane
Farleigh Green
Gallants Lane
Kettle Lane
East Farleigh School
Gallants Farm
West Farleigh
Tutsham Hall
EWELL LANE
153
Ew
Gallants
Lane
ITH'S HILL
1
2
3
4
5
6
7
8

B3
1 Hambledon Ct
B2
1 Gainsborough Dr
B1
1 Fordingbridge Cl
2 Hawkwood
3 Montpelier Ga
4 Rosslyn Gn
5 The Russets
6 Shearwater
7 The Thatchers
8 Watermill Cl
9 Wedgewood Cl
A3
1 Catherine Cl
2 Nicholas Cl
B4
1 Burghclere Dr
2 Knowlton Gdns
3 Portsdown Cl
4 St Margarets Cl
C3
1 Stanford Dr
C4
1 Farnborough Cl
2 The Laurels
D1
1 Elvington Cl
D2
1 Amherst Cl
2 Deerhurst Gdns
3 Somerfield Cl
D3
1 Manor House Dr
2 Poppy Cl
D4
1 Flood Hatch
2 Flume End
3 The Spillway
4 The Stampers
E1
1 Doddington Ct
2 Lesley Pl
E2, E3
Street names for these grid squares are listed at the back of the index
E4
1 Beaconsfield Rd
2 The Laxey
3 The Meadows
4 St Stephen's Sq
E5
1 The Quern
110
131
154
6
Barming Station
Barming Heath
Maidstone Hospital
Oakwood Hospital
ME16
Fant
Tovil
River Medway
East Farleigh
East Farleigh Station
Dean Street
TONBRIDGE ROAD
LOWER ROAD
1 grid square represents 500 metres

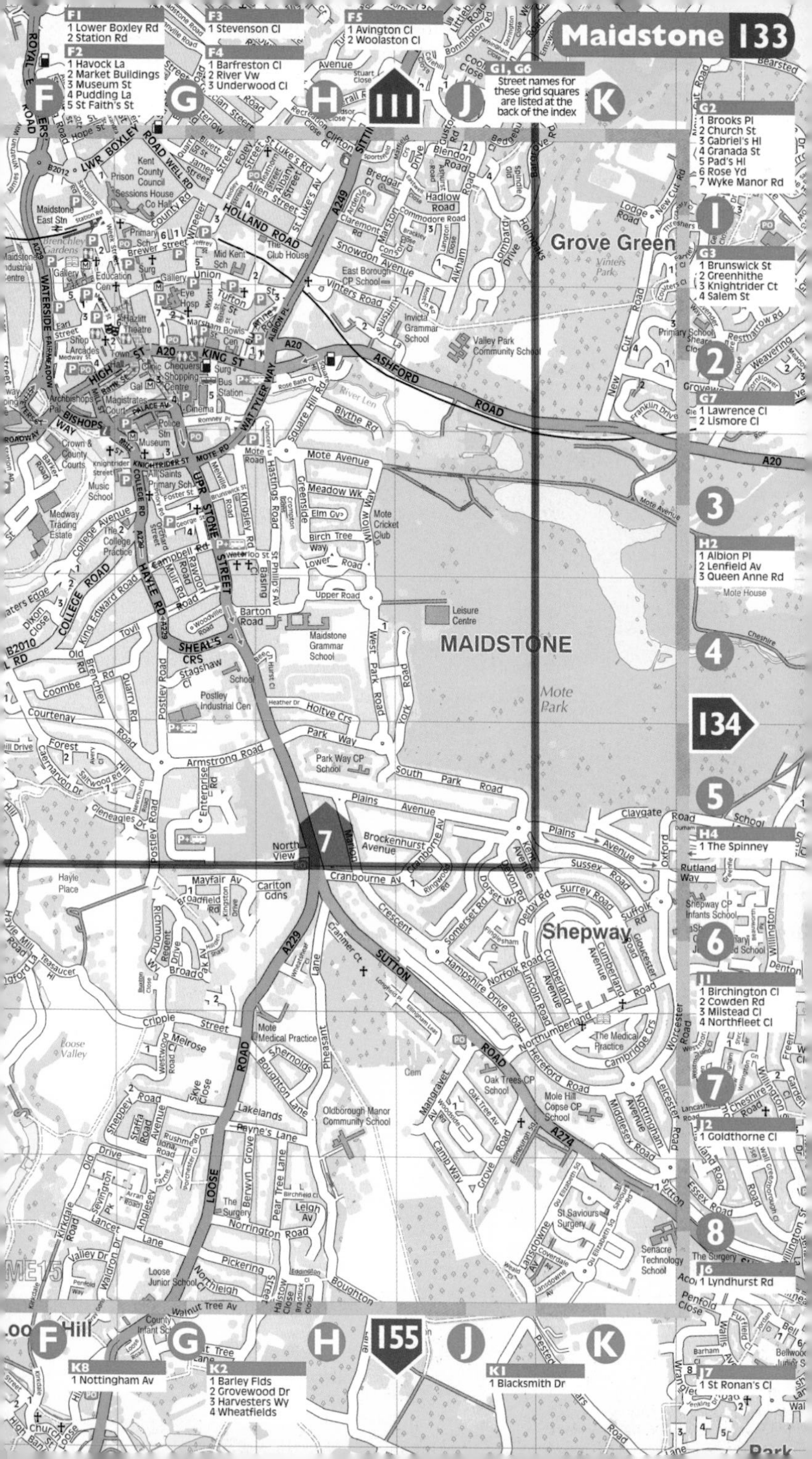
F1
1 Lower Boxley Rd
2 Station Rd
F2
1 Havock La
2 Market Buildings
3 Museum St
4 Pudding La
5 St Faith's St
F3
1 Stevenson Cl
F4
1 Barfreston Cl
2 River Vw
3 Underwood Cl
F5
1 Avington Cl
2 Woolaston Cl
G1, G6
Street names for these grid squares are listed at the back of the index
G2
1 Brooks Pl
2 Church St
3 Gabriel's Hl
4 Granada St
5 Pad's Hl
6 Rose Yd
7 Wyke Manor Rd
G3
1 Brunswick St
2 Greenhithe
3 Knightrider Ct
4 Salem St
G7
1 Lawrence Cl
2 Lismore Cl
H2
1 Albion Pl
2 Lenfield Av
3 Queen Anne Rd
H4
1 The Spinney
J1
1 Birchington Cl
2 Cowden Rd
3 Milstead Cl
4 Northfleet Cl
J2
1 Goldthorne Cl
J6
1 Lyndhurst Rd
J7
1 St Ronan's Cl
K8
1 Nottingham Av
K2
1 Barley Flds
2 Grovewood Dr
3 Harvesters Wy
4 Wheatfields
K1
1 Blacksmith Dr
111
134
155
MAIDSTONE
Grove Green
Shepway
Mote Park
Maidstone East Stn
Kent County Council
Prison
Sessions House
Co Hall
Brenchley Gardens
Hazlitt Theatre
Chequers Shopping Centre
Bus Station
Archbishops Pal
Magistrates Court
Police Stn
Museum
Crown & County Courts
Music School
Medway Trading Estate
The College Practice
Maidstone Grammar School
Leisure Centre
Mote Cricket Club
Mote House
Postley Industrial Cen
Park Way CP School
Invicta Grammar School
Valley Park Community School
East Borough CP School
Mote Medical Practice
Oldborough Manor Community School
Oak Trees CP School
Mole Hill Copse CP School
The Medical Practice
Senacre Technology School
St Saviours Surgery
Loose Junior School
Loose Valley
Hayle Place
Shepway CP Infants School
ME15
A20
A229
A249
A274
B2010
B2012
ASHFORD ROAD
HOLLAND ROAD
LWR BOXLEY ROAD
WATERSIDE
BISHOPS WAY
HIGH ST
KING ST
WAT TYLER WAY
UPR STONE STREET
COLLEGE ROAD
HAYLE RD
SHEAL'S CRS
LOOSE ROAD
SUTTON ROAD
Armstrong Road
South Park Road
Plains Avenue
Mote Avenue
Cripple Street
Boughton Lane
Hereford Road
Northumberland Road
Sussex Road
Surrey Road
Cumberland Avenue
Hampshire Drive
Snowdon Avenue
Vinters Road
Sittingbourne Road

A7
1 Huntingdon Wk
2 Spencer Wy
3 Valentine Rd
4 Wiltshire Wy
A5
1 Otterbourne Pl
A2
1 Crownfields
2 Fallowfield Cl
3 Nutwood Cl
4 Vintners Wy
5 Wagoners Cl
A1
1 Bilberry Cl
2 Harebell Cl
3 Henbane Cl
4 Horseshoe Cl
5 The Maltings
6 Speedwell Cl
112
B1
1 Baron Cl
2 Mamignot Cl
3 Maxton Cl
4 Penhurst Cl
5 Wytherling Cl
6 Yarrow Ct
B2
1 Barncroft Cl
2 Coltsfoot Dr
3 Grovewood Dr
4 Haywain Cl
5 Thistledown
B7
1 Fordcombe Cl
2 Longparish Cl
B3, B8
Street names for these grid squares are listed at the back of the index
133
C1
1 Creve Coeur Cl
2 Longfields Dr
C2
1 The Landway
C3
1 Roseacre Gdns
2 Rosemary Rd
C5
1 Ellenswood Cl
2 Kings Acre
3 Monkdown
4 Pennine Wy
5 Ravens Dane Cl
6 Redsells Cl
D1
1 Sharsted Wy
D2
1 Mount Dr
2 Pimpernel Cl
D4
1 Button La
156
Grove Green
Ware Street
Bearsted Golf Club
Bearsted Station
Weavering Street
Roseacre
A20
ASHFORD ROAD
Mote Park Sailing Club
Mote House
Mote Park
BEARSTED
Willington
Green Hill
Otham
Gore Court
Stoneacre Farm
Holly Farm
Otham Hole
Shepway
SUTTON ROAD
A274
Haslemere Industrial Est
Haslemere Trading Est
Bellwood CP Junior School
Senacre Wood CP School
Senacre Technology School
Shepway CP Infants School
Shepway County Primary Junior Mixed School
Bearsted Green Business Centre
1 grid square represents 500 metres

F
G
H
113
J
K
Broad Street
Water Lane
Longham Wood
M20
Crismill Lane
Roundwell
Crismill Road
Snarkhurst Wood
Woodcut Farm
Tudor Hotel Golf & Country Club
ASHFORD ROAD A20
First Lane
Caring Lane
Junction 8
Musket Lane
Maidstone Service Area
Eyhorne Street
Hollingbourne Station
136
Jarvis Great Danes Hotel & Country Club
River Len
Fulling Mill Farm
Caring Road
Old Mill Road
PENFOLD HILL
B2163
Spout Farm
Merriams Farm
Leeds & Broomfield C of E School
LOWER STREET
Ashbank
Brogden
Forge Lane
Leeds
Wykeham Grove
George Lane
Back Street
Brogden Crescent
Arnold Farm
Farmer Close
Burgess Hall Drive
Avery Lane
UPPER STREET
157
Burberry Lane
Park Barn
Park Barn Farm
1
2
3
4
5
6
7
8

136
Broad Street
Pilgrims Way
North Downs Way
114
A
B
C
D
E
1
2
3
4
5
6
7
8
Allington Farm
Pilgrims Way
Hollingbourne Hill
North Downs Way
Upper Street
PH
Pilgrims Way
Hollingbourne Station
Maidstone Service Area
Eyhorne Street
Hollingbourne County Primary School
Hollingbourne
Musket
Atheistan Green
PO
Eyhorne Street
Tile Fields
Culpeper Close
Greenway
135
Eyhorne Street
Court Road
Oakfield
Harpswood
Green Court
Road
Court Road
PENFOLD HILL
B2163
ASHFORD ROAD
A20(T)
M20
Hospital
Warren Wood
Greenway
Greenway Court
Greenway Forstal
STREET
Ashbank
Leeds Castle
Grove
Lane
Chegworth Road
Broomfield Road
Chegworth Lane
Chegworth
A
B
158
C
D
E
Broomfie
Burberry Lane
Park
Park Barn Farm
1 grid square represents 500 metres

J8
1 The Old Bailey
K8
1 Church Crs
F
G
H
115
J
K
Oorlair
Park Farm
White Post
Marshall's Farm
Hollingbourne House
Morning Dawn
Black Post
Ringlestone
Ringlestone Road
PH
Ringlestone Road
1
2
High Wood
3
Merlewood Farm
Stede Hill
Horsalls
Hogbarn
Hogbarn Lane
4
138
North Downs Way
5
Stede Court
Coles Dane
Stede Hill
6
Pilgrim's Way
Pilgrim's Way
Court Lodge Farm
Goddington
Goddington Lane
7
Marley Road
Harrietsham Station
Harrietsham
Station Road
Holm Mill Lane
Goddington Lane
Pilgrims Lakes
Harrison Drive
St Welcume's Way
Church Lane
Northdown View
Marley Road
Mercer Drive
Dickley Lane
8
Lakelands
Church Road
Old Lain
Downlands
ASHFORD ROAD
A20(T)
M20
West Street
Hook Lane
Quested Way
Forge Meadow
PO
Cricketers Close
Chippendayle Drive
Harrietsham Primary School
Taylor Close
The Surgery
Rectory Lane
Pollhill
F
G
H
159
J
K
Street
Boldrewood Farm

Yewtree Farm
Oorlair
116
A
B
C
D
E
Park Farm
Yoke's Court
1
Madam's Court
Lord's Hill
Ringlestone
2
Ringlestone Road
Wrinsted Court
3
Horsalls
Hogbarn
Hogbarn Lane
Stedehill Wood
4
137
5
West Street
Flint Barn Farm
Flint Lane
Flint Lane
Stede Court
Woods Green
Coles Dane
Stede Hill
6
Marlow Farm
Pilgrim's Way
Lea Farm
Marley Court
Pilgrim's Way
7
Faversham Road
Marley Road
North Downs Way
Marley Road
Dickley
Lane
Ham Lane
Mercer
8
ASHFORD ROAD
A20(T)
Dickley Wood
Cemetery
160
Maidstone
Road
Lenham
Ham
Lane
Hatch Road
Beacon Road
Avenue
Mitchell Close
Malthouse Close
Street
Church Square
The Square
Old
I grid square represents 500 metres

117
F
G
H
J
K
1
2
3
4
5
6
7
8
Timbold Hill
Syndale Bottom
Wichling
Solomons Temple
Temple Farm
Old Lenham Road
Faversham Road
Wichling Wood
Filmer Wood
Lord's Wood
Lady Margaret Manor
Greet
Maitlands Farm
Payden Street
Oakenpole Wood
Slade
Lone Barn Road
Payden Street
Bunker's Hill
Slade Road
Hurstwood
Tophill Farm
Warren Street
Stubblefield House
Warren Street
PH
Great Pivington Farm
Rayners Hill
Waterditch Lane
North Downs Way
Hubbards Hill
161
Highbourne Park
Waterditch Farm
ASHFORD ROAD
Road

OXTED
118
162
E4
1 The Hawthorns
2 Rosemary Cl
E3
1 Nunappleton Wy
A
B
C
D
E
1
2
3
4
5
6
7
8
Barrow Green Rd
Sandy Lane
Wheeler Avenue
St Mary's Cl
Church La
Station Ap
Station Rd
Oxted Station
Alan Carter Gallery
Oxted Health Centre
Snatts Hill
Johnsdale
Granville
DETILLENS
WESTERHAM
Brassey Road
Brassey Hill
Peter Av
The Haywain
Church
WEST HILL A25
Woodhurst Pk
Culver Dr
Old La
Rockfield Road
Uvedale Road
The Priory
Meadowbrook
Brook Hill
High St
Godstone Rd
GODSTONE ROAD
Godstone Road
Bushey Croft
Beadles Lane
Springfield
West Hill Bank
Farley Pk
Wilderness Road
Woodland Rise
Quarry Close
Quarry Road
Greensand Way
St Clair Cl
Neb Lane
Spring La
Woodhurst Lane
Parklands
Icehouse Wood
Icehouse Wd
Wynnstow Pk
Rockfield Cl
Wolf's Hill
Hazelwood Heights
Tandridge Golf Club
Broadham Pl
Hall Hill
The Maltings
Oast Road
Laurel Drive
The Waldrons
Paddock Cl
Paddock Way
Greenhurst Lane
Hurstlands
Church Way
Tanhouse Road
Hurst Green Station
Broadham Green
Greensand Wy
Pollards
Primary School
Greenhurst La
Meldrum Close
Tandridge Court
Hurst Green
Moor House School
Mill Lane
Mill Shaw
Hallsland Wy
Hurst Green Close
Hurst Green Road
Oak
Pollards Crescent
Holland Crs
Greensand Way
Perrysfield Farm
Broadham Green Road
Comforts Farm Av
Orchard Way
Bromford Close
Barnfield Way
Southlands
andridge
Perrysfield
Coltsford Mill
Coldshott
Holland Road
Roseacre
Coltsfoot Lane
Stockett's Manor
Warren Lane
Southlands Lane
Gibbs Brook Lane
Popes Lane
Gincox Farm
Holland Road
Tandridge Lane
Newhouse Farm
Holly Bush Corner
Piper's Wood
River Eden
Foyle Farm
Chathill
Sunt Farm
Crowhurst
whurst
1 grid square represents 500 metres

119
163
142
F
G
H
J
K
1
2
3
4
5
6
7
8
Limpsfield Common
Limpsfield C of E School
Sylvan Close
A25
B269
Wolf's
New Road
Ballards Lane
Stoneswood Road
Brick Kiln Lane
KENT HATCH ROAD
Chapel Road
Ridlands Lane
Ridlands Grove
Ridlands Rise
Stoneleigh Road
Moorhouse Road
St Andrews Way
Mill Lane
Tally Road
Greensand Way
Limpsfield Chart
The High Chart
Pastens Road
Pains Hill
Tenchley's Lane
Tenchleys Park
Caxton Lane
Pollards Wood Road
Boulthurst Farm
Testers Close
Short Lane
Copse
Chestnut
RH8
Greenway
Grants Lane
Itchingwood Common Road
Itchingwood Common
Tenchleys Manor
Trevereux Hill
Trevereux
Vanguard Way
The Moat Farm
Swaynesland Road
Swaynesland
Hurst Farm
Red Lane
LC
Stockenden Farm
Guildables Lane
Foyle Riding
Guildables Wood
Brills Farm
Langhurst
High Ridge Farm
Gaywood
Hole Lane
Staffhurst Wood Road
Black Robins Farm
Staffhurst Wood
Monks Lane
White House Farm
Batchelor's Farm
Troy Town
Caper's Farm

120
141
164
A
B
C
D
E
1
2
3
4
5
6
7
8
Moorhouse Road
Kent County
Surrey County
The High Chart
Greensand Way
Limpsfield Chart
Goodley Stock
Goodley Stock Road
Kent Hatch
Crockhamhill Common
KENT HATCH ROAD
B269
B2026
Horns Hill
Mapleton Road
Froghole
Froghole Lane
Trevereux Hill
Trevereux
Vanguard Way
Crockham Hill
Smiths Lane
Oakdale Lane
Deanery Road
Crockham Hill C of E Primary School
PO
Swaynesland
SPOUT LANE
MAIN ROAD
Hurst Farm
Dairy Lane
Dennettsland Road
Crockham Grange
Redlands
Coakham Farm
Earlylands
Guildables Wood
Rushett
Pootings
Gaywood
Hole Lane
Lane
Homestead Road
Fairmead Road
Swan Lane Farm
Troy Town
1 grid square represents 500 metres

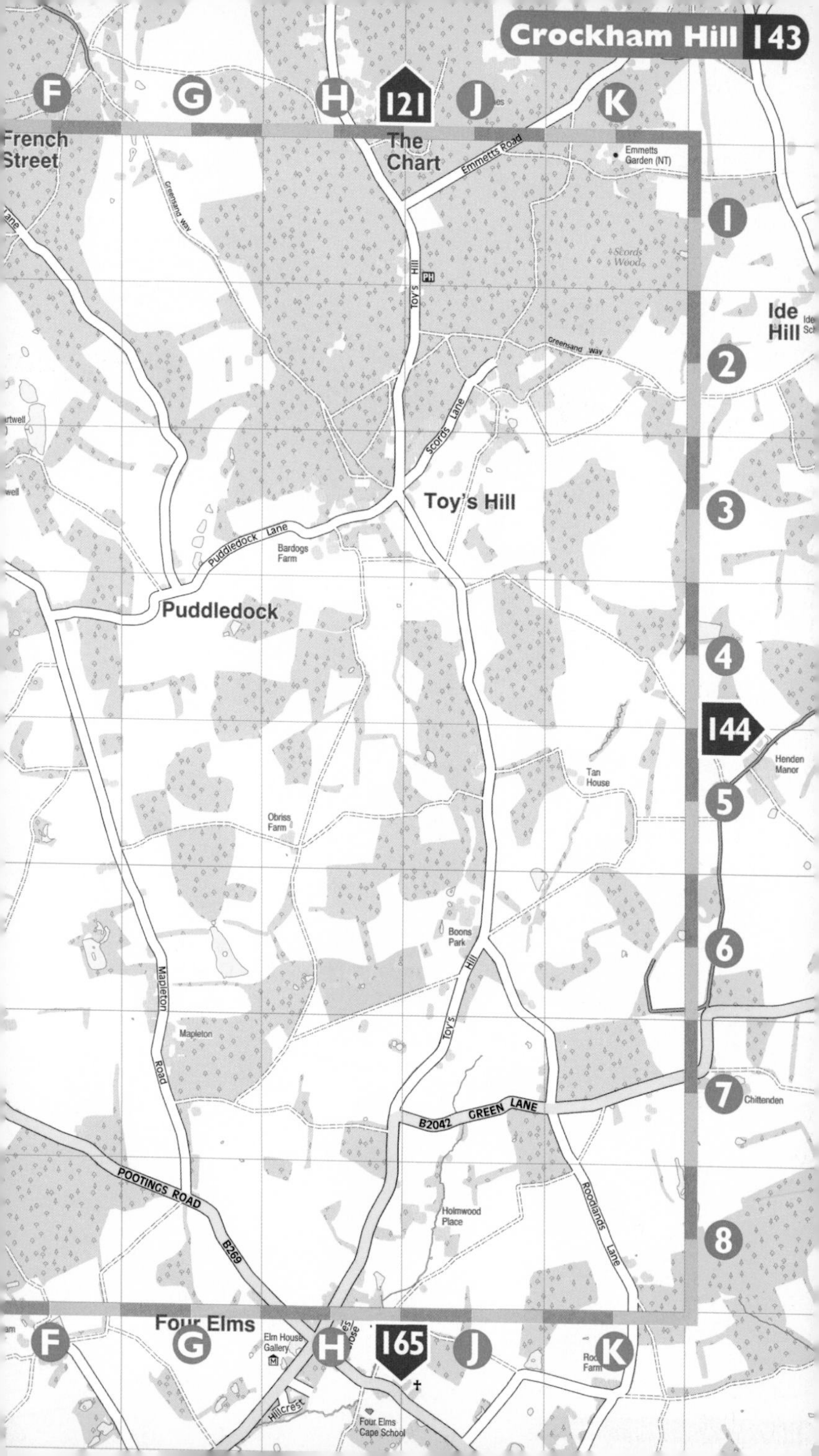
F
G
H
121
J
K
French Street
The Chart
Emmetts Road
Emmetts Garden (NT)
Greensand Way
Toy's Hill
PH
Scords Wood
Ide Hill
Greensand Way
Scords Lane
Toy's Hill
Puddledock Lane
Bardogs Farm
Puddledock
144
Henden Manor
Tan House
Obriss Farm
Boons Park
Toy's Hill
Mapleton Road
Mapleton
B2042 GREEN LANE
Chittenden
POOTINGS ROAD
B269
Holmwood Place
Roodlands Lane
1
2
3
4
5
6
7
8
Four Elms
Elm House Gallery
165
Hillcrest
Four Elms Cape School

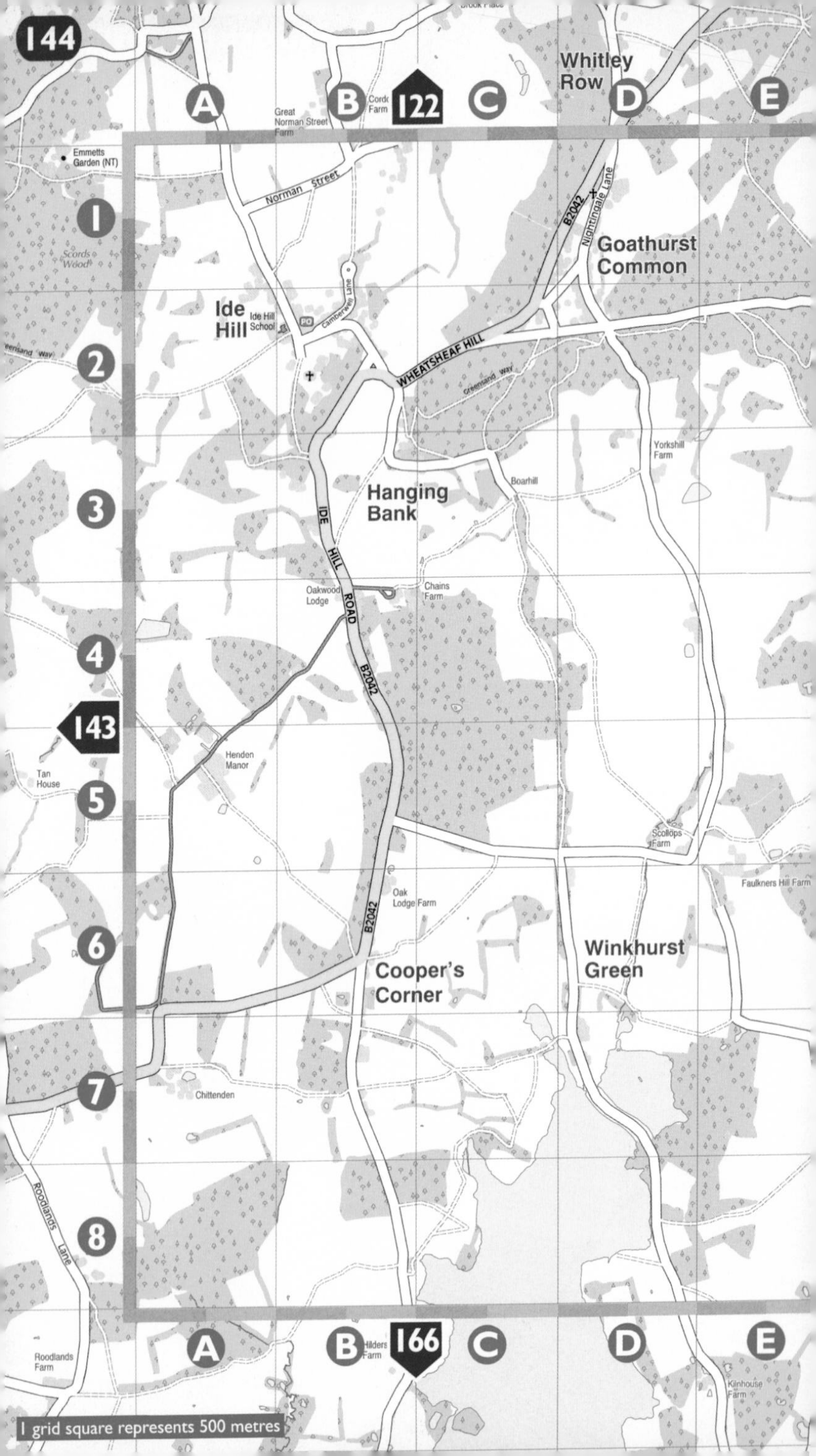

144
Brook Place
Whitley Row
A
B
Cordc Farm
122
C
D
E
Great Norman Street Farm
Emmetts Garden (NT)
Norman Street
B2042
Nightingale Lane
1
Scords Wood
Goathurst Common
Camberwell Lane
Ide Hill
Ide Hill School
PO
Greensand Way
2
WHEATSHEAF HILL
Greensand Way
Yorkshill Farm
Boarhill
3
Hanging Bank
IDE HILL ROAD
Oakwood Lodge
Chains Farm
4
B2042
143
Henden Manor
Tan House
5
Scollops Farm
Faulkners Hill Farm
Oak Lodge Farm
B2042
6
Winkhurst Green
Cooper's Corner
7
Chittenden
Roodlands Lane
8
A
B
Hilders Farm
166
C
D
E
Roodlands Farm
Kilnhouse Farm
1 grid square represents 500 metres

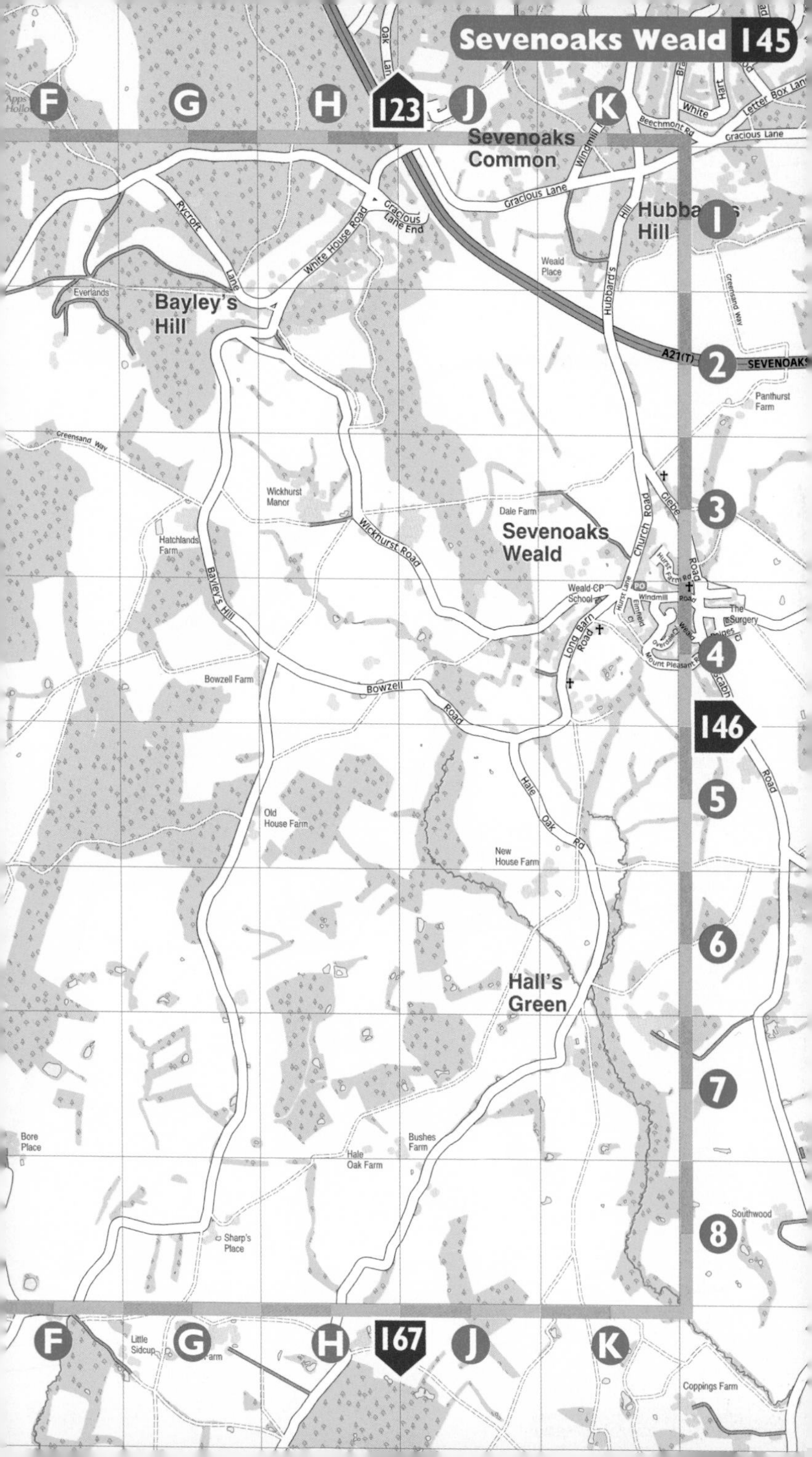
F
G
H
123
J
K
Oak Lane
White Hart
Letter Box Lane
Beechmont Rd
Gracious Lane
Sevenoaks Common
Windmill Hill
Gracious Lane
Rycroft Lane
White House Road
Gracious Lane End
Hubbard's Hill
Hubbard's Hill
1
Weald Place
Everlands
Bayley's Hill
Greensand Way
A21(T)
2
SEVENOAKS
Panthurst Farm
Greensand Way
Wickhurst Manor
Dale Farm
Sevenoaks Weald
Church Road
Glebe Road
3
Hatchlands Farm
Wickhurst Road
Bayley's Hill
Hurst Farm Rd
Weald CP School
Hurst Lane
Elmfield Cl
Windmill Road
The Surgery
Long Barn Road
Overdale Cl
Weald Road
Mount Pleasant Rd
4
Bowzell Farm
Bowzell Road
146
Hale Oak Rd
Road
5
Old House Farm
New House Farm
6
Hall's Green
7
Bore Place
Bushes Farm
Hale Oak Farm
Sharp's Place
Southwood
8
F
Little Sidcup
G
Farm
H
167
J
K
Coppings Farm

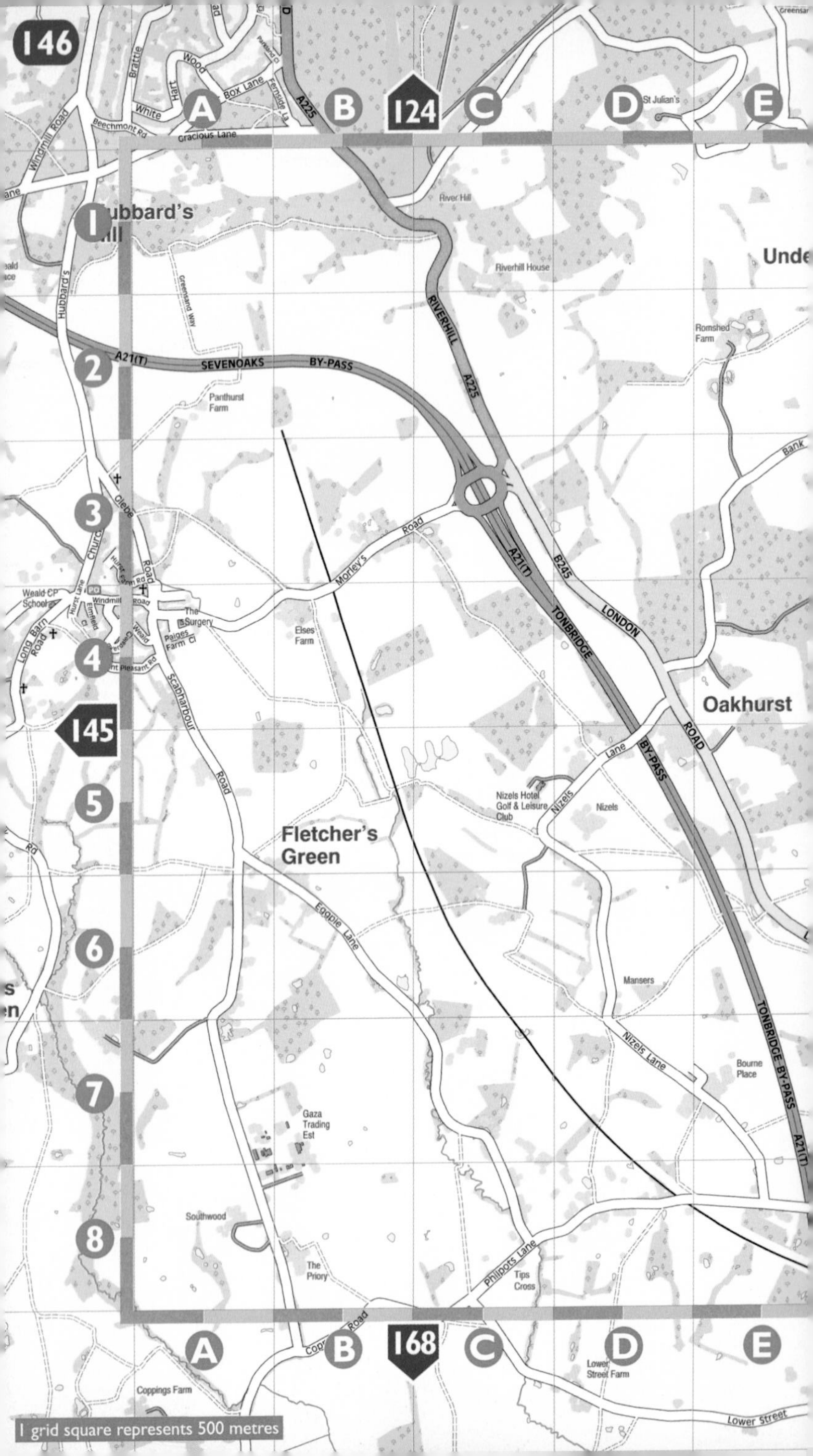

1 grid square represents 500 metres

125
148
169
F
G
H
J
K
1
2
3
4
5
6
7
8
Hill
Rooks Hill
Carter's Hill
Absalom's Farm
St Margarets Old School
Underriver House
Budds Green
Hildenborough Road
Underriver Farm
Underriver House Road
Mill Lane
Marchurst
Tinley Lodge Farm
Fairhill
Riding Lane
Great Hollanden Farm
Great Hollenden Business Centre
Princess Christian's Hospital
Vines Lane
Vines
Alexander House
Hollanden House
Coldharbour Lane
Coldharbo
Horns
Garlands
Trench Farm
The Yews
B245
Hardwick
Fossebank New School
Hildenborough Primary School
Foxbush
Noble Tree Road
Riding Pk
Mount Pleasant
Hardwick Road
Derby Cl
Knowsley Way
Church Rd
Mt Pleasant
Moon
Francis Rd
Sackville School
HILDENBOROUGH
Hilden Brook
TONBRIDGE
Weald Cl
St Marg Primary
Hildenborough Station
Watt's
High Barn Farm
Woodfield Av
The Old Barn
STOCKS GREEN ROAD
B2027
LEIGH RO
Fellowes Wy
Stocks Green CP School
Fairfield Way
Meadway
Wealden
Ashley
Hill View Rd
Park View Av

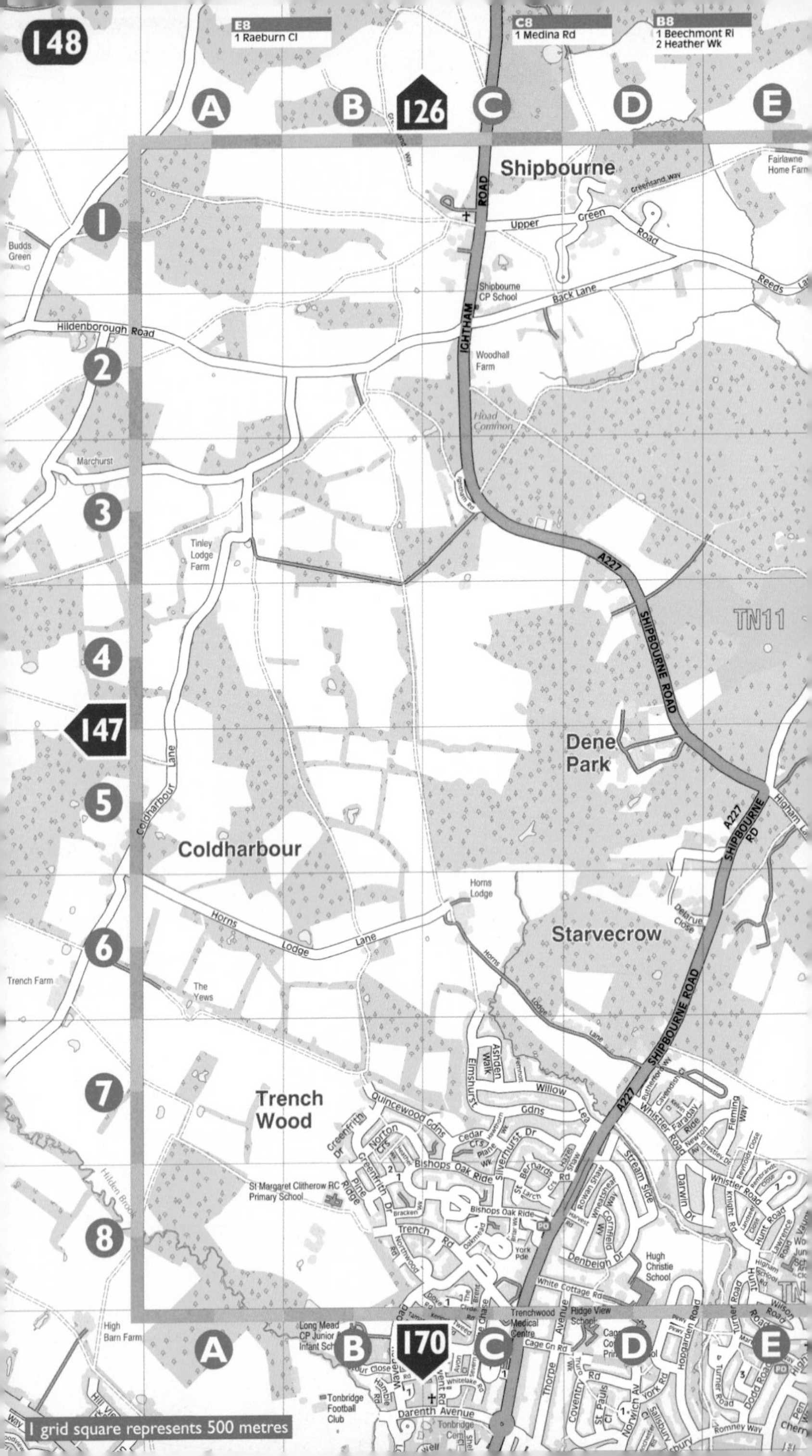
E8
1 Raeburn Cl
C8
1 Medina Rd
B8
1 Beechmont Ri
2 Heather Wk
126
147
170
Shipbourne
Greensand Way
Upper Green Road
Reeds La
Fairlawne Home Farm
Budds Green
Shipbourne CP School
Back Lane
Hildenborough Road
IGHTHAM ROAD
Woodhall Farm
Hoad Common
Marchurst
Tinley Lodge Farm
A227
SHIPBOURNE ROAD
TN11
Dene Park
Coldharbour Lane
Coldharbour
Higham La
Horns Lodge
Horns Lodge Lane
Delarue Close
Starvecrow
Trench Farm
The Yews
Asinden Walk
Elmshurst
Willow Lea
Trench Wood
Quincewood Gdns
Greenfrith Dr
Norton Crs
Cedar Crs
Plane Wk
Silverhurst Dr
Bishops Oak Ride
Pine Ridge
St Bernards Rd
Larch Crs
Hazel Shaw
Rowan Shaw
Wheatsheaf Way
Cornfield Way
Stream Side
Darwin Dr
Whistler Road
Faraday Ride
Fleming Way
Newton Av
Priestley Dr
Reynolds Close
Rembrandt Close
Knight Rd
Hunt Road
Lawrence Road
Hilden Brook
St Margaret Clitherow RC Primary School
Bracken Wk
Trench Rd
Normwood Rd
Oakmead
York Pde
Denbeigh Dr
Hugh Christie School
Higham School Rd
White Cottage Rd
Thorpe Avenue
Ridge View School
Hopgarden Road
Turner Road
Wilson Road
Trenchwood Medical Centre
Cage Gn Rd
High Barn Farm
Long Mead CP Junior & Infant Sch
Hambie Rd
Whitelake Rd
Tonbridge Football Club
Darenth Avenue
Tonbridge Cem
Coventry Rd
St Pauls Ct
Norwich Av
York Rd
Salisbury
Dodd Road
Romney Way
Cherry
1 grid square represents 500 metres

F8
1 Handel Wk
Dunk's Green
Roughway
Hill
F
G
H
127
J
K
Greensand Way
Hamptons Road
Dunk's Green Road
Puttenden Manor Farm
Hamptons
Park Road
Pillar Box La
Hampton's Road
Oxenhoath Road
Lane
Claygate
Hookwood House
River Bourne
Four Wents
Mount Pleasant
Road
Carpenters Lane
The Common
Stallion's Green
Hope Farm
North Frith
High House Lane
Mill Vw
Carpenters Lane
The Freehold
Water Slippe
Twyford Rd
Tainter Rd
Great Elm
Caxton Lane
School Lane
Doctors Surgery
Hadlow CP School
Lane
Pittswood
Bourne Grange Farm
Bourne Grange Lane
Hadlow College
Ashes Lane
HIGH STREET
THE SQUARE
Church Street
A26
Tonbridge Road
River Bourne
Grange Farm
Blackman's Lane
Cuckoo Lane
Parker's Green
Higham Lane
Bourneside Farm
Higham Wood
Hadlow Rd
Road
Barchester Way
Purcell Av
Three Elm Lane
171
Framley Road
Guestwick
Cranford
Allington Dr
Frank Wooley Road
Estridge Way
Godfrey Evans Close
Barclay Avenue
Hadlow Road
Hadlow Place Farm
1
2
3
4
5
6
7
8
150

B6
1 Appletons
A6
1 Dray Ct
2 Hailstone Cl
3 Kenward Ct
4 Maltings Cl
5 Toby Gdns
Gover Hill
Gover Hill
Adams Well Farm
128
West Peckham
Church Road
Wealdway
Greensand Way
Pillar Box La
Road
Oxon Hoath
Park Farm
Matthews Lane
Carpenters Lane
The Common
Common Road
Steers Place
Steer's Place
149
Lonewood Way
Valley Dr
Palmers Brook
A26
MAIDSTONE ROAD
Goose Green
Stanford Lane
Cemetery
The Paddock
Hope Avenue
Marshall Gdns
Hadlow Pk
Great Elms
The Cherry Orch
Hadlow
Spar Close
Twyford Rd
Painter Rd
Brookfields
The Freehold
Water Slippe
Carpenters Lane
Smithers
Doctors Surgery
Caxton Lane
School Lane
Hadlow CP School
Hadlow College
Bourne Grange
HIGH STREET
THE SQUARE
Church Street
The Forstal
Goblands Farm
Cemetery Lane
Court Lane
Court Lane
Bells Farm
River Bourne
Victoria Road
Style Place Farm
Bourneside Farm
Lane
Mill Lane
Pierce
Wealdway
Three Elm Lane
Tithe Ward
172
Golden Green
Kelchers Lane
Three Elm Lane
Tonbridge Road
1 grid square represents 500 metres

G8
1 The Paddocks
2 William Luck Cl
H8
1 Bramley Rd
Nettles
129
Nettlestead Lane
Rock Farm
Forge Farm
Gibbs Hill
MAIDSTONE ROAD
Old Church Road
Park Road
Old Church Lane
Roydon Hall Road
ME18
A228 SEVEN MILE LANE
Moat Wood
Greensand Way
Mount Pleasant Farm
Wealdway
Medway Valley Wk
Greensand
Nettlestead Green
B2015
152
Peckham Place Farm
Martins Lane
Hextall Court
Bells Farm Road
Crowhurst Farm
Yalding Station
HAMPSTEAD
A228
MAIDSTONE RD
Borough's Oak Farm
Maidstone Road
Peckham Bush
Bush Road
Bardsley Close
Hale Court
Pattenden Gdn
Smithers La
Hale Street
Church Lane
East Peckham Primary School
Bullen Farm
Lane
Chidley Cross Road
Drage Road
Pound Road
Pippin Road
Russett Rd
East Peckham
Whitebine Gdns
Henham Gardens
Golding Gdns
Medway Meadows
Westwood Road
Cotman Way
Fell Mead
The Freehold
Orchard Road
Crown Acres
Road
Old Road
Branbridges
Medway Valley Walk
Tonbridge Road
Addlestead Road
Stockenbury
Snoll Hatch Road
Strettitt Gardens
173
Branbridges Industrial Estate
Torbay
F
G
H
J
K
1
2
3
4
5
6
7
8

Nettlestead
Waterside Mews
Wateringbury Station
B2015
Bryant Close
Bishops Cl
130
A
B
C
D
E
Medway Valley Walk
Gibbs Hill
MAIDSTONE ROAD
Bow Hill
Hunt Street
Bow Hill House
Small
1
2
3
4
5
6
7
8
Kenward
Kenward Road
YALDING
Hill Farm
B2010
Medway Valley Wk
Greensand Way
Nettlestead Green
151
Station Rd
Yalding Station
HAMPSTEAD LANE
LC
Cronks Farm
B2162
The Nook
Medway Av
Downs Road
Yalding
Mount Avenue
Blunden Lane
Oast Ct
Maidstone Road
HIGH ST
Yalding C of E Primary School
Vicarage
Cem
River Beult
Acott Flds
The Lees
LEES ROAD
PO
Greensand Way
Lees House
Lyngs Close
MAIDSTONE RD
A228
River Medway
Lees Road
Congelow
BENOVER ROAD
Symonds Lane
Mill Lane
Woodfalls Business Centre
Woodfalls Farm
Mill Place Farm
Branbridges
Gravelly Ways
Manor Farm
174
Hill Lane
Cleavesland
Laddingford
1 grid square represents 500 metres

Green
Lane
Lane
Lane
F
G
H
131
J
K
West Farleigh
Tutsham Hall
B2163
EWELL LANE
Ewell Manor
B2010
SMITH'S HILL
Gallants Farm
Wilsons Lane
Gallants Lane
Hospital Barn Farm
Quarry Wood
Heath Road
Shingle Barn
Fox Pitt
Shingle Barn Lane
Hilltop
B2163
Upper Barn Hill
North Folly Road
Foremans Barn Road
Barn Hill
Upper Hunton Hill
Amst
Buston Manor
Greensand Way
Barn Hill
Hunton Hill
Gennings Farm
154
Lughorse Lane
Cheveney Farm
Cheveney
West Street
East Street
East Street
Hunton
Bensted Close
Hunton Court
Hunton CP School
Bishop's Lane
George St
Water Lane
Elphicks Farm
River Beult
1
2
3
4
5
6
7
8
F
G
H
175
J
K
Benover
BENOVER
Hunton Road
Reed Court Farm

1 grid square represents 500 metres

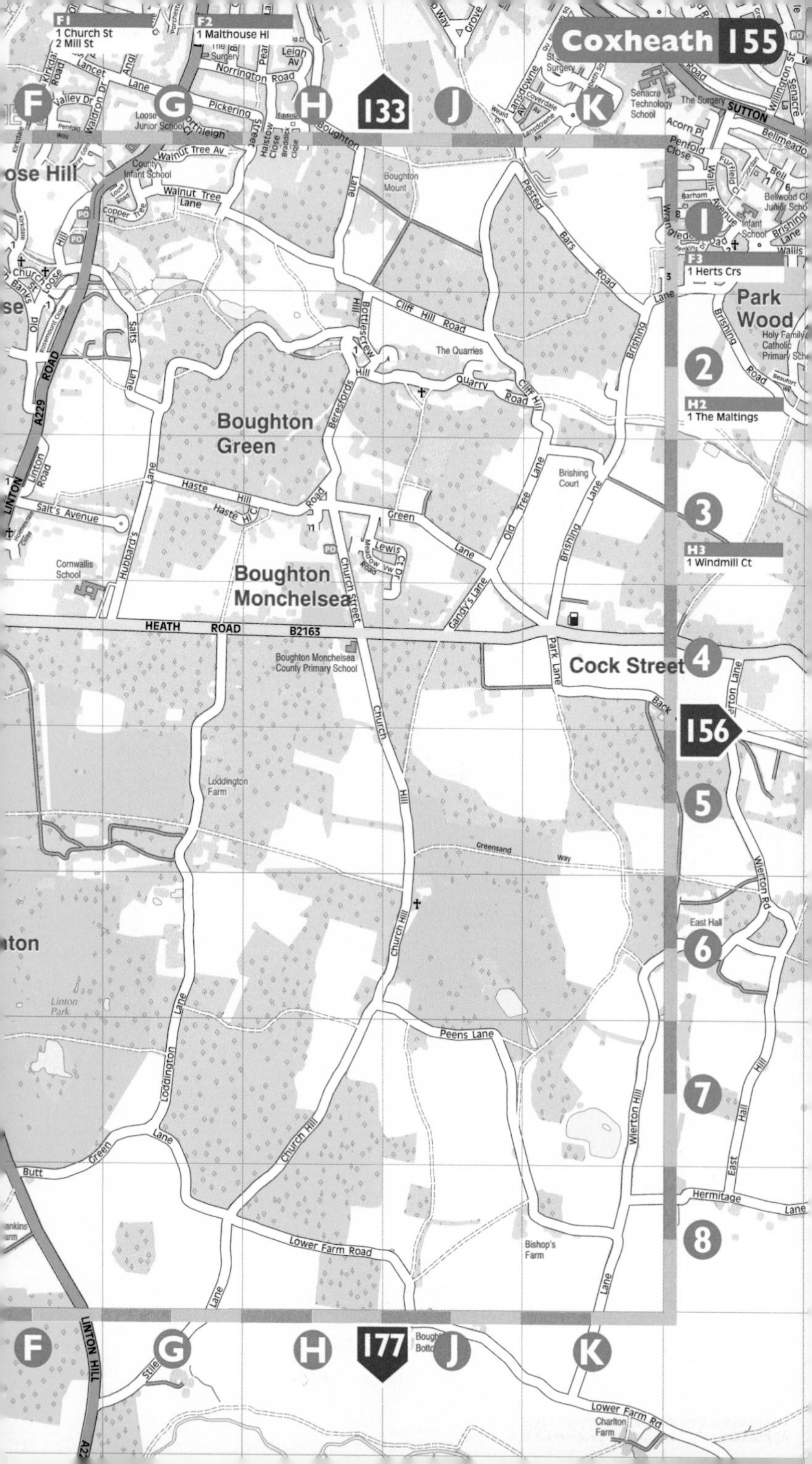
F1
1 Church St
2 Mill St
F2
1 Malthouse Hl
F3
1 Herts Crs
H2
1 The Maltings
H3
1 Windmill Ct
133
156
177
F
G
H
J
K
I
2
3
4
5
6
7
8
Loose Hill
Boughton Green
Boughton Monchelsea
Cock Street
Park Wood
Norrington Road
Pickering Street
Loose Junior School
County Infant School
Walnut Tree Av
Walnut Tree Lane
Copper Tree Ct
Lancet Lane
Valley Dr
Waldron Dr
Penfold Way
Leigh Av
Halstow Close
Braddick Close
Boughton Lane
Boughton Mount
Pested Bars Road
Lansdowne Av
Coverdale Av
Weald Ct
Senacre Technology School
The Surgery
SUTTON
Acorn Pl
Penfold Close
Barham
Wallis Avenue
Wrangleden Road
Furfield Cl
Bell
Bellwood Ct
Junior School
Infant School
Brishing Lane
Brishing Road
Holy Family Catholic Primary Sch
Beaufort Wk
Cliff Hill Road
Bottlescrew Hill
The Quarries
Quarry Road
Cliff Hill
Beresfords Hill
Salts Lane
Old Loose Hill
Rosemount Close
A229
ROAD
LINTON
Linton Road
Salt's Avenue
Haste Hill
Haste Hl Cl
Hubbard's Lane
Cornwallis School
Church Street
Lewis Ct Dr
Meadow Vw Road
Green Lane
Old Tree Lane
Brishing Court
Candy's Lane
HEATH ROAD B2163
Boughton Monchelsea County Primary School
Park Lane
Back
Wierton Lane
Loddington Farm
Church Hill
Greensand Way
Wierton Rd
East Hall
Linton Park
Peens Lane
Loddington Lane
Butt Green Lane
Wierton Hill
Hermitage Lane
East Hall Hill
Bishop's Farm
Lower Farm Road
LINTON HILL
Stile
Lower Farm Rd
Charlton Farm

156
B2
1 Coldred Rd
2 Collington Ter
3 Lymington Ct
4 Somner Wk
B1
1 Connaught Cl
A1
1 Brishing Cl
2 Disraeli Cl
3 Felderland Cl
4 Felderland Dr
5 Felderland Rd
6 Lubbock Cl
7 Wotton Cl
8 Wrangleden Cl
D5
1 Mercer Wy
134
155
178
Sutton Road
Essex Road
Senacre Technology School
Surgery
Acorn Pl
Bellmeadow
Gore Court
White
Honey
Simmonds Lane
Hole
Penfold Close
Furfield Cl
Bell
Walls Avenue
Barham Cl
Bellwood CP Junior School
Infant School
Brishing Lane
Wrangleden Road
Jenkins Dr
Wallis
Haslemere Industrial Est
Haslemere Trading Est
Avenue
Cuxton Road
Longshaw Road
Selby Rd
Bicknor Road
Birchold Road
Park Wood
Holy Family Catholic Primary School
Brishing Road
Beaufort Wk
Heronden Road
Wren Industrial Estate
Parkwood Industrial Estate
Target Business Cen
Birchold Road
Pal Industrial Est
Orchard Industrial Ests
Boxmend Industrial Est
Mount Pleasant Farm
Rumwood Court
New Road
A274
Langley
Langley Park Farm
Brishing Court
Brishing Lane
Tree Lane
Cliff Hill
Pested Bars
Cock Street
Park Lane
Back Lane
Wierton Lane
Brishing Road
Pleasant Farm
Fir Tree Farm
PLOUGH WENT
Lested Lane
Chart Corner
Cobfield
Laxton Drive
Amber Lane
Warmlake Road
Amberfield
Chart Hill Road
Marsham Crs
Way
Wierton Rd
East Hall
Wierton
Greensand Way
Chart Hill Road
Chart Hill
Church Road
Underhill School
Heronden
Wierton
East Hall Hill
Hermitage Lane
Lucks Lane
Chart Hill Road
Rectory Lane
Bishop's Farm
Long Lane
Lamb's Cross
Forge Lane
Chart Sutton
Green Lane
Lower Farm
Chart Bottom Farm
1 grid square represents 500 metres

G7
1 Chapel Rd
2 Southways
Arnold Farm
Avery Lane
Back Street
Farmer Close
135
UPPER STREET
B2163
Burberry Lane
Park Barn Farm
Park Barn Road
Horseshoes Lane
Gullands
Turgis Close
Porters Walk
Lacey Close
Copperfield Drive
Dickens Close
Skinners Way
Heath Road
Forsters
Shepherds Way
Orchard Close
Green Lane
Heathfield
Grasslands
Langley Heath
ROAD
Ulcombe Road
LEEDS
Rectory Farm
Abbey Wood
Five Wents
Collingwood Industrial Estate
Gravelly Bottom Road
Pitt Road
Cross Drive
158
MAIDSTONE ROAD
A274
Chartway Street
Warmlake
NORTH STREET
Charlton Lane
Greensand Way
Workhouse Road
Pleasure House Road
Church Lane
Charlton Court
East Sutton Road
Cobtree Medical Centre
Sutton Valence
Sutton Valence CP School
Sutton Valence School
PO
School Lane
High Street
Broad St
Tumblers Hill
Lower Road
Rectory Lane
The Platt
Baker Lane
East Sutton Road
Pleasure House
West Drive
East Sutton Park
Friday Street
S Bank
South Lane
Boyton Court
Boyton Court Road
Stallance
Captain's Cl
Harbour
179
Heniker Lane
Brook House
Barling Farm
East Sutton Road

C4
1 Heatherwood Cl
136
Chegworth
Broomfield
Burberry Lane
Park Barn Road
Park Barn Farm
Broomfield Road
Kings Wood
Chegworth Road
Water Lane
Charlesford Avenue
Whitehall Drive
Ashford Drive
Elder Close
Chestnut Drive
Laurel Gv
Tall Trees Close
Croft Close
The Wytchlings
Bushy Grove
Holly Tree Close
Bell Way
The Waldens
Cayser Drive
School
Wildwood Close
Kingswood Surgery
Kingswood
Gravelly Bottom Road
Lenham Road
PO
ME17
157
Chartway Street
Ulcombe Hill
Hill Farm
Morry Lane
Morry House
Chariton Lane
Broomes Court
Greensand Way
Church Lane
Charlton Court
West Drive
East Sutton Park
East Sutton Road
Friday Street
The Street
Streetfield
Ulcombe
Ulcombe C of E Primary School
Lodge Gdns
Chestnut Close
Headcorn Road
Brick Kiln Lane
180
1 grid square represents 500 metres

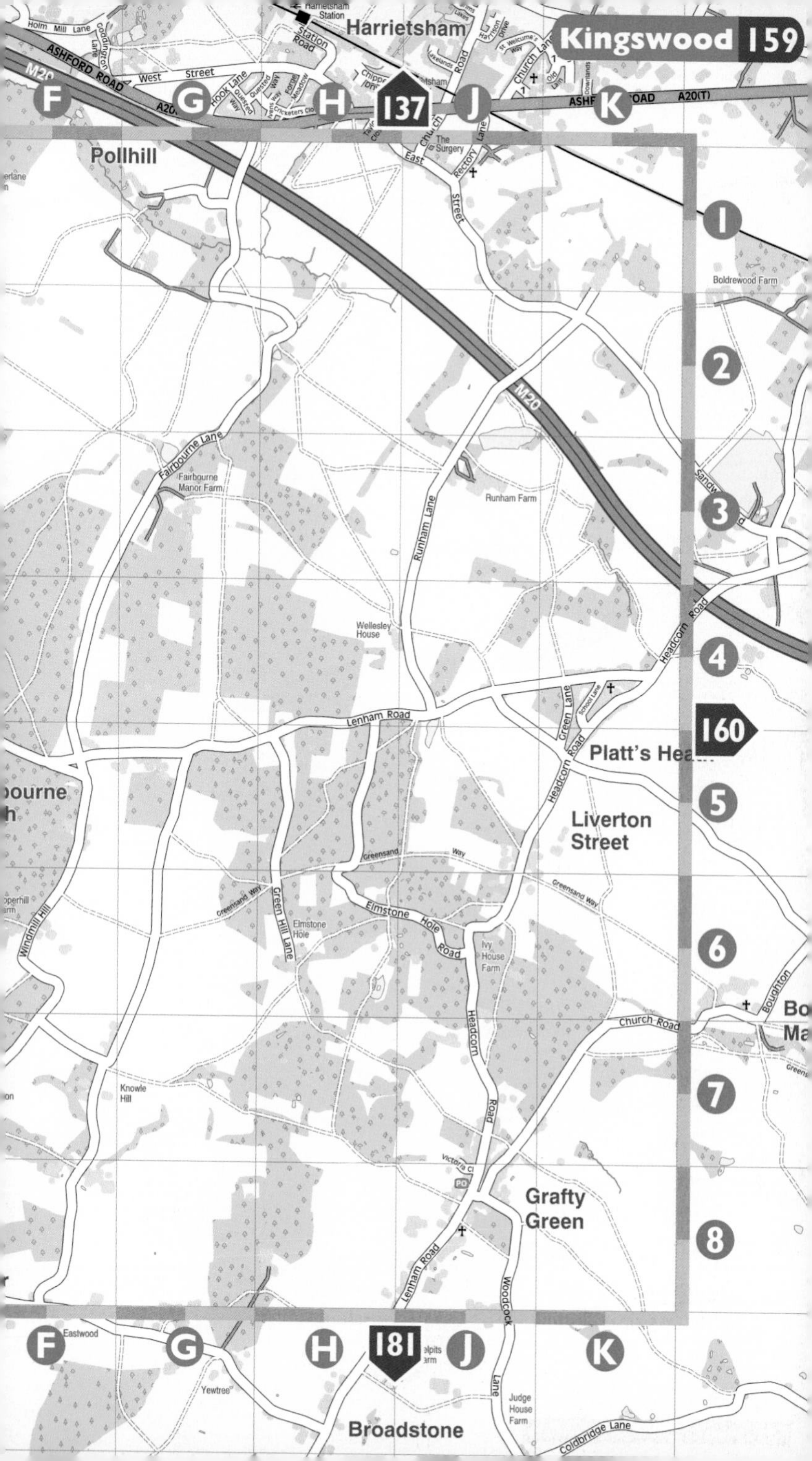

Harrietsham
Harrietsham Station
Station Road
Holm Mill Lane
Coddington Lane
ASHFORD ROAD
M20
West Street
A20
Hook Lane
Quested Way
Forge Meadow
Cricketers Close
Church Lane
St. Welcume's Way
Old Lain
Downlands
Lakelands
Lakelands Road
Church
ASHFORD ROAD A20(T)
F
G
H
J
K
137
Pollhill
The Surgery
East Street
Rectory Lane
Boldrewood Farm
1
2
3
4
5
6
7
8
Fairbourne Lane
Fairbourne Manor Farm
Runham Lane
Runham Farm
Wellesley House
Lenham Road
Headcorn Road
Green Lane
School Lane
160
Platt's Heath
Liverton Street
Greensand Way
Green Hill Lane
Elmstone Hole
Elmstone Hole Road
Ivy House Farm
Windmill Hill
Church Road
Boughton
Knowle Hill
Headcorn Road
Victoria Cl
PO
Grafty Green
Lenham Road
Woodcock Lane
Eastwood
181
Yewtree
Judge House Farm
Broadstone
Coldbridge Lane

160
138
182
159
A
B
C
D
E
1
2
3
4
5
6
7
8
D1
1 Douglas Rd
ASHFORD ROAD
A20(T)
Dickley Lane
Dickley Wood
Ham Lane
Cemetery
Maidstone Road
Ford Road
Royton Avenue
Douglas Road
Chilston Road
Faversham Road
The Square
Groveway
Old
Loder Close
Swadelands Close
Mitchell Close
Hatch Road
Beacon Road
Robins Avenue
Honywood Road
Robins Close
Lenham
Malthouse Close
Church Square
High Street
Croft Gardens
Glebe Gdns
Old School Close
Mill Close
Lenham Station
Boldrewood Farm
Old Ham Lane
Tanyard Farm
Stour Valley Walk
Headcorn Road
Sandway Road
Leadingcross Green
Sandway
Lenham Heath Road
M20
Headcorn Road
Green Lane
School Lane
Platt's Heath
Liverton Street
Lewsome Farm
Boughton Road
Hotel
Chilston Park
Bowley Lane
Bowley Farm
Greensand Way
Church Road
Boughton Malherbe
Pope's Hall
Field Farm
Wellham Wood
Coach
Burscombe
Foxden Wood
House
1 grid square represents 500 metres

F
G
H
139
J
K
North Downs Way
Hubbards Hill
Rayners Hill
Waterditch Lane
Highbourne Park
Waterditch Farm
ASHFORD ROAD
Road
East Lenham
North Downs Way
Cobham Farm
A20(T)
New Shelve Farm
Old Shelve
ASHFORD ROAD
1
2
3
4
5
6
7
8
Lenham Forstal
Mount Castle Lane
Lenham Forstal Road
Rose Lane
Bull Hill
Crabtree Lane
Lenham Forstal Road
Lenham Heath
Lenham Heath Road
Hook St
Burleigh Farm
Tile Lodge
Road
Lodge
Cherry Tree Road
Charing Heath
M20
Church Hill
Tile
Wind Hill
Stour Valley Walk
Great Stour
Swan Street
Heath Farm School
Road
Egerton
Brockton Farm
Lane
Coach Road
Foxen Farm
M20
Hurst Wood
183
Stonebridge Gn Road
Mill Rd
Southfield
Field
Green
Stonebridge Green

140
A
B
C
D
E
1
2
3
4
5
6
7
8
Foyle Farm
Sunt Farm
Chanin
whurst
e End
Tandridge Lane
agham
odge Farm
obbs Farm
Crowhurst Lane
Crowhurst
Stocks and Kingswood Farms
Oldhouse Farm
Lane
Caterfield
Park
Road
Crowhurst Village Road
Pikes Farm
Lane
Pikes
Chellows Lane
Chellows Farm
Chellows Park
Ardenrun
enrun
Bowerland Farm
Bowerland
Lane
Arden Green
Barrow Green Farm
Crowhurst
Road
Haxted Road
Waterside
Sugham Farm
Rushford Farm
B2029
Ray
Lod
Lingfield
Common
Road
Crowhurst Road
Lingfield Common
Rushfords
RH7
Saxbys Lane
Selbys
Grove Rd
Station
ark Farm
Lane
Park
Pond Farm
Haywardens
Little Lullenden
Pauls Md
Ash
Bake
Lane
1 grid square represents 500 metres

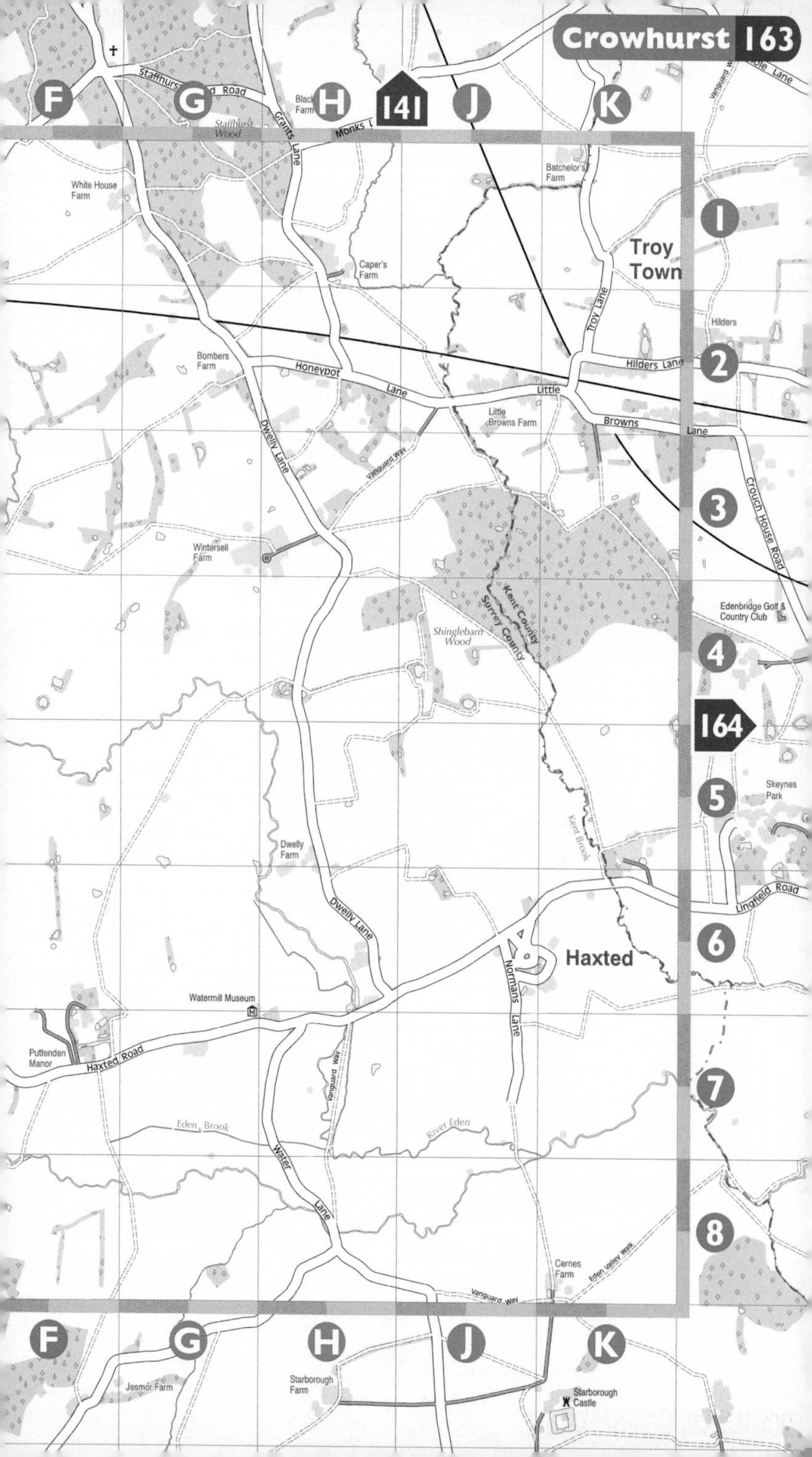
F
G
H
141
J
K
Staffhurst Wood Road
Grants Lane
Black Farm
Monks L
Staffhurst Wood
White House Farm
Batchelor's Farm
1
Troy Town
Caper's Farm
Troy Lane
Hilders
Bombers Farm
Honeypot Lane
Little
Hilders Lane
2
Little Browns Farm
Browns Lane
Dwelly Lane
Vanguard Way
Crouch House Road
3
Wintersell Farm
Kent County
Surrey County
Shinglebarn Wood
Edenbridge Golf & Country Club
4
164
5
Skeynes Park
Kent Brook
Dwelly Farm
Dwelly Lane
Lingfield Road
6
Haxted
Normans Lane
Watermill Museum
Puttenden Manor
Haxted Road
Vanguard Way
7
Eden Brook
River Eden
Water Lane
8
Cernes Farm
Eden Valley Walk
Vanguard Way
F
G
H
J
K
Jesmor Farm
Starborough Farm
Starborough Castle

1 grid square represents 500 metres

POOTINGS ROAD
B269
Holmwood Place
143
F
G
H
J
K
Four Elms
Elm House Gallery
Styles Close
Hillcrest
Four Elms Cape School
Roodlands Farm
FOUR ELMS ROAD
B2027
Broxham House
Hill Court
Five Fields Lane
Furnace House Farm
Owls Court
Prettymans Lane
Lockhurst
LC
Prettymans Lane
CLINTON LANE
B2027
Harbord
Medhurst Row
Brasted Lands
How Green
Whistlers
Eden Valley Walk
How Green Lane
Hever Road
Hever Golf Club
Ascot Hever Golf Club
Hever Castle Farm
Hever Golf Clubhouse
166
1
2
3
4
5
6
7
8
Delaware Farm
Eden Valley Walk
TN8
Hever Road
Polebrook Farm
Hever Castle
Brocas Farm
Lydens Lane
Hever
Hever C of E Primary School
Lydens Farm
Eden Valley Walk
Hever Station
185
Hever Warren
Pigdown

Lane
A
B
144
C
D
E
Roodlands Farm
1
Hilders Farm
Kilnhouse Farm
2
Furnace House Farm
Bough Beech Reservoir
Lakeside Close
Bough Beech Sailing Club
Coles Farm
3
CLINTON LANE
B2027
Harborough
Waterlake
Somerden
Brasted
4
PH
The Close
Bough Beech
How Green
165
Gravelpits
Hever
Hever Golf Club
Hever Golf Clubhouse
5
Mill Farm
6
Chiddingstone
Gilwyns
7
PH
PO
Chiddingstone Church of England
8
Eden Valley Walk
Hill Hoath
A
B
186
C
D
E
1 grid square represents 500 metres

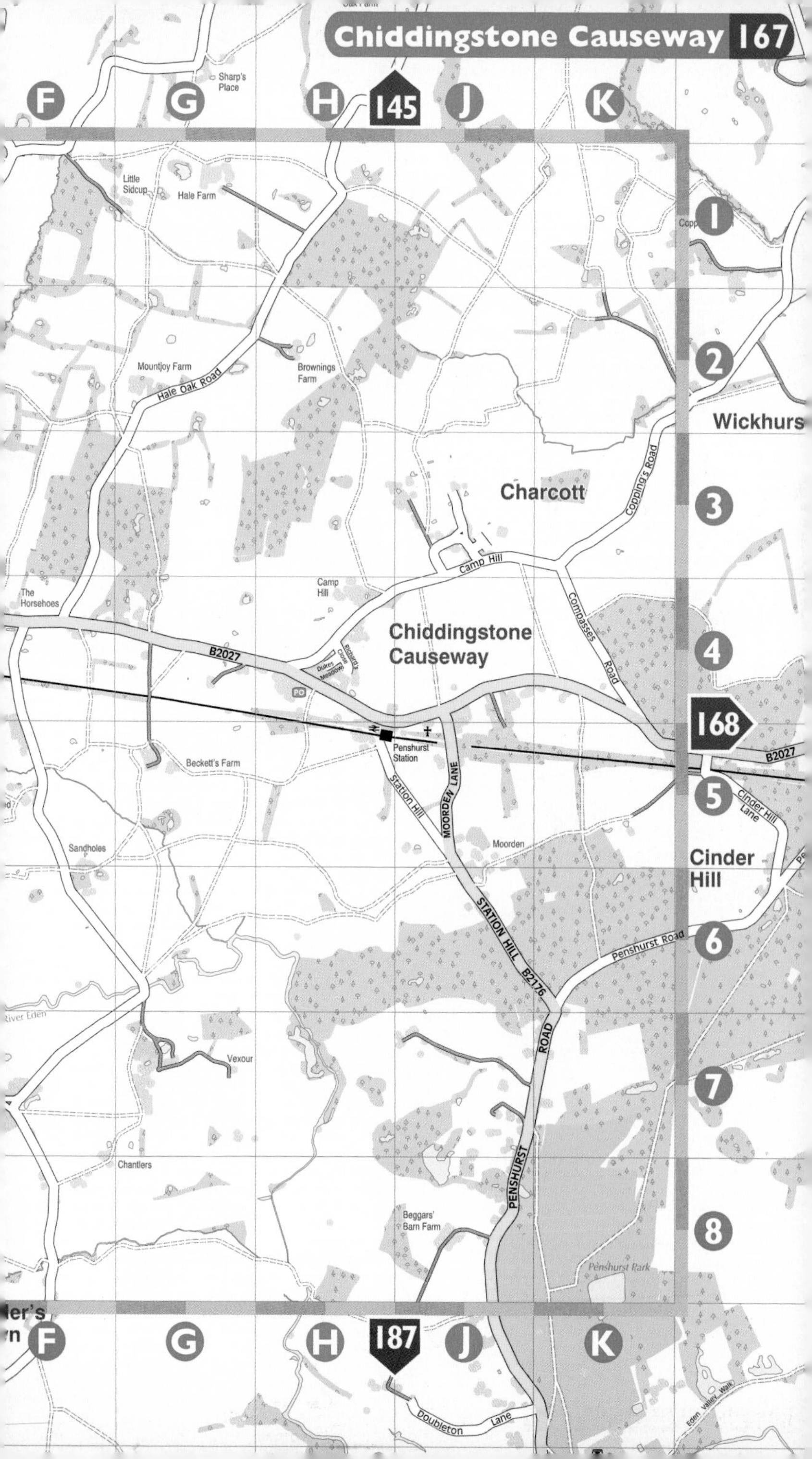
F
G
H
J
K
145
Sharp's Place
Little Sidcup
Hale Farm
1
Mountjoy Farm
Hale Oak Road
Brownings Farm
2
Wickhurs
Charcott
Copping's Road
3
Camp Hill
Camp Hill
The Horsehoes
Compasses Road
Chiddingstone Causeway
4
B2027
Richard's Close
Dukes Meadow
PO
168
B2027
Penshurst Station
Beckett's Farm
Station Hill
MOORDEN LANE
5
Cinder Hill Lane
Moorden
Sandholes
Cinder Hill
STATION HILL
B2176
Penshurst Road
6
River Eden
ROAD
Vexour
7
Chantlers
PENSHURST
Beggars' Barn Farm
8
Penshurst Park
F
G
H
187
J
K
Doubleton Lane
Eden Valley Walk

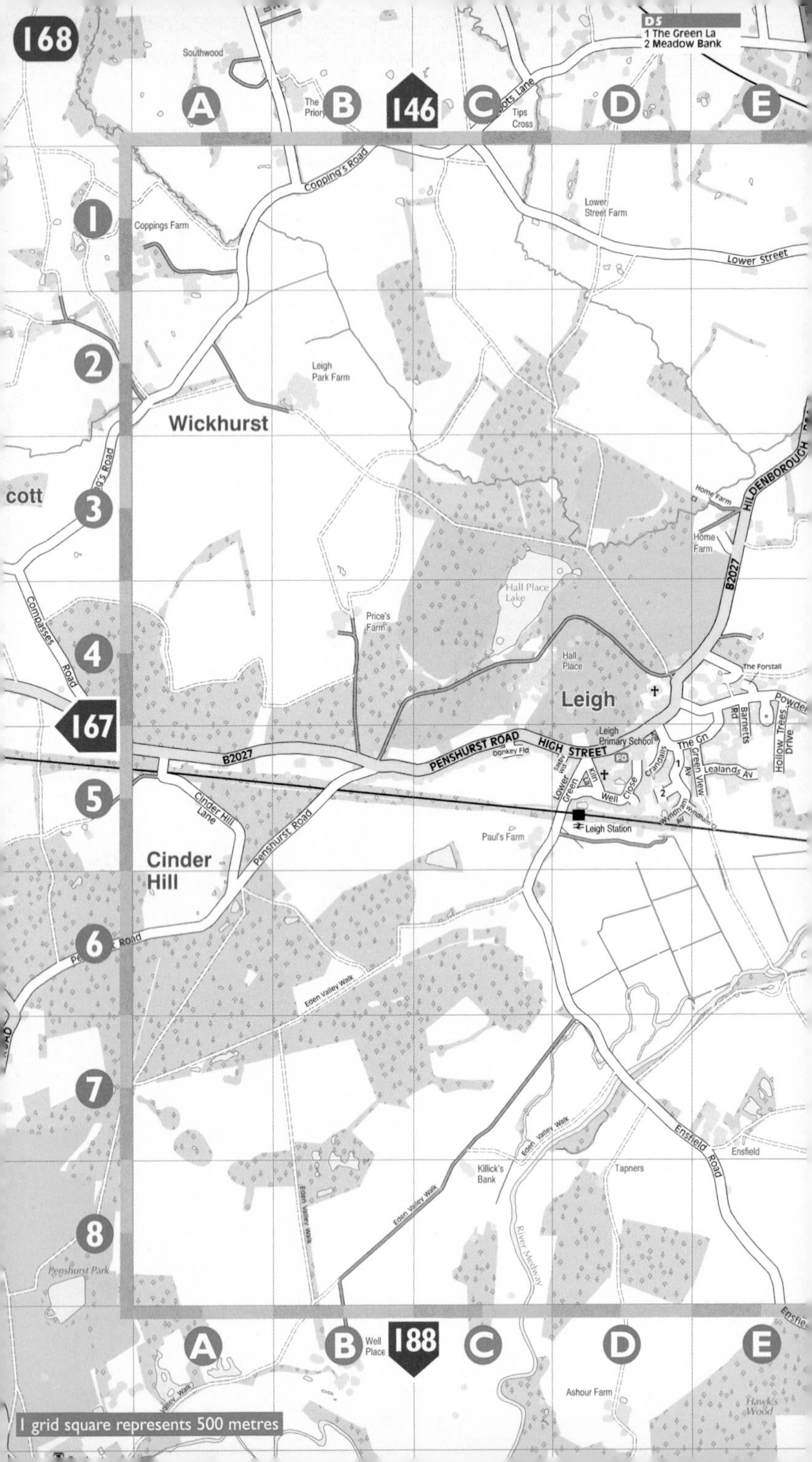
D5
1 The Green La
2 Meadow Bank
Southwood
The Priory
146
Tips Cross
Copping's Road
Coppings Farm
Lower Street Farm
Lower Street
Leigh Park Farm
Wickhurst
cott
Compasses Road
Home Farm Cl
Home Farm
HILDENBOROUGH
B2027
Hall Place Lake
Price's Farm
Hall Place
The Forstall
Leigh
Powder
Barnetts Rd
Hollow Trees Drive
167
Leigh Primary School
PENSHURST ROAD
HIGH STREET
Donkey Fld
B2027
The Gn
Green View
Lealands Av
Crandalls
Kiln La
Well Close
Lower Green
Windham Av
Leigh Station
Paul's Farm
Cinder Hill Lane
Penshurst Road
Cinder Hill
Eden Valley Walk
Killick's Bank
Tapners
Enfield Road
Ensfield
River Medway
Penshurst Park
Well Place
188
Ashour Farm
Hawk's Wood
1 grid square represents 500 metres

HILDENBOROUGH
Hildenborough Station
Sackville School
J1 1 Fir Tree Cl
K4 1 Chestnut Wk
K6 1 Scott Rd
K7 1 Brantingham Cl 2 Leconfield Cl 3 Lockington Cl
F
G
H
J
K
147
170
189
1
2
3
4
5
6
7
8
STOCKS GREEN ROAD
B2027
LEIGH ROAD
TONBRIDGE ROAD
B245
Stocks Green
Stocks Green CP School
The Old Barn
High Barn Farm
Hilden Park
Tonbridge Oast Theatre
Hawden Farm
Selby's Farm
Meopham Bank
Powder Mills
Powder Mill Lane
Powder Ml La
Ramhurst Manor
Eden Valley Walk
River Medway
Barden Park
Haysden Water
Tonbridge Town Sailing Club
Lower Haysden Lane
Lower Haysden
High Weald Wk
Manor Farm
TONBRIDGE BY-PASS
A21(T)
Brook Street
The Judd School
West Kent College of Further Education
Upper Haysden Lane
Fosters Farm
Hayesden Lane
Upper Hayesden
Mabledon
South Frith
A26
ROAD

B4
1 Houselands Rd
B1
1 Speyside
A7
1 Fosse Bank Cl
A5
1 Pembroke Rd
B5
1 Bradford St
2 Holford St
3 Lambert's Yd
4 Northcote Rd
5 Vale Rd
B6
1 Alexandra Rd
2 Bickley Rd
3 Gardyne Ms
4 St Georges Ms
5 Waterloo Pl
B7
1 The Birches
2 White Oak Cl
C1
1 Penfolds Cl
C2
1 Uridge Crs
C3
1 Ashburnham Rd
2 Old London Rd
C4
1 Castle St
2 Church St
3 Kinnings Rw
4 Lime Tree Cl
C5
1 Strawberry V
C6
1 Bishops Ms
2 Fairfield Crs
3 Pembury Gv
D1
1 Canterbury Crs
E1
1 Constable Rd
2 Eastfield Gdns
3 Gainsboro Gdns
148
169
190
TONBRIDGE
Cage Green
Brook Street
Mabledon
TN9
London Road
Shipbourne Road
High Street
Hadlow Road
Cannon Lane
Vale Road
Woodgate Way
Pembury Road
Quarry Hill Road
Tonbridge By-Pass
Vauxhall Lane
Yardley Park Road
Dry Hill Park Rd
Barden Road
Hectorage Road
Tudeley Lane
Tonbridge Stn
Tonbridge Sch
Tonbridge Grammar School for Girls
Weald of Kent School for Girls
Queen Victoria Cottage Hospital
Tonbridge Football Club
Old Judd Rugby Club
Clock House Gallery
Angel Indoor Bowling
Morley Business Centre
Orchard Business Centre
Riverside Business Cen
West Kent College
West Kent College of Further Education
Hayesbrook School
The Judd School
Sussex Road CP School
Slade CP School
Tonbridge Hillview School
St Stephens CP School
Cage Green County Primary School
Long Mead CP Junior & Infant School
Hilden Oaks School
Trenchwood Medical Centre
Warders Medical Centre
Tanyard Farm
Bournemill Farm
Mabledon Farm
Hawden Farm
South Frith
Eden Valley Walk
A26
A227
A2014
A21(T)
B2021
1 grid square represents 500 metres

Parker's Green
Higham Wood
F
G
H
149
J
K
Three Elm Lane
Hadlow Place Farm
Fish Hall
Hadlow Stair
Hartlake Road
Hartlake
Wealdway
River Medway
172
The Postern
Postern Park
Upper Postern
Sherenden Farm
Sherenden Road
Tudeley Hale
Lilley Farm
Cemetery
Five Oak Green Road
B2017
Tudeley Lane
Bank Farm
Tudeley
High Weald Walk
Yardley Court Preparatory School
Crockhurst Street
Alders Road
191
Knowles Bank
Castle

150
A
B
C
D
E
1
2
3
4
5
6
7
8
171
192
Bourneside Farm
Lane
Tithe Ward
Three Elm Lane
Bourne Pk
Golden Green
Kelchers Lane
Goldhill Farm
Hartlake Road
Hartlake
Barnes Street
Wealdway
Pierce Mill Lane
River Bourne
Tonbridge Road
River Medway
Hammer Dyke
Sherenden Farm
Road
Bank Farm
Sherenden Road
Moat Farm
Five Oak Green
Whetsted
Willow Crs
Way
Nortons
Larkfield
Acorn Cl
PO
Falmouth Place
BADSELL ROAD
B2017
FIVE OAK GREEN ROAD
Capel CP School
Peble Close
Sychem Place
Tolhurst Road
Tatlingbury
GREEN ROAD
Alders Road
Lane
Capel
Church
Redwood Park
MAIDSTONE ROAD
Amhurst
Spring Farm
1 grid square represents 500 metres

H7
1 Newton Gdns
H8
1 Apple Ct
2 Keyworth Cl
3 Mount Pleasant
4 Northdown Cl
East Peckham
151
Branbridges
J7
1 Bowls Pl
2 Clavadal Rd
3 Station Ap
J8
1 St Andrews Cl
K8
1 Heather Bank
174
Tonbridge Road
Snoll Hatch Road
Pinkham
Branbridges Industrial Estate
Torbay Road
Beltring Road
Gravelly Way
Beltring Station
Beltring
Hop Farm
BRANBRIDGES ROAD
A228
Medway Valley Walk
Lily Hoo
Beltring House
MAIDSTONE ROAD
Whetsted Road
WHETSTED ROAD
Lindow Lea Farm
Whetsted
Keylands
Lucks Lane
B2160
Transfesa Road
Nursery Road
Nucknow Road
Eldon Way
Henley Rd
Hop Pocket Lane
Paddock Wood Station
Wood Business Centre
The Cedars
Ribston Gdns
Laxton Gdns
Allington Road
Station Rd
Woodlands Health Centre
Commercial Road
Old Kent Road
Kent Close
Church Road
Dimmock Cl
Cemetery
PADDOCK WOOD
Paddock Wood Town Council
Paddock Wood CP School
St Andrews Road
Walnut Close
Bullion Cl
Cogate Road
Tutsham Way
Alliance Way
Warrington Road
Forest Road
New Road
Blackberry Way
Granary
Larch Grove
Eastwell Close
Mercer Close
Fuggles Close
Badsell Manor Farm
Tudsley Brook
BADSELL ROAD
B2017
Ringden Avenue
193
Rowan Close
Clover Way
Green Lane
Linnet Avenue
Redpoll Wk
Mascalls Park
Mascalls
Queen Street
Pearsons
F
G
H
J
K
1
2
3
4
5
6
7
8

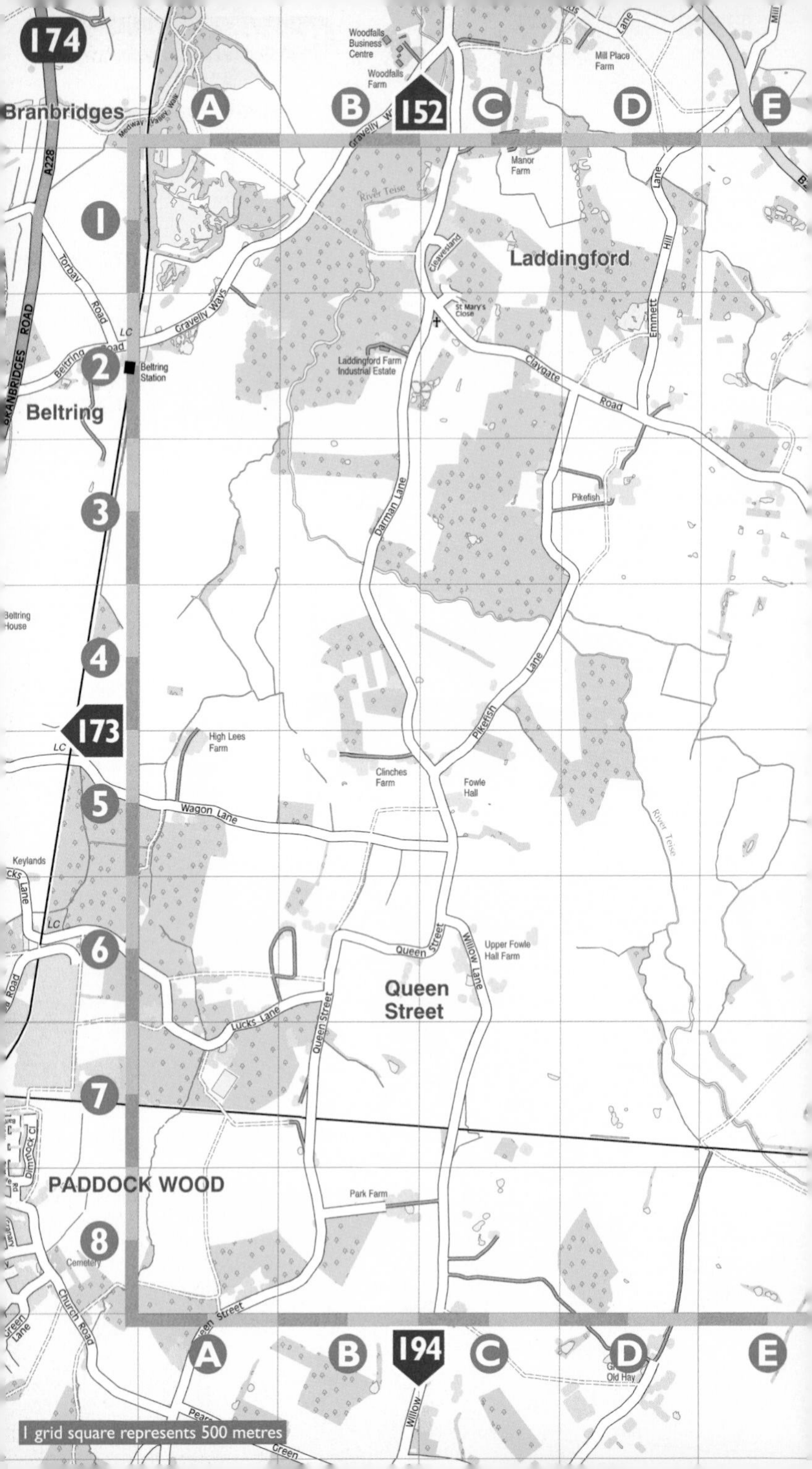
Branbridges
A228
BRANBRIDGES ROAD
Medway Valley Walk
Woodfalls Business Centre
Woodfalls Farm
152
Mill Place Farm
Gravelly Ways
Manor Farm
Lane
River Teise
Torbay Road
LC
Beltring Road
Beltring Station
Beltring
Cleaveland
Laddingford
St Mary's Close
Laddingford Farm Industrial Estate
Claygate Road
Emmett Hill Lane
Darman Lane
Pikefish
Beltring House
173
Pikefish Lane
High Lees Farm
Clinches Farm
Fowle Hall
Wagon Lane
Keylands
Lucks Lane
River Teise
Queen Street
Willow Lane
Upper Fowle Hall Farm
Queen Street
Lucks Lane
Dimmock Cl
PADDOCK WOOD
Park Farm
Cemetery
Church Road
Green Lane
Queen Street
194
Willow
Old Hay
1 grid square represents 500 metres

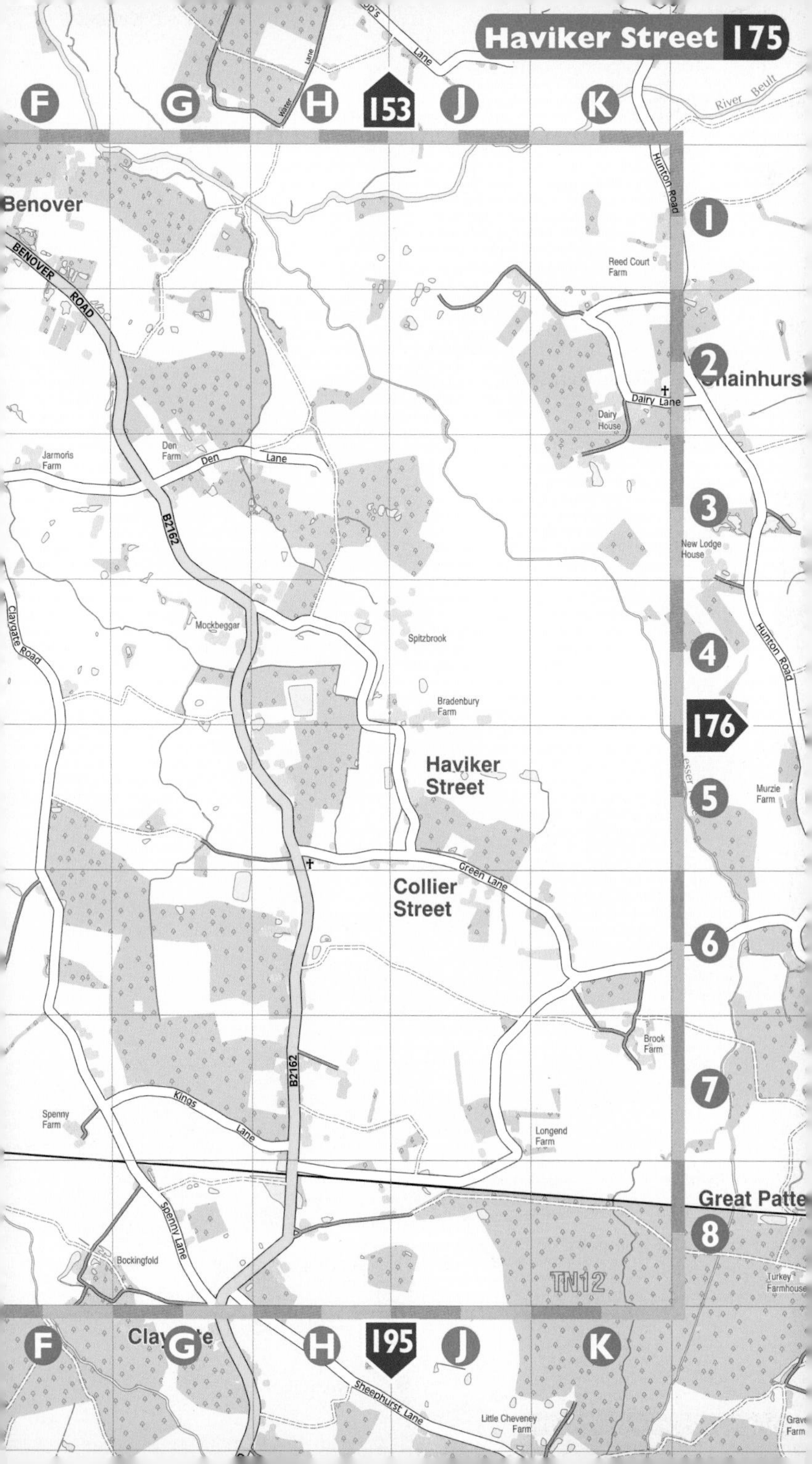
F
G
H
153
J
K
River Beult
Water Lane
Lane
Benover
BENOVER ROAD
Hunton Road
Reed Court Farm
Chainhurst
Dairy Lane
Dairy House
Jarmons Farm
Den Farm
Den Lane
B2162
New Lodge House
Mockbeggar
Spitzbrook
Claygate Road
Hunton Road
Bradenbury Farm
176
Haviker Street
Murzie Farm
Green Lane
Collier Street
Brook Farm
B2162
Kings Lane
Spenny Farm
Longend Farm
Great Patte
Spenny Lane
Bockingfold
TN12
Turkey Farmhouse
Claygate
195
Sheephurst Lane
Little Cheveney Farm
1
2
3
4
5
6
7
8

D8
1 Merchant Pl
C8
1 Barrel Arch Cl
2 Lime Cl
154
A
B
C
D
E
Redwall Lane
River Beult
Hunton Road
1
2
3
4
5
6
7
8
175
Reed Court Farm
Chainhurst
Dairy Lane
Dairy House
Great Tilden
Tilden Lane
Chain Dene Farm
Stilebridge Lane
Little Tilden Farm
New Lodge House
Broad Forstal Farm
Lesser Teise
Murzie Farm
Underlyn Lane
Milebush Lane
Gatehouse Farm
Tilden Lane
Milebush
Little Pattenden
Pattenden Lane
The Grange
Brook Farm
MAIDSTONE ROAD
Wheelbarrow Park Estate
Guardian Industrial Estate
Cemetery
Longend Farm
Church Farm
Great Pattenden
Crest Industrial Estate
Marden Station
Sovereigns Way
B2079
CHURCH GREEN
HIGH ST
Marden Medical Centre
Chantry Rd
Chantry Pl
Ballard Cl
Meadow Way
South Rd
Barnes Walk
Sutton Forge
Roundel Wy
TN12
Turkey Farmhouse
Marden CP School
196
MARDEN
Westfield House
Copper
1 grid square represents 500 metres

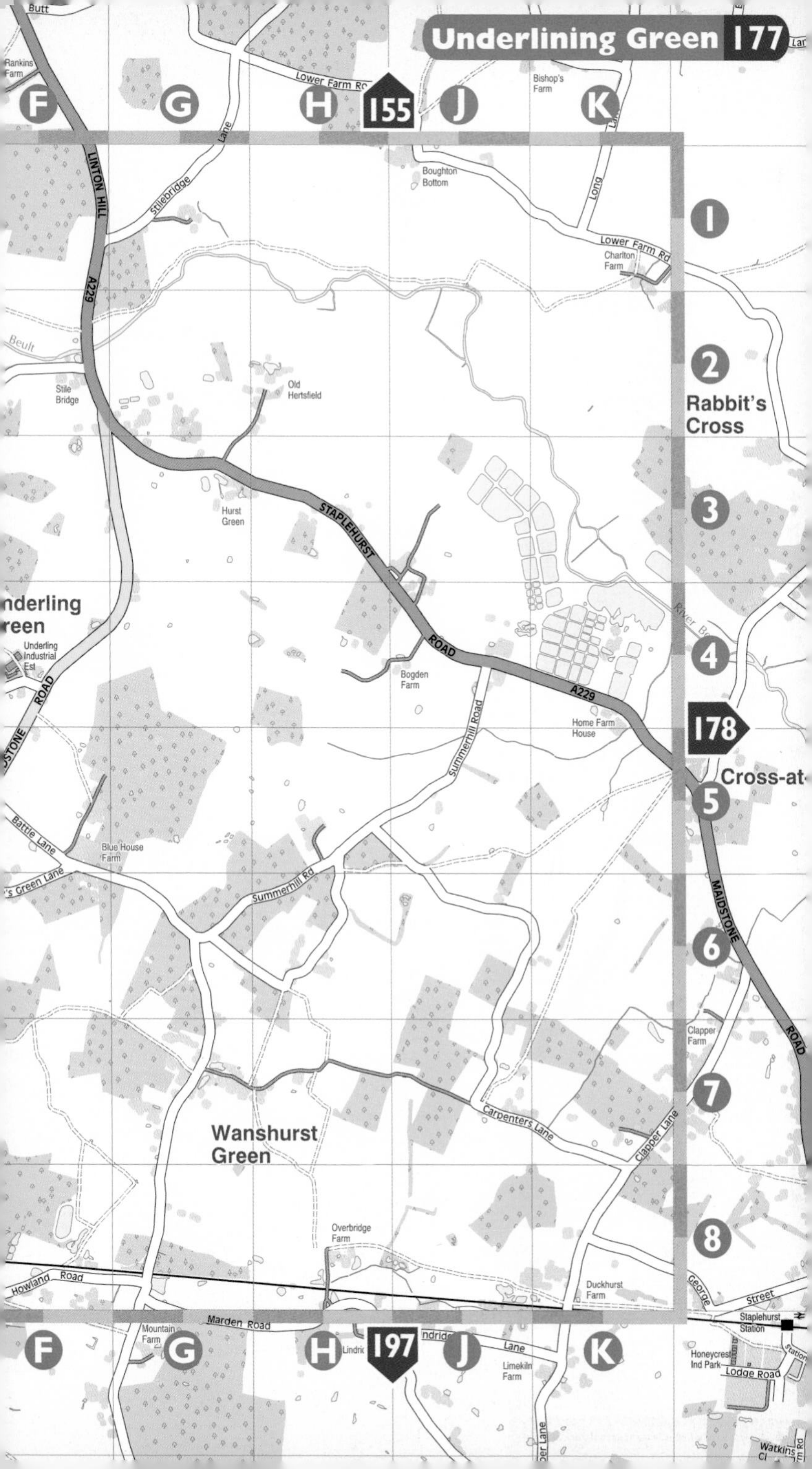

Butt
Rankins Farm
Lower Farm Rd
Bishop's Farm
155
F
G
H
J
K
LINTON HILL
Stilebridge Lane
Boughton Bottom
Long Lane
Lower Farm Rd
Charlton Farm
A229
Beult
Stile Bridge
Old Hertsfield
Rabbit's Cross
Hurst Green
STAPLEHURST ROAD
Underling Green
Underling Industrial Est
River Beult
Bogden Farm
A229
Home Farm House
178
Summerhill Road
Cross-at-
MAIDSTONE ROAD
Battle Lane
Blue House Farm
Summerhill Rd
Clapper Farm
Carpenters Lane
Clapper Lane
Wanshurst Green
Overbridge Farm
Howland Road
Duckhurst Farm
George Street
Staplehurst Station
Marden Road
Mountain Farm
197
Lindridge Lane
Limekiln Farm
Honeycrest Ind Park
Lodge Road
Station
Watkins Cl
1
2
3
4
5
6
7
8

178
Hermitage Lane
Lucks
Bishop's Farm
Long Lane
156
Lamb's Cross
Forge Lane
Chart Sutton
Green Lane
Lower Farm Rd
Charlton Farm
Chart Bottom Farm
Holbrook
Moat Farm
Lake Farm
Green Lane
Rabbit's Cross
Devil's Den
Babylon Lane
Elderden Farm
Ashurst Court
Lower Farm
River Beult
A229
Home House
177
Cross-at-Hand
Dunbury Farm
Babylon
MAIDSTONE ROAD
Bardingley
Clapper Farm
Sweetlands Couchman Green
Couchman Green Lane
Newstead Farm
Clapper Lane
A229
River Beult
Duckhurst Farm
George Street
Staplehurst Station
Honeycrest Ind Park
Station Ap
Lodge Road
Market St
Fishers Rd
Fisher's Farm
Fishers C
Newlyn Dr
198
Headcorn Road
Slaney Place
STATION R
Watkins Cl
1 grid square represents 500 metres
A
B
C
D
E
1
2
3
4
5
6
7
8

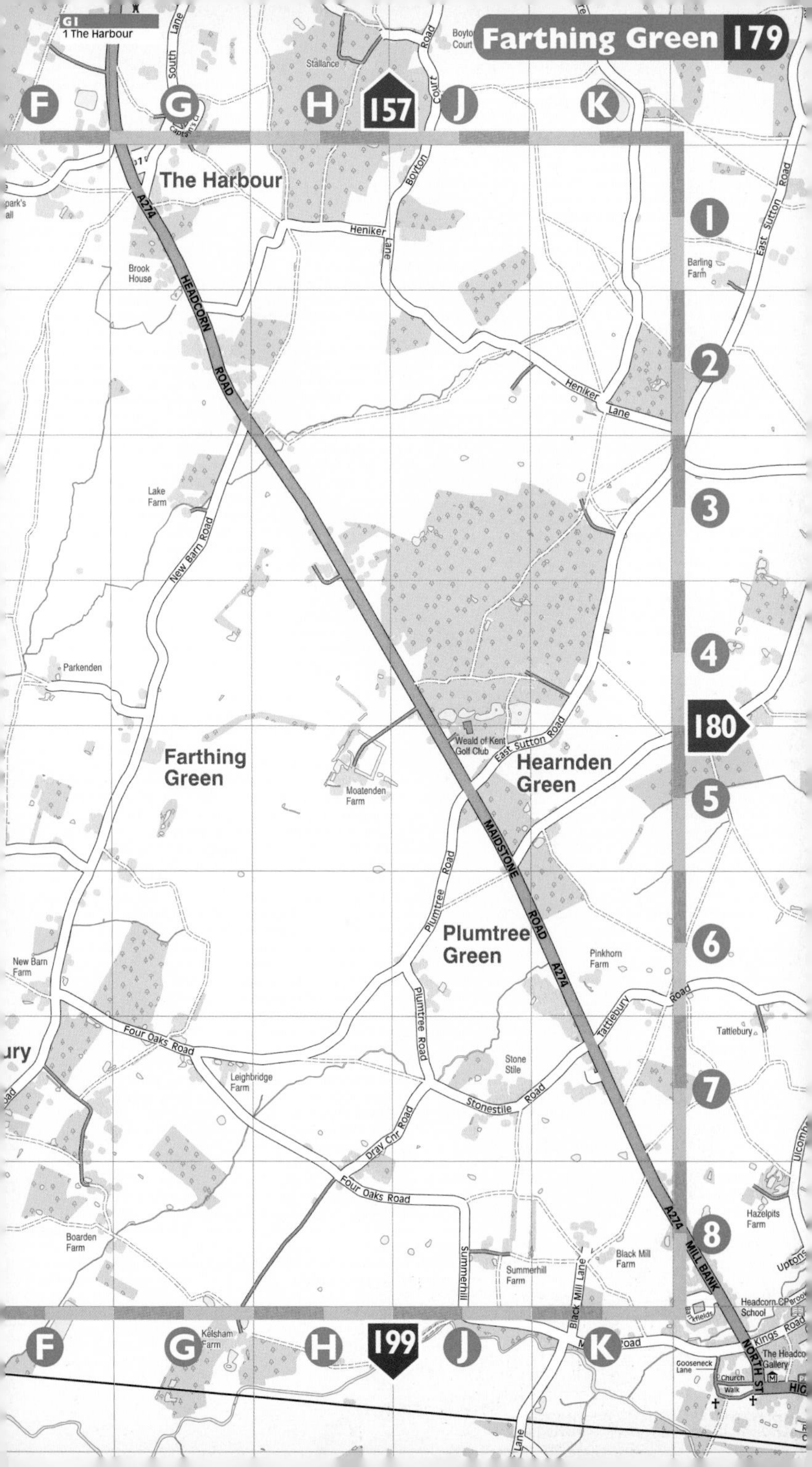
G1
1 The Harbour
F
G
H
157
J
K
South Lane
Stallance
Boyton Court Road
Boyton Court
The Harbour
A274
HEADCORN ROAD
Heniker Lane
Boyton Lane
Brook House
Heniker Lane
East Sutton Road
Barling Farm
1
2
3
4
5
6
7
8
180
Lake Farm
New Barn Road
Parkenden
Farthing Green
Moatenden Farm
Weald of Kent Golf Club
East Sutton Road
Hearnden Green
MAIDSTONE ROAD
A274
Plumtree Road
Plumtree Green
Pinkhorn Farm
New Barn Farm
Four Oaks Road
Plumtree Road
Tattlebury Road
Tattlebury
Leighbridge Farm
Stone Stile
Stonestile Road
Dray Cnr Road
Four Oaks Road
Summerhill
Summerhill Farm
Black Mill Lane
Black Mill Farm
Hazelpits Farm
A274
MILL BANK
Boarden Farm
Kelsham Farm
199
Headcorn C P School
Kings Road
NORTH ST
The Headco Gallery
Gooseneck Lane
Church Walk
Lane

Ulcombe C of E Primary School
PO
Lodge Gdns
Chestnut Close
A
B
158
C
D
E
1
2
3
4
5
6
7
8
179
200
East Sutton Road
Brick Kiln Lane
Headcorn Road
Barling Farm
Heniker Lane
Stickfast Lane
Jubilee Corner
Crump's Lane
Stone Hall
Tilden Road
Sparrow Hall
Tong
earnden
reen
Boy Court Lane
Boy Court
Peckham Farm
Pinkhorn Farm
A274
Tattlebury
Road
Tattlebury
Tilden
Lenham Road
Barling Green Farm
Sunnyside Farm
Baker Lane
Witherden Farm
Ulcombe Road
Hazelpits Farm
Black Mill Farm
A274 MILL BANK
Uptons
Oak Farm Gdns
Brooklands
Thatch Barn Road
HEADCORN
Headcorn CP School
Knight's Way
Forge Mdw
Forge La
Black Mill Lane
Moat Road
Gooseneck Lane
The Headcorn Gallery
Church Walk
Doctors Surg
Chaplin Dr
Becket
New Rd
HIGH ST
STATION RD
WHEELER ST
Sharp's Field
Sherway Close
The Burdens
Orchard Glade
Love Lane
BIDDEND
1 grid square represents 500 metres

Grafty Green
PO
F
G
H
159
J
K
Woodcock Lane
Eastwood
Telpits Farm
Yewtree
Judge House Farm
Broadstone
Coldbridge Lane
1
Blackpit Wood
2
House
Park House
3
Southpark Wood
Woodsden
Barham's Mill Farm
Southernden Road
4
Thornden Farm
182
Coldharbour Farm
5
Wallett Court
Southernden Road
Clark Hill Farm
Southernden
6
Grigg Lane
Sherway Road
Kingsden Farm
7
Gloversbridge Farm
Bedlam Lane
River Sherway
Burnt House
8
F
G
H
201
J
K
Green
Bedlam Lane
Rosemary Lane

A
B
160
C
D
E
1
2
3
4
181
5
6
7
8
202
Coldbridge Lane
Coldbridge Wood
Wellham Wood
Field Farm
Greensand Way
Burscombe Farm
Foxden Wood
House
Egerton
Egerton House
Coldbridge Farm
Hazeldene Farm
Pembles Cross
Barham's Mill Road
Egert
Link House
Link Hill Lane
Chapel Lane
Crocken Hill Road
Barham's Mill Farm
Rock
Little Houses
Potter's Forstal
Rock Hill Road
Coldharbour Farm
Forstal Road
Forge Lane
Egerton Forstal
Ragge Farm House
Munday
Bedlam Lane
Wanden Lane
Newland Green
Clark Hill Farm
Heronsdale
Newland Green Lane
Wanden
Kingsden Farm
Bedlam Lane
Frith Wood
Burnt House
Park Farm
The Quarter
Oaklands
Dering Wood
1 grid square represents 500 metres

F
G
H
161
J
K
Brockton Farm
Foxen Farm
M20
Hurst Wood
Coach Road
Stonebridge Gn Road
Mill Rd
Field
Southfield
Stonebridge Green
Stonebridge Green Road
Iden Lane
Stour Valley Wk
Court Lodge Farm
Barnfield
Glebeland
The St
Iden
PO
Stevens Cl
Elm Cl
Harmers Way
Hill Road
Stone Hill
Greensand Way
New Road
Greenhill Farm
Pivington Lane
Pivington Mill
Stour Valley Walk
Swallow Mill Farm
Chart Court
Greenhill La
Britcher Farm
Egerton Road
Nettlepole Lane
Munday Farm
Greensand Way
Elvey Farm
Mundy Bois
Road
PH
Westfields
Pluckley
The St
Sheerland
Greensand Way
Smarden Road
Pluckley C of E Primary School
Station Road
Pluckley Thorne
The Thorn Estate
Lambden Road
Fir Toll
The Pinnock
Malmains
Smarden Road
203
Rushbrook Farm
1
2
3
4
5
6
7
8

164
A
B
C
D
E
1
2
3
4
5
6
7
8
Gabriel's Manor
Den Cross
Cernes Farm
Eden Valley Walk
MARSH GREEN ROAD B2028
Marsh Green
Little Ray
Chiswell Hall
Shernden Lane
Roman Road
Starborough Castle
Vanguard Way
Christmas Mill
Shernden Farm
Howlets Farm
New Barns Farm
Greybury Lane
Ockhams
Clatfields
Cobhambury Farm
Hoopers Farm
Greybury Farm
Shernden Wood
Moon's Lane
Kent County
Surrey County
Beechenwood Farm
Ludwells Farm
Sussex Border Path
Beeches Farm
Lower Stonehurst Farm
Shepherdsgrove Lane
Basing Farm
Scarletts
Furnace Farm
1 grid square represents 500 metres

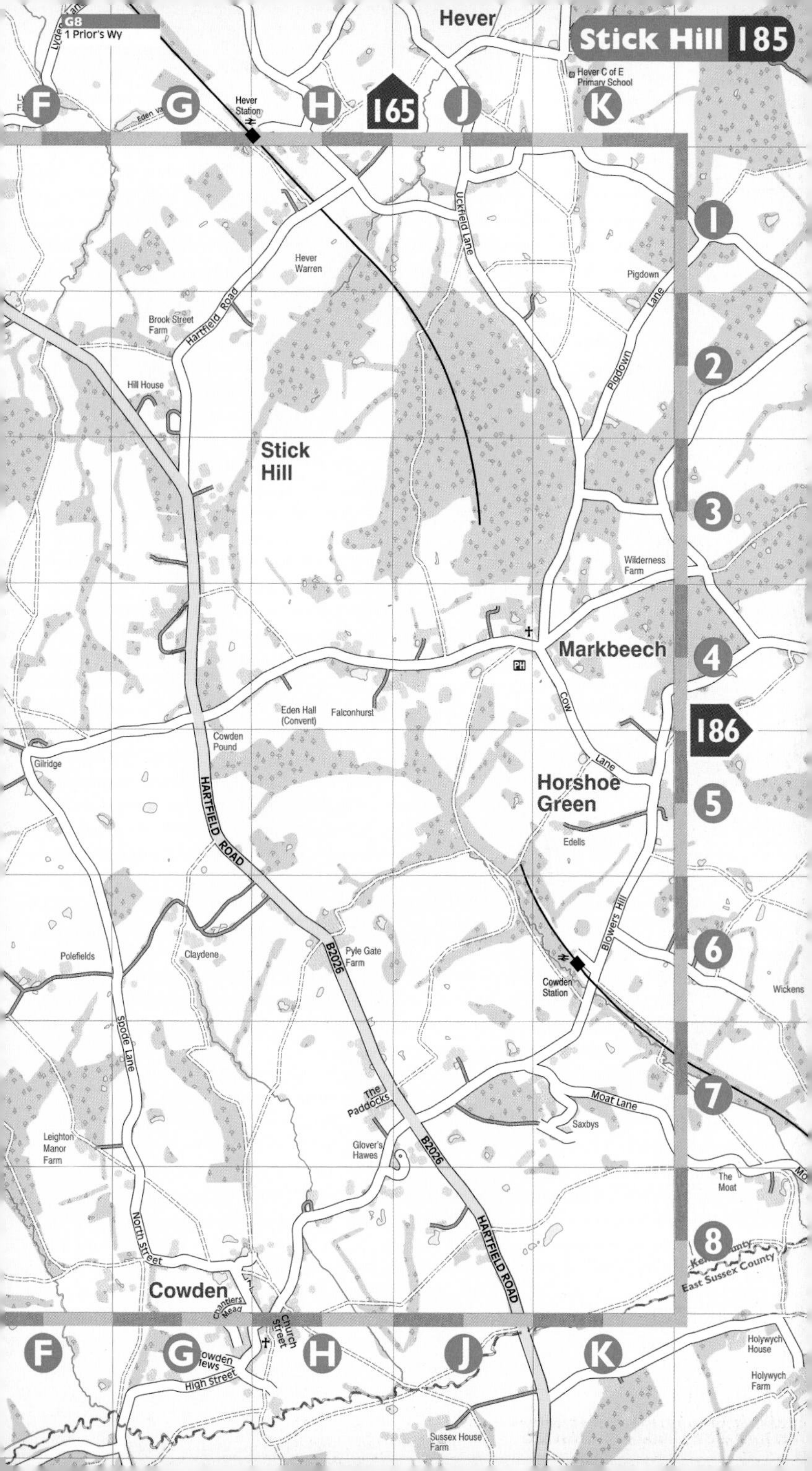
G8
1 Prior's Wy
Hever
Hever C of E Primary School
Hever Station
165
F
G
H
J
K
1
2
3
4
5
6
7
8
186
Uckfield Lane
Hever Warren
Pigdown
Pigdown Lane
Brook Street Farm
Hartfield Road
Hill House
Stick Hill
Wilderness Farm
Markbeech
PH
Cow Lane
Eden Hall (Convent)
Falconhurst
Cowden Pound
Gilridge
Horshoe Green
Edells
HARTFIELD ROAD
B2026
Pyle Gate Farm
Claydene
Polefields
Blowers Hill
Cowden Station
Wickens
Spode Lane
The Paddocks
Moat Lane
Saxbys
Leighton Manor Farm
Glover's Hawes
The Moat
North Street
Cowden
Chantlers Mead
Church Street
Cowden Mews
High Street
East Sussex County
Holywych House
Holywych Farm
Sussex House Farm

186
Hever C of E Primary School
Eden Valley
166
Hill Hoath
A
B
C
D
E
Lockskinners Farm
Eden Valley Wk
1
Pigdown
Lane
2
3
Wilderness Farm
Hoath Corner
Trugger's Farm
Chiddingstone Hoath
Oakenden
Hoath House
4
Cow Lane
185
Oakenden Lane
Stone Park
5
Edells
Blowers Hill
6
Wickens
Bassetts
Bassetts
7
Moat
Saxbys
The Moat
Moat Lane
8
Sussex Border Path
Kent County
East Sussex County
Kent Water
Hobbs Hill Farm
Holywych Farm
1 grid square represents 500 metres

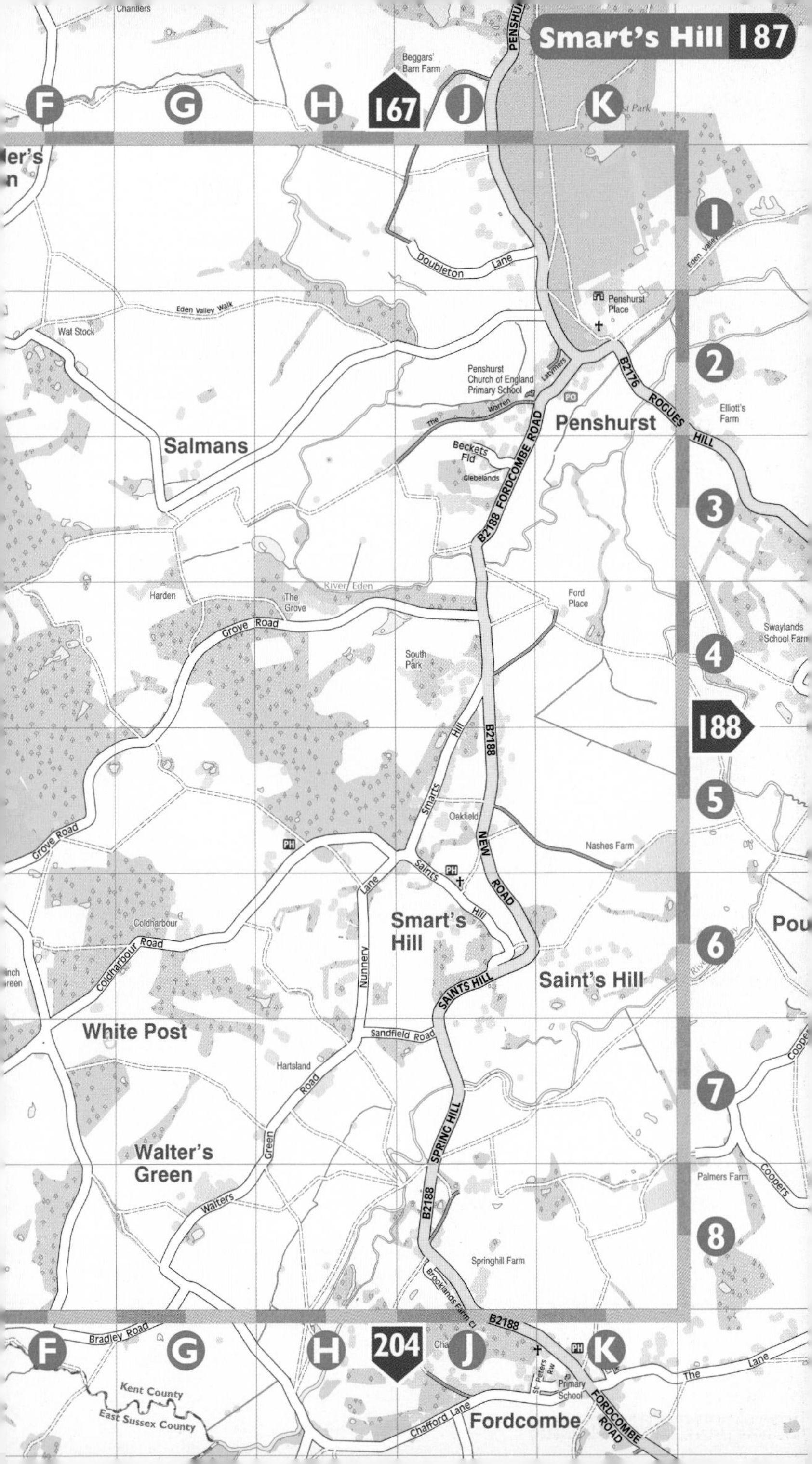
Chantlers
Beggars' Barn Farm
167
F
G
H
J
K
Doubleton Lane
Eden Valley Walk
Wat Stock
Penshurst Place
Penshurst Church of England Primary School
Latymers
The Warren
PO
Penshurst
B2176
ROGUES HILL
Elliott's Farm
Salmans
Beckets Fld
Glebelands
B2188 FORDCOMBE ROAD
River Eden
Harden
The Grove
Grove Road
Ford Place
South Park
Swaylands School Farm
188
Smarts Hill
B2188
Oakfield
NEW ROAD
Nashes Farm
PH
Saints Hill
Grove Road
Coldharbour
Coldharbour Road
Nunnery Lane
Smart's Hill
SAINTS HILL
Saint's Hill
White Post
Sandfield Road
Hartsland
Road
Walter's Green
Green
Walters
SPRING HILL
B2188
Springhill Farm
Brooklands Farm Cl
Palmers Farm
Coopers
1
2
3
4
5
6
7
8
Bradley Road
204
St Peters Rw
Primary School
Kent County
East Sussex County
Chafford Lane
Fordcombe
FORDCOMBE ROAD
The Lane

1 grid square represents 500 metres

K4
1 Ruscombe Cl
2 Still La
K5
1 Breedon Av
2 Summerhill Av
3 Woolley Cl
Upper Haysden Lane
Mabledon
Upper Hayesden
Haysden Lane
169
190
10
206
F
G
H
J
K
1
2
3
4
5
6
7
8
LONDON ROAD
A26
High Weald Walk
Nightingale Farm
Gate Farm Road
Broadfield
B2176
BIDBOROUGH RIDGE
Ridgelands
PO
The Crs
Darnley Drive
Harland Way
Vauxhall Lane
Honnington Farm
The Glebe
High Street
Woodland Way
St Lawrence Avenue
Rectory Dr
Great Bounds Dr
Bounds Oak Way
Smythe Close
Glebelands
Spring Lane
Bidborough
Hardinge Av
Dower House Crs
Brookhurst Gdns
Birchwood Avenue
Bidborough Primary School
Meadows Memorial School
Vicarage Rd
Doon Brae
Fernhurst Crs
Oak End Cl
Frank's Hollow Road
Southborough Cemetery
Church Rd
Constitutional Hill Road
Sheffield Rd
Modest Corner
Victoria Road
Holden Road
Vale Rd
Doric Av
Doric Avenue
Carville Av
St Andrews Medical Centre
St Andrews Park Road
Springfield Road
Prospect Pk
Bedford Rd
Meadow Rd
Crendon Park
Bondfield Cl
The Ridgeway
Bentham Hill
Scriventon
Road
Green
Stockland
Manor Rd
Crundwell Road
Woolley Rd
Edward Street
Western Rd
Forge Rd
Hythe Close
Yew
St David's Pk
Kibbles Lane
Broomhill Park Road
Holden Pk
Taylor St
St Charles
Stockland Green
Keel Gdns
Ladys Gift Rd
TN4
Bright Ridge
Speldhurst Road
Etherington Hill
David Salomon's House
Whitegate
St John's Park
Tunbridge Wells Grammar School for Boys
Broomhill Road
St Gregorys RC School
West Kent College of Further Education
Reynolds Lane
St Augustine School
Leigh Close
Broomhill Bank
Smockham Farm
New England Rd
St John's
Tunbridge Wells Grammar School for Girls
The Barry Clinic
East Cliff Rd
Harwarton
Broomhill Bank School
Lower Green Road
Bennett Memorial Diocesan School
Culverden Av
Huntleys Pk
Down
Culverden Pk Road
Whitefield Rd
Somerset Rd
Infant School
Newcomen Rd
Doctors Surg
Lower Green
Derwent Dr
Culverden
Knightsbridge Cl
Standen St
William St
John St
Thomas St
ST JOHN'S ROAD
Southwood Road
Westwood Road
Tuxford Road
Ashley Gdns
Ashley Park Close
Shirley Gdns
Rydal Cl
Rydal Dr
Kendal Pk
Coniston Av
Byng Road
Park
Woodbury Pk
Culverden Square

A7
1 The Fairways
A6
1 Hillgarth
A5
1 Norton Rd
2 St Andrews Ct
A4
1 Flaxmore Pl
TONBRIDGE BY-PASS
A21(T)
South Frith
Mabledon
Queen Victoria Cottage Hospital
VAUXHALL LANE
170
A8
1 Campbell Rd
2 Kent Rd
3 Newlands Ri
B7
1 Cunningham Cl
2 Newlands Wy
C6
1 Powdermill Cl
C7
1 Denbigh Rd
D5
1 Lambersart Cl
D7
1 Brooklands
2 Orchidhurst
3 Trebilco Cl
D8
1 Lipscombe Rd
E6
1 Hawthorn Wk
LONDON ROAD
A26
Nightingale Farm
Vauxhall Lane
Honnington Farm
High Weald Walk
Forest Farm
Old Forge Farm
Meadows Memorial
Pennington
Fairlight Cl
Pennington Pl
Ridgewaye
Powder Mill Lane
189
The Gallery
Pinewood Gdns
St Andrews Medical Centre
St Andrews Park Road
SOUTHBOROUGH
Doric Avenue
Prospect Pk
Meadow Rd
Western Rd
Forge Rd
Holden Pk
Crendon Park
Yew Tree Road
Brian Crs
Hill Crest
Brokes Way
Blackthorn Av
Hornbeam Av
Dowding Way
North Farm
Industrial Estate
Chalkin Business Park
Longfield Road
Orchard Business Cen
Chapman Way
TN4
High Brooms
Chestnut Avenue
Nursery Rd
South Vw Rd
Powder Mill La
Apple Tree La
Lamberts Road
Caley Road
Rankine
St John's Park
Tunbridge Wells Grammar School for Boys
St Gregorys RC School
West Kent College of Further Education
St Augustine School
Tunbridge Wells Sports Cen
Montgomery Road
Cunningham Rd
Holmewood Rd
Cambrian Rd
High Brooms Station
Clifton Road
Brook Rd
Oak Rd
Laurel Rd
Wiltshire Wy
Milton Dr
Theodore Cl
The Hurst
Greggs Wd Rd
Kemble Close
Malton Way
Oakwood Rise
Birch Cl
Harries Road
Bursiem Rd
Leighton Close
Wilman Road
St Johns Primary School
St Lukes School
Merrion Close
Woodland Rd
St John's
10
11
Tunbridge Wells School
Beltring Rd
All Saints Road
Hopwood Gdns
Impala Gdns
St Luke's Road
Silverdale Road
Stephen's Road
Queen's Road
Doctors Surgery
Dunstan Rd
Somerset Rd
Dilion Way
Sandhurst Road
Sandhurst Park
Friars Way
Primary School
Infant School
Sherwood Rd
Ravenswood Av
Sherwood Park
Culverden Pk
Culverden Down
Connaught Wy
Infant School
Woodbury Park Rd
207
Rochdale Rd
Auckland Rd
Dorking Road
St James' Road
Albion Road
Quarry Rd
Stanley Rd
Tunnel Rd
Sandhurst Road
IDA
Ferndale
Talbot Rd
1 grid square represents 500 metres

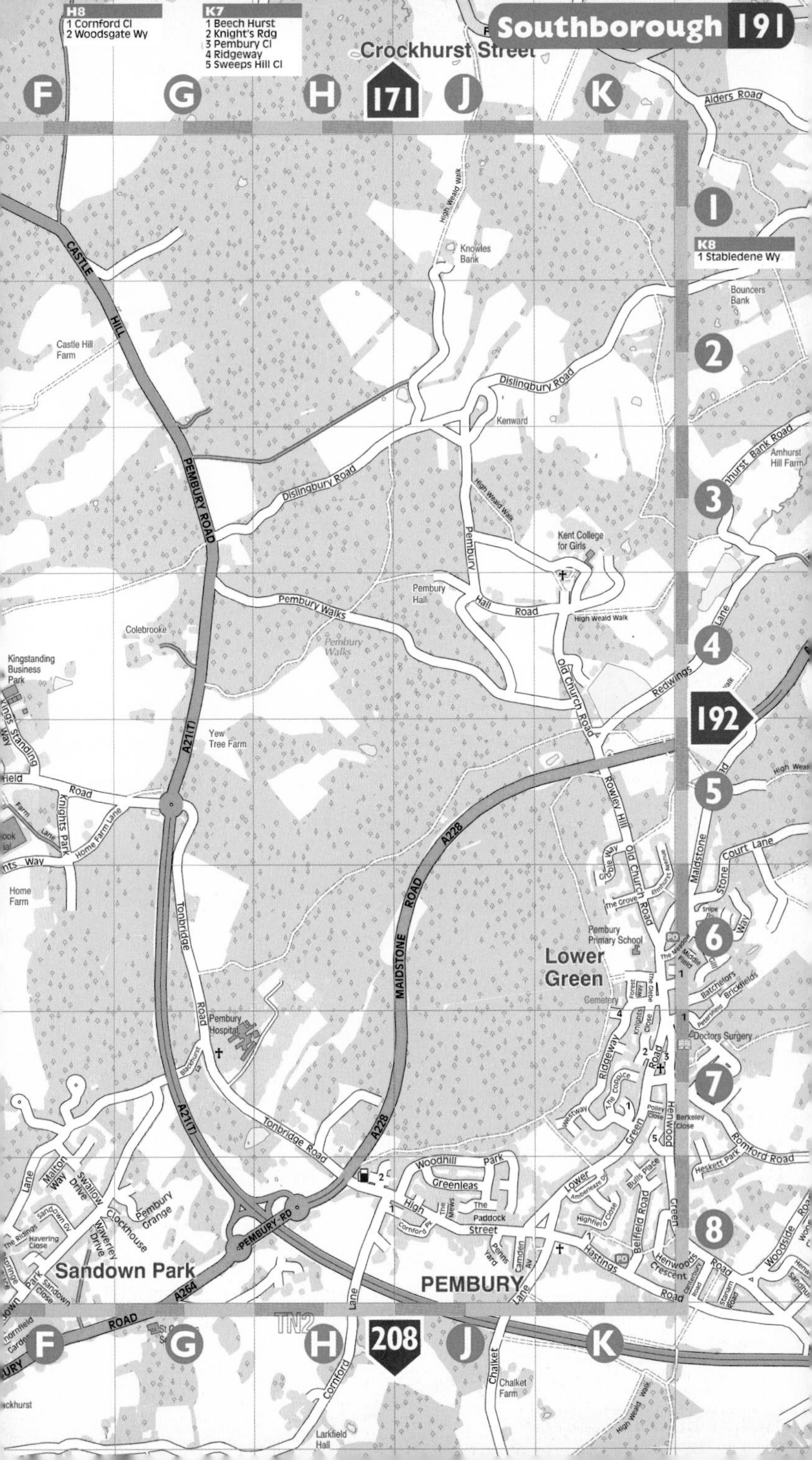
H8
1 Cornford Cl
2 Woodsgate Wy
K7
1 Beech Hurst
2 Knight's Rdg
3 Pembury Cl
4 Ridgeway
5 Sweeps Hill Cl
Crockhurst Street
171
F
G
H
J
K
Alders Road
1
K8
1 Stabledene Wy
Bouncers Bank
2
3
4
5
6
7
8
192
208
Knowles Bank
High Weald Walk
Castle Hill Farm
CASTLE HILL
PEMBURY ROAD
Dislingbury Road
Kenward
Amhurst Bank Road
Amhurst Hill Farm
Kent College for Girls
Pembury Hall
Pembury Hall Road
Pembury Walks
Colebrooke
Kingstanding Business Park
Kings Standing Way
Redwings Lane
Old Church Road
Yew Tree Farm
A21(T)
Road
Knights Park
Home Farm Lane
Home Farm
Rowley Hill
A228
MAIDSTONE ROAD
Maidstone Road
Stone Court Lane
The Grove
Grove Way
Elmhurst Avenue
Pembury Primary School
Lower Green
Cemetery
Forest Way
The Glebe
Knights Close
Ridgeway
The Coppice
Westway
Snipe Way
The Meadow
Middle Field
Gill
Batchelors
Brickfields
Petersfield
Doctors Surgery
Tonbridge Road
Pembury Hospital
Blackhurst La
Polley Close
Henwood Green
Berkeley Close
Romford Road
Heskett Park
Woodhill Park
Greenleas
The Mews
The Paddock
High Street
Cornford Pk
Lower Green
Amberleaze Dr
Bulls Place
Belfield Road
Highfield Close
Penns Yard
Camden Av
Hastings Road
Henwoods Crescent
Canterbury Road
Stanam Road
Woodside Road
PEMBURY RD
Malton Way
Swallow Drive
Pembury Grange
Sandown Gv
The Ridings
Havering Close
Clockhouse
Waverley Drive
Sandown Park
Sandown Close
Park
A264
PEMBURY
ROAD
TN2
Lane
Cornford
Chalket Lane
Chalket Farm
Larkfield Hall
Thornfield Gardens

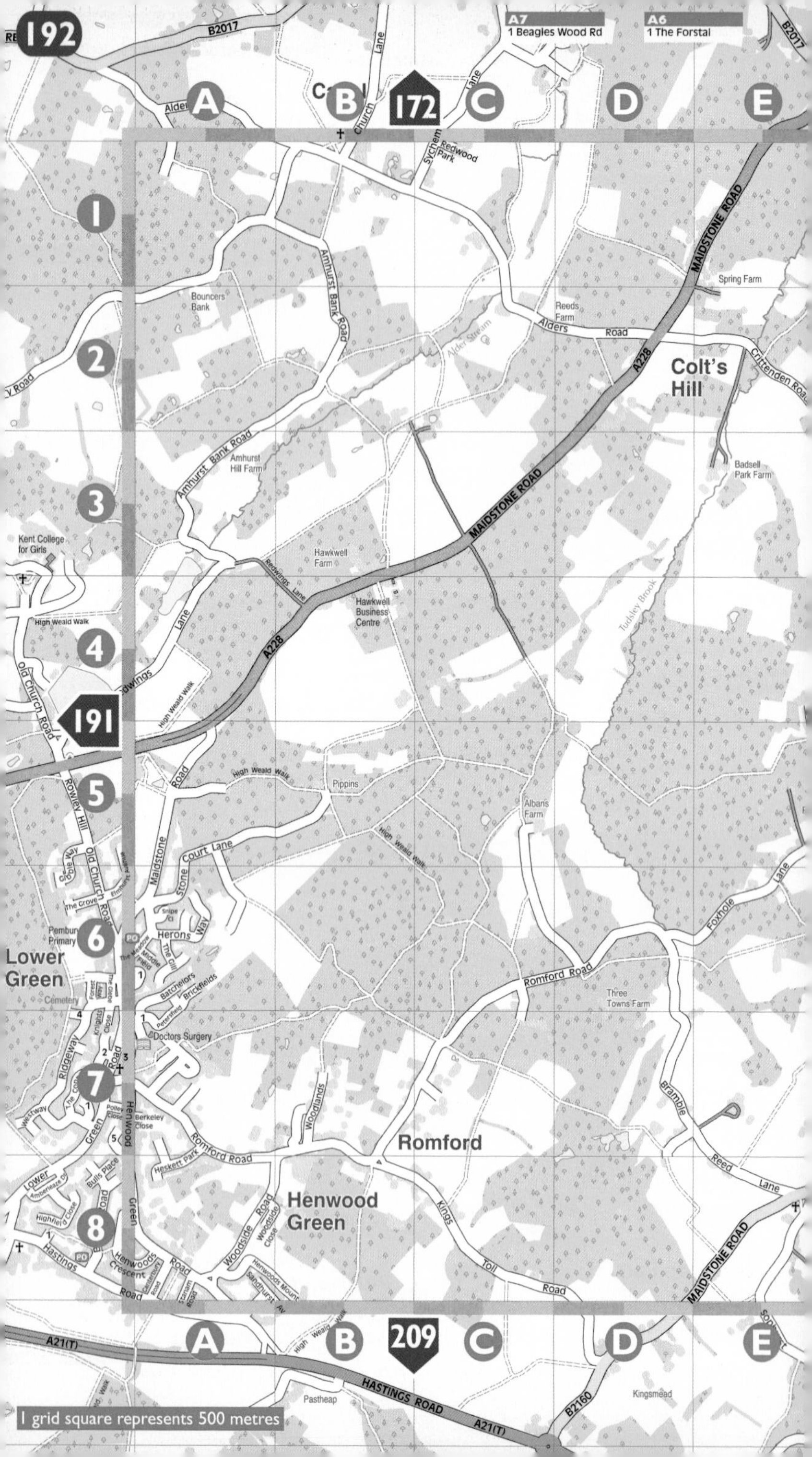
B2017
A7 1 Beagles Wood Rd
A6 1 The Forstal
A
B
172
C
D
E
1
2
3
4
5
6
7
8
Church Lane
Sychem Lane
Redwood Park
Bouncers Bank
Amhurst Bank Road
Alder Stream
Reeds Farm
Alders Road
Spring Farm
MAIDSTONE ROAD
A228
Colt's Hill
Crittenden Road
Badsell Park Farm
Amhurst Hill Farm
Kent College for Girls
High Weald Walk
Hawkwell Farm
Redwings Lane
Hawkwell Business Centre
Tudeley Brook
Old Church Road
191
Rowley Hill
Pippins
Albans Farm
Stone Court Lane
Maidstone Road
The Grove
Pembury Primary
Lower Green
Herons Way
Snipe Cl
The Gill
Batchelors
Brickfields
Petersfield
Cemetery
Doctors Surgery
Ridgeway
Knights Close
Romford Road
Three Towns Farm
Foxhole Lane
Bramble
Reed Lane
Romford
Woodlands
Henwood Green
Heskett Park
Berkeley Close
Westway
Bulls Place
Highfield Close
Hastings Road
Henwoods Crescent
Woodside Road
Woodside Close
Henwoods Mount
Sandhurst Av
Kings Toll Road
209
A21(T)
HASTINGS ROAD
B2160
Pastheap
Kingsmead
1 grid square represents 500 metres

G1
1 Goldings
H1
1 The Greenways
2 Hornbeam Cl
3 Sycamore Gdns
J1
1 Bullfinch Cl
2 Goldfinch Cl
3 Haywain Cl
PADDOCK WOOD
173
194
210
Badsell Manor Farm
BADSELL ROAD
B2017
Ringden Avenue
Tutsham Way
Fuggles Close
Paddock Wood CP School
Walnut Close
Blackberry Way
Church Road
Queen Street
Commercial Road
Kent Close
Ewins Cl
St Andrews Road
Granary
Rowan Close
Oakfield Road
Ashcroft Road
Kiln Way
Bluebell Walk
Clover Way
Primrose Wk
Green Lane
The Bines
Chaffinch Way
Linnet Avenue
Buttercup Close
Siskin Gdns
Redpoll Wk
Mascalls Park
Mascalls
Mascall's Court Road
Mascalls Secondary School
Mascall Court
Mascall's Court Lane
Catts Place
Mile Oak Road
Mile Oak
Knowle
Chantler's Hill
B2160
Crittenden
Crittenden Road
Biggenden
Waterman's Lane
Moatlands
GEDGE'S HILL
Gedges Farm
Crundalls Farm
Prall's Lane
Pixot Hill
Maycotts Lane
Chestnut Lane
Birch Close
Chestnut Lane
MAIDSTONE ROAD
Maynard's Lane
Brenchley Road
Matfield
PO
Brenchley & Matfield C of E Primary School
Holly Bank
The Lawns
High St
Windmill Hill
Broad Oak
Broad Oak Cl
The Noble Clinic
Brenchley
Horsmonden Road
Oakfield Road
Friars
Tibbs Court Lane
Hatmill Lane
Fairman's Lane
Petteridge Lane
Porters Close
Tibb's Court
Petteridge
Chillmill
Kite Lane
Cryals Road
Brattles Grange
Old Cryals
Tong Road
Flightshott Farm
Marle Place Road
F
G
H
J
K
1
2
3
4
5
6
7
8

E8
1 The Manwarings
Park Farm
Cemetery
Church Road
174
193
211
A
B
C
D
E
1
2
3
4
5
6
7
8
Queen Street
Pearsons Green Road
Willow Lane
Great Old Hay
Catts Place
Mascall Court
Mascall's Court Road
Mascall's Court
Mile Oak Road
Mile Oak
Knowle Lane
Knowle Road
Longbrooks Farm
Pearson's Green Road
Pearson's Green
Churn Lane
August Pitts Farm
Lane
The Knowle
Poplars Farm
Hill
Pixot
Castle Hill
Weald View
Crook Road
Yew Tree
Windmill Hill
Broad Oak
Poulhurst Farm
Furnace Lane
Holly Bank
The Lawns
High St
PO
Broad Oak Cl
Palmer's Green
Palmers Green Lane
Church Cl
Brenchley
Horsmonden Road
Hononton Farm
Lane
Furnace Pond
Fairman's Lane
MAIDSTONE RO
Kirkins Close
Gunlands
Gibbet Lane
LAMBERHURST ROAD
Horsmond CP School
Morley
Orchard Crs
Orchard Close
Back La
Orch Wy
Green Rd
Orchard Wy
Oast Vw
Burrs Hill
Shirrenden
Brenchley Road
Angley Ct
The Surgery
Spout Lane
Farm
B2162
1 grid square represents 500 metres

F
G
H
175
J
K
Bockingfold
Spenny La
TN12
Turkey Farmhou
Claygate
Sheephurst Lane
Little Cheveney Farm
Little Cheveney
MAIDSTONE ROAD
River Teise
Bennetts Farm
B2162
Beech Road
1
2
3
4
196
5
6
7
8
Baybrooks Cottages
Rams Hill
Road
Mill Lane
Great Cheveney
Lesser Teise
The Corner
Northiam Farm
River Teise
Tanner House
School House Farm
Haymans Hill Farm
Haymans Hill
School House Lane
Ash Farm
Grovehurst
orsmonden
Lane
212
Grovehurst
B2079
Capel Cross
Finchurst Farm

Great Pattenden
Crest Industrial Estate
Marden Station
D1
1 Jewell Gv
2 Napoleon Dr
3 Oak Tree Cl
4 Stella Cl
5 Sunburst Cl
TN12
Turkey Farmhouse
176
Marden Medical Centre
Chantry Pl
Sutton Forge
Barnes Walk
Meadow Way
South Rd
Marden CP School
GOUDHURST ROAD
Maynards
Sutton Ct
Roundel Wy
Albion Road
South Road
MARDEN
Copper
Gravelpit Farm Cotts
Westfield House
The Plain
Plain Road
Beech Road
Marden Beech
Beale Farm
Springfield
195
B2079
Great Cheveney
Lesser Teise
River Teise
Sherenden Lane
Loves Farm
Tanner House
Winchet Hill
213
Lane
1 grid square represents 500 metres

Overbridge Farm
177
Marden Road
Mountain Farm
Lindridge
Lindridge Lane
Limekiln Farm
George Street
Staplehurst Station
Honeycrest Ind Park
Lodge Road
Watkins Cl
Clapper Lane
Marden Road
Park House
Park Road
Pagehurst Road
Pagehurst
Aydehurst Farm
Oliver Road
Bathurst Road
Gybbon Rise
Offen's Dr
Bell Lane
Marden Thorn
South Bank
Hammer Way
198
Pinnock Lane
Brattle Farm Museum
Five Oak Lane
Saynden Farm
Ely Court
Goudhurst Road
Pristling Lane
Plain Farm
Snoad Lane
Bletchingley Farm
Chapmans Farm
Cork Lane
Lovehurst Manor
Snoad Wood
Hushheath Manor
Mathurst Farm
214
Paley Farm
Bounds End Farm
F
G
H
J
K
1
2
3
4
5
6
7
8

B2
1 Benden Cl
B1
1 Winch's Garth
A2
1 Barn Meadow
2 Corner Farm Rd
178
A
B
C
D
E
1
2
3
4
5
6
7
8
197
215
River
Duckhurst Farm
George Street
Staplehurst Station
Honeycrest Ind Park
Lodge Road
Station Ap
Willow Cres
Market St
Fishers Rd
Fishers Cl
Newlyn Dr
Fisher's Farm
STATION ROAD
Headcorn Road
Slaney Place
Pile Lane
Watkins Cl
Tomlin Cl
Corner Farm Rd
Lime Trees
N Down
Brooks Cl
Hurst Cl
Guelder Rose Medical Centre
Doctors Surgery
Marden Road
Cradducks
Spills Hill Farm
Marden Rd
Bathurst Cl
Chestnut Av
Jeffrey Cl
Staney Cl
Oliver Road
Pope Dr
Butch Cl
Reeves Cl
Thatcher Rd
Alen Sq
Cornforth Cl
Poyntell Rd
Weavers
Slaney Rd
Weld Cl
Marian Square
STAPLEHURST
Lane
Aydehurst Farm
Bathurst Road
Surrenden Road
Crowther Close
HIGH STREET
Staple Dr
Gybbon Rise
Fletcher Road
Staplehurst CP School
Offen's Dr
Usborne Cl
Chapel Lane
Fir Tree Close
Rose Cottage Surgery
Spilsill Court
Cradducks Lane
Bell Lane
Jaggard Way
Vine Wk
McCabe Cl
South Bank
Exhurst Manor
Cradducks Lane
Church Gn
Frittenden Road
Frittenden Rd
Hanmer Way
Iden Cres
Hallwards
Brattle Farm Museum
Henhurst Farm
Pinnock Lane
Park Wood Lane
Five Oak Lane
Staplehurst Manor
Broadla
Ely Court
Maplehurst
Mill
Goudhurst Road
Cork Lane
Iden Grange
Lovehurst Manor
A229
Bromley Barn
CRANBROOK
Little Wadd Farm
Hill Top
Castle Bank
Great Wadd Farm
ROAD
Knox Bridge
Rock Farm
Waller Hill
Grandshore Lane
Grandshore Lane
ROCKS HILL
Paley Farm
Tolehurst Farm
1 grid square represents 500 metres

Four Oaks Road
Boarden Farm
F
G
H
179
J
K
Summerhill Farm
Black Mill Farm
Black Mill Lane
MILL BANK
Uptons
Headcorn CP School
Kings Road
NORTH ST
The Headcorn Gallery
Kelsham Farm
Moat Road
Goosens Lane
1
Church Walk
Water Lane
Waterlane Farm
Place Farm
Chickenden Farm
Lane
2
New House Farm
3
4
Appleton Farm
200
Sinkhurst Green
5
Little Brookwood
6
Bubhurst
Cherry Tree Farm
Mill Lane
Frittenden
Cemetery
PO
Peasridge Farm
Bubhurst Lane
7
Frittenden Primary School
Chestnut Close
The Street
Pond Farm
8
Sand Lane
Tanyard
Buckhurst
216
Catherine Wheel

C1
1 Gibbs Hl
2 Hydes Orch
B1
1 Bramleys
2 Kingsland Gv
3 Knowles Gdns
4 Woodcocks
A1
1 Clerks Fld
180
199
217
A
B
C
D
E
1
2
3
4
5
6
7
8
A274
MILL BANK
Black Mill Farm
Black Mill Lane
Moat Road
Uptons
Oak Farm Gdns
Headcorn CP School
Banfields
Kings Road
Forge Mdw
Knight's Way
Knaves Acre
Thatch Barn Road
Forge La
Oak Lane
NORTH ST
The Headcorn Gallery
Gooseneck Lane
Church Walk
Doctors Surg
Chaplin Dr
New Rd
HIGH ST
STATION RD
WHEELER ST
Sharp's Field
Downs Cl
Sherway Close
Rushford Close
The Burdens
Orchard Glade
Tollgate Place
BIDDENDEN LANE
Headcorn Station
Smarden Road
Love Lane
LC
Wick Farm
New House Farm
Bletchenden
Waterman Quarter
Lashenden (Headcorn) Airfield
The Hall
BIDDENDEN ROAD
Shenley Farm
Lane
Cold Harbour
Tile Barn Farm
Ayleswade
Bubhurst
Bubhurst Lane
Wick Hill
Bell Lane
Peasridge Farm
HEADCORN ROAD
Lashenden
Pond Farm
Ibornden Farm
Weeks
1 grid square represents 500 metres

River Sherway
F
G
H
181
J
K
Swift's Green
Rosemary Lane
Bedlam Lane
I
st End
2
Headcorn Road
Marley Farm
Marley
Watch House
Hegg Hill Farm
Beult
TN27
3
New House Farm
Bell Lane
PH
Smarden Bell
Water Lane
Ash Farm
Mill Lane
4
Hadman's Place
Ashenden
The Acorns
202
Haylands Farm
High
CP School
Green Lane
Vesper Court
West Hoy Farm
5
Sm
Beult Meadow
Cage Lane
Burnthouse Lane
Vesper Hawk Farm
Barnden Farm
Walford House
Obeden Farm
Biddenden Road
Snughorne Lane
6
Bethersden Road
The Cut
Haffen
Quarte
7
Lime Kiln Farm
Monks Hill
Gillham
Smarden Road
Roberts Farm
8
Bethersden Ro
Vane Court
F
G
H
218
J
K
en
Great Omenden Farm
Pook Lane
Pook Lane

Frith Wood
B4
1 Haslewood Cl
A
B
182
C
D
E
1
2
3
4
5
6
7
8
The Quarter
Oaklands
Dering Wood
Lewd Lane
Berry Court
New House Farm
Ash Farm
Mill Lane
Pluckley Road
Dering Farm
Romden Road
Mainey Wood
Ashenden
201
Glebe Cl
Biddenden Green
Smarden CP School
High Street
Green Lane
Cressenden La
Vesper Court
PH
PO
Smarden
Beult Meadow
Cage Lane
Vesper Hawk Farm
Romden Road
Romden Castle
Walford House
Road
Bethersden Road
Romden Wood
Buckman Green Farm
Haffenden Quarter
Luckhurst Farm
Hamden
Langley
Bethersden Road
219
Tearnden Farm
Bethersden
Hegg Hill Farm
Lane

1 grid square represents 500 metres

Pluckley Thorne
The Thorn
183
Fir Toll
The Pinnock
Road
Malmains
F
G
H
J
K
1
2
3
4
5
6
7
8
Rose Farm
Smarden Road
Rushbrook Farm
Cooper Farm
Station Road
Pluckley Road
Dering Close
Chamber's Green
PH
Pluckley Station
an's
The Forest
Newhouse Farm
Stanford Bridge Farm
Pimphurst
Tuesnoad
Buss Farm
Barnhurst Farm
Oakdene Farm
Frid Farm
Wissenden
Runsell Grange
Baylisden
Pluckley Road
Lane
Mill Farr
Mill Road
Norton
Bethersden County Primary School
PO
The Street
Church Hill
Forgefield
Chester Avenue
The Dene
Forge Hill
Bethersde
Lovelace
Lovelace Court
The Surgery

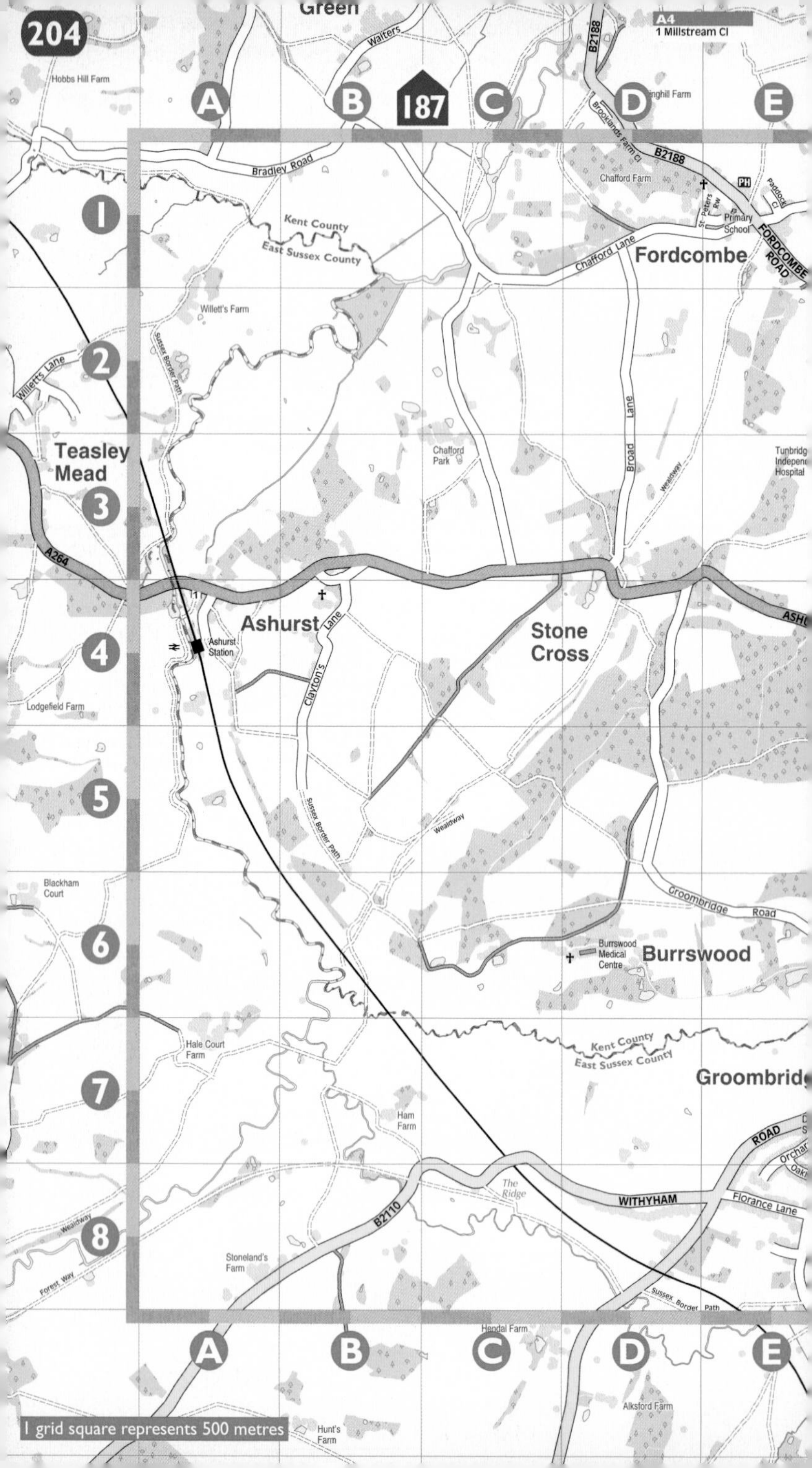

Green
Walters
B2188
A4
1 Millstream Cl
Hobbs Hill Farm
A
B
187
C
D
E
nghill Farm
Brooklands Farm Cl
B2188
Bradley Road
Chafford Farm
PH
Paddock Cl
St Peters Rw
Primary School
FORDCOMBE ROAD
Kent County
East Sussex County
Chafford Lane
Fordcombe
1
Willett's Farm
Sussex Border Path
2
Willetts Lane
Chafford Park
Broad Lane
Wealdway
Teasley Mead
3
A264
Ashurst
Clayton's Lane
Stone Cross
ASHU
4
Ashurst Station
Lodgefield Farm
5
Sussex Border Path
Wealdway
Blackham Court
6
Groombridge Road
Burrswood Medical Centre
Burrswood
Hale Court Farm
Kent County
East Sussex County
7
Groombridg
Ham Farm
ROAD
Orchar
Oak
The Ridge
WITHYHAM
Florance Lane
B2110
Wealdway
8
Forest Way
Stoneland's Farm
Sussex Border Path
Hendal Farm
Alksford Farm
1 grid square represents 500 metres
Hunt's Farm

F6
1 Bird In Hand St
F7
1 Gromenfield
2 The Homestead
188
F8
1 The Close
H2
1 Winstone Scott Av
H3
1 Birchetts Av
2 Lampington Rw
3 Sherwood Pl
206
J3
1 Gipps Cross La
2 Hazelbank
3 Little Mallett
4 Upton Quarry
5 Widbury Cl
K2
1 Forstall
K3
1 Farnham Cl
Langton Green
Birchden
Park Corner
Hickman's Farm
Wealdway
Poundsbridge Hill
Old House Lane
Leggs' Lane
High Weald Walk
Speldhurst Road
Burnt House Lane
Ewehurst Lane
Farnham Lane
Ashurst Place
Langton Green CP School
Fernchase Manor
Rushetts
Great Footway
Langholm Rd
Stonewall Park Road
Homewood Rd
First Street
Third St
Knowle Close
The Green
Gibbetts
Great Courtlands
Mercers
Newlands
Bushy Gill
Ryders
Upper Profit
Long Slip
Ox Lea
Upper Stephens
Monteith Close
Dornden Drive
Asher
Reeds
Farnham Beeches
Farnham Pl
LANGTON ROAD
A264
Holmewood Ridge
Broom Park
Broomlands
Barrow Lane
Hither Chantlers
Holmewood House School
Crockers Hatch Corner
B2188
B2110
The Hollonds
Broom Lane
Top Hill Farm
GROOMBRIDGE HILL
Pokehill
River Grom
Spa Valley Railway
Broadwater Forest
The Warren
Station Road
Newton Willows
Lealands
Lealands Cl
Lynwood
St Thomas C of E Primary School
Endge Road
Cemetery
Rusthall Medical Centre
Junior School
Fremlin Close
Nellington Road
The Boundary
Southwood Road
Tuxford Road

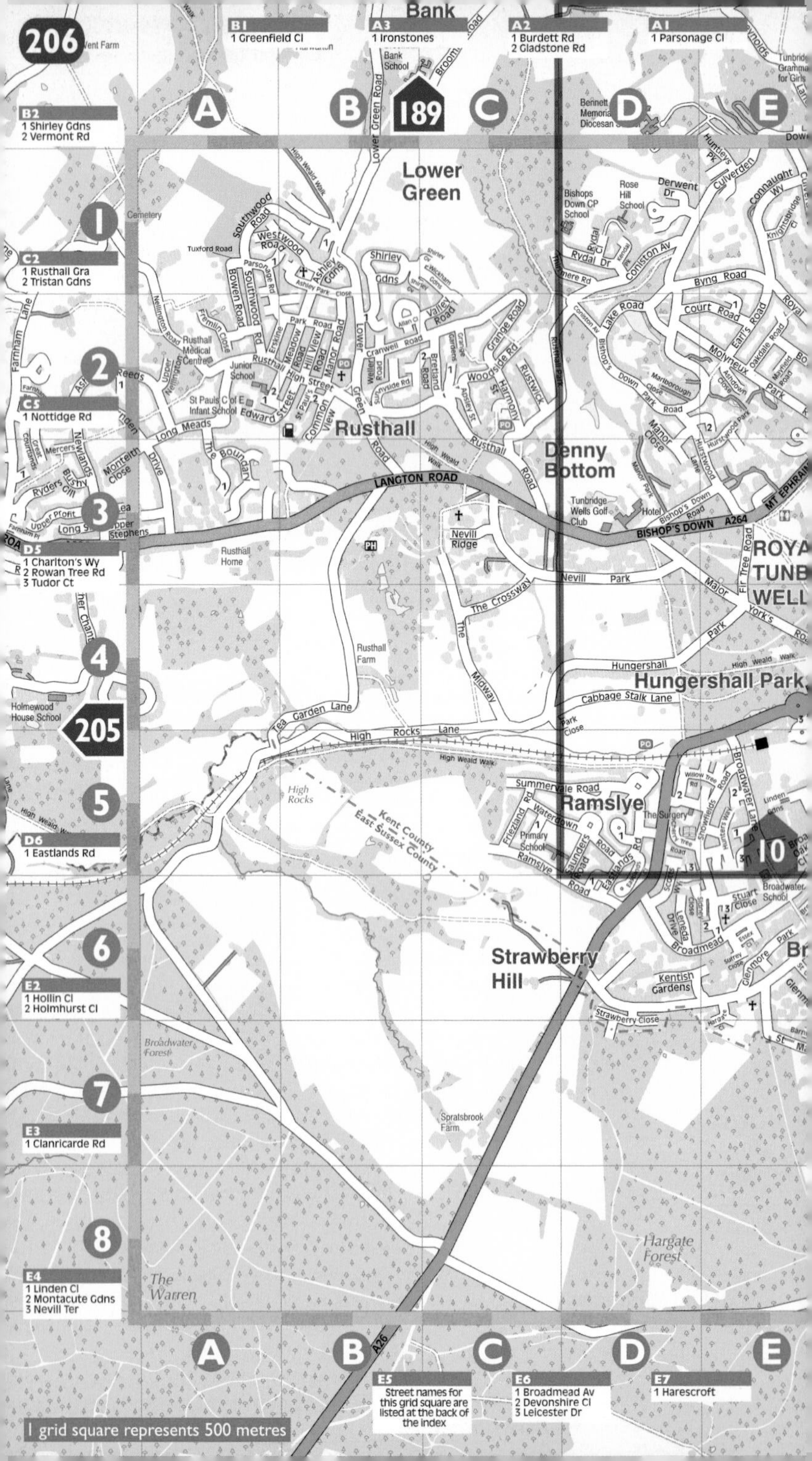
B1
1 Greenfield Cl
A3
1 Ironstones
A2
1 Burdett Rd
2 Gladstone Rd
A1
1 Parsonage Cl
B2
1 Shirley Gdns
2 Vermont Rd
C2
1 Rusthall Gra
2 Tristan Gdns
C5
1 Nottidge Rd
D5
1 Charlton's Wy
2 Rowan Tree Rd
3 Tudor Ct
D6
1 Eastlands Rd
E2
1 Hollin Cl
2 Holmhurst Cl
E3
1 Clanricarde Rd
E4
1 Linden Cl
2 Montacute Gdns
3 Nevill Ter
E5
Street names for this grid square are listed at the back of the index
E6
1 Broadmead Av
2 Devonshire Cl
3 Leicester Dr
E7
1 Harescroft
189
205
10
Lower Green
Rusthall
Denny Bottom
Hungershall Park
Ramslye
Strawberry Hill
LANGTON ROAD
BISHOP'S DOWN A264
MT EPHRAIM
A26
Kent County
East Sussex County
High Rocks
Broadwater Forest
Hargate Forest
The Warren
Spratsbrook Farm
Rusthall Farm
Rusthall Home
Nevill Ridge
Tunbridge Wells Golf Club
1 grid square represents 500 metres

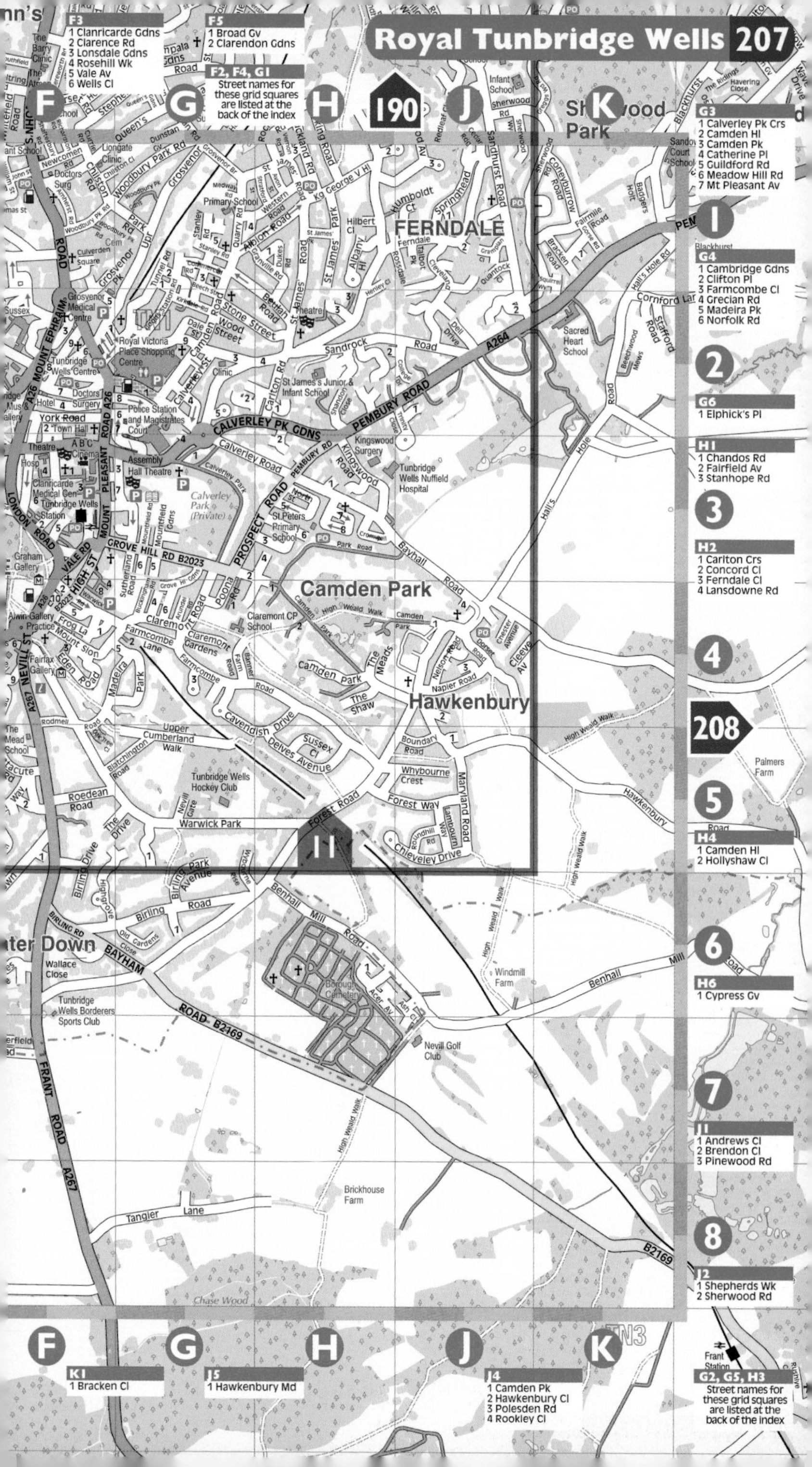
F3
1 Clanricarde Gdns
2 Clarence Rd
3 Lonsdale Gdns
4 Rosehill Wk
5 Vale Av
6 Wells Cl
F5
1 Broad Gv
2 Clarendon Gdns
F2, F4, G1
Street names for these grid squares are listed at the back of the index
190
G3
1 Calverley Pk Crs
2 Camden Hl
3 Camden Pk
4 Catherine Pl
5 Guildford Rd
6 Meadow Hill Rd
7 Mt Pleasant Av
G4
1 Cambridge Gdns
2 Clifton Pl
3 Farmcombe Cl
4 Grecian Rd
5 Madeira Pk
6 Norfolk Rd
G6
1 Elphick's Pl
H1
1 Chandos Rd
2 Fairfield Av
3 Stanhope Rd
H2
1 Carlton Crs
2 Concord Cl
3 Ferndale Cl
4 Lansdowne Rd
208
H4
1 Camden Hl
2 Hollyshaw Cl
H6
1 Cypress Gv
J1
1 Andrews Cl
2 Brendon Cl
3 Pinewood Rd
J2
1 Shepherds Wk
2 Sherwood Rd
K1
1 Bracken Cl
J5
1 Hawkenbury Md
J4
1 Camden Pk
2 Hawkenbury Cl
3 Polesden Rd
4 Rookley Cl
G2, G5, H3
Street names for these grid squares are listed at the back of the index
FERNDALE
Camden Park
Hawkenbury
Sherwood Park
Royal Victoria Place Shopping Centre
Tunbridge Wells Centre
Calverley Park (Private)
Tunbridge Wells Hockey Club
Borough Cemetery
Nevill Golf Club
Windmill Farm
Brickhouse Farm
Palmers Farm
Chase Wood
Tunbridge Wells Borderers Sports Club
PEMBURY ROAD
A264
CALVERLEY PK GDNS
PROSPECT ROAD
GROVE HILL RD B2023
MOUNT PLEASANT ROAD A26
A26 MOUNT EPHRAIM
LONDON ROAD
FRANT ROAD
A267
BAYHAM ROAD B2169
B2169
Forest Road
Tangier Lane
Benhall Mill Road
Warwick Park
Cavendish Drive
Delves Avenue
Sandrock Road
Bayhall Road
Hawkenbury Road
Birling Road
Frant Station
TN3
F G H J K
1 2 3 4 5 6 7 8

1 grid square represents 500 metres

Henwood Green
Woodside Road
Woodside Close
Henwoods Mount
Sandhurst Av
Kings
Road
192
MAIDSTONE ROAD
Reed
Sophurst
Lane
High Weald Walk
Pastheap
HASTINGS ROAD
A21(T)
B2160
Kingsmead
Cryals Road
Old Cryals
Fletchers Farm
Dundale Road
Kipping's Cross
Cryals Road
Beech Lane
Key's Green
Elmhurst Farm
Old Farm
Great Sandhurst Wood
Lamberhurst
Dundale Farm
210
The Grange
Perch
Sandhurst Farm
Clay Hill Cotts
Clay Hill
Rear Wood
Tollslye
Bayham Abbey
Bayham Lake
River Teise
Hoathly Farm
220
Clay Hill Road
F
G
H
J
K
1
2
3
4
5
6
7
8

210
193
209
221
A
B
C
D
E
1
2
3
4
5
6
7
8
Petteridge
Chillmill
Petteridge Lane
Porters Close
Tibb's Court
Court
Kite Lane
Lane
Fairman's
Cryals Road
Sophurst
Lane
Brattles Grange
Spout
Tong Road
Marle Place
Old Cryals
Old Tong Farm
Road
Beech Lane
Key's Green
Old Farm
Tong Lane
Cuckoo Lane
Lamberhurst Quarter
Little Dunks Farm
Coldharbour
A21(T)
Perch Lane
The Grange
Lindridge Lodge Farm
Clay Hill Cotts
Clay Hill Road
Windmill Farm
Owl House
Grantham Hall
Mount Pleasant
Hoathly Farm
Mount Pleasant Lane
Parsonage Lane
SCHOOL HILL
Lamberhurst C of E School
Furnace Mill
Brewer Street
Lamberhurst Surgery
PO
HIGH STREET
Pearse Place
1 grid square represents 500 metres

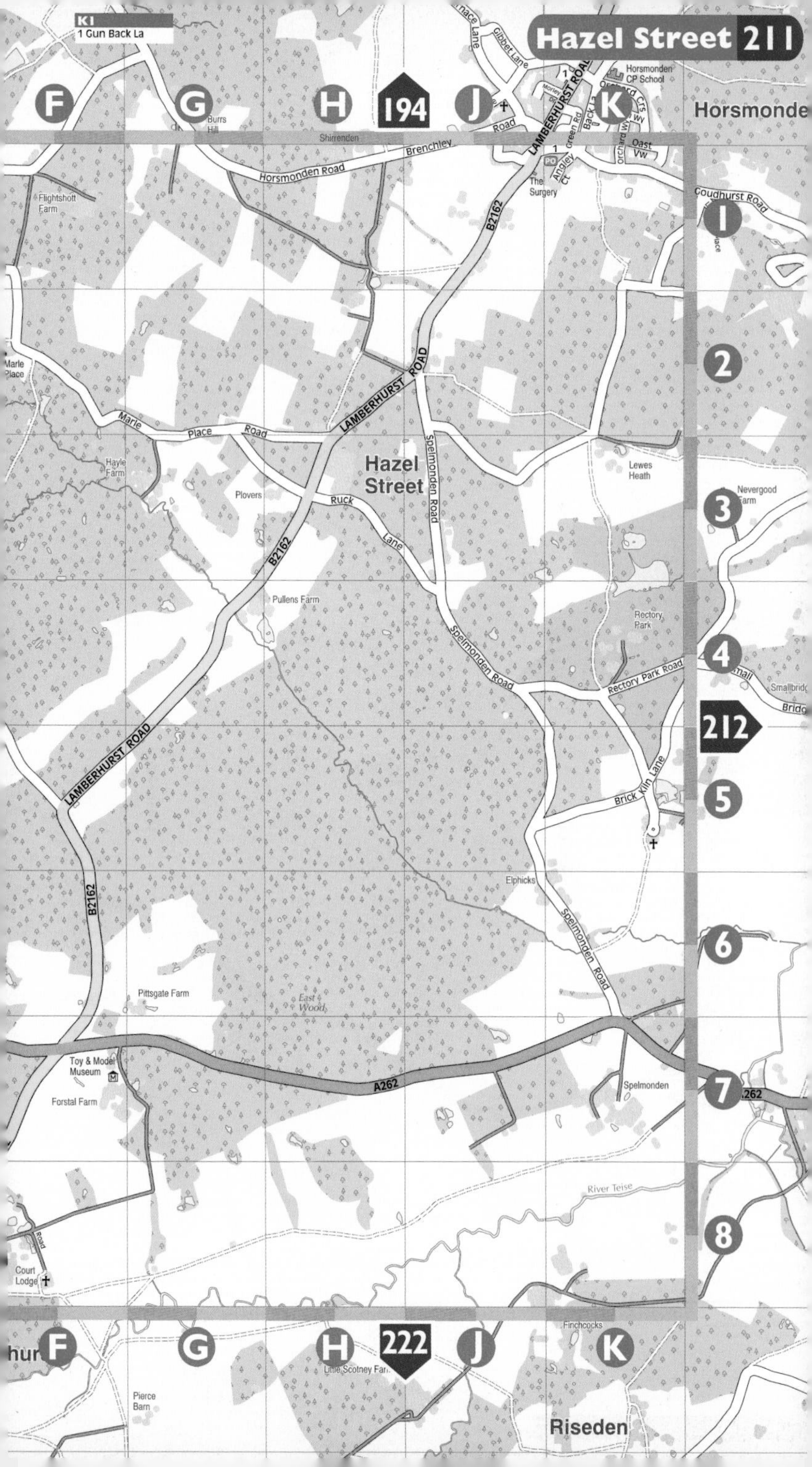
K1
1 Gun Back La
F
G
H
194
J
K
Horsmonden
Horsmonden CP School
Gibbet Lane
Furnace Lane
Morley
Orchard Crs
Back La
Orchard Wy
Oast Vw
Burrs Hill
Shirrenden
Brenchley Road
Horsmonden Road
LAMBERHURST ROAD
Green Rd
Angley Ct
PO
The Surgery
Goudhurst Road
1
B2162
Flightshott Farm
2
Marle Place
Marle Place Road
Hayle Farm
Plovers
Hazel Street
Ruck Lane
Spelmonden Road
Lewes Heath
Nevergood Farm
3
Pullens Farm
Rectory Park
4
Rectory Park Road
Smallbridge
212
Brick Kiln Lane
5
Elphicks
6
Pittsgate Farm
East Wood
A262
7
Toy & Model Museum
Forstal Farm
Spelmonden
River Teise
8
Road
Court Lodge
Finchcocks
222
Little Scotney Farm
Pierce Barn
Riseden

212
Horsmonden CP School
Orchard Crs
Back La
Orch Wy
Orchard Wy
Green Rd
Oast Vw
Horsmonden
195
Grovehurst
Goudhurst Road
Lamberts Place
Capel Cross
Goudhurst Road
Broad Ford
Brick Kiln Lane
Finchurst Farm
B2079
Gore Lane
Gore Court
Swan Farm
Swan Lane
Lewes Heath
Nevergood Farm
Share Farm
Brandfold
Rectory Park
Rectory Park Road
Lidwells House
Small Bridge Road
Smallbridge
211
Trottenden Farm
Lidwells Lane
Blind Lane
NORTH ROAD
Lovers Lane
Trowswell
B2084
Spelmonden Road
Crowbourne Farm
CHURCH ROAD
HIGH ST
WEST ROAD
BALCOMBES HILL
CLAYHILL
Back Lane
Beaman Close
Goudhurst and K C of E Primary S
Maypole
Goudhurst
High Ridge
Mary Day's
Bankfield Wy
Culpepers
Lurkins Rise
A262
STATION ROAD
Blue Coat Lane
Ranters Lane
Peasley Lane
River Teise
Smugley Farm
Pattenden Farm
Finchcocks
223
Trillinghurst Farmhouse
1 grid square represents 500 metres
A B C D E
1 2 3 4 5 6 7 8

Winchet Hill
F
G
H
196
J
K
Curtisden Green
Bethany School
Jarvis Lane
Great Horden Farm
Hill Top
Blantyre House
Worms Hill
Combourne Farm
Round Green
Bockingfold Farm
Blue Barn Farm
Ladham Road
Jarvis Lane
Ladham House
Green
214
Old Park Wood
Mile Lane
Jarvis Lane
Frog's Hole
CRANBROOK ROAD
Iden Green
Four Wents
Lime Tree Farm
A262
PH
Chalk Lane
Flishin
Glassenbury House
Glassenbury
B2085
224
1
2
3
4
5
6
7
8

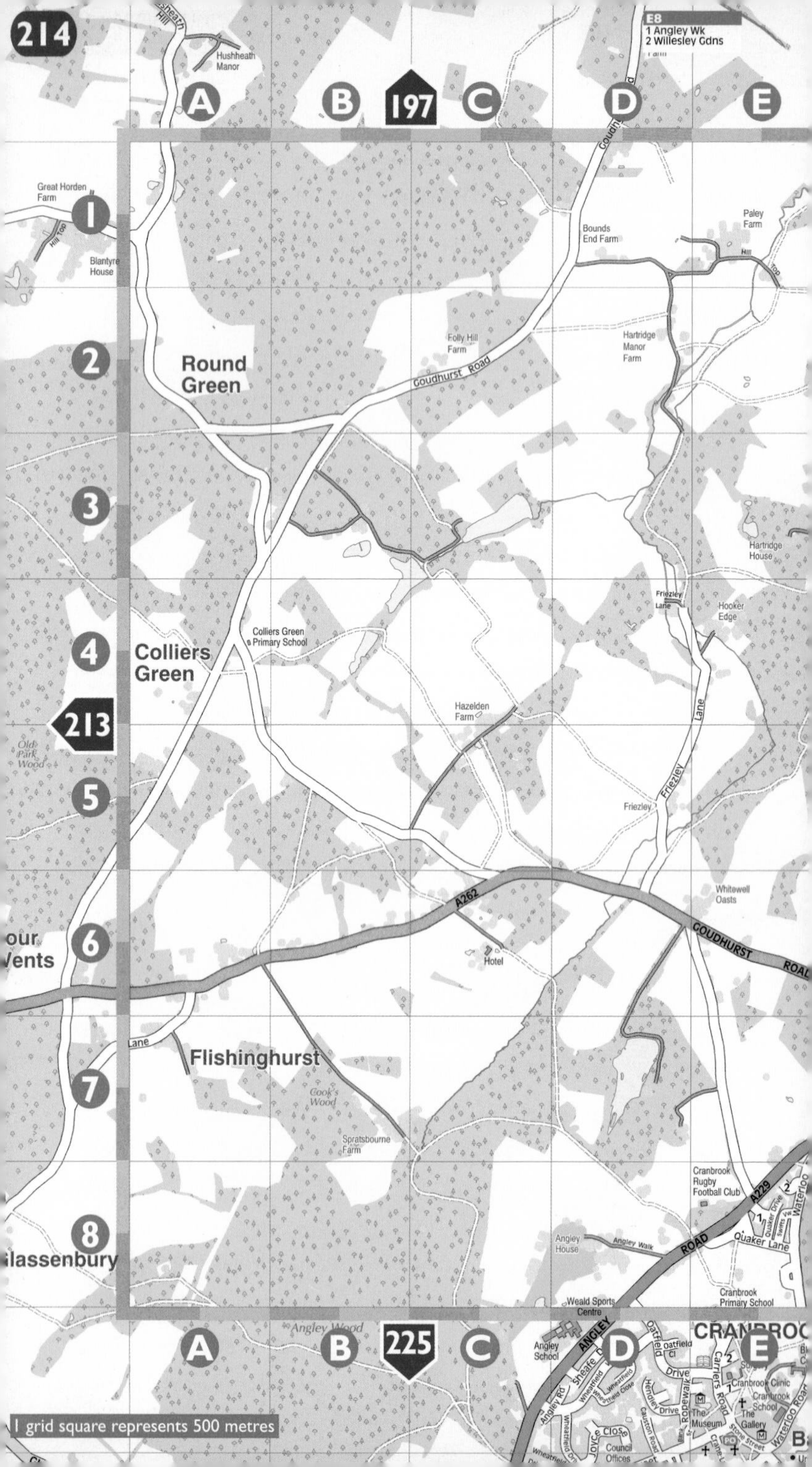
197
A
B
C
D
E
1
2
3
4
5
6
7
8
213
225
E8
1 Angley Wk
2 Willesley Gdns
Hushheath Manor
Great Horden Farm
Hill Top
Blantyre House
Round Green
Goudhurst Road
Bounds End Farm
Paley Farm
Folly Hill Farm
Hartridge Manor Farm
Hartridge House
Friezley Lane
Hooker Edge
Colliers Green
Colliers Green Primary School
Old Park Wood
Hazelden Farm
Friezley
Friezley Lane
Whitewell Oasts
A262
GOUDHURST ROAD
Hotel
Four Wents
Lane
Flishinghurst
Cook's Wood
Spratsbourne Farm
Glassenbury
Cranbrook Rugby Football Club
A229
Waterloo
Quaker Drive
Quaker Lane
Angley House
Angley Walk
ROAD
Cranbrook Primary School
Weald Sports Centre
Angley Wood
Angley School
ANGLEY
Angley Rd
Sheafe Dr
Oatfield
Oatfield Cl
Drive
Hendley Drive
Rope Walk
Carriers Road
Cranbrook Clinic
Cranbrook School
The Museum
The Gallery
Stone Street
Waterloo Road
Council Offices
Joyce Close
CRANBROOK
1 grid square represents 500 metres

H6
1 Hop Pocket Cl
Castle Bank
Little Wadd
Knox Bridge
198
Hill Top
ROAD
Rock Farm
Grandshore Lane
ROCKS HILL
Tolehurst Farm
Waller Hill
Grandshore Lane
Tanyard
Whitsunden
Brewers Wood
Park Farm
A229
Comenden Manor
Camden Hill
London Lane
Convalescent Lane
Cranbrook Common
ROCKS HILL
216
Spongs Lane
Sissinghurst Castle Garden
Common Road
Roundshill Park Wood
Wilsley Pound
Skinner Gardens
Cleavers
Hovendens
Sissinghurst
Cemetery
Mill Lane
Cramptons
Milk House Cottages
Sissinghurst Primary Sch.
A262
THE STREET
PO
SISSINGHURST
Buckhurst Farm
Chapel Lane
Great Swifts
Golford
226
Middleton Farm
Golford Road
Cemetery
s Cross
F
G
H
J
K
1
2
3
4
5
6
7
8

Chestnut Close
School
Pond Farm
A
B
199
C
D
E
Tanyard
Sand Lane
Catherine Wheel
1
Grandshore Lane
Whitsunden
Brissenden Farm
Sand Lane
2
Lowland Farm
Park
3
Digdog Lane
Hammer Stream
White House Farm
4
PH
Frogs Hole Farm
A262
215
Three Chimney
5
Sissinghurst Castle Garden (NT)
Roundshill Park Wood
6
A262
SISSINGHURST ROAD
Hammer Wood
7
Branden
Roger's Wood
Cranbrook Road
8
High Tilt
Middle Farm
A
B
227
C
D
E
1 grid square represents 500 metres
Causton Wood

J4
1 The Meadows
K4
1 Cloth Hall Gdns
F
G
H
200
J
K
Ibornden Farm
Chart Hills Golf Club
Buckhurst
Vane Court
Stand
1
Weeks Lane
Pook Lane
Smarden Road
A274
Newcastle Farm
2
HEADCORN ROAD
Hareplain
Ibornden Park
Cot Lane
Curteis' Corn
3
NORTH STREET
Ongley
Elmstone
Mansion House Close
4
Biddenden
Church View
Spinners
Cheeselands
Chulkhurst
Glebelands
Townland Cl
The Weavers
218
SISSINGHURST ROAD
HIGH ST
A262
PO
John Mayne C of E Primary School
Biddenden Club House
5
High Halden Rd
Worsenden Farm
Dashmonden
6
TENTERDEN ROAD
Fosten Lane
Goose Green
Randolph's
Castweazel Oast
Woolpack Corner
A262
7
Birchley House
Duesden
8
Bargate
Fosten
Clapper
F
G
H
228
J
K
Little Whatmans
Birchwood Farm
Gribble Bridge
Biddenden

1 grid square represents 500 metres

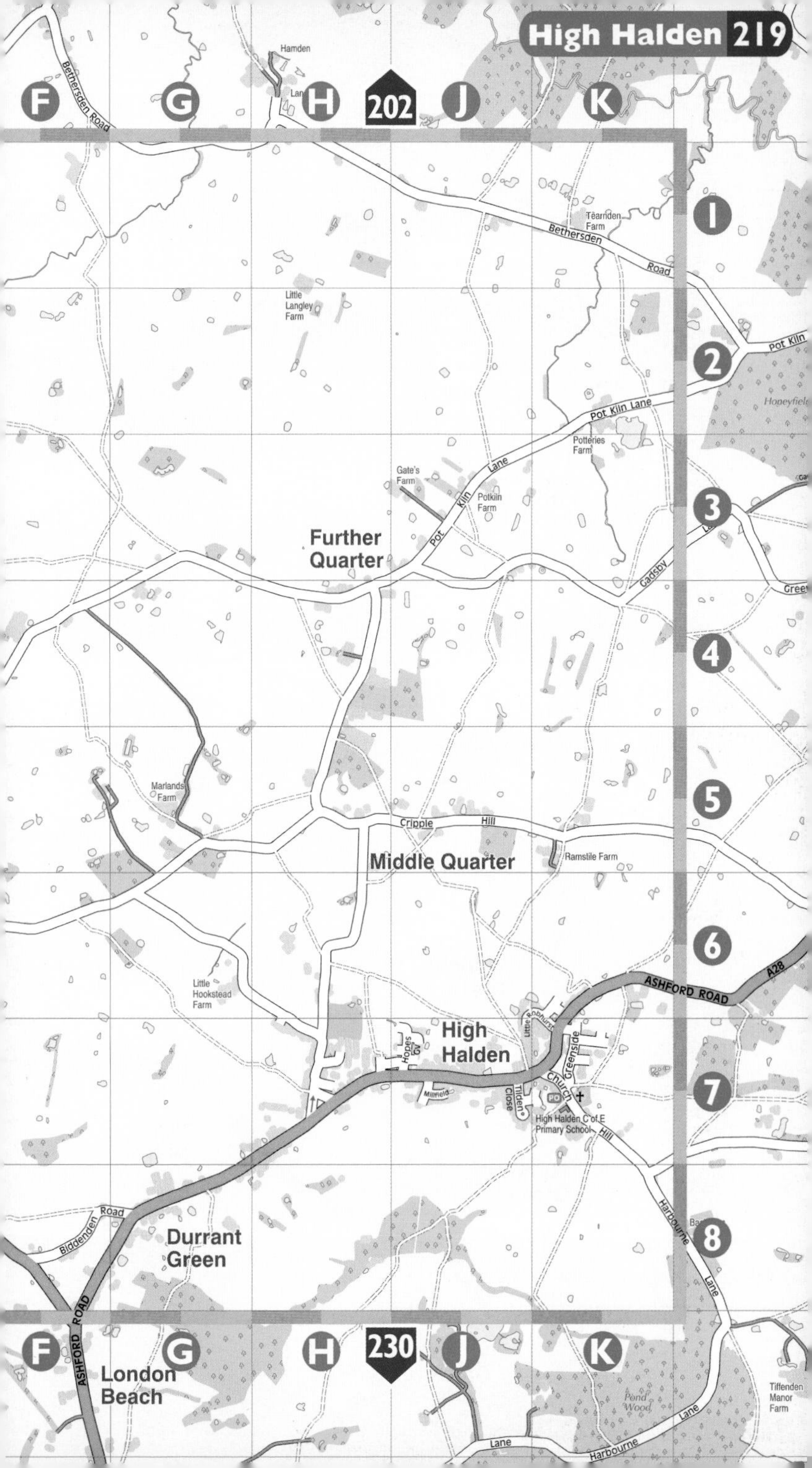
F
G
H
202
J
K
Hamden
Bethersden Road
Tearnden Farm
Bethersden
Road
Little Langley Farm
Pot Kiln
Honeyfield
Pot Kiln Lane
Potteries Farm
Gate's Farm
Lane
Kiln
Pot
Potkiln Farm
Further Quarter
Gadsby
Marlands Farm
Cripple
Hill
Middle Quarter
Ramstile Farm
ASHFORD ROAD
A28
Little Hookstead Farm
High Halden
Little Robhurst
Greenside
Hopes Gv
Millfield
Tilden Close
Church
PO
High Halden C of E Primary School
Hill
Harbourne
Lane
Road
Biddenden
Durrant Green
ASHFORD ROAD
230
London Beach
Pond Wood
Tiffenden Manor Farm
Lane
Harbourne
Lane
1
2
3
4
5
6
7
8

209
Bayham Abbey
Bayham Lake
Jews Wood
B2169
Bartley Mill Road
Little Bayham
Wickhurst Farm
Kent County
East Sussex County
Free Heath Road
Buss's Green
Stiver's Wood
Free Heath
Great Shoesmiths Farm
Sussex Border Path
Buckland Hill Farm
Monks Park
Newbury Lane
Windmill Lane
White Gates Farm
Wood's Green
Monks Lane
Osmers Hill
Rockrobin
Pell Green
Great Butts
Turner's Green
Old Station Road
Turners Green Road
Balaclava Lane
Hollydene Road
Deepdene
Pell Close
Weald View
COUSLEY WOOD ROAD
Southfields
Western Road
Gloucester Rd
South View Road
B2100
B2099
ROAD
Queens Cottages
Jonas Drive
Blackmount Lane
Sparrow's Green
Wadhurst C of E Primary School
Green Square
Bankside
Mayfield Park
HIGH STREET
The Marlpit
Blacksmith's Lane
Little Pell Farm
Baldock Road
School
Close
Walk
Lane
1 grid square represents 500 metres

Mount Pleasant
Hoathly
F
G
H
210
J
K
Mount Pleasant Lane
Parsonage Lane
Church Road
Lamberhurst Golf Club
Court Lodge
Lamberhurst C of E School
Lamberhurst
1
Furnace Mill
Brewer Street
Lamberhurst Surgery
PO
A21(T)
Morland Drive
HIGH STREET
Pearse Place
B2100
TOWN HILL
SPRAY HILL
2
FURNACE
LANE
ook Green
Furnace Farm
Sand Road
B2169
The Priory
Down Avenue
Furnace Avenue
Spray Hill
Nellis Road
THE SLADE
3
The Down
Wiseacre
A21(T)
Owls Castle Farm
Hoghole Lane
4
Kent County
East Sussex County
Wiskett's Wood
222
Sweetings Lane
B2100
5
Markwicks
Ladymeads Farm
COUSLEY WOOD ROAD
6
Hook Farm
Lower Cousley Wood
Sussex Border Path
7
Bewl Water
Sussex Border Path
Little Butts Farm
Bryant's Farm
Hook Hill
Hook Hill
Beaumans
8
Sussex Border Path
Ward's Lane
F
G
H
J
K
Claphatch Lane

222
211
221
232
A
B
C
D
E
1
2
3
4
5
6
7
8
Lamberhurst
Riseden
Kildow
Stonecrouch
River Teise
School Hill
Church Road
Lamberhurst Golf Club
Court Lodge
Parsonage Lane
Lamberhurst C of E School
Morland Drive
A21(T)
Spray Hill
The Priory
Finchcocks
Little Scotney Farm
Pierce Barn
Rante
Twysden
Scotney Castle Garden (NT)
River Bewl
Kilndown Wood
West Road
Church Road
Rogers
Rough
Chicks Lane
Wiskett's
Bewl Bridge Farm
Bewlbridge Lane
Shearn Wood
Cats Wood
Chingley Wood
Chingley Manor
Sussex Border Path
Rosemary Farmhouse
Rosemary Lane
Hazelhurst Farm
1 grid square represents 500 metres

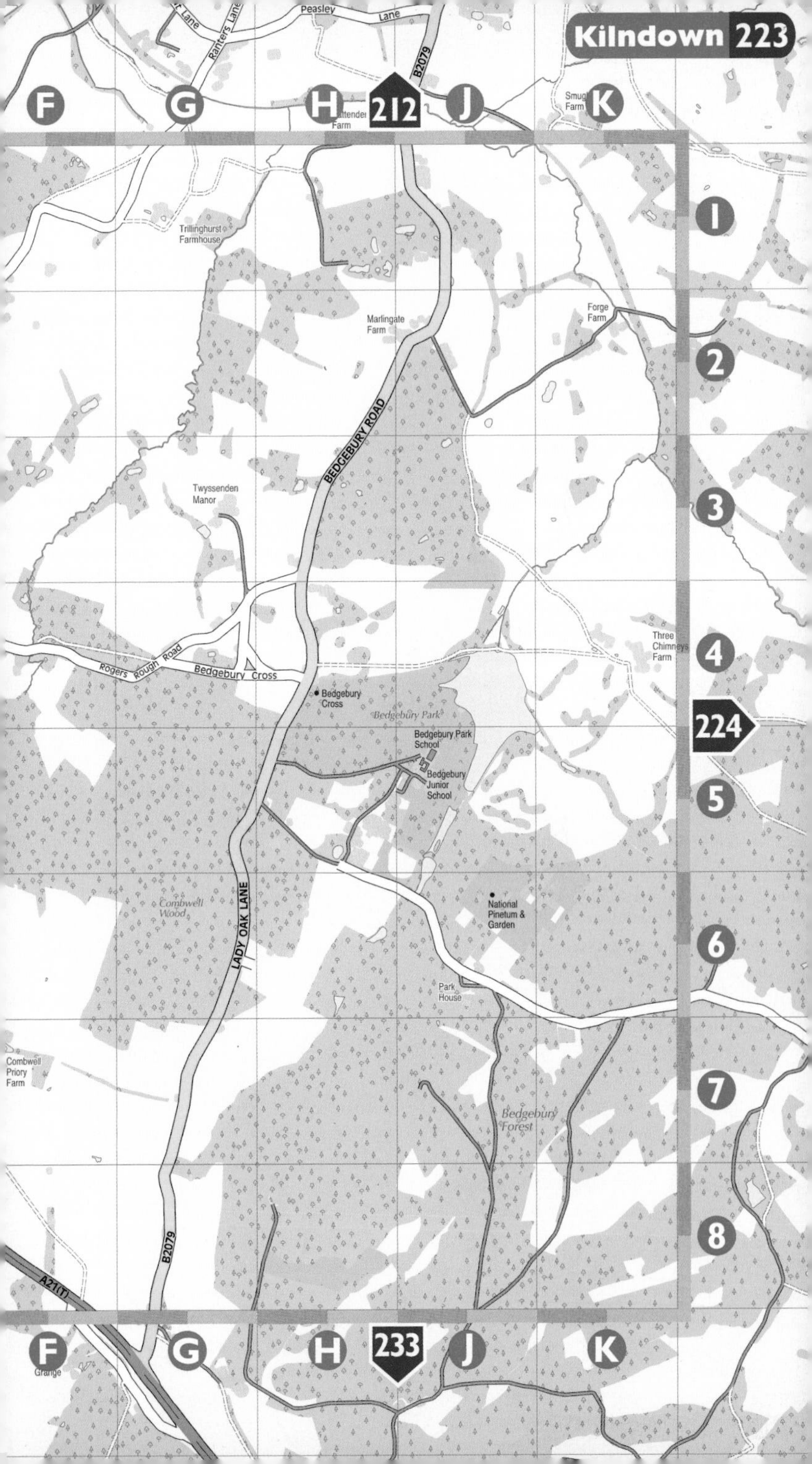
Peasley Lane
Ranters Lane
B2079
F
G
H
J
K
212
Trillinghurst Farmhouse
Marlingate Farm
Forge Farm
Twyssenden Manor
BEDGEBURY ROAD
Rogers Rough Road
Bedgebury Cross
Bedgebury Park
Bedgebury Park School
Bedgebury Junior School
Three Chimneys Farm
224
National Pinetum & Garden
Combwell Wood
LADY OAK LANE
Park House
Combwell Priory Farm
Bedgebury Forest
A21(T)
Grange
233
1
2
3
4
5
6
7
8

Smugley Farm
A
B
213
C
D
E
B2085
GLASSENBURY
1
Forge Farm
2
Blackbush Wood
3
Furnace Farm
Three Chimneys Farm
4
223
5
6
Whitelimes
Louisa Lodge
Park Lane
7
8
Frith Farm
Trenley Farm
Tanyard Farm
234

1 grid square represents 500 metres

G3
1 Hartley Ct Gdns
K1
1 Jockey La
2 Rectory Flds
K2
1 Huntington Cl
2 Norman Ri
3 Pennyfields
4 The Tanyard
F
G
H
214
J
K
1
2
3
4
5
6
7
8
226
235
CRANBROOK
Baker
Angley Wood
Weald Sports Centre
Angley School
Cranbrook Primary School
The Crane Surgery
Cranbrook Clinic
Cranbrook School
The Museum
The Gallery
Council Offices
Union Mill
Blubery House Cranbrook School
Goddard's Green
ANGLEY ROAD
Angley Walk
Quaker Lane
Oatfield Drive
Oatfield Cl
Sheafe Dr
Wheatfield Way
Wheatfield Close
Wheatfield Drive
Angley Rd
Hendley Drive
Ropewalk
Carriers Road
Causton Road
Joyce Close
Stone Street
Waterloo Road
Crane Lane
High Street
New Road
Goddards Greenway
Orchard Way
The Hill
Bakers Cross
Way
Brickenden Road
Brookside
Doctor
Rammell Mews
Bramley Drive
Frythe Cl
Frythe Wk
Frythe
Dorothy Avenue
Turner Avenue
Kirby Cl
Broadcloth
Pear Tree Cl
Winch Cl
Freight Lane
Mount Ephraim
TN17
Huggin's Hall
Turnden Road
Hartley House
The Heathers
Campion Crescent
HARTLEY ROAD
A229
Hancock's Farm
Tilsden
Tilsden Lane
Lane
artley
Westfield Ter
The Meads
SWATTENDEN LANE
B2086
Pricklegate
CRANBROOK
Robin's Wood
Tubslake
Water Lane
Baretilt Farm
HAWKHURST ROAD
Osborne's
Attwaters Lane
Netter's Hall Farm
Nineveh Lane
Rose's Farm
Potter's Farm
Potter's Lane
Four Wents
The Forest
Gill's Green
Tilden Farm

226
Wilsley Green
Great Swifts
Quaker Lane
Waterloo
215
A
B
C
D
E
Lane
Golford
Cranbrook Primary School
CRANBROOK
The Crane Surgery
Blubery House Cranbrook School
Crowden House Cranbrook School
Stream Farm
Carriers Road
Cranbrook
Cranbrook School
The Gallery
Museum
Stone Street
Waterloo Road
Golford Road
Cemetery
Baker's Cross
Union Mill
Crane Lane
The Hill
Dulwich College Preparatory School
Bakers Cross
Doctor
Brickenden Road
Brookside
Bramley Drive
Dorothy Avenue
Frythe
Turner Avenue
Coursehorn
Old Cloth Hall
Broadcloth
Pear Tree
Winch Cl
Hancock's Farm
1
2
3
4
5
6
7
8
Tilsden
Tilsden Lane
Little Coursehorne
Chitter Farm
225
B2086
Doves Farm
Pricklegate
Crabtree Farm
Chequertree Farm
CRANBROOK ROAD
School Farm
Benenden School
The Moat
Mount's Farm
Crit Hall
B2086
MOUNTS HILL
B2086
MOUNTS HILL
Netter's Hall Farm
Nineveh Lane
Little Nineveh
Babbes Farm
Babb's Lane
The Forest
Scullsgate House
236
Stream Farm
Tilden Farm
Great Nineveh
Coldharbour
Sarnden
1 grid square represents 500 metres

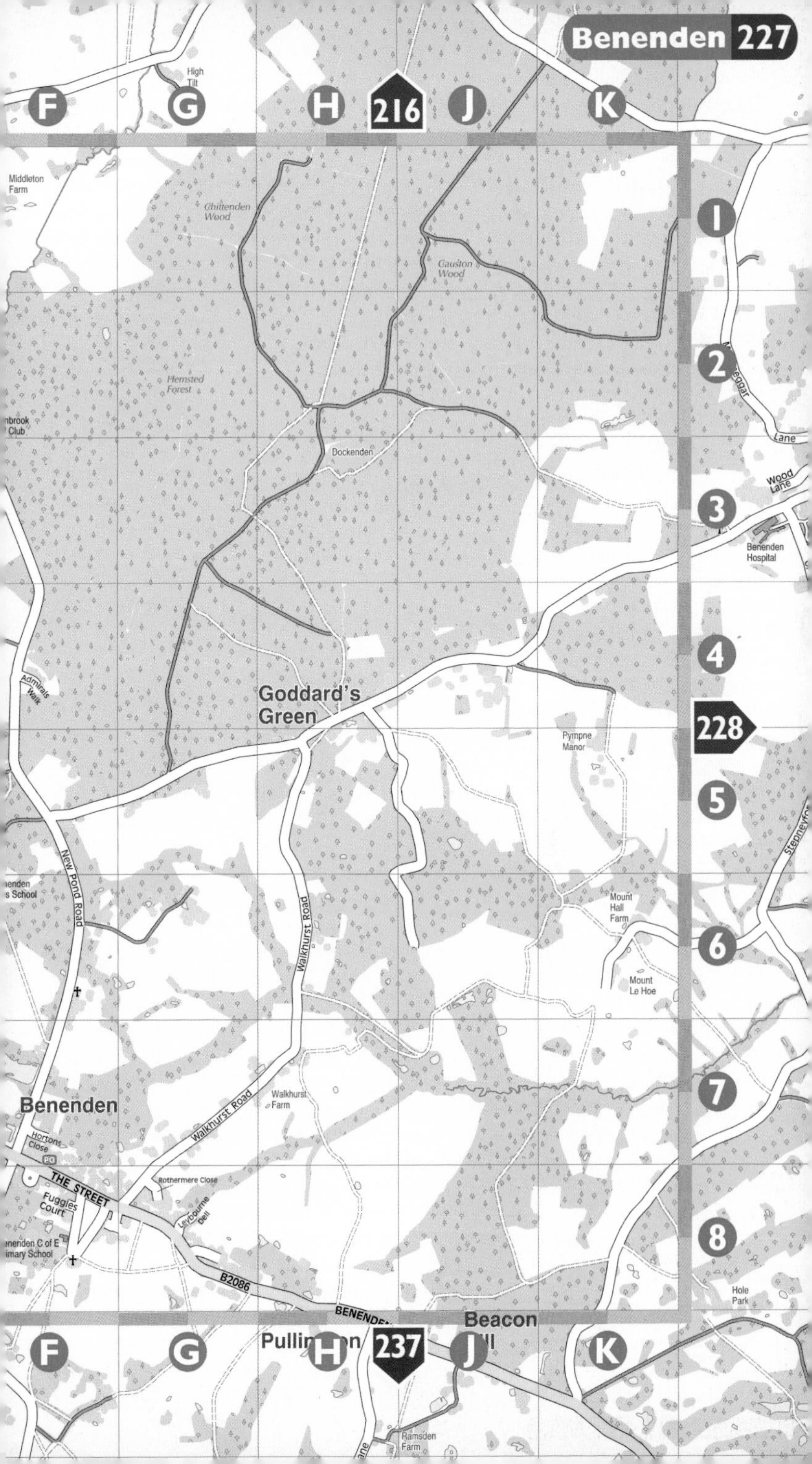
216
F
G
H
J
K
High Tilt
Middleton Farm
Chittenden Wood
Causton Wood
Hemsted Forest
nbrook Club
Dockenden
Goddard's Green
Pympne Manor
Benenden Hospital
Wood Lane
Lane
228
Admirals Walk
New Pond Road
Walkhurst Road
Mount Hall Farm
Mount Le Hoe
Walkhurst Farm
Benenden
Hortons Close
PO
THE STREET
Fuggles Court
Rothermere Close
Leybourne Dell
B2086
BENENDEN
Beacon
Pullin
237
Hole Park
Ramsden Farm
1
2
3
4
5
6
7
8

1 grid square represents 500 metres

K7
1 Caxton Cl
2 Old Tannery Cl
3 Smallhythe Rd
218
A262
BIDDENDEN ROAD
Biddenden Rd
ASHFORD ROAD
Bugglesden
Haffenden Farm
Nortons Lane
Bugglesden Road
Gribble Bridge Lane
London Beach Golf Club
Brook Farm
Reader's Bridge Road
Penhill
Shoreham Lane
Orchard Road
Grange Road
Grange Crs
Millpond Lane
Parkgate
Twisden Farm
Chennell Park Road
Meadows
230
Goodshill Farm
Pott's Farm
Coombe Farm
Cranbrook Road
Little Halden Place
Watermill House
Goods Hill
TENTERDEN
Eastwell
New Barn Farm
LC
Rogersmead
Coombe La
Station Road
Town Hall
Church Rd
PH
Bridewell Lane
Highbury Lane
Cemetery
Hurst Cl
Lawn Close
W Cross Gdns
Westwell Court
WEST CROSS
Malt House La
Woodbury Lane
Longfield
A28
Plummer Lane
Heronden Hall
B2082
Cold Harbour
West View Hospital
ROLVENDEN HILL
239
Strood
Puddingcake Lane
Puddingcake
Morghew

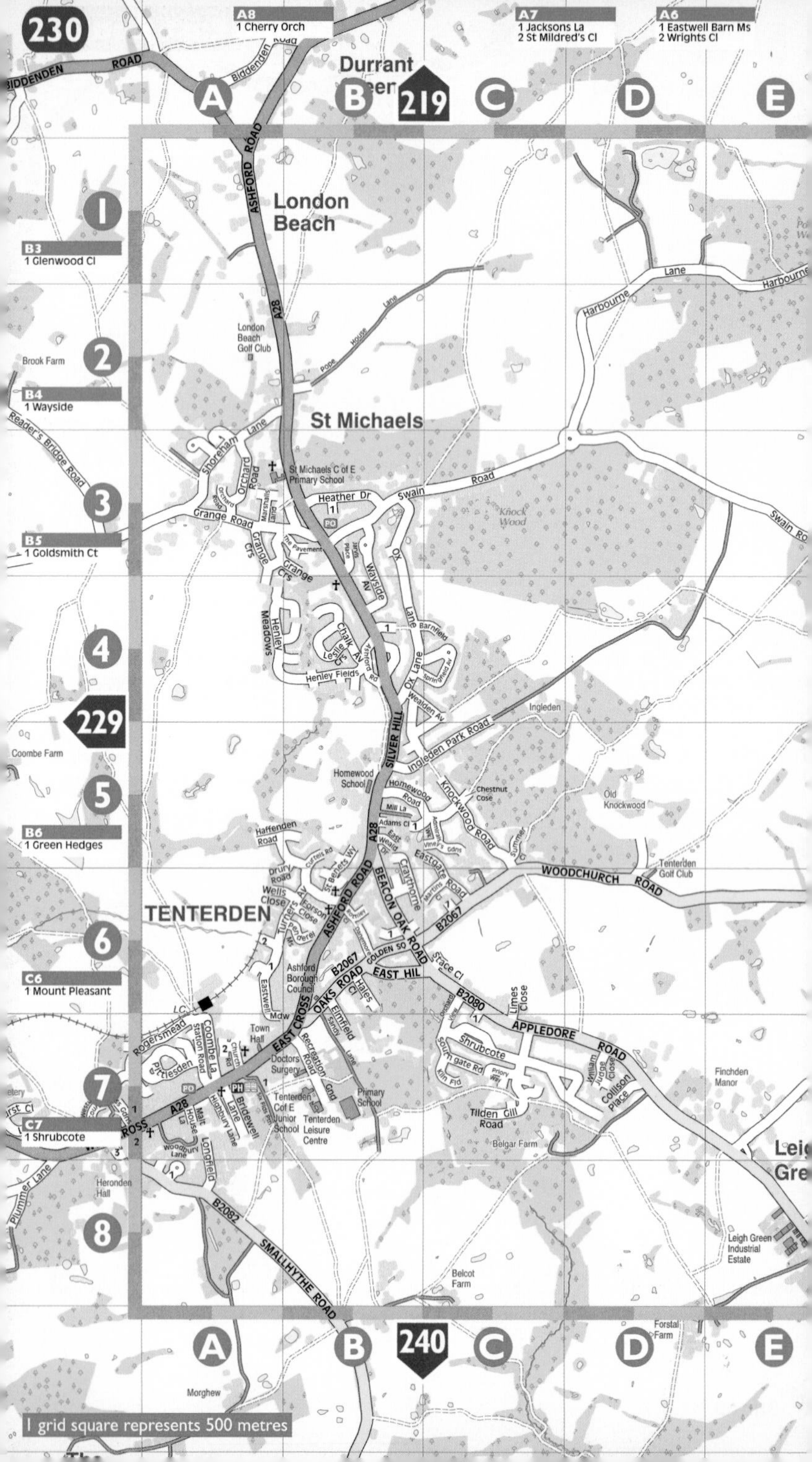
A8
1 Cherry Orch
A7
1 Jacksons La
2 St Mildred's Cl
A6
1 Eastwell Barn Ms
2 Wrights Cl
B3
1 Glenwood Cl
B4
1 Wayside
B5
1 Goldsmith Ct
B6
1 Green Hedges
C6
1 Mount Pleasant
C7
1 Shrubcote
219
229
240
Durrant Green
London Beach
London Beach Golf Club
St Michaels
St Michaels C of E Primary School
Knock Wood
Ingleden
Old Knockwood
TENTERDEN
Homewood School
Ashford Borough Council
Town Hall
Doctors Surgery
Primary School
Tenterden C of E Junior School
Tenterden Leisure Centre
Tenterden Golf Club
Finchden Manor
Belgar Farm
Belcot Farm
Forstal Farm
Leigh Green Industrial Estate
Brook Farm
Coombe Farm
Heronden Hall
Morghew
BIDDENDEN ROAD
ASHFORD ROAD
A28
Pope House Lane
Harbourne Lane
Swain Road
Shoreham Lane
Orchard Road
Grange Road
Grange Crs
Heather Dr
Wayside Av
Ox Lane
Henley Meadows
Henley Fields
Chalk Av
Leslie Crs
Barnfield
Springfield Av
Wealden Av
SILVER HILL
Ingleden Park Road
Homewood Road
Mill La
Adams Cl
Knockwood Road
Chestnut Close
Haffenden Road
Drury Road
Wells Close
Forson Close
Turners Av
St Benets Wy
BEACON OAK ROAD
Craythorne
Eastgate Road
WOODCHURCH ROAD
B2067
GOLDEN SQ
EAST HILL
Stace Cl
B2080
Limes Close
APPLEDORE ROAD
OAKS ROAD
Elmfield Cl
Hales Cl
Eastwell Mdw
EAST CROSS
Recreation Road
Shrubcote
Southgate Rd
Priory Way
Klin Fld
William Judge Close
Collison Place
Tilden Gill Road
Rogersmead
Pittlesden
Coombe La
Station Road
Church Rd
Bridewell Lane
Highbury Lane
Malt House La
Longfield
Woodbury Lane
B2082
SMALLHYTHE ROAD
Reader's Bridge Road
Plummer Lane
1 grid square represents 500 metres

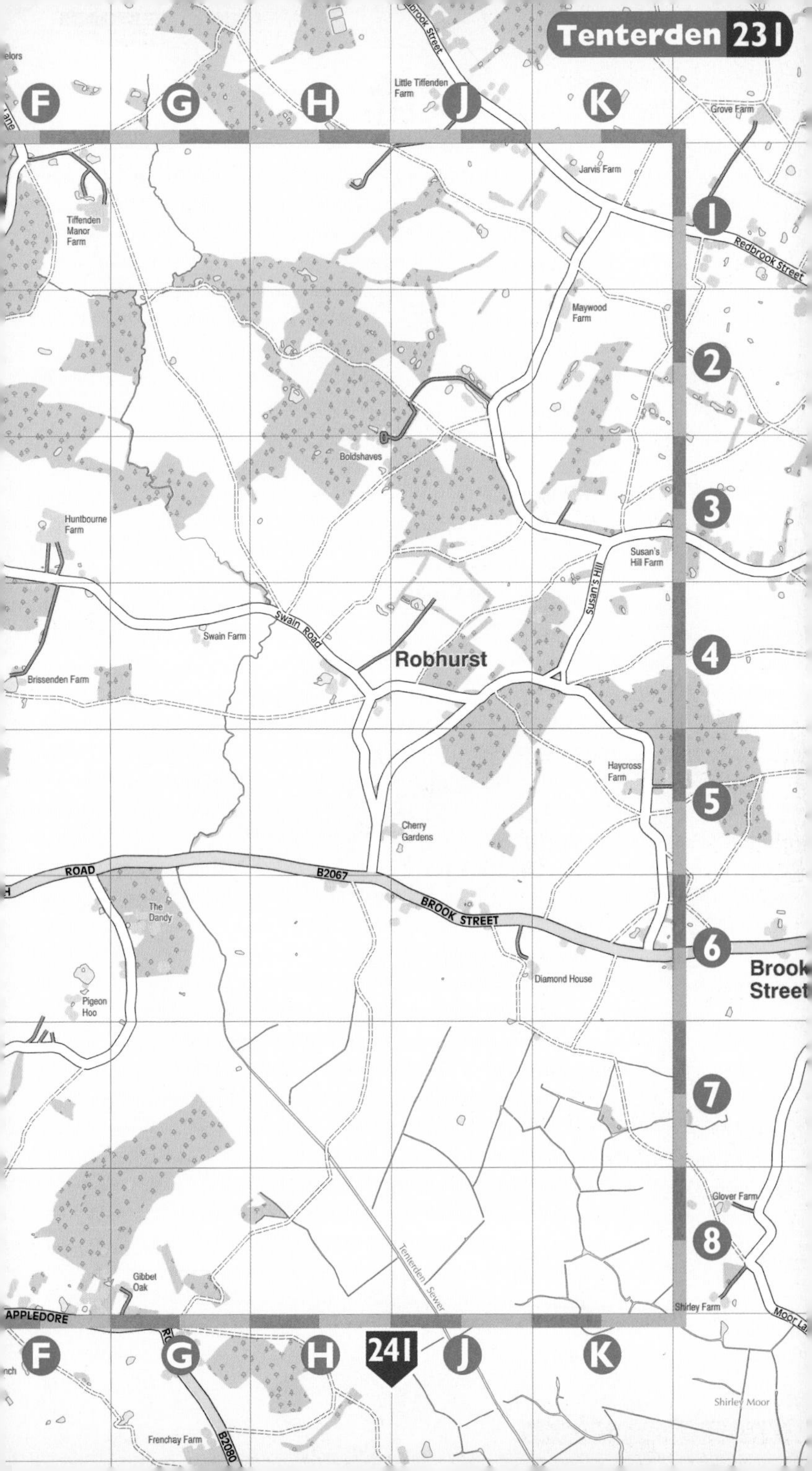
F
G
H
J
K
1
2
3
4
5
6
7
8
Little Tiffenden Farm
Grove Farm
Jarvis Farm
Redbrook Street
Tiffenden Manor Farm
Maywood Farm
Boldshaves
Huntbourne Farm
Susan's Hill Farm
Susan's Hill
Swain Road
Swain Farm
Robhurst
Brissenden Farm
Haycross Farm
Cherry Gardens
ROAD
B2067
BROOK STREET
The Dandy
Diamond House
Brook Street
Pigeon Hoo
Glover Farm
Tenterden Sewer
Gibbet Oak
Shirley Farm
Moor La
APPLEDORE
241
Shirley Moor
Frenchay Farm
B2080

C5
1 Lavender Gdns
2 Reeves Ter
222
A
B
C
D
E
1
2
3
4
5
6
7
8
East Sussex County
Kent County
Sussex Border Path
Rosemary Farmhouse
Rosemary Lane
Hazelhurst Farm
Huntley Mill Road
Overy's Farm
Ketley Farm
Rowley
Lower Hazelhurst
Pinton Hill
Boarders Lane
PH
Tinkers Lane
Downash House
Three Leg Cross
Three Leg Cross Road
Berne Hill
B2087
Lodge Lane
Dale Hill
Ticehurst
Broomden
Vineyard Lane
Burnt Lodge Lane
Ridgeway Farm
Ticehurst House
Cross Lane Gardens
Pickforde Lane
Dale Hill Hotel & Golf Club
B2099
Brick Kiln Farm
Hillbury Gardens
The Surgery
Farthing Hill
The Warren
Steellands Rise
PO
HIGH STREET
Springfields
Acres Rise
LOWER PLATTS
Horsegrove Avenue
St Mary's Lane
St Mary's Close
Doctors Surgery
Ticehurst C of E Primary School
Birchenwood Farm
Oakover
Wardsbrook Road
Gibbs Reed Farm
Wedd's Farm
Wardsbrook Farm
Chestnutfield Wood
Myskyns
Cottenden
1 grid square represents 500 metres

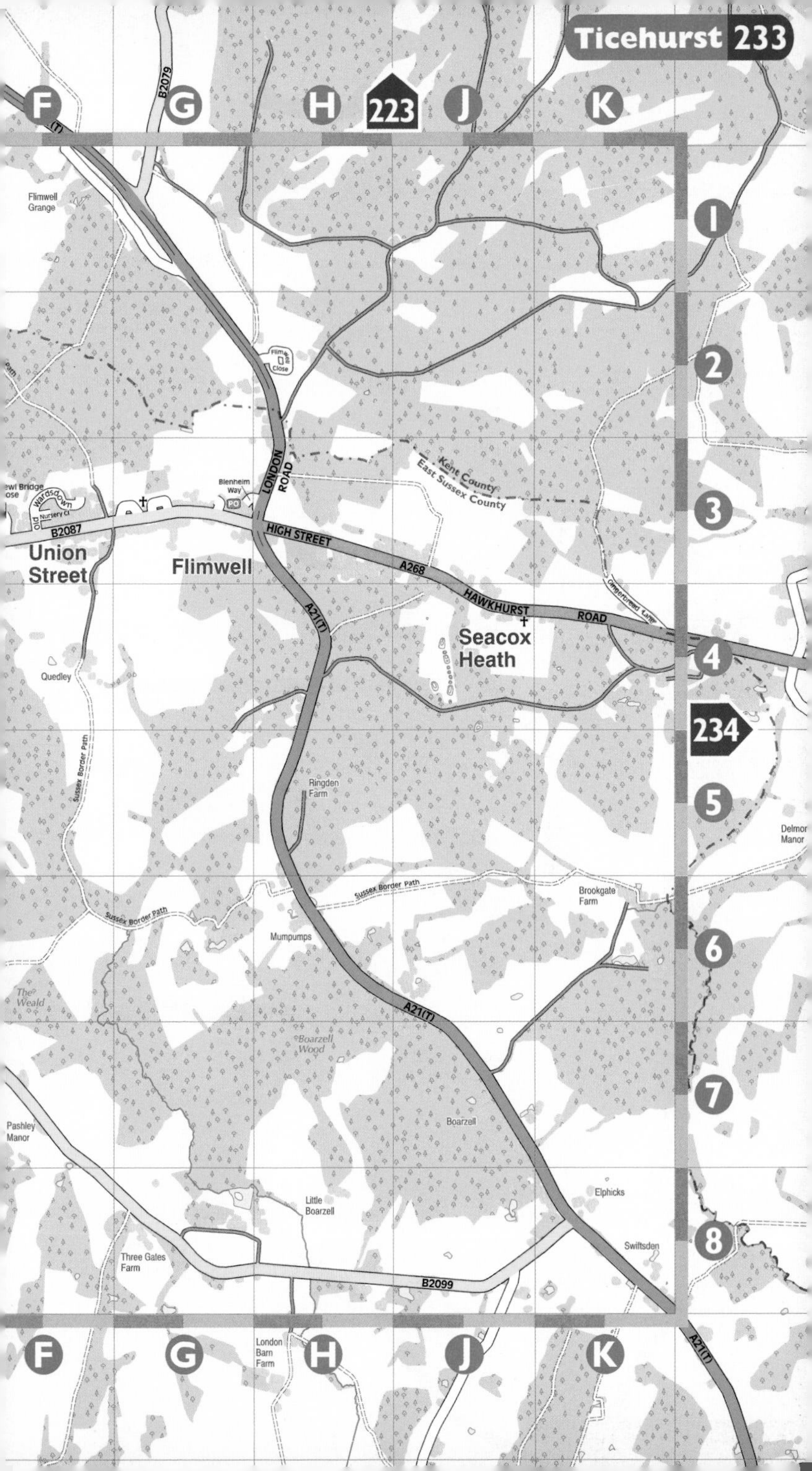
F
G
H
223
J
K
B2079
Flimwell Grange
Flimwell Close
Kent County
East Sussex County
LONDON ROAD
Blenheim Way
PO
Wardsdown
Old Nursery Cl
B2087
HIGH STREET
A268
HAWKHURST
ROAD
Union Street
Flimwell
A21(T)
Seacox Heath
Gingerbread Lane
234
Quedley
Sussex Border Path
Ringden Farm
Delmor Manor
Brookgate Farm
Mumpumps
The Weald
Boarzell Wood
Boarzell
Pashley Manor
Elphicks
Little Boarzell
Swiftsden
Three Gates Farm
B2099
London Barn Farm
1
2
3
4
5
6
7
8

A
B
224
C
D
E
Frith Farm
Trenley Farm
Tanyard Farm
1
Soper's Lane
Siseley Farm
2
3
Little Pix Hall Farm
Gingerbread Lane
ROAD
High Street
Slip Mill Road
Slip Mill Rd
4
Hospital
A268
HIGH
Elm Hill House
233
Delmonden Road
North Hill Road
5
Delmonden Manor
Sussex Border Path
Brookgate Farm
Delmonden House
6
Horns Road
Delmonden Road
A229
HORNS
ROAD
Avards Close
Cowden Close
Red Oak
Horns Corner
Bokes Farm
7
Cowden Lane
Cowden
Elphicks
8
Kent County
East Sussex County
A229
A21(T)
A
B
C
D
E
Merriments Lane
Merriments Farm
Stone House Farm
1 grid square represents 500 metres

F4
1 Northgrove Rd
2 Post Office Rd
G4
1 Hammonds
2 Murton-neale Cl
Four Wents
225
236
242
Gill's Green
Merry Mead Farm
Tilden Farm
Paul's Farm
Water Lane
Ellenden Farm
Beal's Green
Park Farm
Ockley Lane
Heartenoak Road
Ockley
CRANBROOK ROAD
A229
Springfield Industrial Estate
Gun Green
White's Lane
Highgate
Fowler's Park
Dickens Way
Hotel
Pipsden
RYE ROAD
A268
Doctors Surgery
Mercers
Highfield Cl
Oaklands Rd
Copthall Avenue
Fieldways
HIGHGATE HILL
Oakfield
Theobalds
Western Road
Queen's Road
Winchester Rd
Woodbury
Barretts Road
Ockley Road
All Saints Road
Smugglers Mews
Tongswood Dr
Four Throws
Foxhole Lane
Clayhill
Risden
Hall House
Hawkhurst C of E Primary School
MOOR HILL
The Moor
Stream Lane
Risden Lane
TN18
Collingwood House
Thorpes
Little Conghurst
Conghurst Lane
B2244
HASTINGS ROAD
East Heath
Sussex Border Path
Cemetery
The Forest
Conghurst Farm

Nineveh Lane
Little Nineveh
Babbes Farm
Babb's Lane
226
A
B
C
D
E
The Forest
Scullsgate House
Stream Farm
Great Nineveh
Coldharbour Road
Sarnden
Coldharbour Chapel Road
Woodsden
Diprose
Park Farm
Hinksden Road
Mill Street
The Paper Mill
Eaglesden
235
Pipsden
Foxhole Lane
Foxhole
Sponden Lane
A268
Clayhill
Rye Road
Risden
Beeches Farm
Sponden House
Field Green
Lane
TN18
Alderden Manor
Megrims Hill
Downgate
Queen Street
Sandhurst CP School
Back Road
Stream Pit La
Old Orchard
Oaks Forstal
Burnt House Close
243
Sandhurst
1
2
3
4
5
6
7
8
1 grid square represents 500 metres

F
G
H
227
J
K
STREET
Fuggles Court
Leybourne Dell
Benenden C of E Primary School
B2086
Hole Park
BENENDEN ROAD
Pullington
Beacon Hill
I
Ramsden Farm
Ramsden Lane
B2086
2
BENENDEN RO
Moor Wood
Sandhurst Road
Woodcock Lane
Standen Wood
Dingleden
3
Standen Street
4
Old Standen
Dingleden Lane
238
Standen Street
Springhill Farm
Cattsford
Sandhurst Road
Devenden
5
Hopehouse Lane
Standen Street
Kensham Farm
Crouch Lane
Hope House
6
A28
Hopehouse Lane
7
ROAD
Hexden Farm
8
HASTINGS
Lane
Hoad's Farm
F
G
H
244
J
K
Stone pit Lane
Lomas
A268

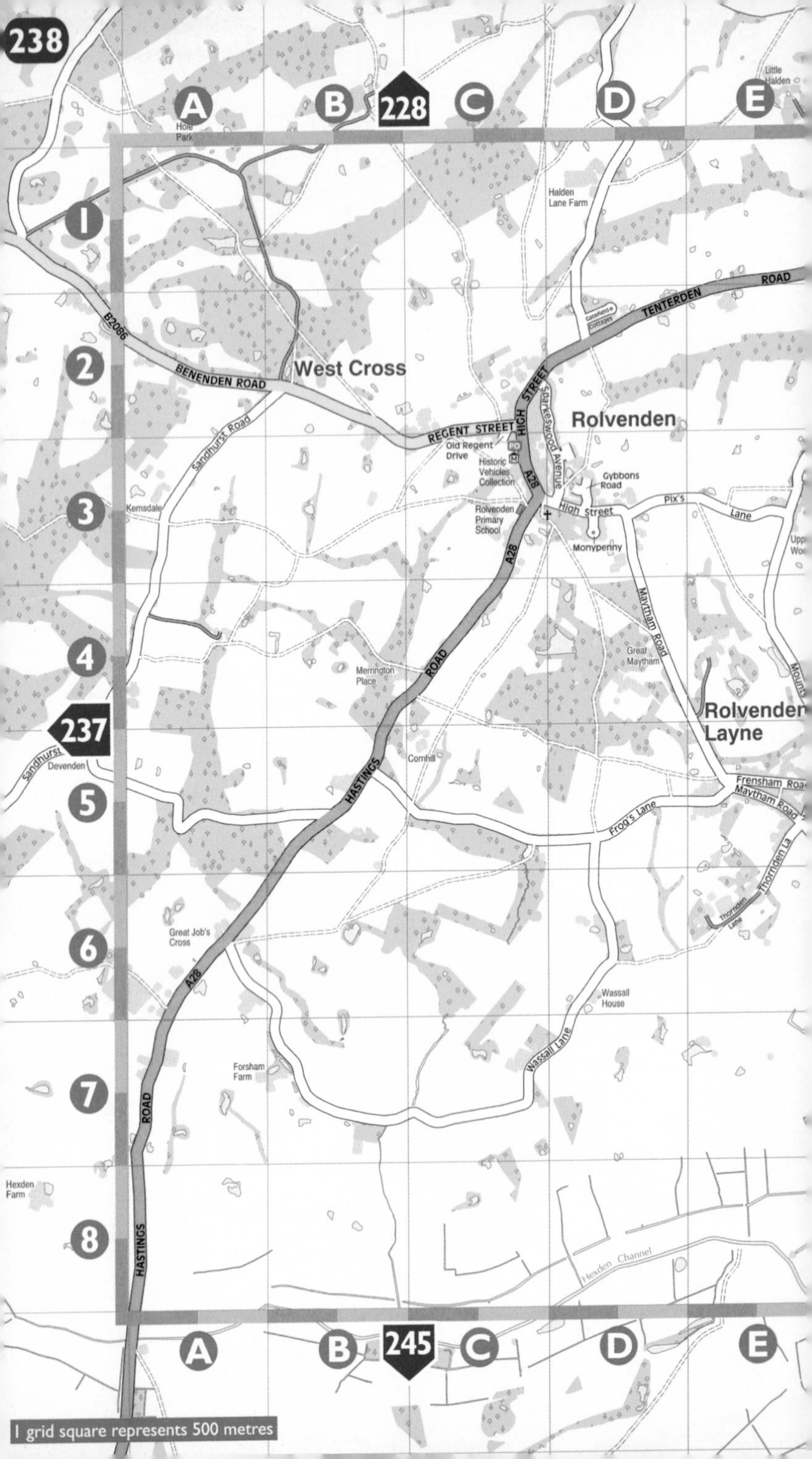
A
B
228
C
D
E
Hole Park
Little Halden
Halden Lane Farm
1
2
3
4
5
6
7
8
B2086
BENENDEN ROAD
West Cross
TENTERDEN ROAD
Gatefield Cottages
HIGH STREET
Sparkeswood Avenue
Rolvenden
REGENT STREET
Old Regent Drive
Historic Vehicles Collection
A28
Gybbons Road
Sandhurst Road
Kemsdale
Rolvenden Primary School
High Street
Pix's Lane
Monypenny
Maytham Road
Great Maytham
Merrington Place
HASTINGS ROAD
Rolvenden Layne
237
Sandhurst
Devenden
Cornhill
Frensham Road
Maytham Road
Frog's Lane
Thornden Lane
Great Job's Cross
Wassall House
Wassall Lane
Forsham Farm
Hexden Farm
Hexden Channel
245
1 grid square represents 500 metres

F
G
H
J
K
229
240
246
2
3
4
5
6
7
8
LC
Cold Harb
West View Hospital
ROLVENDEN HILL
Strood
Puddingcake Lane
Puddingcake
Winton Farm
The Quarter
Lower Woolwich
Kent & East Sussex Railway
Morghew Farm
Friezingham Farm
Hillgate Farm
Britcher Farm
Lambsland Farm
Maytham Road
Newmill Channel
Maytham Farm
Plastre Court
Potman's Heath
East Sussex Railway

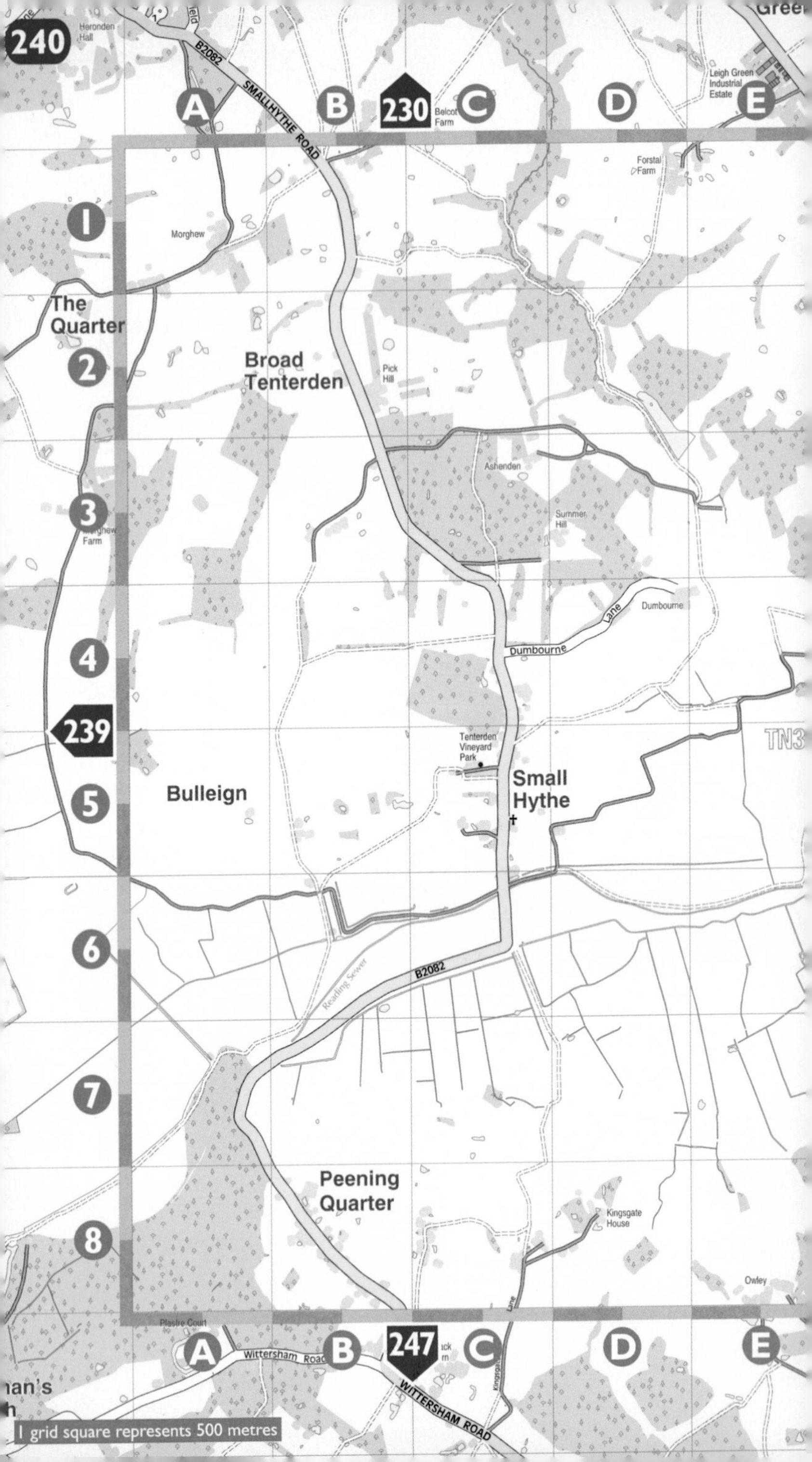

Heronden Hall
B2082
SMALLHYTHE ROAD
A
B
230
Belcot Farm
C
D
E
Leigh Green Industrial Estate
Forstal Farm
1
Morghew
The Quarter
2
Broad Tenterden
Pick Hill
Ashenden
Summer Hill
3
Morghew Farm
Dumbourne
Dumbourne Lane
4
239
Tenterden Vineyard Park
Small Hythe
5
Bulleign
6
B2082
Reading Sewer
7
Peening Quarter
Kingsgate House
8
Owley
Line
Plastre Court
A
Wittersham Road
B
247
C
D
E
WITTERSHAM ROAD

1 grid square represents 500 metres

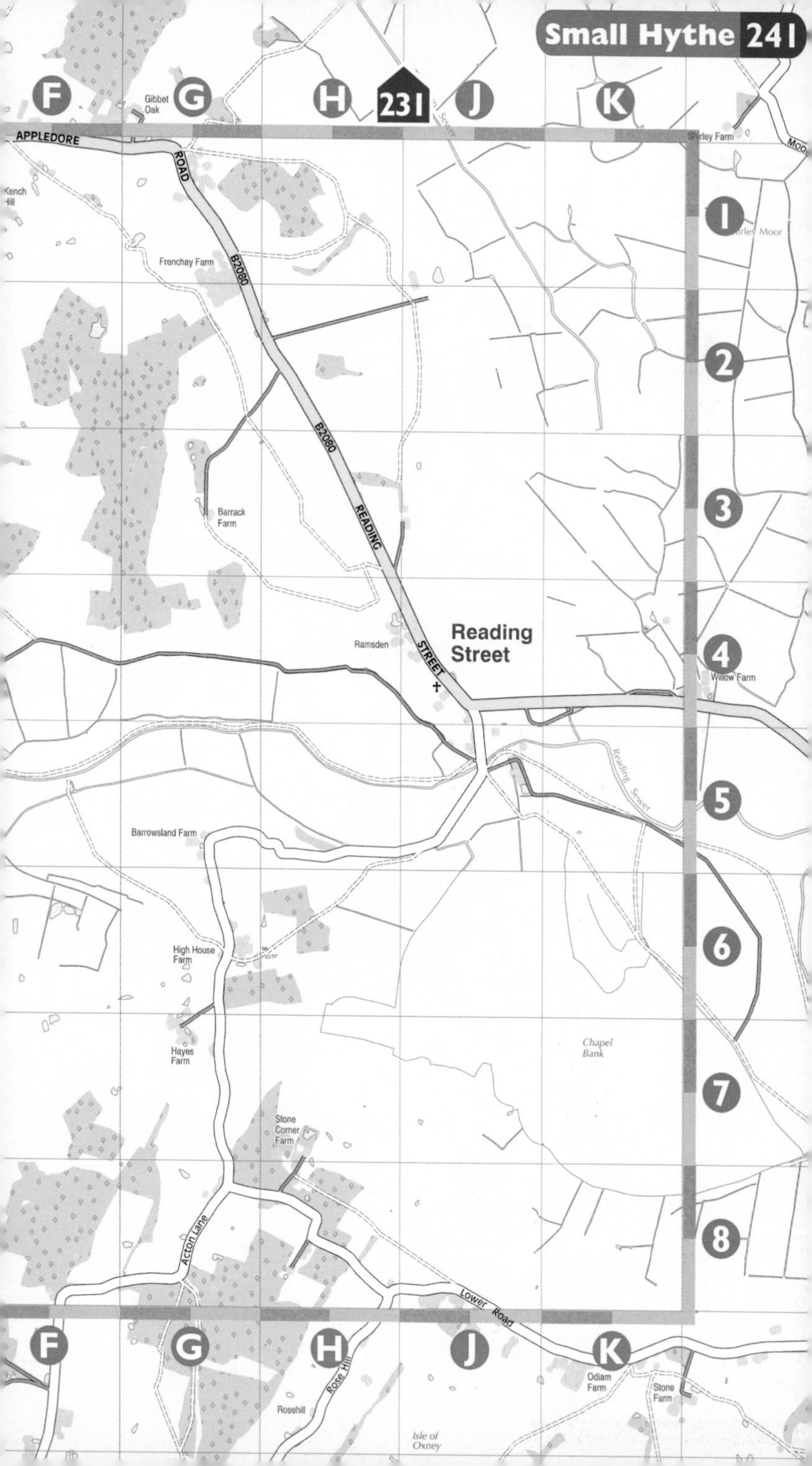
F
G
H
231
J
K
Gibbet Oak
APPLEDORE
ROAD
Shirley Farm
Kench Hill
Shirley Moor
Frenchay Farm
B2080
B2080
READING
STREET
Barrack Farm
Ramsden
Reading Street
Willow Farm
Reading Sewer
Barrowsland Farm
High House Farm
Hayes Farm
Chapel Bank
Stone Corner Farm
Acton Lane
Lower Road
Rose Hill
Rosehill
Odiam Farm
Stone Farm
Isle of Oxney
1
2
3
4
5
6
7
8
F
G
H
J
K

East Heath
Sussex Border
235
A
B
C
D
E
1
2
3
4
5
6
7
8
Merriments Farm
Conghurst Lane
Sussex Border Path
Conghurst Farm
Sussex Border Path
Brickhurst Wood
Northlands
Sussex Border Path
B2244
JUNCTION ROAD
High Wigsell
Climsett's Farm
Neals
Elms Farm
Boarsney Farm
South Park
Castle Hurst
B2244
Bourne Lane
Bourne Farm
New House
Haiselman's Farm
JUNCTION ROAD
Park Farm
Rocks Hill
Higham House
Moat Farm
B2244
1 grid square represents 500 metres

Megrims Hill
Downgate
236
Queen Street
Stream Pit La
Poundfield
Tanyard
Old Orchard
PO
Sandhurst CP School
Rope Wk
Back Road
Sandhurst
Silverden
Oaks Forstal
Burnt House Close
Crouch
A268
Silverdale Lane
Bodiam Road
Church Road
Sandhurst Cross
Boxhurst
Marsh Quarter Lane
Old Place Farm
Marsh Quarter Farm
244
Kent County
East Sussex County
Kent Ditch
Sussex Border Path
Court Lodge
Bodiam
Bodiam Castle (NT)
River Rother
Padgham
Kent & East Sussex Railway
Bodiam Bridge
Ockham
PH
Dagg Lane
Ewhurst Green
Sempstead Wood
Snagshall
F G H J K
1 2 3 4 5 6 7 8

237
243
A
B
C
D
E
1
2
3
4
5
6
7
8
Hexden Farm
Hoad's Farm
Crouch Lane
Stone Pit Lane
Lomas Lane
QUEEN ST
Oaks Forstal
Burnt House Close
A268
Linkhill
Lamberden
Heronden Farm
Boxhurst
Ethnam Lane
Ethnam
River Rother
Kent & East Sussex Ra
Kent County
East Sussex County
Weights Wood
Dixter Wood
Crockers Lane
Dixter Lane
Coplands Rise
Spring Hi
Wilderness Gdns
Strawberry Fields
High Park
High Meadow
Chapel Field
Northridge
Higham Lane
Dixter Road
A28
The Paddock
Frewen Close
Beales
Thyssel Lane
PO
Northia
MAIN STREET
Cem
Ewhurst Lane
Park View
The Plat
Fulle
The Surg
Padgham
Sussex Border Path
Spital Wood
Sempstead Wood
1 grid square represents 500 metres

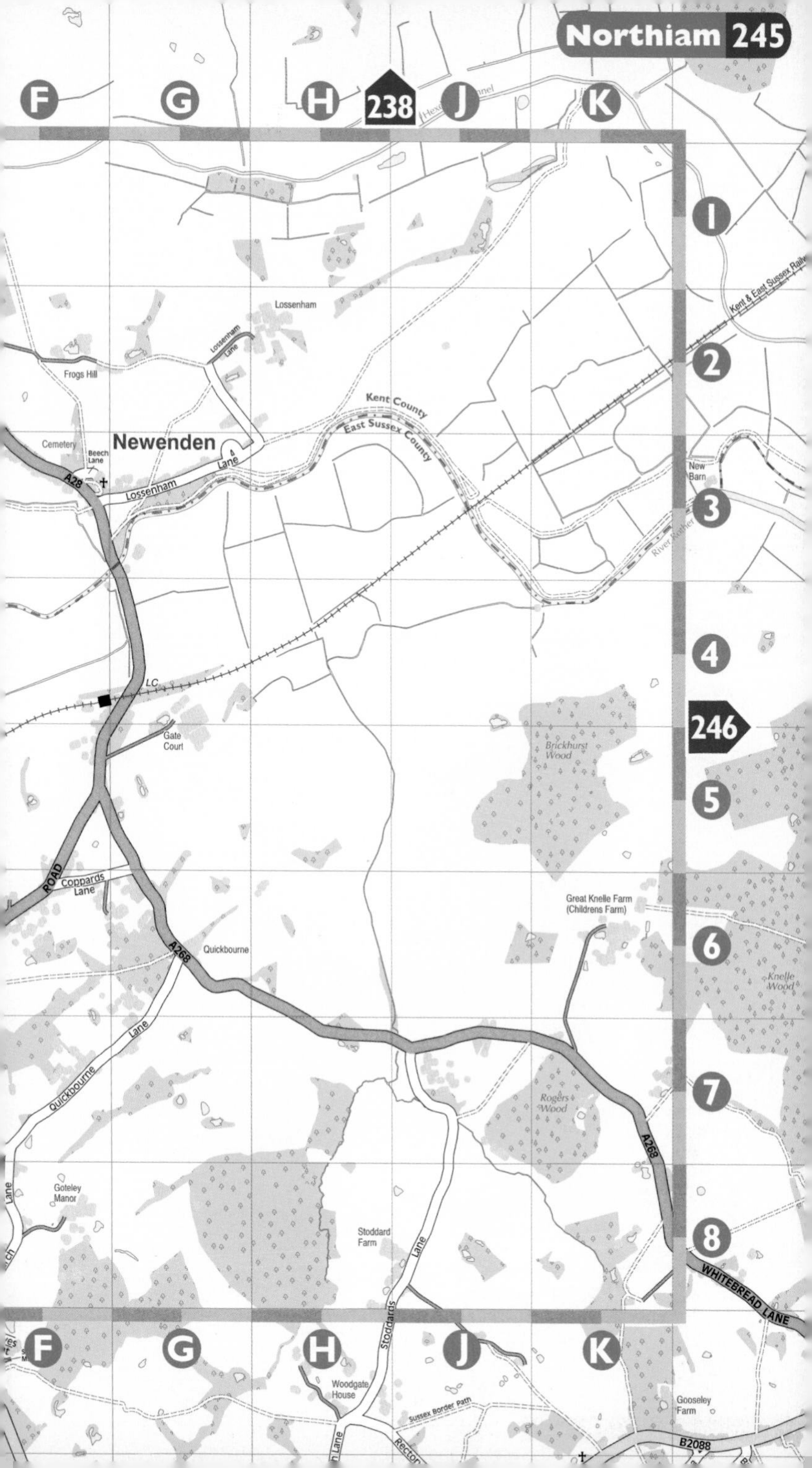
F
G
H
238
J
K
Hexden Channel
1
Kent & East Sussex Railway
2
Lossenham
Lossenham Lane
Frogs Hill
Kent County
East Sussex County
Newenden
Cemetery
Beech Lane
A28
Lossenham
Lane
New Barn
3
River Rother
4
LC
Gate Court
246
Brickhurst Wood
5
ROAD
Coppards Lane
Great Knelle Farm (Childrens Farm)
6
Knelle Wood
A268
Quickbourne
Quickbourne
Lane
7
Rogers Wood
A268
Goteley Manor
Lane
Stoddard Farm
Lane
8
WHITEBREAD LANE
F
G
H
J
K
Stoddards
Woodgate House
Sussex Border Path
Gooseley Farm
B2088

239
245
A
B
C
D
E
1
2
3
4
5
6
7
8
Maytham Farm
Potman's Heath
Kent & East Sussex Railway
Wittersham Road
Maytham Wharf
New Barn
River Rother
Methersham
Wet Level
Otter Channel
Brickhurst Wood
Great Knelle Farm (Childrens Farm)
Knelle Wood
Bellhurst Farms
Oxenbridge
Rogers Wood
A268
Hobbs Lane
Sussex Border Path
WHITEBREAD LANE
Kitchenour Lane
Gooseley Farm
Four Oaks
Kitchenour
B2088
Beckley
1 grid square represents 500 metres

Peening Quarter
Kingsgate House
240
F
G
H
J
K
Plastre Court
Wittersham Road
Black Barn
Kingsgate Lane
WITTERSHAM ROAD
1
Rugden
Coombe Lands
B2082
Lloyds Gn
Acton
2
Woodland View
Jubilee Field
Forge Meads
PO
Moon's Green
Swan Street
Swan Cottages
Wittersham
POPLAR ROAD
B2082
STOCKS ROAD
3
Swan Street
Cemetery
The Street
Wittersham Manor
Wittersham Primary School
Budd's Lane
4
Blackbrook Farm
Budd's Farm
Ham Green
5
River Rother
6
Kent County
East Sussex County
Sussex Border Path
Sussex Border Path
7
Sussex Border Path
Kitchenham
8
Farm
Readers Lane
Baron's Grange
Moat Farm
F
G
H
J
K

Abbey Gate 111 F3
Addington 107 F4
Allhallows 19 G7
Allhallows-on-Sea 19 J4
Allington 110 D6
Aperfield 97 K4
Ash 81 K1
Ashbank 135 K7
Ashurst 204 A4
Aylesford 109 K3
Badgers Mount 77 J4
Baker's Cross 225 K1
Bapchild 95 F3
Barden Park 169 K5
Barming Heath 131 K3
Barnehurst 22 A2
Barnes Cray 22 E3
Barnes Street 172 C2
Barnfield 183 J2
Basted 127 F2
Bayley's Hill 145 G2
Beacon Hill 237 J1
Beal's Green 235 G2
Bean 43 G1
Bearsted 134 D4
Beltring 173 K2
Benenden 227 F7
Benover 175 F1
Berner's Hill 232 E4
Berry's Green 98 A3
Bessels Green 123 F3
Betsham 44 A2
Bexon 116 B2
Bicknor 115 G4
Bidborough 189 H3
Biddenden 217 H4
Biddenden Green 202 B4
Biggin Hill 97 F4
Birchden 205 G8
Birling 84 E8
Bitchet Green 125 H5
Blue Bell Hill 87 H5
Bluetown 117 H5
Bobbing 73 G7
Bodiam 243 F6
Borden 93 F4
Borough Green 105 G6
Borstal 2 B6
Bottom Pond 116 D4
Bough Beech 166 B4
Boughton Green 155 G2
Boughton Malherbe 160 A6
Boughton Monchelsea 155 G3
Bowmans 22 C6
Boxley 111 K4
Branbridges 151 K8
Brasted 121 K3
Brasted Chart 121 H7
Breach 71 J6
Bredgar 116 A1
Bredhurst 89 J5
Brenchley 194 A6
Broad Ford 212 B2
Broadham Green 140 A3
Broadstone 181 H1
Broad Street 50 D2
Broad Street 113 K8
Broad Tenterden 240 A2
Broadwater Down 206 E6
Brompton 4 B2
Brook Street 170 A7
Broomfield 158 A1
Broom Hill 56 A4
Broomhill Bank 189 G7
Buckhurst 217 F1
Bulleign 240 A5
Burham 86 E5
Burham Court 86 C5
Burrswood 204 D6
Cage Green 170 C2
Camden Hill 215 G4
Camden Park 11 E5
Camer 63 K3
Capel 172 B8
Capel Cross 212 B1
Capstone 68 E7
Castle Hill 194 C5
Cellarhill 95 K5
Chainhurst 176 A2
Chalk 28 D7
Chalkwell 93 H2
Chamber's Green 203 J2
Charcott 167 J3
Chart Corner 156 D5
Chart Hill 156 D6
Chart Sutton 178 C1
The Chart 143 H1
Chatham 3 F5
Chattenden 49 K1
Chegworth 136 D8
Chelsfield 77 F1
Chesley 91 K3
Chestnut Street 92 D2
Chevening 100 B6
Chiddingstone 166 C6
Chiddingstone Causeway 167 H4
Chiddingstone Hoath 186 C4
Childsbridge 102 D6
Chillmill 193 J8
Chipstead 122 E1
Church Street 30 C5
Cinder Hill 168 A5
Clapper Hill 228 D1
Claygate 149 F2
Claygate 195 G1
Claygate Cross 127 G3
Clement Street 41 G4
Cliffe 15 H8
Cliffe Woods 31 H7
Cobham 64 C1
Cock Street 155 K4
Coldblow 40 C2
Cold Harbour 72 E8
Coldharbour 148 A5
Colliers Green 214 A4
Collier Street 175 J6
Colt's Hill 192 D2
Comp 106 B8
Congelow 152 C7
Cooling 32 A1
Cooling Street 31 J5
Coomb Hill 64 B8
Cooper's Corner 144 B6
The Corner 195 F6
Cousley Wood 220 E7
Cowden 185 G8
Coxheath 154 D3
Cranbrook 225 K1
Cranbrook Common 215 H4
Crayford 22 D4
Crit Hall 226 B7
Crockenhill 58 A4
Crockham Hill 142 C4
Crockhurst Street 171 H8
Cross-at-Hand 178 A5
Cross Keys 8 B6
Crouch 127 H2
Crowdleham 103 H4
Crowhurst 162 B3
Cudham 98 D2
Culverstone Green 83 F4
Curteis' Corner 217 K3
Curtisden Green 213 H1
Cuxton 66 B4
Dale Hill 232 D4
Danaway 92 B4
Darenth 42 B3
Dartford 23 F6
David Street 83 H1
Dean Bottom 43 G8
Deans Bottom 115 G1
Deans Hill 92 C8
Dean Street 132 D8
Dene Park 148 D5
Denny Bottom 206 C3
Denton 28 B6
Derry Downs 56 E3
Detling 112 D5
Dingleden 237 H3
Ditton 109 G4
Downe 74 E6
The Down 221 H3
Dryhill 122 D3
Dungate 117 H3
Dunk's Green 127 G8
Dunn Street 89 H6
Dunton Green 101 G6
Durrant Green 219 G8
East Barming 131 J5
East End 200 E2
East End 228 B3
East Farleigh 132 B7
East Hill 80 A4
East Malling 109 F8
East Malling Heath 130 C3
East Peckham 151 H8
Eccles 110 A1
Edenbridge 164 D4
Egerton 182 E3
Egerton Forstal 182 D5
Eyhorne Street 135 K4
Eynsford 59 H6
Fairbourne Heath 158 E5
Fairseat 82 D7
Fant 6 A4
Farleigh Green 131 J8
Farnborough 75 G1
Farningham 59 K4
Farthing Corner 90 B3
Farthing Green 179 G5
Fawkham Green 61 G7
Fenn Street 33 H3
Ferndale 11 E2
Field Green 236 A7
Fir Toll 183 J8
Five Oak Green 172 C6
Five Wents 157 G4
Fleet Downs 24 A8
Fletcher's Green 146 B5
Flimwell 233 G3
Flishinghurst 214 A7
Foots Cray 38 C4
Force Green 120 E3
Fordcombe 204 D1
Forstal 110 C4
Fosten Green 228 B1
Four Elms 165 G1
Four Throws 235 J6
Four Wents 213 K6
Four Wents 225 H8
Foxendown 63 K6
French Street 143 F1
Frindsbury 49 H6
Frinigham 113 H5
Frinsted 116 C7
Frittenden 199 H7
Froghole 142 D3
Further Quarter 219 H3
Gadshill 48 B4
Gillingham 5 E5
Gill's Green 235 F1
Glassenbury 213 K8
Goathurst Common 144 D1
Goddard's Green 227 H4
Godden Green 125 F4
Goddington 56 D7
Golden Green 172 B1
Golford 215 H8
Goodley Stock 142 B1
Goose Green 150 D4
Goose Green 217 H6
Goudhurst 212 E6
Gover Hill 128 A8
Grafty Green 159 J8
Grain 21 H8
Grange 51 J8
Gravesend 27 K5
Great Buckland 84 D2
Great Cheveney 196 A5
Greatness 102 B7
Great Pattenden 176 A8
Green Hill 134 D6
Greenhithe 25 G4
Green Street Green 43 F4
Green Street Green 75 K3
Greet 139 K3
Grigg 180 E8
Groombridge 204 D7
Grove End 93 H7
Grove Green 133 K1
Grubb Street 43 G6
Gun Green 235 J4
Hadlow 150 B5
Hadlow Stair 171 G2
Haffenden Quarter 202 A7
Hale 68 E6
Hale Street 151 J7
Halling 86 A1
Hall's Green 145 J6
Halstead 77 H7
Ham Green 53 J8
Ham Green 247 H5
Ham Hill 85 K8
Hamptons 149 H1
Hanging Bank 144 B3
Harbourland 111 H5
The Harbour 179 G1
Hareplain 217 F3
Harman's Corner 93 G4
Harrietsham 137 H8
Hartley 62 A2
Hartley 225 F4

Hartley Green 61 K2
Hartlip 91 G1
Harvel 83 K3
Haviker Street 175 J5
Hawkenbury 11 F5
Hawkenbury 178 E7
Hawkhurst 234 E5
Hawley 41 H3
Haxted 163 K6
Hazel Street 114 E3
Hazel Street 211 H3
Hazelwood 75 H6
Headcorn 180 B8
Hearnden Green 179 J5
Hearts Delight 93 G5
Heath Side 22 C8
Heaverham 103 J4
Hempstead 89 F1
Henhurst 46 B6
Henley Street 64 C3
Henwood Green 192 B8
Herne Pound 129 G4
Hever 165 J8
Hextable 40 D5
Higham 48 B2
Higham Wood 149 F8
High Brooms 190 C6
Highgate 235 G4
High Halden 219 J7
High Halstow 33 F3
Highsted 94 A7
High Street 234 D4
Hildenborough 147 J8
Hilden Park 169 J2
Hill Green 91 F5
Hill Hoath 166 D8
Hill Park 120 B2
Hoath Corner 186 D3
Hockenden 39 J8
Hodsoll Street 82 D4
Holborough 85 K4
Holland 140 E4
Hollingbourne 136 C4
Hollybushes 117 G6
Holt Hill 109 H6
Hook Green 40 C2
Hook Green 44 A4
Hook Green 63 H3
Hook Green 221 F2
Hoo St Werburgh 32 D8
Horns Green 98 E4
Horn Street 85 H8
Horsalls 137 K4
Horshoe Green 185 K5
Horsmonden 195 F8
Horton Kirby 60 C1
Hosey Hill 120 E7
How Green 165 K4
Howt Green 73 J5
Hubbard's Hill 145 K1
Hucking 114 C5
Hulberry 58 E6
Hungershall Park 10 A5
Hunton 153 J6
Hurst Green 140 C3
Ide Hill 144 A2
Iden Green 213 H6
Iden Green 237 F2
Ightham 126 D1
Igtham Common 126 A3
Istead Rise 45 F5
Ivy Hatch 126 B4
Iwade 73 J2
Kemsing 102 D4
Kemsley Street 89 K5
Kent Street 129 H4
Kettle Corner 131 K6
Kevingtown 57 G3
Keycol 72 D8
Key's Green 209 K2
Key Street 93 F1
Kilndown 222 E4
Kingsdown 117 K2
Kings Farm 45 K1
Kingswood 158 C4
Kipping's Cross 209 H2
Kippington 8 C5
Kit's Coty 87 H6
Knatts Valley 80 D5
Knockhall 25 G4
Knockholt 99 G4
Knockmill 80 D7
Knox Bridge 198 C8
Laddingford 174 C1
Lamberhurst 221 K1
Lamberhurst Quarter 210 A4
Lamb's Cross 156 B8
Lane End 42 C3
Langley 156 E2
Langley Heath 157 H2
Langton Green 205 J2
Larkfield 108 E4
Leadingcross Green 160 C3
Leaves Green 74 C6
Leeds 135 J7
Leigh 168 D4
Leigh Green 230 E7
Lenham 160 D1
Lenham Forstal 161 H5
Lenham Heath 161 H6
Lett's Green 99 F3
Leybourne 108 C3
Lidsing 89 F5
Limpsfield 118 D6
Limpsfield Chart 141 K2
Limpsfield Common 141 F1
Lingfield Common 162 B8
Linkhill 244 B2
Linton 155 F6
Little Bayham 220 B2
Little Cheveney Fm 195 J2
Little Mill 173 F1
Little Pattenden 176 C6
Little Preston 110 A5
Liverton Street 159 K5
Livesey Street 130 E4
London Beach 230 A1
Longfield 44 A8
Longfield Hill 62 E1
Longford 101 F7
Loose 155 F2
Loose Hill 155 F1
Lords Wood 88 D4
Lower Bitchet 125 G5
Lower Bush 65 J3
Lower Cousley Wood 221 G6
Lower Cox Street 90 A8
Lower Green 191 K6
Lower Green 206 B1
Lower Halstow 72 B3
Lower Hartlip 91 H2
Lower Haysden 169 J6
Lower Higham 30 C8
Lower Rainham 70 B3
Lower Stoke 35 F1
Lower Twydall 69 K1
Lower Upnor 50 A3
Luddesdown 64 C5
Lunsford 108 C2
Luton 68 C5
Luxted 98 A1
Lynsted 95 H8
Mabledon 169 K8
Maidstone 7 F5
Maltman's Hill 202 E3
Maplescombe 80 A1
Marden 196 C1
Marden Beech 196 B3
Marden Thorn 197 G4
Markbeech 185 K4
Marlpit Hill 164 B2
Marsh Green 184 B1
Matfield 193 G6
Maypole 22 B7
Maypole 77 G2
Medhurst Row 165 H4
Meopham 63 G6
Meopham Green 63 H7
Meopham Station 63 J2
Meresborough 90 B1
Mereworth 128 E6
Merle Common 140 E7
Middle Quarter 219 H5
Middle Stoke 35 F2
Milebush 176 E6
Mile Oak 194 A2
Millhall 109 G4
Mill Street 108 C7
Milstead 116 E4
Milton 28 A5
Milton Regis 93 H1
Mockbeggar 49 F1
Modest Corner 189 J4
Monks Hill 201 G7
Moon's Green 247 F3
Moorhouse Bank 120 A7
Moor Street 70 E7
The Moor 235 F6
Mowshurst 164 E2
Mundy Bois 182 D6
Mundy Bois 183 F6
Murston 94 D2
Nash 74 A2
Nash Street 45 H7
Nettlestead 130 A8
Nettlestead Green 151 K4
New Ash Green 62 B6
New Barn 44 C7
Newenden 245 G3
New House 27 F8
New Hythe 109 F2
Newington 72 B8
New Street 82 E1
New Town 23 J5
New Town 65 K8
New Town 107 K5
Noah's Arks 102 E6
Noke Street 49 H2
North Cray 39 H1
Northfleet 26 D4
Northfleet Green 44 D3
North Halling 65 K7
Northiam 244 E8
North Street 34 B4
Oad Street 92 D5
Oakhurst 146 E4
Offham 107 F6
Oldbury 104 B8
Old Cryals 210 A1
Orpington 56 A7
Otford 101 J4
Otham 134 C7
Otham Hole 134 E8
Otterham Quay 71 F4
Oxted 118 B8
Paddlesworth 85 G5
Paddock Wood 173 K8
Pains Hill 141 G2
Palmer's Green 194 B6
Parker's Green 149 G8
Parkgate 229 F4
Park Wood 89 K3
Park Wood 156 A2
Parrock Farm 46 A1
Payden Street 139 J6
Pearson's Green 194 C3
Peckham Bush 151 F6
Peening Quarter 240 B8
Pell Green 220 D7
Pembles Cross 182 C3
Pembury 191 J8
Penenden Heath 111 J7
Penshurst 187 K2
Perry Street 27 G6
Petteridge 193 H8
Pettings 82 C3
Pipsden 235 K5
Pittswood 149 G6
Pizien Well 129 K7
Platt 105 J7
Platt's Heath 159 K5
Plaxtol 127 F6
Pluckley 183 J7
Pluckley Thorne 183 G8
Plumtree Green 179 J6
Pollhill 159 F1
Pootings 142 E7
Potman's Heath 246 D1
Potter's Forstal 182 B4
Poundsbridge 188 A6
Poverest 56 B1
Powder Mills 169 J3
Pratling Street 110 B2
Pratt's Bottom 76 C5
Priestwood 83 J1
Priestwood Green 83 K1
Printstile 188 E3
Puddledock 40 A4
Puddledock 143 G4
Pullington 237 H1
Purfleet 12 E6
Pye Corner 158 E8
The Quarter 202 B1
The Quarter 239 K2
Queen Street 174 B6
Rabbit's Cross 178 A2
Radfield 95 H4
Rainham 70 D7
Ramsden 56 D5
Ramslye 206 C5
Reading Street 241 J4
Red Hill 130 D5

Ridley 82 C2
Ringlestone 110 D7
Ringlestone 137 K2
Riseden 222 E1
Riverhead 123 F1
Riverview Park 46 D2
Robhurst 231 J4
Rochester 2 B2
The Rocks 130 E1
Rodmersham 94 E6
Rodmersham Green 94 C7
Rolvenden 238 D2
Rolvenden Layne 238 E4
Romford 192 B7
Romney Street 79 J7
Rooks Hill 125 G7
Roseacre 134 C2
Rosherville 27 G4
Roughway 127 H8
Round Green 214 A2
Round Street 64 A1
Royal British Legion Village 109 K6
Royal Tunbridge Wells 10 B4
Rushmore Hill 76 D8
Rusthall 206 B2
Ruxley 39 F4
Ryarsh 107 J2
St John's 8 C1
St John's 10 B1
St Leonard's Street 107 J7
St Mary Cray 56 D2
St Mary's Hoo 17 K8
St Michaels 230 B2
St Paul's Cray 38 B7
Saint's Hill 187 K6
Salmans 187 G3
Sandhurst 243 H1
Sandhurst Cross 243 F2
Sandling 111 F5
Sandown Park 191 F8
Sandway 160 B3
Scragged Oak 90 A7
Seacox Heath 233 J4
Seal 102 E8
Sevenoaks 9 F3
Sevenoaks Common 123 J8
Sevenoaks Weald 145 J3
Sharnal Street 33 H5
Shepway 133 K6
Sherwood Park 190 E8
Shipbourne 148 C1
Shoreham 78 B6
Shorne 47 H3
Shorne Ridgeway 47 G5
Sidcup 38 C2
Silver Street 92 E8
Singlewell 45 K4
Sinkhurst Green 199 G5
Sissinghurst 215 H6
Sittingbourne 94 B4
Slade Green 22 D1
Small Hythe 240 C5
Smarden 202 A5
Smarden Bell 201 J4
Smart's Hill 187 H6
Snipeshill 94 D3
Snodland 86 A7
Sole Street 63 K2
Southborough 190 A5
South Darenth 42 C6
Southfleet 44 C4
South Green 114 E1
South Street 83 F2
South Street 91 G7
South Street 97 K6
Speed Gate 60 E6
Speldhurst 188 E7
Spitals Cross 164 C3
Standen 217 K1
Standen Street 237 F5
Stanstead 81 K6
Staplehurst 198 B2
Starvecrow 148 C6
Stede Quarter 218 D5
Stick Hill 185 H3
Stiff Street 92 E7
Stockbury 91 H6
Stockland Green 189 G6
Stocks Green 169 F2
Stoke 34 D3
Stone 24 E4
Stonebridge Green 183 G1
Stone Cross 204 C4
Stonecrouch 222 C7
Stonehill Green 39 K4
Stone Street 125 J4
Stonewood 43 J1
Strawberry Hill 206 C6
Strood 48 E7
Strood 239 F1
Styants Bottom 103 K8
Sundridge 122 B3
Sutton at Hone 41 K5
Sutton Valence 157 G7
Swanley 40 D8
Swanley Village 40 D7
Swanscombe 25 J5
Swanton Street 115 K3
Swift's Green 201 J1
Tatsfield 97 H7
Temple Hill 23 G3
Tenterden 230 A6
Teston 130 E7
Teynham 95 K3
Thong 46 D4
Three Chimneys 216 E5
Three Leg Cross 232 B3
Thurnham 112 E6
Ticehurst 232 C4
Timberden Bottom 78 B5
Titsey 119 G4
Tonbridge 170 C5
Tong 180 A4
Tovil 6 B5
Toy's Hill 143 J3
Trench Wood 148 A7
Trottiscliffe 106 C1
Troy Town 2 B4
Troy Town 163 K1
Tubslake 225 F6
Tudeley 171 J7
Tudeley Hale 171 J5
Tunbridge Hill 34 A5
Tunstall 93 J6
Turner's Green 220 A8
Twitton 101 G3
Twydall 69 J4
Ulcombe 158 C7
Underlining Green 177 F4
Underriver 146 E1
Union Street 233 F3
Upchurch 71 J2
Upper Bush 65 J4
Upper Halling 85 G1
Upper Hayesden 169 F8
Upper Rodmersham 94 D8
Upper Upnor 49 K5
Vigo Village 83 G6
Wainscott 49 H4
Walderslade 88 A3
Walter's Green 187 G7
Wanshurst Green 177 G7
Ware Street 134 D1
Warmlake 157 F6
Warren Street 139 K7
Wateringbury 130 B6
Waterman Quarter 200 B4
Waterside 162 D7
Wayfield 68 C7
Weavering Street 134 B2
Weller's Town 186 E1
Well Hill 77 J1
Well Street 108 C8
West Court 28 B8
West Cross 238 B2
Wested Fm 58 B4
West End 117 K7
Westerham 120 D6
West Farleigh 131 F8
Westfield Sole 88 D7
West Kingsdown 80 D4
West Malling 107 K7
West Peckham 128 D8
West Street 31 F1
West Street 138 E5
Westwood 43 H5
West Yoke 61 J7
Wetham Green 71 J1
Whetsted 173 G5
White Oak 40 B7
White Post 187 F7
Whitley Row 122 D8
Wichling 139 J1
Wick Hill 200 D6
Wickhurst 168 A2
Wierton 156 B6
Wigmore 89 K2
Wildernesse 124 C1
Willington 134 B5
Wilmington 40 E2
Wilsley Green 214 E8
Wilsley Pound 215 F6
Winchet Hill 196 B8
Windmill Hill 71 F3
Winkhurst Green 144 D6
Wissenden 203 F7
Wittersham 247 J3
Woodlands 80 B8
Woodsden 236 A2
Wood's Green 220 B6
Woodside Green 138 E6
Woodstock 93 K8
Worms Hill 213 G2
Wormshill 116 A7
Wouldham 86 B1
Wrotham 105 G3
Wrotham Heath 106 A5
Yalding 152 E5
Yelsted 90 D5
Yopps Green 126 E5

USING THE STREET INDEX

Street names are listed alphabetically. Each street name is followed by its postal town or area locality, the Postcode District, the page number, and the reference to the square in which the name is found.

Example: **Acorn Wharf Rd** *ROCH* ME1..................**2** C2 1

Some entries are followed by a number in a blue box. This number indicates the location of the street within the referenced grid square. The full street name is listed at the side of the map page.

GENERAL ABBREVIATIONS

ACC	ACCESS
ALY	ALLEY
AP	APPROACH
AR	ARCADE
ASS	ASSOCIATION
AV	AVENUE
BCH	BEACH
BLDS	BUILDINGS
BND	BEND
BNK	BANK
BR	BRIDGE
BRK	BROOK
BTM	BOTTOM
BUS	BUSINESS
BVD	BOULEVARD
BY	BYPASS
CATH	CATHEDRAL
CEM	CEMETERY
CEN	CENTRE
CFT	CROFT
CH	CHURCH
CHA	CHASE
CHYD	CHURCHYARD
CIR	CIRCLE
CIRC	CIRCUS
CL	CLOSE
CLFS	CLIFFS
CMP	CAMP
CNR	CORNER
CO	COUNTY
COLL	COLLEGE
COM	COMMON
COMM	COMMISSION
CON	CONVENT
COT	COTTAGE
COTS	COTTAGES
CP	CAPE
CPS	COPSE
CR	CREEK
CREM	CREMATORIUM
CRS	CRESCENT
CSWY	CAUSEWAY
CT	COURT
CTRL	CENTRAL
CTS	COURTS
CTYD	COURTYARD
CUTT	CUTTINGS
CV	COVE
CYN	CANYON
DEPT	DEPARTMENT
DL	DALE
DM	DAM
DR	DRIVE
DRO	DROVE
DRY	DRIVEWAY
DWGS	DWELLINGS
E	EAST
EMB	EMBANKMENT
EMBY	EMBASSY
ESP	ESPLANADE
EST	ESTATE
EX	EXCHANGE
EXPY	EXPRESSWAY
EXT	EXTENSION
F/O	FLYOVER
FC	FOOTBALL CLUB
FK	FORK
FLD	FIELD
FLDS	FIELDS
FLS	FALLS
FLS	FLATS
FM	FARM
FT	FORT
FWY	FREEWAY
FY	FERRY
GA	GATE
GAL	GALLERY
GDN	GARDEN
GDNS	GARDENS
GLD	GLADE
GLN	GLEN
GN	GREEN
GND	GROUND
GRA	GRANGE
GRG	GARAGE
GT	GREAT
GTWY	GATEWAY
GV	GROVE
HGR	HIGHER
HL	HILL
HLS	HILLS
HO	HOUSE
HOL	HOLLOW
HOSP	HOSPITAL
HRB	HARBOUR
HTH	HEATH
HTS	HEIGHTS
HVN	HAVEN
HWY	HIGHWAY
IMP	IMPERIAL
IN	INLET
IND EST	INDUSTRIAL ESTATE
INF	INFIRMARY
INFO	INFORMATION
INT	INTERCHANGE
IS	ISLAND
JCT	JUNCTION
JTY	JETTY
KG	KING
KNL	KNOLL
L	LAKE
LA	LANE
LDG	LODGE
LGT	LIGHT
LK	LOCK
LKS	LAKES
LNDG	LANDING
LTL	LITTLE
LWR	LOWER
MAG	MAGISTRATE
MAN	MANSIONS
MD	MEAD
MDW	MEADOWS
MEM	MEMORIAL
MKT	MARKET
MKTS	MARKETS
ML	MALL
ML	MILL
MNR	MANOR
MS	MEWS
MSN	MISSION
MT	MOUNT
MTN	MOUNTAIN
MTS	MOUNTAINS
MUS	MUSEUM
MWY	MOTORWAY
N	NORTH
NE	NORTH EAST
NW	NORTH WEST
O/P	OVERPASS
OFF	OFFICE
ORCH	ORCHARD
OV	OVAL
PAL	PALACE
PAS	PASSAGE
PAV	PAVILION
PDE	PARADE
PH	PUBLIC HOUSE
PK	PARK
PKWY	PARKWAY
PL	PLACE
PLN	PLAIN
PLNS	PLAINS
PLZ	PLAZA
POL	POLICE STATION
PR	PRINCE
PREC	PRECINCT
PREP	PREPARATORY
PRIM	PRIMARY
PROM	PROMENADE
PRS	PRINCESS
PRT	PORT
PT	POINT
PTH	PATH
PZ	PIAZZA
QD	QUADRANT
QU	QUEEN
QY	QUAY
R	RIVER
RBT	ROUNDABOUT
RD	ROAD
RDG	RIDGE
REP	REPUBLIC
RES	RESERVOIR
RFC	RUGBY FOOTBALL CLUB
RI	RISE
RP	RAMP
RW	ROW
S	SOUTH
SCH	SCHOOL
SE	SOUTH EAST
SER	SERVICE AREA
SH	SHORE
SHOP	SHOPPING
SKWY	SKYWAY
SMT	SUMMIT
SOC	SOCIETY
SP	SPUR
SPR	SPRING
SQ	SQUARE
ST	STREET
STN	STATION
STR	STREAM
STRD	STRAND
SW	SOUTH WEST
TDG	TRADING
TER	TERRACE
THWY	THROUGHWAY
TNL	TUNNEL
TOLL	TOLLWAY
TPK	TURNPIKE
TR	TRACK
TRL	TRAIL
TWR	TOWER
U/P	UNDERPASS
UNI	UNIVERSITY
UPR	UPPER
V	VALE
VA	VALLEY
VIAD	VIADUCT
VIL	VILLA
VIS	VISTA
VLG	VILLAGE
VLS	VILLAS
VW	VIEW
W	WEST
WD	WOOD
WHF	WHARF
WK	WALK
WKS	WALKS
WLS	WELLS
WY	WAY
YD	YARD
YHA	YOUTH HOSTEL

POSTCODE TOWNS AND AREA ABBREVIATIONS

BFN/LL	Blackfen/Longlands
BGR/WK	Borough Green/West Kingsdown
BH/WHM	Biggin Hill/Westerham
BUR/ETCH	Burwash/Etchingham
BXLY	Bexley
BXLYHN	Bexleyheath north
CHAT	Chatham
CHST	Chislehurst
CRBK	Cranbrook
CTHM	Caterham
DART	Dartford
DIT/AY	Ditton/Aylesford
E/WMAL	East & West Malling
EDEN	Edenbridge
EGRIN	East Grinstead
ERITH	Erith
EYN	Eynsford
GDST	Godstone
GILL	Gillingham
GRH	Greenhithe
GVE	Gravesend east
GVW	Gravesend west
HART	Hartley
HAWK	Hawkhurst
HAYES	Hayes
HDCN	Headcorn
HOO/HM	Hoo St Werburgh/Higham
HRTF	Hartfield
LING	Lingfield
MAID/BEAR	Maidstone/Bearsted
MAID/SHEP	Maidstone/Shepway
MAIDW	Maidstone west
MEO	Meopham
ORP	Orpington
OXTED	Oxted
PUR	Purfleet

QBOR ... Queenborough
RAIN ... Rainham (Gt Lon)
RASHW ... Rural Ashford west
RBTBR ... Robertsbridge
RDART ... Rural Dartford
RHAM ... Rainham (Kent)
RMAID ... Rural Maidstone
ROCH ... Rochester
RRTW ... Rural Royal Tunbridge Wells
RSEV ... Rural Sevenoaks
RSIT ... Rural Sittingbourne
RTON ... Rural Tonbridge
RTW ... Royal Tunbridge Wells
RTWE/PEM ... Royal Tunbridge Wells east/Pembury
RYE ... Rye
SCUP ... Sidcup
SEV ... Sevenoaks
SIT ... Sittingbourne
SNOD ... Snodland
SOCK/AV ... South Ockendon/Aveley
STH/RUST ... Southborough/Rusthall
STMC/STPC ... St Mary Cray/St Paul's Cray
STPH/PW ... Staplehurst/Paddock Wood
STRD ... Strood
SWCM ... Swanscombe
SWLY ... Swanley
TENT ... Tenterden
TIL ... Tilbury
TON ... Tonbridge
TONN ... Tonbridge north
WADH ... Wadhurst
WALD ... Walderslade
WARL ... Warlingham
WBY/YAL ... Wateringbury/Yalding
WTHK ... West Thurrock

Abb - Ari

Index - streets

A

Abbey Rd GRH DA9 25 H4
GVE DA12 28 B7
RHAM ME8 69 H4
STRD ME2 48 E6
Abbey Wood Rd E/WMAL ME19 129 J1
Abbots Court Rd HOO/HM ME3 51 G2
Abbots Fld MAIDW ME16 132 B4
Abbott Rd BGR/WK TN15 105 F7
Abbotts Cl ROCH ME1 2 B5
SWLY BR8 58 D1
Abigail Crs WALD ME5 88 B5
Abingdon Rd MAIDW ME16 131 K4
Abingdon Wy ORP BR6 56 C8
Abinger Dr WALD ME5 88 E4
Acacia Rd DART DA1 23 F7
GRH DA9 24 D5
Academy Dr GILL ME7 69 G6
Acer Av RTWE/PEM TN2 207 H6
Acer Rd BH/WHM TN16 97 H3
Achilles Rd WALD ME5 88 D4
Acorn Cl STPH/PW TN12 172 D7
Acorn Gv DIT/AY ME20 109 H6
Acorn Pl MAID/SHEP ME15 134 A8
Acorn Rd GILL ME7 5 F4
The Acorns HDCN TN27 201 K5
SEV TN13 8 C2
Acorn Wharf Rd ROCH ME1 2 C2 1
Acott Flds WBY/YAL ME18 152 D5
Acre Cl CHAT ME4 67 K5
Acre Gv STRD ME2 85 K2
Acres Ri WADH TN5 232 C5
Acton La TENT TN30 241 G8
Adam Cl RMAID ME17 154 D3
Adams Cl TENT TN30 230 B5
Addington La E/WMAL ME19 106 C2
Addington Rd SIT ME10 93 K3
Addison Cl E/WMAL ME19 108 D5
Addlestead Rd STPH/PW TN12 151 G8
Adelaide Dr SIT ME10 93 H2
Adelaide Rd GILL ME7 4 C4
The Adelaide HOO/HM ME3 30 B8 1
Adisham Dr MAIDW ME16 110 B7
Admers Wy MEO DA13 83 J6 1
Admiral Cl STMC/STPC BR5 56 E1 1
Admirals Wk CRBK TN17 227 F4
GRH DA9 25 G4 1
TENT TN30 230 C5
Admiralty Rd STRD ME2 50 A5 1
Admiralty Ter STRD ME2 50 A5 2
Admiral Wy WBY/YAL ME18 129 J5
Afghan Rd CHAT ME4 3 E4
Aintree Cl GVE DA12 45 J1
Aintree Rd WALD ME5 88 D3
Airedale Cl RDART DA2 24 B7
Aisher Wy SEV TN13 101 G8
Ajax Rd ROCH ME1 67 H7
Alamein Av WALD ME5 68 A7
Alamein Gdns RDART DA2 24 C6
Alamein Rd SWCM DA10 25 J5
Alanbrooke GVE DA12 27 K6
Alan Cl DART DA1 23 F3
Alban Crs EYN DA4 59 K5
Albany Cl TON TN9 170 D7
Albany Hl RTWE/PEM TN2 11 E2
Albany Rd CHAT ME4 4 B6
GILL ME7 5 D4
ROCH ME1 2 C4
SIT ME10 93 K3
Albany St MAID/BEAR ME14 7 E2
Albany Ter CHAT ME4 3 E4
Albatross Av STRD ME2 48 B8
Albemarle Rd WALD ME5 88 D4
Albert Dr MAID/SHEP ME15 154 B2
Albert Murray Cl GVE DA12 27 K6 1
Albert Pl STRD ME2 2 B1 1
Albert Rd CHAT ME4 4 A5
GILL ME7 4 C4
ORP BR6 76 B1
RDART DA2 41 F1
ROCH ME1 2 C5
STMC/STPC BR5 56 C3
SWCM DA10 26 A5
TON TN9 170 B5
Albert St MAID/BEAR ME14 6 C1
Albion Pl MAID/BEAR ME14 7 E3 1
Albion Rd GVE DA12 27 K6
RTW TN1 11 D2
STPH/PW TN12 196 D1
WALD ME5 88 C4
Albion Ter GVE DA12 27 K5
Albion Wy EDEN TN8 164 C2
Albury Cl WALD ME5 88 E4
Alder Cl RTWE/PEM TN2 190 C5
Aldershot Rd WALD ME5 68 B7
Alders Meadow TON TN9 169 K4
Alders Rd RTON TN11 172 A8
The Alders WBY/YAL ME18 129 F7
Alder Wy SWLY BR8 40 A7
Aldington Cl WALD ME5 88 C1
Aldington La MAID/BEAR ME14 113 F6
Aldington Rd MAID/BEAR ME14 134 B2
Aldon Cl MAID/BEAR ME14 7 F1
Aldon La E/WMAL ME19 106 D6
Alen Sq STPH/PW TN12 198 B2
Alexander Rd GRH DA9 25 H4
Alexandra Av GILL ME7 5 E4
Alexandra Cl SIT ME10 73 K7 1
SWLY BR8 40 B7
Alexandra Gln WALD ME5 88 B5
Alexandra Rd BH/WHM TN16 97 F6
CHAT ME4 4 B6
GVE DA12 28 B6
TIL RM18 27 G1 1
TON TN9 170 B6 1
Alexandra St MAID/BEAR ME14 6 C1
Alfred Cl CHAT ME4 4 B6
Alfred Pl GVW DA11 27 G7
Alfred Rd GVW DA11 27 J8
RDART DA2 41 J2
SOCK/AV RM15 13 G1 1
Alkerden La GRH DA9 25 H5
Alkham Rd MAID/BEAR ME14 7 F2
Allan Cl STH/RUST TN4 206 B2
Allandale Pl ORP BR6 56 E7
Allandale Rd RTWE/PEM TN2 11 F1
Allard Cl STMC/STPC BR5 56 D4
Allenby Rd BH/WHM TN16 97 J4
Allen Cl WALD ME5 68 D8 1
Allendale Cl RDART DA2 24 C7 1
Allens La BGR/WK TN15 127 G7
Allen St MAID/BEAR ME14 7 D2
Allhallows Rd HOO/HM ME3 35 F1
Alliance Wy STPH/PW TN12 173 H8
Allington Dr STRD ME2 48 D6
TONN TN10 171 G1
Allington Gdns WBY/YAL ME18 130 B7
Allington Rd RHAM ME8 69 H3
STPH/PW TN12 173 H7
Allington Wy MAIDW ME16 110 B8
Allison Av GILL ME7 69 F5
Allnutt Mill Cl MAID/SHEP ME15 6 B5
Allotment La SEV TN13 9 E1
All Saints Cl SWCM DA10 26 A4
All Saints' Rd GVW DA11 27 G7
HAWK TN18 235 G5
SIT ME10 94 D2
STH/RUST TN4 10 C1
Allsworth Cl RSIT ME9 72 A8
Alma Pl STRD ME2 2 A1
Alma Rd DIT/AY ME20 86 E8 1
E/WMAL ME19 107 J6
SCUP DA14 38 B1
STMC/STPC BR5 56 E6
SWCM DA10 25 K4
Almond Dr SWLY BR8 40 A8
Almond Gv GILL ME7 89 H2
Almond Rd RDART DA2 24 B6
The Almonds MAID/BEAR ME14 134 C2
Almon Pl ROCH ME1 3 D3
Alpha Cl HOO/HM ME3 34 A7
Amanda Cl WALD ME5 87 K3
Amber La RMAID ME17 156 C5
Amberleaze Dr RTWE/PEM TN2 191 K8
Amberley Cl ORP BR6 76 A1
Amberley Ct SCUP DA14 38 D
Ambleside SIT ME10 94 D
Ambley Gn GILL ME7 69 H
Ambley Rd GILL ME7 69 H
Ambrose Cl DART DA1 22 C
ORP BR6 56 A7
Ambrose Hl WALD ME5 4 C
Ames Av MAID/BEAR ME14 134 C
Ames Rd SWCM DA10 25 K
Amethyst Av WALD ME5 67 K
Amherst Cl MAIDW ME16 6 A3
STMC/STPC BR5 56 B
Amherst Dr STMC/STPC BR5 56 A
Amherst Hl SEV TN13 8 A
Amherst Redoubt GILL ME7 4 A
Amherst Rd ROCH ME1 3 D
SEV TN13 9 D
STH/RUST TN4 10 C
Amhurst Bank Rd
RTWE/PEM TN2 192 A
Ampleforth Cl ORP BR6 56 D8
Amsbury Rd MAID/SHEP ME15 154 A
Amy Rd OXTED RH8 118 C
Anchorage Cl HOO/HM ME3 35 F3
Anchor Bvd GRH DA9 24 B
Anchor Rd ROCH ME1 67 H
Andrew Broughton Wy
MAID/BEAR ME14 7 E
Andrew Cl DART DA1 22 A
Andrew Rd STH/RUST TN4 190 C
Andrews Cl RTWE/PEM TN2 11 F2
STMC/STPC BR5 38 E8
Anerley Cl MAIDW ME16 110 D
Angel La TON TN9 170 B
Anglesea Pl GVE DA12 27 J
GVW DA11 27 J
Anglesea Rd STMC/STPC BR5 56 D
Anglesey Av MAID/SHEP ME15 133 G
Anglesey Cl WALD ME5 68 C
Angley Ct STPH/PW TN12 211 K
Angley Rd CRBK TN17 225 J
Angley Wk CRBK TN17 214 E8
Anne of Cleves Rd DART DA1 23 G
Annetts Hall BGR/WK TN15 105 G
Annie Rd SNOD ME6 85 J8
Ansell Av CHAT ME4 4 A
Anselm Cl SIT ME10 93 K
Anson Av E/WMAL ME19 129 H
Anson Cl WALD ME5 68 D
Anthony Cl SEV TN13 101 G8
Anthonys La SWLY BR8 40 D
Anthonys Wy STRD ME2 49 K
Aperfield Rd BH/WHM TN16 97 J
Appleby Cl ROCH ME1 67 J
Apple Cl SNOD ME6 85 J
Apple Ct STPH/PW TN12 173 H8
Applecross Cl ROCH ME1 2 B
Appledore Rd RHAM ME8 69 H
TENT TN30 230 C
Applegarth Dr DART DA1 23 H
Apple Orch SWLY BR8 58 A1
Appleshaw Cl GVW DA11 45 H3
Appleton Dr RDART DA2 40 E
Appletons RTON TN11 150 B6
Apple Tree Cl MAIDW ME16 131 K4
Apple Tree La RTWE/PEM TN2 190 D
Approach Rd WARL CR6 119 F
The Approach ORP BR6 56 A
April Cl ORP BR6 76 A
Apsley St STH/RUST TN4 206 C
Arbrook Cl STMC/STPC BR5 38 B
Arcadia Rd MEO DA13 45 G
Archer Rd STMC/STPC BR5 56 B
WALD ME5 68 C
Archer Wy SWLY BR8 40 C
Archery Cl HOO/HM ME3 31 G
Ardenlee Dr MAID/BEAR ME14 7 E
Arden St GILL ME7 4 C2
Arethusa Rd ROCH ME1 67 H
Argles Cl GRH DA9 25 F4
Argyle Cl ROCH ME1 67 K7
Argyle Rd SEV TN13 9 D4
STH/RUST TN4 190 A4
Ariel Cl GVE DA12 46 C2

Arkwright Rd *TIL* RM18 ..... **27** H1
Arlott Cl *MAID/BEAR* ME14 ..... **6** C1
Armada Wy *CHAT* ME4 ..... **3** F5 1
Armor Rd *PUR* RM19 ..... **13** H4
Armoury Dr *GVE* DA12 ..... **27** K6
Armstrong Cl *RSEV* TN14 ..... **100** D2
Armstrong Rd *MAID/SHEP* ME15 ..... **7** D6
Armytage Cl *HOO/HM* ME3 ..... **51** F2
Arne Cl *TONN* TN10 ..... **148** E8
Arne Gv *ORP* BR6 ..... **56** A7
Arnhem Av *SOCK/AV* RM15 ..... **13** G1
Arnhem Dr *WALD* ME5 ..... **68** A7
Arnold Av *MEO* DA13 ..... **63** J6
Arnolde Cl *STRD* ME2 ..... **3** E1
Arnold Rd *GVE* DA12 ..... **27** K8
Arnolds La *RDART* DA2 ..... **41** K4
Arran Rd *MAID/SHEP* ME15 ..... **133** G8
Artemis Cl *GVE* DA12 ..... **28** B6
Arterial Road Purfleet *PUR* RM19 ..... **13** G4
Arterial Road West Thurrock
WTHK RM20 ..... **13** K3
Arthur Rd *BH/WHM* TN16 ..... **97** G2
RHAM ME8 ..... **70** B6
ROCH ME1 ..... **3** D5
Arthur St *GVW* DA11 ..... **27** H6
SIT ME10 ..... **93** K2 1
Artillery Rw *GVE* DA12 ..... **27** K6
Arundel Av *SIT* ME10 ..... **93** K5
Arundel Cl *TON* TN9 ..... **170** A6
WALD ME5 ..... **88** E5
Arundel Dr *ORP* BR6 ..... **76** C1
Arundel Rd *DART* DA1 ..... **23** F3
RTW TN1 ..... **11** D5
Arundel St *MAID/BEAR* ME14 ..... **6** C1
Ascot Cl *BGR/WK* TN15 ..... **105** H7
WALD ME5 ..... **88** D4
Ascot Rd *GVW* DA11 ..... **45** J1
STMC/STPC BR5 ..... **56** A1
Ashbee Cl *SNOD* ME6 ..... **85** K7
Ashburnham Rd
MAID/BEAR ME14 ..... **111** H6 1
TONN TN10 ..... **170** C3 1
Ashby Cl *STRD* ME2 ..... **85** K2 1
Ashby's Cl *EDEN* TN8 ..... **164** D6 1
Ash Cl *DIT/AY* ME20 ..... **109** J5
EDEN TN8 ..... **164** B5
RHAM ME8 ..... **69** J3
RTWE/PEM TN2 ..... **207** J6
SCUP DA14 ..... **38** C1
SWLY BR8 ..... **39** K7
WALD ME5 ..... **68** D5
Ashcombe Dr *EDEN* TN8 ..... **164** B2
Ash Crs *HOO/HM* ME3 ..... **48** A3
Ashcroft Rd *STPH/PW* TN12 ..... **193** H1
Ashden Wk *TONN* TN10 ..... **148** C7
Ashdown Cl *MAIDW* ME16 ..... **6** A4
STH/RUST TN4 ..... **10** B3
Ashdown Rd *RSIT* ME9 ..... **139** F3
Ashenden *HDCN* TN27 ..... **201** K4
Ashenden Cl *STRD* ME2 ..... **49** H4
Ashenden Wk *RTWE/PEM* TN2 ..... **190** E6
Ashen Dr *DART* DA1 ..... **22** D5
Ashen Grove Rd *EYN* DA4 ..... **80** A5
Asher Reeds *RRTW* TN3 ..... **205** K2
Ashes La *RTON* TN11 ..... **149** H6
Ashford Dr *RMAID* ME17 ..... **158** B4
Ashford Rd *MAID/BEAR* ME14 ..... **7** E3
MAID/BEAR ME14 ..... **135** G3
RASHW TN26 ..... **219** K6
RMAID ME17 ..... **136** B6
RMAID ME17 ..... **161** F1
TENT TN30 ..... **230** B6
TENT TN30 ..... **230** A1
Ash Gv *MAIDW* ME16 ..... **110** C8
Ashgrove Rd *SEV* TN13 ..... **8** C6
SEV TN13 ..... **123** K7
Ashington Cl *SIT* ME10 ..... **93** H1 1
Ash Keys *MEO* DA13 ..... **83** J6
Ash La *BGR/WK* TN15 ..... **81** H6
Ashleigh Cl *MEO* DA13 ..... **83** G5
Ashleigh Gdns *HDCN* TN27 ..... **180** B8
Ashley Cl *SEV* TN13 ..... **9** D3
Ashley Gdns *ORP* BR6 ..... **75** K1
STH/RUST TN4 ..... **206** B1
Ashley Park Cl *STH/RUST* TN4 ..... **206** B1
Ashley Rd *RHAM* ME8 ..... **69** K4
RTON TN11 ..... **169** J1
SEV TN13 ..... **9** D3
Ashmead Cl *WALD* ME5 ..... **88** D3
Ashmore Gdns *GVW* DA11 ..... **44** E1 1
Ashmore La *HAYES* BR2 ..... **74** B6
Ash Platt Rd *BGR/WK* TN15 ..... **102** C8
Ash Rd *BGR/WK* TN15 ..... **61** J8
BH/WHM TN16 ..... **120** D4
DART DA1 ..... **23** G7
GVE DA12 ..... **45** K2
HART DA3 ..... **43** K8
HART DA3 ..... **61** K7
ORP BR6 ..... **76** B3
RDART DA2 ..... **41** J2
STRD ME2 ..... **48** E8
Ashtead Dr *RSIT* ME9 ..... **94** E4
Ashton Wy *E/WMAL* ME19 ..... **108** A8
Ash Tree Cl *BGR/WK* TN15 ..... **80** E4 1
Ash Tree Dr *BGR/WK* TN15 ..... **80** E4
Ash Tree La *WALD* ME5 ..... **5** D6
Ashurst Cl *DART* DA1 ..... **22** C2
Ashurst Rd *MAID/BEAR* ME14 ..... **7** F2
RRTW TN3 ..... **204** E4
Ashwood Cl *HOO/HM* ME3 ..... **31** H7
Aspdin Rd *GVW* DA11 ..... **44** E1
Aspen Cl *ORP* BR6 ..... **76** B1
SWLY BR8 ..... **40** A6 1
Aspen Wy *RTWE/PEM* TN2 ..... **190** C5
Aspian Dr *RMAID* ME17 ..... **154** D4
Asquith Rd *RHAM* ME8 ..... **69** K8
Aster Rd *HOO/HM* ME3 ..... **51** F3 1
Astley St *MAID/BEAR* ME14 ..... **7** D3
Aston Cl *SCUP* DA14 ..... **38** B1
WALD ME5 ..... **88** B4
Astor Rd *BGR/WK* TN15 ..... **80** D2
Astra Dr *GVE* DA12 ..... **46** B3
Athelstan Gn *RMAID* ME17 ..... **136** A4
Athelstan Rd *CHAT* ME4 ..... **3** F6 1
Athelstan Wy *STMC/STPC* BR5 ..... **38** B6
Atkinson Cl *ORP* BR6 ..... **76** B1 1
Atlas Rd *DART* DA1 ..... **23** J2
Atterbury Cl *BH/WHM* TN16 ..... **120** D5
Attlee Dr *DART* DA1 ..... **23** K4
Attlee Wy *SIT* ME10 ..... **73** K7
Attwaters La *HAWK* TN18 ..... **225** J8
Auckland Cl *TIL* RM18 ..... **27** H1
Auckland Dr *SIT* ME10 ..... **93** H3
Auckland Rd *RTW* TN1 ..... **11** E1
Auden Rd *DIT/AY* ME20 ..... **108** E2
Audley Av *GILL* ME7 ..... **69** F5
TON TN9 ..... **169** K4
Audley Cl *MAIDW* ME16 ..... **132** B1
Audley Ri *TON* TN9 ..... **169** K5
Auger Cl *RSIT* ME9 ..... **91** H1
Augusta Cl *GILL* ME7 ..... **4** C1 1
Augustine Rd *GVE* DA12 ..... **27** K6
STMC/STPC BR5 ..... **38** E8
Austen Cl *GRH* DA9 ..... **25** H5 1
TIL RM18 ..... **27** K1 1
Austen Wy *DIT/AY* ME20 ..... **108** D2
Austin Cl *GILL* ME7 ..... **5** E6 1
Austin Rd *GVW* DA11 ..... **27** G7
STMC/STPC BR5 ..... **56** B3
Austral Cl *BFN/LL* DA15 ..... **38** A1
Autumn Gld *MAID/BEAR* ME14 ..... **88** E6
Avalon Cl *ORP* BR6 ..... **56** E6
Avalon Rd *ORP* BR6 ..... **56** D6
Avards Cl *HAWK* TN18 ..... **234** E6
Avebury Av *TON* TN9 ..... **170** B5
Aveling Cl *HOO/HM* ME3 ..... **32** E8
Avenue La *GRH* DA9 ..... **25** H5
Avenue Le Puy *TON* TN9 ..... **170** C5
Avenue of Remembrance
SIT ME10 ..... **94** A3
Avenue Rd *BH/WHM* TN16 ..... **97** J7
SEV TN13 ..... **9** E3
The Avenue *BGR/WK* TN15 ..... **105** G6
BH/WHM TN16 ..... **119** K1
DIT/AY ME20 ..... **109** J5
GVW DA11 ..... **27** H7
ORP BR6 ..... **56** A6
STMC/STPC BR5 ..... **38** C5
TON TN9 ..... **170** B4
Averenches Rd *MAID/BEAR* ME14 ..... **134** B1
Avery Cl *HOO/HM* ME3 ..... **19** G6 1
MAID/SHEP ME15 ..... **6** C6
Avery La *MAID/SHEP* ME15 ..... **134** E8
Avery Wy *HOO/HM* ME3 ..... **19** G6
Aviemore Gdns *MAID/BEAR* ME14 ..... **134** B2
Avington Cl *MAID/SHEP* ME15 ..... **6** C6 1
Avon Cl *GVE* DA12 ..... **28** A8
TONN TN10 ..... **170** C1
Avondale Rd *GILL* ME7 ..... **5** D3 1
Avonmouth Rd *DART* DA1 ..... **23** G4
Avon St *RTW* TN1 ..... **11** E2
Axtaine Rd *STMC/STPC* BR5 ..... **56** E4
Axtane Cl *EYN* DA4 ..... **42** B7 1
Ayelands *HART* DA3 ..... **61** K6 1
Ayelands La *HART* DA3 ..... **61** K7
Aylesford Crs *RHAM* ME8 ..... **69** H3
Aylewade La *HDCN* TN27 ..... **200** C6
Aynscombe Angle *ORP* BR6 ..... **56** B4 1
Azalea Dr *SWLY* BR8 ..... **58** A1

B

Babb's La *CRBK* TN17 ..... **226** C8
Babylon La *RMAID* ME17 ..... **178** D3
STPH/PW TN12 ..... **178** E5
Backfields *ROCH* ME1 ..... **2** B4
Back La *BGR/WK* TN15 ..... **124** E3
BGR/WK TN15 ..... **126** C3
CRBK TN17 ..... **212** D6
PUR RM19 ..... **13** J4
RMAID ME17 ..... **155** K4
RSEV TN14 ..... **122** D7
RTON TN11 ..... **148** C2
SEV TN13 ..... **123** F3
STPH/PW TN12 ..... **194** E8
Back Rd *HAWK* TN18 ..... **243** J1
SCUP DA14 ..... **38** B2
Back St *RMAID* ME17 ..... **135** G8
Baden Powell Rd *SEV* TN13 ..... **8** A1
Baden Rd *GILL* ME7 ..... **5** D1
Bader Crs *WALD* ME5 ..... **68** B7
Bader Wk *GVW* DA11 ..... **45** F1
Badger Rd *WALD* ME5 ..... **88** D5
Badgers Copse *ORP* BR6 ..... **56** A6
Badgers Holt *RTWE/PEM* TN2 ..... **207** K1
Badgers Ri *RSEV* TN14 ..... **77** H5
Badgers Rd *RSEV* TN14 ..... **77** J5
Badsell Rd *STPH/PW* TN12 ..... **172** D7
Baffin Cl *CHAT* ME4 ..... **3** F6
Bailey Cl *PUR* RM19 ..... **13** H4
Bailey Dr *GILL* ME7 ..... **69** H6
Baker Cl *RSIT* ME9 ..... **95** K3
Baker Hill Cl *GVW* DA11 ..... **45** G2
Baker La *HDCN* TN27 ..... **180** D7
RMAID ME17 ..... **157** H7
Baker Ms *ORP* BR6 ..... **76** A2
Bakers Av *BGR/WK* TN15 ..... **80** D3 1
Bakers Cross *CRBK* TN17 ..... **225** K2
Baker St *ROCH* ME1 ..... **2** C5
ROCH ME1 ..... **86** E5
Baker's Wk *ROCH* ME1 ..... **2** C2
Balaclava La *WADH* TN5 ..... **220** B7
Balcombes Hl *CRBK* TN17 ..... **212** D6
Baldwyn's Pk *BXLY* DA5 ..... **22** A8
Baldwyn's Rd *BXLY* DA5 ..... **22** A8
Balfour Rd *CHAT* ME4 ..... **67** K5
Ballard Cl *STPH/PW* TN12 ..... **176** C8
Ballards La *OXTED* RH8 ..... **119** G8
Ballard Wy *STPH/PW* TN12 ..... **173** K7
Ballens Rd *WALD* ME5 ..... **88** D3
Balmer Cl *RHAM* ME8 ..... **70** A7 1
Balmoral Rd *EYN* DA4 ..... **41** K5
GILL ME7 ..... **5** D3 2
Baltic Rd *TON* TN9 ..... **170** B7
Banbury Vls *MEO* DA13 ..... **44** A4
Banckside *HART* DA3 ..... **61** K1
Bancroft Gdns *ORP* BR6 ..... **56** A5
Bancroft Rd *BGR/WK* TN15 ..... **105** F3
Bangor Rd *STRD* ME2 ..... **48** C8
Bankfields *HDCN* TN27 ..... **200** A1
Bankfield Wy *CRBK* TN17 ..... **212** C7
Bank La *BGR/WK* TN15 ..... **146** E3
Bankside *GVW* DA11 ..... **26** D5
SEV TN13 ..... **101** F8
WALD ME5 ..... **68** C6
Bankside Cl *BH/WHM* TN16 ..... **97** G5 1
RDART DA2 ..... **40** A2
Banks Rd *STRD* ME2 ..... **49** H6
Bank St *CHAT* ME4 ..... **4** B5 1
CRBK TN17 ..... **225** J1
GVE DA12 ..... **27** J5 1
MAID/SHEP ME15 ..... **6** C3
TON TN9 ..... **170** B4
Banky Fields Cl *RHAM* ME8 ..... **70** E5 1
Banky Meadow *MAIDW* ME16 ..... **131** K3
Banner Cl *PUR* RM19 ..... **13** H4
Banner Farm Rd *RTWE/PEM* TN2 ..... **11** D5
Banning St *STRD* ME2 ..... **49** F6
Bannister Gdns *STMC/STPC* BR5 ..... **38** D8 1
Bannister Hl *RSIT* ME9 ..... **93** G4
Bannister Rd *MAID/BEAR* ME14 ..... **111** G7
Bapchild Pl *STMC/STPC* BR5 ..... **56** D1
Barberry Av *WALD* ME5 ..... **87** J1
Barchester Wy *TONN* TN10 ..... **149** F8
Barclay Av *TONN* TN10 ..... **171** F2
Barclay Wy *WTHK* RM20 ..... **13** K5
Barcombe Cl *CHST* BR7 ..... **38** B8 1
Bardell Ter *ROCH* ME1 ..... **3** D3 1
Barden Park Rd *TON* TN9 ..... **170** A5
Barden Rd *RRTW* TN3 ..... **188** D4
TON TN9 ..... **170** A5
Bardsley Cl *STPH/PW* TN12 ..... **151** J7
Barfield *EYN* DA4 ..... **42** A6
Barfleur Mnr *GILL* ME7 ..... **4** A2 1
Barfreston Cl *MAID/SHEP* ME15 ..... **6** C5 1
Bargrove Rd *MAID/BEAR* ME14 ..... **133** K1
Barham Cl *GVE* DA12 ..... **28** C7 1
MAID/SHEP ME15 ..... **156** A1
Barham Rd *DART* DA1 ..... **23** K6
Barham's Mill Rd *HDCN* TN27 ..... **182** B4
Barker Rd *MAIDW* ME16 ..... **6** C4
Barkers Ct *SIT* ME10 ..... **93** J2
Bark Hart Rd *ORP* BR6 ..... **56** C5
Barkis Cl *ROCH* ME1 ..... **67** J7
Barleycorn *E/WMAL* ME19 ..... **108** C5
Barleycorn Dr *RHAM* ME8 ..... **70** B8
Barley Flds *MAID/BEAR* ME14 ..... **133** K2 1
Barleymow Cl *WALD* ME5 ..... **68** D8
Barling Cl *WALD* ME5 ..... **87** H5
Barlow Cl *RHAM* ME8 ..... **90** B1
Barming Rd *E/WMAL* ME19 ..... **130** D4
Barnaby Ter *ROCH* ME1 ..... **2** C6
Barn Cl *RSIT* ME9 ..... **93** F4
Barncroft Cl *MAID/BEAR* ME14 ..... **134** B2 1
Barncroft Dr *GILL* ME7 ..... **89** G2
Barned Ct *MAIDW* ME16 ..... **131** K5
Barn End Dr *RDART* DA2 ..... **41** F2
Barn End La *SWLY* BR8 ..... **41** F4
Barnes Cray Rd *DART* DA1 ..... **22** D3
Barnesdale Crs *STMC/STPC* BR5 ..... **56** B3
Barnes La *RMAID* ME17 ..... **154** D6
Barnes Wk *STPH/PW* TN12 ..... **196** D1
Barnett Cl *ERITH* DA8 ..... **22** C1

Barnetts Cl RTWE/PEM TN2 190 C5
Barnetts Rd RTON TN11 168 E4
Barnett's Shaw OXTED RH8 118 B6
Barnetts Wy STH/RUST TN4 190 C5
Barnfield GVW DA11 27 H8
RTWE/PEM TN2 206 E7
TENT TN30 230 B4
WALD ME5 68 B6
Barnfield Cl GRH DA9 24 E5
HART DA3 44 E8
SWLY BR8 57 K4 1
Barnfield Crs RSEV TN14 102 C4
Barnfield Rd BH/WHM TN16 97 H7
SEV TN13 123 F2
STMC/STPC BR5 38 E8
Barnfield Wy OXTED RH8 140 E4
Barn Hl MAID/SHEP ME15 153 J4
Barnhurst Rd MAID/BEAR ME14 111 G6
Barn Meadow STPH/PW TN12 198 A2 1
STRD ME2 85 H2
Barnsole Rd GILL ME7 5 E4
Barnwell Rd DART DA1 23 J2
Barnwood Cl ROCH ME1 67 G6 1
Baron Cl GILL ME7 5 E1
MAID/BEAR ME14 134 B1 1
Barrack Rd CHAT ME4 50 C6
Barrack Rw GVW DA11 27 H5 1
Barrel Arch Cl STPH/PW TN12 176 C8 1
Barretts Rd HAWK TN18 235 G4
SEV TN13 101 F7
Barrie Dr DIT/AY ME20 108 D2 1
Barrier Rd CHAT ME4 3 F3
Barrington Cl WALD ME5 88 A1
Barrowfields WALD ME5 88 E5
Barrow Green Rd OXTED RH8 118 A8
Barrow Gv SIT ME10 93 J3
Barrow La RRTW TN3 205 J5
Barr Rd GVE DA12 28 C8
Bartholomew Wy SWLY BR8 40 B8
Bartlett Cl WALD ME5 88 D5
Bartlett Rd BH/WHM TN16 120 C5 1
GVW DA11 27 H7
Bartley Mill Rd RRTW TN3 220 A2
Barton Rd EYN DA4 42 A6
MAID/SHEP ME15 7 D5
SCUP DA14 39 F4
STRD ME2 2 A1
Bashford Barn La RSIT ME9 116 A3
Basi Cl STRD ME2 49 H5
Basing Cl MAID/SHEP ME15 7 E4
Basmere Cl MAID/BEAR ME14 7 F1 1
Bassett Rd SIT ME10 93 J2
Bassetts La EDEN TN8 186 E7
Basted La BGR/WK TN15 104 E8
BGR/WK TN15 127 G2
Batchelors RTWE/PEM TN2 192 A6
Batchelor St CHAT ME4 4 A4
Batchwood Gn STMC/STPC BR5 56 B1
Bates Cl DIT/AY ME20 108 E3
Bates Hl BGR/WK TN15 126 C1
Bath Hard ROCH ME1 3 D4
Bath Rd DART DA1 22 E6
Bath St GVW DA11 27 J5 2
Bathurst Cl STPH/PW TN12 198 A2
Bathurst Rd STPH/PW TN12 198 A3
Baton Cl PUR RM19 13 H4
Batteries Cl RSIT ME9 95 J6
Battlefields BGR/WK TN15 105 F3
Battle La STPH/PW TN12 177 F5
Battlesmere Rd HOO/HM ME3 31 G6
Battle St GVE DA12 46 C8
Batt's Rd GVE DA12 64 D2
Baugh Rd SCUP DA14 38 D3
Bay Cl HOO/HM ME3 51 F3 2
Bayford Rd SIT ME10 94 B2
Bayhall Rd RTWE/PEM TN2 11 F4
Bayham Rd RTWE/PEM TN2 207 F6
SEV TN13 9 E2
Bayley's Hl RSEV TN14 145 G3
Bayly Rd DART DA1 23 K5
Bay Manor La WTHK RM20 13 K6
Bayswater Dr RHAM ME8 90 B2
Baywell DIT/AY ME20 108 C5
E/WMAL ME19 108 C4
Bazes Shaw HART DA3 62 A6
Beacon Cl RHAM ME8 70 A7
Beacon Dr RDART DA2 43 H1
Beaconfields SEV TN13 8 B5
Beacon Hl PUR RM19 13 F5
WALD ME5 5 D6
Beacon Hill La HOO/HM ME3 50 A2
Beacon Oak Rd TENT TN30 230 B6
Beacon Ri SEV TN13 8 C5
Beacon Rd RMAID ME17 160 C1
WALD ME5 4 C6
Beaconsfield Av GILL ME7 5 D3
Beaconsfield Rd BXLY DA5 22 B8
CHAT ME4 3 F6
MAID/SHEP ME15 6 B5 1
SIT ME10 94 D3
The Beacons RMAID ME17 154 C4 1
Beadles La OXTED RH8 140 B1
Beagles Cl STMC/STPC BR5 56 E6
Beagles Wood Rd
RTWE/PEM TN2 192 A7 1
Beales La RYE TN31 244 E8
Beaman Cl CRBK TN17 212 E6
Beamish Rd STMC/STPC BR5 56 D4
The Beams MAID/SHEP ME15 134 A5
Bean La RDART DA2 25 G8
RDART DA2 43 G1
Bean Rd GRH DA9 25 G5
Bearsted Cl RHAM ME8 69 J3
Bearsted Rd MAID/BEAR ME14 111 J7
Beaton Cl GRH DA9 25 G3
Beatrice Gdns GVW DA11 27 F8
Beatrice Rd OXTED RH8 118 C7
Beatty Av GILL ME7 5 F5
Beatty Rd ROCH ME1 67 J6
Beaufighter Rd E/WMAL ME19 129 G3
Beaufort Rd STRD ME2 48 D6
Beaufort Wk MAID/SHEP ME15 156 A2
Beaulieu Ri ROCH ME1 67 J5
Beaulieu Rd TONN TN10 170 B2
Beaumont Dr GVW DA11 27 F6
Beaumont Rd GVW DA11 27 F6
MAIDW ME16 132 B4
Beau Nash Wy RTWE/PEM TN2 11 D6 1
Beauworth Pk MAID/SHEP ME15 134 A6
Beaver Rd MAIDW ME16 110 B7
Beblets Cl ORP BR6 76 A1
Beckenham Dr MAIDW ME16 110 D7
Becket Ct HDCN TN27 200 B1
Beckets Fld RTON TN11 187 J3
Becketts Cl ORP BR6 56 A7
Beckley Cl GVE DA12 28 E8 1
Beckley Ms WALD ME5 88 A1
Beckman Cl RSEV TN14 100 E2
Becksbourne Cl
MAID/BEAR ME14 111 G6 1
Becks Rd SCUP DA14 38 B1
Beddington Gn STMC/STPC BR5 38 A6
Beddlestead La WARL CR6 96 D5
Beddow Wy DIT/AY ME20 110 B4
Bedens Rd SCUP DA14 39 F4
Bedford Av RHAM ME8 70 A5
Bedford Pl MAIDW ME16 6 B3
Bedford Rd DART DA1 23 K6
GVW DA11 27 G8
ORP BR6 56 C6
STH/RUST TN4 190 A5
Bedgebury Cl MAID/BEAR ME14 7 F1
ROCH ME1 67 J6
Bedgebury Cross CRBK TN17 223 G4
Bedgebury Rd CRBK TN17 223 H3
Bedlam La HDCN TN27 201 G1
Bedson Wk RHAM ME8 70 E5 2
Bedwin Cl ROCH ME1 67 J7
Beecham Rd TONN TN10 148 E8
Beech Av BH/WHM TN16 97 H6
SWLY BR8 58 C1
Beech Dr MAIDW ME16 132 C1
Beechen Bank Rd WALD ME5 88 B5
Beechenlea La SWLY BR8 58 D1
The Beeches DIT/AY ME20 109 J5
MEO DA13 64 A1
TIL RM18 27 J1
WALD ME5 88 B2 1
Beech Farm Rd WARL CR6 96 B7
Beech Gv HOO/HM ME3 48 A3
SOCK/AV RM15 13 G2
Beech Hurst RTWE/PEM TN2 191 K7 1
Beech Hurst Cl MAID/SHEP ME15 7 E5
Beeching Rd WALD ME5 88 C3 1
Beechings Gn RHAM ME8 69 K3
Beechings Wy RHAM ME8 69 H2
Beechin Wood La BGR/WK TN15 127 J1
Beechlands Cl HART DA3 62 B2
Beech La HAWK TN18 245 F3
STPH/PW TN12 209 K3
Beechmont Ri TONN TN10 148 B8 1
Beechmont Rd SEV TN13 123 K8
Beechmore Dr WALD ME5 88 B4 1
Beech Rd BH/WHM TN16 97 G4
DART DA1 23 G7
E/WMAL ME19 108 D7
HOO/HM ME3 51 F3 3
ORP BR6 76 B3
SEV TN13 9 D4
STPH/PW TN12 195 K3
STRD ME2 48 E8
WBY/YAL ME18 129 F4
Beech St RTW TN1 11 D2
Beech Wk DART DA1 22 D3
Beechwood Av ORP BR6 75 K2
SIT ME10 73 K8
WALD ME5 5 D6
Beechwood Dr MEO DA13 83 H5
Beechwood Gdns MEO DA13 83 H5
Beechwood Ms RTWE/PEM TN2 207 K2
Beechwood Rd MAIDW ME16 131 K3
Beechy Lees Rd RSEV TN14 102 B4
Beesfield La EYN DA4 59 K5
Beggars La BH/WHM TN16 120 D4
Begonia Av RHAM ME8 69 K4
Beke Rd RHAM ME8 90 A2
Beldam Haw RSEV TN14 77 H6
Belfield Rd RTWE/PEM TN2 191 K8
Belgrave Cl STMC/STPC BR5 56 D1
Belgrave Rd RTW TN1 10 C3 1
Belgrave St DIT/AY ME20 86 E
Bell Cl GRH DA9 24 E
Bell Crs ROCH ME1 86 E
Bellefield Rd STMC/STPC BR5 56 C
Belle Friday Cl RSIT ME9 95 K
Belle Vue Rd ORP BR6 75 F
Bell Farm Gdns MAIDW ME16 131 K4
Bell Gdns STMC/STPC BR5 56 D
Bellgrove Ct WALD ME5 88 B6
Bellingham Wy DIT/AY ME20 109 F
Bell La DIT/AY ME20 109 F
HDCN TN27 200 D
MAID/BEAR ME14 88 B
MAID/BEAR ME14 134 C
ROCH ME1 86 E
STPH/PW TN12 198 A
Bellman Av GVE DA12 28 B
Bellmeadow MAID/SHEP ME15 134 A
Bell Rd MAID/SHEP ME15 156 A
SIT ME10 93 K
Bells Farm Rd STPH/PW TN12 151 F
Bell's La HOO/HM ME3 32 E
Bell Wy RMAID ME17 158 C
Bellwood Ct HOO/HM ME3 33 K
Belmont Cl MAIDW ME16 131 K
Belmont Rd GILL ME7 4 C
SIT ME10 93 K
Belnor Av RSIT ME9 72 D
Beltana Dr GVE DA12 46 B
Belton Rd SCUP DA14 38 B
Beltring Rd STH/RUST TN4 10 C
STPH/PW TN12 173 K
Belvedere Cl GVE DA12 27 K7
Belvedere Rd BH/WHM TN16 97 K
Benden Cl STPH/PW TN12 198 B2
Bendon Wy RHAM ME8 70 A
Benedict Cl STRD ME2 86 A2
Benenden Rd CRBK TN17 237 H
HDCN TN27 228 C
STRD ME2 49 H
Benhall Mill Rd RTWE/PEM TN2 207 H
Bennetts Av BGR/WK TN15 81 H
Bennett Wy RDART DA2 42 C
Benover Rd WBY/YAL ME18 152 D
WBY/YAL ME18 175 F
Bensted Cl MAID/SHEP ME15 153 H
Bentham Hl RRTW TN3 189 H
Bentley Cl HART DA3 44 D
WALD ME5 88 E4
Bentley's Meadow BGR/WK TN15 102 D
Bentley St GVE DA12 27 K
Bentlif Cl MAIDW ME16 6 A
Berber Rd STRD ME2 49 G
Berengrave La RHAM ME8 70 B
Berens Rd STMC/STPC BR5 56 D
Berens Wy CHST BR7 56 A
Beresford Av CHAT ME4 3 E
Beresford Rd CRBK TN17 212 E
DIT/AY ME20 87 H
GILL ME7 5 D
GVW DA11 27 F
Beresfords Hl RMAID ME17 155 H
Berkeley Cl ROCH ME1 67 J
RTWE/PEM TN2 192 A
Berkeley Ct SIT ME10 93 J
Berkeley Crs DART DA1 23 J
Berkeley Rd RTW TN1 10 C5
Berkley Rd GVE DA12 27 J5
Berkshire Cl WALD ME5 68 D
Bermuda Rd TIL RM18 27 H
Bernard St GVE DA12 27 J5
Berrylands HART DA3 62 B
ORP BR6 56 D
Berry Rd HOO/HM ME3 51 F3
Berry's Green Rd BH/WHM TN16 98 B
Berry's Hl BH/WHM TN16 98 B
Berry St SIT ME10 94 A
Berwick Wy RSEV TN14 101 K
Berwyn Gv MAID/SHEP ME15 133 G
Bessels Green Rd SEV TN13 123 F
Bessels Meadow SEV TN13 123 F
Best St CHAT ME4 3 F
Beta Rd HOO/HM ME3 34 A
Betenson Av SEV TN13 8 B
Bethel Rd SEV TN13 9 E
Bethersden Rd HDCN TN27 201 K
RASHW TN26 219 K
Betjeman Cl DIT/AY ME20 108 D
Betsham Rd MAID/SHEP ME15 134 B8
MEO DA13 43 J
SWCM DA10 25 K
Bettescombe Rd RHAM ME8 70 A
Beulah Rd RTW TN1 11 E
Beult Meadow HDCN TN27 202 A
Beult Rd DART DA1 22 D
Bevan Pl SWLY BR8 58 C1
Bevans Cl GRH DA9 25 H5
Beverley Cl RHAM ME8 70 C
Beverley Crs TON TN9 169 K
Beverley Rd MAIDW ME16 131 K
Bevis Cl RDART DA2 24 B
Bewl Bridge Cl WADH TN5 233 F
Bewlbridge La RRTW TN3 222 A
Bewley La BGR/WK TN15 126 C
Bexley Cl DART DA1 22 B

Bexley La *DART* DA1 ..... 22 B4
SCUP DA14 ..... 38 D2
Bexon La *RSIT* ME9 ..... 116 C2
Bickley Rd *TON* TN9 ..... 170 B6 2
Bickmore Wy *TON* TN9 ..... 170 C3
Bicknor La *RSIT* ME9 ..... 115 G3
Bicknor Rd *MAID/SHEP* ME15 ..... 156 B2
Bidborough Rdg *STH/RUST* TN4 ..... 189 H2
Biddenden Cl *MAID/SHEP* ME15 ..... 134 B3
Biddenden La *HDCN* TN27 ..... 200 C1
Biddenden Rd *HDCN* TN27 ..... 200 C4
HDCN TN27 ..... 201 J6
HDCN TN27 ..... 218 E8
RASHW TN26 ..... 219 F8
Biddenden Wy *MEO* DA13 ..... 45 F6
Bilberry Cl *MAID/BEAR* ME14 ..... 134 A1 1
Billet Hl *BGR/WK* TN15 ..... 61 H8
Billings *HART* DA3 ..... 62 A3
Bill Street Rd *STRD* ME2 ..... 49 H6
Bilsington Cl *WALD* ME5 ..... 88 C1
Binbury La *MAID/BEAR* ME14 ..... 113 H2
The Bines *STPH/PW* TN12 ..... 193 J1
Bingham Rd *STRD* ME2 ..... 49 H5
Bingley Cl *SNOD* ME6 ..... 85 J6
Bingley Rd *ROCH* ME1 ..... 3 E4
Binland Gv *WALD* ME5 ..... 87 J1
Binnacle Rd *ROCH* ME1 ..... 67 H6
Binney Rd *HOO/HM* ME3 ..... 19 G6
Birch Cl *EYN* DA4 ..... 59 G7
HART DA3 ..... 44 D7
RTON TN11 ..... 169 H2
RTWE/PEM TN2 ..... 190 D7
SEV TN13 ..... 9 D2
STPH/PW TN12 ..... 193 F5
Birch Crs *DIT/AY* ME20 ..... 109 H6
Birch Dr *WALD* ME5 ..... 88 E5
The Birches *SWLY* BR8 ..... 40 B7
TON TN9 ..... 170 B7 1
Birchetts Av *RRTW* TN3 ..... 205 H3 1
Birchfield Cl *MAID/SHEP* ME15 ..... 133 H8
Birchfields *WALD* ME5 ..... 88 B3
Birch Gv *GILL* ME7 ..... 89 H1
Birchin Cross Rd *RSEV* TN14 ..... 102 C2
Birchington Cl *MAID/BEAR* ME14 ..... 7 F2 1
Bircholt Rd *MAID/SHEP* ME15 ..... 156 B2
Birch Pl *GRH* DA9 ..... 24 D5
Birch Rd *HOO/HM* ME3 ..... 51 F3
STPH/PW TN12 ..... 173 J8
Birch Tree Wy *MAID/SHEP* ME15 ..... 7 E4
Birchway *BGR/WK* TN15 ..... 80 E4 2
Birch Wy *RTWE/PEM* TN2 ..... 190 D7
Birchwood Av *SCUP* DA14 ..... 38 C1
STH/RUST TN4 ..... 189 J3
Birchwood Dr *RDART* DA2 ..... 40 B2
Birchwood La *RSEV* TN14 ..... 100 B2
Birchwood Park Av *SWLY* BR8 ..... 40 B8
Birchwood Rd *MAIDW* ME16 ..... 132 C1
RDART DA2 ..... 39 K5
Bird House La *ORP* BR6 ..... 98 A1
Bird In Hand St *RRTW* TN3 ..... 205 F6 1
Birkbeck Rd *SCUP* DA14 ..... 38 B1
Birken Rd *RTWE/PEM* TN2 ..... 11 F1
Birkhall Cl *WALD* ME5 ..... 88 B1
Birling Av *MAID/BEAR* ME14 ..... 134 C2
RHAM ME8 ..... 70 A5
Birling Cl *MAID/BEAR* ME14 ..... 134 B2
Birling Dr *RTWE/PEM* TN2 ..... 207 F6
Birling Hl *MEO* DA13 ..... 84 D5
Birling Pk *E/WMAL* ME19 ..... 108 A1
Birling Park Av *RTWE/PEM* TN2 ..... 207 G6
Birling Rd *E/WMAL* ME19 ..... 107 J2
RTWE/PEM TN2 ..... 207 G6
SNOD ME6 ..... 85 J7
Birling Road Rookery Hl
SNOD ME6 ..... 85 J7
Birnam Sq *MAIDW* ME16 ..... 6 B3 1
Birtrick Dr *MEO* DA13 ..... 63 G2
Bishop Butt Cl *ORP* BR6 ..... 56 A7 2
Bishop La *RSIT* ME9 ..... 71 H3
Bishops Cl *WBY/YAL* ME18 ..... 130 A8
Bishops Ct *GRH* DA9 ..... 24 D4
Bishop's Down *STH/RUST* TN4 ..... 10 A4
Bishop's Down Park Rd
STH/RUST TN4 ..... 10 A3
Bishop's Down Rd
STH/RUST TN4 ..... 10 A4
Bishops La *CRBK* TN17 ..... 224 E4
MAID/SHEP ME15 ..... 153 H7
Bishops Ms *TON* TN9 ..... 170 C6 1
Bishops Oak Ride *TONN* TN10 ..... 148 B8
Bishops Wk *ROCH* ME1 ..... 2 C3
Bishops Wy *MAIDW* ME16 ..... 6 C3
Blackberry Fld *STMC/STPC* BR5 ..... 38 B6 1
Blackberry Wy *STPH/PW* TN12 ..... 173 J8
Black Eagle Cl *BH/WHM* TN16 ..... 120 C6
Blackhall La *BGR/WK* TN15 ..... 124 C2
Black Horse Ms *BGR/WK* TN15 ..... 105 G8
Black Horse Rd *SCUP* DA14 ..... 38 B2 1
Blackhurst La *RTWE/PEM* TN2 ..... 191 G7
Blacklands *E/WMAL* ME19 ..... 108 D6
Blacklands Dr *E/WMAL* ME19 ..... 108 D6
Blackman Cl *HOO/HM* ME3 ..... 32 E7
Blackmans Cl *DART* DA1 ..... 23 F7 1
Blackman's La *RTON* TN11 ..... 149 K7
Blackmanstone Wy *DIT/AY* ME20 ..... 110 B7
Blackmead *SEV* TN13 ..... 101 G8
Black Mill La *HDCN* TN27 ..... 199 K1
Blackness La *HAYES* BR2 ..... 74 C4
Black Rock Gdns *GILL* ME7 ..... 89 J2 1
Blacksmith Dr
MAID/BEAR ME14 ..... 133 K1 1
Blacksmiths La *STMC/STPC* BR5 ..... 56 D2
Blacksole La *BGR/WK* TN15 ..... 105 F3
Blacksole Rd *BGR/WK* TN15 ..... 105 F3 1
Blackthorn Av *RTWE/PEM* TN2 ..... 190 C5
WALD ME5 ..... 88 B3
Blackthorn Cl *BGR/WK* TN15 ..... 80 E4 3
Blackthorn Dr *DIT/AY* ME20 ..... 109 F4
Blackthorne Rd *RHAM* ME8 ..... 70 D6
Blackthorn Rd *BH/WHM* TN16 ..... 97 J3 1
Blair Dr *SEV* TN13 ..... 9 D2
Blake Dr *DIT/AY* ME20 ..... 108 D2
Blake Gdns *DART* DA1 ..... 23 J3
Blakeney Cl *MAID/BEAR* ME14 ..... 134 D2
Blaker Av *ROCH* ME1 ..... 67 K5
Blake Wy *RTWE/PEM* TN2 ..... 190 D7
Blandford Gdns *SIT* ME10 ..... 93 K5
Blatchford Cl *E/WMAL* ME19 ..... 108 D5 1
Blatchington Rd *RTW* TN1 ..... 10 C6
Bleakwood Rd *WALD* ME5 ..... 88 A1
Blean Rd *RHAM* ME8 ..... 69 K4
Blendon Rd *MAID/BEAR* ME14 ..... 7 F2
Blenheim Av *CHAT* ME4 ..... 3 E6
Blenheim Cl *DART* DA1 ..... 23 F5
MAID/SHEP ME15 ..... 134 B3
MEO DA13 ..... 63 J6 1
Blenheim Gdns *SOCK/AV* RM15 ..... 13 F1
Blenheim Gv *GVE* DA12 ..... 27 K6 2
Blenheim Rd *DART* DA1 ..... 23 F5
E/WMAL ME19 ..... 129 H3
ORP BR6 ..... 56 D6
Blenheim Wy *WADH* TN5 ..... 233 G3
Bligh Rd *GVW* DA11 ..... 27 H5
Bligh's Rd *SEV* TN13 ..... 9 D4
Bligh Wy *STRD* ME2 ..... 48 B8
Blind La *CRBK* TN17 ..... 212 D5
GILL ME7 ..... 89 G5
Blind Mary's La *RSIT* ME9 ..... 115 J2
Bliss Wy *TONN* TN10 ..... 170 E1
Blockmakers Ct *CHAT* ME4 ..... 68 C5
Bloors La *RHAM* ME8 ..... 70 A5
Bloors Wharf Rd *GILL* ME7 ..... 70 B2
Blowers Grove Wd *GILL* ME7 ..... 89 J3
Blowers Hl *EDEN* TN8 ..... 185 K6
Bluebell Cl *GILL* ME7 ..... 5 F2
Bluebell Wks *STPH/PW* TN12 ..... 173 J8
Blueberry La *RSEV* TN14 ..... 99 J3
Blue Boar La *ROCH* ME1 ..... 3 D3
Blue Coat La *CRBK* TN17 ..... 212 B7
Bluehouse Gdns *OXTED* RH8 ..... 118 E7
Bluehouse La *OXTED* RH8 ..... 118 C7
Bluett St *MAID/BEAR* ME14 ..... 7 D2
Bluewater Pkwy *GRH* DA9 ..... 24 E6
Blunden La *WBY/YAL* ME18 ..... 152 E5
Blythe Hl *STMC/STPC* BR5 ..... 38 A6
Blythe Rd *MAID/SHEP* ME15 ..... 7 E3
Boakes Meadow *RSEV* TN14 ..... 78 C6
Boarders La *WADH* TN5 ..... 232 A3
Boarley La *MAID/BEAR* ME14 ..... 111 F5
Bobbing Hl *RSIT* ME9 ..... 93 F1
Bockingford La *MAID/SHEP* ME15 ..... 132 E6
Bodiam Cl *RHAM* ME8 ..... 69 K4
Bodiam Rd *HAWK* TN18 ..... 243 G4
Bodle Av *SWCM* DA10 ..... 25 K5
Bodmin Cl *STMC/STPC* BR5 ..... 56 D5
Bodsham Crs *MAID/SHEP* ME15 ..... 134 D3
Bogle Rd *RSIT* ME9 ..... 95 K7
Boley Hl *ROCH* ME1 ..... 2 C2
Boleyn Rd *RSEV* TN14 ..... 102 C4
Boleyn Wy *SWCM* DA10 ..... 25 K6
Bolner Cl *WALD* ME5 ..... 88 A4
Bombers La *BH/WHM* TN16 ..... 98 D7
Bonaventure Ct *GVE* DA12 ..... 46 C2
Bond Cl *RSEV* TN14 ..... 99 K2
Bondfield Cl *STH/RUST* TN4 ..... 190 A5
Bondfield Rd *E/WMAL* ME19 ..... 108 D6
Bond Rd *RHAM* ME8 ..... 90 B2
Boneashe La *BGR/WK* TN15 ..... 105 K8
Bonflower La *RMAID* ME17 ..... 154 C7
Bonham Dr *SIT* ME10 ..... 94 B1
Bonney Wy *SWLY* BR8 ..... 40 B7
Bonnington Rd *MAID/BEAR* ME14 ..... 7 F1
Bootham Cl *STRD* ME2 ..... 66 C2
Booth Rd *CHAT* ME4 ..... 3 F6
Borden La *RSIT* ME9 ..... 93 G4
Bordyke *TON* TN9 ..... 170 C4
Borkwood Pk *ORP* BR6 ..... 56 A8
Borland Cl *GRH* DA9 ..... 25 F4 1
Borough Green Rd *BGR/WK* TN15 ..... 104 D8
Borough Rd *BH/WHM* TN16 ..... 97 H8
GILL ME7 ..... 5 D4
Borstal Rd *ROCH* ME1 ..... 2 B5
Borstal St *ROCH* ME1 ..... 2 A6
Bostall Rd *STMC/STPC* BR5 ..... 38 C5
Boston Gdns *RHAM* ME8 ..... 69 K5
Boston Rd *WALD* ME5 ..... 88 C4
Bosville Dr *SEV* TN13 ..... 8 C2
Bosville Rd *SEV* TN13 ..... 8 C2
Boswell Cl *STMC/STPC* BR5 ..... 56 D3 1
Botany *TON* TN9 ..... 170 C5
Botany Wy *PUR* RM19 ..... 13 F5
Botsom La *BGR/WK* TN15 ..... 80 B2
Bottlescrew Hl *RMAID* ME17 ..... 155 H2
Bottles La *RSIT* ME9 ..... 117 G1
Bottom Pond Rd *RSIT* ME9 ..... 116 E2
Bott Rd *RDART* DA2 ..... 41 J2
Boucher Dr *GVW* DA11 ..... 45 G1
Boughton La *MAID/SHEP* ME15 ..... 133 H7
Boughton Rd *RMAID* ME17 ..... 160 B5
Boulthurst Wy *OXTED* RH8 ..... 140 E3
Boundary Rd *ROCH* ME1 ..... 3 E5
RTWE/PEM TN2 ..... 11 F6
The Boundary *RRTW* TN3 ..... 206 A3
Bounds Oak Wy *STH/RUST* TN4 ..... 189 J3
The Bounds *DIT/AY* ME20 ..... 109 J5
Bourne Cl *TON* TN9 ..... 170 D3
Bourne Grange La *RTON* TN11 ..... 149 K6
Bourne Gv *SIT* ME10 ..... 93 H1
Bourne La *BGR/WK* TN15 ..... 127 F4
RBTBR TN32 ..... 242 A6
TON TN9 ..... 170 C3
Bourne Pk *RTON* TN11 ..... 172 B1
Bourne Rd *GVE* DA12 ..... 28 C8
Bourne V *BGR/WK* TN15 ..... 127 G6
Bourne Wy *SWLY* BR8 ..... 39 K8
Bournewood Cl *MAID/SHEP* ME15 ..... 134 B5
Bournewood Rd *STMC/STPC* BR5 ..... 56 C4
Bournville Av *CHAT* ME4 ..... 68 A5
Bow Arrow La *DART* DA1 ..... 23 K5
RDART DA2 ..... 24 A5
Bowen Rd *STH/RUST* TN4 ..... 206 A1
Bower Cl *MAIDW* ME16 ..... 6 B3
Bowerland La *LING* RH7 ..... 162 B6
Bower La *EYN* DA4 ..... 59 H7
EYN DA4 ..... 79 K3
MAIDW ME16 ..... 6 B5
Bower Mount Rd *MAIDW* ME16 ..... 6 A4
Bower Pl *MAIDW* ME16 ..... 6 B4
Bower Rd *SWLY* BR8 ..... 40 D5
Bowers Av *GVW* DA11 ..... 45 G2
Bowers Rd *RSEV* TN14 ..... 78 C6
Bower St *MAIDW* ME16 ..... 6 B3
Bowesden La *GVE* DA12 ..... 47 J5
STRD ME2 ..... 47 J6
Bowes Rd *STRD* ME2 ..... 49 G6
Bowes Wd *HART* DA3 ..... 62 A7
Bow Hl *WBY/YAL* ME18 ..... 152 C1
Bowley La *RMAID* ME17 ..... 160 E6
Bowls Pl *STPH/PW* TN12 ..... 173 J7 1
Bowman Cl *WALD* ME5 ..... 88 D1
Bowmans Rd *DART* DA1 ..... 22 C6
Bown Cl *TIL* RM18 ..... 27 J1 1
Bow Rd *WBY/YAL* ME18 ..... 130 C7
Bow Ter *WBY/YAL* ME18 ..... 130 C7
Bowzell Rd *RSEV* TN14 ..... 145 H4
Boxley Cl *MAID/BEAR* ME14 ..... 111 H6
Boxley Rd *MAID/BEAR* ME14 ..... 7 D1
MAID/BEAR ME14 ..... 88 D7
WALD ME5 ..... 88 C5
Boxted La *RSIT* ME9 ..... 71 K5
Boyces Hl *RSIT* ME9 ..... 72 C8
Boy Court La *HDCN* TN27 ..... 180 C5
Boyne Pk *STH/RUST* TN4 ..... 10 B3
Boyton Court Rd *RMAID* ME17 ..... 179 J1
Brabourne Av *RHAM* ME8 ..... 69 K2
Bracken Cl *RTWE/PEM* TN2 ..... 207 K1 1
Brackendene *BXLY* DA5 ..... 40 B2
Bracken Hl *WALD* ME5 ..... 88 B5
Bracken Lea *WALD* ME5 ..... 68 D5
Bracken Rd *RTWE/PEM* TN2 ..... 207 K1
The Brackens *ORP* BR6 ..... 76 B1
Bracken Wk *TONN* TN10 ..... 148 B8
Brackley Cl *MAID/BEAR* ME14 ..... 7 F2
Brackwood Cl *RHAM* ME8 ..... 90 A1 1
Bracondale Av *MEO* DA13 ..... 45 G6 1
Bradbourne La *DIT/AY* ME20 ..... 109 F5
Bradbourne Park Rd *SEV* TN13 ..... 8 C2
Bradbourne Pkwy *DIT/AY* ME20 ..... 108 E5
Bradbourne Rd *SEV* TN13 ..... 9 D1
Bradbourne Vale Rd *SEV* TN13 ..... 8 B1
Braddick Cl *MAID/SHEP* ME15 ..... 155 H1
Bradfields Av *WALD* ME5 ..... 68 A8
Bradfields Av West *WALD* ME5 ..... 88 A1 1
Bradford St *TON* TN9 ..... 170 B5 1
Bradley Dr *SIT* ME10 ..... 93 K4
Bradley Rd *RRTW* TN3 ..... 204 A1
STRD ME2 ..... 85 H1
Bradshaw Cl *RSIT* ME9 ..... 71 H3
Braeside Av *SEV* TN13 ..... 8 B3
Braeside Cl *SEV* TN13 ..... 8 B2
The Braes *HOO/HM* ME3 ..... 48 B3
Brake Av *WALD* ME5 ..... 87 K1
Brakefield Rd *MEO* DA13 ..... 44 C4
Brakes Pl *BGR/WK* TN15 ..... 80 D2
Bramble Av *RDART* DA2 ..... 43 H1
Bramble Bank *MEO* DA13 ..... 83 G7 1
Bramble Cl *MAIDW* ME16 ..... 132 B3
RTON TN11 ..... 169 K2
Brambledown *HART* DA3 ..... 62 A1
WALD ME5 ..... 68 C6
Bramblefield Cl *HART* DA3 ..... 43 J8
Bramblefield La *SIT* ME10 ..... 73 K5
Bramble La *SEV* TN13 ..... 123 K7
Bramble Reed La *STPH/PW* TN12 ..... 192 D7
Brambletree Crs *ROCH* ME1 ..... 66 E4

Bramley Cl *MEO* DA13 45 G5 1
RHAM ME8 70 E6 1
SWLY BR8 58 B1
Bramley Ct *STPH/PW* TN12 176 B8
Bramley Crs *MAID/SHEP* ME15 134 B3
Bramley Dr *CRBK* TN17 225 K2
Bramley Gdns *RMAID* ME17 154 D3
STPH/PW TN12 173 G7
Bramley Pl *DART* DA1 22 D3
Bramley Ri *STRD* ME2 48 D6
Bramley Rd *SNOD* ME6 85 K6
STPH/PW TN12 151 H8 1
Bramleys *HDCN* TN27 200 B1 1
Bramley Wy *WBY/YAL* ME18 129 J4
Bramshott Cl *MAIDW* ME16 110 C8 1
Branbridges Rd *STPH/PW* TN12 173 K1
Brandon Rd *DART* DA1 23 K6
Brandon St *GVW* DA11 27 J6
Brands Hatch Rd *BGR/WK* TN15 61 F7
Bransell Cl *SWLY* BR8 57 K3
Bransgore Cl *RHAM* ME8 70 A7
Brantingham Cl *TON* TN9 169 K7 1
Branton Rd *GRH* DA9 24 E5
Brantwood Wy *STMC/STPC* BR5 38 D8
Brasenose Rd *GILL* ME7 5 E5
Brassey Dr *DIT/AY* ME20 109 H6
Brassey Hl *OXTED* RH8 118 E8
OXTED RH8 140 E1
Brassey Rd *OXTED* RH8 118 E8
Brasted Ct *STRD* ME2 49 F5
Brasted Hl *RSEV* TN14 99 G7
Brasted Hill Rd *BH/WHM* TN16 121 J1
Brasted La *RSEV* TN14 99 G6
Brasted Rd *BH/WHM* TN16 120 E5
Brattle Wd *SEV* TN13 124 A8
Braunstone Dr *MAIDW* ME16 110 D7
Bray Gdns *MAID/SHEP* ME15 155 F1
Breach La *RSIT* ME9 71 J6
Breach Rd *WTHK* RM20 13 K6
Breakneck Hl *GRH* DA9 25 G4
Breakspears Dr *STMC/STPC* BR5 38 B6
Bredgar Cl *MAID/BEAR* ME14 7 E2
Bredgar Rd *RHAM* ME8 69 H2
Bredhurst Rd *RHAM* ME8 89 J3
Breedon Av *STH/RUST* TN4 189 K5 1
Bremner Cl *SWLY* BR8 58 D1 1
Brenchley Av *GVW* DA11 45 J3
Brenchley Cl *ROCH* ME1 3 D6
Brenchley Rd *MAID/SHEP* ME15 6 C5
RHAM ME8 69 J4
SIT ME10 94 A4
STPH/PW TN12 193 G5
STPH/PW TN12 211 J1
Brendon Av *WALD* ME5 88 B2
Brendon Cl *RTWE/PEM* TN2 11 F2 2
Brennan Rd *TIL* RM18 27 J1
Brent Cl *RDART* DA2 24 A5
WALD ME5 87 K1
Brentfield Rd *DART* DA1 23 K5
Brentlands Dr *DART* DA1 23 K7
Brent La *DART* DA1 23 J6
The Brent *DART* DA1 24 A6
TONN TN10 148 C8
Brent Wy *DART* DA1 24 A5
Brenzett Cl *WALD* ME5 88 C1
Bretland Rd *STH/RUST* TN4 206 C2
Breton Rd *ROCH* ME1 2 C6
Brevet Cl *PUR* RM19 13 H4
Brewer Rd *HOO/HM* ME3 31 G7
Brewers Fld *RDART* DA2 41 F2
Brewers Rd *GVE* DA12 47 F6
Brewer St *MAID/BEAR* ME14 7 D2
RRTW TN3 221 J1
Brewery Rd *SIT* ME10 73 K8
Brewhouse Yd *GVE* DA12 27 J5 5
Brian Crs *STH/RUST* TN4 190 B6
Briar Cl *DIT/AY* ME20 108 E4
Briar Dl *HOO/HM* ME3 48 A3
Briar Flds *MAID/BEAR* ME14 134 A1
Briar Rd *BXLY* DA5 40 A1
The Briars *BGR/WK* TN15 80 C2
Briars Wy *HART* DA3 62 B2
Briarswood Wy *ORP* BR6 76 A1
Briar Wk *TONN* TN10 148 C8
Briary Ct *SCUP* DA14 38 C3
Brice Rd *HOO/HM* ME3 48 A3
Brickenden Rd *CRBK* TN17 225 K2
Brickfields *E/WMAL* ME19 107 K5
RTWE/PEM TN2 192 A6
Brick Field Vw *STRD* ME2 49 H5
Brick Kiln La *OXTED* RH8 141 G1
RMAID ME17 180 B1
STPH/PW TN12 211 K5
Brickworks Cl *TON* TN9 170 A7
Bridewell La *TENT* TN30 230 A7
Bridge Cl *GRH* DA9 24 C2
TON TN9 170 C6
Bridge Mill Wy *MAID/SHEP* ME15 6 A5
Bridge Rd *GILL* ME7 4 C1
ROCH ME1 2 C6
STMC/STPC BR5 56 C3
Bridges Dr *DART* DA1 24 A4
Bridge St *MAID/SHEP* ME15 155 F1
Bridgewater Pl *E/WMAL* ME19 108 C4
Bridlington Cl *BH/WHM* TN16 97 F6
Brier Cl *WALD* ME5 68 D6
Brier Rd *SIT* ME10 93 F1
Brightlands *GVW* DA11 45 F2 1
Bright Rdg *STH/RUST* TN4 189 J6
Bright Rd *CHAT* ME4 4 B6
Brimfield Rd *PUR* RM19 13 H4
The Brimp *HOO/HM* ME3 19 G5
Brimstone Cl *ORP* BR6 76 D3
Brimstone Hl *MEO* DA13 63 K6
Brindle's Fld *TON* TN9 169 K7
Brindle Wy *WALD* ME5 88 D5
Brionne Gdns *TON* TN9 170 D6
Brisbane Av *SIT* ME10 93 H2
Brisbane Rd *CHAT* ME4 4 A5
Brishing Cl *MAID/SHEP* ME15 156 A1 1
Brishing La *MAID/SHEP* ME15 156 A1
RMAID ME17 155 K3
Brishing Rd *RMAID* ME17 156 A2
Brissenden Cl *STRD* ME2 50 B3
Bristol Cl *STRD* ME2 66 C1
Bristol Rd *GVE* DA12 46 A1
Britannia Cl *SIT* ME10 73 K7
STRD ME2 85 K2 2
Britannia Dr *GVE* DA12 46 C3
Brittains La *SEV* TN13 8 B3
Britten Cl *TONN* TN10 149 F8
Britton St *GILL* ME7 4 B3
Broadcloth *CRBK* TN17 225 K3
Broadcroft *RTWE/PEM* TN2 206 E6
Broad Ditch Rd *MEO* DA13 44 D5
Broader La *MAID/BEAR* ME14 112 D4
Broadfield Rd *MAID/SHEP* ME15 133 G6
Broad Gv *RTWE/PEM* TN2 10 C6 1
Broadham Green Rd *OXTED* RH8 140 B4
Broadham Pl *OXTED* RH8 140 B3
Broadlands Dr *WALD* ME5 88 C2
Broad La *RDART* DA2 40 E2
RRTW TN3 204 D3
Broadmead *RTWE/PEM* TN2 206 D6
Broadmead Av *RTWE/PEM* TN2 206 E6 1
Broadoak *E/WMAL* ME19 108 B4 1
Broad Oak *RRTW* TN3 204 E8
STPH/PW TN12 194 A6
Broadoak Av *MAID/SHEP* ME15 133 G6
Broadoak Cl *RDART* DA2 41 K4
Broad Oak Cl *RTWE/PEM* TN2 10 B6
STMC/STPC BR5 38 B7
STPH/PW TN12 194 A6
Broadoak Rd *RSIT* ME9 93 J7
Broad Rd *SWCM* DA10 25 K5
Broad St *RMAID* ME17 157 G7
Broad Street Hl *RMAID* ME17 114 B7
Broadview Av *RHAM* ME8 70 B6
Broad Wk *BGR/WK* TN15 124 C7
ORP BR6 56 E7
Broadwater Down
RTWE/PEM TN2 206 E6
Broadwater La *RTWE/PEM* TN2 10 B6
Broadwater Ri *RTWE/PEM* TN2 10 B6
Broadwater Rd *E/WMAL* ME19 108 B8
Broadway *MAIDW* ME16 6 C4
RHAM ME8 69 H4
TIL RM18 27 G1 2
The Broadway *RRTW* TN3 221 K1
Broadwood *GVW* DA11 45 J3 1
Broadwood Rd *HOO/HM* ME3 50 A2
Brockenhurst Av *MAID/SHEP* ME15 7 E6
Brockenhurst Cl *RHAM* ME8 69 K7
Brockway *BGR/WK* TN15 105 G8
Brockwell Cl *STMC/STPC* BR5 56 A2
Brogden Crs *RMAID* ME17 135 H7
Broke Farm Dr *ORP* BR6 76 D4
Brokes Wy *STH/RUST* TN4 190 C5
Bromford Cl *OXTED* RH8 140 E4
Bromley Cl *WALD* ME5 88 C2
Brompton Farm Rd *STRD* ME2 48 E5
Brompton Hl *CHAT* ME4 3 F2
Brompton La *STRD* ME2 49 F6
Brompton Rd *GILL* ME7 4 B2
Bronington Cl *WALD* ME5 88 B1
Bronte Cl *DIT/AY* ME20 108 D3
TIL RM18 27 K1 2
Bronte Gv *DART* DA1 23 J3
Bronte Vw *GVE* DA12 27 K7
Brook *CHAT* ME4 4 A4
Brookbank *MAID/BEAR* ME14 111 G6
Brooke Dr *GVE* DA12 28 E7
Brookes Pl *RSIT* ME9 72 A8
Brookfield *RSEV* TN14 102 C4
Brookfield Av *DIT/AY* ME20 108 E2
Brookfields *RTON* TN11 150 A5
Brook Hl *OXTED* RH8 140 A1
Brookhurst Gdns *STH/RUST* TN4 189 J3
Brooklands *DART* DA1 23 H7
HDCN TN27 180 A8
RTWE/PEM TN2 190 D7 1
Brooklands Farm Cl *RRTW* TN3 187 J8
Brooklands Rd *DIT/AY* ME20 108 E3
Brook La *BGR/WK* TN15 127 G6
SNOD ME6 85 K8
TON TN9 170 D4
Brooklyn Paddock *GILL* ME7 5 D2 1
Brookmead *RTON* TN11 169 J2
Brookmead Cl *ORP* BR6 56 C4 1
Brookmead Rd *HOO/HM* ME3 31 G7
Brookmead Wy *ORP* BR6 56 C3
Brook Rd *DIT/AY* ME20 108 C2
GVW DA11 27 F7
RTWE/PEM TN2 190 C7
SWLY BR8 40 A8
Brooks Cl *STPH/PW* TN12 198 A2
Brookside *CRBK* TN17 225 K2
HOO/HM ME3 51 F1
ORP BR6 56 A4
Brookside Rd *MEO* DA13 45 G5
Brooks Pl *MAID/BEAR* ME14 7 D3 1
Brook St *RASHW* TN26 231 J6
SNOD ME6 86 A6
TON TN9 169 K6
Broom Av *STMC/STPC* BR5 38 C7
Broom Bank *WARL* CR6 96 A6
Broomcroft Rd *RHAM* ME8 70 C4
Broome Pl *SOCK/AV* RM15 13 H1 1
Broomes Ct *RMAID* ME17 158 A6
Broomfield Rd *RMAID* ME17 158 A3
SEV TN13 8 B1
SWCM DA10 25 K5
Broomfields *HART* DA3 61 K2
Broomhill Park Rd *STH/RUST* TN4 189 J6
Broomhill Rd *DART* DA1 22 E5
ORP BR6 56 B4
RRTW TN3 189 H8
Broom Hill Rd *STRD* ME2 48 E6
Broomlands La *OXTED* RH8 119 J6
Broom La *RRTW* TN3 205 J5
Broom Pk *RRTW* TN3 205 H3
Broom Rd *SIT* ME10 94 D1
Broomshaw Rd *MAIDW* ME16 131 K3
Broomwood Cl *BXLY* DA5 22 A8
Broomwood Rd *STMC/STPC* BR5 38 C7
Brow Cl *STMC/STPC* BR5 56 E4
Brow Crs *STMC/STPC* BR5 56 D5
Browndens Rd *STRD* ME2 85 H2
Brownelow Copse *WALD* ME5 88 B5
Brownhill Cl *WALD* ME5 88 B2
Browning Cl *DIT/AY* ME20 108 D2 2
Browning Rd *DART* DA1 23 J3
Brownings *EDEN* TN8 164 C2
Brownings Orch *RSIT* ME9 94 B7
Brown Rd *GVE* DA12 28 B8
Brown St *RHAM* ME8 70 B5
Broxbourne Rd *ORP* BR6 56 A5
Bruce Gv *ORP* BR6 56 B5
The Brucks *WBY/YAL* ME18 130 C7
Brunel Cl *TIL* RM18 27 J1
Brunel Wy *CHAT* ME4 50 B6
Brunswick St *MAID/SHEP* ME15 7 D4 1
Brunswick St East
MAID/SHEP ME15 7 D4
Brunswick Wk *GVE* DA12 28 A5 1
Bryanston Rd *TIL* RM18 27 K1
Bryant Cl *WBY/YAL* ME18 130 B8
Bryant Rd *STRD* ME2 49 F6
Bryant St *CHAT* ME4 3 F5
Bubblestone Rd *RSEV* TN14 101 K3
Bubhurst La *CRBK* TN17 199 K7
Buchanan Cl *SOCK/AV* RM15 13 G1 2
Buckham Thorns Rd
BH/WHM TN16 120 C5
Buckhole Farm Rd *HOO/HM* ME3 32 D2
Buckhurst La *SEV* TN13 9 E4
Buckhurst Rd *BH/WHM* TN16 98 B7
Buckingham Rd *GILL* ME7 5 D3 3
GVW DA11 26 E6 1
RTW TN1 11 D5
Buckingham Rw
MAID/SHEP ME15 134 A7
Buckland Cl *WALD* ME5 88 B4 2
Buckland Hl *MAIDW* ME16 6 B2
Buckland La *MAIDW* ME16 6 A1
Buckland Rd *HOO/HM* ME3 30 E7
MAIDW ME16 6 B3
MEO DA13 64 D7
Bucklers Cl *RTWE/PEM* TN2 11 E4 1
Buckley Cl *DART* DA1 22 C1
Bucks Cross Rd *GVW* DA11 45 G1
ORP BR6 77 F1
Budd's La *TENT* TN30 247 K4
Budgin's Hl *ORP* BR6 76 C7
Bugglesden Rd *HDCN* TN27 229 H1
Bulldog Rd *WALD* ME5 88 C4
Buller Rd *CHAT* ME4 3 F6
Bullers Cl *SCUP* DA14 39 F3
Bull Flds *SNOD* ME6 85 K6
Bullfinch Cl *SEV* TN13 123 F1
STPH/PW TN12 193 J1 1
Bullfinch Dene *SEV* TN13 123 F1
Bullfinch La *SEV* TN13 8 A1
Bull Hl *RMAID* ME17 161 G5
Bullingstone La *RRTW* TN3 188 D7
Bullion Cl *STPH/PW* TN12 173 G8
Bullivant Cl *GRH* DA9 25 F4
Bull La *BGR/WK* TN15 105 G3
DIT/AY ME20 87 F8
DIT/AY ME20 109 K3
HOO/HM ME3 30 C7
RSIT ME9 91 H5
Bull Orch *MAIDW* ME16 131 K4
Bull Rd *E/WMAL* ME19 108 A1
Bulls Pl *RTWE/PEM* TN2 191 K8

Bulrush Cl *WALD* ME5 88 A3
Bumbles Cl *ROCH* ME1 67 J6
Bunkers Hl *SCUP* DA14 39 G1
Bunters Hill Rd *HOO/HM* ME3 49 F1
Burberry La *RMAID* ME17 157 K1
The Burdens *HDCN* TN27 200 B1
Burdett Av *GVE* DA12 47 H2
Burdett Cl *SCUP* DA14 39 F3
Burdett Rd *STH/RUST* TN4 206 A2 1
Burgate Cl *DART* DA1 22 C2
Burgess Hall Dr *RMAID* ME17 135 H8
Burgess Rd *STRD* ME2 2 B1 2
Burghclere Dr *MAIDW* ME16 132 B4 1
Burghfield Rd *MEO* DA13 45 G5
Burham Rd *ROCH* ME1 66 D7
Burial Ground La *MAID/SHEP* ME15 6 B6
Burleigh Cl *STRD* ME2 48 D6 1
Burleigh Dr *MAID/BEAR* ME14 111 F5
Burley Rd *SIT* ME10 93 K2
Burlings La *RSEV* TN14 99 F4
Burman Cl *RDART* DA2 24 B6
Burmarsh Cl *WALD* ME5 88 C1
Burma Wy *WALD* ME5 68 A8
Burnaby Rd *GVW* DA11 27 F6
Burnett Rd *ERITH* DA8 12 B6
Burnham Cl *SIT* ME10 73 K6
Burnham Crs *DART* DA1 23 F3
Burnham Rd *DART* DA1 23 G4
Burnham Wk *RHAM* ME8 90 B3
Burnley Rd *WTHK* RM20 13 K8
Burns Crs *TON* TN9 170 A7
Burn's Rd *GILL* ME7 4 C1
  MAIDW ME16 132 C4
Burnt House Cl *HAWK* TN18 243 K1
  STRD ME2 49 H4
Burnthouse La *HDCN* TN27 201 H5
Burnt House La *RDART* DA2 41 H2
  RRTW TN3 205 J1
Burnt Oak Ter *GILL* ME7 4 C2
Burntwick Dr *RSIT* ME9 72 A3
Burntwood Gv *SEV* TN13 9 D6
Burntwood Rd *SEV* TN13 123 K7
Burrfield Dr *STMC/STPC* BR5 56 E2
Burrows La *HOO/HM* ME3 35 F3
The Burrs *SIT* ME10 94 A3 1
Burrstock Wy *RHAM* ME8 70 E4
Burslem Rd *RTWE/PEM* TN2 190 E8
Burston Rd *RMAID* ME17 154 B4
Burton Cl *HOO/HM* ME3 49 H3
Burwash Cl *STMC/STPC* BR5 56 D2 1
Busbridge Rd *MAID/SHEP* ME15 154 E1
  SNOD ME6 85 H7
Bush Cl *RSIT* ME9 115 K1
Bushey Cft *OXTED* RH8 140 A1
Bushmeadow Rd *RHAM* ME8 70 C4
Bush Rd *STPH/PW* TN12 151 G6
  STRD ME2 66 A4
Bush Rw *DIT/AY* ME20 110 A4
Bushy Gill *RRTW* TN3 205 K3
Bushy Gv *RMAID* ME17 158 B4
Busty La *BGR/WK* TN15 104 D8
Butcher Cl *STPH/PW* TN12 198 A3
Butchers La *BGR/WK* TN15 61 J6
  WBY/YAL ME18 129 F5
Butchers Yd *ORP* BR6 75 F6
Buttercup Cl *STPH/PW* TN12 193 J1
Butterfly Av *DART* DA1 23 J8
Buttermere Cl *GILL* ME7 5 F3
Buttermere Rd *STMC/STPC* BR5 56 E1 2
Butt Green La *RMAID* ME17 155 F8
Butt Haw Cl *HOO/HM* ME3 51 F1
Button Dr *HOO/HM* ME3 35 F1
Button La *MAID/SHEP* ME15 134 D4 1
Button St *SWLY* BR8 59 F1
Butts La *WADH* TN5 220 E7
The Butts *RSEV* TN14 101 K4
  SIT ME10 94 A2
Buttway La *HOO/HM* ME3 15 F8
Buxton Cl *MAID/SHEP* ME15 133 G6
  WALD ME5 88 E5
Byng Rd *STH/RUST* TN4 10 A2
Byrneside *RTON* TN11 169 J2
Byron Rd *DART* DA1 24 A3
  GILL ME7 4 C5
  MAID/BEAR ME14 111 H7
Bythorne Ct *RHAM* ME8 70 E5 3

C

Cabbage Stalk La *STH/RUST* TN4 10 A5
Cacket's La *RSEV* TN14 98 D2
Cade La *SEV* TN13 124 A7
Cadlocks Hl *RSEV* TN14 77 G5
Cadnam Cl *STRD* ME2 48 D6
Cadogan Av *RDART* DA2 24 C6
Caerleon Cl *SCUP* DA14 38 D3
Caernarvon Dr *MAID/SHEP* ME15 6 C6
Cage Green Rd *TONN* TN10 170 C1
Cage La *HDCN* TN27 201 K5
Cairns Cl *DART* DA1 23 G4
Caistor Rd *TON* TN9 170 A5
Calcutta Rd *TIL* RM18 27 G1
Caldecote Cl *RHAM* ME8 70 E4 1
Calder Rd *MAID/BEAR* ME14 110 E7
Calderwood *GVE* DA12 46 B4
Caldew Av *RHAM* ME8 69 K5
Caldew Gv *SIT* ME10 94 B3
Calehill Cl *MAID/BEAR* ME14 7 F1
Caley Rd *RTWE/PEM* TN2 190 D6
Calfstock La *EYN* DA4 59 H1
Caling Cft *HART* DA3 62 A5
Caliph Cl *GVE* DA12 46 C1
Callaways La *RSIT* ME9 72 A8
Calverley Ct *RTWE/PEM* TN2 11 E4 2
Calverley Pk *RTWE/PEM* TN2 11 D4
Calverley Park Crs
  RTWE/PEM TN2 11 D4 1
Calverley Park Gdns *RTW* TN1 11 D4
Calverley Rd *RTW* TN1 11 D3 1
  RTWE/PEM TN2 11 D4
Calverley St *RTW* TN1 11 D3
Calvert Cl *SCUP* DA14 39 F4 1
Calvin Cl *STMC/STPC* BR5 38 E8
Camberwell La *RSEV* TN14 144 B2
Camborne Rd *SCUP* DA14 38 D1
Cambray Rd *ORP* BR6 56 A4
Cambria Av *ROCH* ME1 66 E4
Cambria Crs *GVE* DA12 46 B2
Cambrian Gv *GVW* DA11 27 H6
Cambrian Rd *STH/RUST* TN4 190 C7
Cambridge Crs *MAID/SHEP* ME15 133 K7
Cambridge Gdns
  RTWE/PEM TN2 11 D5 1
Cambridge Rd *RHAM* ME8 69 K8
  SIT ME10 94 C4
  STRD ME2 49 F6
Cambridge St *RTWE/PEM* TN2 11 E4 3
Cambridge Ter *CHAT* ME4 3 F4 1
Camden Av *RTWE/PEM* TN2 191 J8
Camden Cl *GVW* DA11 26 D7
  WALD ME5 88 C1
Camden Hl *RTWE/PEM* TN2 11 D4 2
  RTWE/PEM TN2 11 E5 1
Camden Pk *RTWE/PEM* TN2 11 D4 3
  RTWE/PEM TN2 11 F5 1
Camden Rd *GILL* ME7 5 D1 1
  RTW TN1 11 D3
  SEV TN13 9 D1
Camden St *MAID/BEAR* ME14 7 D2 1
Camellia Cl *RHAM* ME8 70 A7
Camelot Cl *BH/WHM* TN16 97 G3
Cameron Cl *BXLY* DA5 40 A1
  WALD ME5 68 C6 1
Camer Park Rd *MEO* DA13 63 J4
Camer Rd *MEO* DA13 63 K3
Camer St *MEO* DA13 63 K3
Campbell Rd *GVW* DA11 27 G7
  MAID/SHEP ME15 7 D4
  STH/RUST TN4 10 C1 1
Camp Hl *RTON* TN11 167 J3
Campion Cl *GVW* DA11 45 F2 2
  WALD ME5 87 K3
Campion Crs *CRBK* TN17 225 F4
Campleshon Rd *RHAM* ME8 90 A1
Campus Wy *GILL* ME7 69 H6
Camp Wy *MAID/SHEP* ME15 133 J7
Canada Farm Rd *EYN* DA4 61 G2
Canadian Av *GILL* ME7 5 E4
Canal Basin *GVE* DA12 28 A5
Canal Rd *GVE* DA12 28 A5
  HOO/HM ME3 30 A6
  STRD ME2 2 B1
Canberra Gdns *SIT* ME10 93 H2
Canberra Sq *TIL* RM18 27 H1 1
Canbury Pth *STMC/STPC* BR5 56 B1
Canning St *MAID/BEAR* ME14 7 D1
Cannon La *TON* TN9 170 D4
Canon Cl *ROCH* ME1 2 B6
Canon La *WBY/YAL* ME18 130 A5
Canterbury Cl *DART* DA1 23 K6
Canterbury Crs *TONN* TN10 170 D1 1
Canterbury La *RHAM* ME8 71 F5
Canterbury Rd *GVE* DA12 27 K8 1
  RTWE/PEM TN2 192 A8
  SIT ME10 94 C3
Canterbury St *GILL* ME7 4 C3
Canterbury Wy *DART* DA1 24 B3
  WTHK RM20 13 J7
Capel Cl *RHAM* ME8 89 K1
Capell Cl *RMAID* ME17 154 C3
Capel Pl *RDART* DA2 41 F2
Capel Rd *SIT* ME10 93 K4
Capstan Ct *GRH* DA9 24 B3
Capstone Rd *GILL* ME7 69 F7
  WALD ME5 68 E5
Captain's Cl *RMAID* ME17 157 G8
The Caravan Site *SOCK/AV* RM15 13 H3
Cardens Rd *HOO/HM* ME3 31 G6
Cardinal Cl *TON* TN9 170 D6
Cardine Cl *SIT* ME10 73 K7
Carey's Fld *SEV* TN13 101 G7 1
Caring La *RMAID* ME17 135 G6
Caring Rd *MAID/SHEP* ME15 135 F5
Carisbrooke Dr *MAIDW* ME16 6 A2
Carisbrooke Rd *STRD* ME2 48 D6
Carleton Pl *EYN* DA4 60 B1
Carleton Rd *DART* DA1 23 K6
Carlisle Rd *DART* DA1 23 K5
Carlton Av *GILL* ME7 5 E4
  GRH DA9 24 D5
Carlton Crs *RTWE/PEM* TN2 11 E3 1
  WALD ME5 68 E6
Carlton Gdns *MAID/SHEP* ME15 133 H6
Carlton Rd *RTWE/PEM* TN2 11 E3
  SCUP DA14 38 A3
Carmelite Wy *HART* DA3 62 A2
Carnation Cl *E/WMAL* ME19 108 E5 1
Carnation Crs *E/WMAL* ME19 108 D6
Carnation Rd *STRD* ME2 48 C7
Caroline Crs *MAIDW* ME16 110 D7
Carolyn Dr *ORP* BR6 56 B7
Carpeaux Cl *CHAT* ME4 4 A4
Carpenters Cl *ROCH* ME1 3 E6
Carpenters La *RTON* TN11 149 K3
  STPH/PW TN12 177 J7
Carpinus Cl *WALD* ME5 88 C5
The Carriageway *RSEV* TN14 121 K3
Carrick Dr *SEV* TN13 9 D2
Carriers Rd *CRBK* TN17 225 K1
Carrington Cl *GILL* ME7 5 F2
Carrington Rd *DART* DA1 23 J5
Carroll Cl *STRD* ME2 85 K2 3
Carroll Gdns *DIT/AY* ME20 108 D3
Carsington Gdns *DART* DA1 23 G8
Cartel Cl *PUR* RM19 13 H4
Carter's Hl *BGR/WK* TN15 147 F1
Carter's Hill La *MEO* DA13 83 G4
Carton Cl *ROCH* ME1 3 D6
Carton Rd *HOO/HM* ME3 48 A3
Carville Av *STH/RUST* TN4 189 K5
Carvoran Wy *RHAM* ME8 89 K1
Cascade Cl *STMC/STPC* BR5 38 D8
Casstine Cl *SWLY* BR8 40 C6
Castle Av *ROCH* ME1 2 C4
Castle Dene *MAID/BEAR* ME14 110 E6
Castle Dr *RSEV* TN14 102 C4
Castle Farm Rd *RSEV* TN14 78 C4
Castlefields *MEO* DA13 45 G6
Castle Hl *HART* DA3 61 J2
  MAID/BEAR ME14 113 F5
  ROCH ME1 2 C2
  RTON TN11 191 F1
Castle Hurst *RBTBR* TN32 242 C6
Castle La *GVE* DA12 28 E8
Castlemaine Av *GILL* ME7 5 E2
Castle Rd *CHAT* ME4 4 A6
  EYN DA4 78 E2
  MAIDW ME16 110 D6
  SIT ME10 94 C1
  STH/RUST TN4 10 B4
  SWCM DA10 26 A5
Castle St *GRH* DA9 25 F4
  ROCH ME1 86 B2 1
  RTW TN1 10 C5 2
  STH/RUST TN4 189 K4
  STRD ME2 49 K5
  SWCM DA10 26 A5
  TON TN9 170 C4 1
Castle View Rd *STRD* ME2 48 E7
Castle Wy *DIT/AY* ME20 108 C1
  E/WMAL ME19 108 C3
Caterfield La *LING* RH7 162 D4
Catherine Cl *MAIDW* ME16 132 A3 1
Catherine Pl *RTW* TN1 11 D4 4
Catherine St *ROCH* ME1 3 D5
Catkin Cl *WALD* ME5 88 A5
Catlyn Cl *E/WMAL* ME19 108 E6
Catterick Rd *WALD* ME5 88 E4
Causeway Br *SOCK/AV* RM15 13 J3
Causton Rd *CRBK* TN17 225 J1
Cave Hl *MAID/SHEP* ME15 6 C6
Cavell Crs *DART* DA1 23 K3
Cavell Wy *SIT* ME10 93 J1
Cavendish Av *GILL* ME7 5 E2
  SEV TN13 8 C1
Cavendish Cl *TONN* TN10 148 D7
Cavendish Dr *RTWE/PEM* TN2 11 D5
Cavendish Rd *ROCH* ME1 3 D5
Cavendish Sq *HART* DA3 43 J8
Cavendish Wy *MAID/SHEP* ME15 134 C3
Caversham Cl *RHAM* ME8 70 C5 1
Caxton Cl *HART* DA3 62 A1
  TENT TN30 229 K7 1
Caxton La *OXTED* RH8 141 J2
  RTON TN11 150 A6
Cayser Dr *RMAID* ME17 158 C4
Cazeneuve St *ROCH* ME1 2 C3 1
Cecil Av *RHAM* ME8 69 H4
  STRD ME2 49 G6
Cecil Rd *GVW* DA11 27 G7
  ROCH ME1 2 C5
Cedar Av *GVE* DA12 45 K2
Cedar Cl *DIT/AY* ME20 109 H6
  MEO DA13 63 H3 1
  SIT ME10 94 C4 1
  SWLY BR8 39 K7
Cedar Crs *TONN* TN10 148 C7
Cedar Dr *EDEN* TN8 164 B4
  EYN DA4 42 A7
  MAIDW ME16 131 J4
Cedar Gv *GILL* ME7 89 H1
Cedar Rdg *RTWE/PEM* TN2 11 F1
Cedar Rd *DART* DA1 23 G7

HOO/HM ME3 51 F3
STRD ME2 48 E8
The Cedars STPH/PW TN12 173 J7
Cedar Terrace Rd SEV TN13 9 E2
Celestine Cl WALD ME5 88 B5
Cellar Hl RSIT ME9 95 K6
Cemetery La RTON TN11 150 C6
Cemetery Rd SNOD ME6 85 J5
STRD ME2 85 K2
Centenary Walk - Maidstone
DIT/AY ME20 87 F8
MAID/BEAR ME14 6 B1
MAID/BEAR ME14 110 E1
MAID/BEAR ME14 111 H2
Centenary Walk - Rochester
ROCH ME1 2 A5
Central Av GVE DA12 27 J8
SIT ME10 94 A3
SOCK/AV RM15 13 G2
WTHK RM20 13 K5
Central Park Gdns ROCH ME1 3 E6
Central Rd DART DA1 23 H4
DIT/AY ME20 109 F2
STRD ME2 2 A1
Central Ter HOO/HM ME3 32 A8
Central Wy OXTED RH8 118 B6
Centre Rd HART DA3 61 K7
Centurion Cl GILL ME7 69 G5
Centurion Wy PUR RM19 12 D4
Century Rd RHAM ME8 70 A6
Cerne Rd GVE DA12 46 B2
Cervia Wy GVE DA12 46 C1
Chada Av GILL ME7 5 E5
Chadwick Cl GVW DA11 27 F8
Chaffe's La RSIT ME9 71 H4
Chaffinch Cl WALD ME5 68 B7
Chaffinch Wy STPH/PW TN12 193 H1
Chafford La RRTW TN3 204 D1
Chalet Cl RDART DA2 40 A2
Chalfont Dr RHAM ME8 70 A8
Chalice Wy GRH DA9 24 D4
Chalk Av TENT TN30 230 B4
Chalkenden Av RHAM ME8 69 H4
Chalket La RTWE/PEM TN2 208 D1
Chalk La CRBK TN17 213 K7
Chalk Pit Av STMC/STPC BR5 38 D8
Chalk Pit Hl CHAT ME4 4 A5 1
Chalkpit La OXTED RH8 118 A6
Chalkpit Wd OXTED RH8 118 B6
Chalk Rd GVE DA12 28 D7
HOO/HM ME3 30 B8
Chalkways RSEV TN14 102 C3
Chalkwell Rd SIT ME10 93 J2
Chalky Bank GVW DA11 45 H2
Chalky Bank Rd RHAM ME8 70 C4
Chalky Rd RSIT ME9 91 F8
Challenge Cl GVE DA12 46 C2
Challenger Cl SIT ME10 73 K7
STPH/PW TN12 173 H8
Challock Cl BH/WHM TN16 97 G3
Chamberlain Av MAIDW ME16 132 B4
Chamberlain Ct RHAM ME8 89 J1
Chamberlain Rd CHAT ME4 4 B6 1
Chambers Cl GRH DA9 24 E4
Chancel Cl BGR/WK TN15 80 D3
Chancery La MAID/SHEP ME15 7 E3
Chancery Rd HOO/HM ME3 31 G1
Chandler's Hl MEO DA13 63 K8
MEO DA13 83 K1
Chandler's Rd MEO DA13 83 K1
Chandos Rd RTW TN1 11 E2 1
Chantler's Hl STPH/PW TN12 193 H3
Chantrey Cl SCUP DA14 39 F3 1
Chantry Av HART DA3 61 K3
Chantry Pl STPH/PW TN12 196 C1
Chantry Rd STPH/PW TN12 196 C1
Chapel Cl DART DA1 22 B4
E/WMAL ME19 107 H1
Chapel Fld RYE TN31 244 D7
Chapel Hl DART DA1 22 B3
Chapel La CRBK TN17 215 J7
CRBK TN17 236 E2
GILL ME7 89 H2
GILL ME7 89 H4
HDCN TN27 182 B3
MAID/BEAR ME14 134 C1
STPH/PW TN12 198 B3
STRD ME2 85 F2
Chapel Rd HOO/HM ME3 37 F1
OXTED RH8 141 G1
RMAID ME17 157 G7 1
SNOD ME6 85 K6
Chapel Rw BGR/WK TN15 104 C8
HOO/HM ME3 35 F2
Chapel St E/WMAL ME19 107 H2
E/WMAL ME19 108 E8
Chapel Wd HART DA3 61 K6
Chapel Wood Rd HART DA3 61 K6
Chaplin Cl HOO/HM ME3 49 H3
Chaplin Dr HDCN TN27 200 B1
Chapman Av MAID/SHEP ME15 134 B5
Chapman's Hl BGR/WK TN15 83 F2
Chapman's La STMC/STPC BR5 38 E7
SWLY BR8 39 H7
Chapmans Rd RSEV TN14 122 A3
Chapman Wy E/WMAL ME19 108 D6
RTWE/PEM TN2 190 C6
Chappell Wy SIT ME10 73 J8
Chapter Rd STRD ME2 48 E7
Charing Cl ORP BR6 56 A8
Charing Rd RHAM ME8 69 J3
Chariot Wy STRD ME2 66 D3
Charlbury Cl MAIDW ME16 132 C3
Charles Cl SCUP DA14 38 C2
SNOD ME6 85 K6 1
Charles Dickens Av STRD ME2 48 B4
Charles Dr STRD ME2 66 A3
Charlesford Av RMAID ME17 158 B3
Charles Rd RSEV TN14 77 J5
Charles St CHAT ME4 3 E5
GRH DA9 24 E4
MAIDW ME16 6 B4
STH/RUST TN4 190 A6
STRD ME2 2 A1
Charlock Cl MAIDW ME16 110 D6 1
Charlotte Cl WALD ME5 68 C8
Charlotte Dr RHAM ME8 69 K5
Charlotte St SIT ME10 93 K1
Charlton Dr BH/WHM TN16 97 H4
Charlton La MAID/SHEP ME15 131 H7
RMAID ME17 158 A6
Charlton St MAIDW ME16 132 C4
Charlton's Wy STH/RUST TN4 10 A6 1
Charmwood La ORP BR6 76 C5
The Charne RSEV TN14 101 J4
Charnock SWLY BR8 58 B1
Charterhouse Dr SEV TN13 8 C2
Charterhouse Rd ORP BR6 56 B7
Charter St CHAT ME4 3 F6
GILL ME7 4 C1
Chart Hill Rd RMAID ME17 156 C8
Chart La BH/WHM TN16 121 J4
Chart Pl RHAM ME8 89 K3
Chart Rd RMAID ME17 156 E7
Chart Vw BGR/WK TN15 102 E4
Chartway BGR/WK TN15 9 E3
Chartway St RMAID ME17 157 H5
Chartwell Cl STRD ME2 49 G5
Chartwell Dr ORP BR6 75 J1
Chartwell Gv SIT ME10 93 H3 1
Chase Sq GVE DA12 27 J5 6
The Chase ORP BR6 76 B6
RHAM ME8 69 H4
ROCH ME1 3 D6
RSEV TN14 102 C3
TONN TN10 170 C1
Chastilian Rd DART DA1 22 D6
Chatfield Wy DIT/AY ME20 109 F5
Chatham Gv CHAT ME4 68 A5
Chatham Hl CHAT ME4 4 B5
Chatham Hill Rd RSEV TN14 102 A8
Chatham Rd DIT/AY ME20 87 J8
MAID/BEAR ME14 110 E2
WALD ME5 87 J5
Chatsworth Dr SIT ME10 93 G1
STRD ME2 49 G5
Chatsworth Rd DART DA1 23 F3 1
GILL ME7 4 C2 2
Chattenden Ct MAID/BEAR ME14 111 H7
Chattenden La HOO/HM ME3 50 A2
Chaucer Cl STRD ME2 49 K6 1
TIL RM18 27 K1
Chaucer Gdns TON TN9 169 K7
Chaucer Pk DART DA1 23 J6
Chaucer Rd GILL ME7 4 C5
GVW DA11 44 E1
SIT ME10 93 J3
Chaucer Wy DART DA1 23 K3
DIT/AY ME20 108 D3
Chave Rd DART DA1 41 H1
Cheeselands HDCN TN27 217 J4
Chegwell Dr WALD ME5 88 C2 1
Chegworth Gdns SIT ME10 93 K5
Chegworth La RMAID ME17 136 D8
Chegworth Rd RMAID ME17 136 D7
Chellows La LING RH7 162 D4
Chelmar Rd CHAT ME4 4 B4
Chelmsford Rd STRD ME2 48 C8
Chelsfield Hl ORP BR6 76 D4
Chelsfield La ORP BR6 56 E8
ORP BR6 77 H3
RSEV TN14 77 K4
STMC/STPC BR5 56 E4
Chelsfield Rd STMC/STPC BR5 56 D3
Chelsham Court Rd WARL CR6 96 B5
Cheltenham Cl GVE DA12 45 K3
MAID/SHEP ME15 134 B8 2
Cheltenham Rd ORP BR6 56 B7
Cheney Cl RHAM ME8 90 A1
Cheney Hl RSIT ME9 117 G2
Chenies Cl RTWE/PEM TN2 207 F6
The Chenies RDART DA2 40 B2
Chennell Park Rd TENT TN30 229 J5
Chequers Cl MEO DA13 45 F7
STMC/STPC BR5 56 A1 1
WALD ME5 88 B5
Chequers Ct STRD ME2 49 F5
Cherbourg Crs WALD ME5 68 A7
Cheriton Rd RHAM ME8 70 A7
Cheriton Wy MAIDW ME16 110 C7
The Cherries MAIDW ME16 131 K4
Cherry Amber Cl RHAM ME8 70 C6 1
Cherry Av SWLY BR8 40 A8
Cherry Cl SIT ME10 73 J8
Cherry Flds SIT ME10 93 F1
Cherry Gdns RSIT ME9 95 K4
Cherry Gv TONN TN10 170 E1
Cherry Orch DIT/AY ME20 109 G6
TENT TN30 230 A8 1
Cherry Orchard Cl
STMC/STPC BR5 56 D2
The Cherry Orch RTON TN11 150 A5
Cherry Orchard Wy MAIDW ME16 132 B3
Cherry Rd HOO/HM ME3 51 F3 5
Cherry Tree Gv EYN DA4 80 A5
Cherry Tree La RDART DA2 40 C1
Cherry Tree Rd RHAM ME8 70 C6
RTWE/PEM TN2 10 A6
Cherry Trees HART DA3 62 A3
Cherrywood Dr GVW DA11 45 F2
Chervilles MAIDW ME16 132 A4
Cherwell Cl TONN TN10 170 B2
Chesham Dr RHAM ME8 70 B8
Cheshire Rd MAID/SHEP ME15 134 A4
Cheshunt Cl MEO DA13 63 H3
Chessenden La HDCN TN27 202 A5
Chester Av RTWE/PEM TN2 11 F5
Chester Cl STRD ME2 48 C8
Chesterfield Cl STMC/STPC BR5 56 E1
Chesterfield Dr DART DA1 22 E4
SEV TN13 123 F1
Chester Rd GILL ME7 5 D6
Chesterton Rd DIT/AY ME20 108 D2
HOO/HM ME3 31 G1 1
Chestfield Cl RHAM ME8 70 B4 1
Chestnut Av BH/WHM TN16 119 H1
GRH DA9 24 E6
STH/RUST TN4 190 B6
STPH/PW TN12 198 A2
WALD ME5 87 K3
Chestnut Cl CRBK TN17 199 G8
E/WMAL ME19 129 J4
EDEN TN8 164 B4 1
GVW DA11 27 G5 1
ORP BR6 76 B1
RMAID ME17 158 D8
STH/RUST TN4 190 B6
TENT TN30 230 C5
Chestnut Copse OXTED RH8 141 F4
Chestnut Dr RMAID ME17 154 B3
RMAID ME17 158 B4
Chestnut Gv RDART DA2 40 A3
Chestnut La MEO DA13 83 J6
SEV TN13 9 D3
STPH/PW TN12 193 G5
Chestnut Rd DART DA1 23 G7
STRD ME2 48 D8
The Chestnuts E/WMAL ME19 106 E3
HAWK TN18 234 E6
Chestnut St RSIT ME9 92 D2
Chestnut Wk BGR/WK TN15 124 D7
TON TN9 169 K4 1
Chestnut Wood La RSIT ME9 92 D2
Cheswick Cl DART DA1 22 C3
Chetney Cl STRD ME2 48 B7
Chevening Cl WALD ME5 88 B1
Chevening La RSEV TN14 100 A3
Chevening Rd RSEV TN14 100 B6
The Chevenings SCUP DA14 38 C1
Cheviot Cl BXLYHN DA7 22 B1
TON TN9 170 C2
Cheviot Gdns MAID/SHEP ME15 134 C5
Cheyne Wk MEO DA13 63 H6
Chicago Av GILL ME7 5 E3
Chichele Rd OXTED RH8 118 C7
Chichester Cl RHAM ME8 70 D6
SOCK/AV RM15 13 G1
Chichester Dr SEV TN13 8 B4
Chichester Ri GVE DA12 46 A2
Chichester Rd GRH DA9 24 E4
TON TN9 170 A6
Chickenden La STPH/PW TN12 198 E2
Chickfield Gdns WALD ME5 4 C6 1
Chicks La CRBK TN17 222 E4
Chiddingstone Cl
MAID/SHEP ME15 134 B8 3
Chidley Cross Rd STPH/PW TN12 151 G8
Chieftain Cl GILL ME7 69 J5
Chieftan Dr PUR RM19 12 E4
Chieveley Dr RTWE/PEM TN2 11 E6
Chiffinch Gdns GVW DA11 45 F1
Childsbridge La RSEV TN14 102 C5
Childsbridge Wy BGR/WK TN15 102 D7
Childs Crs SWCM DA10 25 J5
Childscroft Rd RHAM ME8 70 C4
Childs Wy BGR/WK TN15 105 F3
Chilham Cl CHAT ME4 3 E5 1
Chilham Rd MAIDW ME16 110 C7
RHAM ME8 69 H3
Chillington St MAID/BEAR ME14 6 C1
Chilliwack Rd HOO/HM ME3 50 A1
Chilston Cl STH/RUST TN4 10 C2
Chilston Rd RMAID ME17 160 D1
STH/RUST TN4 10 C2
Chiltern Cl MAID/SHEP ME15 134 B5

Chiltern Rd *GVW* DA11 45 F1
Chiltern Wy *TON* TN9 170 C2
Chilton Av *SIT* ME10 94 B3
Chilton Ct *RHAM* ME8 70 B5
Chilton Dr *HOO/HM* ME3 48 A3
Chippendale Cl *WALD* ME5 88 A5
Chippendayle Dr *RMAID* ME17 137 H8
Chipperfield Rd *STMC/STPC* BR5 38 B7
Chipstead Cl *MAIDW* ME16 6 A1
Chipstead La *SEV* TN13 123 F1
Chipstead Pk *SEV* TN13 123 F1
Chipstead Park Cl *SEV* TN13 123 F1
Chipstead Rd *RHAM* ME8 90 A2
Chislehurst Cl *MAID/SHEP* ME15 134 B8 4
Chislehurst Rd *ORP* BR6 56 B4
SCUP DA14 38 B3
Chorleywood Crs *STMC/STPC* BR5 38 A7
Christchurch Rd *BFN/LL* DA15 38 A2
DART DA1 23 F6
Christ Church Rd *GVE* DA12 27 K6 3
Christian Fields Av *GVE* DA12 45 K2
Christie Cl *WALD* ME5 68 C8
Christie Dr *DIT/AY* ME20 108 D2
Christies Av *RSEV* TN14 77 H5
Christmas La *HOO/HM* ME3 33 F3
Christmas St *GILL* ME7 5 E1
Christy Rd *BH/WHM* TN16 97 G2
Chulkhurst *HDCN* TN27 217 H4
Church Av *SCUP* DA14 38 B3
Church Cl *HOO/HM* ME3 15 G8
STPH/PW TN12 194 A6
WBY/YAL ME18 129 F6
Church Crs *RMAID* ME17 137 K8 1
Church Farm Cl *HOO/HM* ME3 51 F2
Church Farm Rd *RSIT* ME9 71 H3
Church Fld *DART* DA1 23 G8
EDEN TN8 164 D5
SEV TN13 8 B1
SNOD ME6 86 A5
Church Flds *E/WMAL* ME19 107 K6
Churchfields Ter *ROCH* ME1 2 B4 1
Church Gn *STPH/PW* TN12 176 C8
STPH/PW TN12 198 A4
STRD ME2 49 H6
Church Hl *BGR/WK* TN15 126 E6
BH/WHM TN16 119 H1
DART DA1 22 B3
DART DA1 41 G1
GRH DA9 24 D4
HDCN TN27 161 J6
ORP BR6 56 B4
RASHW TN26 219 K7
RMAID ME17 155 H7
RMAID ME17 155 H4
RSEV TN14 98 C2
RSIT ME9 91 J7
WALD ME5 4 C6
Church Hill Wd *STMC/STPC* BR5 56 A2
Church Hollow *PUR* RM19 12 E5 1
Churchill Av *WALD* ME5 68 A8
Churchill Cl *DART* DA1 24 A7 1
Churchill Rd *EYN* DA4 60 B1
GVW DA11 27 G7
Churchill Sq *E/WMAL* ME19 129 J3
Church La *BGR/WK* TN15 103 F4
CHAT ME4 3 F2
E/WMAL ME19 106 C1
GVE DA12 29 F8
MAID/SHEP ME15 131 H7
OXTED RH8 118 C8
PUR RM19 12 E5
RMAID ME17 137 J8
RMAID ME17 157 K6
RSIT ME9 72 A8
RSIT ME9 91 H6
RTON TN11 172 B8
RYE TN31 245 F8
STPH/PW TN12 151 H7
TON TN9 170 C4
WARL CR6 96 A3
Church Ms *RHAM* ME8 70 C6
Church Pth *GILL* ME7 5 E2
GRH DA9 24 E5 1
GVW DA11 26 D5
Church Rd *BGR/WK* TN15 80 D3
BGR/WK TN15 102 D8
BGR/WK TN15 125 J2
BH/WHM TN16 97 H4
BH/WHM TN16 121 H3
CRBK TN17 212 D6
CRBK TN17 222 D4
E/WMAL ME19 107 G5
E/WMAL ME19 107 H3
EYN DA4 41 K4
GRH DA9 24 D4
GVE DA12 45 K4
HART DA3 62 A2
HAWK TN18 243 G2
HAYES BR2 74 C3
MAID/BEAR ME14 114 B5
MAID/SHEP ME15 6 B5
MAID/SHEP ME15 134 B6
MEO DA13 45 K6
ORP BR6 75 H1
ORP BR6 76 E2
RMAID ME17 156 E6
RMAID ME17 159 K7
RMAID ME17 159 J1
RRTW TN3 210 E8
RSEV TN14 122 A5
RSEV TN14 145 K3
RSIT ME9 95 F2
RTON TN11 147 H8
SCUP DA14 38 B2
SIT ME10 94 C1
STH/RUST TN4 10 B4
STH/RUST TN4 189 K4
STPH/PW TN12 173 K8
SWCM DA10 26 A5
SWLY BR8 41 G6
SWLY BR8 58 A4
TENT TN30 230 A7
WBY/YAL ME18 128 C8
Churchside *MEO* DA13 83 H6
Churchside Cl *BH/WHM* TN16 97 G5
Church Sq *RMAID* ME17 160 D1
Church St *BGR/WK* TN15 102 E7
CHAT ME4 4 A4 1
EDEN TN8 164 D5
GILL ME7 5 E2
GVW DA11 27 J5
HOO/HM ME3 30 B7
HOO/HM ME3 31 G1
HOO/HM ME3 51 F1
MAID/BEAR ME14 7 D3 2
MAID/SHEP ME15 6 B5
MAID/SHEP ME15 155 F1 1
MEO DA13 44 B3
RMAID ME17 155 H3
ROCH ME1 3 D4
ROCH ME1 86 D6
RSEV TN14 78 C6
RSIT ME9 94 D7
RTON TN11 150 A6
SIT ME10 93 K2 2
TON TN9 170 C4 2
WBY/YAL ME18 130 E7
Church Ter *WALD* ME5 4 C6
Church Vw *HDCN* TN27 217 J4
SOCK/AV RM15 13 G2
Church Wk *DART* DA1 41 G1
E/WMAL ME19 108 E7
GVE DA12 28 A6
HDCN TN27 200 A1
Church Wy *OXTED* RH8 140 D3
Churn La *STPH/PW* TN12 194 D3
Chute Cl *RHAM* ME8 90 A2 1
Chyngton Cl *BFN/LL* DA15 38 A1
Cimba Wd *GVE* DA12 46 B2
Cinder Hill La *RTON* TN11 168 A5
Cinnabar Cl *WALD* ME5 88 B5 1
Cirrus Crs *GVE* DA12 46 B3
City Wy *ROCH* ME1 3 D4
Civic Sq *TIL* RM18 27 H1
Clacket La *BH/WHM* TN16 119 J3
Clandon Rd *WALD* ME5 88 E5
Clanricarde Gdns *RTW* TN1 10 C4 1
Clanricarde Rd *STH/RUST* TN4 10 B4 1
Clapper La *STPH/PW* TN12 197 K2
Clare Av *TON* TN9 169 K5
Clare La *E/WMAL* ME19 108 C6
Claremont Crs *DART* DA1 22 B3
Claremont Gdns *RTW* TN1 11 D5
Claremont Rd *MAID/BEAR* ME14 7 E2
RTW TN1 11 D5
SWLY BR8 40 B5
Claremont Wy *CHAT* ME4 3 F5 2
Clarence Ct *MAID/BEAR* ME14 134 A2
Clarence Crs *SCUP* DA14 38 C1
Clarence Pl *GVE* DA12 27 J6
Clarence Rd *BH/WHM* TN16 97 K5
CHAT ME4 4 B6
RTW TN1 10 C4 2
SCUP DA14 38 C1
Clarence Rw *GVE* DA12 27 J6
RTW TN1 10 C3 2
Clarendon Cl *MAID/BEAR* ME14 134 C2
SIT ME10 94 A5
STMC/STPC BR5 38 B8 2
Clarendon Gdns *RDART* DA2 24 C7
RTWE/PEM TN2 10 C6 2
STRD ME2 49 F5
Clarendon Gn *STMC/STPC* BR5 38 B8
Clarendon Gv *STMC/STPC* BR5 56 B1 1
Clarendon Pth *STMC/STPC* BR5 56 B1
Clarendon Pl *RDART* DA2 40 A3
Clarendon Rd *GVE* DA12 27 K5
SEV TN13 8 C3
Clarendon Wy *CHST* BR7 38 A8
RTWE/PEM TN2 10 B6
Clare Wy *SEV* TN13 124 A7
Clarewood Dr *E/WMAL* ME19 108 C6
Claridge Cl *GILL* ME7 89 G2
Clarkes Green Rd *BGR/WK* TN15 102 E1
Clark Ms *DIT/AY* ME20 109 K5
Clarks La *RSEV* TN14 77 G7
WARL CR6 119 F2
Claston Cl *DART* DA1 22 B3
Clavadal Rd *STPH/PW* TN12 173 J7 2
Clavell Cl *RHAM* ME8 90 A3
Claxfield Rd *RSIT* ME9 95 H7
Claygate *MAID/SHEP* ME15 133 K5
Claygate Cross *BGR/WK* TN15 127 G3
Claygate La *RTON* TN11 149 F1
Claygate Rd *STPH/PW* TN12 175 F4
WBY/YAL ME18 174 C2
Clayhill *CRBK* TN17 212 C7
Clay Hill Rd *RRTW* TN3 210 A6
Clayton Croft Rd *RDART* DA2 22 D8
Clayton's La *RRTW* TN3 204 B4
Claywood La *RDART* DA2 43 J1
Clearway *BGR/WK* TN15 106 C5
Cleave Av *ORP* BR6 75 K2
Cleave Rd *GILL* ME7 5 E6
Cleavers *CRBK* TN17 215 H6
Cleavesland *WBY/YAL* ME18 174 C1
Cleeve Av *RTWE/PEM* TN2 11 F5
Clematis Av *RHAM* ME8 89 J1
Clement Ct *MAIDW* ME16 6 A2
Clement St *SWLY* BR8 41 G4
Clenches Farm Rd *SEV* TN13 8 C5
Clerks Fld *HDCN* TN27 200 A1 1
Clermont Cl *GILL* ME7 89 H2
Cleveland *RTWE/PEM* TN2 11 F2
Cleveland Rd *GILL* ME7 5 D2 2
Cleve Rd *SCUP* DA14 38 E1
Cleves Rd *RSEV* TN14 102 C4
Clewson Ri *MAID/BEAR* ME14 111 H6 2
Cliffe Rd *STRD* ME2 49 G6
Cliff Hl *RMAID* ME17 155 J2
Cliff Hill Rd *RMAID* ME17 155 J2
Cliff Reach *GRH* DA9 24 D5
Clifton Cl *MAID/BEAR* ME14 7 E1
ORP BR6 75 H1
STRD ME2 48 E7
Clifton Gv *GVW* DA11 27 J6
Clifton Marine Pde *GVW* DA11 27 H5
Clifton Pl *RTW* TN1 11 D5 2
Clifton Rd *GILL* ME7 4 C1
GVW DA11 27 H5
RTWE/PEM TN2 190 C7
Clinch St *HOO/HM* ME3 33 G1
Clinton Av *STRD* ME2 48 C6
Clinton Cl *RMAID* ME17 154 B3
Clinton La *EDEN* TN8 165 K3
Clipper Bvd *GRH* DA9 24 D3
Clipper Bvd West *GRH* DA9 24 C2
Clipper Cl *STRD* ME2 3 E1
Clipper Crs *GVE* DA12 46 C2
Clive Av *DART* DA1 22 C5
Clive Rd *GVW* DA11 27 J5
ROCH ME1 2 C5
SIT ME10 93 G1
Clockhouse *RTWE/PEM* TN2 191 F8
Cloisterham Rd *ROCH* ME1 67 J7
Cloonmore Av *ORP* BR6 76 A1
The Close *BGR/WK* TN15 104 D8
BGR/WK TN15 105 G6
E/WMAL ME19 107 K1
EDEN TN8 166 C4
HART DA3 44 C7 1
RDART DA2 41 F1
ROCH ME1 2 C4
RRTW TN3 205 F8 1
SCUP DA14 38 C3
SEV TN13 8 A3
Cloth Hall Gdns *HDCN* TN27 217 K4 1
Cloudesley Cl *ROCH* ME1 67 G5
Clovelly Wy *ORP* BR6 56 A3
Clover Bank Vw *WALD* ME5 68 C8
Clover Lay *RHAM* ME8 70 E4
Clover Rd *HOO/HM* ME3 51 F3 6
The Clovers *GVW* DA11 45 F2
Clover St *CHAT* ME4 3 F4
Clover Wy *STPH/PW* TN12 193 J1
Clyde Rd *TONN* TN10 170 C1
The Coach Dr *MEO* DA13 83 F7 1
Coach Rd *BGR/WK* TN15 126 A3
HDCN TN27 160 E8
Coalpit La *RSIT* ME9 117 G8
Cobb Cl *STRD* ME2 48 C6
Cobbets Wy *EDEN* TN8 164 C6
Cobbett Cl *E/WMAL* ME19 108 D6 1
Cobbett's Ride *RTWE/PEM* TN2 10 B6 1
Cobblestones *GILL* ME7 89 G1
Cobbs Cl *STPH/PW* TN12 173 H8
WBY/YAL ME18 130 C7
Cob Cl *BGR/WK* TN15 104 C8
Cobden Rd *SEV* TN13 9 E2
Cobdown Cl *DIT/AY* ME20 109 F4
Cobdown Gv *RHAM* ME8 70 D4 1
Cob Dr *GVE* DA12 47 H3
Cobfield *RMAID* ME17 156 C5
Cobham Av *SIT* ME10 93 K5
Cobhambury Rd *GVE* DA12 64 D1
Cobham Cl *MAIDW* ME16 6 B3
STRD ME2 48 D7
Cobhams *RRTW* TN3 188 E6
Cobham St *GVW* DA11 27 H6
Cobtree Cl *WALD* ME5 68 D6
Cobtree Rd *RMAID* ME17 154 C3
Cockerhurst Rd *RSEV* TN14 78 B4
Cockmannings La *STMC/STPC* BR5 56 E5
Cockmannings Rd *STMC/STPC* BR5 56 E4
Cockmount La *WADH* TN5 220 A8

Cocksett Av ORP BR6 75 K2
Cocksure La SCUP DA14 39 H2
Codrington Crs GVE DA12 45 K3
Codrington Gdns GVE DA12 46 A3 1
Cogate Rd STPH/PW TN12 173 G8
Colchester Cl WALD ME5 68 A7
Cold Arbor Rd SEV TN13 123 F3
Cold Blow Crs BXLY DA5 22 A7
Coldblow La MAID/BEAR ME14 113 J5
Coldbridge La RMAID ME17 181 K1
Coldharbour La DIT/AY ME20 110 A5
MAID/BEAR ME14 113 K5
Cold Harbour La RSIT ME9 72 E8
Coldharbour La RTON TN11 147 J8
Coldharbour Rd CRBK TN17 236 C1
GVW DA11 27 F8
RTON TN11 187 F6
Coldred Rd MAID/SHEP ME15 156 B2 1
Coldrum La E/WMAL ME19 106 E1
Coldshott OXTED RH8 140 E4
Colebrook Rd STH/RUST TN4 190 C7
Colegate Dr MAID/BEAR ME14 134 E2
Coleridge Cl DIT/AY ME20 108 E2 1
Coleridge Rd DART DA1 23 K3
TIL RM18 27 K1
Coleridge Wy ORP BR6 56 B3 1
Coleshall Cl MAID/SHEP ME15 134 B8
Coles La BH/WHM TN16 121 J2
Colets Orch RSEV TN14 101 K3 1
Colewood Dr STRD ME2 48 A6
Colin Blythe Rd TONN TN10 171 F1
Colin Chapman Wy HART DA3 60 E7
Colin Cl RDART DA2 24 A5
College Av GILL ME7 4 B4
MAID/SHEP ME15 6 C4
TON TN9 170 A7
College Dr RTWE/PEM TN2 11 F3
College Rd CHAT ME4 4 A1
DIT/AY ME20 109 F3
GVW DA11 26 C4
MAID/SHEP ME15 6 C5
SIT ME10 93 J3
SWLY BR8 40 B5
College Yd ROCH ME1 2 C2
Coller Crs RDART DA2 42 D3
Collet Rd RSEV TN14 102 C4
Collet Wk RHAM ME8 90 A2
Colliers Wd HAYES BR2 74 C1 1
Collington Cl GVW DA11 27 F6 1
Collington Ter
MAID/SHEP ME15 156 B2 2
Collingwood Rd DIT/AY ME20 87 H7
Collison Pl TENT TN30 230 D7
Collis St STRD ME2 49 F6
Colne Rd TONN TN10 170 B1
Colney Rd DART DA1 23 J5
Colonel's Wy STH/RUST TN4 190 A4
Coltsfoot Dr MAID/BEAR ME14 134 B2 2
Coltsfoot La OXTED RH8 140 D4
Coltstead HART DA3 61 K6 2
Columbine Cl E/WMAL ME19 108 D5 2
STRD ME2 48 D7
Columbine Rd E/WMAL ME19 108 D5
STRD ME2 48 D7
Colyer Rd GVW DA11 26 E8
Combe Bank Dr RSEV TN14 122 A2
Comet Cl PUR RM19 12 E4
Comforts Farm Av OXTED RH8 140 D4
Command Rd MAID/BEAR ME14 111 F6
Commercial Pl GVE DA12 27 K5
Commercial Rd RTW TN1 11 D2
STPH/PW TN12 173 H8
STRD ME2 2 B1
TON TN9 170 C6
Commissioner's Rd STRD ME2 49 H6
Commodore Rd MAID/BEAR ME14 7 F2
Common La HOO/HM ME3 15 H8
RDART DA2 22 D8
Common Rd BGR/WK TN15 126 B2
CRBK TN17 215 G5
HOO/HM ME3 49 G2
ROCH ME1 87 G4
RTON TN11 150 A4
Common Vw STH/RUST TN4 206 B3
Common Wall HOO/HM ME3 15 J8
Commonwealth Cl SIT ME10 94 C3
Commority Rd MEO DA13 83 J6
Compass Cl ROCH ME1 67 H5
Compasses Rd RTON TN11 167 K4
Comp La BGR/WK TN15 105 J8
E/WMAL ME19 106 C7
Compton Cl WALD ME5 88 E4 2
Concord Av WALD ME5 87 K1
Concord Cl RTWE/PEM TN2 11 E3 2
STPH/PW TN12 173 G8
Coneyburrow Rd RTWE/PEM TN2 207 K1
Conghurst La HAWK TN18 242 B1
Conifer Av HART DA3 61 K3
Conifer Dr MEO DA13 83 G4
WALD ME5 88 E5
Conifer Wy SWLY BR8 39 K6
Coniston Av STH/RUST TN4 10 A3
Coniston Cl DART DA1 22 E7
GILL ME7 51 H8
Connaught Cl MAID/SHEP ME15 156 B1 1
Connaught Rd CHAT ME4 4 B6
GILL ME7 5 D3 4
SIT ME10 93 K3
Connaught Wy STH/RUST TN4 10 B2
Conrad Cl RHAM ME8 90 A2 2
Consort Cl MAID/BEAR ME14 7 E2
Constable Rd GVW DA11 45 F1
TONN TN10 170 E1 1
Constitutional Hill Rd
STH/RUST TN4 189 J5
Constitution Hl GVE DA12 27 K7
SNOD ME6 85 J6
WALD ME5 4 B5 2
Constitution Rd WALD ME5 4 B5
Contessa Cl ORP BR6 75 K1
Convalescent La CRBK TN17 215 F4
Conway Cl STRD ME2 48 D5 1
Conway Ms GILL ME7 4 A2
Conway Rd MAIDW ME16 110 C8
Conyerd Rd BGR/WK TN15 105 F7
Cooden Cl RHAM ME8 70 D4
Cook Cl WALD ME5 68 D8
Cookham Hl ROCH ME1 2 A6
Cookham Rd SWLY BR8 39 H6
Cookham Wood Rd ROCH ME1 67 G6
Cooks La SIT ME10 73 K8
Cooling Cl MAID/BEAR ME14 7 F1
Cooling Common HOO/HM ME3 31 H6
Cooling Rd HOO/HM ME3 31 J2
STRD ME2 49 G4
Cooling St HOO/HM ME3 31 J4
Coombe Av RSEV TN14 101 K7
Coombe Cl SNOD ME6 85 K7
WALD ME5 88 C3
Coombe Dr SIT ME10 94 D2
Coombe Farm La HOO/HM ME3 18 B8
Coombe Lands TENT TN30 247 J2
Coombe La TENT TN30 230 A7
Coombe Rd GVE DA12 27 K8
HOO/HM ME3 51 F1
MAID/SHEP ME15 6 C5
RSEV TN14 102 A2
Coomb Fld EDEN TN8 164 C6
Coombfield Dr RDART DA2 42 C2
Cooper Cl GRH DA9 24 D4
Cooper Rd SNOD ME6 85 J8
WALD ME5 88 B3
Coopers Cl EYN DA4 42 B6
Coopers La RRTW TN3 188 A8
Cooper's Rd GVW DA11 27 F7
Copenhagen Rd GILL ME7 4 C4
Coplands Ri RYE TN31 244 E7
Coppards La RYE TN31 245 F6
Copper Beech Cl GVE DA12 28 A6 1
STMC/STPC BR5 56 D2 2
Copperfield Cl GVE DA12 28 D7
Copperfield Crs STRD ME2 48 B4
Copperfield Dr RMAID ME17 157 G2
Copperfield Rd ROCH ME1 2 C6
Copperfields BGR/WK TN15 102 D4
Copperfields Wk BGR/WK TN15 102 D4
Coppergate GILL ME7 89 G1
Copperhouse La GILL ME7 51 J8 1
Copperhouse Rd STRD ME2 48 B7
Copper La STPH/PW TN12 196 E1
Copperpenny Dr GILL ME7 89 J3
Copper Tree Ct MAID/SHEP ME15 155 G1
Coppice Ct GILL ME7 89 J2 2
Coppice Rd WALD ME5 88 D4
The Coppice BGR/WK TN15 125 H5
DIT/AY ME20 109 J5
MEO DA13 83 J6
RTWE/PEM TN2 191 K7
Coppice Vw MAID/BEAR ME14 112 A8
Copping's Rd RTON TN11 167 K3
Coppins La RSIT ME9 93 G4
Copse Bank BGR/WK TN15 102 D7
Copse Cl CHAT ME4 67 K5
Copsehill DIT/AY ME20 108 C4
Copse Rd RTON TN11 169 J2
Copse Side HART DA3 43 K8
The Copse HOO/HM ME3 51 F3
Copsewood Wy MAID/SHEP ME15 134 C3
Copthall Av HAWK TN18 235 F5
Copt Hall Rd BGR/WK TN15 126 A2
MEO DA13 63 J1
Cordelia Crs ROCH ME1 66 E4
Cork La STPH/PW TN12 197 K6
Cork St DIT/AY ME20 86 E8
Corkwell St CHAT ME4 3 E5
Cormorant Cl STRD ME2 48 B7 1
Cornell Cl SCUP DA14 39 F4
Corner Farm Rd STPH/PW TN12 198 A2 2
Cornfield Wy TONN TN10 148 D8
Cornflower Cl MAID/BEAR ME14 134 A2
Cornford Cl RTWE/PEM TN2 191 H8 1
Cornford La RTWE/PEM TN2 207 K2
RTWE/PEM TN2 208 C1
Cornford Pk RTWE/PEM TN2 191 J8
Cornforth Cl STPH/PW TN12 198 B2
Corn Mill Dr ORP BR6 56 A4
Cornwall Cl MAID/SHEP ME15 134 A7
Cornwall Crs ROCH ME1 86 B2
Cornwall Dr STMC/STPC BR5 38 D5
Cornwallis Av CHAT ME4 67 K5
GILL ME7 5 F4
RMAID ME17 154 E6
TONN TN10 170 E2
Cornwallis Rd MAIDW ME16 6 A3
Cornwall Rd DART DA1 23 J2
GILL ME7 4 C2 3
ROCH ME1 2 C5
Cornwell Av GVE DA12 45 K1
Corona Ter SNOD ME6 85 J8 2
Coronation Rd HOO/HM ME3 37 G1
WALD ME5 4 C6 2
Corporation Rd GILL ME7 5 D2
Corporation St ROCH ME1 2 C2
Corral Cl WALD ME5 5 D6
Corrance Gn MAID/SHEP ME15 133 G6 1
Correnden Rd RTON TN11 170 A3
Cortland Cl SIT ME10 73 K8 1
Cortland Ms SIT ME10 73 K8 2
Cossack St ROCH ME1 2 C5
Cossington Rd WALD ME5 88 C5
Costells Meadow BH/WHM TN16 120 D5
Cot La HDCN TN27 218 A3
Cotmandene Crs STMC/STPC BR5 38 C7
Cotman's Ash La BGR/WK TN15 103 H2
Cotman Wy STPH/PW TN12 151 G8
Cotswold Gdns MAID/SHEP ME15 134 C5
Cotswold Ri ORP BR6 56 A3 1
Cotswold Rd GVW DA11 45 F1
Cottage Rd CHAT ME4 3 F2
Cottages Crs SEV TN13 101 G7
Cottall Av CHAT ME4 3 F6
Cottenham Cl E/WMAL ME19 108 D7
Cotton La GRH DA9 24 B4
Couchman Green La
STPH/PW TN12 178 B7
Coulman St GILL ME7 5 D3
Coulters Cl MAID/BEAR ME14 133 K2
Coulton Av GVW DA11 27 F6
Council Av GVW DA11 26 D5
County Gv E/WMAL ME19 107 K6
County Rd MAID/BEAR ME14 7 D2
Court Crs SWLY BR8 58 B1
Court Dr MAIDW ME16 6 A2
Courtenay Rd MAID/SHEP ME15 6 C5
Courteney Rd RHAM ME8 69 J6
Courtfield Av WALD ME5 88 D3
Courthope STPH/PW TN12 173 J8
Courtlands RTON TN11 170 A3
WBY/YAL ME18 130 E6
Court La MAID/BEAR ME14 112 E1
RTON TN11 150 C6
Court Lodge Rd GILL ME7 5 F2
Court Rd RDART DA2 42 D3
ROCH ME1 86 C5
SIT ME10 73 K7
STH/RUST TN4 10 A3
Court Road (Orpington By-pass)
ORP BR6 56 C7
Cousley Wood Rd WADH TN5 220 C8
Coutts Av GVE DA12 47 H2
Coventry Cl STRD ME2 48 C8 1
Coventry Rd TONN TN10 170 D1
Coverdale Av MAID/SHEP ME15 133 K8
Coverdale Cl WALD ME5 68 C7
The Covert MEO DA13 83 F7
WALD ME5 88 C5 1
Covet Wood Cl STMC/STPC BR5 56 A3
Covey Hall Rd SNOD ME6 85 K6
Cowbeck Cl RHAM ME8 70 A8 1
Cowden Cl HAWK TN18 234 E6
Cowden La HAWK TN18 234 E7
Cowden Rd MAID/BEAR ME14 7 F2 2
ORP BR6 56 A4
Cowdrey Cl MAIDW ME16 132 B5
ROCH ME1 2 B6
Cowdrey Ct DART DA1 22 E6
Cow La EDEN TN8 185 K4
Cowley Av GRH DA9 24 E4
Cowper Rd GILL ME7 5 D5
SIT ME10 94 C2
Cowstead Rd RSIT ME9 91 G3
Cox's Cl SNOD ME6 85 J6
Cox St MAID/BEAR ME14 112 E2
Cozenton Cl RHAM ME8 70 B5
Crabbs Croft Cl ORP BR6 75 H1 1
Crabtree Cl E/WMAL ME19 129 J4
Crabtree La RMAID ME17 161 H6
Crabtree Rd RHAM ME8 70 A6
Craddock Wy RHAM ME8 90 A1 2
Cradducks La STPH/PW TN12 198 D2
Cradles Rd RSIT ME9 91 F5
Cramptons CRBK TN17 215 G6
Crampton's Rd RSEV TN14 101 K7
Cranborne Av MAID/SHEP ME15 133 J6
Cranbourne Av MAID/SHEP ME15 133 H6
Cranbrook Cl MAID/SHEP ME15 134 B7
RHAM ME8 69 K3 1
Cranbrook Dr SIT ME10 93 J5
Cranbrook Rd CRBK TN17 213 F6
CRBK TN17 226 A5
HAWK TN18 235 F2
HDCN TN27 216 C7
STPH/PW TN12 198 B7
TENT TN30 229 J6
Crandalls RTON TN11 168 D5

Crane La *CRBK* TN17 225 K1
Cranford Cl *RHAM* ME8 70 A5
Cranford Rd *DART* DA1 23 H7
TONN TN10 171 G1
Cranleigh Cl *ORP* BR6 56 B7
Cranleigh Dr *SWLY* BR8 58 B1
Cranleigh Gdns *MAIDW* ME16 110 C7 1
ROCH ME1 3 D5
Cranmer Ct *MAID/SHEP* ME15 133 H6
Cranmere Ct *STRD* ME2 49 H6
Cranmer Rd *SEV* TN13 8 A2
Cranwell Rd *STH/RUST* TN4 206 B2
Craven Rd *ORP* BR6 56 E7
Crawfords *SWLY* BR8 40 B5
Crawshay Cl *SEV* TN13 8 C2
Cray Av *STMC/STPC* BR5 56 C2
Craybrooke Rd *SCUP* DA14 38 C2
Crayburne *MEO* DA13 44 A3
Cray Cl *DART* DA1 22 D4
Crayford Cl *MAID/BEAR* ME14 7 F1 2
Crayford High St *DART* DA1 22 B3
Crayford Rd *DART* DA1 22 C4
Crayford Wy *DART* DA1 22 D3
Craylands *STMC/STPC* BR5 38 D8
Craylands La *SWCM* DA10 25 J4
Craylands Sq *SWCM* DA10 25 J4 1
Cray Rd *SCUP* DA14 38 D4
SWLY BR8 57 K3
Craythorne *TENT* TN30 230 B5
Cray Valley Rd *STMC/STPC* BR5 56 B2
The Creek *GVW* DA11 26 C4
Cremers Rd *SIT* ME10 94 C1
Cremorne Rd *GVW* DA11 27 G6 1
Crendon Pk *STH/RUST* TN4 190 A5
Crescent Gdns *SWLY* BR8 39 K7
Crescent Rd *BFN/LL* DA15 38 A1
SOCK/AV RM15 13 G2 1
The Crescent *BGR/WK* TN15 105 G6
CHAT ME4 50 C5
GRH DA9 25 H5
GVW DA11 27 G8
HART DA3 43 K8
MAID/BEAR ME14 111 F6
SCUP DA14 38 A2
SEV TN13 9 F1
STH/RUST TN4 189 J2
TON TN9 170 B4
Crescent Wk *SOCK/AV* RM15 13 G2
Crescent Wy *ORP* BR6 75 K1
SOCK/AV RM15 13 H1
WALD ME5 87 J1
Cressey Ct *CHAT* ME4 3 E4
Crest Cl *RSEV* TN14 77 J6 1
Crest Rd *ROCH* ME1 67 H5
Crest Vw *GRH* DA9 25 F3 1
Crestway *WALD* ME5 68 C6
Crete Hall Rd *GVW* DA11 26 E5
Creve Coeur Cl
MAID/BEAR ME14 134 C1 1
Cricketers Cl *RMAID* ME17 137 H8
Cricketers Dr *MEO* DA13 63 H7
Cripple Hl *RASHW* TN26 219 J5
Cripple St *MAID/SHEP* ME15 133 G7
Crismill La *MAID/BEAR* ME14 135 H2
Crismill Rd *MAID/BEAR* ME14 135 G3
Crispe Cl *RHAM* ME8 90 A2
Crispin Ct *RMAID* ME17 154 C3 1
Crispin Rd *STRD* ME2 48 D6
Crispin Wy *E/WMAL* ME19 129 J3
Crittenden Rd *STPH/PW* TN12 192 E2
Crockenhall Wy *MEO* DA13 45 F6
Crockenhill Hl *STMC/STPC* BR5 56 E2
Crockenhill La *SWLY* BR8 58 D4
Crocken Hill Rd *HDCN* TN27 182 C4
Crockenhill Rd *STMC/STPC* BR5 56 E3
Crockers La *RYE* TN31 244 E6
Croft Cl *RMAID* ME17 158 B4
TONN TN10 171 F1
WALD ME5 88 D5
Croft Ct *EDEN* TN8 164 C5
The Crofters *RHAM* ME8 70 C7
Croft Gdns *RMAID* ME17 160 D1
Croft La *EDEN* TN8 164 C5
Croft Rd *BH/WHM* TN16 120 B5
Croftside *MEO* DA13 83 H6 1
The Croft *E/WMAL* ME19 108 C4
SWLY BR8 39 K8
Croft Wy *SEV* TN13 8 B4
Cromer Rd *SIT* ME10 93 K6
STRD ME2 49 G6
Cromer St *TON* TN9 170 A5
Crompton Gdns *MAID/SHEP* ME15 7 E4
Cromwell Rd *MAID/BEAR* ME14 7 D2 2
RTWE/PEM TN2 11 E4
Cromwell Ter *CHAT* ME4 4 A5
Cronin Cl *DIT/AY* ME20 108 D2
Crooked La *GVE* DA12 27 J5
Crook Rd *STPH/PW* TN12 194 A5
Crosier Ct *RSIT* ME9 71 H3
Crosley Rd *GILL* ME7 5 D6
Cross Dr *RMAID* ME17 157 K5
Cross Keys *MAID/BEAR* ME14 134 E2
Cross La *SIT* ME10 73 K8 3
Cross La East *GVE* DA12 27 J8
Cross Lane Gdns *WADH* TN5 232 B5
Cross La West *GVW* DA11 27 J8
Crossley Cl *BH/WHM* TN16 97 H2
Cross Rd *DART* DA1 23 F5
GVW DA11 27 G5
RDART DA2 41 J2
SCUP DA14 38 C2 1
STMC/STPC BR5 56 C2 1
Cross St *CHAT* ME4 4 A4
GILL ME7 4 C2
MAID/BEAR ME14 7 D1
STRD ME2 49 G6
Cross Wy *ROCH* ME1 2 B5
Crossway *WALD* ME5 67 K8
Crossways *BH/WHM* TN16 97 G7
SIT ME10 93 K5
Crossways Bvd *GRH* DA9 24 D4
The Crossway *STH/RUST* TN4 206 C4
Crouch Hill Ct *RSIT* ME9 72 B3 1
Crouch House Rd *EDEN* TN8 164 A3
Crouch La *BGR/WK* TN15 105 G8
HAWK TN18 237 H6
Crow Dr *RSEV* TN14 100 E2
Crow Hill Rd *BGR/WK* TN15 105 G7
Crowhurst La *BGR/WK* TN15 81 G1
BGR/WK TN15 126 E2
LING RH7 162 B1
Crowhurst Rd *BGR/WK* TN15 105 F8
LING RH7 162 B8
Crowhurst Village Rd *LING* RH7 162 C4
Crowhurst Wy *STMC/STPC* BR5 56 D2
Crow La *ROCH* ME1 2 C3
Crown Acres *STPH/PW* TN12 151 J8
Crown Cl *ORP* BR6 56 B8
Crownfields *MAID/BEAR* ME14 134 A2 1
SEV TN13 9 D4
Crown Gn *GVE* DA12 47 H3 1
Crown La *GVE* DA12 47 H2
Crown Quay La *SIT* ME10 94 A2 1
Crown Rd *EDEN* TN8 164 D3
ORP BR6 76 B1
RSEV TN14 78 C5
SIT ME10 93 K1
Crown St *GILL* ME7 5 D2 3
Crowther Cl *STPH/PW* TN12 198 A2
Croxley Cl *STMC/STPC* BR5 38 C7
Croxley Gn *STMC/STPC* BR5 38 C6
Croydon Cl *WALD* ME5 88 D2
Croydon Rd *BH/WHM* TN16 120 B5
WARL CR6 118 B1
Cruden Rd *GVE* DA12 46 C1
Crump's La *RMAID* ME17 180 C3
Crundale Rd *RHAM* ME8 69 K3
Crundwell Rd *STH/RUST* TN4 189 K5
Crusader Cl *GILL* ME7 69 H6
PUR RM19 12 E4
Crutches La *STRD* ME2 48 A6
Cryalls La *RSIT* ME9 93 G3
SIT ME10 93 H2
Cryals Rd *STPH/PW* TN12 209 K2
Cuckolds Green Rd *HOO/HM* ME3 34 D1
Cuckoo La *RTON* TN11 149 G7
STPH/PW TN12 210 D4
Cuckoowood Av
MAID/BEAR ME14 111 F5
Cudham Cl *MAID/BEAR* ME14 7 F1
Cudham La North *RSEV* TN14 98 C1
Cudham La South *RSEV* TN14 98 C2
Cudham Park Rd *RSEV* TN14 75 K5
Cudham Rd *BH/WHM* TN16 97 J6
ORP BR6 75 F6
Cugley Rd *RDART* DA2 24 B6
Culcroft *HART* DA3 62 A1
Culpeper Cl *RMAID* ME17 136 B4
STRD ME2 3 D1
Culpepers *CRBK* TN17 212 D7
Culpepper Rd *RHAM* ME8 90 A2
RMAID ME17 154 B3
Culverden Av *STH/RUST* TN4 10 B1
Culverden Down *STH/RUST* TN4 10 B2
Culverden Pk *STH/RUST* TN4 10 B2
Culverden Park Rd *STH/RUST* TN4 10 B1
Culverden Sq *STH/RUST* TN4 10 C2
Culverden St *RTW* TN1 10 C3 3
Culver Dr *OXTED* RH8 140 C1
Culvey Cl *HART* DA3 61 K2
Cumberland Av *GVE* DA12 27 K6 4
MAID/SHEP ME15 133 K6
Cumberland Dr *DART* DA1 23 J6
RSIT ME9 72 A3
Cumberland Rd *GILL* ME7 4 C1
Cumberland Yd *RTW* TN1 10 C5 3
Cumbrian Av *BXLYHN* DA7 22 B1
Cunningham Cl *STH/RUST* TN4 190 B7 1
Cunningham Crs *WALD* ME5 68 B6
Cunningham Rd *STH/RUST* TN4 190 B7
Curlew Av *RSIT* ME9 72 A3
Curlew Crs *STRD* ME2 48 B8
The Curlews *GVE* DA12 28 A8
Currie Rd *STH/RUST* TN4 10 C1
Curteis Rd *TENT* TN30 230 B6
Curtismill Cl *STMC/STPC* BR5 38 C8
Curtismill Wy *STMC/STPC* BR5 38 C8
Curzon Rd *CHAT* ME4 3 F5
MAID/BEAR ME14 7 D1
Cutmore St *GVW* DA11 27 J6
Cutter Ridge Rd *MEO* DA13 64 D5
The Cut *HDCN* TN27 201 H7
Cutty Sark Ct *GRH* DA9 25 F4 2
Cuxton Rd *MAID/SHEP* ME15 156 B1
STRD ME2 2 A2
Cyclamen Rd *SWLY* BR8 58 A1
Cygnet Cl *DIT/AY* ME20 108 E4
Cygnet Rd *WALD* ME5 88 D4
Cygnet Vw *WTHK* RM20 13 K3
Cypress Av *HOO/HM* ME3 51 F3 2
Cypress Cl *GILL* ME7 5 F2
Cypress Gv *RTWE/PEM* TN2 207 H6 1
Cypress Rd *STRD* ME2 49 H5
Cyril Rd *ORP* BR6 56 B4

D

Dacre Av *SOCK/AV* RM15 13 H1
Dacre Crs *SOCK/AV* RM15 13 H1
Daffodil Rd *STRD* ME2 48 D7
Dagmar Rd *CHAT* ME4 4 B6
Dahlia Dr *SWLY* BR8 40 C7
Dairy Cl *EYN* DA4 42 A5
Dairy La *EDEN* TN8 142 B5
STPH/PW TN12 175 K2
Dale Cl *DART* DA1 22 C5
Dale Rd *DART* DA1 22 C5
MEO DA13 44 B2
ROCH ME1 2 C5
SWLY BR8 39 K8
Daleside *ORP* BR6 76 B1
Daleside Cl *ORP* BR6 76 B2
Dale St *CHAT* ME4 3 E6
RTW TN1 11 D3
Dale Vw *ERITH* DA8 22 D1
Dalewood *SIT* ME10 94 B4
Dalison Ct *STRD* ME2 86 A2
Daltons Rd *SWLY* BR8 57 K6
Dalton St *GILL* ME7 4 C2 4
Damiem Cl *CHAT* ME4 4 A6 1
Damigos Rd *GVE* DA12 28 C7
Damon Cl *SCUP* DA14 38 C1
Damson Dr *HOO/HM* ME3 51 F3 8
Dane Cl *ORP* BR6 75 J1
RSIT ME9 91 G1
WALD ME5 88 D4
Dane Ct *RMAID* ME17 154 C4
Dane La *RSIT* ME9 91 G1
Danemore *TENT* TN30 230 B6
Dane Rd *SEV* TN13 101 G4
Danes Cl *GVW* DA11 44 D1
Danes Hl *GILL* ME7 51 H8
Danes Md *SIT* ME10 73 K4
Danns La *WBY/YAL* ME18 129 J6
Danson Wy *RHAM* ME8 70 A5
Danvers Rd *TON* TN9 170 B5
Darby Gdns *HOO/HM* ME3 48 A3
Darent Cl *SEV* TN13 122 E1
Darenth Av *TONN* TN10 170 B1
Darenth Dr *GVE* DA12 28 E7
Darenth Gdns *BH/WHM* TN16 120 D5 1
Darenth Hl *RDART* DA2 42 A3
Darenth La *SEV* TN13 101 G8
Darenth Park Av *RDART* DA2 24 C8
Darenth Ri *WALD* ME5 88 C3
Darenth Rd *DART* DA1 23 J7
Darenth Rd South *RDART* DA2 42 A2
Darenth Wy *RSEV* TN14 78 D6
Darenth Wood Rd *RDART* DA2 24 D7
Darent Md *EYN* DA4 42 A6
Darent Valley Pth *DART* DA1 12 B8
EYN DA4 60 A2
RSEV TN14 101 J2
SEV TN13 100 D8
Dargate Cl *MAIDW* ME16 110 C7
Dargets Rd *WALD* ME5 88 B3
Darland Av *GILL* ME7 5 E6
Darlton Cl *DART* DA1 22 C1
Darman La *STPH/PW* TN12 174 B3
Darnets Fld *RSEV* TN14 101 H4
Darnley Cl *STRD* ME2 48 C8
Darnley Dr *STH/RUST* TN4 189 J2
Darnley Rd *GVW* DA11 27 H5 2
STRD ME2 48 D8
Darnley St *GVW* DA11 27 H6
Darns Hl *SWLY* BR8 57 K4
Dart Cl *STRD* ME2 48 E7
Dartford Rd *DART* DA1 22 D5
EYN DA4 59 J3
SEV TN13 9 E3
Darwin Cl *ORP* BR6 75 J1
Darwin Dr *TONN* TN10 148 D8
Dashmonden Cl *STRD* ME2 49 H4
Dashwood Rd *GVW* DA11 27 H7
Davenport Av *GILL* ME7 5 E2
Davis Av *GVW* DA11 27 F7
Davis Cl *SEV* TN13 9 E1
Davis Rd *SOCK/AV* RM15 13 H1
Davy's Pl *GVE* DA12 46 B4
Dawell Dr *BH/WHM* TN16 97 G4
Dawes Cl *GRH* DA9 24 E4
Dawes St *GILL* ME7 4 C3
Dawson Av *STMC/STPC* BR5 38 C7

Dawson Dr *SWLY* BR8 ... 40 B5
Dayton Dr *ERITH* DA8 ... 12 B5
Deacon Cl *STRD* ME2 ... 48 D6 2
Deakin Leas *TON* TN9 ... 170 B7
Deakins Ter *ORP* BR6 ... 56 B4 2
Deanery Rd *EDEN* TN8 ... 142 C5
Dean La *MEO* DA13 ... 64 A7
Dean Rd *SIT* ME10 ... 73 K8
STRD ME2 ... 48 D6
Deans Hill Rd *RSIT* ME9 ... 115 J1
Dean St *MAID/SHEP* ME15 ... 132 D6
Deanwood Dr *RHAM* ME8 ... 70 A8
Decoy Hill Rd *HOO/HM* ME3 ... 17 G8
Deepdene *WADH* TN5 ... 220 B8
Deerhurst Cl *HART* DA3 ... 44 D8 1
Deerhurst Gdns *MAIDW* ME16 ... 6 A3 2
Deerleap La *RSEV* TN14 ... 76 E8
Defiant Cl *WALD* ME5 ... 68 C8
Defoe Cl *WALD* ME5 ... 68 C8 1
Delagarde Rd *BH/WHM* TN16 ... 120 C5
De Lapre Cl *STMC/STPC* BR5 ... 56 E4
Delarue Cl *RTON* TN11 ... 148 D6
Delce Rd *ROCH* ME1 ... 3 D4
Del Gdns *SNOD* ME6 ... 85 K6 2
Delius Dr *TONN* TN10 ... 149 F8
Dell Dr *RTWE/PEM* TN2 ... 11 F3
The Dell *BXLY* DA5 ... 22 B7
Delmonden Rd *HAWK* TN18 ... 234 C6
Delves Av *RTWE/PEM* TN2 ... 11 E6
De Mere Cl *RHAM* ME8 ... 70 A8
Denbeigh Dr *TONN* TN10 ... 148 D8
Denberry Dr *SCUP* DA14 ... 38 C1
Denbigh Av *RHAM* ME8 ... 70 A5
Denbigh Cl *SIT* ME10 ... 73 K7
Denbigh Rd *STH/RUST* TN4 ... 190 C7 1
Dene Cl *RDART* DA2 ... 40 B2
Dene Dr *HART* DA3 ... 44 C7
ORP BR6 ... 56 C7
Dene Holm Rd *GVW* DA11 ... 44 E1
Dene Lodge Cl *BGR/WK* TN15 ... 105 F7
Dene Rd *DART* DA1 ... 23 J6
Denesway *MEO* DA13 ... 63 H3
The Dene *SEV* TN13 ... 9 D5
Dene Wk *HART* DA3 ... 43 K8
Dene Wy *RRTW* TN3 ... 188 E7
Denham Rd *RSIT* ME9 ... 72 A7
Denison Ms *HOO/HM* ME3 ... 35 F2 1
Den La *STPH/PW* TN12 ... 175 G3
Dennettsland Rd *EDEN* TN8 ... 142 C5
Dennis Rd *GVW* DA11 ... 45 H1
Denton Cl *MAID/SHEP* ME15 ... 134 A6
Denton Court Rd *GVE* DA12 ... 28 B7
Denton Rd *BXLY* DA5 ... 22 B7
DART DA1 ... 22 B6
Denton St *GVE* DA12 ... 28 B6
Denver Rd *DART* DA1 ... 22 D6
Derby Cl *RTON* TN11 ... 147 J8
SIT ME10 ... 73 J8
Derby Rd *MAID/SHEP* ME15 ... 133 J6
WALD ME5 ... 5 E6
Dering Cl *HDCN* TN27 ... 203 J2
Dering Wy *GVE* DA12 ... 28 C7
Deringwood Dr *MAID/SHEP* ME15 ... 134 B5
Dernier Rd *TON* TN9 ... 170 C2
Derry Downs *STMC/STPC* BR5 ... 56 D3
Derwent Cl *DART* DA1 ... 22 E7
Derwent Dr *STH/RUST* TN4 ... 10 A2
Derwent Rd *TONN* TN10 ... 170 C1
Derwent Wy *RHAM* ME8 ... 70 A6
Detillens La *OXTED* RH8 ... 118 E8
Detling Cl *RHAM* ME8 ... 69 K4
Detling Hl *MAID/BEAR* ME14 ... 112 C5
Detling Rd *GVW* DA11 ... 26 E7
Devon Cl *RHAM* ME8 ... 70 C5
WALD ME5 ... 68 D7
Devon Rd *EYN* DA4 ... 42 A6
MAID/SHEP ME15 ... 7 F6
Devonshire Av *DART* DA1 ... 22 E5
Devonshire Cl *RTWE/PEM* TN2 ... 206 E6 2
Devonshire Rd *GILL* ME7 ... 5 D1 2
GVW DA11 ... 27 J7
ORP BR6 ... 56 B4 3
Dewlands Av *RDART* DA2 ... 24 A6
Dhekelia Cl *MAID/BEAR* ME14 ... 111 G7
Dial Cl *GILL* ME7 ... 5 F2
GRH DA9 ... 25 H4
Dial Rd *GILL* ME7 ... 5 F2
Dibden La *RSEV* TN14 ... 8 A6
Dickens Av *DART* DA1 ... 23 K3
Dickens Cl *HART* DA3 ... 61 K2
RMAID ME17 ... 157 G2
Dickens Dr *E/WMAL* ME19 ... 108 D5
Dickensian Cl *HOO/HM* ME3 ... 34 D3
Dickens Rd *GVE* DA12 ... 28 B7
MAID/BEAR ME14 ... 110 E7
ROCH ME1 ... 2 C6
Dickens Wy *HAWK* TN18 ... 235 G5
Dickley La *RMAID* ME17 ... 138 A8
Digdog La *CRBK* TN17 ... 216 B3
Dignals Cl *RHAM* ME8 ... 70 C4
Dillon Wy *RTWE/PEM* TN2 ... 11 F1
Dillywood La *HOO/HM* ME3 ... 48 D4
Dimmock Cl *STPH/PW* TN12 ... 173 K8
Dingleden La *CRBK* TN17 ... 237 H4
Dippers Cl *BGR/WK* TN15 ... 102 D4
Discovery Dr *E/WMAL* ME19 ... 129 J3
Dislingbury Rd *RTON* TN11 ... 191 H3
Disraeli Cl *MAID/SHEP* ME15 ... 156 A1 2
Ditton Court Cl *DIT/AY* ME20 ... 109 F5 1
Ditton Pl *DIT/AY* ME20 ... 109 F5
Dixon Cl *MAID/SHEP* ME15 ... 6 C5
Dixter La *RYE* TN31 ... 244 D7
Dixter Rd *RYE* TN31 ... 244 D7
Dixwell Cl *RHAM* ME8 ... 90 A1
Dobbie Cl *SIT* ME10 ... 73 K8
Dobson Rd *GVE* DA12 ... 46 B3
Dock Rd *CHAT* ME4 ... 3 F3
Doctor Hope's Rd *CRBK* TN17 ... 225 K2
Doddington Ct *MAIDW* ME16 ... 6 B2 1
Doddington Rd *RHAM* ME8 ... 69 K4
Dodd Rd *TONN* TN10 ... 170 E1
Doggets Cl *EDEN* TN8 ... 164 C6 1
Doggetts Rw *HOO/HM* ME3 ... 21 G8 1
Doggett's Sq *STRD* ME2 ... 2 B1 3
Dogwood Cl *GVW* DA11 ... 45 G2
WALD ME5 ... 88 E5 1
Dolphin Dr *RHAM* ME8 ... 90 B1
Dolphin Rd *SIT* ME10 ... 94 C1
Dombey Cl *HOO/HM* ME3 ... 48 B3
ROCH ME1 ... 2 C5 1
Donald Moor Av *RSIT* ME9 ... 95 K4
Doncaster Cl *MAID/SHEP* ME15 ... 134 B8 5
Donet Cl *RHAM* ME8 ... 89 K1
Dongola Rd *STRD* ME2 ... 49 F5
Donkey Fld *RTON* TN11 ... 168 C5
Donkey La *EYN* DA4 ... 60 A6
Doon Brae *STH/RUST* TN4 ... 190 A4
Dorado Gdns *ORP* BR6 ... 56 E7
Dorchester Cl *DART* DA1 ... 23 J6
HOO/HM ME3 ... 31 G7 1
STMC/STPC BR5 ... 38 C5 1
Dorchester Rd *GVE* DA12 ... 46 A1
Doric Av *STH/RUST* TN4 ... 189 K5
Doric Cl *STH/RUST* TN4 ... 189 K5
Dorking Rd *RTW* TN1 ... 11 E1
Dormers Dr *MEO* DA13 ... 63 J4 1
Dornden Dr *RRTW* TN3 ... 205 K2
Dornden Gdns *WALD* ME5 ... 88 C4
Dorney Ri *STMC/STPC* BR5 ... 56 A1
Dorothy Av *CRBK* TN17 ... 225 K2
Dorrit Wy *ROCH* ME1 ... 3 D6
Dorset Crs *GVE* DA12 ... 46 B2
Dorset Rd *RTWE/PEM* TN2 ... 11 F5
Dorset Sq *RHAM* ME8 ... 70 A5
Dorset Wy *MAID/SHEP* ME15 ... 133 J6
Dotterel Cl *WALD* ME5 ... 88 E5
Doubleday Dr *RSIT* ME9 ... 94 E4
Doubleton La *RTON* TN11 ... 187 J1
Douglas Rd *MAIDW* ME16 ... 6 B4
RMAID ME17 ... 160 D1 1
TON TN9 ... 170 A6
Doust Wy *ROCH* ME1 ... 3 D4
Dove Cl *WALD* ME5 ... 68 C8
Dovedale Rd *RDART* DA2 ... 24 B7 1
Doveney Cl *STMC/STPC* BR5 ... 56 E1
Dove Rd *TONN* TN10 ... 148 C8
Dover Rd *GVW* DA11 ... 26 E6
Dover Rd East *GVW* DA11 ... 27 F6
Dover St *MAIDW* ME16 ... 132 C4
SIT ME10 ... 93 K2 3
Doves Cft *RSIT* ME9 ... 93 H7
Dowding Rd *BH/WHM* TN16 ... 97 H2
Dowding Wy *RTWE/PEM* TN2 ... 190 E5
Dower House Crs *STH/RUST* TN4 ... 189 J3
Dowgate Cl *TON* TN9 ... 170 D7
Dowlerville Rd *ORP* BR6 ... 76 A2
Dowling Cl *SNOD* ME6 ... 85 H7 1
The Downage *GVW* DA11 ... 27 H8
Down Av *RRTW* TN3 ... 221 J3
Downderry Wy *DIT/AY* ME20 ... 109 F5
Downe Av *RSEV* TN14 ... 75 H7
Downer Ct *ROCH* ME1 ... 67 K6
Downe Rd *HAYES* BR2 ... 74 D4
RSEV TN14 ... 98 C1
Downlands *RMAID* ME17 ... 137 K8
Downs Av *DART* DA1 ... 23 K6
Downs Cl *HDCN* TN27 ... 200 C1
MAID/BEAR ME14 ... 111 G6 2
SIT ME10 ... 93 J4
Downside *STRD* ME2 ... 2 A1
Downs Rd *MAID/BEAR* ME14 ... 111 H6
MEO DA13 ... 44 E3
WBY/YAL ME18 ... 152 E5
The Downs *WALD* ME5 ... 87 J5
Downs Va *HART* DA3 ... 61 K1
Downs Vw *ROCH* ME1 ... 86 E5
Downsview *E/WMAL* ME19 ... 83 H8
WALD ME5 ... 68 D6
Downs View Cl *ORP* BR6 ... 76 D5
Downsview Cl *SWLY* BR8 ... 40 C8 1
Downs View Rd *MAID/BEAR* ME14 ... 111 G6
Downsview Rd *SEV* TN13 ... 8 B4
Downsway *ORP* BR6 ... 75 K1 1
Downs Wy *OXTED* RH8 ... 118 C6
Downs Wd *MEO* DA13 ... 83 G6
Drage Rd *STPH/PW* TN12 ... 151 G8
Drake's Av *STRD* ME2 ... 48 E6
Drakes Cl *RSIT* ME9 ... 71 H4
Draper St *STH/RUST* TN4 ... 189 K4
Dray Corner Rd *HDCN* TN27 ... 179 H7
Dray Ct *RTON* TN11 ... 150 A6
Dray's Fld *RSIT* ME9 ... 116 A
Drayton Cl *HOO/HM* ME3 ... 33 F
Drayton Rd *TON* TN9 ... 170 C
Drewery Dr *RHAM* ME8 ... 89 K
Driffield Gdns *STH/RUST* TN4 ... 169 J
The Drive *CHST* BR7 ... 38 A
GVE DA12 ... 46 A
HART DA3 ... 44 C
ORP BR6 ... 56 A
RTWE/PEM TN2 ... 10 C
SCUP DA14 ... 38 C
SEV TN13 ... 9 D
TON TN9 ... 170 B
The Drove Wy *MEO* DA13 ... 45 F
Drudgeon Wy *RDART* DA2 ... 43 G
Drury Rd *TENT* TN30 ... 230 A
Dry Bank Ct *TONN* TN10 ... 170 B
Dryden Wy *ORP* BR6 ... 56 B
Dryhill La *RSEV* TN14 ... 122 D
Dry Hill Park Crs *TONN* TN10 ... 170 C
Dry Hill Park Rd *TONN* TN10 ... 170 B
Dry Hill Rd *TONN* TN10 ... 170 B
Dryland Av *ORP* BR6 ... 56 A
Dryland Rd *BGR/WK* TN15 ... 105 F
SNOD ME6 ... 85 J
Duchess Cl *STRD* ME2 ... 48 D
Duchess of Kent Dr *WALD* ME5 ... 88 C
Duchess' Wk *BGR/WK* TN15 ... 124 C
Ducketts Rd *DART* DA1 ... 22 C
Dudely Rd *GVW* DA11 ... 27 F
Dudley Rd *RTW* TN1 ... 10 C3
Dudsbury Rd *DART* DA1 ... 22 E
Dukes Meadow *RTON* TN11 ... 167 H
Dukes Meadow Dr *GILL* ME7 ... 69 G
Dukes Rd *RTW* TN1 ... 11 E
Dully Rd *RSIT* ME9 ... 117 K
Dumbourne La *TENT* TN30 ... 240 C
Duncan Rd *GILL* ME7 ... 5 D
Dundale Rd *RRTW* TN3 ... 209 F
Dunedin Cl *SIT* ME10 ... 93 H
Dunera Dr *MAID/BEAR* ME14 ... 111 F
Dunkin Rd *DART* DA1 ... 23 K
Dunkirk Cl *GVE* DA12 ... 45 K
Dunkirk Dr *WALD* ME5 ... 68 A
Dunk's Green Rd *RTON* TN11 ... 149 G
Dunning's La *ROCH* ME1 ... 2 C4
The Dunnings *MAIDW* ME16 ... 132 A
Dunn Street Rd *GILL* ME7 ... 89 H
Dunstan Gv *STH/RUST* TN4 ... 11 D
Dunstan Rd *STH/RUST* TN4 ... 11 D
Durant Rd *SWLY* BR8 ... 40 D
Durham Cl *MAID/SHEP* ME15 ... 133 K
Durham Rd *RHAM* ME8 ... 69 K
SCUP DA14 ... 38 C
Durley Gdns *ORP* BR6 ... 56 C
Durndale La *GVW* DA11 ... 45 F
Durrant Wy *ORP* BR6 ... 75 J
SWCM DA10 ... 25 K
Durrell Gdns *WALD* ME5 ... 68 D5
Duval Dr *ROCH* ME1 ... 67 K
Dux Court Rd *HOO/HM* ME3 ... 32 D
Dux Hl *BGR/WK* TN15 ... 127 F
Dux La *BGR/WK* TN15 ... 127 F
Dwelly La *LING* RH7 ... 163 G
Dyke Dr *STMC/STPC* BR5 ... 56 D
Dykewood Cl *BXLY* DA5 ... 40 A
Dynes Rd *RSEV* TN14 ... 102 C
Dynevor Rd *STH/RUST* TN4 ... 190 C
Dyngley Cl *SIT* ME10 ... 73 K8

E

Eagle Cl *DIT/AY* ME20 ... 108 E
Eagles Cl *SIT* ME10 ... 94 D
Eagles Dr *BH/WHM* TN16 ... 97 H
Eagles Rd *GRH* DA9 ... 25 G
Eaglestone Cl *BGR/WK* TN15 ... 105 G6
Eagle Wy *GVW* DA11 ... 26 B
Ealing Cl *WALD* ME5 ... 88 C
Eardemont Cl *DART* DA1 ... 22 C
Eardley Rd *SEV* TN13 ... 9 D
Earl Cl *WALD* ME5 ... 88 C
Earl Rd *GVW* DA11 ... 27 F
Earl's Rd *STH/RUST* TN4 ... 10 B
Earl St *MAID/BEAR* ME14 ... 6 C
MAIDW ME16 ... 6 C
East Cliff Rd *STH/RUST* TN4 ... 10 C
Eastcote *ORP* BR6 ... 56 A
Eastcourt Gn *RHAM* ME8 ... 69 J
Eastcourt La *GILL* ME7 ... 69 K
RHAM ME8 ... 69 J
East Cross *TENT* TN30 ... 230 A
East Dr *STMC/STPC* BR5 ... 56 C
Easterfields *E/WMAL* ME19 ... 131 G
Eastern Av *SOCK/AV* RM15 ... 13 G
WTHK RM20 ... 13 K
Eastern Rd *GILL* ME7 ... 5 F
Eastern Vw *BH/WHM* TN16 ... 97 G
Eastfield Gdns *TONN* TN10 ... 170 E1
Eastgate *ROCH* ME1 ... 2 C
Eastgate Rd *TENT* TN30 ... 230 B
Eastgate Ter *ROCH* ME1 ... 2 C3

East Hall Hl RMAID ME17 156 A8
East Hall La SIT ME10 94 D1
East Hall Rd STMC/STPC BR5 57 F4
East Hl BH/WHM TN16 97 F5
DART DA1 23 J6
EYN DA4 42 C6
OXTED RH8 118 D8
TENT TN30 230 B6
East Hill Dr DART DA1 23 J6 1
East Hill Rd BGR/WK TN15 80 A7
OXTED RH8 118 C8
East Kent Av GVW DA11 26 D5
Eastlands Cl OXTED RH8 118 B6
STH/RUST TN4 206 D6
Eastlands Rd STH/RUST TN4 206 D6 1
Eastlands Wy OXTED RH8 118 B6
Eastling Cl RHAM ME8 70 A3
East Milton Rd GVE DA12 28 A6
East Park Rd DIT/AY ME20 110 A5
East Rochester Wy DART DA1 22 A6
East Rw ROCH ME1 2 C3
Eastry Cl MAIDW ME16 110 C7
East St CHAT ME4 4 A5
E/WMAL ME19 107 F4
GILL ME7 5 D2
MAID/SHEP ME15 153 K6
RMAID ME17 159 J1
SIT ME10 94 B2
SNOD ME6 86 A6
TON TN9 170 C4
East St (North) E/WMAL ME19 107 F3
East Sutton Rd HDCN TN27 179 J5
RMAID ME17 157 H7
East Ter GVE DA12 27 K5
East Weald Dr TENT TN30 230 B5
Eastwell Barn Ms TENT TN30 230 A6 1
Eastwell Cl MAID/BEAR ME14 7 F2
STPH/PW TN12 173 G7
Eastwell Mdw TENT TN30 230 A6
Eastwood Rd SIT ME10 93 J1
Eccles Rw DIT/AY ME20 86 E8
Eccleston Rd MAID/SHEP ME15 6 C5
Echo Cl MAID/SHEP ME15 134 B8
Echo Ct GVE DA12 27 K8
Eclipse Dr SIT ME10 73 K6
Eddington Cl MAID/SHEP ME15 133 H8
Eden Av WALD ME5 68 A7
Edenbridge Cl STMC/STPC BR5 56 E2
Eden Cl BXLY DA5 40 A2
Eden Pl GVE DA12 27 J6
Eden Rd BXLY DA5 39 K2
HOO/HM ME3 33 F2
RTW TN1 10 C5
Eden Valley Wk EDEN TN8 163 K8
RTON TN11 168 C7
Edgar Cl SWLY BR8 40 C8
Edgar Rd BH/WHM TN16 97 H8
RSEV TN14 102 C4
Edgefield Cl DART DA1 24 A7 2
Edgehill Gdns MEO DA13 45 G6
Edgeler Ct SNOD ME6 85 J7
Edgewood Dr ORP BR6 76 A1
Edgington Wy SCUP DA14 38 D5
Edinburgh Ms TIL RM18 27 J1 2
Edinburgh Rd CHAT ME4 4 C6
GILL ME7 5 D3 5
HOO/HM ME3 37 F1
Edinburgh Sq MAID/SHEP ME15 133 J8
Edith Rd ORP BR6 76 B1
Ediva Rd MEO DA13 63 H2
Edmund Cl MAIDW ME16 132 A3
MEO DA13 63 H2
Edmund Rd STMC/STPC BR5 56 D3
Edmunds Av STMC/STPC BR5 38 E8
Edna Rd MAID/BEAR ME14 111 F7
Edward Rd BH/WHM TN16 97 J5
Edwards Cl RHAM ME8 89 K1
Edwards Gdns SWLY BR8 58 A1 2
Edward St CHAT ME4 4 A6
STH/RUST TN4 189 K5
STRD ME2 2 B1
Edward Wk E/WMAL ME19 108 D6
Edwin Petty Pl RDART DA2 24 B6 1
Edwin Rd RDART DA2 40 E1
RHAM ME8 69 K5
Edwin St GVE DA12 27 J6
Egerton Av SWLY BR8 40 C6
Egerton Cl DART DA1 22 E7
Egerton House Rd HDCN TN27 182 E2
Egerton Rd HDCN TN27 161 J8
MAID/BEAR ME14 110 E7
Eggpie La RTON TN11 146 B6
Eglantine La EYN DA4 60 A3
Eglinton Rd SWCM DA10 26 A5
Egremont Rd MAID/SHEP ME15 134 B4
Egret Cl CHAT ME4 50 C4
Elaine Av STRD ME2 48 D7
Elder Cl HOO/HM ME3 51 F3 9
RMAID ME17 158 B4
Elder Ct RHAM ME8 69 J8 1
Eldon St CHAT ME4 4 A4
Eldon Wy STPH/PW TN12 173 H7
Eldred Dr STMC/STPC BR5 56 E6
Elford Rd HOO/HM ME3 31 G1
Elgal Cl ORP BR6 75 G1
Elgar Cl TONN TN10 148 E8
Elham Cl RHAM ME8 69 J4
Eliot Rd DART DA1 24 A4
Elizabeth Cl TIL RM18 27 J1 3
Elizabeth Ct RHAM ME8 69 K5 1
Elizabeth St GRH DA9 24 D4
Elizabeth Wy STMC/STPC BR5 56 D2
Ellenborough Rd SCUP DA14 38 E4
Ellenswood Cl
MAID/SHEP ME15 134 C5 1
Ellerman Rd TIL RM18 27 G1 3
Ellice Rd OXTED RH8 118 D8
Ellingham Leas MAID/SHEP ME15 133 J6
Elliotts La BH/WHM TN16 121 J3
Elliott St GVE DA12 28 A6
Ellison Wy RHAM ME8 70 D4
Ellis Waterton Cl SWLY BR8 58 A1 3
Ellis Wy DART DA1 23 J8 1
Elm Av CHAT ME4 67 K5
HOO/HM ME3 50 B2
Elm Cl DART DA1 23 F7
HDCN TN27 183 F3
HOO/HM ME3 48 B3
Elm Crs E/WMAL ME19 108 D6
Elmcroft Rd ORP BR6 56 B4
Elm Dr SWLY BR8 40 A7
Elmfield RHAM ME8 69 H3
TENT TN30 230 B6
Elmfield Cl GVW DA11 27 J7
RSEV TN14 145 K4
Elm Gv MAID/SHEP ME15 7 E4
ORP BR6 56 A5
RTON TN11 169 K2
SIT ME10 94 C2
Elmhurst Av RTWE/PEM TN2 191 K6
Elmhurst Gdns ROCH ME1 3 D5
Elm La TON TN9 170 C3
Elm Rd BH/WHM TN16 120 E4
DART DA1 23 G7
GILL ME7 5 E2
GRH DA9 24 D5
GVE DA12 45 K1
HOO/HM ME3 51 F3 10
ORP BR6 76 B3
SCUP DA14 38 B2
SOCK/AV RM15 13 H1
STH/RUST TN4 189 K5
Elmshurst Gdns TONN TN10 148 C7
Elmstone Cl MAIDW ME16 132 B4
Elmstone Hole Rd RMAID ME17 159 H6
Elmstone La MAIDW ME16 132 A4
Elmstone Rd RHAM ME8 70 A7
Elm Tree Dr ROCH ME1 2 A6
Elm Wk DIT/AY ME20 109 J5
Elmwood Rd HOO/HM ME3 32 A8
Elphick's Pl RTWE/PEM TN2 207 G6 1
Elvington Cl MAIDW ME16 6 A2 1
Elwill Wy MEO DA13 45 G6
Ely Cl ERITH DA8 22 C1
RHAM ME8 70 B4
Ely Gdns TON TN9 170 D2
Embassey Ct SCUP DA14 38 C1
Embassy Cl GILL ME7 69 G5 1
Emerald Cl ROCH ME1 67 J7
Emersons Av SWLY BR8 40 C5
Emily Rd WALD ME5 68 C8
Emmett Hill La WBY/YAL ME18 174 D2
Emmetts Rd BH/WHM TN16 143 J1
Empress Rd GVE DA12 28 B6
Emsworth Gv MAID/BEAR ME14 111 K8
Englefield Cl STMC/STPC BR5 56 A1 2
Englefield Crs HOO/HM ME3 31 G7
STMC/STPC BR5 56 B2
Englefield Pth STMC/STPC BR5 56 B1 2
Ensfield Rd RTON TN11 168 D7
Enterprise Cl STRD ME2 49 J6
Enterprise Rd MAID/SHEP ME15 7 D6
Epaul La ROCH ME1 2 C2 2
Epps Rd SIT ME10 93 K3
Epsom Cl E/WMAL ME19 107 K6
MAID/SHEP ME15 134 B8 6
Eridge Green Cl STMC/STPC BR5 56 D5
Eridge Rd RRTW TN3 205 G8
STH/RUST TN4 10 B5
Erith Cl MAID/BEAR ME14 111 G6
Erith Ct PUR RM19 12 E4
Ernest Dr MAIDW ME16 132 B1
Ernest Rd CHAT ME4 4 A5
Erskine Park Rd STH/RUST TN4 206 A2
Erskine Rd MEO DA13 83 J6
Eshcol Rd HOO/HM ME3 33 K8
Eskdale Cl RDART DA2 24 B8
Esplanade ROCH ME1 2 B2
Essex Cl RTWE/PEM TN2 206 E6
Essex Rd DART DA1 23 G5 1
GVW DA11 27 H7
HART DA3 43 J7
MAID/SHEP ME15 134 A8
STRD ME2 85 K1
Estelle Cl ROCH ME1 67 J7
Esther Ct SIT ME10 73 K6
Estridge Wy TONN TN10 171 F1
Etfield Gv SCUP DA14 38 C3
Ethelbert Rd ROCH ME1 2 C4
STMC/STPC BR5 38 E8
Ethelbery Rd RDART DA2 41 H2
Etherington Hl RRTW TN3 189 G6
Ethnam La HAWK TN18 244 B3
Eton Cl WALD ME5 88 A2
Eton Rd ORP BR6 56 C8
Eton Wy DART DA1 23 F3
Euclid Wy WTHK RM20 13 K4
Eurolink Wy SIT ME10 94 B2
Evans Cl GRH DA9 25 F4
Eva Rd GILL ME7 5 D5
Evelyn Cl STRD ME2 49 H6
Evelyn Rd MAIDW ME16 6 B4
RSEV TN14 102 A3
Evenden Rd MEO DA13 63 H4
Everest Cl GVW DA11 45 F1 1
Everest Dr HOO/HM ME3 51 F2
Everest La STRD ME2 49 G5
Everest Ms HOO/HM ME3 51 F2
Everest Pl SWLY BR8 58 A1
Everglade BH/WHM TN16 97 H5
Everglade Cl HART DA3 62 A1 1
The Everglades GILL ME7 69 G8
Evergreen Cl E/WMAL ME19 108 C4 1
GILL ME7 89 H1
HOO/HM ME3 47 K3
RSIT ME9 73 J2
Eversley Av BXLYHN DA7 22 B1
Eversley Cl MAIDW ME16 110 C8 2
Eversley Cross BXLYHN DA7 22 B1
Evesham Rd GVE DA12 28 A8 1
Evry Rd SCUP DA14 38 D4
Ewart Rd CHAT ME4 67 K5
Ewehurst La RRTW TN3 188 D8
Ewell Av E/WMAL ME19 107 J6
Ewell La MAID/SHEP ME15 153 H1
Ewins Cl STPH/PW TN12 173 J8
Exedown Rd BGR/WK TN15 104 C2
Exeter Cl TON TN9 170 D2
Exeter Rd GVE DA12 46 A1
Exmouth Rd GILL ME7 4 C1 2
Exton Cl WALD ME5 88 D4
Exton Gdns MAID/BEAR ME14 134 B1
Eyhorne St RMAID ME17 136 A5
Eynsford Ri EYN DA4 59 G8
Eynsford Rd EYN DA4 59 J5
GRH DA9 25 H4
MAIDW ME16 110 D7
SWLY BR8 58 B3
Eynswood Dr SCUP DA14 38 C3

F

Fackenden La BGR/WK TN15 79 K8
Factory Rd GVW DA11 26 D5
Faesten Wy BXLY DA5 40 B1
Fagus Cl WALD ME5 88 C5
Fairbourne La RMAID ME17 159 G3
Fairby La HART DA3 61 K3
Fairchildes Rd WARL CR6 96 B2
Fairfax Cl RHAM ME8 90 A1
Fairfield GVE DA12 46 B3
Fairfield Av RTWE/PEM TN2 11 E2 2
Fairfield Cl BGR/WK TN15 102 E5
Fairfield Crs TON TN9 170 C6 2
Fairfield Rd BGR/WK TN15 105 F6
Fairfield Wy RTON TN11 169 J1
Fairhurst Dr MAID/SHEP ME15 154 B2
Fairlawn Cl WBY/YAL ME18 130 E6
Fairlead Rd ROCH ME1 67 J5
Fairleas SIT ME10 94 C4
Fairlight Cl STH/RUST TN4 190 A4
Fairlight Cross HART DA3 44 C8
Fairman's La STPH/PW TN12 193 K8
Fairmeadow MAID/BEAR ME14 6 C2
MAIDW ME16 6 C3
Fairmead Rd EDEN TN8 164 B1
Fairmile Rd RTWE/PEM TN2 207 K1
Fairseat La BGR/WK TN15 82 B5
BGR/WK TN15 105 H2
Fairtrough Rd ORP BR6 76 C8
Fairview HAWK TN18 235 F4
Fairview Av RHAM ME8 89 J1
Fairview Cl RTON TN11 170 B8
Fairview Dr HOO/HM ME3 48 A2
Fairview Gdns MEO DA13 63 J2
Fairview Rd MEO DA13 44 E5
SIT ME10 94 B3
Fairway Cl ROCH ME1 67 H5
Fairway Dr RDART DA2 24 A6
The Fairways STH/RUST TN4 190 A7 1
The Fairway GVW DA11 27 H8
ROCH ME1 67 H5
SIT ME10 93 K5
Falcon Cl DART DA1 23 J4
Falcon Ms GVW DA11 27 F7 1
Falcons Cl BH/WHM TN16 97 H4
Falkland Pl WALD ME5 87 K5
Fallowfield RDART DA2 43 G1
SIT ME10 94 B4
WALD ME5 68 C6
Fallowfield Cl MAID/BEAR ME14 134 A2 2
Falmouth Pl STPH/PW TN12 172 E7
Fanconi Rd WALD ME5 88 C3

Fane Wy RHAM ME8 90 A2
Fanns Ri PUR RM19 12 E4
Fans La RSIT ME9 73 J2
Fant La MAIDW ME16 132 B4
Faraday Ride TONN TN10 148 D7
Faraday Rd MAID/BEAR ME14 111 J7
Faraday Wy STMC/STPC BR5 56 C1
Farleigh Court Rd WARL CR6 96 A2
Farleigh Hl MAID/SHEP ME15 6 B6
Farleigh La MAIDW ME16 132 A4
Farley Cl WALD ME5 88 E4
Farleycroft BH/WHM TN16 120 B5
Farley La BH/WHM TN16 120 B6
Farley Nursery BH/WHM TN16 120 C6
Farley Pk OXTED RH8 140 B1
Farley Rd GVE DA12 28 C6
Farlow Cl GVW DA11 45 G1
Farm Av SWLY BR8 39 K8
Farmcombe Cl RTW TN1 11 D5 3
Farmcombe La RTW TN1 11 D5
Farmcombe Rd RTW TN1 11 D5
Farm Crs SIT ME10 94 B4
Farmcroft GVW DA11 27 H8
Farmdale ROCH ME1 66 E3 1
Farmdale Av ROCH ME1 66 E4
Farmer Cl RMAID ME17 135 J8
Farm Ground Cl TON TN9 170 E6
Farm Holt HART DA3 62 A5
Farm La RTON TN11 170 A2
Farm Pl DART DA1 22 D3
Farm Rd RSEV TN14 102 A7
WALD ME5 87 K3
Farmstead Dr EDEN TN8 164 D3
Farnaby Dr SEV TN13 8 B5
Farnborough Cl MAIDW ME16 132 C4 1
Farnborough Hl ORP BR6 75 J1
Farnborough Wy ORP BR6 75 K2
Farne Cl MAID/SHEP ME15 133 G8
Farnham Beeches RRTW TN3 205 K2
Farnham Cl RHAM ME8 70 E5
RRTW TN3 205 K3 1
Farnham La RRTW TN3 205 K2
Farnham Pl RRTW TN3 205 K3
Farningham Cl MAID/BEAR ME14 7 F1
Farningham Hill Rd SWLY BR8 59 F2
Farnol Rd DART DA1 23 K4 1
Farraday Cl ROCH ME1 67 J6
Farrant Cl ORP BR6 76 B3 1
Farrier Cl MAID/BEAR ME14 133 K1
Farriers Cl GVE DA12 28 C7 2
Farriers Ct RHAM ME8 71 F6
Farrington Av STMC/STPC BR5 38 C8
Fartherwell Av E/WMAL ME19 107 J6
Fartherwell Rd E/WMAL ME19 107 H7
Farthingfield BGR/WK TN15 105 G3 1
Farthing Hl WADH TN5 232 C5
Farthing St ORP BR6 74 E3
Farwell Rd SCUP DA14 38 C2
Fauchon's Cl MAID/BEAR ME14 134 B3
Fauchon's La MAID/BEAR ME14 134 B3
Faversham Rd RMAID ME17 138 E7
Fawkes Av DART DA1 23 J8
Fawkham Av HART DA3 44 D8 2
Fawkham Green Rd HART DA3 61 G7
Fawkham Rd BGR/WK TN15 60 E8
HART DA3 61 J1
Fawley Cl MAID/BEAR ME14 110 E7 1
Featherbed La RSIT ME9 73 K4
Featherby Rd GILL ME7 69 H1
RHAM ME8 69 H3
Felderland Cl RMAID ME17 156 A1 3
Felderland Dr RMAID ME17 156 A1 4
Felderland Rd RMAID ME17 156 A1 5
Feldspar Cl WALD ME5 88 A5 1
Fell Md STPH/PW TN12 151 H8
Fellowes Wy RTON TN11 169 J1
Felstead Rd ORP BR6 56 B6
Felton Lea SCUP DA14 38 A3
Fen Meadow BGR/WK TN15 104 C6
Fennel Cl MAIDW ME16 132 B3
ROCH ME1 2 B5
Fen Pond Rd BGR/WK TN15 104 D7
Fens Wy SWLY BR8 40 D4
Ferbies RRTW TN3 188 E7 1
Ferguson Av GVE DA12 45 K2
Fernbank Cl WALD ME5 87 K5
Ferndale RTWE/PEM TN2 11 F2
Ferndale Cl RTWE/PEM TN2 11 E3 3
RTWE/PEM TN2 11 E3 3
Ferndale Rd GILL ME7 5 E3
GVE DA12 27 J8
Ferndale Wy ORP BR6 75 J1
Ferndell Av BXLY DA5 40 A1
Ferndene HART DA3 44 E8
Fern Down MEO DA13 83 J6
Ferndown Cl GILL ME7 89 H1
Fernheath Wy RDART DA2 40 A3
Fernhill Rd MAIDW ME16 132 A4
Fernholt TONN TN10 148 C7
Fernhurst Crs STH/RUST TN4 190 A4
Fernleigh Ri DIT/AY ME20 109 F4
Fernside La SEV TN13 124 A8
The Ferns BGR/WK TN15 105 J7
DIT/AY ME20 109 F5
RTW TN1 11 D3 2
Ferrier Cl RHAM ME8 90 B2
Ferry La ROCH ME1 86 B2
Ferry Rd RSIT ME9 73 K2
STRD ME2 86 A2 2
TIL RM18 27 H1
Festival Av HART DA3 44 E8
Ffinch Cl DIT/AY ME20 109 H6
Fiddlers Cl GRH DA9 25 G3
Field Cl WALD ME5 67 K8
Field Ct OXTED RH8 118 C7
Field Dr EDEN TN8 164 D3
Fielding Dr DIT/AY ME20 108 E3
The Fieldings SIT ME10 93 K4
Field Mill Rd HDCN TN27 183 G1
Field Rd BGR/WK TN15 83 F1
MEO DA13 63 G8
SOCK/AV RM15 13 G1
Fields La WBY/YAL ME18 130 C7
Fieldways HAWK TN18 235 G5
Fieldworks Rd CHAT ME4 4 A1
Fiennes Wy SEV TN13 9 E6
Filborough Wy GVE DA12 28 E7
Filey Cl BH/WHM TN16 97 F6
Filmer La RSEV TN14 102 C8
Filston La RSEV TN14 78 B8
The Finches SIT ME10 94 B3
Finchley Cl DART DA1 23 K5
Findlay Cl RHAM ME8 90 A1
Finglesham Cl STMC/STPC BR5 56 E5 1
Finglesham Ct MAID/SHEP ME15 133 J6
Fintonagh Dr MAID/BEAR ME14 111 H7
Finucane Dr STMC/STPC BR5 56 D4
Finwell Rd RHAM ME8 70 D4
Fircroft Wy EDEN TN8 164 C3
Firecrest Cl HART DA3 44 C8 1
Firethorn Cl GILL ME7 5 E2 1
Firmingers Rd ORP BR6 77 J1
Firmin Rd DART DA1 23 F4
Firs Cl DIT/AY ME20 109 J5
First Av CHAT ME4 4 C6
GILL ME7 5 E6
GVW DA11 27 F7
The Firs BXLY DA5 22 A7
First La MAID/SHEP ME15 135 G4
First St RRTW TN3 205 J3
Fir Tree Cl ORP BR6 76 A1
RTON TN11 169 J1 1
STPH/PW TN12 198 B3
Fir Tree Gv GILL ME7 89 J5
WALD ME5 88 E5
Fir Tree Rd STH/RUST TN4 10 B5
Fishermen's Hl GVW DA11 26 C4 1
Fisher Rd WALD ME5 68 C7
Fishers Cl STPH/PW TN12 198 B1
Fishers Rd STPH/PW TN12 198 B1
Fisher St MAID/BEAR ME14 7 D1
Fishponds Rd HAYES BR2 74 C1
Fitzwilliam Rd MAID/BEAR ME14 134 B1
Fiveash Rd GVW DA11 27 G6
Five Bells La ROCH ME1 3 D4 1
Five Fields La EDEN TN8 165 J2
Five Oak Green Rd RTON TN11 171 J8
TON TN9 171 F7
Five Oak La STPH/PW TN12 197 G5
Five Wents SWLY BR8 40 D7
Flack Gdns HOO/HM ME3 51 F1
Flamborough Cl BH/WHM TN16 97 F6
Flamingo Cl WALD ME5 68 B7 1
Flaxman Dr MAIDW ME16 110 C8
Flaxmans Ct GILL ME7 4 A2 2
Flaxmore Pl STH/RUST TN4 190 A4 1
Fleet Av RDART DA2 24 B7
Fleet Rd GVW DA11 44 D1
RDART DA2 24 B7
ROCH ME1 67 J5
Fleming Wy TONN TN10 148 E7
Fletcher Rd STPH/PW TN12 198 A3
Flimwell Cl WADH TN5 233 H2
Flint Cl ORP BR6 76 A2 1
Flint Down Cl STMC/STPC BR5 38 B6 2
Flint Gn WALD ME5 88 D4
Flint La RMAID ME17 138 D6
The Floats SEV TN13 101 G8
Flood Hatch MAID/SHEP ME15 6 A5 1
Florance La RRTW TN3 204 E8
Florence Rd MAIDW ME16 6 B4
Florence St STRD ME2 49 G6 1
Florin Dr ROCH ME1 2 B4
Flowerfield RSEV TN14 101 H4
Flowerhill Wy MEO DA13 45 F5
Flume End MAIDW ME16 6 A5 2
The Flyers Wy BH/WHM TN16 120 D5
Foalhurst Cl TONN TN10 170 E2
Foley Rd BH/WHM TN16 97 H5
Foley St MAID/BEAR ME14 7 D2
Fontwell Cl MAID/SHEP ME15 134 B8 7
Foord Cl RDART DA2 24 D8
Foord Rd RMAID ME17 160 D1
Foord St ROCH ME1 2 C4
Footbury Hill Rd ORP BR6 56 B4
Foots Cray High St SCUP DA14 38 D4
Force Green La BH/WHM TN16 120 D3
Fordcombe Cl
MAID/SHEP ME15 134 B7 1
Fordcombe Rd RRTW TN3 204 E1
RTON TN11 187 J3
Fordcroft Rd STMC/STPC BR5 56 C2
Fordingbridge Cl MAIDW ME16 132 B1 1
Ford La BGR/WK TN15 106 B4
Ford Rd GVW DA11 26 C4 2
Fordwich Cl MAIDW ME16 110 B7
ORP BR6 56 A4
Foremans Barn Rd
MAID/SHEP ME15 153 K3
Forestdale Rd WALD ME5 88 B6
Forest Dr WALD ME5 88 A4
Foresters Cl WALD ME5 88 A4
Forest Gv TONN TN10 170 C1
Forest Hl MAID/SHEP ME15 6 C6
Forest Rd RTWE/PEM TN2 11 E6
STPH/PW TN12 173 H8
Forest Wy E/WMAL ME19 129 J3
RTWE/PEM TN2 11 E6
RTWE/PEM TN2 191 K6
STMC/STPC BR5 56 B2
Forge Cft EDEN TN8 164 C5
Forgefield BH/WHM TN16 97 H3
Forge La BGR/WK TN15 81 F5
EYN DA4 60 B1
GILL ME7 5 E2
GILL ME7 89 H5
GVE DA12 28 C8
GVE DA12 47 H3
HDCN TN27 182 C5
HDCN TN27 200 B1
HOO/HM ME3 32 E3
HOO/HM ME3 48 B3
MAID/BEAR ME14 111 J3
MAID/SHEP ME15 132 B7
RMAID ME17 135 H7
RMAID ME17 178 B1
RSIT ME9 71 J3
WBY/YAL ME18 128 C8
WBY/YAL ME18 174 E2
Forge Meadow RMAID ME17 137 H8
Forge Mdw HDCN TN27 200 B1
Forge Meads TENT TN30 247 K3
Forge Rd SIT ME10 73 K8
STH/RUST TN4 189 K5
Forge Wy RSEV TN14 78 C6
STPH/PW TN12 173 J7
Formby Rd STRD ME2 65 K8
Forsham La RMAID ME17 178 E1
Forson Cl TENT TN30 230 B6
Forstall RRTW TN3 205 K2 1
Forstal La RMAID ME17 154 D2
The Forstall RTON TN11 168 E4
Forstal Rd DIT/AY ME20 110 A4
HDCN TN27 182 C5
The Forstal RTON TN11 150 A6
RTWE/PEM TN2 192 A6 1
Forsters RMAID ME17 157 G2
Forsyth Cl DIT/AY ME20 108 E5 2
Fort Pitt Hl ROCH ME1 3 E4
Fort Pitt St CHAT ME4 3 E5
Fort Rd RSEV TN14 100 E2
TIL RM18 27 J3
Fortrye Cl GVW DA11 27 F8
Fort St ROCH ME1 3 D4
Forward Wy ROCH ME1 67 H8
Fosse Bank TON TN9 170 A7
Fosse Bank Cl TON TN9 170 A7 1
Fosse Rd TON TN9 170 B4
Fosten La HDCN TN27 217 H6
Foster St MAID/SHEP ME15 7 D4
Fostington Wy WALD ME5 88 A5
Foulds Cl RHAM ME8 89 J2
Fountain La MAIDW ME16 132 A4
Fountain Rd STRD ME2 48 D5
Fountain St SIT ME10 93 K2 2
Fountain Wk GVW DA11 27 F5
Four Elms Hl HOO/HM ME3 49 K3
Four Elms Rd EDEN TN8 165 F2
Four Oaks Rd STPH/PW TN12 179 G7
Fourth Av GILL ME7 5 E4
Fourwents Rd HOO/HM ME3 32 E8
Fowey Cl WALD ME5 88 D1
Fowler Cl RHAM ME8 89 K3
SCUP DA14 39 F3
Foxburrow Cl RHAM ME8 90 A1
Foxbury Cl ORP BR6 76 B1 2
Foxbury Dr ORP BR6 76 B2
Foxbush RTON TN11 147 G8
Fox Cl ORP BR6 76 B1
Foxden Dr MAID/SHEP ME15 134 B5
Foxearth Cl BH/WHM TN16 97 J5
Foxendown La MEO DA13 63 J5
Foxglove Crs WALD ME5 87 K2
Foxglove Ri MAID/BEAR ME14 110 E7
Foxgrove SIT ME10 73 K7
Fox Hl SIT ME10 94 E3
Foxhole La HAWK TN18 235 K6
STPH/PW TN12 192 E6
Fox La HAYES BR2 74 A1
Fox St GILL ME7 4 C2
Foxwood Gv GVW DA11 27 F7
ORP BR6 76 D5
Foxwood Rd RDART DA2 43 G1
Foxwood Wy HART DA3 44 D7
Framley Rd TONN TN10 171 F1

Francis Dr WALD ME5 88 B4
Francis La MAID/SHEP ME15 156 B1
Francis Rd DART DA1 23 G4
RTON TN11 147 H8
STMC/STPC BR5 38 E8
Frankapps Cl RSIT ME9 72 A8 1
Frankfield Ri RTWE/PEM TN2 10 B6
Franklin Dr MAID/BEAR ME14 133 K2
Franklin Rd GILL ME7 5 D3
GVE DA12 46 A3
Franks Ct RHAM ME8 69 J5
Frank's Hollow Rd RRTW TN3 189 G5
Franks La EYN DA4 60 A2
Frank Woolley Rd TONN TN10 171 F1
Frant Fld EDEN TN8 164 D5
Frant Rd RTWE/PEM TN2 207 F7
Frederick Rd GILL ME7 4 C4
Frederick St SIT ME10 93 K2
Free Heath Rd RRTW TN3 220 E3
The Freehold RTON TN11 149 K5
STPH/PW TN12 151 H8
Freelands Rd SNOD ME6 85 H6
Freeman Gdns CHAT ME4 3 F6 2
Freeman Rd GVE DA12 46 B1
Freeman Wy MAID/SHEP ME15 134 A7
Freesia Cl GILL ME7 5 F2
ORP BR6 76 A1 1
Freight La CRBK TN17 225 J3
Fremlin Cl STH/RUST TN4 206 A2
Fremlins Rd MAID/BEAR ME14 134 E2
Frensham Cl SIT ME10 94 C2
Frensham Rd CRBK TN17 238 E5
Frensham Wk WALD ME5 88 A5 2
Freshland Rd MAIDW ME16 132 B2
Freshwater Rd WALD ME5 68 C7
Frewen Cl RYE TN31 244 E7
Friar Rd STMC/STPC BR5 56 B2
Friars Av WALD ME5 88 A4
Friars Wy RTWE/PEM TN2 11 F1
Friary Pl STRD ME2 2 B1
Friday St RMAID ME17 157 K7
Friezland Rd STH/RUST TN4 206 C5
Friezley La CRBK TN17 214 D4
Frimley Ct SCUP DA14 38 D3
Frindsbury Hl STRD ME2 49 H5
Frindsbury Rd STRD ME2 49 G6
Frinstead Cl STMC/STPC BR5 56 E1
Frinstead Wk MAIDW ME16 110 B7
Frinsted Cl RHAM ME8 69 K3 2
Frinsted Rd RSIT ME9 116 E5
Friston Wy ROCH ME1 67 J6
Frithwood Cl MAID/SHEP ME15 134 B5
Frittenden Rd STPH/PW TN12 198 B4
STRD ME2 49 J5
Frobisher Cl SIT ME10 73 K8 5
Frobisher Gdns ROCH ME1 2 C6 1
Frobisher Wy GRH DA9 25 G3
GVE DA12 46 B3
Froghole La EDEN TN8 142 E3
Frog La E/WMAL ME19 108 A6
RTW TN1 10 C5
Frognal Av SCUP DA14 38 B4
Frognal Cl RSIT ME9 95 J4
Frognal Gdns RSIT ME9 95 J4
Frognal La RSIT ME9 95 J4
Frognal Pl SCUP DA14 38 B3
Frogs Hole La CRBK TN17 228 B4
Frog's La CRBK TN17 238 D5
Frost Crs WALD ME5 68 B7
Froyle Cl MAIDW ME16 110 C8
Fruiterer's Cl RSIT ME9 94 B7
Fry Cl HOO/HM ME3 21 F8 1
Frythe Cl CRBK TN17 225 K2
Frythe Crs CRBK TN17 225 K2
Frythe Wk CRBK TN17 225 K2
Frythe Wy CRBK TN17 225 K2
Fuggles Cl STPH/PW TN12 173 G8
Fuggles Ct CRBK TN17 227 F8
Fulbert Dr MAID/BEAR ME14 134 B1
Fuller Cl ORP BR6 76 A1
Fullers Cl MAID/BEAR ME14 134 C2
Fullers Hl BH/WHM TN16 120 D5
Fullers La RYE TN31 244 E8
Fulmar Rd STRD ME2 66 C1
Fulston Pl SIT ME10 94 B3
Fulwich Rd DART DA1 23 J5
Furfield Cl MAID/SHEP ME15 156 A1
Furnace Av RRTW TN3 221 H3
Furnace La RRTW TN3 221 F2
STPH/PW TN12 194 C5
Furner Cl DART DA1 22 C2
Furrell's Rd ROCH ME1 3 D3 2
Furzefield Av RRTW TN3 188 E6
Furzehill Sq STMC/STPC BR5 56 C1 1

G

Gabion Av PUR RM19 13 H4
Gable Cl DART DA1 22 D4
The Gables HART DA3 44 D7
Gabriel Gdns GVE DA12 46 B3
Gabriel's Hl MAID/SHEP ME15 7 D3 3
Gabriel Spring Rd EYN DA4 60 C6
Gabriel Spring Rd (East) EYN DA4 60 D6
Gadby Rd SIT ME10 93 H1
Gadsby La RASHW TN26 219 K4
Gainsborough Av DART DA1 23 F4
Gainsborough Cl RHAM ME8 70 A8
SIT ME10 93 G1 1
Gainsborough Dr GVW DA11 44 E1
MAIDW ME16 132 B2 1
Gainsborough Gdns TONN TN10 170 E1 3
Galahad Av STRD ME2 48 D8
Galena Cl WALD ME5 88 B5 2
Gallants La MAID/SHEP ME15 131 K8
Galleon Bvd GRH DA9 24 C3
Galleon Cl ROCH ME1 67 H6
Galley Hill Rd SWCM DA10 26 A4
The Gallops MEO DA13 83 G6
Gamma Rd HOO/HM ME3 34 A7
Gandy's La RMAID ME17 155 J4
Garden Cl MAID/SHEP ME15 134 A7
Gardenia Cl STRD ME2 49 G5
Garden Pl RDART DA2 41 G1
Garden Rd RTW TN1 11 D3 3
SEV TN13 9 F1
TON TN9 170 D4
Garden Rw GVW DA11 45 G1 1
Garden St GILL ME7 4 A2
RTW TN1 11 D3 4
Garden Wy WBY/YAL ME18 129 H4
Gardiner Cl STMC/STPC BR5 38 D7
Gardiner St GILL ME7 4 C2
Gardyne Ms TON TN9 170 B6 3
Garfield Rd GILL ME7 5 D2
Garlands RTON TN11 147 H6
Garlinge Rd STH/RUST TN4 190 A5
Garner Dr E/WMAL ME19 108 E5
Garrick St GVW DA11 27 J5 7
Garrington Cl MAID/BEAR ME14 7 F1
Garrolds Cl SWLY BR8 40 A7
Garrow HART DA3 44 C8
Garth Rd SEV TN13 124 A7
Garvock Dr SEV TN13 8 C5
Gascoyne Dr DART DA1 22 C2
Gasson Rd SWCM DA10 25 K5
Gassons Rd SNOD ME6 85 H6 1
Gatcombe Cl MAIDW ME16 132 B1
WALD ME5 88 B1
Gate Farm Rd RRTW TN3 189 G2
Gatefield Cottages CRBK TN17 238 D2
Gatland La MAIDW ME16 132 B4
Gattons Wy SCUP DA14 39 G2
Gatwick Rd GVE DA12 27 J8
Gault Cl MAID/SHEP ME15 134 C4
Gayhurst Cl RHAM ME8 70 A8
Gayhurst Dr SIT ME10 93 H1
Gaze Hill Av SIT ME10 94 B3
Gazelle Gld GVE DA12 46 C3
Gean Cl WALD ME5 88 B5
Gedge's Hl STPH/PW TN12 193 H4
Genesta Cl SIT ME10 73 K7
Genesta Gld GVE DA12 46 D3
Geneva Av RHAM ME8 69 H4
Gentian Cl MAID/BEAR ME14 134 A1
George La RMAID ME17 135 J7
ROCH ME1 2 C2 3
Georges Cl STMC/STPC BR5 38 D8
George's Rd BH/WHM TN16 97 H7
George St MAID/SHEP ME15 7 D4
MAID/SHEP ME15 154 A8
SIT ME10 94 C3 1
STPH/PW TN12 178 A8
TON TN9 170 B6
George Summers Cl STRD ME2 49 K6
Georgian Dr RMAID ME17 154 D3
Georgian Wy RHAM ME8 89 K2
Gerald Av CHAT ME4 3 F6
Gerald Rd GVE DA12 28 B6
Gerdview Dr RDART DA2 41 F2
Gerrard Av ROCH ME1 67 J6
Gerrards Dr SIT ME10 94 A4
Ghyll Side Rd RYE TN31 244 E7
Gibbet La STPH/PW TN12 194 D8
Gibbetts RRTW TN3 205 J3
Gibbons Rd SIT ME10 93 G1
Gibbs Brook La OXTED RH8 140 B7
Gibbs Hl HDCN TN27 200 C1 1
WBY/YAL ME18 151 K1
Gibraltar Av GILL ME7 4 A1
Gibraltar Hl CHAT ME4 3 F4
Gibraltar La MAID/BEAR ME14 110 E6
Gibson Cl GVW DA11 45 G1
Gibson Dr E/WMAL ME19 129 H2
Gibson St SIT ME10 93 K2
Giddyhorn La MAIDW ME16 132 C2
Gifford Cl GILL ME7 69 K2
Giggs Hl STMC/STPC BR5 38 B7
Gighill Rd DIT/AY ME20 108 D3
Gilbert Cl GILL ME7 89 H1
SWCM DA10 25 J5
Gildenhill Rd SWLY BR8 41 F5
Gill Av STRD ME2 49 J3
Gill Crs GVW DA11 45 G1
Gilletts La E/WMAL ME19 108 E8
Gillies Rd BGR/WK TN15 80 D1
Gillingham Gn GILL ME7 5 E2
Gillingham Rd GILL ME7 5 D3
Gillmans Rd STMC/STPC BR5 56 C5
Gill's Rd EYN DA4 42 D6
The Gill RTWE/PEM TN2 192 A6
Gilroy Wy STMC/STPC BR5 56 C4
Gimble Wy RTWE/PEM TN2 191 K6
Gingerbread La HAWK TN18 233 K3
Ginsbury Cl STRD ME2 3 D2
Gipps Cross La RRTW TN3 205 J3 1
The Glades GVE DA12 46 A4
The Glade SEV TN13 9 D2
WALD ME5 88 B4
Gladstone Dr SIT ME10 94 D3
Gladstone Rd CHAT ME4 3 E6
DART DA1 23 J5
MAID/BEAR ME14 7 D1
ORP BR6 75 H1
STH/RUST TN4 206 A2 2
TON TN9 170 B5
Gladwyn Cl RHAM ME8 90 A2 3
Glamford Rd STRD ME2 66 C1
Glamis Cl WALD ME5 88 B1
Glanville Rd GILL ME7 5 D3 6
STRD ME2 2 A1
Glassenbury Rd CRBK TN17 224 E2
Glastonbury Cl STMC/STPC BR5 56 D5
Gleaming Wood Dr
MAID/BEAR ME14 88 E6
Gleaners Cl MAID/BEAR ME14 134 A2
Glebe Cl HDCN TN27 202 B4
The Glebefield SEV TN13 8 B2
Glebe Gdns RMAID ME17 160 E1
Glebeland HDCN TN27 183 F2
Glebelands DART DA1 22 C3
HDCN TN27 217 J5
RRTW TN3 189 G3
RTON TN11 187 J3
Glebe La MAIDW ME16 131 K5
SEV TN13 9 D5
SIT ME10 94 C4
Glebe Meadow WBY/YAL ME18 130 B7
Glebe Pl EYN DA4 60 B1
Glebe Rd GILL ME7 5 E5
GVW DA11 27 G7
RSEV TN14 145 K3
The Glebe RTWE/PEM TN2 191 K6
STH/RUST TN4 189 H3
STRD ME2 66 B4
Gleeson Dr ORP BR6 76 A1
Glenbrook Gv SIT ME10 73 K7
Glencoe Rd CHAT ME4 4 A6
Glendale SWLY BR8 58 C2
Glendale Rd GVW DA11 45 F2
Glendower Crs ORP BR6 56 B3
Gleneagles Dr MAID/SHEP ME15 6 C6
Glenmore Pk RTWE/PEM TN2 206 E6
Glenrosa Gdns GVE DA12 46 C3
Glentrammon Av ORP BR6 76 A2
Glentrammon Cl ORP BR6 76 A2
Glentrammon Gdns ORP BR6 76 A2
Glentrammon Rd ORP BR6 76 A2
Glen Vw GVE DA12 27 K7
Glenwood Cl GILL ME7 69 G7
MAIDW ME16 132 C1
TENT TN30 230 B3 1
WALD ME5 68 D5
Glistening Gld RHAM ME8 70 B8
Gload Crs STMC/STPC BR5 56 E6
Globe La CHAT ME4 3 F3
Gloucester Cl RHAM ME8 70 D6 1
Gloucester Rd DART DA1 22 E5
GVE DA12 45 K2
MAID/SHEP ME15 133 K6
WADH TN5 220 B8
Gloxinia Rd MEO DA13 44 C4
Glyn Davies Cl SEV TN13 101 G7
Glyn Dr SCUP DA14 38 C2
Goad Av WALD ME5 88 C3
Goatsfield Rd BH/WHM TN16 97 G7
Goddards Cl CRBK TN17 225 H2
Godden Cl RYE TN31 244 E6
Godden Rd SNOD ME6 85 J6
Goddings Dr ROCH ME1 2 A5
Goddington Cha ORP BR6 56 C8
Goddington La ORP BR6 56 D7
RMAID ME17 137 F8
Goddington Rd STRD ME2 49 G6
Godfrey Evans Cl TONN TN10 171 F1
Godstone Rd OXTED RH8 140 A1
Golden Sq TENT TN30 230 B6
Golden Wood Cl WALD ME5 88 E6
Goldfinch Cl DIT/AY ME20 108 E4
ORP BR6 76 B1
STPH/PW TN12 193 J1 2
Golding Cl DIT/AY ME20 109 G5
Golding Gdns STPH/PW TN12 151 J8
Golding Rd SEV TN13 9 E1
Goldings STPH/PW TN12 193 G1 1
Goldings Cl E/WMAL ME19 129 J4
The Goldings RHAM ME8 69 K6
Goldsel Rd SWLY BR8 58 B1
Goldsmid Rd TON TN9 170 C7
Goldsmith Ct TENT TN30 230 B5 1
Goldsmith Rd RHAM ME8 90 B1
Goldstone Wk WALD ME5 88 B5 3
Gold St GVE DA12 64 B2

Goldsworth Dr STRD ME2 49 F5 1
Goldthorne Cl MAID/BEAR ME14 7 F3 1
Golf Links Av GVW DA11 45 J3
Golford Rd CRBK TN17 226 B1
Gooch Cl MAIDW ME16 110 D6
Goodall Cl RHAM ME8 90 B1
Goodbury Rd BGR/WK TN15 80 A8
Goodley Stock Rd EDEN TN8 120 B8
Goodmead Rd ORP BR6 56 B4
Goodnestone Rd SIT ME10 94 C3
Goods Hl TENT TN30 229 H6
Goods Station Rd RTW TN1 11 D3
Goodwin Dr MAID/BEAR ME14 111 H6
Goodwin Rd HOO/HM ME3 31 G7
The Goodwins RTWE/PEM TN2 10 B6 2
Goodwood Cl HOO/HM ME3 33 F3
MAID/SHEP ME15 134 B8 3
Goodwood Crs GVE DA12 45 K4
Goodworth Rd BGR/WK TN15 105 F3
Goose Cl WALD ME5 68 B7 2
Goose Green Cl STMC/STPC BR5 38 B7
Gooseneck La HDCN TN27 200 A1
Gordon Cl SIT ME10 94 D2 1
Gordon Pl GVE DA12 27 K5 1
Gordon Rd CHAT ME4 4 A6
DART DA1 23 G6
GILL ME7 4 A1 1
GVW DA11 27 F6
HOO/HM ME3 50 E1
SEV TN13 9 D4
STH/RUST TN4 190 C7
STRD ME2 49 F6
Gordons Wy OXTED RH8 118 B7
Gordon Ter ROCH ME1 2 C4
Gore Court Rd MAID/SHEP ME15 156 B1
SIT ME10 93 K4
Gore Green Rd HOO/HM ME3 30 C7
Gore La CRBK TN17 212 D3
Gore Rd RDART DA2 24 C8
RSIT ME9 115 K1
Gorham Cl SNOD ME6 85 J7
Gorham Dr MAID/SHEP ME15 134 C5
TON TN9 170 D6
Gorringe Av EYN DA4 42 C7
Gorse Av WALD ME5 87 K2
Gorse Crs DIT/AY ME20 109 H6
Gorse Rd RTWE/PEM TN2 207 K1
SIT ME10 94 D1
STMC/STPC BR5 57 H6
STRD ME2 48 E6
Gorse Wy HART DA3 62 A2
Gorse Wood Rd HART DA3 62 A2
Goss Hl SWLY BR8 41 F4
Gothic Cl DART DA1 41 G1
Goudhurst Cl MAIDW ME16 6 B3 2
Goudhurst Rd CRBK TN17 214 E6
RHAM ME8 69 J3
STPH/PW TN12 196 B1
STPH/PW TN12 212 A1
Gouge Av GVW DA11 27 F7
Gould Rd WALD ME5 88 C3
Gover Hl WBY/YAL ME18 128 A8
Gover Vw WBY/YAL ME18 128 A7
Grace Av MAIDW ME16 6 A1
Gracious La SEV TN13 145 J1
Gracious Lane End RSEV TN14 145 H1
Grafton Av ROCH ME1 67 K6
Grafton Rd SIT ME10 94 A2
Grainey Fld RSIT ME9 91 H2
Grain Rd HOO/HM ME3 34 E3
RHAM ME8 89 K3
Grampian Cl ORP BR6 56 A3
RTWE/PEM TN2 11 F2
Grampian Wy MAID/SHEP ME15 134 C5
Granada St MAID/SHEP ME15 7 D3 4
Granary STPH/PW TN12 173 K8
Granary Cl MAID/BEAR ME14 134 A1
RHAM ME8 70 C5
Granby Rd GVW DA11 26 E5
Grandshore La CRBK TN17 215 H1
Grandsire Gdns HOO/HM ME3 33 F8
Grand View Av BH/WHM TN16 97 G4
Grange Cl BFN/LL DA15 38 B1
BH/WHM TN16 120 D5 2
E/WMAL ME19 108 A4
EDEN TN8 164 C5 1
Grange Crs RDART DA2 24 A5
TENT TN30 230 A3
Grange Dr ORP BR6 76 D4
Grange Gdns STH/RUST TN4 206 C2
Grange Hl BGR/WK TN15 126 E6
WALD ME5 4 B5
Grange La HART DA3 62 C4
MAID/BEAR ME14 111 H5
Grange Rd BGR/WK TN15 105 J7
GILL ME7 5 E2
GVW DA11 27 H6
SEV TN13 8 C6
SOCK/AV RM15 13 G1
STH/RUST TN4 206 C2
STRD ME2 2 B1
TENT TN30 229 K3
The Grange BGR/WK TN15 80 E4
E/WMAL ME19 108 E7
EYN DA4 42 C6
Grange Wy HART DA3 62 A3
ROCH ME1 2 C5
Grangeways Cl GVW DA11 45 G2 1
Grant Cl GILL ME7 69 J5
Granton Rd SCUP DA14 38 C4
Grant Rd HOO/HM ME3 49 H3
Grants La OXTED RH8 141 H8
Granville Ms SCUP DA14 38 B2
Granville Rd BH/WHM TN16 120 C5
GILL ME7 5 E3
GVW DA11 27 G6
MAID/BEAR ME14 7 D1
OXTED RH8 118 D8
RTW TN1 11 D2
SCUP DA14 38 B2
SEV TN13 8 C3
Grapple Rd MAID/BEAR ME14 111 G7
Grasmere Gv STRD ME2 49 H4
Grassington Rd SCUP DA14 38 B2
Grasslands RMAID ME17 157 G2
Grassmere DIT/AY ME20 108 C5
Grassy Gld GILL ME7 69 J8
Grassy La SEV TN13 9 D6
Gravelly Bottom Rd RMAID ME17 157 K4
Gravelly Ways STPH/PW TN12 174 A2
Gravel Pit Wy ORP BR6 56 B6
Gravel Rd EYN DA4 42 A5
Gravel Wk ROCH ME1 3 D3 3
Graveney Cl HOO/HM ME3 31 H7
Graveney Rd MAID/SHEP ME15 134 B7
Gravesend Rd BGR/WK TN15 83 F6
GVE DA12 47 J2
HOO/HM ME3 48 B4
STRD ME2 48 E6
Graylings Ct SIT ME10 93 H4
Grayne Av HOO/HM ME3 37 G1
Grays Farm Rd STMC/STPC BR5 38 C6
Grayshott Cl SIT ME10 94 A3
Grays Rd BH/WHM TN16 98 B8
Great Bounds Dr STH/RUST TN4 189 J3
Great Brooms Rd STH/RUST TN4 190 B6
Great Courtlands RRTW TN3 205 K3
Great Elms RTON TN11 150 A5
Great Footway RRTW TN3 205 J2
Great Lines GILL ME7 4 B3
Greatness La RSEV TN14 102 A8
Greatness Rd RSEV TN14 102 A8
Great Queen St DART DA1 23 J5
Great South Av CHAT ME4 68 B5
Great Till Cl RSEV TN14 101 G3
Grebe Cl HOO/HM ME3 35 F2 2
Grecian Rd RTW TN1 11 D5 4
Grecian St MAID/BEAR ME14 7 D1
Greenacre Cl SWLY BR8 58 B1 1
WALD ME5 88 B1 1
Greenacres OXTED RH8 118 C6
Greenbank WALD ME5 68 C6 2
Green Bank Cl GILL ME7 89 H1 1
Greenbanks DART DA1 23 H8
Greenborough Cl
MAID/SHEP ME15 134 A8
Green Cl ROCH ME1 3 D6
Green Court Rd SWLY BR8 58 A2
Green Farm Cl ORP BR6 76 A1
Green Farm La GVE DA12 47 H1
Greenfield EDEN TN8 164 D5
Greenfield Cl DIT/AY ME20 87 F8
STH/RUST TN4 206 B1 1
Greenfield Rd GILL ME7 5 D2
RDART DA2 40 A3
Greenfields MAID/SHEP ME15 134 A6
Greenfields Cl HOO/HM ME3 49 J3 1
Greenfinches GILL ME7 69 G8
HART DA3 44 C8
Greenfrith Dr TONN TN10 148 B7
Green Gdns ORP BR6 75 H1
Green Hedges TENT TN30 230 B6 1
Green Hl MAID/SHEP ME15 134 D5
ORP BR6 74 D7
Greenhill La HDCN TN27 182 E7
Green Hill La RMAID ME17 159 H6
Greenhill Rd GVW DA11 27 G8 1
RSEV TN14 102 A2
Greenhithe MAID/SHEP ME15 7 D4 2
Greenhurst La OXTED RH8 140 D3
Greenlands BGR/WK TN15 105 H7
Green Lands GVE DA12 64 A2
Green La CRBK TN17 228 A3
E/WMAL ME19 106 C1
EDEN TN8 143 J7
HDCN TN27 202 A5
HOO/HM ME3 15 G8
HOO/HM ME3 21 G8
MEO DA13 63 J4
RMAID ME17 155 J3
RMAID ME17 157 G3
RMAID ME17 159 K5
RMAID ME17 178 B1
RSIT ME9 91 J5
RSIT ME9 94 C7
STPH/PW TN12 175 J5
STPH/PW TN12 193 J1
The Green La RTON TN11 168 D5 1
Greenleas RTWE/PEM TN2 191 J8
Greenleigh Av STMC/STPC BR5 56 C1
Greenoak Ri BH/WHM TN16 97 G5
Green Rd STPH/PW TN12 211 K1
Greensand Rd MAID/SHEP ME15 134 C4
Green Sands MAID/BEAR ME14 88 D6
Greensand Wy EDEN TN8 142 C2
HDCN TN27 183 F4
MAID/SHEP ME15 153 J4
OXTED RH8 118 C5
OXTED RH8 140 C2
RMAID ME17 155 J5
RSEV TN14 145 F3
RTON TN11 149 F1
WBY/YAL ME18 151 J3
Greenside MAID/SHEP ME15 7 E4
RASHW TN26 219 K7
SWLY BR8 40 A7 1
Green St GILL ME7 4 C3
Green Street Green Rd DART DA1 23 K7
RDART DA2 42 B1
The Green BH/WHM TN16 120 D5
RDART DA2 24 C8
RRTW TN3 205 H3
RSIT ME9 72 A3 1
RTON TN11 168 D5
SCUP DA14 38 B3
SEV TN13 9 F1
STMC/STPC BR5 38 C5
Greentrees Av TONN TN10 171 F1
Greenvale Gdns RHAM ME8 69 J4
Green View Av RTON TN11 168 E5
Greenview Crs RTON TN11 169 J2
Green Wk DART DA1 22 C3
Green Wy HART DA3 61 K2
MAIDW ME16 132 B3
RTWE/PEM TN2 190 E6
Greenway BH/WHM TN16 97 G7
CRBK TN17 225 H2
WALD ME5 67 J8
Greenway Court Rd RMAID ME17 136 D7
Greenway La RMAID ME17 136 E7
Greenways HART DA3 44 E8
MAID/BEAR ME14 134 B1
SIT ME10 94 C3
The Greenways STPH/PW TN12 193 H1 1
The Greenway OXTED RH8 140 E4
Greenwich Cl MAIDW ME16 6 A3
WALD ME5 88 C2 2
Greenwood Rd BXLY DA5 40 A2
Greenwood Wy SEV TN13 8 B4
Greggs Wood Rd RTWE/PEM TN2 190 E7
Gregory Cl RHAM ME8 90 B2
Grenadier Cl RHAM ME8 70 E4
Grenville Cl MEO DA13 63 H7
Gresham Av HART DA3 62 A2
Gresham Cl OXTED RH8 118 D8
RHAM ME8 70 C5 2
Gresham Rd OXTED RH8 118 D8
RMAID ME17 154 D3
Gresswell Cl SCUP DA14 38 B1
Greybury La EDEN TN8 184 B3
Greyfriars Cl MAIDW ME16 6 A2
Greyhound Wy DART DA1 22 B4
Greys Park Cl HAYES BR2 74 B1
Greystone Pk RSEV TN14 122 A4
Greystones Cl RSEV TN14 102 C4
Greystones Rd MAID/SHEP ME15 134 C4
Grey Wethers MAID/BEAR ME14 110 E2
Gribble Bridge La HDCN TN27 229 F1
Grice Av BH/WHM TN16 74 A8
Grieves Rd GVW DA11 45 G1
Griffin Wk GRH DA9 24 E4
Grigg La HDCN TN27 181 H7
Griggs Wy BGR/WK TN15 105 G7
Grizedale Cl ROCH ME1 67 J6
Gromenfield RRTW TN3 205 F7 1
Groombridge Hl RRTW TN3 205 F6
Groombridge Rd RRTW TN3 204 D6
Groombridge Sq
MAID/SHEP ME15 134 B8 9
Grosvenor Av ROCH ME1 3 E5
Grosvenor Br STH/RUST TN4 11 D2
Grosvenor Crs DART DA1 23 G4
Grosvenor Pk RTW TN1 10 C2
Grosvenor Rd GILL ME7 69 G5
Grosvenor Wk RTW TN1 10 C3 5
Grove Av RTW TN1 10 C5 4
Grove Green La MAID/BEAR ME14 134 A1
Grove Green Rd MAID/BEAR ME14 134 B1
Groveherst Rd DART DA1 23 J2
Grove Hill Gdns RTW TN1 11 D5
Grove Hill Rd RTW TN1 10 C4
Grovehurst La STPH/PW TN12 212 B1
Grovehurst Rd RSIT ME9 73 K3
SIT ME10 73 K5
Grovelands RMAID ME17 160 E1
Grovelands Rd STMC/STPC BR5 38 B5
Grove Park Av SIT ME10 93 F1
Grove Rd BGR/WK TN15 124 E1
BH/WHM TN16 97 G7
CHAT ME4 4 B6
EDEN TN8 187 F5
GILL ME7 51 H8
GVW DA11 26 C4
MAID/SHEP ME15 133 J8
RSEV TN14 102 A8

STRD ME2 49 G6
The Groves SNOD ME6 85 J7
The Grove BGR/WK TN15 80 E5
BH/WHM TN16 97 H5
GVE DA12 27 J6
MAID/BEAR ME14 134 C3
RTWE/PEM TN2 191 K6
SCUP DA14 39 F3
SWCM DA10 25 K4
SWLY BR8 40 C8 2
Grovewood Dr
MAID/BEAR ME14 133 K2 2
MAID/BEAR ME14 134 B2 3
Grub St OXTED RH8 119 G8
Guardian Ct RHAM ME8 69 K5
Guestwick TONN TN10 171 F1
Guildables La EDEN TN8 141 J7
OXTED RH8 141 J5
Guildford Gdns STRD ME2 48 B8 1
Guildford Rd RTW TN1 11 D4 5
Gullands RMAID ME17 157 G2
Gun Back La STPH/PW TN12 211 K1 1
Gundulph Rd CHAT ME4 3 E4
Gundulph Sq ROCH ME1 2 C2 4
Gunfleet Cl GVE DA12 28 B6
Gunlands STPH/PW TN12 194 E8
Gun La STRD ME2 2 B1
Gunnis Cl RHAM ME8 89 K2
Gunn Rd SWCM DA10 25 K5
Guston Rd MAID/BEAR ME14 7 F2
Gwynn Rd GVW DA11 26 D8
Gybbon Ri STPH/PW TN12 198 A3
Gybbons Rd CRBK TN17 238 D3

H

Hackney Rd MAIDW ME16 132 C4
Haddon Rd STMC/STPC BR5 56 D2
Hadleigh Ct GILL ME7 89 H3
Hadley Cl MEO DA13 63 J6
Hadlow Pk RTON TN11 150 A5
Hadlow Rd MAID/BEAR ME14 7 F2
SCUP DA14 38 B2
TON TN9 170 C4
TONN TN10 170 E2
Hadlow Stair Rd TONN TN10 171 F2
Hadlow Wy MEO DA13 45 F5 1
Haffenden Cl STPH/PW TN12 176 D8
Haffenden Rd TENT TN30 230 A5
Haig Av CHAT ME4 4 A6
CHAT ME4 67 J5
GILL ME7 5 E4
Haig Gdns GVE DA12 27 K6
Haig Rd BH/WHM TN16 97 J4
Haileybury Rd ORP BR6 56 B8
Hailstone Cl RTON TN11 150 A6 2
Haldane Gdns GVW DA11 26 D7
Halden Cl MAID/SHEP ME15 134 B8
Halden La CRBK TN17 228 C5
Hale Ct STPH/PW TN12 151 J7
Hale La RSEV TN14 101 H4
Hale Oak Rd EDEN TN8 167 G2
RSEV TN14 145 J5
Hale Rd HOO/HM ME3 31 H7
Hales Cl TENT TN30 230 B6
Hales Rd SIT ME10 93 J5
Hale St STPH/PW TN12 151 J7
Haleys Pl ROCH ME1 87 F6 1
Half Moon La RTON TN11 147 H8
Halfpence La GVE DA12 46 E7
Halfpenny Cl MAIDW ME16 132 A4
Halfway Ct PUR RM19 12 E4
Halifax Cl WALD ME5 68 C8
Hall Av SOCK/AV RM15 13 G1
Hall Cl SIT ME10 73 K8
Hall Crs SOCK/AV RM15 13 G2
Hallford Wy DART DA1 23 F5
Hall Hl BGR/WK TN15 125 F2
OXTED RH8 140 B3
Hall Rd DART DA1 23 J3
DIT/AY ME20 109 K5
GVW DA11 26 E8
HOO/HM ME3 17 K8
ROCH ME1 86 B3
SOCK/AV RM15 13 G2
WALD ME5 88 D3
Hallsfield Rd WALD ME5 87 J3
Hall's Hole Rd RTWE/PEM TN2 207 K3
Hallsland Wy OXTED RH8 140 D4
Hall Ter SOCK/AV RM15 13 H2
Hallwards STPH/PW TN12 198 A4
Hallwood Cl RHAM ME8 90 A1
Halstead La RSEV TN14 100 A2
Halstow Cl MAID/SHEP ME15 155 H1
Hambledon Ct MAIDW ME16 132 B3 1
Hamble Rd TONN TN10 170 B1
Hamelin Rd GILL ME7 69 G6
Hamerton Rd GVW DA11 26 C4 5
Hamfield Cl OXTED RH8 118 A6
Hamilton Crs SIT ME10 93 H3
Hamilton Rd BFN/LL DA15 38 B2
GILL ME7 5 D1
Ham La GILL ME7 89 F3
RMAID ME17 160 B1
Hamlin Rd SEV TN13 101 G8
Hammonds HAWK TN18 235 G4 1
Hammonds Sq SNOD ME6 85 K6
Hamond Hl CHAT ME4 3 E4 1
Hampshire Cl WALD ME5 68 D7 1
Hampshire Drive Rd
MAID/SHEP ME15 133 J6
Hampson Wy MAID/BEAR ME14 134 C2
Hampstead La WBY/YAL ME18 152 A5
Hampton Cl WALD ME5 88 B1
Hampton Crs GVE DA12 28 B8
Hampton Rd MAID/BEAR ME14 7 F1
Hamptons Rd RTON TN11 149 F1
Ham River Hl HOO/HM ME3 31 F8
Ham Shades Cl BFN/LL DA15 38 A1
Hamwick Gn WALD ME5 88 D5
Hanbury Cl WBY/YAL ME18 130 C7
Hanbury Dr BH/WHM TN16 74 A8
Hancock Cl STRD ME2 49 G5
Handel Wk TONN TN10 149 F8 1
Hanford Rd SOCK/AV RM15 13 G1 3
Hang Grove Hl ORP BR6 75 G8
Hanmer Wy STPH/PW TN12 198 A4
Hanover Cl SIT ME10 93 K4
Hanover Dr RHAM ME8 89 K2
Hanover Rd RMAID ME17 154 C3
RTW TN1 10 C3 6
Hanway RHAM ME8 69 H4
Harbledown Pl STMC/STPC BR5 56 D1 1
Harbourland Cl
MAID/BEAR ME14 111 H6 3
Harbourne La RASHW TN26 230 E2
TENT TN30 230 D2
The Harbour RMAID ME17 179 G1 1
Harcourt Gdns RHAM ME8 90 B2
Harden Rd GVW DA11 27 G8
Hardie Cl E/WMAL ME19 108 D5 3
Hardinge Av STH/RUST TN4 189 J3
Hardinge Cl RHAM ME8 89 K2
Hards Town CHAT ME4 4 A4
Hardwick Crs DART DA1 24 A5 1
Hardwick Rd RTON TN11 147 J8
Hardy Av GVW DA11 27 F8
Hardy Cl WALD ME5 68 C8
Hardy Gv DART DA1 23 K3
Hardy St MAID/BEAR ME14 7 D1
Harebell Cl MAID/BEAR ME14 134 A1 2
Haredale Cl ROCH ME1 67 J7
Harescroft RTWE/PEM TN2 206 E7 1
Harfst Wy SWLY BR8 39 K6
Hargate Cl RTWE/PEM TN2 206 E7
Harland Wy STH/RUST TN4 189 K3
Harlech Cl STRD ME2 48 E5
Harman Av GVW DA11 45 J3
Harmer Rd SWCM DA10 26 A5
Harmer St GVE DA12 27 K5
Harmers Wy HDCN TN27 183 F3
Harmony St STH/RUST TN4 206 C2
Harold Av GILL ME7 5 E4
Harold Rd RDART DA2 41 J2
SIT ME10 94 C2
STRD ME2 66 A3
Harp Farm Rd MAID/BEAR ME14 88 D7
Harple La MAID/BEAR ME14 112 B5
Harptree Dr WALD ME5 88 A1
Harrier Dr SIT ME10 94 B4
Harries Rd RTWE/PEM TN2 190 D7
Harris Cl GVW DA11 45 F1
Harrison Dr HOO/HM ME3 33 F2
RMAID ME17 137 J8
Harrison Rd BGR/WK TN15 105 F7
Harrisons Whf PUR RM19 12 E5
Harrison Wy SEV TN13 8 C1
Harrowby Gdns GVW DA11 27 F8 1
Harrow Ct RSIT ME9 91 G6
Harrow Gdns ORP BR6 56 C8
Harrow Rd GILL ME7 69 G8
RSEV TN14 100 A2
Harrow Wy MAID/BEAR ME14 134 A1
Harrys Rd RSIT ME9 95 K3
Hart Dyke Rd STMC/STPC BR5 56 D5 1
SWLY BR8 40 A8
Hartfield Cl TONN TN10 170 E1
Hartfield Pl GVW DA11 26 E6 2
Hartfield Rd EDEN TN8 185 G2
Hartington Cl ORP BR6 75 H1
Hartington St CHAT ME4 4 A5
Hartlake Rd RTON TN11 171 J6
Hartley Bottom Rd HART DA3 62 C5
Hartley Cl MAID/SHEP ME15 134 B8
Hartley Court Gdns CRBK TN17 225 G3 1
Hartley Hl HART DA3 62 B5
Hartley Rd BH/WHM TN16 120 D4
CRBK TN17 225 G4
HART DA3 43 K7
Hartlip Hl RSIT ME9 71 H7
Hartnokes HAWK TN18 235 G4
Hartnup St MAIDW ME16 132 C4
Hartpiece Cl RHAM ME8 70 C4 1
Hart Shaw HART DA3 44 C7
Hartshill Rd GVW DA11 27 G8
Hartsland Rd SEV TN13 9 E2
Hart St MAIDW ME16 6 C4
Harty Av RHAM ME8 89 J3
Harvel Av STRD ME2 48 D7
Harvel Cl CHST BR7 38 B8
Harvel La MEO DA13 83 J3
Harvel Rd MEO DA13 83 F7
Harvel St MEO DA13 83 K3
Harvesters Cl RHAM ME8 70 B8
Harvesters Wy
MAID/BEAR ME14 133 K2 3
Harvest Rdg E/WMAL ME19 108 B4
Harvest Rd TONN TN10 148 D8
Harvest Wy SWLY BR8 57 K4
Harvey Dr SIT ME10 94 B4
Harvey Rd RHAM ME8 70 B6
Harvill Rd SCUP DA14 38 E3
Harwood Rd RHAM ME8 70 E5 4
Hasletts Cl STH/RUST TN4 11 D1
Haslewood Cl HDCN TN27 202 B4 1
Hasted Cl GRH DA9 25 H5
Hasted Rd RSIT ME9 72 A7
Hasteds RMAID ME17 136 A4
Haste Hill Cl MAID/SHEP ME15 155 G3
Haste Hill Rd MAID/SHEP ME15 155 G3
Hastings Rd CRBK TN17 238 B5
HAWK TN18 235 F7
MAID/SHEP ME15 7 E4
RTWE/PEM TN2 191 K8
STPH/PW TN12 209 G1
Hatches La RTON TN11 151 F8
Hatch Rd RMAID ME17 160 C1
Hatfield Rd STRD ME2 49 F6
Hatham Green La BGR/WK TN15 81 J5
Hathaway Ct ROCH ME1 2 B3
Hatherall Rd MAID/BEAR ME14 7 E1
Hatherley Rd SCUP DA14 38 B1
Hatmill La STPH/PW TN12 193 J7
Hatton Cl GVW DA11 45 F1
Hatton Rd WALD ME5 88 D3
Havelock Rd DART DA1 22 E6
GVW DA11 27 G7
TON TN9 170 B3
Haven Cl MEO DA13 45 G6
ROCH ME1 2 C6
SCUP DA14 38 D4
SWLY BR8 40 C7
Havengore Av GVE DA12 28 B6
Haven Hl BGR/WK TN15 82 B2
Haven St HOO/HM ME3 49 H1
Haven Wy CHAT ME4 50 C5
Havering Cl RTWE/PEM TN2 191 F8
Havisham Cl ROCH ME1 3 D6 1
Havisham Rd GVE DA12 28 D7
Havock La MAID/BEAR ME14 6 C3 1
Hawbeck Rd RHAM ME8 89 K3
Hawden Cl RTON TN11 169 K2
Hawden La RTON TN11 169 K3
Hawden Rd TON TN9 170 B4
Hawfield Bank ORP BR6 56 E7 1
Hawkenbury Cl RTWE/PEM TN2 11 F5 2
Hawkenbury Md
RTWE/PEM TN2 11 F6 1
Hawkenbury Rd RTWE/PEM TN2 207 K5
STPH/PW TN12 178 E8
Hawkes Pl SEV TN13 8 C6
Hawkes Rd DIT/AY ME20 109 K1
Hawkhurst Rd BUR/ETCH TN19 233 J4
HAWK TN18 225 F7
RHAM ME8 69 H3
Hawkins Av GVE DA12 45 K2
Hawkins Cl CHAT ME4 4 A2
SIT ME10 73 K8
Hawkwood MAIDW ME16 132 B1 2
Hawkwood Cl ROCH ME1 3 D4 2
Hawley Rd DART DA1 23 H8
Hawser Rd ROCH ME1 67 H5
Hawstead La ORP BR6 77 G1
Hawthorn Cl EDEN TN8 164 C4 1
GVE DA12 45 J2
Hawthorne Av BH/WHM TN16 97 H2
RHAM ME8 69 K4
Hawthorn Rd DART DA1 23 G8
SIT ME10 93 K2
STRD ME2 48 E8
Hawthorns HART DA3 62 A1
WALD ME5 88 A5 3
The Hawthorns DIT/AY ME20 109 J5
OXTED RH8 140 E4 1
Hawthorn Wk RTWE/PEM TN2 190 E6 1
TONN TN10 148 C7
Haxted Rd LING RH7 162 C7
Haydens Cl STMC/STPC BR5 56 D4
Haydens Ms TON TN9 170 C3
The Haydens TON TN9 170 C3
Hayes Cl HOO/HM ME3 48 B3
Hayesden La RRTW TN3 188 E2
Hayes La RSIT ME9 91 J8
Hayes Rd RDART DA2 24 D6
Hayfield E/WMAL ME19 108 B4
Hayfield Rd STMC/STPC BR5 56 B2
Hayfields WALD ME5 88 E4
Hayle Mill Rd MAID/SHEP ME15 133 F6
Hayle Rd MAID/SHEP ME15 7 D4
Hayley Cl STRD ME2 66 B4
Haymans Hl STPH/PW TN12 195 F7
Hayman Wk DIT/AY ME20 86 E8 2
Haymen St CHAT ME4 3 E5

Haynes Rd *GVW* DA11 **45** G1
Hayrick Cl *MAID/BEAR* ME14 **134** A1
Haysel *SIT* ME10 **94** B4
Haywain Cl *MAID/BEAR* ME14 **134** B2 4
STPH/PW TN12 **193** J1 3
The Haywain *OXTED* RH8 **140** B1
Hayward Av *STRD* ME2 **49** G6
Hayward Cl *DART* DA1 **22** A4
Haywood Ri *ORP* BR6 **75** K1
Hazel Av *HOO/HM* ME3 **50** E3
MAIDW ME16 **132** C1
Hazelbank *RRTW* TN3 **205** J3 2
Hazelden Cl *BGR/WK* TN15 **81** F4
Hazel End *SWLY* BR8 **58** B2 1
Hazel Gv *WALD* ME5 **68** C6
Hazel Rd *DART* DA1 **23** G8
Hazel Shaw *TONN* TN10 **148** C8
The Hazels *RHAM* ME8 **89** J1
Hazel Street Rd *RSIT* ME9 **114** E2
Hazelwood Cl *RTWE/PEM* TN2 **190** D6
Hazelwood Dr *MAIDW* ME16 **132** B2
Hazelwood Hts *OXTED* RH8 **140** E2
Hazelwood Rd *OXTED* RH8 **141** F3
RSEV TN14 **75** J7
Hazlemere Dr *GILL* ME7 **69** H1
Hazlitt Dr *MAIDW* ME16 **6** A2
Headcorn Rd *HDCN* TN27 **200** D7
RHAM ME8 **69** J2 1
RMAID ME17 **159** J6
STPH/PW TN12 **198** C2
Headingley Rd *MAIDW* ME16 **110** B8
The Head Race *MAIDW* ME16 **6** A5
Healy Dr *ORP* BR6 **56** A7
Heansill La *HAWK* TN18 **234** E6
Heard Wy *SIT* ME10 **94** C1
Hearns Cl *STMC/STPC* BR5 **56** D1
Hearns Rd *STMC/STPC* BR5 **56** D1
Heartenoak Rd *HAWK* TN18 **235** G2
Hearts Delight Rd *RSIT* ME9 **93** G5
Heath Cl *STMC/STPC* BR5 **56** D3
SWLY BR8 **40** B7 1
Heathclose Av *DART* DA1 **22** E6
Heathclose Rd *DART* DA1 **22** D7
Heathcote Cl *DIT/AY* ME20 **109** K4
Heathend Rd *BXLY* DA5 **22** B7
Heather Bank *STPH/PW* TN12 **173** K8 1
Heatherbank Cl *DART* DA1 **22** B5
Heather Cl *SIT* ME10 **94** B3
WALD ME5 **88** A2
Heather Dr *DART* DA1 **22** D6
MAID/SHEP ME15 **7** E5
TENT TN30 **230** B3
Heather End *SWLY* BR8 **58** A2 1
Heatherside Rd *SCUP* DA14 **38** D1
The Heathers *CRBK* TN17 **225** G3
Heather Wk *TONN* TN10 **148** B8 2
Heatherwood Cl *RMAID* ME17 **158** C4 1
Heathfield *RMAID* ME17 **157** G2
Heathfield Av *MAID/BEAR* ME14 **111** J7
Heathfield Cl *HAYES* BR2 **74** B1 1
MAID/BEAR ME14 **111** H7
WALD ME5 **68** C7
Heathfield Rd *HAYES* BR2 **74** B1
MAID/BEAR ME14 **111** H7
SEV TN13 **8** B1
Heath Gv *MAIDW* ME16 **132** A4
Heathlands Ri *DART* DA1 **22** E6
Heath La *DART* DA1 **22** E7
Heathlee Rd *DART* DA1 **22** B5
Heathorn St *MAID/BEAR* ME14 **7** E2
Heath Rd *DART* DA1 **22** C5
MAID/SHEP ME15 **153** J2
MAIDW ME16 **131** K3
RMAID ME17 **157** G2
Heathside Av *RMAID* ME17 **154** C2
Heath St *DART* DA1 **23** G6
The Heath *E/WMAL* ME19 **130** C1
Heathview Av *DART* DA1 **22** B5
Heathview Crs *DART* DA1 **22** D6
Heathwood Gdns *SWLY* BR8 **39** K7
Heathwood Wk *BXLY* DA5 **22** B7
Heaverham Rd *BGR/WK* TN15 **103** F4
Hectorage Rd *TON* TN9 **170** C6
Hedge Place Rd *GRH* DA9 **24** D5
The Hedgerows *GVW* DA11 **27** F8
The Hedgerow *MAID/BEAR* ME14 **134** A1
The Hedges *MAID/BEAR* ME14 **111** G7 1
Hedley St *MAID/BEAR* ME14 **7** D2
Helen Cl *DART* DA1 **22** E6
Helen Thompson Cl *RSIT* ME9 **73** K2
Hellyar Ct *ROCH* ME1 **2** C4 2
Hempstead La *RSIT* ME9 **95** F3
Hempstead Rd *GILL* ME7 **69** H8
Hempstead Valley Dr *GILL* ME7 **69** H8
Henbane Cl *MAID/BEAR* ME14 **134** A1 3
Henderson Dr *DART* DA1 **23** K3
Henderson Rd *BH/WHM* TN16 **74** B7
Hendley Dr *CRBK* TN17 **225** J1
Hendy Rd *SNOD* ME6 **86** A6
Henham Gdns *STPH/PW* TN12 **151** J8
Henhurst Rd *MEO* DA13 **46** A7
Heniker La *RMAID* ME17 **179** H1
Henley Cl *RHAM* ME8 **70** A6
RTWE/PEM TN2 **11** E3
WALD ME5 **68** B8
Henley Deane *GVW* DA11 **45** F2
Henley Flds *MAID/BEAR* ME14 **112** A8
TENT TN30 **230** B4
Henley Mdw *TENT* TN30 **230** A4
Henley Rd *STPH/PW* TN12 **173** J7
Henley St *MEO* DA13 **64** C3
Henry St *CHAT* ME4 **4** B5
RHAM ME8 **70** D5
Henwood Green Rd
RTWE/PEM TN2 **191** K7
Henwoods Crs *RTWE/PEM* TN2 **191** K8
Henwoods Mt *RTWE/PEM* TN2 **192** A8
Herbert Rd *CHAT* ME4 **4** A5
RHAM ME8 **70** B6
SWCM DA10 **26** A5
SWLY BR8 **40** E4
Herdsdown *HOO/HM* ME3 **50** E1
Hereford Rd *MAID/SHEP* ME15 **133** J7
Heritage Dr *GILL* ME7 **69** G5
Heritage Hl *HAYES* BR2 **74** B1
Heritage Rd *WALD* ME5 **68** B8
Herman Ter *CHAT* ME4 **4** A5
Hermitage Ct *MAIDW* ME16 **131** K1
Hermitage La *DIT/AY* ME20 **109** K7
MAID/BEAR ME14 **112** D3
MAIDW ME16 **109** K8
RMAID ME17 **156** A8
Hermitage Rd *HOO/HM* ME3 **48** B3
Herne Rd *RHAM* ME8 **69** K4
Heron Cl *RSIT* ME9 **72** A3
Heronden Rd *MAID/SHEP* ME15 **156** B2
Herongate Rd *SWLY* BR8 **40** B4
Heron Hill La *MEO* DA13 **83** J2
Heron Rd *DIT/AY* ME20 **108** D5
Herons Wy *RTWE/PEM* TN2 **192** A6
Heron Wy *HOO/HM* ME3 **35** F2
WALD ME5 **68** B8
Herts Crs *MAID/SHEP* ME15 **155** F3 1
Herying Cl *STRD* ME2 **86** A2
Hesiers Hl *WARL* CR6 **96** C4
Hesiers Rd *WARL* CR6 **96** C3
Hesketh Av *RDART* DA2 **24** A7
Heskett Pk *RTWE/PEM* TN2 **192** A8
Hever Av *BGR/WK* TN15 **80** D2
Hever Cl *MAID/SHEP* ME15 **134** B8
Hever Court Rd *GVE* DA12 **45** K4
Hever Cft *STRD* ME2 **66** E1
Hever Gdns *MAIDW* ME16 **6** B4 1
Hever Pl *SIT* ME10 **93** H3
Hever Rd *BGR/WK* TN15 **80** D2
EDEN TN8 **165** G7
Hever Wood Rd *BGR/WK* TN15 **80** D3
Hewett Pl *SWLY* BR8 **58** A1
Hewitt Cl *GILL* ME7 **5** F2
Hewitts Rd *ORP* BR6 **77** G3
Hextable Cl *MAIDW* ME16 **110** C7 2
Hibbs Cl *SWLY* BR8 **40** A7
Hibernia Dr *GVE* DA12 **46** C1
Hickory Dell *GILL* ME7 **89** H1
Higham Cl *MAID/SHEP* ME15 **6** A5
Higham Gdns *TONN* TN10 **171** F1
Higham La *RTON* TN11 **148** E5
RYE TN31 **244** D8
TONN TN10 **149** F8
Higham Rd *HOO/HM* ME3 **31** F2
HOO/HM ME3 **49** H3
Higham School Rd *TONN* TN10 **148** E8
Higham Vw *MAID/BEAR* ME14 **110** E2 1
High Bank *ROCH* ME1 **3** D6
High Banks *MAID/SHEP* ME15 **155** F1
High Beeches *ORP* BR6 **76** B2
RTWE/PEM TN2 **11** F1
SCUP DA14 **39** F3
Highberry *E/WMAL* ME19 **108** C4 2
Highbourne Pk *RMAID* ME17 **161** J1
High Brooms Rd *STH/RUST* TN4 **190** C6
Highbury La *TENT* TN30 **230** A7
High Cross Rd *BGR/WK* TN15 **126** B5
Highcross Rd *MEO* DA13 **43** J4
High Dewar Rd *RHAM* ME8 **70** D6
High Elms *RHAM* ME8 **70** B4
High Elms Rd *ORP* BR6 **75** H4
Highfield Av *ORP* BR6 **76** A2
Highfield Cl *HAWK* TN18 **235** G5
RHAM ME8 **70** A7 2
RTWE/PEM TN2 **191** K8
Highfield Rd *BH/WHM* TN16 **97** G4
DART DA1 **23** G6
RHAM ME8 **70** A7
RSEV TN14 **102** C3
STH/RUST TN4 **190** C7
STMC/STPC BR5 **38** A8
Highfield Rd South *DART* DA1 **23** G6
Highfields Rd *EDEN* TN8 **164** C1
High Firs *SWLY* BR8 **58** B1
Highgate Hl *HAWK* TN18 **235** F5
Highgrove *RTWE/PEM* TN2 **207** F6
Highgrove Rd *WALD* ME5 **88** B1
High Halden Rd *HDCN* TN27 **217** K5
High Hilden Cl *RTON* TN11 **170** A2
High House La *RTON* TN11 **149** H5
Highland Rd *MAID/SHEP* ME15 **134** A7
RSEV TN14 **77** J6
Highlands Cl *STRD* ME2 **48** C8
Highlands Hl *SWLY* BR8 **40** D7
Highlands Pk *BGR/WK* TN15 **102** C8
Highlands Rd *STMC/STPC* BR5 **56** C4
High Meadow *RYE* TN31 **244** D7
High Oak Hl *RSIT* ME9 **72** D6
High Pk *RYE* TN31 **244** D7
High Rdg *CRBK* TN17 **212** C7
Highridge *GILL* ME7 **69** G5 2
Highridge Cl *MAID/BEAR* ME14 **134** B1
High Rd *RDART* DA2 **40** E1
High Rocks La *RRTW* TN3 **206** B5
Highsted Rd *RSIT* ME9 **94** A7
High St *BGR/WK* TN15 **102** E4
BGR/WK TN15 **102** D8
BGR/WK TN15 **105** G3
BGR/WK TN15 **105** F7
BH/WHM TN16 **120** C6
BH/WHM TN16 **121** J3
CHAT ME4 **3** F4
CHAT ME4 **4** A4
CRBK TN17 **212** D6
CRBK TN17 **225** J2
CRBK TN17 **238** D3
DART DA1 **23** H5
DIT/AY ME20 **109** K3
E/WMAL ME19 **107** K6
E/WMAL ME19 **108** E8
EDEN TN8 **164** C5
EYN DA4 **59** J3
EYN DA4 **59** H6
GILL ME7 **4** C2 5
GILL ME7 **4** A2
GRH DA9 **25** G3
GVE DA12 **27** J5
GVW DA11 **26** C5
HAWK TN18 **234** D4
HDCN TN27 **200** A1
HDCN TN27 **202** A5
HDCN TN27 **217** J5
HOO/HM ME3 **21** G8
HOO/HM ME3 **35** F2 3
MAID/BEAR ME14 **6** C3
ORP BR6 **56** B4
ORP BR6 **75** F6
ORP BR6 **75** H1
OXTED RH8 **119** F7
OXTED RH8 **140** B1
RDART DA2 **43** G1
RHAM ME8 **70** C6
RMAID ME17 **157** G7
RMAID ME17 **160** D2
ROCH ME1 **2** C2
ROCH ME1 **86** B2
RRTW TN3 **221** J2
RSEV TN14 **78** C5
RSEV TN14 **101** J3
RSIT ME9 **72** A8
RTON TN11 **150** A6
RTON TN11 **168** C5
RTW TN1 **10** C5
RTWE/PEM TN2 **191** J8
SCUP DA14 **38** B2
SEV TN13 **9** E4
SEV TN13 **122** E1
SIT ME10 **73** K8
SNOD ME6 **85** K6
SOCK/AV RM15 **13** G1
STH/RUST TN4 **189** G3
STMC/STPC BR5 **56** D3
STPH/PW TN12 **176** D8
STPH/PW TN12 **193** K6
STPH/PW TN12 **198** B3
STRD ME2 **2** B1
STRD ME2 **50** A4
SWCM DA10 **26** A4
SWLY BR8 **40** B8
TENT TN30 **230** A7
TON TN9 **170** C5
TONN TN10 **170** C4
WADH TN5 **233** H3
WBY/YAL ME18 **152** D5
High Vw *HOO/HM* ME3 **48** B2
Highview *MEO* DA13 **83** J6
Highview Dr *WALD* ME5 **87** J1
Highview Rd *SCUP* DA14 **38** C2
The Highway *ORP* BR6 **76** C1
High Weald Wk *RRTW* TN3 **189** F7
RTON TN11 **191** J3
RTWE/PEM TN2 **207** K6
STH/RUST TN4 **10** B5
TON TN9 **170** E7
Highwoods Cl *HOO/HM* ME3 **48** B2 1
High Woods La *RTWE/PEM* TN2 **208** A4
Hilary Gdns *ROCH* ME1 **66** E4
Hilbert Cl *RTW* TN1 **11** E2
Hilborough Wy *ORP* BR6 **75** J1
Hilda May Av *SWLY* BR8 **40** B8
Hilda Rd *CHAT* ME4 **4** A5
Hilden Av *RTON* TN11 **169** K2
Hildenborough Crs *MAIDW* ME16 **110** B7
Hildenborough Rd *RTON* TN11 **147** K2
RTON TN11 **168** E3
Hilden Park Rd *RTON* TN11 **169** K2
Hilders Cl *EDEN* TN8 **164** B2
Hilders La *EDEN* TN8 **163** K2
Hillary Av *GVW* DA11 **45** F1

Hillary Rd *MAID/BEAR* ME14 .... 111 G7
Hillborough Gv *WALD* ME5 .... 88 B3
Hill Brow *DART* DA1 .... 22 C5
MAID/BEAR ME14 .... 134 C1
SIT ME10 .... 93 J4
Hillbrow Cl *BXLY* DA5 .... 40 A2
Hillbury Gdns *WADH* TN5 .... 232 B5
Hill Cha *WALD* ME5 .... 87 K3
Hill Cl *MEO* DA13 .... 45 F5
Hill Ct *HOO/HM* ME3 .... 50 A2
Hillcrest *EDEN* TN8 .... 165 H1
Hill Crest *SEV* TN13 .... 8 C1
STH/RUST TN4 .... 190 B6
Hillcrest Dr *GRH* DA9 .... 25 F4
RTWE/PEM TN2 .... 190 D7
STRD ME2 .... 66 B4
Hillcrest Rd *BH/WHM* TN16 .... 97 H3
CHAT ME4 .... 3 F6 3
DART DA1 .... 22 B6
EDEN TN8 .... 164 C2
ORP BR6 .... 56 B6
Hillden Shaw *MAID/SHEP* ME15 .... 133 G6
Hill End *ORP* BR6 .... 56 A6
Hill Farm Av *STRD* ME2 .... 48 E5
Hillfield Rd *SEV* TN13 .... 101 G7
Hillgarth *STH/RUST* TN4 .... 190 A6 1
Hill Green Rd *RSIT* ME9 .... 91 F6
Hill House Rd *RDART* DA2 .... 24 B6
Hillingdale *BH/WHM* TN16 .... 97 F5
Hillingdon Av *SEV* TN13 .... 102 A8
Hillingdon Ri *SEV* TN13 .... 9 F1
Hillingdon Rd *GVW* DA11 .... 27 J8
Hill Ri *RDART* DA2 .... 42 C3
Hill Rd *DART* DA1 .... 23 H8
ROCH ME1 .... 2 A6
ROCH ME1 .... 86 D1
Hill Shaw *HART* DA3 .... 62 A3
Hillshaw Crs *STRD* ME2 .... 66 C1
Hillside *EYN* DA4 .... 59 J4
RDART DA2 .... 42 D3
TON TN9 .... 170 A7
Hillside Av *GVE* DA12 .... 28 A8
STRD ME2 .... 49 G6
Hillside Ct *SWLY* BR8 .... 58 D1
WBY/YAL ME18 .... 130 C7
Hillside Dr *GVE* DA12 .... 28 A8
Hillside Rd *BH/WHM* TN16 .... 97 J6
CHAT ME4 .... 4 A4 2
DART DA1 .... 22 D5
RSEV TN14 .... 102 D4
SEV TN13 .... 9 F2
The Hillside *ORP* BR6 .... 76 C4
Hills La *BGR/WK* TN15 .... 80 A7
Hill's Ter *CHAT* ME4 .... 3 F5
Hill St *RTW* TN1 .... 11 D2 1
The Hill *CRBK* TN17 .... 225 K2
GVW DA11 .... 26 D5
Hill Top *CRBK* TN17 .... 213 K1
Hilltop *MAID/SHEP* ME15 .... 153 H3
TON TN9 .... 170 B7
Hilltop Gdns *DART* DA1 .... 23 J4
Hilltop Rd *STRD* ME2 .... 49 H5
Hill Vw *BGR/WK* TN15 .... 105 G7
Hill View Cl *BGR/WK* TN15 .... 105 G7
Hill View Rd *HART* DA3 .... 44 C8
ORP BR6 .... 56 A5
RTON TN11 .... 169 K1
STH/RUST TN4 .... 206 B2
Hill View Wy *WALD* ME5 .... 87 K1
Hillydeal Rd *RSEV* TN14 .... 102 A2
Hillyfield Cl *STRD* ME2 .... 48 E5 1
Hilton Dr *SIT* ME10 .... 73 G8
Hilton Rd *HOO/HM* ME3 .... 31 G7
Hinksden Rd *CRBK* TN17 .... 236 B3
Hinton Crs *GILL* ME7 .... 69 H8
Hitchen Hatch La *SEV* TN13 .... 8 C2
Hither Chantlers *RRTW* TN3 .... 205 K3
Hive La *GVW* DA11 .... 26 C4
Hoath Cl *GILL* ME7 .... 69 H7
Hoath La *RHAM* ME8 .... 69 J7
Hoath Wy *RHAM* ME8 .... 69 J7 1
Hobart Gdns *SIT* ME10 .... 93 H2
Hobbs La *RYE* TN31 .... 246 C8
Hockenden La *SWLY* BR8 .... 39 H8
Hockers Cl *MAID/BEAR* ME14 .... 112 C6
Hockers La *MAID/BEAR* ME14 .... 112 B7
Hodgson Crs *SNOD* ME6 .... 85 K5 1
Hodsoll St *BGR/WK* TN15 .... 82 E4
Hodson Crs *STMC/STPC* BR5 .... 56 E2 1
Hogbarn La *RMAID* ME17 .... 137 K4
Hoghole La *RRTW* TN3 .... 221 G4
Hog La *MEO* DA13 .... 44 E1
Hognore La *BGR/WK* TN15 .... 82 E8
Hogtrough Hl *BH/WHM* TN16 .... 121 G1
Holborough Rd *SNOD* ME6 .... 85 K6
Holcombe Cl *BH/WHM* TN16 .... 120 D5
Holcombe Rd *CHAT* ME4 .... 3 F6
ROCH ME1 .... 2 C5
Holden Cnr *STH/RUST* TN4 .... 189 J5
Holden Park Rd *STH/RUST* TN4 .... 189 K6
Holden Rd *STH/RUST* TN4 .... 189 K5
Holder Cl *WALD* ME5 .... 68 D8
Holding St *RHAM* ME8 .... 70 B5
Hole La *EDEN* TN8 .... 142 A8
Holford St *TON* TN9 .... 170 B5 2
Holland Crs *OXTED* RH8 .... 140 E4
Holland La *OXTED* RH8 .... 140 E4
Holland Rd *MAID/BEAR* ME14 .... 7 D2
OXTED RH8 .... 140 E6
WALD ME5 .... 87 K2
Hollands Cl *GVE* DA12 .... 47 H3
The Hollies *GVE* DA12 .... 46 A4
HART DA3 .... 44 D8
Hollin Cl *STH/RUST* TN4 .... 10 B3 1
Hollingbourne Hl *RMAID* ME17 .... 136 D2
Hollingbourne Rd *RHAM* ME8 .... 69 K3
Hollingworth Rd
MAID/SHEP ME15 .... 156 B1
Hollingworth Wy
BH/WHM TN16 .... 120 D5 3
Hollow La *RSIT* ME9 .... 91 G1
SNOD ME6 .... 85 J7
Hollow Trees Dr *RTON* TN11 .... 168 E5
Holly Bank *STPH/PW* TN12 .... 193 K6
Hollybush Cl *SEV* TN13 .... 9 E3
Hollybush La *ORP* BR6 .... 77 H2
Holly Bush La *SEV* TN13 .... 9 E3 1
Hollybush Rd *GVE* DA12 .... 27 K8
Holly Cl *GILL* ME7 .... 5 E2
WALD ME5 .... 68 D5
Hollydene Rd *WADH* TN5 .... 220 B8
Holly Farm Rd *MAID/SHEP* ME15 .... 134 E8
Holly Hl *MEO* DA13 .... 84 D4
Holly Rd *DART* DA1 .... 23 G7
ORP BR6 .... 76 B3
STRD ME2 .... 48 D8
STRD ME2 .... 49 J4
Hollyshaw Cl *RTWE/PEM* TN2 .... 11 E5 2
Hollytree Av *SWLY* BR8 .... 40 B7
Holly Tree Cl *RMAID* ME17 .... 158 C4
Hollytree Dr *HOO/HM* ME3 .... 48 A3
Hollywood La *BGR/WK* TN15 .... 80 E6
STRD ME2 .... 49 H4
Holmes Cl *HOO/HM* ME3 .... 33 F3
Holmesdale Cl *MAID/SHEP* ME15 .... 155 F3
Holmesdale Hl *EYN* DA4 .... 42 C6
Holmesdale Rd *EYN* DA4 .... 42 B6
Holmewood Rdg *RRTW* TN3 .... 205 J3
Holmewood Rd *STH/RUST* TN4 .... 190 C7
Holmhurst Cl *STH/RUST* TN4 .... 10 B3 2
Holmleigh Av *DART* DA1 .... 23 F3
Holm Mill La *RMAID* ME17 .... 137 F8
Holmoaks *MAID/BEAR* ME14 .... 7 F2
RHAM ME8 .... 70 B4
Holmsdale Gv *BXLYHN* DA7 .... 22 B1
Holmside *GILL* ME7 .... 5 E6
Holt Wood Av *DIT/AY* ME20 .... 109 H6
Holtwood Cl *RHAM* ME8 .... 90 A1
Holtye Crs *MAID/SHEP* ME15 .... 7 E5
Holyoake Ter *SEV* TN13 .... 8 C3
Holywell La *RSIT* ME9 .... 71 J4
Homedean Rd *SEV* TN13 .... 122 E1
Home Farm Cl *RTON* TN11 .... 168 E3
Home Farm La *RTWE/PEM* TN2 .... 190 E6
Homefield Cl *STMC/STPC* BR5 .... 56 C1 2
SWLY BR8 .... 40 C8
Homefield Dr *RHAM* ME8 .... 70 E4
Homefield Ri *ORP* BR6 .... 56 B5
Homefield Rd *SEV* TN13 .... 8 A1
Home Gdns *DART* DA1 .... 23 H5
Home Hl *SWLY* BR8 .... 40 C5
Home Lea *ORP* BR6 .... 76 A1
Home Mead Cl *GVE* DA12 .... 27 J6
Home Pk *OXTED* RH8 .... 140 E2
Homestead Rd *EDEN* TN8 .... 164 B1
ORP BR6 .... 76 C3
The Homestead *DART* DA1 .... 23 F5
RRTW TN3 .... 205 F7 2
Homestead Vw *RSIT* ME9 .... 93 G4
Homeview *SIT* ME10 .... 94 C2 1
Homewards Rd *HOO/HM* ME3 .... 18 E6
Homewood Av *SIT* ME10 .... 93 J3
Homewood Rd *RRTW* TN3 .... 205 J3
TENT TN30 .... 230 B5
Hone St *STRD* ME2 .... 49 G6
Honeyball Wk *RSIT* ME9 .... 95 K4
Honey Bee Gld *RHAM* ME8 .... 70 B8 1
Honey Cl *GILL* ME7 .... 89 H1
Honeycrock Hl *RSIT* ME9 .... 91 J6
Honeyden Rd *SCUP* DA14 .... 39 F4
Honey La *MAID/SHEP* ME15 .... 134 D8
Honeypot Cl *STRD* ME2 .... 49 G6
Honeypot La *BGR/WK* TN15 .... 82 D4
BGR/WK TN15 .... 103 G6
LING RH7 .... 163 H2
Honeysuckle Cl *GILL* ME7 .... 89 G2 1
Honywood Rd *RMAID* ME17 .... 160 C1
Hoo Common *HOO/HM* ME3 .... 50 B2
Hood Av *STMC/STPC* BR5 .... 56 C2
Hook Cl *WALD* ME5 .... 87 K1
Hookfields *GVW* DA11 .... 45 F1
Hook Green La *RDART* DA2 .... 40 C1
Hook Green Rd *MEO* DA13 .... 44 A5
Hook Hl *WADH* TN5 .... 221 J8
Hook La *RMAID* ME17 .... 137 G8
Hook Rd *SNOD* ME6 .... 85 J6
Hook St *RMAID* ME17 .... 161 F6
Hookwood Cnr *OXTED* RH8 .... 119 F7
Hookwood Rd *ORP* BR6 .... 76 D6
Hoopers La *HOO/HM* ME3 .... 34 C1
Hooper's Rd *ROCH* ME1 .... 2 C4 3
Hoo Rd *STRD* ME2 .... 49 J3
Hope Av *RTON* TN11 .... 150 A5
Hopehouse La *CRBK* TN17 .... 237 H5
HAWK TN18 .... 237 G7
Hope Rd *SWCM* DA10 .... 26 A5
Hopes Gv *RASHW* TN26 .... 219 J7
Hope St *CHAT* ME4 .... 4 A5 2
MAID/BEAR ME14 .... 6 C2
Hopewell Dr *GVE* DA12 .... 46 C3
WALD ME5 .... 68 D6
Hopgarden La *SEV* TN13 .... 123 J7
Hopgarden Rd *TONN* TN10 .... 170 D1
Hop Pocket Cl *CRBK* TN17 .... 215 H6 1
Hop Pocket La *STPH/PW* TN12 .... 173 H7
Hopwood Gdns *STH/RUST* TN4 .... 10 C1
Horizon Cl *STH/RUST* TN4 .... 190 B6
Hornbeam Av *RTWE/PEM* TN2 .... 190 D5
WALD ME5 .... 88 C4 1
Hornbeam Cl *DIT/AY* ME20 .... 109 F5
STPH/PW TN12 .... 193 H1 2
Hornbeams *MEO* DA13 .... 83 J6
Horn Hl *RSIT* ME9 .... 116 E4
Horns La *WBY/YAL* ME18 .... 129 F4
Horns Lodge La *RTON* TN11 .... 148 C6
Horn's Oak Rd *MEO* DA13 .... 63 J8
Horns Rd *HAWK* TN18 .... 234 D6
Horn Yd *GVE* DA12 .... 27 J5 3
Horsecroft Cl *ORP* BR6 .... 56 C5 1
Horsegrove Av *WADH* TN5 .... 232 D5
Horsell Rd *STMC/STPC* BR5 .... 38 B6
Horseshoe Cl *GILL* ME7 .... 89 G1
MAID/BEAR ME14 .... 134 A1 1
Horseshoes La *RMAID* ME17 .... 157 F2
Horsfield Cl *RDART* DA2 .... 24 B6 2
Horsham La *RHAM* ME8 .... 71 G3
Horsley Rd *ROCH* ME1 .... 2 B4
Horsmonden Cl *ORP* BR6 .... 56 A4 1
Horsmonden Rd *STPH/PW* TN12 .... 194 A7
Horsted Av *CHAT* ME4 .... 67 K5
Horsted Wy *ROCH* ME1 .... 67 J7
Horton Downs *MAID/SHEP* ME15 .... 134 B5
Horton Pl *BH/WHM* TN16 .... 120 D5
Horton Rd *EYN* DA4 .... 42 B8
Hortons Cl *CRBK* TN17 .... 227 F7
Hortons Wy *BH/WHM* TN16 .... 120 D5
Horton Wy *EYN* DA4 .... 59 J4
Horwood Cl *ROCH* ME1 .... 67 G6 2
Hoselands Vw *HART* DA3 .... 61 K1
Hosey Common La
BH/WHM TN16 .... 142 E1
Hosey Common Rd
BH/WHM TN16 .... 120 E8
Hosey Hl *BH/WHM* TN16 .... 120 E6
Hoskins Rd *OXTED* RH8 .... 118 C8
Hospital Rd *RMAID* ME17 .... 136 C6
SEV TN13 .... 102 A8
Hostier Cl *STRD* ME2 .... 86 A2
Hotel Rd *RHAM* ME8 .... 69 H4
Hotham Cl *EYN* DA4 .... 41 K5
SWLY BR8 .... 40 E6
Hothfield Rd *RHAM* ME8 .... 70 C5
Hottsfield *HART* DA3 .... 43 K8
Houghton Av *GILL* ME7 .... 89 J3
Houselands Rd *TON* TN9 .... 170 B4 1
Hovendens *CRBK* TN17 .... 215 H6
Howard Av *ROCH* ME1 .... 3 D5
SIT ME10 .... 73 J8
Howard Dr *MAIDW* ME16 .... 110 B8
Howard Rd *DART* DA1 .... 23 K5
E/WMAL ME19 .... 108 D6
Howbury La *ERITH* DA8 .... 22 D1
Howbury Rd *DART* DA1 .... 22 D1
Howells Cl *BGR/WK* TN15 .... 80 D2 1
How Green La *EDEN* TN8 .... 165 J5
Howick Cl *DIT/AY* ME20 .... 109 K6
Howland Rd *STPH/PW* TN12 .... 177 F8
Howlsmere Cl *STRD* ME2 .... 86 A3
Hubbards Hl *RMAID* ME17 .... 161 H1
SEV TN13 .... 145 K2
Hubbard's La *MAID/SHEP* ME15 .... 155 G3
Hubble Dr *MAID/SHEP* ME15 .... 134 A7
Huckleberry Cl *WALD* ME5 .... 88 C3 2
Hudson Cl *RHAM* ME8 .... 69 K5
Hughes Dr *STRD* ME2 .... 49 J4
Hugh Price Cl *SIT* ME10 .... 94 D1
Hulsewood Cl *RDART* DA2 .... 40 E1
Humber Crs *STRD* ME2 .... 48 E7
Humber Rd *DART* DA1 .... 23 G4
Humboldt Ct *RTWE/PEM* TN2 .... 11 F2
Hume Av *TIL* RM18 .... 27 J2
Hume Cl *TIL* RM18 .... 27 H2
Hungershall Pk *STH/RUST* TN4 .... 10 A5
Hunsdon Dr *SEV* TN13 .... 9 D2
Hunstanton Cl *RHAM* ME8 .... 90 B3
Hunters Cl *BXLY* DA5 .... 40 B1
Huntersfield Cl *WALD* ME5 .... 88 D5 1
Hunters Wk *RSEV* TN14 .... 100 A1
Hunters Wy *GILL* ME7 .... 69 F5
RTWE/PEM TN2 .... 10 B6
Hunters Wy West *WALD* ME5 .... 5 D6
Huntingdon Wk
MAID/SHEP ME15 .... 134 A7 1
Huntingfield Rd *MEO* DA13 .... 63 H4
Huntington Cl *CRBK* TN17 .... 225 K2 1

Huntington Rd *RMAID* ME17 .... **154** B3
Huntley Av *GVW* DA11 .... **26** C5
Huntley Mill Rd *WADH* TN5 .... **232** B3
Huntleys Pk *STH/RUST* TN4 .... **10** B1
Hunton Hl *MAID/SHEP* ME15 .... **153** K5
Hunton Rd *STPH/PW* TN12 .... **175** K1
Hunt Rd *GVW* DA11 .... **45** F1
TONN TN10 .... **148** E8
Hunts Farm Cl *BGR/WK* TN15 .... **105** G7
Huntsman La *BGR/WK* TN15 .... **106** A5
MAID/BEAR ME14 .... **7** E3
Huntsmans Cl *CHAT* ME4 .... **67** K5 1
Hunt St *WBY/YAL* ME18 .... **152** C2
Hurlfield *RDART* DA2 .... **41** F1
Huron Cl *ORP* BR6 .... **76** A2 2
Hurricane Rd *E/WMAL* ME19 .... **129** H3
Hurst Cl *STPH/PW* TN12 .... **198** B2
TENT TN30 .... **229** J7
WALD ME5 .... **67** K8
Hurst Farm Rd *RSEV* TN14 .... **145** K3
Hurst Green Cl *OXTED* RH8 .... **140** E3
Hurst Green Rd *OXTED* RH8 .... **140** E3
Hurst Hl *WALD* ME5 .... **87** K4
The Hurstings *MAIDW* ME16 .... **6** A5
Hurstlands *OXTED* RH8 .... **140** E3
Hurst La *RSEV* TN14 .... **145** K4
Hurst Pl *RHAM* ME8 .... **70** C6
The Hurst *RTWE/PEM* TN2 .... **190** E7
Hurst Wy *MAIDW* ME16 .... **131** K4
SEV TN13 .... **9** E6
Hurstwood *WALD* ME5 .... **87** K2
Hurstwood La *STH/RUST* TN4 .... **10** A4
Hurstwood Pk *STH/RUST* TN4 .... **10** B4
Hurstwood Rd *GILL* ME7 .... **89** J5
MAID/BEAR ME14 .... **89** J7
Husheath Hl *CRBK* TN17 .... **197** F8
Hutsford Cl *RHAM* ME8 .... **90** A1 3
Hyacinth Rd *STRD* ME2 .... **48** C8
Hybrid Cl *ROCH* ME1 .... **67** J5
Hyde Dr *STMC/STPC* BR5 .... **56** C1
Hyde Rd *MAIDW* ME16 .... **110** D7
Hydes Orch *HDCN* TN27 .... **200** C1 2
Hyperion Dr *STRD* ME2 .... **48** E5 2
Hythe Cl *STH/RUST* TN4 .... **190** A5
STMC/STPC BR5 .... **56** D1 2
Hythe Rd *SIT* ME10 .... **93** J1
Hythe St *DART* DA1 .... **23** H4

I

Icehouse Wd *OXTED* RH8 .... **140** C2
Ide Hill Rd *RSEV* TN14 .... **144** B3
Iden Crs *STPH/PW* TN12 .... **198** A4
Iden La *HDCN* TN27 .... **183** H2
Iden Rd *STRD* ME2 .... **49** H5
Idenwood Cl *RHAM* ME8 .... **70** A8
Idleigh Court Rd *HART* DA3 .... **62** C6
Ifield Cl *MAID/SHEP* ME15 .... **134** B6
Ifield Wy *GVE* DA12 .... **46** A4
Ightham By-pass *BGR/WK* TN15 .... **104** C8
Ightham Rd *RTON* TN11 .... **148** C3
Illustrious Cl *WALD* ME5 .... **88** B1
Impala Gdns *STH/RUST* TN4 .... **11** D1
Imperial Dr *GVE* DA12 .... **46** C3
Imperial Rd *GILL* ME7 .... **4** C5
Impton La *WALD* ME5 .... **88** A6
Ingleden Park Rd *TENT* TN30 .... **230** B5
Ingle Rd *CHAT* ME4 .... **3** F6
Inglewood Rd *BXLYHN* DA7 .... **22** A3
Ingoldsby Rd *GVE* DA12 .... **28** B7
Ingram Rd *DART* DA1 .... **23** H7
GILL ME7 .... **5** E3
Institute Rd *CHAT* ME4 .... **4** A4
Instone Rd *DART* DA1 .... **23** G6
Invicta Rd *RDART* DA2 .... **24** A5
Iona Cl *WALD* ME5 .... **88** E5
Iona Rd *MAID/SHEP* ME15 .... **133** G7
Irene Rd *ORP* BR6 .... **56** A4
Iris Cl *WALD* ME5 .... **88** B6
Iron Mill La *DART* DA1 .... **22** C3
Iron Mill Pl *DART* DA1 .... **22** C3
Ironside Cl *WALD* ME5 .... **68** B6
Ironstones *RRTW* TN3 .... **206** A3 1
Irvine Rd *HOO/HM* ME3 .... **48** A3
Irvine Wy *ORP* BR6 .... **56** A4
Irving Wy *SWLY* BR8 .... **40** A7
Island Wy East *CHAT* ME4 .... **50** C5
Island Wy West *CHAT* ME4 .... **50** C4
Islingham Rd *HOO/HM* ME3 .... **49** H3
Ismays Rd *BGR/WK* TN15 .... **126** B4
Istead Ri *MEO* DA13 .... **45** G5
Itchingwood Common Rd
OXTED RH8 .... **141** G4
Ivens Wy *RMAID* ME17 .... **137** H8
Iversgate Cl *RHAM* ME8 .... **70** C4
Ives Rd *TON* TN9 .... **169** K5
Ivy Bower Cl *GRH* DA9 .... **25** G4
Ivy Cl *DART* DA1 .... **23** K5
GVE DA12 .... **45** K2
RMAID ME17 .... **158** B4
Ivy House La *SEV* TN13 .... **101** F4
Ivy La *RSEV* TN14 .... **100** A3
Ivy St *RHAM* ME8 .... **70** C6

J

Jackass La *HAYES* BR2 .... **74** A2
Jacklin Cl *WALD* ME5 .... **88** A3
Jackson Av *ROCH* ME1 .... **67** K6
Jackson Cl *GRH* DA9 .... **24** E4
RHAM ME8 .... **69** K5
Jacksons La *TENT* TN30 .... **230** A7 1
Jacob's La *HOO/HM* ME3 .... **33** J8
Jaggard Wy *STPH/PW* TN12 .... **198** A3
Jagger Cl *RDART* DA2 .... **24** B6
Jail La *BH/WHM* TN16 .... **97** H2
James Rd *DART* DA1 .... **22** D6
STRD ME2 .... **66** A4
James St *CHAT* ME4 .... **3** F4 2
GILL ME7 .... **4** C2
MAID/BEAR ME14 .... **7** D2
ROCH ME1 .... **2** C4
James Whathan Wy
MAID/BEAR ME14 .... **6** C2
Japonica Cl *WALD* ME5 .... **88** D4 1
Jarrett Av *STRD* ME2 .... **49** J4 1
Jarvis La *CRBK* TN17 .... **213** F5
Jarvis Pl *TENT* TN30 .... **230** B3
Jasmine Cl *E/WMAL* ME19 .... **108** D6
Jasmine Rd *E/WMAL* ME19 .... **108** D6
Jasper Av *ROCH* ME1 .... **2** C6
Javelin Rd *E/WMAL* ME19 .... **129** H3
Jefferson Dr *RHAM* ME8 .... **69** K5
Jeffery St *GILL* ME7 .... **4** C2
Jeffrey Cl *STPH/PW* TN12 .... **198** A2
Jeffrey St *MAID/BEAR* ME14 .... **7** D2
Jellicoe Av *GVE* DA12 .... **45** K1
Jenkins' Dl *CHAT* ME4 .... **3** F5
Jenkins Dr *MAID/SHEP* ME15 .... **156** A1
Jenner Rd *ROCH* ME1 .... **2** C4
Jenner Wy *DIT/AY* ME20 .... **86** E8
Jerome Rd *DIT/AY* ME20 .... **108** D2
Jersey Rd *STRD* ME2 .... **49** F6
Jeskyns Rd *MEO* DA13 .... **46** A7
Jessamine Pl *RDART* DA2 .... **24** B6
Jessica Ms *SIT* ME10 .... **73** K7
Jetty Rd *HOO/HM* ME3 .... **34** A7
Jewell Gv *STPH/PW* TN12 .... **196** D1 1
Jeyes Rd *GILL* ME7 .... **4** C4
Jezreels Rd *GILL* ME7 .... **5** D5
Jiniwin Rd *ROCH* ME1 .... **67** J7
Jockey La *CRBK* TN17 .... **225** K1 1
Jodrell Wy *WTHK* RM20 .... **13** K5
Johns Cl *HART* DA3 .... **62** A2
Johnsdale *OXTED* RH8 .... **118** D8
Johnson Av *GILL* ME7 .... **4** C1
Johnson Cl *GVW* DA11 .... **44** E1
Johnson Rd *SIT* ME10 .... **93** J2
Johnsons Av *RSEV* TN14 .... **77** J5
Johnsons Wy *GRH* DA9 .... **25** H5 3
John's Rd *BH/WHM* TN16 .... **97** H7
MEO DA13 .... **63** G2
John St *MAID/BEAR* ME14 .... **7** D1
ROCH ME1 .... **2** C4
STH/RUST TN4 .... **10** C2
Joiners Ct *CHAT* ME4 .... **4** B6
Jordan Cl *MAID/SHEP* ME15 .... **156** A1
Joslin Rd *PUR* RM19 .... **13** G5
Joyce Cl *CRBK* TN17 .... **225** J2
Joyce Green La *DART* DA1 .... **12** B8
Joyden's Wood Rd *BXLY* DA5 .... **40** A2 1
Joy Rd *GVE* DA12 .... **27** K7
Jubilee Cl *GRH* DA9 .... **25** H5
Jubilee Crs *BGR/WK* TN15 .... **104** C8
GVE DA12 .... **28** B8
Jubilee Fld *TENT* TN30 .... **247** K2
Jubilee Ri *BGR/WK* TN15 .... **102** D8
Jubilee Rd *ORP* BR6 .... **77** H2
Jubilee St *SIT* ME10 .... **93** K1
Jubilee Ter *GILL* ME7 .... **4** C2 6
Judd Rd *TON* TN9 .... **170** B7
Judeth Gdns *GVE* DA12 .... **46** B3
Judkins Cl *WALD* ME5 .... **68** D8 2
Juglans Rd *ORP* BR6 .... **56** B5
Julian Rd *ORP* BR6 .... **76** B2
Julians Cl *SEV* TN13 .... **8** C6
Julians Wy *SEV* TN13 .... **8** C6
Juliette Wy *PUR* RM19 .... **12** D2
Junction Rd *DART* DA1 .... **23** G5
GILL ME7 .... **5** D4
RBTBR TN32 .... **242** B4
Juniper Cl *BH/WHM* TN16 .... **97** J4
MAIDW ME16 .... **110** B8
RTWE/PEM TN2 .... **190** D5
WALD ME5 .... **88** B2
Jury St *GVE* DA12 .... **27** J5 3
Jutland Cl *HOO/HM* ME3 .... **19** G7

K

Katherine Rd *EDEN* TN8 .... **164** C6
Keary Rd *SWCM* DA10 .... **26** A6
Keats Gdns *TIL* RM18 .... **27** J1
Keats Rd *DIT/AY* ME20 .... **108** D3
Kedleston Dr *STMC/STPC* BR5 .... **56** A3
Keefe Cl *WALD* ME5 .... **87** J5
Keel Gdns *STH/RUST* TN4 .... **189** J6
Keith Av *EYN* DA4 .... **42** A4
Keith Park Crs *BH/WHM* TN16 .... **74** B7
Kelchers La *RTON* TN11 .... **172** B1
Kellaway Rd *WALD* ME5 .... **88** B4
Kelly Dr *GILL* ME7 .... **4** C1
Kelsey Rd *STMC/STPC* BR5 .... **38** C7
Kelso Dr *GVE* DA12 .... **46** C2
Kelvin Cl *TONN* TN10 .... **148** D7
Kelvin Rd *TIL* RM18 .... **27** H1
Kemble Cl *RTWE/PEM* TN2 .... **190** E7
Kembleside Rd *BH/WHM* TN16 .... **97** G5
Kemp Cl *WALD* ME5 .... **87** J2
Kempton Cl *WALD* ME5 .... **88** D3
Kemsing Rd *BGR/WK* TN15 .... **104** B4
Kemsley Cl *GRH* DA9 .... **25** G5
GVW DA11 .... **45** G2
Kemsley Rd *BH/WHM* TN16 .... **97** H6
Kemsley Street Rd
MAID/BEAR ME14 .... **89** K5
Kendal Dr *TON* TN9 .... **170** C4
Kendal Pk *STH/RUST* TN4 .... **10** A2
Kendal Wy *RHAM* ME8 .... **70** A6
Kenilworth Ct *SIT* ME10 .... **93** H1
Kenilworth Dr *RHAM* ME8 .... **70** A8
Kennard Cl *ROCH* ME1 .... **66** E4
Kennedy Gdns *SEV* TN13 .... **9** E2
Kennel Barn Rd *RSIT* ME9 .... **115** F2
Kennet Rd *TONN* TN10 .... **170** C1
Kennington Cl *MAID/SHEP* ME15 .... **134** B6
RHAM ME8 .... **69** J2
Kent Av *MAID/SHEP* ME15 .... **7** F6
SIT ME10 .... **93** J3
Kent Cl *ORP* BR6 .... **75** K2
ROCH ME1 .... **67** H6
STPH/PW TN12 .... **173** J8
Kent Hatch Rd *OXTED* RH8 .... **141** G1
Kentish Gdns *RTWE/PEM* TN2 .... **206** D6
Kent Rd *DART* DA1 .... **23** G5
GVW DA11 .... **27** H7
HART DA3 .... **43** J7
SNOD ME6 .... **85** K8
STH/RUST TN4 .... **10** C1
STMC/STPC BR5 .... **56** C3
STRD ME2 .... **65** K8
Kent St *WBY/YAL* ME18 .... **129** G4
Kent Ter *RHAM* ME8 .... **71** F4
Kent Vw *SOCK/AV* RM15 .... **13** G2
Kenward Ct *RTON* TN11 .... **150** A6
Kenward Rd *MAIDW* ME16 .... **132** C1
WBY/YAL ME18 .... **152** C3
Kenwood Av *HART* DA3 .... **44** D8
WALD ME5 .... **88** B2
Kenwyn Rd *DART* DA1 .... **23** G4
Kerry Av *PUR* RM19 .... **12** D2
Kesteven Cl *STRD* ME2 .... **85** K1
Keston Av *HAYES* BR2 .... **74** B1
Kestrel Cl *SIT* ME10 .... **94** B4
Kestrel Rd *WALD* ME5 .... **88** D4
Keswick Cl *TON* TN9 .... **170** C4
Keswick Dr *MAIDW* ME16 .... **132** C1
Keswick Rd *ORP* BR6 .... **56** A5
SIT ME10 .... **94** D3
Ketridge La *WBY/YAL* ME18 .... **130** B4
Kettle La *MAID/SHEP* ME15 .... **131** J8
Kettlewell Ct *SWLY* BR8 .... **40** C7
Kevington Cl *STMC/STPC* BR5 .... **56** A1
Kevington Dr *CHST* BR7 .... **56** A1
Kewlands *MAID/BEAR* ME14 .... **7** F1
Keycol Hl *RSIT* ME9 .... **92** D1
Keyes Av *CHAT* ME4 .... **3** F6
Keyes Gdns *TON* TN9 .... **169** K7
Keyes Rd *DART* DA1 .... **23** K3
Keymer Cl *BH/WHM* TN16 .... **97** G3
Key St *SIT* ME10 .... **93** F1
Keyworth Cl *STPH/PW* TN12 .... **173** H8
Khartoum Rd *CHAT* ME4 .... **3** F2
Khyber Rd *GILL* ME7 .... **4** B1
Kibbles La *STH/RUST* TN4 .... **189** J6
Killewarren Wy *STMC/STPC* BR5 .... **56** D4
Killick Cl *SEV* TN13 .... **101** G8
Killick Rd *HOO/HM* ME3 .... **50** E1
Kiln Barn Rd *DIT/AY* ME20 .... **109** G6
Kiln Cl *SIT* ME10 .... **94** B3
Kilndown *GVE* DA12 .... **45** K4
Kilndown Cl *MAIDW* ME16 .... **110** C7
Kiln Fld *TENT* TN30 .... **230** C7
Kiln La *RTON* TN11 .... **168** D5
Kiln Wy *STPH/PW* TN12 .... **193** J1
Kilnwood *RSEV* TN14 .... **77** G8
Kimberley Rd *GILL* ME7 .... **5** D5
Kincraig Dr *SEV* TN13 .... **8** C2
King Arthur's Dr *STRD* ME2 .... **49** F5
King Edward Av *DART* DA1 .... **23** G5
King Edward Rd *CHAT* ME4 .... **3** F6
GILL ME7 .... **5** F2
GRH DA9 .... **25** F4
MAID/SHEP ME15 .... **6** C5
ROCH ME1 .... **2** C3
Kingfisher Cl *RSIT* ME9 .... **73** K2
STMC/STPC BR5 .... **56** E1

Kingfisher Dr WALD ME5 68 D7
Kingfisher Rd DIT/AY ME20 108 D4
King George Rd WALD ME5 87 K2
King George V Hl RTW TN1 11 E2
King Henry Ms ORP BR6 76 A1
King Hl E/WMAL ME19 129 J1
Kings Acre MAID/SHEP ME15 134 C5 2
King's Av ROCH ME1 2 C5
King's Bastion GILL ME7 4 A3
Kings Cl DART DA1 22 B3
Kingsdown Cl GILL ME7 89 H2
GVE DA12 28 C7 3
MAIDW ME16 6 B3 3
Kingsdown Rd RSIT ME9 117 J3
Kings Dr GVE DA12 45 J1
Kingsgate Cl MAIDW ME16 132 C2
STMC/STPC BR5 38 D7
Kingsgate La TENT TN30 247 H1
Kings Hill Av E/WMAL ME19 129 J2
Kingshill Dr HOO/HM ME3 32 E8
Kingsingfield Cl BGR/WK TN15 80 D3 2
Kingsingfield Rd BGR/WK TN15 80 D4
Kingsland Gv HDCN TN27 200 B1 2
Kingsland La HDCN TN27 182 E5
Kings La STPH/PW TN12 175 G7
Kingsley Av DART DA1 23 K4
Kingsley Rd MAID/SHEP ME15 7 D4
ORP BR6 76 A2
Kingsmead BH/WHM TN16 97 H3
Kings Mill Cl SIT ME10 93 K1 1
Kingsnorth Rd RHAM ME8 69 K2
King's Orch ROCH ME1 2 C3
Kingsridge Gdns DART DA1 23 G5
Kings Rd BH/WHM TN16 97 G4
HDCN TN27 200 A1
ORP BR6 56 A8
TON TN9 170 C7
WALD ME5 68 E5
Kings Standing Wy
RTWE/PEM TN2 191 F4
Kings Toll Rd RTWE/PEM TN2 192 C8
Kingston Ct GVW DA11 26 C5 1
Kingston Crs WALD ME5 88 C2
Kingston Dr MAID/SHEP ME15 133 G6
King St CHAT ME4 4 A4
E/WMAL ME19 107 K6
GVE DA12 27 J5
MAID/BEAR ME14 7 D3
ROCH ME1 2 C4
SIT ME10 93 K1
Kingsway GILL ME7 69 F5
WALD ME5 68 E5
Kingswear Gdns STRD ME2 2 C1 1
Kingswood Av CHAT ME4 3 F6 4
SWLY BR8 58 C1
Kingswood Cl DART DA1 23 F5
Kingswood Rd GILL ME7 5 D2
ROCH ME1 87 J6
RTWE/PEM TN2 11 E4
SEV TN13 101 G8
King William Rd GILL ME7 4 C1 3
Kinnings Rw TON TN9 170 C4 3
Kinross Cl WALD ME5 68 C7 1
Kipling Dr DIT/AY ME20 108 D2
Kipling Rd DART DA1 24 A4 1
Kippington Cl SEV TN13 8 B3
Kippington Rd SEV TN13 8 C4
Kirby Cl CRBK TN17 225 K2
Kirby Rd HOO/HM ME3 49 K1
RDART DA2 24 B6
Kirkdale MAID/SHEP ME15 155 F1
Kirkdale Cl WALD ME5 88 E5
Kirkdale Rd MAID/SHEP ME15 133 F8
RTW TN1 11 D3
Kirkins Cl STPH/PW TN12 194 E8
Kitchener Av CHAT ME4 68 A5
GVE DA12 45 K2
Kitchener Rd HOO/HM ME3 50 A2
STRD ME2 49 F6
Kite La STPH/PW TN12 193 J8
Kit Hill Av WALD ME5 87 K3
Knatts La BGR/WK TN15 80 D6
Knatts Valley Rd EYN DA4 80 B2
Knaves Acre HDCN TN27 200 B1
Knave Wood Rd RSEV TN14 102 C4
Knight Av GILL ME7 5 D2
Knighton Rd RSEV TN14 101 H4
Knightrider Ct MAID/SHEP ME15 7 D4 3
Knightrider St MAID/SHEP ME15 6 C4
Knight Rd STRD ME2 2 A3
TONN TN10 148 E8
Knightsbridge Cl STH/RUST TN4 10 B2
Knights Cl HOO/HM ME3 51 F1
RTWE/PEM TN2 191 K7
Knights Cft HART DA3 62 A7
Knightsfield Rd SIT ME10 73 J8
Knights Manor Wy DART DA1 23 J5
Knights Pk RTWE/PEM TN2 191 F5
Knights Rdg ORP BR6 76 C1 1
RTWE/PEM TN2 191 K7 2
Knights Rd HOO/HM ME3 32 E8
Knight's Wy HDCN TN27 200 B1
RTWE/PEM TN2 191 F6
Knockhall Cha GRH DA9 25 H4
Knockhall Rd GRH DA9 25 H5
Knockholt Rd RSEV TN14 100 B1
Knock Mill La BGR/WK TN15 81 F8
Knockwood Rd TENT TN30 230 C5
Knole La BGR/WK TN15 9 E5
Knole Rd DART DA1 22 D6
SEV TN13 9 F2
WALD ME5 88 D4
The Knole MEO DA13 45 F5
Knole Wy BGR/WK TN15 9 E4
Knoll Ri ORP BR6 56 A5
Knoll Rd SCUP DA14 38 C3
Knott Ct MAID/BEAR ME14 7 D1
Knotts Pl SEV TN13 8 C3
Knowle Cl RRTW TN3 205 H3
Knowle La STPH/PW TN12 194 A2
Knowle Rd MAID/BEAR ME14 7 D1
ROCH ME1 86 B2
STPH/PW TN12 194 B4
Knowles Gdns HDCN TN27 200 B1 3
Knowlton Gdns MAIDW ME16 132 B4 2
Knowsley Wy RTON TN11 147 H8
Koonowla Cl BH/WHM TN16 97 H2
Kyetop Wk RHAM ME8 70 A8 2
Kynaston Rd STMC/STPC BR5 56 C4

L

Labour-in-vain Rd BGR/WK TN15 81 J8
Laburnum Av DART DA1 23 F7
SWLY BR8 40 A8
Laburnum Dr DIT/AY ME20 108 E4
Laburnum Gv GVW DA11 26 E6
Laburnum Pl SIT ME10 93 K2 5
Laburnum Rd STRD ME2 66 D1
Lacey Cl RMAID ME17 157 G2
Laceys La RMAID ME17 154 C7
Lacy Cl MAIDW ME16 110 D7 1
Ladbrooke Crs SCUP DA14 38 E1
Ladds La SNOD ME6 85 K4
Ladds Wy SWLY BR8 58 A1
Ladham Rd CRBK TN17 213 F4
Ladyclose Av HOO/HM ME3 31 F7
Ladycroft Gdns ORP BR6 75 H1 2
Ladycroft Wy ORP BR6 75 H1
Ladyfields GVW DA11 45 G2
WALD ME5 88 E4 3
Ladyfields Cl RSIT ME9 92 E1
Lady Oak La CRBK TN17 223 G6
Lady's Gift Rd STH/RUST TN4 189 K6
Ladywood Rd RDART DA2 42 D3
STRD ME2 66 A4
Lagonda Wy DART DA1 23 F3
Lake Dr HOO/HM ME3 30 B8
Lakelands MAID/SHEP ME15 133 G7
RMAID ME17 137 J8
Lake Rd DIT/AY ME20 109 J6
STH/RUST TN4 10 A3
Laker Rd ROCH ME1 67 H8
Lakeside RTWE/PEM TN2 190 E8
SNOD ME6 85 J8
Lakeside Cl EDEN TN8 166 B2
Lakes Rd HAYES BR2 74 B1
Lakeview Cl SNOD ME6 85 K8
Lake View Rd SEV TN13 8 C2
Lakewood Dr RHAM ME8 69 K8
Lambarde Cl STRD ME2 85 K2 4
Lambarde Dr SEV TN13 8 C2
Lambarde Rd SEV TN13 8 C1
Lambardes HART DA3 62 A7
Lamb Cl TIL RM18 27 K1
Lambden Rd HDCN TN27 183 H8
Lamberhurst Cl STMC/STPC BR5 56 E5 2
Lamberhurst Gn RHAM ME8 69 J4
Lamberhurst Rd STPH/PW TN12 211 F5
Lambersart Cl RTWE/PEM TN2 190 D5 1
Lambert Cl BH/WHM TN16 97 H3
Lambert Ms SNOD ME6 85 K6 3
Lamberts Pl STPH/PW TN12 212 A1
Lamberts Rd RTWE/PEM TN2 190 D6
Lambert's Yd TON TN9 170 B5 3
Lambeth Cl WALD ME5 88 C2
Lambfrith Gv GILL ME7 89 J3
Lambourne Dr E/WMAL ME19 129 H4
Lambourne Pl RHAM ME8 70 D4
Lambourn Wy RTWE/PEM TN2 11 F6
WALD ME5 88 D4
Lambs Bank TON TN9 170 B7
Lambsfrith Gv GILL ME7 89 J3
Lammas Dr SIT ME10 73 K8
Lamorna Av GVE DA12 28 A8
Lamorna Cl ORP BR6 56 B4 4
Lampington Rw RRTW TN3 205 H3 2
Lamplighters Cl DART DA1 23 J5 1
GILL ME7 89 G2
Lancashire Rd MAID/SHEP ME15 134 A7
Lancaster Ct RHAM ME8 69 K7
Lancaster Wy E/WMAL ME19 129 H3
Lancelot Av STRD ME2 48 D7
Lancelot Cl STRD ME2 48 D8
Lances Cl MEO DA13 63 H4 1
Lancet La MAID/SHEP ME15 133 F8
Lancing Rd ORP BR6 56 C6
Landale Gdns DART DA1 23 F7
Landau Wy ERITH DA8 12 B5
Landor Ct GILL ME7 89 H3
Landrail Rd RSIT ME9 72 A3
Landseer Av GVW DA11 44 E1
Landseer Cl TONN TN10 148 E8
Landway BGR/WK TN15 102 D7
Land Wy HOO/HM ME3 48 C1
The Landway BGR/WK TN15 102 E4
BGR/WK TN15 105 F7
MAID/BEAR ME14 134 C2 1
STMC/STPC BR5 38 D8
Lanes Av GVW DA11 45 G1
The Lane RRTW TN3 205 F1
Langafel Cl HART DA3 43 K7
Langdale Cl RHAM ME8 70 A5
Langdale Ri MAIDW ME16 132 C1
Langdon Rd ROCH ME1 2 C4 4
Langdon Shaw SCUP DA14 38 A3
Langford Pl SCUP DA14 38 B1
Langham Gv MAIDW ME16 132 C2
Langholm Rd RRTW TN3 205 J3
Langlands Dr RDART DA2 42 D3
Langton Cl MAID/BEAR ME14 7 F2
Langton Rd RRTW TN3 188 E7
Langworth Cl RDART DA2 41 G1
Lankester Parker Rd ROCH ME1 67 H8 1
Lansbury Crs DART DA1 23 K4
Lansdowne Av MAID/SHEP ME15 133 J8
Lansdowne Rd CHAT ME4 3 E6
RTW TN1 11 E3 4
SEV TN13 9 F2
TON TN9 170 B4
TONN TN10 170 B3
Lansdowne Sq GVW DA11 27 G5
RTW TN1 11 D3 5
Lansdown Rd GVW DA11 27 G7 1
SCUP DA14 38 C1
SIT ME10 94 D2
TIL RM18 27 G1
Lapins La WBY/YAL ME18 129 H4
Lapis Cl GVE DA12 28 E7
Lapwing Dr RSIT ME9 72 A3
Lapwing Rd HOO/HM ME3 37 G1
Lapwings HART DA3 44 C8
Lapworth Cl ORP BR6 56 D6
Larch Cl DIT/AY ME20 109 F4
Larch Crs HOO/HM ME3 51 F3 11
TONN TN10 148 C8
Larchcroft WALD ME5 88 B2
The Larches HOO/HM ME3 48 B3 1
Larch Gv STPH/PW TN12 173 H8
Larch Rd DART DA1 23 G7
Larch Wood Cl WALD ME5 88 E5
Larkfield STPH/PW TN12 172 C7
Larkfield Av GILL ME7 5 E4
SIT ME10 73 K8
Larkfield Cl DIT/AY ME20 108 E5
Larkfield Rd DIT/AY ME20 108 E5
SCUP DA14 38 A1
SEV TN13 122 E2
Larkfields GVW DA11 45 F1
Larkin Cl STRD ME2 49 G4
Larking Dr MAIDW ME16 110 D7
Larks Fld HART DA3 62 A1
Larkspur Cl E/WMAL ME19 108 E5 3
ORP BR6 56 D6 1
Larkspur Rd E/WMAL ME19 108 D5
WALD ME5 87 K2
Larkwell La HART DA3 62 A1
Laser Quay STRD ME2 3 D2
Latham Cl BH/WHM TN16 97 G3
Latimer Pl GILL ME7 4 C1 4
Latona Dr GVE DA12 46 C3
Latymers RTON TN11 187 K2
Launder Wy MAID/SHEP ME15 6 B5
Laura Dr SWLY BR8 40 D5
Laura Pl ROCH ME1 66 E4 1
Laurel Av GVE DA12 27 K8
Laurel Bank STH/RUST TN4 190 B6
Laurel Cl DART DA1 23 F7
SCUP DA14 38 B1
Laurel Dr OXTED RH8 140 D2
Laurel Gv RMAID ME17 158 B4
Laurel Rd GILL ME7 4 C1
RTWE/PEM TN2 190 D7
The Laurels HART DA3 44 D8
MAIDW ME16 132 C4 2
Laurie Gray Av WALD ME5 87 J5
Lavenda Cl GILL ME7 89 H2
Lavender Cl E/WMAL ME19 108 D6
Lavender Ct SIT ME10 94 B3
Lavender Gdns WADH TN5 232 C5 1
Lavender Hl SWLY BR8 40 A8
TON TN9 170 C6
Lavender Rd E/WMAL ME19 108 D6
Lavenders Rd E/WMAL ME19 108 A7
Laverstoke Rd MAIDW ME16 110 C6
Lavinia Rd DART DA1 23 J5
Lawford Gdns DART DA1 23 F4
Lawn Cl CHAT ME4 4 B6
SWLY BR8 39 K7
TENT TN30 229 K7
Lawn Pk SEV TN13 9 D6
Lawn Rd GVW DA11 26 D5
TON TN9 170 B6

The Lawns SCUP DA14 38 C2 2
STPH/PW TN12 193 K6
Lawrence Cl MAID/SHEP ME15 133 G7 1
Lawrence Dr GVE DA12 64 D1
Lawrence Hill Gdns DART DA1 23 F5 1
Lawrence Hill Rd DART DA1 23 F5
Lawrence Rd TONN TN10 148 E8
Lawrence St GILL ME7 4 C3 1
Lawson Gdns DART DA1 23 G4
Lawson Rd DART DA1 23 G3
Laxey Rd ORP BR6 76 A2
The Laxey MAID/SHEP ME15 6 B5 2
Laxton Cl MAID/SHEP ME15 134 B3 1
Laxton Dr RMAID ME17 156 C5
Laxton Gdns STPH/PW TN12 173 G7
Laxton Wy SIT ME10 73 J8
Layfield Rd GILL ME7 5 F1
Leafield La SCUP DA14 39 G2
Leafy Gld RHAM ME8 69 J8
Leafy Gv HAYES BR2 74 B1
Leafy La MEO DA13 83 H2
Lealands Av RTON TN11 168 E5
Lealands Cl RRTW TN3 205 F7
Leaman Cl HOO/HM ME3 33 F2
Leander Dr GVE DA12 46 C2
Leander Rd ROCH ME1 67 H7
Lea Rd SEV TN13 9 E6
Leas Gn CHST BR7 38 A4
The Leas WADH TN5 220 C8
Leather Cl EDEN TN8 164 C6
Lea V DART DA1 22 A3
Leaves Green Crs HAYES BR2 74 B6
Leaves Green Rd HAYES BR2 74 C6
Lebanon Gdns BH/WHM TN16 97 H4
Leconfield Cl TON TN9 169 K7 2
Leechcroft Av SWLY BR8 40 C8
Leeds Cl ORP BR6 56 E6
Leeds Rd RMAID ME17 157 G3
Leeds Sq RHAM ME8 69 J3
Lee Gn STMC/STPC BR5 56 B2
Lee Green Rd HOO/HM ME3 49 J2
Lee Rd SNOD ME6 85 K6
Leesons Wy STMC/STPC BR5 38 A7
Lees Rd WBY/YAL ME18 152 C7
Leet Cl GILL ME7 5 E2
Leeward Rd ROCH ME1 67 H5
Leewood Pl SWLY BR8 58 A1 4
Legge La E/WMAL ME19 85 G7
Leggs' La RRTW TN3 205 H1
Leicester Dr RTWE/PEM TN2 206 E6 3
Leicester Rd MAID/SHEP ME15 133 K7
Leigh Av MAID/SHEP ME15 133 H8
Leigh Rd GVW DA11 27 J8
HOO/HM ME3 49 H3
RTON TN11 169 H4
Leighton Cl STH/RUST TN4 190 A7
Leith Hl STMC/STPC BR5 38 B6
Leith Park Rd GVW DA11 27 J7
Lendon Rd BGR/WK TN15 105 F8
Leneda Dr RTWE/PEM TN2 206 D6
Leney Rd WBY/YAL ME18 130 C7
Lenfield Av MAID/BEAR ME14 7 E3 2
Lenham Forstal Rd RMAID ME17 161 H6
Lenham Heath Rd RMAID ME17 160 B3
Lenham Rd HDCN TN27 180 E6
RMAID ME17 158 D4
Lennard Rd SEV TN13 101 G7
Lennox Av GVW DA11 27 H5
Lennox Rd GVW DA11 27 G5
Lennox Rd East GVW DA11 27 H6
Lenside Dr MAID/SHEP ME15 134 C4
Leonard Av RSEV TN14 101 K2
SWCM DA10 25 K6
Leonard Cl MAIDW ME16 110 B8
Leonard Rd CHAT ME4 4 B5 3
Leopold Rd CHAT ME4 4 A5
Lesley Cl MEO DA13 45 G6
SWLY BR8 40 A8
Lesley Pl MAIDW ME16 6 B2 2
Leslie Crs TENT TN30 230 B4
Leslie Rd GILL ME7 5 D1
Lested La RMAID ME17 156 D4
Lester Rd CHAT ME4 4 A5
Letchworth Av CHAT ME4 68 A5
Le Temple Rd STPH/PW TN12 173 K7
Letter Box La SEV TN13 124 A8
Levett Cl HOO/HM ME3 21 G8 2
Levetts La RBTBR TN32 242 E5
Lewd La HDCN TN27 202 A2
Lewis Av RHAM ME8 69 J4
Lewis Court Dr RMAID ME17 155 H3
Lewis Rd MEO DA13 45 G6
SCUP DA14 38 D1
SWCM DA10 25 K5
Leybank RTON TN11 169 J2
Leybourne Cl WALD ME5 88 B4 3
Leybourne Dell CRBK TN17 227 G8
Leybourne Rd STRD ME2 48 E6
Leybourne Wy DIT/AY ME20 108 D2
Leydenhatch La SWLY BR8 40 A6
Leyhill Cl SWLY BR8 58 B2 2
Leyton Av GILL ME7 69 F5
Leyton Cross Rd RDART DA2 40 C1
Leywood Rd MEO DA13 84 A3
Lezayre Rd ORP BR6 76 A2
Lidsing Rd GILL ME7 89 G4
MAID/BEAR ME14 111 J2
Lidwells La CRBK TN17 212 B5
Lilac Crs STRD ME2 48 D8
Lilac Gdns SWLY BR8 40 A8
Lilac Gn E/WMAL ME19 108 E6
Lilac Pl MEO DA13 63 J4
Lilac Rd STRD ME2 66 D1
Lila Pl SWLY BR8 58 B1 2
Lillechurch Rd HOO/HM ME3 30 E7
Lillieburn E/WMAL ME19 108 B4
Lillie Rd BH/WHM TN16 97 H5
Lime Av GVW DA11 26 E6
Lime Cl STPH/PW TN12 176 C8 2
Lime Ct RHAM ME8 89 K3
Lime Crs E/WMAL ME19 108 E7
Lime Gv SIT ME10 94 B2
Lime Hill Rd RTW TN1 10 C3 7
Lime Pit La RSEV TN14 100 E4
Lime Rd SWLY BR8 40 A8
Limes Cl TENT TN30 230 C7
Limes Gv HAWK TN18 235 F1
Limes Rw ORP BR6 75 G1
The Limes EDEN TN8 164 C5
PUR RM19 12 E5
Lime Tree Av GRH DA9 25 F7
Lime Tree Cl TON TN9 170 C4 4
Limetree Cl WALD ME5 68 C7
Lime Trees STPH/PW TN12 198 A2
Lime Tree Wk SEV TN13 9 D4
Linclon Cl ERITH DA8 22 C1
Lincoln Green Rd STMC/STPC BR5 56 A2
Lincoln Rd ERITH DA8 22 C1
MAID/SHEP ME15 133 J6
SCUP DA14 38 C3
Lincon Rd GILL ME7 5 D1 3
Linden Av DART DA1 23 F7
Linden Cha SEV TN13 9 D1
Linden Cl ORP BR6 76 B1
PUR RM19 13 G6
RTWE/PEM TN2 10 B5 1
SIT ME10 93 J3
STPH/PW TN12 173 J8
Linden Gdns RTWE/PEM TN2 10 B6
Linden Park Rd RTWE/PEM TN2 10 B6
Linden Rd GILL ME7 5 E3
RMAID ME17 154 C2
Linden Sq SEV TN13 8 A1 1
The Lindens DIT/AY ME20 109 J4 1
Lindisfarne Cl GVE DA12 28 B8 1
Lindridge La STPH/PW TN12 197 J1
Lineacre Cl RHAM ME8 70 A8
Lines Ter CHAT ME4 4 A4
Lingfield Av RDART DA2 24 A6
Lingfield Rd BGR/WK TN15 105 G7
EDEN TN8 164 A6
GVE DA12 27 J8
Lingley Dr STRD ME2 49 H4
Link Hill La HDCN TN27 182 C4
The Links E/WMAL ME19 107 G4
WALD ME5 68 C6
Links Vw DART DA1 23 F7
Linkway DIT/AY ME20 109 G5
RSIT ME9 73 J2
Link Wy RTWE/PEM TN2 190 E6
Linnet Av STPH/PW TN12 193 J1
Linnet Wy PUR RM19 13 F5
Linslade Rd ORP BR6 76 B2
Linton Dann Cl HOO/HM ME3 32 E8
Linton Gore RMAID ME17 154 C3
Linton Hl RMAID ME17 154 E6
Linton Rd MAID/SHEP ME15 155 F3
Linwood Av STRD ME2 48 D6
Lionel Rd TON TN9 170 A6
Liphook Wy MAIDW ME16 110 C6
Lipscombe Rd RTWE/PEM TN2 11 F1 1
Liptraps La RTWE/PEM TN2 190 D7
Lipwell Hl HOO/HM ME3 32 C2
Lisle Cl GVE DA12 28 E8
Lismore Cl MAID/SHEP ME15 133 G7 2
Lister Cl E/WMAL ME19 108 D6
Lister Rd TIL RM18 27 H1
Listmas Rd CHAT ME4 4 B5
Little Aly EDEN TN8 184 B1
Little Boundes Cl STH/RUST TN4 189 J3
Littlebourne Av RHAM ME8 69 J2
Littlebourne Rd MAID/BEAR ME14 7 F1
Littlebrook Manor Wy DART DA1 23 K4
Little Browns La EDEN TN8 163 J2
Little Buckland Av MAIDW ME16 6 A1
Littlecourt Rd SEV TN13 8 C3 1
Littlecroft MEO DA13 45 F5
Littlefield Rd RHAM ME8 70 E4 2
Little Footway RRTW TN3 205 J3
Little Glovers SIT ME10 94 A3
Little John Av WALD ME5 88 A4
Littlejohn Rd STMC/STPC BR5 56 B3
Little Julians Hl SEV TN13 8 C6
Little Mallett RRTW TN3 205 J3 3
Little Market Rw E/WMAL ME19 108 C4
Little Mount Sion RTW TN1 10 C5 5
Little Oakham Ct HOO/HM ME3 35 F2 4
Little Orch RMAID ME17 154 D3
Little Oxley DIT/AY ME20 108 C4
Little Queen St DART DA1 23 J6
Little Robhurst RASHW TN26 219 J
Little Wd SEV TN13 9 E
Little Wood Cl STMC/STPC BR5 38 B6
Livesey St WBY/YAL ME18 130 D
Livingstone Gdns GVE DA12 46 A
Livingstone Rd GILL ME7 5 E
GVE DA12 46 A
Lloyds Gn TENT TN30 247 J
Loampits Cl TON TN9 170 D
Lobelia Cl GILL ME7 5 E2
Locarno Av RHAM ME8 69 H
Lochat Rd HOO/HM ME3 31 K
Lockesley Dr STMC/STPC BR5 56 A
Lockington Cl TON TN9 169 K7
Lockington Gv ROCH ME1 2 C
Lock La MAIDW ME16 110 D
Lockside TON TN9 170 C
Locksley Cl WALD ME5 87 K
Lock St GILL ME7 4 B
Lockswood MAIDW ME16 110 D7
Lockyer Rd PUR RM19 13 G
Lockyers Hl MEO DA13 84 B
Loddington La RMAID ME17 155 G
Loder Cl RMAID ME17 160 B
Lodge Av DART DA1 23 F
Lodge Cl ORP BR6 56 C
WBY/YAL ME18 130 B
Lodge Ct GVE DA12 47 H
Lodge Crs ORP BR6 56 C
Lodge Gdns RMAID ME17 158 D
Lodge Hill La HOO/HM ME3 32 A
Lodge La BH/WHM TN16 120 C6
GVE DA12 64 E
Lodge Oak La TON TN9 170 D
Lodge Rd MAID/BEAR ME14 133 K
STPH/PW TN12 198 A
TON TN9 170 B
Lomas La HAWK TN18 244 D
Lomas Rd SIT ME10 94 E
Lombard St EYN DA4 60 B
Lombardy Cl GILL ME7 69 H
Lombardy Dr MAID/BEAR ME14 7 F
London La CRBK TN17 215 H
London Rd BGR/WK TN15 81 G
BH/WHM TN16 120 D
DART DA1 22 A
DIT/AY ME20 109 F
E/WMAL ME19 106 E
EYN DA4 59 G
GRH DA9 24 D
GVW DA11 26 E
RDART DA2 24 B
RHAM ME8 70 D
RSEV TN14 77 G
RSIT ME9 71 J
SEV TN13 8 B
SIT ME10 93 H
SOCK/AV RM15 12 E
STH/RUST TN4 10 C
STRD ME2 2 A
SWCM DA10 25 K
SWLY BR8 39 K
SWLY BR8 40 B8
TIL RM18 27 J
TONN TN10 170 B
WADH TN5 233 H
London Road Purfleet PUR RM19 13 F
London Road Rocky Hl
MAIDW ME16 6 B
London Road West Thurrock
WTHK RM20 13 K
Lone Barn Rd RMAID ME17 139 H
Lonewood Wy RTON TN11 150 B
Long Acre STMC/STPC BR5 56 E
Long Barn Rd RSEV TN14 145 K
Longbury Cl STMC/STPC BR5 38 C
Longbury Dr STMC/STPC BR5 38 C
Long Catlis Rd RHAM ME8 90 A
Long Ct PUR RM19 12 E
Longfellow Rd GILL ME7 4 C
Longfield TENT TN30 230 A
Longfield Av HART DA3 44 D
HOO/HM ME3 33 F
Longfield Pl MAID/SHEP ME15 133 H
Longfield Rd MEO DA13 63 F
RTWE/PEM TN2 190 E
Longfields Dr MAID/BEAR ME14 134 C1
Longford Cl RHAM ME8 70 D6
Longham Copse
MAID/SHEP ME15 134 B
Longhill Av GILL ME7 4 B
Longhurst Dr WALD ME5 88 A
Long La RMAID ME17 177 K
Longley Rd RHAM ME8 70 C
ROCH ME1 2 C
Longmarsh Vw EYN DA4 42 A
Longmeadow SEV TN13 101 F
Long Meads RRTW TN3 206 A
Long Mead Wy TONN TN10 170 B
Long Mill La BGR/WK TN15 127 G
Longparish Cl MAID/SHEP ME15 134 B7
Long Rede La MAIDW ME16 131 K
Longridge SIT ME10 94 C
Longshaw Rd MAID/SHEP ME15 156 B
Long Slip RRTW TN3 205 K

Longview Wy RTWE/PEM TN2 190 D6
Longwalk MEO DA13 45 F6
Longwood WALD ME5 88 C5
Lonsdale Crs RDART DA2 24 B8
Lonsdale Dr RHAM ME8 70 B8
SIT ME10 93 H1
Lonsdale Gdns RTW TN1 10 C4 3
Loose Rd MAID/SHEP ME15 133 G8
Lord Chatham's Ride RSEV TN14 99 J4
Lords Cl RSIT ME9 95 F4
Lord St GVE DA12 27 J6
Lordswood Cl RDART DA2 42 D2
Lords Wood Cl WALD ME5 88 C4
Lords Wood La WALD ME5 88 C1
Lorton Cl GVE DA12 28 B8
Lossenham La HAWK TN18 245 G2
Lotus Rd BH/WHM TN16 97 K5
Louisville Av GILL ME7 5 D4
Louvain Rd RDART DA2 24 D6
Lovelace Cl BGR/WK TN15 80 D2 2
RHAM ME8 90 A1
Love La HDCN TN27 200 E1
ROCH ME1 2 C3
SOCK/AV RM15 13 G2
WBY/YAL ME18 130 B7
Lovers La CRBK TN17 212 D5
GRH DA9 25 J3
Low Cl GRH DA9 25 F4
Lower Bell La DIT/AY ME20 109 F4
Lower Bloors La RHAM ME8 70 B4
Lower Boxley Rd
MAID/BEAR ME14 6 C2 1
Lower Cft SWLY BR8 58 C1
Lower Fant Rd MAIDW ME16 6 B4
Lower Farm Rd RMAID ME17 155 H8
Lower Gn RTON TN11 168 D5
Lower Green Rd RRTW TN3 206 B1
RTWE/PEM TN2 191 K8
STH/RUST TN4 206 B2
Lower Hartlip Rd RSIT ME9 91 G2
Lower Haysden La TON TN9 169 H6
Lower Higham Rd GVE DA12 28 C7
Lower Platts WADH TN5 232 C5
Lower Rainham Rd GILL ME7 69 K1
RHAM ME8 70 E3
Lower Range Rd GVE DA12 28 B6
Lower Rd GVE DA12 29 H8
GVW DA11 26 B3
MAID/SHEP ME15 7 E4
MAID/SHEP ME15 131 G7
RMAID ME17 157 G7
RSIT ME9 95 G3
STMC/STPC BR5 56 C3
SWLY BR8 40 E5
TENT TN30 241 J8
TIL RM18 27 H3
Lower Rochester Rd HOO/HM ME3 30 C8
Lower Station Rd DART DA1 22 B5
Lower St RMAID ME17 135 J7
RTON TN11 168 E1
Lower Tovil MAID/SHEP ME15 6 B5
Lower Twydall La GILL ME7 69 K2
RHAM ME8 69 J2
Lower Warren Rd WALD ME5 87 K8
Lower Woodlands Rd GILL ME7 5 F2
Lowfield St DART DA1 23 H6
Lowlands Rd SOCK/AV RM15 13 G1
Low Meadow STRD ME2 85 K1
Loxwood Cl STMC/STPC BR5 56 E6
Lubbock Cl MAID/SHEP ME15 156 A1 6
Lucas Rd SNOD ME6 85 H7
Lucerne Rd ORP BR6 56 A5
Lucerne St MAID/BEAR ME14 7 D2 3
Lucilina Dr EDEN TN8 164 C6 2
Lucknow Rd STPH/PW TN12 173 J6
Lucks Hl E/WMAL ME19 108 B6
Lucks La RMAID ME17 156 B8
STPH/PW TN12 173 J5
Lucks Wy STPH/PW TN12 176 B8
Luddenham Cl MAID/BEAR ME14 7 F1 4
Luddesdown Rd MEO DA13 64 D5
Lughorse La WBY/YAL ME18 152 E4
Lullarook Cl BH/WHM TN16 97 G3
Lullingstone Av SWLY BR8 40 C8
Lullingstone Cl GILL ME7 89 J3
STMC/STPC BR5 38 C5 2
Lullingstone Crs STMC/STPC BR5 38 B5
Lullingstone La EYN DA4 59 F7
Lullingstone Rd MAIDW ME16 110 C7
Lumsden Ter CHAT ME4 3 E4 2
Lunar Cl BH/WHM TN16 97 H3
Lunedale Rd RDART DA2 24 B7
Lunsford La DIT/AY ME20 108 D4
Lurkins Ri CRBK TN17 212 C7
Lushington Rd MAID/BEAR ME14 110 E7
Lusted Hall La BH/WHM TN16 97 G7
Luton High St WALD ME5 4 C6
Luton Rd CHAT ME4 4 B5
SCUP DA14 38 D1
Luxon Rd MEO DA13 84 B2
Luxted Rd ORP BR6 75 F7
Lyall Wy RHAM ME8 90 A2
Lychfield Dr STRD ME2 49 F5
Lych Gate Rd ORP BR6 56 B5
Lydbrook Cl SIT ME10 93 H2
Lydd Rd WALD ME5 88 C1 1
Lydens La EDEN TN8 165 F8
Lyle Cl STRD ME2 49 G6
Lyle Ct MAIDW ME16 132 C2
Lyle Pk SEV TN13 9 D2
Lyminge Cl RHAM ME8 69 K4
SCUP DA14 38 A2
Lymington Ct MAID/SHEP ME15 156 B2 3
Lynden Wy SWLY BR8 39 K8
Lyndhurst Av RHAM ME8 69 K7
Lyndhurst Dr SEV TN13 8 A3
Lyndhurst Gv SIT ME10 93 K4
Lyndhurst Rd MAID/SHEP ME15 133 J6 1
Lyndhurst Wy MEO DA13 45 F6
Lynette Av STRD ME2 49 F5
Lyngs Cl WBY/YAL ME18 152 D6
Lynmead Cl EDEN TN8 164 B2 1
Lynmouth Ri STMC/STPC BR5 56 C1
Lynne Cl ORP BR6 76 A2 3
Lynors Av STRD ME2 49 F4
Lynsted La RSIT ME9 95 J7
Lynsted Rd RHAM ME8 69 J3
Lynton Av STMC/STPC BR5 56 C1
Lynton Dr WALD ME5 88 C3
Lynton Rd GVW DA11 27 H7
Lynton Rd South GVW DA11 27 H7
Lynwood RRTW TN3 205 F8
Lyons Crs TON TN9 170 C4
Lysander Rd E/WMAL ME19 129 H3

M

Mabel Rd SWLY BR8 40 D4
Mabledon Rd TON TN9 170 A6
Macaulay Cl DIT/AY ME20 108 E2
Macdonald Rd GILL ME7 5 D2 4
Mace La RSEV TN14 75 J8
Mackenders Cl DIT/AY ME20 86 E8
Mackenders La DIT/AY ME20 87 F8
Mackenzie Wy GVE DA12 46 A4
Macklands Wy RHAM ME8 70 D4
Madan Rd BH/WHM TN16 120 D4
Madden Av WALD ME5 87 K1
Madden Cl SWCM DA10 25 K5 1
Maddocks Cl SCUP DA14 38 E4
Madeira Pk RTW TN1 11 D5 5
Madginford Cl MAID/SHEP ME15 134 C4
Madginford Rd MAID/SHEP ME15 134 B4
Madison Wy SEV TN13 8 B2
Maesmaur Rd BH/WHM TN16 97 H8
Mafeking Rd WALD ME5 88 A3
Magdalen Cl GILL ME7 89 H2
Magdelan Gv ORP BR6 56 C8
Magnolia Av RHAM ME8 89 J1
Magnolia Dr BH/WHM TN16 97 H3
Magpie Cl DIT/AY ME20 108 E5 4
Magpie Hall Rd CHAT ME4 68 A6
Magpie La MAID/BEAR ME14 90 C5
Magwitch Cl ROCH ME1 2 B4 2
Maida Rd CHAT ME4 4 B6
Maida Vale Rd DART DA1 22 D5
Maiden La DART DA1 22 D2
Maidstone Rd BGR/WK TN15 125 F1
CHAT ME4 67 K6
GILL ME7 89 J4
HDCN TN27 179 J5
RHAM ME8 89 K3
RMAID ME17 157 G4
ROCH ME1 67 H6
RSIT ME9 92 C3
RTON TN11 150 A6
RTWE/PEM TN2 191 J6
SCUP DA14 38 E4
SIT ME10 73 F8
STPH/PW TN12 176 E7
SWLY BR8 39 J6
WALD ME5 87 J5
WBY/YAL ME18 151 K4
The Mailyns RHAM ME8 69 K7
Main Gate Rd CHAT ME4 3 F1
Main Rd BH/WHM TN16 74 B8
EDEN TN8 142 C5
EYN DA4 42 A4
EYN DA4 59 H3
HART DA3 43 K7
HOO/HM ME3 34 A7
HOO/HM ME3 50 C1
HOO/HM ME3 50 A2
RDART DA2 43 H6
RSEV TN14 99 G5
STMC/STPC BR5 38 D8
SWLY BR8 40 C6
SWLY BR8 57 K3
Main Road Gorse Hl EYN DA4 60 A5
Main St RYE TN31 244 E8
Major York's Rd STH/RUST TN4 10 B4
Malan Cl BH/WHM TN16 97 J4
Malden Dr MAID/BEAR ME14 111 F6
Mallard Cl DART DA1 23 J4
Mallards Wy MAID/SHEP ME15 134 C5
Mallard Wy HOO/HM ME3 34 E2
Mallingdene Cl HOO/HM ME3 31 G6 1
Malling Rd DIT/AY ME20 108 C1
SNOD ME6 85 K7
WBY/YAL ME18 129 G5
Mallings Dr MAID/BEAR ME14 134 E2
Mallings La MAID/BEAR ME14 134 E2
Malling Ter MAIDW ME16 132 C2
Mallow Cl GVW DA11 45 F2 3
The Mallows MAID/BEAR ME14 110 E7
Mallys Pl EYN DA4 42 B6 1
Malmaynes Hall Rd HOO/HM ME3 33 K3
Malta Av WALD ME5 68 B7
Malta Rd TIL RM18 27 G1
Maltby Cl ORP BR6 56 B5
Malthouse Cl RMAID ME17 160 D1
Malthouse Hl MAID/SHEP ME15 155 F2 1
Malthouse La GVE DA12 47 H3
Malt House La TENT TN30 230 A7
Malthouse Rd BGR/WK TN15 82 A4
Maltings Cl RTON TN11 150 A6 4
The Maltings MAID/BEAR ME14 134 A1 5
ORP BR6 56 A5
OXTED RH8 140 D2
RHAM ME8 70 D6
RMAID ME17 155 H2 1
Malton Wy RTWE/PEM TN2 191 F8
Malus Cl WALD ME5 88 B5
Malvern Rd GILL ME7 5 E6
ORP BR6 56 C8
Malvina Av GVE DA12 27 J8
Malyons Rd SWLY BR8 40 C5
Mamignot Cl MAID/BEAR ME14 134 B1 2
Manchester Cl WALD ME5 68 D8 3
Mangravet Av MAID/SHEP ME15 133 J7
Manning Rd STMC/STPC BR5 56 E2
Manning St SOCK/AV RM15 13 G1
Mannock Rd DART DA1 23 J2 1
Mann Sq TON TN9 170 D7
Manor Cl DART DA1 22 A3
GVE DA12 28 E8 2
MAID/BEAR ME14 134 D3
RDART DA2 40 D1
SOCK/AV RM15 13 G1
STH/RUST TN4 10 A3
Manor Ct MAID/BEAR ME14 134 D3
MEO DA13 64 A2
Manor Dr HART DA3 62 B3
Manor Fld GVE DA12 47 H3
Manorfields Cl CHST BR7 38 A8
Manor Forstal HART DA3 62 A7
Manor Gdns WALD ME5 88 A2
Manor Gv SIT ME10 93 K3
TONN TN10 170 C3
Manor House Dr MAIDW ME16 6 A4 1
Manor House Gdns EDEN TN8 164 C5
Manor La HART DA3 61 H4
HART DA3 62 B3
ROCH ME1 66 E3
Manor Pk STH/RUST TN4 10 A4
Manor Ri MAID/BEAR ME14 134 D3
Manor Rd BFN/LL DA15 38 A1
BH/WHM TN16 97 J7
CHAT ME4 3 F4
DART DA1 22 B3
EDEN TN8 164 B5
GVE DA12 27 J5 10
HART DA3 62 D2
MEO DA13 63 K2
RSEV TN14 121 K3
RSIT ME9 117 F5
STH/RUST TN4 189 J5
SWCM DA10 25 J5
TIL RM18 27 H1
Manor St GILL ME7 4 A2
Manor Wy BXLYHN DA7 22 A2
GVW DA11 26 B2
SWCM DA10 25 K3
Mansel Dr ROCH ME1 2 A6
Manse Wy SWLY BR8 58 D1
Mansfield Cl STMC/STPC BR5 56 E4
Mansfield Rd SWLY BR8 40 B4
Mansion House Cl HDCN TN27 217 J4
Mansion Rw GILL ME7 4 A2 3
The Manwarings
STPH/PW TN12 194 E8 1
Manwood Cl SIT ME10 94 A4
Maple Av GILL ME7 5 E3
MAIDW ME16 110 C8
Maple Cl DIT/AY ME20 108 E4
SWLY BR8 40 B7 2
Maple Rd DART DA1 23 F7
GVE DA12 45 K2
HOO/HM ME3 51 F3 12
STRD ME2 48 E8
Maplescombe La EYN DA4 59 K7
Maplesden Cl MAIDW ME16 131 K3 1
The Maples HART DA3 44 C8 2
Mapleton Rd BH/WHM TN16 142 E1
EDEN TN8 143 G6
Maplins Cl RHAM ME8 70 C5 3
Marathon Paddock GILL ME7 5 D4 1
Marcet Rd DART DA1 23 F4
Marconi Rd GVW DA11 44 E1
Marcus Rd DART DA1 22 D6
Mardale Cl RHAM ME8 70 D5
Marden Rd STPH/PW TN12 197 G1
STRD ME2 49 H5

Margate Cl GILL ME7 5 E2
Margetts La ROCH ME1 86 C5
Margetts Pl STRD ME2 50 B3
Marian Sq STPH/PW TN12 198 B2
Marina Dr DART DA1 23 K7
GVW DA11 27 G6
Marine Ct PUR RM19 12 D4
Marine Dr HOO/HM ME3 51 F3 13
Marine Vw CHAT ME4 50 C5
Marion Cl WALD ME5 88 B4
Marion Crs MAID/SHEP ME15 7 E6
STMC/STPC BR5 56 C2
Maritime Cl GRH DA9 25 G4
STRD ME2 49 J6
Maritime Wy CHAT ME4 50 B6
Market Buildings
MAID/BEAR ME14 6 C3 2
Market Meadow
STMC/STPC BR5 56 D1 3
Market Pl DART DA1 23 H6 1
Market Sq BH/WHM TN16 120 C6
Market St DART DA1 23 H6
MAID/BEAR ME14 6 C3
RTWE/PEM TN2 10 C5 6
STPH/PW TN12 198 B1
Market Wy BH/WHM TN16 120 D5 4
Mark La GVE DA12 28 B6
Marks Sq GVW DA11 45 G2
Marlborough Cl ORP BR6 56 A3 2
STH/RUST TN4 10 A3
Marlborough Crs SEV TN13 8 A3
Marlborough Rd DART DA1 23 F5 2
GILL ME7 4 B4
Marle Place Rd STPH/PW TN12 210 E1
Marley La HDCN TN27 201 G2
Marley Rd HOO/HM ME3 32 E8
RMAID ME17 137 K8
Marley Wy ROCH ME1 2 C6
Marlhurst EDEN TN8 164 B2
Marling Wy GVE DA12 46 B3
Marlow Av PUR RM19 12 E4
Marlow Copse WALD ME5 88 A5
Marlowe Rd DIT/AY ME20 108 D3
The Marlowes DART DA1 22 A3
Marlpit Cl EDEN TN8 164 C2
Marquis Dr GILL ME7 89 J3
Marriott Rd DART DA1 23 K6
Marsden Wy ORP BR6 56 A8
Marshall Gdns RTON TN11 150 A5
Marshall Rd RHAM ME8 69 K5
Marshalls Land TENT TN30 230 A3
Marsham Crs RMAID ME17 156 D5
Marsham St MAID/BEAR ME14 7 D3
Marsham Wy STRD ME2 85 K1 1
Marsh Crs HOO/HM ME3 33 F2
Marsh Green Rd EDEN TN8 184 B2
Marshland Vw HOO/HM ME3 35 F1
Marsh La HOO/HM ME3 15 G8
Marsh Quarter La HAWK TN18 243 K2
Marsh Rd STRD ME2 86 A1
Marsh St DART DA1 23 K2
STRD ME2 2 B1 4
Marsh Wy DIT/AY ME20 108 E2
Marstan Cl RSIT ME9 71 H4
Marston Cl WALD ME5 87 K3
Marston Dr MAID/BEAR ME14 7 E2
Martin Ct GILL ME7 89 H3 1
Martindale Av ORP BR6 76 B1
Martin Hardie Wy TONN TN10 170 E1
Martin Rd RDART DA2 41 F1
SOCK/AV RM15 13 H1
STRD ME2 49 G6 2
Martins Cl HOO/HM ME3 30 C8
STMC/STPC BR5 38 E8
TENT TN30 230 C6
Martins La STPH/PW TN12 151 G4
Martin Sq DIT/AY ME20 108 E5 5
Martin's Shaw SEV TN13 122 E1
Marwell BH/WHM TN16 120 B5
Mary Day's CRBK TN17 212 D7
Maryfield Cl BXLY DA5 40 B1
Maryland Ct RHAM ME8 90 B1
Maryland Dr MAIDW ME16 131 K4
Maryland Rd RTWE/PEM TN2 11 F6
Mascall's Court La STPH/PW TN12 193 K2
Mascall's Court Rd
STPH/PW TN12 193 K2
Mascalls Pk STPH/PW TN12 193 H1
Masefield Dr HOO/HM ME3 31 G6 2
Masefield Rd DART DA1 24 A4
GVW DA11 44 E1
Masefield Wy TON TN9 169 K6
Master Cl OXTED RH8 118 C8
Masters La E/WMAL ME19 107 K1
Masthead Cl GRH DA9 24 B3
Matfield Crs MAID/BEAR ME14 7 F2
Matilda Cl GILL ME7 69 J6
Matterdale Gdns MAIDW ME16 131 J4
Matthews La RTON TN11 150 B3
Mattinson Pl RSIT ME9 115 K7
Matts Hill Rd RSIT ME9 90 B4
Maude Rd SWLY BR8 40 D4
Maunders Cl WALD ME5 68 D6 1
Maximilian Dr STRD ME2 86 A2
Maxim Rd DART DA1 22 B4
Maxton Cl MAID/BEAR ME14 134 B1 3
Maxwell Dr MAIDW ME16 110 B8
Maxwell Gdns ORP BR6 56 A7
Maxwell Rd GILL ME7 4 A3
May Av GVW DA11 27 G7
STMC/STPC BR5 56 C2
Maybury Av RDART DA2 24 B7 2
Maycotts La STPH/PW TN12 193 F5
Mayes Cl SWLY BR8 58 D1
Mayfair STRD ME2 49 H5 1
Mayfair Av MAID/SHEP ME15 133 G6
Mayfair Rd DART DA1 23 G4
Mayfield SWCM DA10 25 K5 2
Mayfield Av ORP BR6 56 A5
Mayfield Cl RHAM ME8 70 B4
WALD ME5 88 B5
Mayfield Rd GVW DA11 27 G7
STH/RUST TN4 10 B3
Mayfly Cl STMC/STPC BR5 56 E1 4
Mayford Rd WALD ME5 88 E4
Maylands Dr SCUP DA14 38 E1
Maynard Pl WALD ME5 5 D6
Maynards STPH/PW TN12 196 C1
Maynard's La STPH/PW TN12 193 G5
Mayplace Av DART DA1 22 D3
Maypole Crs ERITH DA8 12 B6
Maypole La CRBK TN17 212 D6
Maypole Rd GVE DA12 28 C7 4
ORP BR6 77 G2
May Rd GILL ME7 4 B4
RDART DA2 41 J2
ROCH ME1 2 C5
May St SNOD ME6 86 A6
STRD ME2 66 A4
May Ter GILL ME7 4 A1 2
Maytham Rd CRBK TN17 238 D4
Mayweed Av WALD ME5 87 K2
Mcalpine Crs MAID/SHEP ME15 155 F3
Mccabe Cl STPH/PW TN12 198 A4
Mccudden Rd DART DA1 23 J2
Mcdermott Rd BGR/WK TN15 105 F7
Mckenzie Cl DIT/AY ME20 109 K6
Mc Kenzie Rd WALD ME5 88 B3
Mcmillan Cl GVE DA12 45 K2 1
Mead Cl SWLY BR8 58 D2 1
Mead Crs DART DA1 23 G7
Meades Cl STPH/PW TN12 176 B8
Meadfield Rd MEO DA13 63 H6 1
Meadow Bank E/WMAL ME19 108 A6
RTON TN11 168 D5 2
Meadow Bank Cl BGR/WK TN15 80 E4 4
Meadowbank Rd CHAT ME4 4 A4 3
Meadowbrook OXTED RH8 140 A1
Meadow Cl RSIT ME9 73 J2 1
SEV TN13 8 C2
STRD ME2 85 H2
WALD ME5 88 A1
Meadow Ct BGR/WK TN15 105 F3
RHAM ME8 69 J4
Meadow Crs STRD ME2 85 H2
Meadowdown MAID/BEAR ME14 134 A2
Meadowdown Cl GILL ME7 89 H2
Meadow Hill Rd RTW TN1 11 D4 6
Meadowlands BGR/WK TN15 102 D7
OXTED RH8 140 E5
Meadow La EDEN TN8 164 B2
MEO DA13 83 G5
Meadow Ri RSIT ME9 73 J2
Meadow Rd GVW DA11 26 D7
GVW DA11 27 H8
RRTW TN3 204 E7
STH/RUST TN4 189 K5
TON TN9 170 A6
Meadowside DART DA1 23 H7 1
The Meadows HDCN TN27 217 J4 1
MAID/SHEP ME15 6 B5 3
ORP BR6 76 D2
RSEV TN14 77 G8
SIT ME10 94 A4
Meadowsweet View CHAT ME4 50 C4 1
The Meadow RTWE/PEM TN2 191 K6
Meadow View Rd RMAID ME17 155 H3
Meadow Wk MAID/SHEP ME15 7 E4
RDART DA2 41 F2
SNOD ME6 85 J7
Meadow Wy RDART DA2 24 B6
STPH/PW TN12 176 D8
Mead Rd DART DA1 23 G7
EDEN TN8 164 D7
GVW DA11 27 J8
The Meads Av SIT ME10 73 J7
Meadside Wk WALD ME5 68 A8
The Meads CRBK TN17 225 F5
RTWE/PEM TN2 11 E5
The Mead E/WMAL ME19 108 C4
HART DA3 61 K6
Mead Wall HOO/HM ME3 14 C6
Meadway RSEV TN14 77 G8
RTON TN11 169 J1
The Meadway ORP BR6 76 C1
SEV TN13 8 B1
Meath Cl STMC/STPC BR5 56 C2
Medbury Rd GVE DA12 28 C7
Medhurst Crs GVE DA12 46 C1
Medhurst Gdns GVE DA12 46 C1
Medina Rd DIT/AY ME20 109 G
TONN TN10 148 C8
Medlar Cl RSIT ME9 93 F
Medlar Gv GILL ME7 89 H
The Medlars MAID/BEAR ME14 111 K
MEO DA13 63 H3
Medway Av HOO/HM ME3 33 F
WBY/YAL ME18 152 D
Medway Br STRD ME2 66 D
Medway Cl SIT ME10 93 J
Medway Gdns CHAT ME4 3 F
Medway Mdw STPH/PW TN12 151 J
Medway Rd DART DA1 22 D
GILL ME7 4 B
RTW TN1 11 D
Medway St CHAT ME4 3 F
MAIDW ME16 6 C
Medway Valley Wk DIT/AY ME20 109 H
MAIDW ME16 110 D
ROCH ME1 2 C3
STPH/PW TN12 173 C
WBY/YAL ME18 130 E
Medway Wharf Rd TON TN9 170 C
Meeting House La CHAT ME4 3 F
Megrims Hl HAWK TN18 236 C
Meirscourt Rd RHAM ME8 90 B
Melbourne Rd CHAT ME4 4 A5
Meldrum Cl OXTED RH8 140 D
STMC/STPC BR5 56 D3
Melford Dr MAIDW ME16 132 B
Melliker La MEO DA13 63 G
Melody Cl RHAM ME8 89 K
Melody Rd BH/WHM TN16 97 C
Melrose Cl MAID/SHEP ME15 133 C
Melrose Rd BH/WHM TN16 97 C
Melville Rd MAID/SHEP ME15 7 D
Mercer Dr RMAID ME17 137 K
Mercers HAWK TN18 235 C
RRTW TN3 205 K
Mercers Cl STPH/PW TN12 173 C
Mercers Pl WBY/YAL ME18 129 J4
Mercer St RTW TN1 11 D2
Mercer Wy RMAID ME17 156 D5
Merchant Pl STPH/PW TN12 176 D8
Mercury Cl ROCH ME1 2 A
Meresborough La RHAM ME8 90 D
Meresborough Rd RHAM ME8 90 C
Mereworth Cl RHAM ME8 69 H3
Mereworth Rd STH/RUST TN4 10 C
WBY/YAL ME18 128 E
Merivale Gv WALD ME5 88 C
Merle Common Rd OXTED RH8 140 E
Merlin Av DIT/AY ME20 108 D
Merlin Cl SIT ME10 94 B
TONN TN10 170 E
Mermaid Cl WALD ME5 68 B
Mermerus Gdns GVE DA12 46 C2
Merrals Wood Rd STRD ME2 66 C
Merrion Cl STH/RUST TN4 190 B
Merrion Wy STH/RUST TN4 190 B
Merry Boys Rd HOO/HM ME3 31 G
Merryfields STRD ME2 49 F
Merryfields Cl HART DA3 62 A1
Merryhills Cl BH/WHM TN16 97 H
Merryweather Cl DART DA1 23 J5
Mersey Rd TONN TN10 170 B
Merton Av HART DA3 61 K
Merton Cl WALD ME5 88 D
Merton Rd MAID/SHEP ME15 134 B
Mesne Wy RSEV TN14 78 C
Meteor Cl SIT ME10 73 K
Meteor Rd E/WMAL ME19 129 H
Mewsend BH/WHM TN16 97 H
The Mews RTWE/PEM TN2 191 J
SIT ME10 94 A
STRD ME2 48 E7
Micawber Cl WALD ME5 88 B5
Michael Gdns GVE DA12 46 B
Michaels La HART DA3 61 G
Mickleham Cl STMC/STPC BR5 38 A
Mickleham Rd STMC/STPC BR5 38 A
Middle Fld RTWE/PEM TN2 192 A
Middlefields RHAM ME8 70 D6
Middle La BGR/WK TN15 102 D
Middle Mill Rd E/WMAL ME19 108 D
Middlesex Rd MAID/SHEP ME15 133 K
Middle St GILL ME7 4 A
Middleton Av SCUP DA14 38 D
Middleton Cl RHAM ME8 90 B2
Middletune Av SIT ME10 73 K
Middle Wk RTWE/PEM TN2 190 E
Middle Wy SIT ME10 94 C
The Middlings SEV TN13 8 B
Middlings Wd SEV TN13 8 B
Midfield Av SWLY BR8 40 D
Midfield Wy STMC/STPC BR5 38 C
Midley Cl MAIDW ME16 110 C
Midsummer Rd SNOD ME6 85 H
The Midway STH/RUST TN4 206 C
Mierscourt Cl RHAM ME8 70 D
Mierscourt Rd RHAM ME8 70 C
Milbourne Gv SIT ME10 73 K
Milburn Rd GILL ME7 4 C
Mildmay Pl RSEV TN14 78 C
Mildred Cl DART DA1 23 K

Milebush La STPH/PW TN12 ... 176 E5
Mile La CRBK TN17 ... 213 G5
Mile Oak Rd STPH/PW TN12 ... 194 A4
Miles Pl ROCH ME1 ... 3 D5 1
Mile Stone Rd RDART DA2 ... 24 A5
Milford Cl MAIDW ME16 ... 132 C1
Military Rd CHAT ME4 ... 3 F3 1
Milk House Cottages CRBK TN17 ... 215 H6
Milking La ORP BR6 ... 74 D7
Mill Bank HDCN TN27 ... 180 A8
Millbro SWLY BR8 ... 40 D6 1
Millbrook E/WMAL ME19 ... 108 B5
Millbrook Cl MAID/SHEP ME15 ... 6 C5
Mill Brook Rd STMC/STPC BR5 ... 56 D1
Mill Cl RMAID ME17 ... 160 C2
STRD ME2 ... 49 G5
Mill Crs TON TN9 ... 170 D4
Millcroft Rd HOO/HM ME3 ... 31 G2
Millen Rd SIT ME10 ... 93 K1
Miller Rd GVE DA12 ... 28 D8
Millers Wk MEO DA13 ... 63 H6
Miller Wy STRD ME2 ... 49 H4
Millfield HART DA3 ... 61 K6
RASHW TN26 ... 219 J7
SIT ME10 ... 94 A3
Millfield Dr GVW DA11 ... 27 F8
Millfield La HART DA3 ... 61 K6
Millfield Rd BGR/WK TN15 ... 80 C2
Millfields WALD ME5 ... 88 E4
Millfields Cl STMC/STPC BR5 ... 56 C1
Millfordhope Rd STRD ME2 ... 48 B7
Millhall DIT/AY ME20 ... 109 H4
Mill Hall Rd DIT/AY ME20 ... 109 F3
Mill Hl EDEN TN8 ... 164 D7
Mill Hill La GVE DA12 ... 47 G3
Millhouse La E/WMAL ME19 ... 107 F3
Mill La BGR/WK TN15 ... 126 D1
BGR/WK TN15 ... 147 F3
BH/WHM TN16 ... 120 C6
CRBK TN17 ... 199 G7
CRBK TN17 ... 215 G6
EYN DA4 ... 59 H5
HDCN TN27 ... 201 K4
ORP BR6 ... 75 F5
OXTED RH8 ... 140 D3
OXTED RH8 ... 141 K2
RMAID ME17 ... 154 D3
RSEV TN14 ... 78 C5
RSEV TN14 ... 102 A8
RSIT ME9 ... 71 H8
RTON TN11 ... 147 F6
SNOD ME6 ... 86 A6
STPH/PW TN12 ... 195 F5
STPH/PW TN12 ... 198 E5
TENT TN30 ... 230 B5
TON TN9 ... 170 C4
WALD ME5 ... 68 D5
WALD ME5 ... 87 J5
WBY/YAL ME18 ... 130 B6
WBY/YAL ME18 ... 152 E8
Mill Pl DART DA1 ... 22 D3
Mill Pond Cl SEV TN13 ... 102 B8
Millpond Cl STRD ME2 ... 49 G6 3
Millpond La HDCN TN27 ... 229 F4
Mill Pond Rd DART DA1 ... 23 H5
Mill Rd GILL ME7 ... 4 C2
GVW DA11 ... 27 F6
PUR RM19 ... 13 F6
RDART DA2 ... 41 J2
SEV TN13 ... 101 G8
STRD ME2 ... 49 G6
Mills Crs BGR/WK TN15 ... 102 D7
Mill Shaw OXTED RH8 ... 140 D3
Mills Rd DIT/AY ME20 ... 109 J7
Mills Ter CHAT ME4 ... 4 A5
Mill Stone Cl EYN DA4 ... 42 B7 2
Millstone Ms EYN DA4 ... 42 B6
Millstream Cl RRTW TN3 ... 204 A4 1
Mill St BH/WHM TN16 ... 120 D6
CRBK TN17 ... 236 E3
E/WMAL ME19 ... 108 D7
HAWK TN18 ... 236 D4
MAID/BEAR ME14 ... 6 C3
MAID/SHEP ME15 ... 7 D4
MAID/SHEP ME15 ... 155 F1 2
SIT ME10 ... 93 K1
SNOD ME6 ... 86 A6
Mill Vw RTON TN11 ... 149 K5
Mill Wk MAIDW ME16 ... 132 A3
Millwood Rd STMC/STPC BR5 ... 38 D8
Milner Rd GILL ME7 ... 5 D1
Milroy Av GVW DA11 ... 27 F8
Milstead Cl MAID/BEAR ME14 ... 7 F2 3
Milsted Rd RHAM ME8 ... 69 K4
Milton Av GVE DA12 ... 28 A7
HOO/HM ME3 ... 31 G6
RSEV TN14 ... 77 J5
Milton Dr RTWE/PEM TN2 ... 190 D7
Milton Gdns TON TN9 ... 169 K7
Milton Hall Rd GVE DA12 ... 28 A7
Milton Pl GVE DA12 ... 27 K5
Milton Rd GILL ME7 ... 4 C5
GVE DA12 ... 27 K5 2
SEV TN13 ... 101 G8
SIT ME10 ... 93 K2
SWCM DA10 ... 25 K5
Milton St MAIDW ME16 ... 132 C4
SWCM DA10 ... 25 J5
Mimosa Cl ORP BR6 ... 56 D6 2
Mincers Cl WALD ME5 ... 88 D4 2
Minerva Rd STRD ME2 ... 49 F6
Minster Rd RHAM ME8 ... 69 K3 3
Mintching Wood La RSIT ME9 ... 117 F4
Minterne Av SIT ME10 ... 93 H4
Minters Orch BGR/WK TN15 ... 105 H7
Miskin Rd DART DA1 ... 23 F6
HOO/HM ME3 ... 50 E1
Miskin Wy GVE DA12 ... 46 A4
Mitchell Av CHAT ME4 ... 3 F6
GVW DA11 ... 26 E8
Mitchell Cl DART DA1 ... 23 H8
RMAID ME17 ... 160 C1
Mitchell Rd E/WMAL ME19 ... 129 H4
ORP BR6 ... 56 A8
Mitchem Cl BGR/WK TN15 ... 80 D3
Mitre Ct TON TN9 ... 170 C4
Mitre Rd ROCH ME1 ... 2 B4 3
Moat Cl ORP BR6 ... 76 A2
Moat Farm RTWE/PEM TN2 ... 207 F7
Moat Farm Rd HOO/HM ME3 ... 17 K8
Moat La EDEN TN8 ... 185 K7
Moat Rd HDCN TN27 ... 199 K1
Mockbeggar La CRBK TN17 ... 228 A2
Molash Rd STMC/STPC BR5 ... 56 E1
Molescroft Wy TON TN9 ... 169 K7
Moles Md EDEN TN8 ... 164 C4
Mollison Ri GVE DA12 ... 46 B3
Molyneux Park Rd STH/RUST TN4 ... 10 B3
Monarch Cl TIL RM18 ... 27 J1
WALD ME5 ... 68 B8
Monckton's Av MAID/BEAR ME14 ... 110 E7
Monckton's Dr
MAID/BEAR ME14 ... 110 E7 2
Monckton's La MAID/BEAR ME14 ... 110 E7
Moncrif Cl MAID/BEAR ME14 ... 134 D2
Monkdown MAID/SHEP ME15 ... 134 C5 3
Monks La OXTED RH8 ... 141 H8
WADH TN5 ... 220 D7
Monks Orch DART DA1 ... 23 F8
Monks Wk MEO DA13 ... 44 B4
Monks Wy RYE TN31 ... 244 E6
Monkton Rd BGR/WK TN15 ... 105 F7
Monkwood Cl ROCH ME1 ... 67 G6 3
Monmouth Cl RHAM ME8 ... 70 A4
Monson Rd RTW TN1 ... 11 D3 6
Monson Wy RTW TN1 ... 11 D3 7
Montacute Gdns
RTWE/PEM TN2 ... 10 B5 2
Montacute Rd RTWE/PEM TN2 ... 10 C6
Montague Cl SWLY BR8 ... 58 C1
Montbretia Cl STMC/STPC BR5 ... 56 D1 4
Monteith Cl RRTW TN3 ... 205 K3
Montfort Dr WBY/YAL ME18 ... 129 J4
Montfort Rd RSEV TN14 ... 102 C4
STRD ME2 ... 2 A1
WALD ME5 ... 87 K4
Montgomery Av WALD ME5 ... 68 B7
Montgomery Rd EYN DA4 ... 42 C6
GILL ME7 ... 4 C5
STH/RUST TN4 ... 190 B7
Montpelier Ga MAIDW ME16 ... 132 B1 3
Montreal Rd SEV TN13 ... 8 A2
TIL RM18 ... 27 H2
Montrose Av WALD ME5 ... 5 E6
Mont St Aignan Wy EDEN TN8 ... 164 C5
Monypenny CRBK TN17 ... 238 D3
Moonstone Dr WALD ME5 ... 88 C4 2
Moorden La RTON TN11 ... 167 J5
Moore Av TIL RM18 ... 27 J1
Moore Rd SWCM DA10 ... 25 K5
Moore St STRD ME2 ... 49 F6
Moorfield Rd ORP BR6 ... 56 B4
Moor Hl HAWK TN18 ... 235 F6
Moorhouse Rd OXTED RH8 ... 141 K1
Mooring Rd ROCH ME1 ... 67 J5
Moor Park Cl RHAM ME8 ... 70 D6
The Moor Rd RSEV TN14 ... 101 K7
Moor St RHAM ME8 ... 70 E6
The Moor HAWK TN18 ... 235 F6
Morants Court Rd RSEV TN14 ... 100 E5
Morden St ROCH ME1 ... 2 C4 5
Morel Ct SEV TN13 ... 9 D1
Morello Cl RSIT ME9 ... 95 K4 1
SWLY BR8 ... 58 A1
Morement Rd HOO/HM ME3 ... 32 E8
Moreton Ct DART DA1 ... 22 B2
Morewood Cl SEV TN13 ... 8 B2
Morgan Dr RDART DA2 ... 24 D6
Morgan Rd STRD ME2 ... 49 F6 1
Morhen Cl SNOD ME6 ... 85 H7
Morland Av DART DA1 ... 22 E4
Morland Dr RRTW TN3 ... 221 K1
STRD ME2 ... 49 F5
Morley Dr STPH/PW TN12 ... 194 D8
Morley Rd TON TN9 ... 170 D5
Morley's Rd RSEV TN14 ... 146 B4
Mornington Ct BXLY DA5 ... 22 A7
Morris Cl E/WMAL ME19 ... 108 D5 4
Morris Court Cl RSIT ME9 ... 94 E4
Morris Gdns DART DA1 ... 23 K4
Morry La RMAID ME17 ... 158 B6
Mortimer Rd BH/WHM TN16 ... 74 B7
ORP BR6 ... 56 B5 1
Mortimers Av HOO/HM ME3 ... 31 F6
Moselle Rd BH/WHM TN16 ... 97 J5
Mosquito Rd E/WMAL ME19 ... 129 H3
Mossbank WALD ME5 ... 88 B3 1
Moss Wy RDART DA2 ... 42 C2
Mossy Gld RHAM ME8 ... 70 B8
Mostyn Rd MAID/BEAR ME14 ... 7 F3
Mosyer Dr STMC/STPC BR5 ... 56 E6
Mote Av MAID/SHEP ME15 ... 7 E4
MAID/SHEP ME15 ... 133 K3
Mote Rd BGR/WK TN15 ... 126 A7
MAID/SHEP ME15 ... 7 D4
Motney Hill Rd RHAM ME8 ... 70 D2
Mouchotte Cl BH/WHM TN16 ... 74 A7
Moultain Hl SWLY BR8 ... 58 D1
Mount Av WBY/YAL ME18 ... 152 E5
Mountbatten Av HOO/HM ME3 ... 48 B2
WALD ME5 ... 68 B7
Mount Castle La RMAID ME17 ... 161 F5
Mount Cl SEV TN13 ... 8 B2
Mount Culver Av SCUP DA14 ... 38 E4
Mount Dr MAID/BEAR ME14 ... 134 D2 1
Mount Edgcumbe Rd
STH/RUST TN4 ... 10 C4
Mount Ephraim RTW TN1 ... 10 C3
Mount Ephraim Rd RTW TN1 ... 10 C3 8
Mountfield BGR/WK TN15 ... 105 G7
Mountfield Cl MEO DA13 ... 83 F4
Mountfield Gdns RTWE/PEM TN2 ... 11 D4
Mountfield Pk TON TN9 ... 170 C6
Mountfield Rd RTWE/PEM TN2 ... 11 D4
Mountfield Wy STMC/STPC BR5 ... 56 D1
Mount Harry Rd SEV TN13 ... 9 D2
Mount La MAID/BEAR ME14 ... 134 D2
RSIT ME9 ... 91 G2
Mount Pleasant BH/WHM TN16 ... 97 H4
DIT/AY ME20 ... 110 A3
RTON TN11 ... 147 H8
STPH/PW TN12 ... 173 H8 3
TENT TN30 ... 230 C6 1
Mount Pleasant Av
RTWE/PEM TN2 ... 11 D4 7
Mount Pleasant Dr
MAID/BEAR ME14 ... 134 C1
Mount Pleasant La RRTW TN3 ... 210 C8
Mount Pleasant Rd DART DA1 ... 23 J5
RSEV TN14 ... 145 K4
RTW TN1 ... 10 C4
Mount Rd CHAT ME4 ... 3 F5
DART DA1 ... 22 C5
ROCH ME1 ... 2 A6
Mountsfield Cl MAIDW ME16 ... 6 A2
Mounts Hl CRBK TN17 ... 226 C7
Mount Sion RTW TN1 ... 10 C5
Mounts La CRBK TN17 ... 238 E4
Mounts Rd GRH DA9 ... 25 G5
Mountview RSIT ME9 ... 93 G4
Mountview Rd ORP BR6 ... 56 B4
Moyle Cl RHAM ME8 ... 90 A2
Mozart Ct CHAT ME4 ... 3 E5 2
Muir Rd MAID/SHEP ME15 ... 7 D4
Mulberry Cl GILL ME7 ... 89 H2
MEO DA13 ... 63 J3
RTWE/PEM TN2 ... 190 D5
Mulberry Dr PUR RM19 ... 12 D4
Mulberry Rd GVW DA11 ... 45 F2
Multon Rd BGR/WK TN15 ... 80 D2
Munday Bois Rd HDCN TN27 ... 182 E5
Munford Dr SWCM DA10 ... 26 A6
Mungo Park Rd GVE DA12 ... 46 A3
Mungo Park Wy STMC/STPC BR5 ... 56 D4
Munn's La RSIT ME9 ... 71 H8
Munsgore La RSIT ME9 ... 92 D4
Murrain Dr MAID/SHEP ME15 ... 134 C5
Murray Rd STMC/STPC BR5 ... 38 C8
STRD ME2 ... 49 H6 1
Murston Rd SIT ME10 ... 94 C3
Murton-neale Cl HAWK TN18 ... 235 G4 2
Museum St MAID/BEAR ME14 ... 6 C3 3
Musket La RMAID ME17 ... 135 J4
Mussenden La EYN DA4 ... 60 C3
Mustang Rd E/WMAL ME19 ... 129 H3 1
Mynn Crs MAID/BEAR ME14 ... 134 C2
Myrtle Crs WALD ME5 ... 88 A1
Myrtle Gv SOCK/AV RM15 ... 13 G2
Myrtle Pl RDART DA2 ... 24 C7
Myrtle Rd DART DA1 ... 23 G8

N

Nag's Head La ROCH ME1 ... 3 D4
Nansen Rd GVE DA12 ... 46 A2
Napier Cl SIT ME10 ... 93 H2
Napier Rd GILL ME7 ... 5 D4
GVW DA11 ... 27 G7
RTWE/PEM TN2 ... 11 F5
Napoleon Dr STPH/PW TN12 ... 196 D1 2
Napwood Cl RHAM ME8 ... 70 A8 3
Nares Rd RHAM ME8 ... 90 A2
Nash Bank MEO DA13 ... 45 G7

Nash Cl *WALD* ME5 **88** D4
Nash Cft *MEO* DA13 **45** F2
Nashenden La *ROCH* ME1 **66** E4
Nash St *MEO* DA13 **45** H7
Natal Rd *CHAT* ME4 **4** A6
Nativity Cl *SIT* ME10 **93** K2
Neale St *CHAT* ME4 **3** F6
Neal Rd *BGR/WK* TN15 **80** D2
Neb La *OXTED* RH8 **140** A2
Neills Rd *RRTW* TN3 **221** F4
Nellington Rd *RRTW* TN3 **206** A2
Nelson Av *TON* TN9 **170** A5
Nelson Cl *BH/WHM* TN16 **97** J4
Nelson Pl *SCUP* DA14 **38** B2
Nelson Rd *DART* DA1 **23** F5
GILL ME7 **5** D4
GVW DA11 **27** G8
ROCH ME1 **86** B2
RTWE/PEM TN2 **11** F5
SCUP DA14 **38** B2 2
Nelson Ter *WALD* ME5 **68** D5
Nepicar La *BGR/WK* TN15 **105** J2
Neptune Cl *STRD* ME2 **3** E1
Neptune Wy *STRD* ME2 **3** E2
Nestor Ct *WBY/YAL* ME18 **130** E6
Netley Cl *MAID/BEAR* ME14 **111** K8 1
Nettlestead La *WBY/YAL* ME18 **129** J8
Nevill Ct *E/WMAL* ME19 **108** A5
Neville Cl *BFN/LL* DA15 **38** A2
MAID/BEAR ME14 **111** H6
Neville Rd *CHAT* ME4 **3** E6
Nevill Ga *RTWE/PEM* TN2 **11** D6
Nevill Pk *STH/RUST* TN4 **10** A4
Nevill Pl *SNOD* ME6 **85** K7 1
Nevill Rdg *STH/RUST* TN4 **206** C3
Nevill Rd *SNOD* ME6 **85** K7
Nevill St *RTWE/PEM* TN2 **10** C5
Nevill Ter *RTWE/PEM* TN2 **10** B5 3
Newark Yd *STRD* ME2 **2** B1
Newbarn La *RSEV* TN14 **98** D3
New Barn Rd *HART* DA3 **44** C8
MEO DA13 **44** D3
RMAID ME17 **179** G4
SWLY BR8 **40** B6
New Barns Rd *MAID/BEAR* ME14 **111** G6
Newbridge Av *SIT* ME10 **73** K7
Newbury Av *MAIDW* ME16 **6** A1
Newbury Cl *HOO/HM* ME3 **31** G6 3
Newbury La *WADH* TN5 **220** E6
Newchurch Rd *MAID/SHEP* ME15 **7** D6
Newcomen Rd *STH/RUST* TN4 **10** C2
New Covenant Pl *ROCH* ME1 **3** D4 3
New Cut *CHAT* ME4 **3** E4
MAID/SHEP ME15 **132** D7
New Cut Rd *MAID/BEAR* ME14 **133** K1
Newenden Cl *MAID/BEAR* ME14 **111** K8 2
Newenden Rd *STRD* ME2 **49** H4
New England Rd *STH/RUST* TN4 **190** A7
New Gardens Rd *RSIT* ME9 **95** K4
New Hall Farm La *HOO/HM* ME3 **18** E8
New House La *GVW* DA11 **45** G1
New Hythe La *DIT/AY* ME20 **108** E4
Newitt Rd *HOO/HM* ME3 **50** E1
Newland Green La *HDCN* TN27 **182** D6
Newlands *RRTW* TN3 **205** K2
Newlands Av *SIT* ME10 **93** G2
Newlands Farm Rd *HOO/HM* ME3 **33** J1
Newlands La *MEO* DA13 **83** G5
Newlands Ri *STH/RUST* TN4 **10** C1 3
Newlands Rd *STH/RUST* TN4 **11** D1
Newlands Wy *STH/RUST* TN4 **190** B7 2
New Lodge Dr *OXTED* RH8 **118** D7
Newlyn Dr *STPH/PW* TN12 **198** B1
Newman's Rd *GVW* DA11 **27** G8
New Mill Rd *STMC/STPC* BR5 **38** D6
Newnham Cl *RHAM* ME8 **69** K4 1
Newnham St *CHAT* ME4 **4** A5
New Pond Rd *CRBK* TN17 **226** E8
Newports *SWLY* BR8 **58** A4
New Pound La *WBY/YAL* ME18 **128** E4
New Rd *CHAT* ME4 **3** F5
CRBK TN17 **225** H2
DIT/AY ME20 **109** G5
E/WMAL ME19 **108** E5
EYN DA4 **42** B7
GVW DA11 **27** J5
GVW DA11 **27** H5 3
HDCN TN27 **183** G4
HDCN TN27 **200** B1
HOO/HM ME3 **31** F2
MEO DA13 **63** G2
ORP BR6 **56** B4
OXTED RH8 **141** F1
RMAID ME17 **156** E1
ROCH ME1 **3** D4
ROCH ME1 **86** E6
RSEV TN14 **121** K3
RTON TN11 **187** J5
STPH/PW TN12 **173** J8
SWLY BR8 **40** C8
SWLY BR8 **40** C5
New Road Av *CHAT* ME4 **3** E4
New Road Hl *HAYES* BR2 **74** D4
New Stairs *CHAT* ME4 **3** F2
New St *BGR/WK* TN15 **82** E2
BH/WHM TN16 **120** C6
CHAT ME4 **3** E5
New Street Rd *BGR/WK* TN15 **62** D7
New Swan Yd *GVE* DA12 **27** J5 11
Newton Abbot Rd *GVW* DA11 **27** G8
Newton Av *TONN* TN10 **148** D7
Newton Cl *MAIDW* ME16 **6** B4
WALD ME5 **88** D4 3
Newton Gdns *STPH/PW* TN12 **173** H7 1
Newton Rd *RTW* TN1 **11** D3 8
TIL RM18 **27** H1
Newton's Ct *GRH* DA9 **24** C3
Newton Willows *RRTW* TN3 **205** F7
New Wharf Rd *TON* TN9 **170** B4
New Years La *RSEV* TN14 **99** F2
Nicholas Cl *MAIDW* ME16 **132** A3 2
Nicklaus Dr *WALD* ME5 **88** A3
Nickleby Cl *ROCH* ME1 **2** C6
Nickleby Rd *GVE* DA12 **28** D7
Nicolson Rd *STMC/STPC* BR5 **56** D4
Nightingale Cl *BH/WHM* TN16 **97** G2
DIT/AY ME20 **108** D4
GVW DA11 **45** F2 4
RHAM ME8 **70** C7 1
Nightingale La *RSEV* TN14 **144** D1
Nightingale Rd *RSEV* TN14 **102** B4
The Nightingales *CRBK* TN17 **216** C6
Nightingale Wy *SWLY* BR8 **40** B8
Nile Rd *GILL* ME7 **4** C4
Nine Acres Rd *STRD* ME2 **65** K3
Nine Elms Gv *GVW* DA11 **27** H6
Ninehams Rd *BH/WHM* TN16 **97** H8
Nineveh La *HAWK* TN18 **226** A8
Niven Cl *HOO/HM* ME3 **49** H3
Nizels La *RTON* TN11 **146** D7
Noah's Ark *BGR/WK* TN15 **103** F5
Nobel Cl *RSIT* ME9 **95** K4
Noble Tree Rd *RTON* TN11 **147** F8
The Nook *WBY/YAL* ME18 **152** D4
Norah La *HOO/HM* ME3 **48** A2
Nore Cl *GILL* ME7 **69** F5
Norfield Rd *RDART* DA2 **39** K2
Norfolk Cl *DART* DA1 **23** K5
WALD ME5 **88** D3
Norfolk Rd *GVE* DA12 **28** A5
MAID/SHEP ME15 **133** J6
RTW TN1 **11** D5 6
TON TN9 **170** A5
Norheads La *BH/WHM* TN16 **96** E5
Norman Cl *MAID/BEAR* ME14 **7** E1
RHAM ME8 **89** J2
RSEV TN14 **102** B4
STRD ME2 **66** E2
Normanhurst Rd *BGR/WK* TN15 **105** G7
STMC/STPC BR5 **38** C7
Norman Ri *CRBK* TN17 **225** K2 2
Norman Rd *DART* DA1 **23** H7
E/WMAL ME19 **107** J5
RTW TN1 **11** D2 3
SNOD ME6 **85** K8
Normans Cl *GVW* DA11 **27** H6
Normans La *EDEN* TN8 **163** J6
Norman St *RSEV* TN14 **144** A1
Norreys Rd *RHAM* ME8 **70** B7
Norrington Rd *MAID/SHEP* ME15 **133** G8
Norris Wy *DART* DA1 **22** C2
Norstead Gdns *STH/RUST* TN4 **190** B7
Norsted La *ORP* BR6 **76** C6
North Ash Rd *HART* DA3 **62** A7
North Bank Cl *STRD* ME2 **66** E1
Northbourne Rd *RHAM* ME8 **69** J2
Northcote Rd *GVW* DA11 **27** G7
STRD ME2 **2** A1
TON TN9 **170** B5 4
North Cray Rd *SCUP* DA14 **39** F4
North Crs *RMAID* ME17 **154** D2
North Dane Wy *WALD* ME5 **88** D1
North Down *STPH/PW* TN12 **198** A2
Northdown Cl *MAID/BEAR* ME14 **111** H7
STPH/PW TN12 **173** H8 4
Northdown Rd *HART* DA3 **43** K7
RSEV TN14 **102** C4
North Downs Wy *BGR/WK* TN15 **104** E2
MAID/BEAR ME14 **112** A2
OXTED RH8 **118** E2
RMAID ME17 **114** B8
RMAID ME17 **138** D7
RMAID ME17 **161** K2
SEV TN13 **101** F5
STRD ME2 **65** J5
Northdown Vw *RMAID* ME17 **137** K8
North End La *ORP* BR6 **75** G4
North Farm La *RTWE/PEM* TN2 **190** D6
North Farm Rd *STH/RUST* TN4 **190** C7
Northfield *HART* DA3 **44** A8
Northfield Av *STMC/STPC* BR5 **56** D3
Northfields *MAIDW* ME16 **131** K4
RRTW TN3 **188** E6
Northfleet Cl *MAID/BEAR* ME14 **7** F2 4
North Folly Rd *MAID/SHEP* ME15 **153** K3
Northgate *ROCH* ME1 **2** C2 5
Northgrove Rd *HAWK* TN18 **235** F4 1
North Hill Rd *HAWK* TN18 **234** C5
North Kent Av *GVW* DA11 **26** D5
North Kent Aveune *GVW* DA11 **26** D5
Northleigh Cl *MAID/SHEP* ME15 **133** G
North Meadow *E/WMAL* ME19 **107** F
North Pasley Rd *CHAT* ME4 **4** B
North Pole Rd *WBY/YAL* ME18 **131** F
Northridge *RYE* TN31 **244** D
Northridge Rd *GVE* DA12 **45** K
North Riding *HART* DA3 **44** E
North Rd *CHAT* ME4 **50** C
CRBK TN17 **212** D
DART DA1 **22** C
GILL ME7 **4** A
HOO/HM ME3 **15** G
PUR RM19 **13** G
North St *DART* DA1 **23** G
EDEN TN8 **185** G
GVE DA12 **27** J6
HDCN TN27 **200** A
HDCN TN27 **217** K
MAIDW ME16 **131** J
RMAID ME17 **157** G
RTWE/PEM TN2 **11** E
SIT ME10 **73** K
STRD ME2 **2** B
North Ter *HOO/HM* ME3 **32** A
Northumberland Av *RHAM* ME8 **70** B
Northumberland Rd
MAID/SHEP ME15 **133** J
MEO DA13 **45** G
North Vw *MAID/SHEP* ME15 **7** E
Northview *SWLY* BR8 **40** B
North View Rd *SEV* TN13 **102** A
North Wy *MAID/BEAR* ME14 **111** H
Northwood Av *HOO/HM* ME3 **33** F
Northwood Dr *SIT* ME10 **94** A
Northwood Rd *TONN* TN10 **148** B
Norton Crs *TONN* TN10 **148** B
Norton Gv *WALD* ME5 **87** K
Norton Rd *RMAID* ME17 **156** E
STH/RUST TN4 **190** A5
Nortons La *TENT* TN30 **229** J
Nortons Wy *STPH/PW* TN12 **172** C
Norwich Av *TONN* TN10 **170** D
Norwich Cl *STRD* ME2 **48** C8
Norwood Cl *HOO/HM* ME3 **31** G
Norwood La *MEO* DA13 **63** J
Nottidge Rd *STH/RUST* TN4 **206** C5
Nottingham Av
MAID/SHEP ME15 **133** K8
Novar Cl *ORP* BR6 **56** A
The Nower *RSEV* TN14 **99** F
Nuffield Rd *SWLY* BR8 **40** D
Nunappleton Wy *OXTED* RH8 **140** E3
Nunnery La *RTON* TN11 **187** H
Nursery Av *MAID/BEAR* ME14 **134** D
MAIDW ME16 **110** B
Nursery Cl *ORP* BR6 **56** A
RDART DA2 **24** B
SEV TN13 **9** E
SWLY BR8 **39** K7
TONN TN10 **170** E
WADH TN5 **233** F
Nursery Gdns *HOO/HM* ME3 **51** F1
Nursery Pl *SEV* TN13 **123** F
Nursery Rd *DIT/AY* ME20 **109** G
MEO DA13 **63** H
RHAM ME8 **70** A
STH/RUST TN4 **190** B
STPH/PW TN12 **173** H
Nurstead Av *HART* DA3 **44** E
Nurstead Church La *MEO* DA13 **63** H
Nurstead La *HART* DA3 **62** E
Nutfield Cl *WALD* ME5 **68** C
Nutfields *BGR/WK* TN15 **126** B
SIT ME10 **94** C
Nuthatch *HART* DA3 **44** C
Nutley Cl *SWLY* BR8 **40** C
Nut Tree Cl *ORP* BR6 **56** E
Nutwood Cl *MAID/BEAR* ME14 **134** A2

O

Oakapple La *MAIDW* ME16 **132** A
Oak Av *GILL* ME7 **5** E
SEV TN13 **123** K
Oak Cl *DART* DA1 **22** B
HOO/HM ME3 **51** F3
Oakdale La *EDEN* TN8 **142** C
Oakdale Rd *STH/RUST* TN4 **10** B
Oakdene Rd *SEV* TN13 **8** C
STMC/STPC BR5 **56** B
Oak Dr *DIT/AY* ME20 **108** E
HOO/HM ME3 **48** A
Oak End Cl *STH/RUST* TN4 **190** A
Oakenden La *EDEN* TN8 **186** D
Oakenden Rd *MEO* DA13 **64** B
Oak Farm Gdns *HDCN* TN27 **180** B
Oak Farm La *BGR/WK* TN15 **83** F
Oakfield *HAWK* TN18 **235** F
Oakfield Court Rd
RTWE/PEM TN2 **11** E4
Oakfield La *RDART* DA2 **22** D
Oakfield Park Rd *DART* DA1 **23** G
Oakfield Pl *DART* DA1 **23** G

Oakfield Rd EDEN TN8 164 B2
STPH/PW TN12 193 F6
Oakfields SEV TN13 9 D5
SIT ME10 93 H3 2
Oakhill Rd ORP BR6 56 A6
PUR RM19 13 F5
Oak Hill Rd SEV TN13 8 C4
Oakhurst Cl WALD ME5 88 A3
Oaklands Cl BGR/WK TN15 80 D2
Oaklands La BH/WHM TN16 97 G2
Oaklands Rd GVW DA11 45 G2
HAWK TN18 235 F5
RDART DA2 24 A7
RRTW TN3 204 E8
Oaklands Wy RTON TN11 169 K2
Oak La HDCN TN27 200 B1
RSIT ME9 71 G5
SEV TN13 8 C6
SEV TN13 123 H8
Oaklea Rd STPH/PW TN12 173 H8
Oakleigh Cl SWLY BR8 40 B8
WALD ME5 87 K4
Oak Lodge La BH/WHM TN16 120 D4
Oakmead MEO DA13 63 H6 2
TONN TN10 148 C8
Oakmore Gdns STMC/STPC BR5 56 D1
Oak Rd BH/WHM TN16 120 D4
GRH DA9 24 D5
GVE DA12 45 J1
HOO/HM ME3 51 F3 15
ORP BR6 76 B3
RTWE/PEM TN2 190 D7
SIT ME10 94 D1
STPH/PW TN12 172 D7
STRD ME2 48 D8
Oaks Dene WALD ME5 88 A5
Oaks Forstal HAWK TN18 243 K1
Oakshaw OXTED RH8 118 B6
Oaks Rd TENT TN30 230 B7
The Oaks DIT/AY ME20 109 J5
SWLY BR8 40 B7
Oak Tree Auenue GRH DA9 24 E6
Oak Tree Av MAID/SHEP ME15 133 J7
Oak Tree Cl RTW TN1 10 C6
STPH/PW TN12 196 D1 3
Oakum Ct CHAT ME4 4 B6
Oak Vw EDEN TN8 164 B4
Oakwood Cl DART DA1 24 A7
Oakwood Ct MAIDW ME16 6 A4
Oakwood Ri HART DA3 43 K8
RTWE/PEM TN2 190 E7
Oakwood Rd MAIDW ME16 132 C3
Oast Cl RTWE/PEM TN2 190 D7
Oast Ct SIT ME10 93 K4
WBY/YAL ME18 152 D5
Oast House Wy STMC/STPC BR5 56 C1
Oast La RTON TN11 170 A2
Oast Rd OXTED RH8 140 D2
Oastview RHAM ME8 70 D6
Oast Vw STPH/PW TN12 194 E8
Oast Wy HART DA3 61 K3
Oatfield Cl CRBK TN17 225 J1
Oatfield Dr CRBK TN17 225 J1
Oatfield Rd ORP BR6 56 A5
Ocelot Ct CHAT ME4 4 B5 4
Ockham Dr STMC/STPC BR5 38 B5 1
Ockley La HAWK TN18 235 G2
Ockley Rd HAWK TN18 235 G4
Octavia Ct WALD ME5 88 C3 3
Odiham Dr MAIDW ME16 110 C7
Offen's Dr STPH/PW TN12 198 A3
Offham Rd E/WMAL ME19 107 J7
Officers Ter CHAT ME4 3 F1
Old Ashford Rd RMAID ME17 160 E1
The Old Bailey RMAID ME17 137 J8 1
Old Barn Cl BGR/WK TN15 102 E4
GILL ME7 69 G8
TON TN9 169 K6
Old Barn Rd E/WMAL ME19 108 B4
Old Barn Wy BXLYHN DA7 22 A3
Old Bexley La BXLY DA5 22 A8
Oldbury Cl STMC/STPC BR5 56 E1
Oldbury La BGR/WK TN15 126 B1
The Old Carriageway GILL ME7 89 G3
SEV TN13 122 E2
Old Chapel Rd SWLY BR8 57 K4
Old Chatham Rd DIT/AY ME20 87 J8
MAID/BEAR ME14 110 E5
Old Church La WBY/YAL ME18 151 G1
Old Church Rd ROCH ME1 86 C5
RTWE/PEM TN2 191 K5
WBY/YAL ME18 151 F1
Old Coach Rd BGR/WK TN15 104 E1
Old Dartford Rd EYN DA4 59 J3
Old Downs HART DA3 61 K2
Old Dr MAID/SHEP ME15 133 F8
Old Farm Gdns SWLY BR8 40 C8 3
Old Ferry Rd RSIT ME9 55 K8
Oldfield Cl MAID/SHEP ME15 134 A5
RHAM ME8 70 A6
Old Forge La RSIT ME9 114 D2
Old Forge Wy SCUP DA14 38 C2
Old Gardens Cl RTWE/PEM TN2 207 G6
The Old Gdn SEV TN13 123 F2
Old Hadlow Rd TONN TN10 170 E2
Old Ham La RMAID ME17 160 B2
Old Hl ORP BR6 75 K2
Old House La RRTW TN3 205 G1
Old House Rd RSIT ME9 91 H2
Old Kent Rd STPH/PW TN12 173 H8
Old Lain RMAID ME17 137 K8
Old La BGR/WK TN15 126 B2
BH/WHM TN16 97 H8
OXTED RH8 140 D1
Old Lenham Rd RSIT ME9 139 K1
Old London Rd BGR/WK TN15 105 F2
RSEV TN14 77 H5
TONN TN10 170 C3 2
Old Loose Hl MAID/SHEP ME15 155 F2
Old Maidstone Rd SCUP DA14 39 G5
Old Manor Wy BXLYHN DA7 22 A1
Old Mill Cl EYN DA4 59 H5
Old Mill La DIT/AY ME20 110 C3
Old Mill Rd RMAID ME17 135 H6
Old Orch HAWK TN18 243 J1
Old Orchard La E/WMAL ME19 108 B5
The Old Orch RHAM ME8 70 C6
Old Otford Rd RSEV TN14 101 K5
Old Pattens La ROCH ME1 3 D6
Old Perry St GVW DA11 27 F8
Old Regent Dr CRBK TN17 238 C3
Old Rd CHAT ME4 3 F4
DART DA1 22 A3
STPH/PW TN12 151 H8
WBY/YAL ME18 129 K7
Old Rd East GVE DA12 28 A7
Old Rd West GVW DA11 27 G7
Old School Cl RMAID ME17 160 D2
Old School Ct HDCN TN27 183 F3
HOO/HM ME3 50 A2 1
Old School La E/WMAL ME19 107 H2
Old Soar Rd BGR/WK TN15 127 H6
Old Station Rd WADH TN5 220 A8
Old Tannery Cl TENT TN30 229 K7 2
Old Terry's Lodge Rd
BGR/WK TN15 103 K3
Old Tovil Rd MAID/SHEP ME15 6 C5
Old Trafford Cl MAIDW ME16 110 B8
Old Tree La RMAID ME17 155 J3
Old Tye Av BH/WHM TN16 97 J3
The Old Wk RSEV TN14 101 K4
Old Wardsdown WADH TN5 233 F3
Old Watling St STRD ME2 48 A6
The Old Yews HART DA3 44 C8
Oleander Cl ORP BR6 75 J1
Oliver Cl CHAT ME4 4 B6
WTHK RM20 13 K7
Oliver Crs EYN DA4 59 J4
Olive Rd DART DA1 23 G7
Oliver Rd STPH/PW TN12 198 A3
SWLY BR8 40 A8
WTHK RM20 13 K8
Oliver Twist Cl ROCH ME1 2 B4
Olivine Cl WALD ME5 88 B6
Olliffe Cl WALD ME5 88 A4 1
Onslow Dr SCUP DA14 38 E1
Onslow Rd ROCH ME1 3 D5
Orache Dr MAID/BEAR ME14 134 A1
Orange Court La ORP BR6 75 F4
Orange Ter ROCH ME1 3 D3
Orbit Cl WALD ME5 88 B6
Orchard Av DART DA1 22 E6
DIT/AY ME20 109 J5
GVW DA11 45 J3
STRD ME2 48 E5 3
Orchard Cl EDEN TN8 164 B4
HART DA3 44 C7
RMAID ME17 154 C3
RMAID ME17 157 G2
RSEV TN14 102 A8
RTWE/PEM TN2 190 D7
STPH/PW TN12 194 D8
Orchard Crs STPH/PW TN12 194 E8
Orchard Dr EDEN TN8 164 B4
MEO DA13 63 G2
RSIT ME9 91 K1
TONN TN10 170 E1
Orchard Gld HDCN TN27 200 B1
Orchard Gv DIT/AY ME20 109 F4
ORP BR6 56 A6
Orchard Hl DART DA1 22 B4
Orchard Pl MAIDW ME16 6 B4
SIT ME10 94 B3
Orchard Ri RRTW TN3 204 E7
Orchard Rd GVW DA11 26 D8
MAID/BEAR ME14 134 A2
ORP BR6 75 G1
ORP BR6 76 D4
RSEV TN14 101 H3
SEV TN13 8 A1
STPH/PW TN12 151 J8
SWCM DA10 25 K4
TENT TN30 230 A3
Orchard St DART DA1 23 H5
MAID/SHEP ME15 7 D4
RHAM ME8 70 B7
The Orchard MAID/BEAR ME14 134 D2
SEV TN13 101 G8 2
SWLY BR8 40 A7 2
Orchard Vw MAID/BEAR ME14 112 C6
RSIT ME9 95 K3
TENT TN30 230 C7
Orchard Wy BGR/WK TN15 102 E4
CRBK TN17 225 H2
OXTED RH8 140 E4
RDART DA2 41 G1
SNOD ME6 85 J7
STPH/PW TN12 194 E8
Orchid Cl STRD ME2 48 B8
Orchidhurst RTWE/PEM TN2 190 D7 2
Ordnance Rd GVE DA12 27 K5
Ordnance St CHAT ME4 3 E5
Ordnance Ter CHAT ME4 3 E4 3
Oriole Wy DIT/AY ME20 108 D4
Orion Rd ROCH ME1 67 H7
Orlestone Gdns ORP BR6 77 F1 1
Orlick Rd GVE DA12 28 E8
The Orpines WBY/YAL ME18 130 D7
Orpington By-pass RSEV TN14 77 H4
Orwell Cl DIT/AY ME20 108 D3
Orwell Spike E/WMAL ME19 129 J1
Osborne Rd GILL ME7 5 D3 7
Osbourne Rd RDART DA2 24 A5
Osgood Av ORP BR6 76 A1
Osgood Gdns ORP BR6 76 A1
Osmers Hl WADH TN5 220 B7
Osney Wy GVE DA12 28 C8
Osprey Av WALD ME5 5 E6
Osprey Ct SIT ME10 94 B3
Osprey Wk DIT/AY ME20 108 D5
Ospringe Pl RTWE/PEM TN2 191 F8
Osterberg Rd DART DA1 23 J3
Ostlers Ct SNOD ME6 85 K6 4
Otford La RSEV TN14 77 G8
Otford Rd RSEV TN14 101 K8
Otham La MAID/SHEP ME15 134 E4
Otham St MAID/SHEP ME15 134 D7
Otlinge Cl STMC/STPC BR5 56 E1 5
Ottawa Rd TIL RM18 27 H1
Otterbourne Pl
MAID/SHEP ME15 134 A5 1
Otterham Quay La RHAM ME8 70 E6
Otteridge Rd MAID/BEAR ME14 134 C3
Otters Cl STMC/STPC BR5 56 E1 6
Otway St CHAT ME4 4 A5
Otway Ter CHAT ME4 4 A5
The Oval HART DA3 44 D8
Ovenden Rd RSEV TN14 99 K7
Overcliffe GVW DA11 27 H5
Overdale RSEV TN14 145 K4
Overmead SWLY BR8 58 B2 3
Over Minnis HART DA3 62 A7
Overy St DART DA1 23 J5
Owen Cl E/WMAL ME19 108 D6 2
Owens Wy GILL ME7 51 H8
Oxenden Wood Rd ORP BR6 76 C2
Oxenhill Rd RSEV TN14 102 C4
Oxenhoath Rd RTON TN11 149 J2
Oxford Cl GVE DA12 28 C8 1
Oxford Rd GILL ME7 5 D5
MAID/SHEP ME15 133 K5
SCUP DA14 38 C3
Oxford St SNOD ME6 85 K6
Ox La TENT TN30 230 B4
Ox Lea RRTW TN3 205 K3
Oxley Shaw La E/WMAL ME19 108 C4
Oyster Cl SIT ME10 73 K8 6

P

Packer Pl WALD ME5 68 B6
Packham Rd GVW DA11 45 G1
Packhorse Rd SEV TN13 122 E2
Padbrook OXTED RH8 118 E8
Paddlesworth Rd SNOD ME6 85 F5
Paddock Cl BGR/WK TN15 105 J8
EYN DA4 42 B6
OXTED RH8 140 D2
RRTW TN3 204 E1
Paddocks Cl STMC/STPC BR5 56 E6
The Paddocks EDEN TN8 185 H7
GILL ME7 89 H1
STPH/PW TN12 151 G8 1
The Paddock BH/WHM TN16 120 C5
CHAT ME4 3 F4
MEO DA13 83 G7
RTON TN11 150 A5
RTWE/PEM TN2 191 J8
RYE TN31 244 E7
Paddock Wy OXTED RH8 140 D2
Pad's Hl MAID/SHEP ME15 7 D3 5
Page Cl RDART DA2 43 H1
Pagehurst Rd STPH/PW TN12 197 J3
Paget St GILL ME7 4 C3
Pagitt St CHAT ME4 3 E6
Paiges Farm Cl RSEV TN14 146 A4
Pains Hl OXTED RH8 141 G3
Painters Ash La GVW DA11 44 E1
Palace Av MAID/SHEP ME15 7 D3
Palace Rd BH/WHM TN16 98 A8
Palewell Cl STMC/STPC BR5 38 C7
Palmar Rd MAIDW ME16 6 A1
Palmarsh Cl STMC/STPC BR5 56 E1 7

Palm Av *SCUP* DA14 38 E4
Palmer Av *GVE* DA12 46 A2
Palmers Brook *RTON* TN11 150 B4
Palmers Green La *STPH/PW* TN12 194 B5
Palmers Orch *RSEV* TN14 78 C6 1
Palmerston Rd *CHAT* ME4 68 A5
Pankhurst Rd *HOO/HM* ME3 32 E8
Pannell Rd *HOO/HM* ME3 21 F8
Panteny La *RSIT* ME9 95 F4
Panter's *SWLY* BR8 40 C5
The Pantiles *RTWE/PEM* TN2 10 C5 7
Panton Cl *WALD* ME5 88 D2
Papion Gv *WALD* ME5 87 K4
The Parade *STRD* ME2 48 D6
Parham Rd *CHAT* ME4 3 F6 5
Park Av *EDEN* TN8 164 B4
GILL ME7 5 D6
GVE DA12 27 K7
GVW DA11 27 F7
MAID/BEAR ME14 7 E1
ORP BR6 56 B7
RMAID ME17 154 E4
RTON TN11 169 K1
SIT ME10 93 K4
Park Barn Rd *RMAID* ME17 157 K1
Park Cl *STH/RUST* TN4 10 A5
Park Corner Rd *MEO* DA13 26 B8
Park Crs *CHAT* ME4 68 A6
Park Dr *HART* DA3 43 K8 1
SIT ME10 93 J5
Parker Cl *RHAM* ME8 90 B1
Park Farm Rd *E/WMAL* ME19 84 B7
Parkfield *BGR/WK* TN15 124 D2
Parkfield Rd *RHAM* ME8 70 C4
Parkfields *STRD* ME2 48 B7
Parkgate Rd *ORP* BR6 57 K8
Park Hl *MEO* DA13 63 F1
Park Hill Rd *RSEV* TN14 102 C4
Park House Gdns *STH/RUST* TN4 190 A5
Parkland Cl *SEV* TN13 124 A8
Parklands *OXTED* RH8 140 C2
Park La *BGR/WK* TN15 102 E5
BGR/WK TN15 124 E2
HAWK TN18 224 D7
MAID/BEAR ME14 111 F7
RMAID ME17 155 K4
SEV TN13 9 E3
SOCK/AV RM15 13 H1
SWLY BR8 41 F7
Park Pl *GVE* DA12 27 K5
SEV TN13 123 F2
Park Rd *DART* DA1 23 K6
E/WMAL ME19 106 E3
E/WMAL ME19 108 B3
GVW DA11 27 J8
LING RH7 162 C3
OXTED RH8 118 D7
RTON TN11 149 J1
SIT ME10 93 K3
STH/RUST TN4 11 D2
STMC/STPC BR5 56 D3
STPH/PW TN12 197 G3
SWCM DA10 25 K5
SWLY BR8 58 C1
WBY/YAL ME18 151 H1
Parkside *HOO/HM* ME3 31 G7
RSEV TN14 77 F8
Parkside Av *BXLYHN* DA7 22 A1
TIL RM18 27 J1
Parkside Cross *BXLYHN* DA7 22 B1
Park St *RTWE/PEM* TN2 11 E4 5
Park Ter *GRH* DA9 25 G4
The Park *SCUP* DA14 38 A3
Park Vw *RYE* TN31 244 D8
SOCK/AV RM15 13 H1
Park View Cl *EDEN* TN8 164 B4
Park Wallis *GVW* DA11 26 C4
Park Wy *BXLY* DA5 40 C1
MAID/SHEP ME15 7 E6
RMAID ME17 154 C3
Parkway *TONN* TN10 170 D1
Parkwood Cl *RTWE/PEM* TN2 11 F1
Park Wood La *STPH/PW* TN12 198 E4
Parkwood Rd *BH/WHM* TN16 97 J8
Parr Av *GILL* ME7 5 D2
Parrock Av *GVE* DA12 27 K7
Parrock Rd *GVE* DA12 27 K6
Parrock St *GVE* DA12 27 J5 12
Parrs Haed Ms *ROCH* ME1 2 C2 6
Parsonage Cl *STH/RUST* TN4 206 A1 1
Parsonage La *EYN* DA4 42 A4
RRTW TN3 210 E8
RSIT ME9 73 F6
SCUP DA14 39 G2
STRD ME2 49 H6
Parsonage Rd *STH/RUST* TN4 206 A1
Parsons La *BGR/WK* TN15 81 K5 1
RDART DA2 40 E1
Partridge Av *DIT/AY* ME20 108 D3
Partridge Dr *CHAT* ME4 50 C5 1
Pasley Rd *GILL* ME7 4 A1
Pasley Rd East *CHAT* ME4 4 A1
Pastens Rd *OXTED* RH8 141 G2
Pastime Cl *SIT* ME10 73 K6 1
The Patch *SEV* TN13 8 A1
Patrixbourne Av *RHAM* ME8 69 K4
Pattenden Gdns *STPH/PW* TN12 151 J7
Pattenden La *STPH/PW* TN12 176 B6
Pattens La *CHAT* ME4 67 K5
Patterdale Rd *RDART* DA2 24 B7
Paulinus Cl *STMC/STPC* BR5 38 D7
The Pavement *TENT* TN30 230 A3
Pavilion La *WBY/YAL* ME18 129 J6
Payden St *RMAID* ME17 139 K6
RSIT ME9 139 J4
Paynesfield Rd *BH/WHM* TN16 97 G7
Payne's La *MAID/SHEP* ME15 133 G7
Peach Cft *GVW* DA11 45 F1
Peacock St *GVE* DA12 27 K6
Peal Cl *HOO/HM* ME3 51 F1
Pearman Cl *RHAM* ME8 70 D5 1
Pearse Pl *RRTW* TN3 221 J1
Pearsons Green Rd
STPH/PW TN12 194 A1
STPH/PW TN12 194 C2
Pearson Wy *DART* DA1 23 J8
Pear Tree Av *DIT/AY* ME20 109 G6
Pear Tree Cl *CRBK* TN17 225 K3
SWLY BR8 40 A7 3
Pear Tree La *GILL* ME7 69 F7
MAID/SHEP ME15 133 H8
Peartree La *STRD* ME2 47 K4
Pease Hl *BGR/WK* TN15 82 A2
Peasley La *CRBK* TN17 212 C8
Peat Wy *HOO/HM* ME3 20 C7
Peckham Cl *STRD* ME2 49 H6 2
Peel Dr *SIT* ME10 94 D2
Peel St *MAID/BEAR* ME14 7 D1
Peens La *RMAID* ME17 155 J7
Pegasus Ct *GVE* DA12 45 K1
Peggoty Cl *HOO/HM* ME3 48 A3
Pelham Rd *GVW* DA11 27 G6
Pelham Rd South *GVW* DA11 27 G7
Pelican Cl *STRD* ME2 48 B8
Pell Cl *WADH* TN5 220 C8
Pells La *BGR/WK* TN15 81 F6
Pemberton Gdns *SWLY* BR8 40 B8 2
Pemble Cl *STPH/PW* TN12 172 C7
Pembroke *CHAT* ME4 50 B6
Pembroke Gdns *RHAM* ME8 90 B2 2
Pembroke Pl *EYN* DA4 42 A6 1
Pembroke Rd *RMAID* ME17 154 C3
SEV TN13 9 D4
TON TN9 170 A5 1
Pembury Cl *RTWE/PEM* TN2 191 K7 3
Pembury Gdns *MAIDW* ME16 6 A4
Pembury Gra *RTWE/PEM* TN2 191 G8
Pembury Gv *TON* TN9 170 C6 3
Pembury Hall Rd *RTWE/PEM* TN2 191 J3
Pembury Rd *RTON* TN11 191 G3
RTWE/PEM TN2 11 E4
TON TN9 170 B6
Pembury St *SIT* ME10 93 K2 6
Pembury Wks *RTON* TN11 191 H4
Pembury Wy *RHAM* ME8 70 B4 2
Pencroft Dr *DART* DA1 23 F6
Pendennis Rd *ORP* BR6 56 D6
SEV TN13 9 D2
Penderel Ms *TENT* TN30 230 B6
Penenden *HART* DA3 62 A6
Penenden Heath Rd
MAID/BEAR ME14 111 H7
Penenden St *MAID/BEAR* ME14 7 D1 1
Penfield La *RSIT* ME9 117 G2
Penfold Cl *MAID/SHEP* ME15 134 A8
WALD ME5 68 C7 2
Penfold Hl *RMAID* ME17 135 K6
Penfolds Cl *TONN* TN10 170 C1 1
Penfold Wy *MAID/SHEP* ME15 133 F8
Penguin Cl *STRD* ME2 48 C8 3
Penhurst Cl *MAID/BEAR* ME14 134 B1 4
Penlee Cl *EDEN* TN8 164 C4
Pennant Rd *ROCH* ME1 67 H7
Penn Cl *SIT* ME10 94 C4
Penney Cl *DART* DA1 23 G6
Pennine Wy *GVW* DA11 45 F1
MAID/SHEP ME15 134 C5 4
Pennington Pl *STH/RUST* TN4 190 B4
Pennington Rd *STH/RUST* TN4 190 A4
Penn La *RSEV* TN14 122 A6
Penns Yd *RTWE/PEM* TN2 191 J8
Pennyfields *CRBK* TN17 225 K2 3
Penshurst Cl *BGR/WK* TN15 80 D2 3
HART DA3 44 E7 1
RHAM ME8 70 A4
Penshurst Rd *RTON* TN11 167 K6
RTON TN11 188 B4
Penshurst Wy *STMC/STPC* BR5 56 D1 5
The Penstocks *MAIDW* ME16 6 A5
Pen Wy *TONN* TN10 170 E1
Pepingstraw Cl *E/WMAL* ME19 107 F7
Pepper Hl *GVW* DA11 44 D1
Pepys Cl *GVW* DA11 44 E1
Pepys Ri *ORP* BR6 56 A5
Pepy's Wy *STRD* ME2 48 E6
Perch La *RRTW* TN3 210 A5
Peregrine Dr *SIT* ME10 94 B3
Peregrine Rd *WBY/YAL* ME18 129 J4
Perimeter Rd *DIT/AY* ME20 109 G3
Periwinkle Cl *SIT* ME10 93 K1
Perkins Cl *GRH* DA9 24 E4
Perran Cl *HART* DA3 62 A1 3
Perryfield St *MAID/BEAR* ME14 6 C1
Perry Gv *DART* DA1 23 K3
Perry Hall Cl *ORP* BR6 56 B4
Perry Hall Rd *ORP* BR6 56 A3
Perry Hl *HOO/HM* ME3 31 H5
Perrys La *ORP* BR6 76 C8
Perry St *CHAT* ME4 3 E5
CHST BR7 38 A4
DART DA1 22 B2
GVW DA11 27 F7
MAID/BEAR ME14 6 C1
Perth Gdns *SIT* ME10 93 H2 1
Pescot Av *HART* DA3 44 B8
Pested Bars Rd *RMAID* ME17 155 J1
Peter Av *OXTED* RH8 118 B8
Petersfield *RTWE/PEM* TN2 192 A7
Petersham Dr *STMC/STPC* BR5 38 A7
Petersham Gdns
STMC/STPC BR5 38 A7 1
Petham Gn *RHAM* ME8 69 K4
Petten Cl *STMC/STPC* BR5 56 E5
Petten Gv *STMC/STPC* BR5 56 D5
Petteridge La *STPH/PW* TN12 193 G8
Pett La *RSIT* ME9 91 K6
Peverel Dr *MAID/BEAR* ME14 134 B1
Pheasant La *MAID/SHEP* ME15 133 H7
Pheasant Rd *CHAT* ME4 4 C6 3
Phelps Cl *BGR/WK* TN15 80 D2
Phillip Av *SWLY* BR8 58 A1
Phillippa Ct *SIT* ME10 73 K7
Phillips Cl *DART* DA1 22 E5
Phillips Ct *RHAM* ME8 69 J4
Philpots La *RTON* TN11 146 C8
Phoenix Dr *WBY/YAL* ME18 130 C8
Phoenix Pl *DART* DA1 23 G6
Phoenix Rd *WALD* ME5 88 C4
Pickering St *MAID/SHEP* ME15 133 G8
Pickforde La *WADH* TN5 232 C5
Pickle's Wy *HOO/HM* ME3 15 F8
Pickwick Crs *ROCH* ME1 2 C6
Pickwick Gdns *GVW* DA11 44 E1
Pier Approach Rd *GILL* ME7 5 D1
Pierce Mill La *RTON* TN11 172 D1
Pier Rd *GILL* ME7 5 D1
GRH DA9 25 G3
GVW DA11 27 G5
Pigdown La *EDEN* TN8 185 K2
Pigsdean Rd *MEO* DA13 64 E4
Pikefish La *STPH/PW* TN12 174 C5
Pikes La *LING* RH7 162 C5
Pikey La *E/WMAL* ME19 130 B1
Pile La *STPH/PW* TN12 198 C2
Pilgrims Ct *DART* DA1 23 K4
Pilgrims Lakes *RMAID* ME17 137 J8
Pilgrims La *OXTED* RH8 119 G3
Pilgrims Rd *STRD* ME2 65 J7
SWCM DA10 25 K3
Pilgrims Vw *GRH* DA9 25 H5
MAID/BEAR ME14 110 E3 1
Pilgrims Wy *BGR/WK* TN15 105 F2
DART DA1 24 A7
DIT/AY ME20 87 G8
E/WMAL ME19 83 G8
MAID/BEAR ME14 111 J2
RMAID ME17 136 D3
RMAID ME17 137 K7
ROCH ME1 86 D2
RSEV TN14 102 C3
SNOD ME6 84 E5
STRD ME2 66 B3
STRD ME2 85 G3
Pilgrims Wy East *RSEV* TN14 102 A3
Pilgrims Wy West *RSEV* TN14 101 H3
Pillar Box La *RTON* TN11 149 K1
Pillar Box Rd *BGR/WK* TN15 125 J1
Pilot Rd *ROCH* ME1 67 H6
Pilots Pl *GVE* DA12 27 K5
Pimpernel Cl *MAID/BEAR* ME14 134 D2 2
Pimpernel Wy *WALD* ME5 87 K2 1
Pinchbeck Rd *ORP* BR6 76 A2
Pincroft Wd *HART* DA3 62 D1
Pine Av *GVE* DA12 28 A7
Pine Cl *DIT/AY* ME20 108 E4
SWLY BR8 58 C1 2
Pine Gv *EDEN* TN8 164 B4
GILL ME7 89 H1
MAID/BEAR ME14 7 E1
Pinehurst *RSEV* TN14 102 C8
Pineneedle La *SEV* TN13 9 D2
Pine Pl *MAID/SHEP* ME15 6 B6
Pine Rdg *TONN* TN10 148 B8
Pine Ri *MEO* DA13 63 H3
Pine Rd *STRD* ME2 48 E8
Pinesfield La *E/WMAL* ME19 83 J8
Pine Tree La *BGR/WK* TN15 126 A4
Pine Vw *BGR/WK* TN15 105 J7 1
Pinewood Av *SEV* TN13 102 B8
Pinewood Cl *STPH/PW* TN12 173 H8
Pinewood Dr *MAID/BEAR* ME14 88 E6
ORP BR6 75 K1
Pinewood Gdns *STH/RUST* TN4 190 A5
Pinewood Rd *RTWE/PEM* TN2 11 F2 3
Pinkham *STPH/PW* TN12 173 J1

Pinks Hl SWLY BR8 58 B2
Pinnock La STPH/PW TN12 198 A5
Pinnock's Av GVW DA11 27 J7
Pintail Cl HOO/HM ME3 21 G8 3
The Pintails CHAT ME4 50 C5
Pioneer Wy SWLY BR8 40 B8
Piper's Green Rd BH/WHM TN16 121 G7
Pipers La BH/WHM TN16 121 H6
Pippin Cl RMAID ME17 154 B4
SIT ME10 73 J8 1
Pippin Cft GILL ME7 69 H8
Pippin Rd STPH/PW TN12 151 H8
The Pippins MEO DA13 63 H3
Pippin Wy WBY/YAL ME18 129 J4
Pirbright Cl WALD ME5 88 E4 4
Pirrip Cl GVE DA12 28 C7
Pitchfont La OXTED RH8 118 E5
Pitfield HART DA3 62 A1
Pitfield Dr MEO DA13 63 G7
Pit La EDEN TN8 164 C2
Pitstock Rd RSIT ME9 117 H2
Pittlesden TENT TN30 230 A7
Pitt Rd MAIDW ME16 132 B5
RMAID ME17 157 J4
Pivington La HDCN TN27 183 H4
Pixot Hl STPH/PW TN12 193 K5
Pix's La CRBK TN17 238 D3
Pizien Well Rd WBY/YAL ME18 129 J8
Place La RSIT ME9 91 G1
Plain Rd STPH/PW TN12 196 C3
Plains Av MAID/SHEP ME15 7 E6
Plane Av GVW DA11 26 E6
Plane Wk TONN TN10 148 C7
Plantation Dr STMC/STPC BR5 56 E5
Plantation La MAID/BEAR ME14 134 C2
Plantation Rd GILL ME7 51 H8
SWLY BR8 40 D5
Platt Common BGR/WK TN15 105 J7
The Platters RHAM ME8 69 K6
The Plat EDEN TN8 164 D5
RYE TN31 244 E8
Platt House La BGR/WK TN15 82 D8
The Platt RMAID ME17 157 G7
Plaxdale Green Rd BGR/WK TN15 81 J7
Plaxtol La BGR/WK TN15 126 C6
Playstool Cl RSIT ME9 72 A8
Playstool Rd RSIT ME9 71 K8
Pleasance Rd STMC/STPC BR5 38 C7
Pleasant Valley La
MAID/SHEP ME15 154 B2
Pleasant Vw ORP BR6 75 H1
Pleasure House Rd RMAID ME17 157 J7
Plomley Cl RHAM ME8 90 A2
Plough Hl BGR/WK TN15 127 F2
Ploughmans Wy RHAM ME8 70 B8
WALD ME5 88 B5
Plough Wents Rd RMAID ME17 156 E4
Plover Cl WALD ME5 88 E5
Plover Rd DIT/AY ME20 108 D4
Plowenders Cl E/WMAL ME19 107 F3
Pluckley Cl RHAM ME8 69 K3
Pluckley Rd HDCN TN27 202 B4
Plug La MEO DA13 84 A1
Plummer La TENT TN30 229 K8
Plumtree Gv GILL ME7 89 H2
Plum Tree La RSIT ME9 90 E6
Plumtree Rd HDCN TN27 179 J6
Plumtrees MAIDW ME16 132 A4
Plymouth Dr BGR/WK TN15 9 E3
Plymouth Pk BGR/WK TN15 9 E3
Poachers Cl WALD ME5 88 D1
Podkin Wd WALD ME5 88 A6
Polesden Rd RTWE/PEM TN2 11 F5 3
Polesteeple Hl BH/WHM TN16 97 H4
The Poles RSIT ME9 71 H2
Polhill RSEV TN14 100 E2
Polhill Dr WALD ME5 88 A4
Police Station Rd E/WMAL ME19 108 A6
Pollards Oak Crs OXTED RH8 140 E3
Pollards Oak Rd OXTED RH8 140 E3
Pollards Wood Hl OXTED RH8 140 E1
Pollards Wood Rd OXTED RH8 141 F2
Polley Cl RTWE/PEM TN2 191 K7
Pollyhaugh EYN DA4 59 H7
Polperro Cl ORP BR6 56 A3
Pond Dr SIT ME10 94 B4
Pond Farm Rd RMAID ME17 114 B5
RSIT ME9 92 E5
Pondfield La GVE DA12 47 H5
Pond Hl HOO/HM ME3 15 G8
Pond La BGR/WK TN15 125 J4
Pook La HDCN TN27 218 B2
Poona Rd RTWE/PEM TN2 11 D5
Pootings Rd EDEN TN8 142 D6
Poot La RSIT ME9 53 H8
Pope Dr STPH/PW TN12 198 A2
Pope House La TENT TN30 230 B2
Popes La OXTED RH8 140 D6
Pope St MAIDW ME16 132 C4
Poplar Av GVE DA12 45 K2
Poplar Cl HOO/HM ME3 51 F3
STRD ME2 66 E1
Poplar Gv MAIDW ME16 132 C1
Poplar Rd STRD ME2 66 D1
TENT TN30 247 J2
Poplars Cl HART DA3 44 D8
Poplar Wk MEO DA13 63 J3
Poplicans Rd STRD ME2 66 A3
Poppy Cl GILL ME7 5 E3
MAIDW ME16 6 A4 2
Porchester Cl HART DA3 62 A1
MAID/SHEP ME15 133 G8
Porchfield Cl GVE DA12 27 K8
Port Av GRH DA9 25 G5
Port Cl MAID/BEAR ME14 134 B1
WALD ME5 88 C3 4
Porters Cl STPH/PW TN12 193 H8
Porters Wk RMAID ME17 157 G2
Port Hl ORP BR6 76 C7
Portland Av GVE DA12 27 J8
SIT ME10 94 D2
Portland Pl SNOD ME6 85 K6 5
Portland Rd GILL ME7 5 E2
GVW DA11 26 E5
ROCH ME1 86 B2
Portland St CHAT ME4 4 B6
Portman Cl BXLY DA5 22 B7
Portman Pk TON TN9 170 C3
Port Ri CHAT ME4 3 F5
Portsdown Cl MAIDW ME16 132 B4 3
Portsmouth Cl STRD ME2 48 C8
Port Victoria Rd HOO/HM ME3 37 H3
Portway Rd HOO/HM ME3 31 G6
Post Barn Rd CHAT ME4 3 F6
Postern La TON TN9 170 D4
TON TN9 171 F6
Postley Rd MAID/SHEP ME15 7 D6
Postmill Dr MAID/SHEP ME15 6 C6
Post Office Rd HAWK TN18 235 F4 2
Potash La BGR/WK TN15 105 J8
Pot Kiln La RASHW TN26 219 J3
Potter's La HAWK TN18 225 G8
Pottery Rd HOO/HM ME3 50 E1
Poulters Wd HAYES BR2 74 C1
Pound Bank Cl BGR/WK TN15 80 E4 5
Poundfield Rd HAWK TN18 243 J1
Pound La RSEV TN14 99 K2
SEV TN13 9 E3
Pound Rd STPH/PW TN12 151 G8
Poundsbridge Hl RRTW TN3 188 B8
Pounsley Rd SEV TN13 101 G8
Pout Rd SNOD ME6 85 J7
Poverest Rd STMC/STPC BR5 56 A2
Povey Av STRD ME2 49 H4
Powdermill Cl RTWE/PEM TN2 190 C6 1
Powder Mill La DART DA1 23 H8
RTON TN11 168 E4
STH/RUST TN4 190 B7
Powell Cl DIT/AY ME20 110 A3
Powerscroft Rd SCUP DA14 38 D4
Powlett Rd STRD ME2 49 H5
Poynings Cl ORP BR6 56 D6 3
Poyntell Rd STPH/PW TN12 198 B2
Prall's La STPH/PW TN12 193 G4
Pratling St DIT/AY ME20 110 B3
Premier Pl DIT/AY ME20 109 J5
Prentis Cl SIT ME10 93 H1
Prentis Quay SIT ME10 93 K1 2
Prestley Dr TONN TN10 148 D7
Preston Av GILL ME7 69 F5
Preston Rd GVW DA11 27 F7
TON TN9 170 A5
Pretoria Rd CHAT ME4 3 F6 6
GILL ME7 5 D5
Prettymans La EDEN TN8 165 G3
Pridmore Rd SNOD ME6 85 J6 1
Priestfield Rd GILL ME7 5 E3
Priestfields ROCH ME1 2 B6
Priest Hl OXTED RH8 119 F8
Priestlands Park Rd BFN/LL DA15 38 A1
Priestley Dr DIT/AY ME20 108 D2
Priestwood Rd MEO DA13 83 J2
Primrose Av RHAM ME8 89 J1
Primrose Cl ROCH ME1 67 K7
Primrose Dr DIT/AY ME20 109 H6
Primrose La RSIT ME9 93 F8
Primrose Rd STRD ME2 85 H1
Primrose Wk STPH/PW TN12 193 J1
Prince Arthur Rd GILL ME7 4 B2
Prince Charles Av EYN DA4 42 C7
SIT ME10 94 C4
WALD ME5 88 C2
Princes Av RDART DA2 24 A7
WALD ME5 68 D7
Princes Cl SCUP DA14 38 E1
Princes Rd DART DA1 22 E6
GVE DA12 45 K2
RDART DA2 24 B7
SWLY BR8 40 D4
Princess Mary Av CHAT ME4 4 B1
Princes St GVW DA11 27 J5
MAID/BEAR ME14 7 D2 4
ROCH ME1 2 C5
RTWE/PEM TN2 11 E4 6
Princes Vw DART DA1 23 K7
Princes Wy MAID/BEAR ME14 112 C5
Prinys Dr RHAM ME8 89 K2
Priorsdean Cl MAIDW ME16 131 J5
Priorsford Av STMC/STPC BR5 56 B1
Prior's Wy EDEN TN8 185 G8 1
Priory Cl DART DA1 23 F4
MAID/SHEP ME15 132 B6
Priory Flds EYN DA4 59 J6
Priory Gdns DART DA1 23 G4
Priory Gv DIT/AY ME20 109 H5
TON TN9 170 B6
Priory Hl DART DA1 23 G5
Priory La EYN DA4 59 J5
Priory Pl DART DA1 23 G5
Priory Rd DART DA1 23 G3
MAID/SHEP ME15 7 D4
RHAM ME8 69 H4
STRD ME2 2 A2
TON TN9 170 C6
Priory St TON TN9 170 B6
Priory Wk TON TN9 170 B6
Priory Wy TENT TN30 230 C7
Pristling La STPH/PW TN12 197 H6
Prospect Av STRD ME2 49 G6
Prospect Gv GVE DA12 28 A6
Prospect Pk STH/RUST TN4 189 K5
Prospect Pl DART DA1 23 H5
GVE DA12 28 A6
MAIDW ME16 6 B4
Prospect Rd RTWE/PEM TN2 11 D4
SEV TN13 9 E2
STH/RUST TN4 189 K5
Prospect Rw CHAT ME4 4 A5
GILL ME7 4 A2
Provender Wy MAID/BEAR ME14 134 A2
Providence La ROCH ME1 2 C3 4
Providence St GRH DA9 25 F4
Puddingcake La CRBK TN17 239 G1
Pudding La MAID/BEAR ME14 6 C3 4
Pudding Rd RHAM ME8 70 C6 2
Puddledock La BH/WHM TN16 143 G3
RDART DA2 40 B3
Puffin Rd HOO/HM ME3 37 G1 1
Pump Cl E/WMAL ME19 108 B5
Pump La GILL ME7 70 A3
RHAM ME8 69 K4
Punch Cft HART DA3 61 K7
Purbeck Rd CHAT ME4 3 E6
Purcell Av TONN TN10 149 F8
Purfleet By-pass PUR RM19 13 G5
Purfleet Rd SOCK/AV RM15 13 F1
Purser Wy GILL ME7 4 C1
Puttenden Rd RTON TN11 149 F4
Pyrus Cl WALD ME5 88 B6

Q

The Quadrant PUR RM19 13 G4
Quaker Cl SEV TN13 9 F2
Quaker Dr CRBK TN17 214 E8
Quaker La CRBK TN17 214 E8
Quakers Cl HART DA3 44 A8
Quaker's Hall La SEV TN13 9 E1
Quantock Cl RTWE/PEM TN2 11 F2
Quantock Rd BXLYHN DA7 22 B1 1
Quarry Bank TON TN9 170 A7
Quarry Cl OXTED RH8 140 C1
Quarry Hl BGR/WK TN15 9 F2
Quarry Hill Rd BGR/WK TN15 104 E8
STH/RUST TN4 170 A8
TON TN9 170 A7
Quarry Ms PUR RM19 12 E4
Quarry Ri TON TN9 170 A7
Quarry Rd MAID/SHEP ME15 7 D5
OXTED RH8 140 C1
RMAID ME17 155 J2
RTW TN1 11 D2
Quarry Sq MAID/BEAR ME14 7 D2
Quarry Wy WTHK RM20 13 K6
Quay La GRH DA9 25 G3
Quayside CHAT ME4 50 C6
Quebec Av BH/WHM TN16 120 D5
Quebec Rd TIL RM18 27 H1
Quebec Sq BH/WHM TN16 120 D5
Queen Anne Rd MAID/BEAR ME14 7 E3 3
Queendown Av RHAM ME8 90 A1
Queen Elizabeth Ii Br GRH DA9 24 D1
Queen Elizabeth Sq
MAID/SHEP ME15 133 K8
The Queen Mother Ct ROCH ME1 2 B4 4
Queen's Av MAIDW ME16 6 A2
SNOD ME6 85 K6
Queens Ct HAWK TN18 235 G4
Queen's Dr RSEV TN14 102 A7
Queen's Farm Rd GVE DA12 29 H8
Queens Gdns RDART DA2 24 A7
STH/RUST TN4 11 D1
Queen's Rd GILL ME7 4 C4
GVE DA12 45 K1
HAWK TN18 235 G4
MAIDW ME16 132 B3
SNOD ME6 85 K6
STH/RUST TN4 11 D1
WALD ME5 68 E5
Queen St CHAT ME4 4 A4
GVE DA12 27 J5
HAWK TN18 236 D8
ROCH ME1 2 C4 6

STPH/PW TN12 .... 194 A1
Queensway *HOO/HM* ME3 .... 19 G5
Queens Wy *MAID/BEAR* ME14 .... 112 C5
Queenswood Rd *DIT/AY* ME20 .... 87 J7
The Quern *MAID/SHEP* ME15 .... 6 B6 1
Quested Wy *RMAID* ME17 .... 137 G8
Quickbourne La *RYE* TN31 .... 245 F7
Quickrells Av *HOO/HM* ME3 .... 31 G1
Quickthorn Crs *WALD* ME5 .... 87 K1
Quilter Rd *STMC/STPC* BR5 .... 56 D5
Quincewood Gdns *TONN* TN10 .... 148 B7
Quinion Cl *WALD* ME5 .... 88 A6
Quinnell St *RHAM* ME8 .... 70 B5
Quinton Rd *RSIT* ME9 .... 73 H7
Quixote Crs *STRD* ME2 .... 49 G5

R

Rabbits Rd *EYN* DA4 .... 42 E7
Racefield Cl *GVE* DA12 .... 47 H4
Radleigh Gdns *CHAT* ME4 .... 67 K5 2
Raeburn Av *DART* DA1 .... 22 E4
Raeburn Cl *TONN* TN10 .... 148 E8 1
Ragge Wy *BGR/WK* TN15 .... 102 D7
Rag Hill Rd *BH/WHM* TN16 .... 97 H8
Ragstone Ct *DIT/AY* ME20 .... 109 G6
Ragstone Rd *MAID/SHEP* ME15 .... 134 C4
Railway Ap *TON* TN9 .... 170 B6
Railway Pl *GVE* DA12 .... 27 J5 13
Railway St *CHAT* ME4 .... 3 F4
GILL ME7 .... 5 D3
GVW DA11 .... 26 B4
Railway Ter *BH/WHM* TN16 .... 120 D4
Rainham Rd *GILL* ME7 .... 4 C5
Raleigh Cl *WALD* ME5 .... 68 B8
Raleigh Ms *ORP* BR6 .... 76 A1 2
Ramillies Cl *WALD* ME5 .... 88 B1
Rammell Ms *CRBK* TN17 .... 225 K2
Rampion Cl *MAID/BEAR* ME14 .... 134 A1
Ramsden Cl *STMC/STPC* BR5 .... 56 D5 2
Ramsden La *CRBK* TN17 .... 237 H2
Ramsden Rd *ORP* BR6 .... 56 C4
STMC/STPC BR5 .... 56 D5
Ramslye Rd *STH/RUST* TN4 .... 206 C5
Ramus Wood Av *ORP* BR6 .... 75 K1
Randall Hill Rd *BGR/WK* TN15 .... 105 F3
Randall Rd *CHAT* ME4 .... 67 K5
Randall St *MAID/BEAR* ME14 .... 6 C1
Randle's La *ORP* BR6 .... 99 K1
Randolph Rd *GILL* ME7 .... 4 C3
Ranelagh Gdns *GVW* DA11 .... 27 G6
Range Rd *GVE* DA12 .... 28 A6
Rangeworth Pl *BFN/LL* DA15 .... 38 A1 1
Rankine Rd *RTWE/PEM* TN2 .... 190 D7
Ranmore Pth *STMC/STPC* BR5 .... 56 B1
Ranscombe Cl *STRD* ME2 .... 66 C1
Ranters La *CRBK* TN17 .... 222 E2
Ranworth Cl *ERITH* DA8 .... 22 B1
Raphael Rd *GVE* DA12 .... 28 A6
Rapier Cl *PUR* RM19 .... 12 D4
Rashleigh Wy *EYN* DA4 .... 60 B1
Raspberry Hill La *RSIT* ME9 .... 55 H8
Ratcliffe Hwy *HOO/HM* ME3 .... 33 H4
Rathmore Rd *GVW* DA11 .... 27 H6
Raven Cl *DIT/AY* ME20 .... 108 E5 6
Ravensbourne Rd *DART* DA1 .... 22 D2
Ravensbury Rd *STMC/STPC* BR5 .... 56 A1
Ravenscourt Rd *STMC/STPC* BR5 .... 38 B8
Ravens Dane Cl
MAID/SHEP ME15 .... 134 C5 5
Ravenswood Av *RTW* TN1 .... 11 E1
STRD ME2 .... 49 G6
Rawdon Rd *MAID/SHEP* ME15 .... 7 D4
Rawlings Cl *ORP* BR6 .... 76 A1
Rawling St *RSIT* ME9 .... 117 F2
Rayfield Ct *SNOD* ME6 .... 85 K5
Rayford Cl *DART* DA1 .... 23 F4
Rayleigh Cl *MAIDW* ME16 .... 110 D7 3
Raymer Rd *MAID/BEAR* ME14 .... 111 H6
Rayners Hl *RMAID* ME17 .... 139 J8
Rays Hl *EYN* DA4 .... 60 B1
Reader's Bridge Rd *TENT* TN30 .... 229 K2
Reading St *TENT* TN30 .... 241 H3
Readscroft Rd *RHAM* ME8 .... 90 A1
Read Wy *GVE* DA12 .... 46 A3
Recreation Av *SNOD* ME6 .... 85 K6 6
Recreation Cl *MAID/BEAR* ME14 .... 7 E1
Recreation Ground Rd *TENT* TN30 .... 230 B7
Rectory Cl *DART* DA1 .... 22 B3
ROCH ME1 .... 86 B1
SCUP DA14 .... 38 C2
SNOD ME6 .... 85 K6
Rectory Dr *STH/RUST* TN4 .... 189 G3
Rectory Flds *CRBK* TN17 .... 225 K1 2
Rectory Gra *ROCH* ME1 .... 2 C6 2
Rectory La *BGR/WK* TN15 .... 126 C1
BH/WHM TN16 .... 119 J2
BH/WHM TN16 .... 121 J3
MAIDW ME16 .... 132 A5
RMAID ME17 .... 156 E8
RMAID ME17 .... 157 G7
RMAID ME17 .... 159 J1
SCUP DA14 .... 38 C2
SEV TN13 .... 9 D5
Rectory La North *E/WMAL* ME19 .... 108 B4
Rectory La South *E/WMAL* ME19 .... 108 C4
Rectory Meadow *MEO* DA13 .... 44 B4
Rectory Park Rd *STPH/PW* TN12 .... 211 K4
Rectory Rd *BGR/WK* TN15 .... 82 D1
HAYES BR2 .... 74 C3
HOO/HM ME3 .... 31 F4
SIT ME10 .... 94 C3
SWCM DA10 .... 25 K6
Redbank *E/WMAL* ME19 .... 108 C4
Redbridge Cl *WALD* ME5 .... 88 D1 1
Redcliffe La *MAID/BEAR* ME14 .... 111 H7
Redding Cl *RDART* DA2 .... 24 D8
Rede Court Rd *STRD* ME2 .... 48 D6
Rede Wood Rd *MAIDW* ME16 .... 131 J3
Redfern Av *GILL* ME7 .... 5 E3
Red Hl *WBY/YAL* ME18 .... 130 C6
Redhill Rd *BGR/WK* TN15 .... 61 K8
Redhill Wd *HART* DA3 .... 62 B8
Red House Gdns *WBY/YAL* ME18 .... 130 B7
Redhouse Rd *BH/WHM* TN16 .... 97 G8
Redland Shaw *CHAT* ME4 .... 67 K5
Redlands Rd *SEV* TN13 .... 8 B3
Red La *OXTED* RH8 .... 141 F7
Redleaf Cl *RTWE/PEM* TN2 .... 11 F1
Red Lion Cl *STMC/STPC* BR5 .... 56 D3
Red Lodge Crs *BXLY* DA5 .... 40 A1
Red Lodge Rd *BXLY* DA5 .... 40 A1
Redmans La *RSEV* TN14 .... 78 C2
Red Oak *HAWK* TN18 .... 234 E6
Redpoll Wk *STPH/PW* TN12 .... 193 J1
Redsells Cl *MAID/SHEP* ME15 .... 134 C5 3
Redshank Rd *CHAT* ME4 .... 50 B5
Red St *MEO* DA13 .... 44 C4
Redvers Rd *CHAT* ME4 .... 4 A6
Redwall La *RMAID* ME17 .... 154 B7
Redwell La *BGR/WK* TN15 .... 126 B2
Redwing Rd *WALD* ME5 .... 68 C8
Redwings La *RTWE/PEM* TN2 .... 191 K4
Redwood Cl *WALD* ME5 .... 88 C4
Redwood Pk *RTON* TN11 .... 192 C1
Reedham Crs *HOO/HM* ME3 .... 31 H7
Reeds La *RTON* TN11 .... 148 E1
Reed St *HOO/HM* ME3 .... 15 G8
Reeves Cl *STPH/PW* TN12 .... 198 A2
Reeves Ct *DIT/AY* ME20 .... 108 E5
Reeves Cresent *SWLY* BR8 .... 40 A8
Reeves Ter *WADH* TN5 .... 232 C5 2
Reform Rd *CHAT* ME4 .... 4 B5
Regency Cl *BGR/WK* TN15 .... 80 D2
RHAM ME8 .... 89 K3
Regency Ct *SIT* ME10 .... 93 J2
Regent Dr *MAID/SHEP* ME15 .... 133 G6
Regent Rd *GILL* ME7 .... 4 B4
Regents Dr *HAYES* BR2 .... 74 C1
Regent St *CRBK* TN17 .... 238 C3
Reginald Av *STRD* ME2 .... 66 B3
Reginald Rd *MAIDW* ME16 .... 6 B4
Reinden Gv *MAID/SHEP* ME15 .... 134 B5
Rembrandt Cl *TONN* TN10 .... 148 E8
Rembrandt Dr *GVW* DA11 .... 44 E1
Renown Rd *WALD* ME5 .... 88 D4
Renton Dr *STMC/STPC* BR5 .... 56 E4
Repton Rd *ORP* BR6 .... 56 B8
Repton Wy *WALD* ME5 .... 88 A2
Resolution Cl *WALD* ME5 .... 88 B1
Restharrow Rd *MAID/BEAR* ME14 .... 134 A2
The Retreat *ORP* BR6 .... 76 C2
Revenge Rd *MAID/BEAR* ME14 .... 88 D6
WALD ME5 .... 88 D5
Reynolds Cl *TONN* TN10 .... 148 E8
Reynolds Flds *HOO/HM* ME3 .... 30 B8
Reynolds La *STH/RUST* TN4 .... 10 B1
Rhode St *CHAT* ME4 .... 3 F4 3
Rhodewood Cl *MAID/SHEP* ME15 .... 134 C5
Rhododendron Av *MEO* DA13 .... 83 H3
Ribblesdale Rd *RDART* DA2 .... 24 B7
Ribston Gdns *STPH/PW* TN12 .... 173 G7
Richard's Cl *RTON* TN11 .... 167 H4
Richardson Cl *GRH* DA9 .... 24 E4
Richardson Rd *STH/RUST* TN4 .... 10 C1
Richard St *CHAT* ME4 .... 3 F4
ROCH ME1 .... 2 C5
Richborough Cl *STMC/STPC* BR5 .... 56 E1 8
Richborough Dr *STRD* ME2 .... 49 F5
Richmond Cl *BH/WHM* TN16 .... 97 F6 1
STRD ME2 .... 50 A5 3
WALD ME5 .... 88 C2 3
Richmond Dr *SIT* ME10 .... 73 K7
Richmond Rd *GILL* ME7 .... 4 C2
Richmond Wy *MAID/SHEP* ME15 .... 133 G6
Ricketts Hill Rd *BH/WHM* TN16 .... 97 H5
Riddlesdale Av *STH/RUST* TN4 .... 10 C1
Riddles Rd *SIT* ME10 .... 93 H3
Ridge Av *DART* DA1 .... 22 C5
Ridgelands *RRTW* TN3 .... 189 G2
Ridge La *MEO* DA13 .... 83 H3
The Ridge *CTHM* CR3 .... 118 C4
Ridge Wy *DART* DA1 .... 22 C5
EDEN TN8 .... 164 C2
Ridgeway *RDART* DA2 .... 42 D3
RTWE/PEM TN2 .... 191 K7 4
Ridgeway Av *GVE* DA12 .... 45 J1
Ridgeway Crs *TONN* TN10 .... 170 D2
The Ridgewaye *STH/RUST* TN4 .... 190 A5
The Ridgeway *CHAT* ME4 .... 67 K7
GILL ME7 .... 4 C1 5
GVE DA12 .... 47 H5
TON TN9 .... 170 D2
Ridgewood *MEO* DA13 .... 44 D6
Ridgway *MAIDW* ME16 .... 132 B4
Riding La *RTON* TN11 .... 147 H7
Riding Pk *RTON* TN11 .... 147 H7
The Ridings *BH/WHM* TN16 .... 97 J4
RTWE/PEM TN2 .... 191 F8
STPH/PW TN12 .... 173 J7
Ridlands Gv *OXTED* RH8 .... 141 J1
Ridlands La *OXTED* RH8 .... 141 J1
Ridlands Ri *OXTED* RH8 .... 141 J1
Ridley Rd *ROCH* ME1 .... 2 B4
Ringden Av *STPH/PW* TN12 .... 193 G1
Ringlestone Crs
MAID/BEAR ME14 .... 111 F6 1
Ringlestone Rd *RMAID* ME17 .... 137 G2
Ringshall Rd *CHST* BR7 .... 38 B8
Rings Hl *RTON* TN11 .... 168 E2
Ringwood Av *ORP* BR6 .... 76 D5
Ringwood Cl *RHAM* ME8 .... 70 A6 1
Ringwood Rd *MAID/SHEP* ME15 .... 133 J6
Ripon Cl *RHAM* ME8 .... 70 A3 1
Risden La *HAWK* TN18 .... 235 J7
The Rise *DART* DA1 .... 22 C3
GILL ME7 .... 89 H3
GVE DA12 .... 46 B2
ROCH ME1 .... 3 D5
RSIT ME9 .... 93 G4
SEV TN13 .... 124 A7
Ritch Rd *SNOD* ME6 .... 85 H7
River Cl *MAID/SHEP* ME15 .... 132 A7
River Dr *STRD* ME2 .... 48 D7
Riverhead Cl *MAIDW* ME16 .... 6 A1
SIT ME10 .... 93 H3
Riverhill *SEV* TN13 .... 146 C2
River Lawn Rd *TON* TN9 .... 170 B5
River Park Vw *ORP* BR6 .... 56 C4
Rivers Cl *WBY/YAL* ME18 .... 130 C7
Riversdale *GVW* DA11 .... 27 F8
Riverside *EDEN* TN8 .... 164 C5
EYN DA4 .... 59 G6
Riverside Cl *STMC/STPC* BR5 .... 38 D7
Riverside Rd *SCUP* DA14 .... 39 F1
Riverside Wy *DART* DA1 .... 23 H4
River St *GILL* ME7 .... 4 A2
River Vw *GILL* ME7 .... 70 A3
MAID/SHEP ME15 .... 6 C5
Riverview Rd *GRH* DA9 .... 25 F4
River Wk *TON* TN9 .... 170 B5
River Wy *DIT/AY* ME20 .... 108 E2
Roach St *STRD* ME2 .... 2 A1
Roan Ct *STRD* ME2 .... 48 E6 1
Roberts Cl *SIT* ME10 .... 73 J7
STMC/STPC BR5 .... 56 D2
Roberts Orchard Rd
MAIDW ME16 .... 131 J3
Roberts Rd *RHAM* ME8 .... 70 B6
SNOD ME6 .... 85 J6
Robin Hood Gn *STMC/STPC* BR5 .... 56 B2
Robin Hood La *WALD* ME5 .... 87 J5
Robin Hood Lane (Lower)
WALD ME5 .... 87 K5
Robin Hood Lane (Upper)
WALD ME5 .... 87 K5
Robinia Av *GVW* DA11 .... 26 E6
Robins Av *RMAID* ME17 .... 160 C2
Robins Cl *RMAID* ME17 .... 160 C2
Robin Wy *STMC/STPC* BR5 .... 38 C8
Robson Dr *DIT/AY* ME20 .... 109 H4
HOO/HM ME3 .... 50 E1
Robyns Cft *GVW* DA11 .... 45 F1
Robyns Wy *EDEN* TN8 .... 164 D6
SEV TN13 .... 8 B1
Rocfort Rd *SNOD* ME6 .... 85 K6
Rochdale Rd *RTW* TN1 .... 11 E1
Rochester Av *ROCH* ME1 .... 2 C4
Rochester Crs *HOO/HM* ME3 .... 32 E8
Rochester Rd *DART* DA1 .... 23 K6
DIT/AY ME20 .... 110 A3
GVE DA12 .... 28 C8
ROCH ME1 .... 86 D3
STRD ME2 .... 66 C3
TONN TN10 .... 170 D2
WALD ME5 .... 87 H2
Rochester St *CHAT* ME4 .... 3 E6
Rochester Wy *DART* DA1 .... 22 B6
Rock Av *GILL* ME7 .... 4 C5
Rockfield Cl *OXTED* RH8 .... 140 D2
Rockfield Rd *OXTED* RH8 .... 140 D1
Rock Hl *ORP* BR6 .... 77 J2
Rock Hill Rd *HDCN* TN27 .... 182 E4
Rock Rd *BGR/WK* TN15 .... 105 F7
MAID/BEAR ME14 .... 111 G7
SIT ME10 .... 93 K2
Rocks Cl *E/WMAL* ME19 .... 108 E8
Rocks Hl *CRBK* TN17 .... 215 G5
The Rocks Rd *E/WMAL* ME19 .... 108 E8
Rock Villa Rd *RTW* TN1 .... 10 C3
Rodmell Rd *RTWE/PEM* TN2 .... 10 C6
Rodney Av *TONN* TN10 .... 170 E2

Roebuck Rd *ROCH* ME1 2 C3
Roedean Cl *ORP* BR6 56 C8
Roedean Rd *RTWE/PEM* TN2 10 C6
Roehampton Cl *GVE* DA12 28 B6
Roffen Rd *ROCH* ME1 2 C6
Rogers Ct *SWLY* BR8 58 D1 2
Rogersmead *TENT* TN30 229 K7
Rogers Rough Rd *CRBK* TN17 222 E3
Rogers Wood La *BGR/WK* TN15 61 F8
Rogues Hl *RTON* TN11 187 K2
Rollo Rd *SWLY* BR8 40 C5
Rolvenden Av *RHAM* ME8 69 K3
Rolvenden Dr *SIT* ME10 93 G1
Rolvenden Hl *CRBK* TN17 239 F1
Rolvenden Rd *STRD* ME2 49 H4
Roman Cl *WALD* ME5 87 J5
Roman Hts *MAID/BEAR* ME14 111 J7
Roman Rd *EDEN* TN8 184 D1
GVW DA11 44 D1
RDART DA2 25 G8
SNOD ME6 85 J6
Roman Sq *SIT* ME10 94 A3
Roman Villa Rd *EYN* DA4 42 B4
Roman Wy *DART* DA1 22 B4
STRD ME2 66 E2
Romany Rd *RHAM* ME8 69 J4
Romden Rd *HDCN* TN27 202 E4
Romford Rd *RTWE/PEM* TN2 192 A7
Romney Cl *MAID/SHEP* ME15 134 C3
Romney Ct *SIT* ME10 93 J1
Romney Pl *MAID/SHEP* ME15 7 D3
Romney Rd *GVW* DA11 45 F1
WALD ME5 88 C1
Romney Wy *TONN* TN10 170 E1
Romsey Cl *STRD* ME2 48 D6
Ronfearn Av *STMC/STPC* BR5 56 E2
Roodlands La *EDEN* TN8 143 K8
Rookery Cl *RSIT* ME9 93 F8
Rookery Crs *HOO/HM* ME3 15 G8
Rookery Gdns *STMC/STPC* BR5 56 D2
Rookery Rd *ORP* BR6 74 E5
Rookesley Rd *STMC/STPC* BR5 56 E4
Rook La *RSIT* ME9 72 E8
Rookley Cl *RTWE/PEM* TN2 11 F5 4
Rooks Hl *BGR/WK* TN15 125 G8
Roonagh Ct *SIT* ME10 93 K4
Roopers *RRTW* TN3 188 E7
Roosevelt Av *WALD* ME5 68 A7
Ropemakers Ct *CHAT* ME4 68 B5
Roper Cl *RHAM* ME8 89 K3
Roper's Green La *HOO/HM* ME3 33 H6
Roper's La *HOO/HM* ME3 33 G6
Rope Wk *CHAT* ME4 4 A4 4
Ropewalk *CRBK* TN17 225 J1
The Rope Wk *HAWK* TN18 243 J1
Roseacre *OXTED* RH8 140 E4
Roseacre Gdns
MAID/BEAR ME14 134 C3 1
Roseacre La *MAID/BEAR* ME14 134 C3
Rose Av *GVE* DA12 28 B7
Rose Bank Cl *MAID/SHEP* ME15 7 E3
Rosebank Gdns *GVW* DA11 27 F7
Roseberry Gdns *DART* DA1 23 F6
Rosebery Cl *SIT* ME10 94 E2
Rosebery Ct *GVW* DA11 27 G7
Rosebery Rd *CHAT* ME4 3 E6
GILL ME7 5 D1
Rosecroft Cl *BH/WHM* TN16 97 K5 1
STMC/STPC BR5 56 D3
Rosedale Cl *RDART* DA2 24 A6
Rosedene Cl *DART* DA1 23 F6
Rosefield *SEV* TN13 8 C3
Rosegarth *MEO* DA13 45 F6
Rosehill Rd *BH/WHM* TN16 97 G4
Rosehill Wk *RTW* TN1 10 C4 4
Roseholme *MAIDW* ME16 6 A5
Rose La *RMAID* ME17 161 H5
Roselare Cl *BH/WHM* TN16 120 D4
Roseleigh Av *MAIDW* ME16 132 C2
Roseleigh Rd *SIT* ME10 93 J5
Rosemary Cl *OXTED* RH8 140 E4 2
Rosemary La *BGR/WK* TN15 82 E4
HDCN TN27 201 J1
WADH TN5 232 E1
Rosemary Rd *E/WMAL* ME19 108 D5
MAID/SHEP ME15 134 C3 2
Rosemount Cl *MAID/SHEP* ME15 155 F2
Rosemount Ct *STRD* ME2 49 F5 2
Rosenheath Cl *ORP* BR6 76 C3
Rose St *GVW* DA11 26 C5
ROCH ME1 3 D5
TON TN9 170 C6
Rosewood *RDART* DA2 40 B2
Rosewood Cl *SCUP* DA14 38 D1 1
Rose Yd *MAID/BEAR* ME14 7 D3 6
Rosherville Wy *GVW* DA11 27 F6
Rossdale *RTWE/PEM* TN2 11 E2
Rossell Rd *TIL* RM18 27 G1 4
Rosslyn Gn *MAIDW* ME16 132 B1 4
Ross Rd *DART* DA1 22 D5
Ross St *ROCH* ME1 3 D4
Rothermere Cl *CRBK* TN17 227 G8
Rother Rd *TONN* TN10 170 B1
Rother V *WALD* ME5 88 D2
Rothley Cl *TENT* TN30 230 B6
Rouge La *GVE* DA12 27 J7
Roughetts Rd *E/WMAL* ME19 107 H3
Roughway La *RTON* TN11 127 H8
Round Ash Wy *HART* DA3 61 K3
The Roundel *SIT* ME10 93 K4
Roundel Wy *STPH/PW* TN12 196 C1
Roundhay *E/WMAL* ME19 108 B5
Roundhill Rd *RTWE/PEM* TN2 11 F6
Roundlyn Gdns *STMC/STPC* BR5 56 C1
Round St *MEO* DA13 45 K8
Roundwell *MAID/BEAR* ME14 135 F2
Round Wood Cl *WALD* ME5 88 B5
Rover Rd *WALD* ME5 88 C4
Rowan Cl *DIT/AY* ME20 109 J5 1
MEO DA13 63 J3
STPH/PW TN12 193 H1
Rowan Crs *DART* DA1 23 F7
Rowan Lea *WALD* ME5 68 C6
Rowan Rd *SWLY* BR8 40 A8
Rowans Cl *HART* DA3 43 J7
Rowan Shaw *TONN* TN10 148 D8
The Rowans *SOCK/AV* RM15 13 G1 4
Rowan Tree Rd *RTWE/PEM* TN2 10 A6 2
Rowbrocke Cl *RHAM* ME8 90 A3
Rowdow La *RSEV* TN14 102 B3
Rowhill Rd *RDART* DA2 40 D3
Rowland Av *GILL* ME7 69 F5
Rowland Cl *WALD* ME5 69 F5
Rowlatt Cl *RDART* DA2 41 F2
Rowley Hl *RTWE/PEM* TN2 191 K5
Rowmarsh Cl *GVW* DA11 44 E1
Rowzill Rd *SWLY* BR8 40 C4
Royal Av *TON* TN9 170 C6
Royal Cha *STH/RUST* TN4 10 B3
Royal Eagle Cl *STRD* ME2 3 E1
Royal Engineers' Rd
MAID/BEAR ME14 6 C1
Royal Pier Rd *GVE* DA12 27 J5
Royal Rd *RDART* DA2 41 K3
SCUP DA14 38 E1
Royal Sovereign Av *CHAT* ME4 4 B1
Royal West Kent Av *TONN* TN10 170 D2
Roydon Hall Rd *WBY/YAL* ME18 151 G1
Royston Rd *DART* DA1 22 C5
MAID/SHEP ME15 134 C3
Roystons Cl *RHAM* ME8 70 C4
Royton Av *RMAID* ME17 160 D1
Ruckinge Wy *RHAM* ME8 69 K3
Ruck La *STPH/PW* TN12 211 H3
Rudge Cl *WALD* ME5 88 E4
Rugby Cl *WALD* ME5 88 A2
Ruggles Cl *HOO/HM* ME3 33 F3
Ruins Barn Rd *RSIT* ME9 116 C2
SIT ME10 93 K6
Rumstead La *MAID/BEAR* ME14 114 A4
RSIT ME9 114 B1
Rumstead Rd *RSIT* ME9 114 B2
Runciman Cl *ORP* BR6 76 D5
Runham La *RMAID* ME17 159 J3
Rural V *GVW* DA11 27 F6
Ruscombe Cl *STH/RUST* TN4 189 K4 1
Rush Cl *WALD* ME5 88 B3
Rushdean Rd *STRD* ME2 66 C1
Rushdene Wk *BH/WHM* TN16 97 H4
Rushet Rd *STMC/STPC* BR5 38 B7
Rushetts *RRTW* TN3 205 J2
Rushetts Rd *BGR/WK* TN15 80 C3
Rushford Cl *HDCN* TN27 200 A1
Rushfords *LING* RH7 162 C8
Rushmead Dr *MAID/SHEP* ME15 133 G7
Rushmere Ct *BGR/WK* TN15 104 D7
Rushmore Hl *ORP* BR6 76 D5
RSEV TN14 99 K1
Rushymead *BGR/WK* TN15 102 E5
Ruskin Cl *E/WMAL* ME19 108 D6 3
Ruskin Gv *DART* DA1 23 K4
Russell Cl *DART* DA1 22 D2
SIT ME10 93 H3
Russell Ct *CHAT* ME4 4 B5
Russell Pl *EYN* DA4 41 K6
Russell Rd *DIT/AY* ME20 87 H7
GVE DA12 28 A5
Russells Av *RHAM* ME8 70 D6
Russet Cl *STRD* ME2 48 D6
The Russets *MAIDW* ME16 132 B1 5
MEO DA13 63 H3
Russett Cl *DIT/AY* ME20 109 J6
ORP BR6 76 C1
Russett Rd *STPH/PW* TN12 151 H8
Russett Wy *SWLY* BR8 40 A7
Russet Wy *E/WMAL* ME19 129 H4
Rusthall Gra *STH/RUST* TN4 206 C2 1
Rusthall High St *STH/RUST* TN4 206 A2
Rusthall Pk *STH/RUST* TN4 206 C2
Rusthall Rd *STH/RUST* TN4 206 C3
Rustwick *STH/RUST* TN4 206 C2
Rutherford Wy *TONN* TN10 148 D7
Rutland Cl *DART* DA1 23 G6 1
Rutland Pl *RHAM* ME8 89 K3
Rutland Wy *MAID/SHEP* ME15 134 A6
STMC/STPC BR5 56 D3
Ruxley Cl *SCUP* DA14 38 E4
Ruxton Cl *SWLY* BR8 40 B8
Ruxton Ct *SWLY* BR8 40 B8 3
Ryan Dr *MAID/SHEP* ME15 134 C4
Ryarsh La *E/WMAL* ME19 107 K5
Ryarsh Rd *E/WMAL* ME19 107 K1
Rycault Cl *MAIDW* ME16 6 B4 2
Rycaut Cl *RHAM* ME8 90 A3
Rycroft La *RSEV* TN14 145 G1
Rydal Cl *STH/RUST* TN4 10 A2
Rydal Dr *STH/RUST* TN4 10 A2
Ryde Cl *WALD* ME5 68 C6
Ryders *RRTW* TN3 205 K3
Rye Crs *STMC/STPC* BR5 56 D5
Ryecroft *GVE* DA12 46 B3 1
HART DA3 62 E1
Ryecroft Rd *RSEV* TN14 101 J4
Ryedale Ct *SEV* TN13 101 G8
Ryegrass Cl *WALD* ME5 68 D8 2
Rye La *RSEV* TN14 101 H6
Rye Rd *HAWK* TN18 235 K6
Rymers Cl *RTWE/PEM* TN2 190 D7
Rysted La *BH/WHM* TN16 120 C5

S

Sackville Cl *SEV* TN13 9 D1
Sackville Rd *DART* DA1 23 G8
Saddington St *GVE* DA12 27 J6
Saddlers Cl *MAID/BEAR* ME14 134 A1
Saddler's Pk *EYN* DA4 59 G7
Sadlers Cl *WALD* ME5 87 J4
Sage Rd *ROCH* ME1 2 A5
Sailmakers Ct *CHAT* ME4 4 B6
St Aidan's Wy *GVE* DA12 46 B1
St Albans Cl *GILL* ME7 5 E1
GVE DA12 46 A1
St Alban's Gdns *GVE* DA12 46 A1
St Alban's Rd *DART* DA1 23 J5
STRD ME2 48 B8
St Andrew Rd *GILL* ME7 5 D1
St Andrew's Cl *MAIDW* ME16 132 A4
STPH/PW TN12 173 J8 1
St Andrews Ct *STH/RUST* TN4 190 A5 2
St Andrews Dr *ORP* BR6 56 C3
St Andrews Park Rd
STH/RUST TN4 190 A5
St Andrew's Rd *GVE* DA12 27 J6 2
MAIDW ME16 132 A4
SCUP DA14 38 E1
STPH/PW TN12 173 J8
TIL RM18 27 F1
St Andrews Wy *OXTED* RH8 141 J2
St Anne Ct *MAIDW* ME16 6 B3
St Ann's Green La *STPH/PW* TN12 177 F6
St Aubyns Cl *ORP* BR6 56 A7
St Aubyns Gdns *ORP* BR6 56 A6
St Barnabas Cl *GILL* ME7 5 D5
MAIDW ME16 110 C6
RTW TN1 11 D2 4
St Bartholomew's La *CHAT* ME4 3 E4 4
St Bartholomew's Ter *ROCH* ME1 3 E4 5
St Benedict Rd *SNOD* ME6 85 H6
St Benedict's Av *GVE* DA12 46 B1
St Benets Wy *TENT* TN30 230 B6
St Benjamins Dr *ORP* BR6 76 D4
St Bernards Rd *TONN* TN10 148 C8
St Botolph Rd *GVW* DA11 44 E1
St Botolph's Av *SEV* TN13 8 C3
St Botolph's Rd *SEV* TN13 9 D3
St Chad's Dr *GVE* DA12 46 B1
St Clair Cl *OXTED* RH8 140 A1
St Clements Cl *GVW* DA11 45 G1 2
St Clements Ct *PUR* RM19 12 E4 1
St Clere Hill Rd *BGR/WK* TN15 80 E7
St Columba's Cl *GVE* DA12 46 B1
St David's Crs *GVE* DA12 46 A2
St David's Rd *HOO/HM* ME3 19 G6
STH/RUST TN4 11 D1
SWLY BR8 40 C4
St Dunstan's Dr *GVE* DA12 46 B1
St Edith's Rd *BGR/WK* TN15 102 E5
St Edmunds Rd *DART* DA1 23 J3
St Faith's La *MAID/BEAR* ME14 134 D2
St Faith's St *MAID/BEAR* ME14 6 C3 5
St Francis Av *GVE* DA12 46 B2
St Francis Rd *MEO* DA13 83 J3
St George's Ct *BGR/WK* TN15 105 F3 2
St George's Crs *GVE* DA12 46 A2
St Georges Ms *TON* TN9 170 B6 4
St George's Pk *RTWE/PEM* TN2 206 E6
St George's Rd *GILL* ME7 4 C2
SCUP DA14 38 E4
SEV TN13 9 D1
SWLY BR8 58 C1 3
St George's Sq *MAIDW* ME16 6 A4
St Giles Cl *ORP* BR6 75 J1
St Gregory's Crs *GVE* DA12 28 B8
St Helens La *MAID/SHEP* ME15 131 J6
St Helens Rd *HOO/HM* ME3 31 G1
St Helier's Cl *MAIDW* ME16 132 B4
St Hildas *BGR/WK* TN15 127 F6
St Hilda's Wy *GVE* DA12 46 A2
St James' La *RDART* DA2 24 D6
St James' Pk *RTW* TN1 11 E2
RTWE/PEM TN2 11 E2
St James Pl *DART* DA1 23 G5 2

St James Rd HOO/HM ME3 .... 21 G8
RTW TN1 .... 11 E2
St James' Rd RTW TN1 .... 11 E3
St James's Av GVW DA11 .... 27 H6
St James's Rd GVW DA11 .... 27 H6
SEV TN13 .... 9 D1
St James's St GVW DA11 .... 27 H5 4
St James Wy SCUP DA14 .... 39 F3
St John's Av SIT ME10 .... 94 C3
St John's Cl HOO/HM ME3 .... 48 B3
St John's Hl SEV TN13 .... 9 E2
St John's La HART DA3 .... 62 A3
St John's Pk STH/RUST TN4 .... 190 A6
St John's Rd GILL ME7 .... 4 C5
GVE DA12 .... 28 A6
HOO/HM ME3 .... 32 E8
HOO/HM ME3 .... 48 B2
RDART DA2 .... 24 B6
SCUP DA14 .... 38 C2
SEV TN13 .... 9 D1
STH/RUST TN4 .... 190 A7
St Johns Wy ROCH ME1 .... 2 A6
St Josephs Cl ORP BR6 .... 56 A8 1
St Justin Cl STMC/STPC BR5 .... 38 E8
St Katherine's La SNOD ME6 .... 85 J7
St Kilda Rd ORP BR6 .... 56 A5
St Laurence Av DIT/AY ME20 .... 110 B6
St Laurence Cl RSIT ME9 .... 94 E4
STMC/STPC BR5 .... 38 E8
St Lawrence Av STH/RUST TN4 .... 189 H3
St Leonards Av CHAT ME4 .... 3 F6
St Leonards Rd MAIDW ME16 .... 110 C6
St Leonard's St E/WMAL ME19 .... 107 K7
St Luke's Av MAID/BEAR ME14 .... 7 E2
St Lukes Cl RDART DA2 .... 42 D3
SWLY BR8 .... 40 A7 4
St Luke's Rd MAID/BEAR ME14 .... 7 E2
STH/RUST TN4 .... 11 D1
St Luke's Wy HOO/HM ME3 .... 19 G6
St Margarets Cl MAIDW ME16 .... 132 B4 4
ORP BR6 .... 56 C8 1
RDART DA2 .... 24 C8
St Margaret's Crs GVE DA12 .... 46 B1
St Margarets Dr RHAM ME8 .... 89 K1
St Margaret's Ms ROCH ME1 .... 2 C3 5
St Margaret's Rd EYN DA4 .... 42 D5
St Margaret's St ROCH ME1 .... 2 B4
St Mark's Av GVW DA11 .... 27 F6
St Marks Ct DIT/AY ME20 .... 86 E8 3
St Mark's Rd RTWE/PEM TN2 .... 206 E7
St Martin's Ct MAID/BEAR ME14 .... 112 C5
St Martins Dr EYN DA4 .... 59 G7
St Martins Meadow
BH/WHM TN16 .... 121 J2
St Martin's Rd DART DA1 .... 23 J5
St Mary's Church Rd RSEV TN14 .... 122 A4
St Mary's Cl BGR/WK TN15 .... 105 J7
GVE DA12 .... 27 K8
OXTED RH8 .... 118 C8
STMC/STPC BR5 .... 38 C7
WADH TN5 .... 232 B5
WBY/YAL ME18 .... 174 C2
St Mary's Ct BH/WHM TN16 .... 120 D5
St Mary's Dr SEV TN13 .... 8 A2
St Mary's Gdns CHAT ME4 .... 4 B1
St Mary's Gn BH/WHM TN16 .... 97 G5
St Mary's Gv BH/WHM TN16 .... 97 G5
St Mary's La RRTW TN3 .... 188 E6
WADH TN5 .... 232 B5
St Marys Rd BGR/WK TN15 .... 105 G4
GILL ME7 .... 4 C2
GRH DA9 .... 24 D4
STRD ME2 .... 2 B1
SWLY BR8 .... 58 A1
TON TN9 .... 170 B7
St Mary's Vw RSIT ME9 .... 72 B8
St Marys Wy HART DA3 .... 43 K8
St Matthews Dr ROCH ME1 .... 2 A6
St Matthew's Wy HOO/HM ME3 .... 19 G6 2
St Michael's Cl CHAT ME4 .... 3 F5
DIT/AY ME20 .... 110 C3
St Michaels Ct STRD ME2 .... 49 G6 4
St Michaels Dr RSEV TN14 .... 102 B3
St Michael's Rd MAIDW ME16 .... 6 A4
SIT ME10 .... 93 K2
STH/RUST TN4 .... 190 B7
St Mildred's Cl TENT TN30 .... 230 A7 2
St Nicholas Gdns STRD ME2 .... 48 E6
St Patrick's Gdns GVE DA12 .... 46 A2
St Paul's Cl STRD ME2 .... 66 C1 1
SWCM DA10 .... 25 K6
TONN TN10 .... 170 D1
St Paul's St SIT ME10 .... 93 K1 5
STH/RUST TN4 .... 206 B2
St Peters Cl DIT/AY ME20 .... 109 F5
SWCM DA10 .... 26 A6
St Peters Pl DIT/AY ME20 .... 86 E8
St Peters Rd DIT/AY ME20 .... 109 F5
St Peters Rw RRTW TN3 .... 204 E1
St Peters St MAIDW ME16 .... 6 C3
RTWE/PEM TN2 .... 11 E4 7
St Peter St ROCH ME1 .... 3 D4
St Philip's Av MAID/SHEP ME15 .... 7 E4
St Ronan's Cl MAID/SHEP ME15 .... 133 J7 1
St Saviours Rd MAID/SHEP ME15 .... 133 K8
Saints Hl RTON TN11 .... 187 J5
St Stephen's Sq MAID/SHEP ME15 .... 6 B5 4
St Stephen's St TON TN9 .... 170 B6
St Stephons Ct RTW TN1 .... 11 D2 5
St Thomas Rd GVW DA11 .... 27 F7 2
St Thomas's Av GVW DA11 .... 27 J8
St Vincents La E/WMAL ME19 .... 106 D4
St Vincents Rd DART DA1 .... 23 K5
St Welcume's Wy RMAID ME17 .... 137 J8
St Werburgh Crs HOO/HM ME3 .... 50 E1
St William's Wy ROCH ME1 .... 3 D5
St Winifred's Rd BH/WHM TN16 .... 97 K5
Saladin Dr PUR RM19 .... 12 E4
Salcote Rd GVE DA12 .... 46 B3 2
Salem Pl GVW DA11 .... 26 E6 3
Salem St MAID/SHEP ME15 .... 7 D4 4
Salisbury Av RHAM ME8 .... 70 A6
SWLY BR8 .... 58 D1
Salisbury Cl SIT ME10 .... 94 D2
TONN TN10 .... 170 D1
Salisbury Rd CHAT ME4 .... 4 A5
DIT/AY ME20 .... 87 H6
GVW DA11 .... 27 G7
MAID/BEAR ME14 .... 7 D1
RDART DA2 .... 24 B7
RRTW TN3 .... 205 J3
STH/RUST TN4 .... 190 C6
TONN TN10 .... 170 D2
Sallows Shaw MEO DA13 .... 63 K2
Sally Port GILL ME7 .... 4 A2
Sally Port Gdns GILL ME7 .... 4 A2
Salmon Rd DART DA1 .... 23 J2
Saltbox Hl BH/WHM TN16 .... 74 A8
Saltings Rd SNOD ME6 .... 85 K7
Salt La HOO/HM ME3 .... 30 E2
Salt's Av MAID/SHEP ME15 .... 155 F3
Salts La MAID/SHEP ME15 .... 155 G2
Saltwood Cl ORP BR6 .... 56 D8
Saltwood Rd MAID/SHEP ME15 .... 6 C6
Samara Cl WALD ME5 .... 88 B5
Samphire Cl MAID/BEAR ME14 .... 134 A2
Sanctuary Cl DART DA1 .... 23 F5
Sanctuary Rd RHAM ME8 .... 69 H3
Sandbanks Hl RDART DA2 .... 43 H4
Sandbourne Dr MAID/BEAR ME14 .... 111 F5
Sandersons Av RSEV TN14 .... 77 H5 1
Sanderson Wy TON TN9 .... 170 E5
Sanderstead Rd STMC/STPC BR5 .... 56 C3 1
Sandfield Rd RTON TN11 .... 187 H7
Sandford Rd SIT ME10 .... 93 G1
Sandgate Ct RHAM ME8 .... 90 C2
Sandhill La HOO/HM ME3 .... 30 C8
Sandhurst Av RTWE/PEM TN2 .... 192 A8
Sandhurst Cl RHAM ME8 .... 69 K3 4
RTWE/PEM TN2 .... 190 C7
Sandhurst Pk RTWE/PEM TN2 .... 11 F1
Sandhurst Rd BFN/LL DA15 .... 38 A1
CRBK TN17 .... 237 K5
ORP BR6 .... 56 B7
RTWE/PEM TN2 .... 190 D7
TIL RM18 .... 27 K1
Sandilands SEV TN13 .... 123 F1
Sand La CRBK TN17 .... 199 J8
Sandling La MAID/BEAR ME14 .... 110 E5
Sandling Rd MAID/BEAR ME14 .... 6 C1
Sandling Wy CHAT ME4 .... 50 C5
Sandown Cl RTWE/PEM TN2 .... 191 F8
Sandown Dr RHAM ME8 .... 70 A7
Sandown Gv RTWE/PEM TN2 .... 191 F8
Sandown Pk RTWE/PEM TN2 .... 208 A1
Sandown Rd E/WMAL ME19 .... 107 K6
GVE DA12 .... 45 K4
Sandpiper Rd WALD ME5 .... 88 D4
The Sandpipers GVE DA12 .... 28 A8
Sandpiper Wy STMC/STPC BR5 .... 56 E1
Sandringham Rd RHAM ME8 .... 90 B2
Sand Rd RRTW TN3 .... 221 J2
Sandrock Rd RTWE/PEM TN2 .... 11 E3
Sandstone Dr SIT ME10 .... 73 K6
Sandstone Ri MAID/BEAR ME14 .... 88 D6 1
Sandway Rd RMAID ME17 .... 160 A3
STMC/STPC BR5 .... 56 D1
Sandy Bank Rd GVE DA12 .... 27 J7
Sandycroft Rd STRD ME2 .... 48 E5 4
Sandy Dell GILL ME7 .... 89 H3
Sandy La BGR/WK TN15 .... 106 B5
BGR/WK TN15 .... 126 B4
BH/WHM TN16 .... 120 D4
E/WMAL ME19 .... 107 J5
MAID/BEAR ME14 .... 111 J5
MAID/BEAR ME14 .... 134 D1
MEO DA13 .... 43 K2
ORP BR6 .... 56 B4
OXTED RH8 .... 118 A8
OXTED RH8 .... 119 F6
RDART DA2 .... 43 J1
SEV TN13 .... 9 E2
SNOD ME6 .... 85 H8
STMC/STPC BR5 .... 38 E5
TENT TN30 .... 230 B7
Sandy Mt MAID/BEAR ME14 .... 134 D1
Sandy Rdg BGR/WK TN15 .... 105 G7
Sapho Pk GVE DA12 .... 46 C2
Saphora Cl ORP BR6 .... 75 J1 1
Saracen Cl GILL ME7 .... 69 H5
Saracen Flds WALD ME5 .... 88 C6
Sara Crs GRH DA9 .... 25 F3
Sara Pk GVE DA12 .... 46 B2 1
Sarsen Hts WALD ME5 .... 88 A5
Sarsens Cl GVE DA12 .... 46 C8 1
Sassoon Cl DIT/AY ME20 .... 108 E2
Satis Av SIT ME10 .... 73 K7
Saunders Cl GVW DA11 .... 27 F8
Saunders Rd STH/RUST TN4 .... 10 A6
Saunders St GILL ME7 .... 4 C2
Saunders Wy DART DA1 .... 23 J8
Savage Rd WALD ME5 .... 88 C3
Savoy Rd DART DA1 .... 23 F4
Sawpit Rd RSIT ME9 .... 117 G3
Sawyers Ct CHAT ME4 .... 4 B6
Saxbys Rd BGR/WK TN15 .... 125 H1
Saxby Wd RTON TN11 .... 168 D5
Saxon Cl GVW DA11 .... 44 D1
RSEV TN14 .... 101 H4
STRD ME2 .... 48 E5
WBY/YAL ME18 .... 129 H4
Saxon Pl EYN DA4 .... 60 B2
Saxon Rd RDART DA2 .... 41 H2
Saxons Dr MAID/BEAR ME14 .... 7 E1
Saxon Shore Wy GILL ME7 .... 51 K8
GVE DA12 .... 27 K5
HOO/HM ME3 .... 29 K3
ROCH ME1 .... 3 D4
RSIT ME9 .... 55 H5
STRD ME2 .... 49 K6
Saxton St GILL ME7 .... 4 C3
Saxville Rd STMC/STPC BR5 .... 38 C8
Sayer Cl GRH DA9 .... 25 F4
Sayes Court Rd STMC/STPC BR5 .... 38 B8
Scabharbour Rd RSEV TN14 .... 146 A4
Scadbury Gdns STMC/STPC BR5 .... 38 B7
Scads Hill Cl ORP BR6 .... 56 A3
Scarborough Cl BH/WHM TN16 .... 97 G5
Scarborough La ROCH ME1 .... 86 C5
Scarlet Cl STMC/STPC BR5 .... 56 C1 3
Scholars Ri STRD ME2 .... 48 B7
Scholey Cl STRD ME2 .... 86 A2
School Ap BGR/WK TN15 .... 105 F7
School Av GILL ME7 .... 5 E4
School Cl DART DA1 .... 22 C3
MEO DA13 .... 63 H4 2
School Fld EDEN TN8 .... 164 C4
School Hl RRTW TN3 .... 210 E8
School House La STPH/PW TN12 .... 195 H7
School La BGR/WK TN15 .... 80 E6
BGR/WK TN15 .... 102 D8
E/WMAL ME19 .... 106 C1
EYN DA4 .... 60 E3
HOO/HM ME3 .... 30 B8
HOO/HM ME3 .... 48 B2
MAID/SHEP ME15 .... 134 A5
MEO DA13 .... 83 H4
RDART DA2 .... 43 H1
RMAID ME17 .... 157 G7
RMAID ME17 .... 159 K4
ROCH ME1 .... 86 C1
RSIT ME9 .... 72 A4
RSIT ME9 .... 72 A7
RSIT ME9 .... 73 H3
RSIT ME9 .... 92 E3
RSIT ME9 .... 94 E4
RTON TN11 .... 126 E8
RTON TN11 .... 150 A6
SWLY BR8 .... 40 E5
School Ri RTWE/PEM TN2 .... 10 B6 3
School Rd GVE DA12 .... 45 K1
SIT ME10 .... 94 C3
School Ter HAWK TN18 .... 235 F4
Schooner Ct GRH DA9 .... 24 B3
Scimitar Cl GILL ME7 .... 69 H5
Scords La BH/WHM TN16 .... 143 J3
Scotby Av WALD ME5 .... 88 C2
Scotland La GVE DA12 .... 46 D6
Scotshall La WARL CR6 .... 96 A2
Scott Av RHAM ME8 .... 70 D6
Scott Cl DIT/AY ME20 .... 109 G6
Scotteswood Av CHAT ME4 .... 3 F6
Scott Rd GVE DA12 .... 46 A3
TON TN9 .... 169 K6 1
Scott's Ter CHAT ME4 .... 3 F5
Scott St MAID/BEAR ME14 .... 6 C1
Scotts Wy RTWE/PEM TN2 .... 206 D6
SEV TN13 .... 8 A1
Scragged Oak Rd
MAID/BEAR ME14 .... 89 J8
Scraps Hl RSIT ME9 .... 95 F2
Scratchers La EYN DA4 .... 60 C7
Scratton Flds GVE DA12 .... 64 A2
Scudders Hl HART DA3 .... 61 H3
Seabrook Rd RTON TN11 .... 170 A3
Seagull Rd STRD ME2 .... 48 C8
Seal Dr BGR/WK TN15 .... 102 D8
Seal Hollow Rd SEV TN13 .... 9 E3
Seal Rd SEV TN13 .... 102 B8
Seaton Rd DART DA1 .... 22 D6
GILL ME7 .... 5 E5
Seaview HOO/HM ME3 .... 37 G1
Seaview Rd GILL ME7 .... 4 C4
Second Av GILL ME7 .... 5 E5
WALD ME5 .... 68 D5

Secretan Rd *ROCH* ME1 **67** G5
Sedcombe Cl *SCUP* DA14 **38** D2 1
Sedge Crs *WALD* ME5 **87** K2
Sedley *MEO* DA13 **44** B3
Sedley Cl *DIT/AY* ME20 **109** J4
HOO/HM ME3 **31** H7
RHAM ME8 **89** K3
Sefton Cl *STMC/STPC* BR5 **56** A1
Sefton Rd *STMC/STPC* BR5 **56** A1
Selah Dr *SWLY* BR8 **39** K6
Selborne Rd *SCUP* DA14 **38** C2
Selbourne Cl *HART* DA3 **62** E1
Selbourne Rd *GILL* ME7 **5** D1
Selbourne Wk *MAID/SHEP* ME15 **134** B8
Selby Rd *MAID/SHEP* ME15 **156** B2
Selstead Cl *RHAM* ME8 **69** J5
Selwyn Rd *TIL* RM18 **27** G1
Senacre La *MAID/SHEP* ME15 **134** A8
Senacre Sq *MAID/SHEP* ME15 **134** B7
Sequoia Gdns *ORP* BR6 **56** A4 2
Sermon Dr *SWLY* BR8 **39** K8
Serpentine Rd *SEV* TN13 **9** E2
Setford Rd *WALD* ME5 **68** D8
Settington Av *WALD* ME5 **68** D5
Seven Acres *SWLY* BR8 **58** A3
Seven Mile La *BGR/WK* TN15 **106** B6
RTON TN11 **151** G2
Sevenoaks By-pass *SEV* TN13 **8** A5
Sevenoaks Rd *BGR/WK* TN15 **104** E7
ORP BR6 **56** A8
RSEV TN14 **77** G4
Sevenoaks Wy *STMC/STPC* BR5 **38** D7
Severn Cl *TONN* TN10 **170** C1
Severn Rd *WALD* ME5 **88** D1
Sevington Pk *MAID/SHEP* ME15 **133** F8
Seymour Rd *GVW* DA11 **27** G7
RHAM ME8 **71** F6
WALD ME5 **4** B5
Seymour Wk *SWCM* DA10 **25** K6
Shacklands Rd *RSEV* TN14 **77** K6
Shackleton Cl *WALD* ME5 **68** C8 2
The Shades *STRD* ME2 **48** A7
Shaftesbury Cl *E/WMAL* ME19 **108** D5 5
Shaftesbury Dr *MAIDW* ME16 **132** C2
Shaftesbury La *DART* DA1 **24** A3
Shaftesbury Rd *STH/RUST* TN4 **10** C1
Shakespeare Av *TIL* RM18 **27** J1
Shakespeare Farm Rd
HOO/HM ME3 **18** C7
Shakespeare Rd *DART* DA1 **23** K3
GILL ME7 **4** C5
SIT ME10 **94** B2
TON TN9 **169** K6
Shamrock Rd *GVE* DA12 **28** B6
Shandon Cl *RTWE/PEM* TN2 **11** E3
Shanklin Cl *WALD* ME5 **68** D6
Sharfleet Dr *STRD* ME2 **48** A7
Sharland Rd *GVE* DA12 **27** K8
Sharman Ct *SCUP* DA14 **38** B2
Sharnal La *SNOD* ME6 **85** K7
Sharnal St *HOO/HM* ME3 **33** H5
Sharon Crs *WALD* ME5 **88** A2
Sharp's Fld *HDCN* TN27 **200** C1
Sharps Gn *GILL* ME7 **70** A1
Sharp Wy *DART* DA1 **23** J2
Sharsted Wy *GILL* ME7 **89** H3
MAID/BEAR ME14 **134** D1 1
Shaw Cl *HOO/HM* ME3 **31** G7
Shaw Rd *BH/WHM* TN16 **97** G7
Shawstead Rd *WALD* ME5 **68** D7
Shaws Wy *ROCH* ME1 **2** B5
The Shaw *RTWE/PEM* TN2 **11** E5
Sheafe Dr *CRBK* TN17 **225** J1
Sheal's Crs *MAID/SHEP* ME15 **7** D5
Shearers Cl *MAID/BEAR* ME14 **134** A2
Shearwater *HART* DA3 **44** C8
MAIDW ME16 **132** B1 6
Shearwater Cl *STRD* ME2 **48** B7 2
Shearwood Cresent *DART* DA1 **22** C2
Sheen Rd *STMC/STPC* BR5 **56** A1
Sheepcote La *STMC/STPC* BR5 **57** H1
Sheephurst La *STPH/PW* TN12 **195** H1
Sheerstone *RSIT* ME9 **73** J3
Sheet Hl *BGR/WK* TN15 **126** D5
Sheffield Rd *STH/RUST* TN4 **189** K4
The Sheilings *BGR/WK* TN15 **102** D7
Shelbury Cl *SCUP* DA14 **38** B1
Shelden Dr *RHAM* ME8 **70** C6
Sheldon Wy *DIT/AY* ME20 **108** E3
Shellbank La *RDART* DA2 **43** G3
Shelldrake Cl *HOO/HM* ME3 **37** G1 2
Shelley Rd *MAIDW* ME16 **132** C4
Shelleys La *RSEV* TN14 **99** G3
Shelton Cl *TONN* TN10 **170** C1
Shenden Cl *SEV* TN13 **124** A7
Shenden Wy *SEV* TN13 **124** A7
Shenley Gv *MAID/BEAR* ME14 **111** F4
Shenley Rd *DART* DA1 **23** K5
Shepherds Cl *ORP* BR6 **56** A7 3
Shepherds Ga *GILL* ME7 **89** G1
Shepherds Gate Dr
MAID/BEAR ME14 **134** A1
Shepherds La *DART* DA1 **22** D7
Shepherd St *GVW* DA11 **26** E6
Shepherds Wk *RTWE/PEM* TN2 **11** F3 1
Shepherds Wy *HOO/HM* ME3 **35** F2
RMAID ME17 **157** G2
Shepperton Cl *WALD* ME5 **88** D2 1
Sheppey Rd *MAID/SHEP* ME15 **133** F7
Sheppey Wy *SIT* ME10 **93** F1
Sheppy Pl *GVE* DA12 **27** J6
Sheraton Ct *WALD* ME5 **88** A5
Sherborne Rd *STMC/STPC* BR5 **56** A2
Sherbourne Cl *BGR/WK* TN15 **80** D2
Sherbourne Dr *MAIDW* ME16 **132** B4
STRD ME2 **49** F5 3
Sherenden La *STPH/PW* TN12 **196** C6
Sherenden Rd *RTON* TN11 **171** J5
Sheridan Cl *MAID/BEAR* ME14 **110** E6
WALD ME5 **68** D7
Sheridan Ct *DART* DA1 **23** K3
Sheriff Dr *WALD* ME5 **88** B4
Sherman Cl *GILL* ME7 **69** J5
Shernden La *EDEN* TN8 **184** C1
Shernolds *MAID/SHEP* ME15 **133** H7
Sherway Cl *HDCN* TN27 **200** C1
Sherway Rd *HDCN* TN27 **181** H7
Sherwood Av *WALD* ME5 **88** B4
Sherwood Pl *RRTW* TN3 **205** H3 3
Sherwood Rd *RTWE/PEM* TN2 **11** F3 2
RTWE/PEM TN2 **11** F1
Sherwood Wy *RTWE/PEM* TN2 **11** F1
The Shieling *MEO* DA13 **83** G5
Shillingheld Cl *MAID/BEAR* ME14 **134** B1
Shingle Barn La *WBY/YAL* ME18 **153** F2
Shipbourne Rd *RTON* TN11 **148** D4
TON TN9 **170** C2
Ship Field Cl *BH/WHM* TN16 **97** G8
Ship Hl *BH/WHM* TN16 **97** H8
Ship La *EYN* DA4 **41** H6
ROCH ME1 **3** E4
SOCK/AV RM15 **13** H2
SWLY BR8 **41** G6
Shipley Hills Rd *MEO* DA13 **63** G5
Shipwrights Av *CHAT* ME4 **4** A6
Shirehall Rd *RDART* DA2 **41** G3
Shire La *ORP* BR6 **74** E3
The Shires *STPH/PW* TN12 **173** J7
Shirley Cl *DART* DA1 **23** F3
GVE DA12 **28** E8 3
Shirley Gdns *STH/RUST* TN4 **206** B2 1
Shirley Gv *STH/RUST* TN4 **206** C1
Shirley Wy *MAID/SHEP* ME15 **134** C3
Sholden Gdns *STMC/STPC* BR5 **56** D2
Sholden Rd *STRD* ME2 **49** H5
Shorefields *RHAM* ME8 **70** D4
Shoregate La *RSIT* ME9 **53** J8
Shoreham La *ORP* BR6 **77** H2
RSEV TN14 **77** H7
SEV TN13 **8** B1
TENT TN30 **230** A3
Shoreham Pl *RSEV* TN14 **78** D7
Shoreham Rd *RSEV* TN14 **101** K2
STMC/STPC BR5 **38** C6
Shorehill La *BGR/WK* TN15 **102** E2
The Shore *GVW* DA11 **26** D4
Shorne Cl *STMC/STPC* BR5 **56** E1
Shorne Ifield Rd *GVE* DA12 **46** E4
Shortlands Rd *SIT* ME10 **94** B2
Short La *OXTED* RH8 **141** F3
Short St *CHAT* ME4 **4** B5 5
Shorts Wy *ROCH* ME1 **2** A6
Shottenden Rd *GILL* ME7 **5** D1
Showfields Rd *RTWE/PEM* TN2 **10** B6
Shropshire Ter *MAID/SHEP* ME15 **134** A7
Shrubbery Rd *EYN* DA4 **42** C6
GVE DA12 **27** J7
Shrubcote *TENT* TN30 **230** C7 1
Shrubsole Dr *MAID/BEAR* ME14 **110** E3
Shurland Av *SIT* ME10 **94** A5
Shurlock Av *SWLY* BR8 **40** A7
Shuttle Rd *DART* DA1 **22** D2
Sidcup Hl *SCUP* DA14 **38** C3
Sidcup Pl *SCUP* DA14 **38** B3
Sidmouth Rd *STMC/STPC* BR5 **56** C2 2
Sidney Cl *RTWE/PEM* TN2 **206** D6
Sidney Gdns *RSEV* TN14 **102** A3
Sidney Rd *GILL* ME7 **4** C1
ROCH ME1 **2** A6
Sidney St *MAIDW* ME16 **132** C4
Silchester Ct *MAID/BEAR* ME14 **111** J7
Silkham Rd *OXTED* RH8 **118** B6
Silk Mills Cl *RSEV* TN14 **102** A8
Silver Bank *WALD* ME5 **68** B8
Silver Birch Av *MEO* DA13 **83** G5
Silver Birch Cl *RDART* DA2 **40** B2
Silver Birches *WALD* ME5 **88** B3
Silver Cl *TON* TN9 **170** B8
Silverdale *HART* DA3 **62** A1 4
MAIDW ME16 **131** K4
Silverdale Dr *RHAM* ME8 **70** B7
Silverdale Gv *SIT* ME10 **93** H3
Silverdale La *HAWK* TN18 **243** G2
STH/RUST TN4 **11** D1
Silverdale Rd *STH/RUST* TN4 **11** D1
STMC/STPC BR5 **38** B8
Silver Hl *CHAT* ME4 **3** F5
ROCH ME1 **66** E4 2
TENT TN30 **230** B5
Silver Hill Gdns *CHAT* ME4 **3** F5 3
Silverhurst Dr *TONN* TN10 **148** C8
Silver Rd *GVE* DA12 **28** B8
Silverspot Cl *RHAM* ME8 **70** C7
Silversted La *BH/WHM* TN16 **98** E7
Silver St *RSIT* ME9 **115** K1
Silver Tree *WALD* ME5 **88** B5
Silverweed Rd *WALD* ME5 **88** A1
Silwood Cl *RTWE/PEM* TN2 **190** E7
Simmonds La *MAID/SHEP* ME15 **134** D8
Simpson Rd *SIT* ME10 **93** H1
SNOD ME6 **85** K8
Sinclair Cl *RHAM* ME8 **90** B1 1
Sinclair Wy *RDART* DA2 **42** C2
Singapore Dr *GILL* ME7 **4** B2 1
Single's Cross La *RSEV* TN14 **99** J2
Single St *BH/WHM* TN16 **98** B2
Singlewell Rd *GVW* DA11 **45** J1
Sirdar Strd *GVE* DA12 **46** C3
Sir David's Pk *STH/RUST* TN4 **189** J5
Sir Evelyn Rd *ROCH* ME1 **67** G6
Sir John Hawkins Wy *CHAT* ME4 **3** F4 4
Sir Thomas Longley Rd *STRD* ME2 **3** E1
Siskin Gdns *STPH/PW* TN12 **193** J1
Sissinghurst Dr *MAIDW* ME16 **132** B2
Sissinghurst Rd *CRBK* TN17 **216** A6
HDCN TN27 **216** E4
Sittingbourne Rd
MAID/BEAR ME14 **7** E2
Six Fields Pth *TENT* TN30 **230** A7
Six Penny Cl *EDEN* TN8 **164** C6
Skeet Hill La *STMC/STPC* BR5 **57** G6
Skene Cl *RHAM* ME8 **70** D5
Skeynes Rd *EDEN* TN8 **164** B5
Skibbs La *ORP* BR6 **57** F7
Skid Hill La *WARL* CR6 **96** D2
Skinner Gdns *CRBK* TN17 **215** H6
Skinners Cl *DIT/AY* ME20 **87** F8
Skinners La *EDEN* TN8 **164** D4
Skinner St *CHAT* ME4 **3** F5
GILL ME7 **4** C2
Skinner's Wy *RMAID* ME17 **157** G2
Skinney La *EYN* DA4 **42** C8
Skippers Cl *GRH* DA9 **25** G4 2
Skye Cl *MAID/SHEP* ME15 **133** G7
Slade Cl *WALD* ME5 **88** C4
Slade Rd *RMAID* ME17 **139** K6
The Slade *RRTW* TN3 **221** J3
TON TN9 **170** B4
Slaney Rd *STPH/PW* TN12 **198** B2
Slatin Rd *STRD* ME2 **49** F6
Sleepers Stile Rd *WADH* TN5 **220** E5
Slicketts Hl *CHAT* ME4 **4** A4 5
Slip Mill Rd *HAWK* TN18 **234** E4
The Slip *BH/WHM* TN16 **120** C5
Slough Rd *RSIT* ME9 **117** G2
Small Bridge Rd *STPH/PW* TN12 **212** A4
Small Grains *HART* DA3 **61** G7
Smallhythe Rd *TENT* TN30 **229** K7 3
Small Profits *WBY/YAL* ME18 **152** E2
Smarden Rd *HDCN* TN27 **200** C2
HDCN TN27 **203** G1
HDCN TN27 **217** K2
Smarts Hl *RTON* TN11 **187** J5
Smarts Rd *GVE* DA12 **45** J1
Smeed Cl *SIT* ME10 **94** C2 2
Smetham Gdns *STRD* ME2 **49** G5 1
Smithers Cl *RTON* TN11 **150** A5
Smithers La *STPH/PW* TN12 **151** J7
Smithfield Rd *HOO/HM* ME3 **37** H1
Smith Rd *WALD* ME5 **88** C3
Smith's Hl *MAID/SHEP* ME15 **153** G2
Smiths La *EDEN* TN8 **142** C4
Smiths Orch *RSIT* ME9 **115** K1
Smith St *STRD* ME2 **2** A2
Smugglers Ms *HAWK* TN18 **235** G5
Smugglers Whf *GRH* DA9 **25** G4
Smythe Cl *STH/RUST* TN4 **189** J3
Smythe Rd *EYN* DA4 **41** K6 1
Snag La *RSEV* TN14 **75** J7
Snatts Hl *OXTED* RH8 **118** D8
Snelling Av *GVW* DA11 **27** G8
Snipe Cl *RTWE/PEM* TN2 **192** A6
Snoad La *STPH/PW* TN12 **197** G6
Snodhurst Av *WALD* ME5 **87** K1
Snodland Rd *E/WMAL* ME19 **85** G7
Snoll Hatch Rd *STPH/PW* TN12 **173** H1
Snowdon Av *MAID/BEAR* ME14 **7** E2
Snowdon Cl *WALD* ME5 **68** C7 3
Snughorne La *HDCN* TN27 **201** G6
Solefields Rd *SEV* TN13 **123** K7
Soleoak Dr *SEV* TN13 **9** D6
Sole St *MEO* DA13 **64** A2
Solomon Rd *RHAM* ME8 **70** C5
Solomons Rd *CHAT* ME4 **3** F4
Somerden Rd *STMC/STPC* BR5 **56** E4
Somerfield Cl *MAIDW* ME16 **6** A3 3
Somerfield La *MAIDW* ME16 **6** A2
Somerfield Rd *MAIDW* ME16 **6** A3
Somerhill Rd *TON* TN9 **170** D6
Somerset Cl *SIT* ME10 **93** H2
WALD ME5 **68** D6
Somerset Rd *DART* DA1 **22** E5
MAID/SHEP ME15 **133** J6
ORP BR6 **56** B4
STH/RUST TN4 **10** C1

Somerville Gdns STH/RUST TN4 .... 10 B3
Somerville Rd DART DA1 .... 23 J5 3
Somner Wk MAID/SHEP ME15 .... 156 B2 4
Soper's La HAWK TN18 .... 234 D2
Sophurst La STPH/PW TN12 .... 209 K1
Sopwith Cl BH/WHM TN16 .... 97 H3
Sorrell Rd WALD ME5 .... 88 A2
Sorrell Wy GVW DA11 .... 45 F2 5
Sortmill Rd SNOD ME6 .... 86 A7
Sounds Ldg SWLY BR8 .... 57 K3 1
South Ash Rd BGR/WK TN15 .... 81 K2
South Av RHAM ME8 .... 69 H4
SIT ME10 .... 94 B3
South Bank BH/WHM TN16 .... 120 D5
HOO/HM ME3 .... 31 G4
RMAID ME17 .... 157 G7
STPH/PW TN12 .... 198 A4
Southbourne Gv WALD ME5 .... 88 B2 2
South Bush La RHAM ME8 .... 70 E8
South Crs RMAID ME17 .... 154 C3
Southdene RSEV TN14 .... 77 G8
South Dr ORP BR6 .... 75 K1
South Eastern Rd STRD ME2 .... 2 C1 2
Southernden Rd HDCN TN27 .... 181 G5
Southern Pl SWLY BR8 .... 58 A1 5
Southey Wy DIT/AY ME20 .... 108 D2
Southfield Rd CHST BR7 .... 38 A8
STH/RUST TN4 .... 10 C1
Southfields ROCH ME1 .... 2 B5
RRTW TN3 .... 188 E7
WADH TN5 .... 220 B8
Southfield Shaw MEO DA13 .... 83 J5
Southfields Rd BGR/WK TN15 .... 80 E3
Southfields Wy STH/RUST TN4 .... 190 B6
Southfleet Av HART DA3 .... 44 C7
Southfleet Rd GVW DA11 .... 27 G7 2
RDART DA2 .... 43 H2
SWCM DA10 .... 26 B6
South Ga PUR RM19 .... 13 G4
Southgate Rd TENT TN30 .... 230 C7
South Green La RSIT ME9 .... 91 J7
South Gv RTW TN1 .... 10 C5 8
South Hall Cl EYN DA4 .... 59 J4
South Hill Rd GVE DA12 .... 27 J7
Southill Rd CHAT ME4 .... 3 F5
South Kent Av GVW DA11 .... 26 D5
South La RMAID ME17 .... 157 G8
Southlees La RSIT ME9 .... 114 D4
South Pk SEV TN13 .... 9 D4
South Park Rd MAID/SHEP ME15 .... 7 E6
South Rd GILL ME7 .... 4 A1
STPH/PW TN12 .... 176 E8
South St GVE DA12 .... 27 J6
MAIDW ME16 .... 131 J6
MEO DA13 .... 63 G8
South Street Rd RSIT ME9 .... 91 H6
Southview Cl SWLY BR8 .... 58 D1 3
South View Rd RDART DA2 .... 41 G1
STH/RUST TN4 .... 190 B6
WADH TN5 .... 220 B8
Southwark Rd STRD ME2 .... 48 C8
South Wy PUR RM19 .... 13 J3
Southways RMAID ME17 .... 157 G7 2
Southwell Rd STRD ME2 .... 48 B8
Southwood MAIDW ME16 .... 131 K4
Southwood Av STH/RUST TN4 .... 10 C1
Southwood Rd STH/RUST TN4 .... 206 A1
Sovereign Bvd GILL ME7 .... 5 E6
Sovereigns Wy STPH/PW TN12 .... 176 B8
Sovereign Wy TON TN9 .... 170 C5
Spade La RSIT ME9 .... 71 F8
Spar Cl RTON TN11 .... 150 B5
Sparepenny La EYN DA4 .... 59 H4
Sparkeswood Av CRBK TN17 .... 238 C2
Spearhead Rd MAID/BEAR ME14 .... 111 F7
Speedgate Hl HART DA3 .... 61 F6
Speedwell Av WALD ME5 .... 87 K2
Speedwell Cl GILL ME7 .... 5 E3
MAID/BEAR ME14 .... 134 A1 6
Spekes Rd GILL ME7 .... 69 H8
Speldhurst Hl RRTW TN3 .... 189 F6
Speldhurst Rd RRTW TN3 .... 205 J1
STH/RUST TN4 .... 189 K6
Spelmonden Rd STPH/PW TN12 .... 211 J2
Spencer Cl WALD ME5 .... 88 B1
Spencer St GVW DA11 .... 27 H6
Spencer Wk TIL RM18 .... 27 H1
Spencer Wy MAID/SHEP ME15 .... 134 A7 2
Spenlow Dr WALD ME5 .... 88 B6 2
Spenny La STPH/PW TN12 .... 175 G8
Speyside TONN TN10 .... 170 B1 1
Spielman Rd DART DA1 .... 23 J3
The Spillway MAID/SHEP ME15 .... 6 A5 3
Spindle Gld MAID/BEAR ME14 .... 7 F2
Spindlewood Cl WALD ME5 .... 88 C3 5
Spinners Cl HDCN TN27 .... 217 J4
The Spinney MAID/SHEP ME15 .... 7 E5 1
SCUP DA14 .... 39 F3
SWLY BR8 .... 40 B7
TON TN9 .... 170 A7
WALD ME5 .... 88 C5 2
Spinney Wy RSEV TN14 .... 75 J6
Spire Cl GVE DA12 .... 27 J7 1
The Spires DART DA1 .... 23 G8
MAIDW ME16 .... 6 A3
STRD ME2 .... 66 C1
Spital St DART DA1 .... 23 G5
Spitfire Cl WALD ME5 .... 68 C8
Spitfire Rd E/WMAL ME19 .... 129 H3
Spode La EDEN TN8 .... 185 G6
Sponden La HAWK TN18 .... 236 B6
Spongs La CRBK TN17 .... 215 H5
Sportsfield MAID/BEAR ME14 .... 7 E2
Spot La MAID/SHEP ME15 .... 134 C4
Spout La EDEN TN8 .... 142 C5
STPH/PW TN12 .... 210 E1
Spray Hl RRTW TN3 .... 221 K2
The Sprig MAID/BEAR ME14 .... 134 C2
Springcroft HART DA3 .... 62 B3
Spring Cross HART DA3 .... 62 B7
Springett Cl DIT/AY ME20 .... 86 E8
Springett Wy RMAID ME17 .... 154 D2
Springfield OXTED RH8 .... 140 B1
Springfield Av MAID/BEAR ME14 .... 6 B1
SWLY BR8 .... 58 C1 4
TENT TN30 .... 230 B4
Springfield Rd DIT/AY ME20 .... 108 D2
EDEN TN8 .... 164 B5
GILL ME7 .... 5 E2
RRTW TN3 .... 205 F7
SIT ME10 .... 93 J1
STH/RUST TN4 .... 189 K5
Springfields WADH TN5 .... 232 C5
Springfield Wy STMC/STPC BR5 .... 38 D8
Spring Gdns BH/WHM TN16 .... 97 G5
ORP BR6 .... 76 C2
Spring Gv GVE DA12 .... 27 J7
Springhead RTWE/PEM TN2 .... 11 F2
Spring Head Rd BGR/WK TN15 .... 102 D4
Springhead Rd GVW DA11 .... 26 D6
Spring Hl RTON TN11 .... 187 J8
RYE TN31 .... 244 E7
Springholm Cl BH/WHM TN16 .... 97 G5
Spring La BGR/WK TN15 .... 126 B1
OXTED RH8 .... 140 B2
STH/RUST TN4 .... 189 H3
Spring Shaw Rd STMC/STPC BR5 .... 38 B6
Spring V GRH DA9 .... 25 H5
MAIDW ME16 .... 6 B3
Springvale RHAM ME8 .... 69 K8
RSIT ME9 .... 73 J2
Spring Vale Cl SWLY BR8 .... 40 C5
Spring V North DART DA1 .... 23 G5 3
Spring V South DART DA1 .... 23 G6 2
Springwell Rd TON TN9 .... 170 B6
Springwood Rd MAIDW ME16 .... 132 A3
Sprotshill Cl SIT ME10 .... 73 K8
Spruce Cl DIT/AY ME20 .... 108 E4
Sprucedale Cl SWLY BR8 .... 40 B7
Spruce Rd BH/WHM TN16 .... 97 H3
Spurrell Av RDART DA2 .... 40 A2
Spur Rd ORP BR6 .... 56 B6
Spurway MAID/BEAR ME14 .... 134 C2
Square Hl MAID/BEAR ME14 .... 7 E3
Square Hill Rd MAID/SHEP ME15 .... 7 E4
The Square BH/WHM TN16 .... 97 G7
RMAID ME17 .... 160 D1
RTON TN11 .... 150 A6
Squerryes Mede
BH/WHM TN16 .... 120 C6 2
Squires Cl STRD ME2 .... 48 A7
Squires Fld SWLY BR8 .... 40 D6
Squires Wy RDART DA2 .... 40 A2
Squirrel Wy RTWE/PEM TN2 .... 207 K1
Stable Cl WALD ME5 .... 88 D1 2
Stabledene Wy RTWE/PEM TN2 .. 191 K8 1
Stace Cl TENT TN30 .... 230 C6
Stacey Cl GVE DA12 .... 46 B3
Stacey Rd RTON TN11 .... 170 A3
Stacklands Cl BGR/WK TN15 .... 80 D2 4
Stack La HART DA3 .... 62 A2
Stack Rd EYN DA4 .... 60 C1
Stadium Wy DART DA1 .... 22 B5
Staffa Rd MAID/SHEP ME15 .... 133 G7
Staffhurst Wood Rd OXTED RH8 .... 141 G8
Stafford Cl GRH DA9 .... 24 E4 1
Stafford Rd RTWE/PEM TN2 .... 207 K2
TON TN9 .... 170 B4
Stafford St GILL ME7 .... 4 C3
Stafford Wy SEV TN13 .... 9 E6
Stag Rd RTWE/PEM TN2 .... 190 D5
WALD ME5 .... 88 C1
Stagshaw Cl MAID/SHEP ME15 .... 7 D5
Stainer Rd TONN TN10 .... 149 F8
Stairfoot La SEV TN13 .... 122 E1
Stair Rd TONN TN10 .... 171 F2
Stake La STRD ME2 .... 65 K8
Staleys Rd BGR/WK TN15 .... 104 E7
Stalham Ct GILL ME7 .... 89 J2 3
Stalin Av WALD ME5 .... 68 C6
The Stampers MAID/SHEP ME15 .... 6 A5 4
Stanam Rd RTWE/PEM TN2 .... 209 F1
Stanbridge Rd EDEN TN8 .... 164 B4
Stanbrook Rd GVW DA11 .... 27 G7
Standard Rd ORP BR6 .... 75 F5
Standen Cl RHAM ME8 .... 90 B2
Standen St CRBK TN17 .... 237 F4
HAWK TN18 .... 237 G6
STH/RUST TN4 .... 10 C2
Stanford Dr MAIDW ME16 .... 132 C3 1
Stanford Gdns SOCK/AV RM15 .... 13 J
Stanford La RTON TN11 .... 150 E
Stanford Wy STRD ME2 .... 66 B
Stangate Rd E/WMAL ME19 .... 84 E
STRD ME2 .... 48 B
Stangrove Rd EDEN TN8 .... 164 C
Stanham Pl DART DA1 .... 22 D
Stanham Rd DART DA1 .... 23 F
Stanhope Av SIT ME10 .... 94 B
Stanhope Cl MAID/BEAR ME14 .... 110 E
Stanhope Rd BFN/LL DA15 .... 38 B
RTW TN1 .... 11 E2
STRD ME2 .... 2 A1
SWCM DA10 .... 26 A
Stanhopes OXTED RH8 .... 119 F
Stanhope Wy SEV TN13 .... 123 F
Stan La WBY/YAL ME18 .... 128 C
Stanley Cl GRH DA9 .... 24 D
STPH/PW TN12 .... 197 K
Stanley Crs GVE DA12 .... 46 A
Stanley Rd GILL ME7 .... 4 C2
ORP BR6 .... 56 A
RTW TN1 .... 11 D
SCUP DA14 .... 38 B
SWCM DA10 .... 26 A
WALD ME5 .... 68 D
Stanley Wy STMC/STPC BR5 .... 56 C
Stansted Cl MAIDW ME16 .... 110 C
Stansted Hl BGR/WK TN15 .... 82 B
Stansted La BGR/WK TN15 .... 81 G
Stanton Cl STMC/STPC BR5 .... 56 D
Staple Cl BXLY DA5 .... 40 A
SIT ME10 .... 73 K
Staple Dr STPH/PW TN12 .... 198 B
Staplehurst Rd RHAM ME8 .... 69 J
SIT ME10 .... 73 H
STPH/PW TN12 .... 177 H
Staplers Ct MAID/BEAR ME14 .... 111 H6
Stapleton Rd ORP BR6 .... 56 A
Starboard Av GRH DA9 .... 25 G5
Star Hl DART DA1 .... 22 B
ROCH ME1 .... 3 D
Star Hill Rd RSEV TN14 .... 100 B
Star La GILL ME7 .... 69 G
STMC/STPC BR5 .... 56 E
Starling Cl HART DA3 .... 44 C
Star Mill La WALD ME5 .... 5 D
Starts Hill Av ORP BR6 .... 75 H1
Starveacre La RSIT ME9 .... 93 H
Station Ap BGR/WK TN15 .... 105 F7
DART DA1 .... 23 H
EDEN TN8 .... 164 C
MAIDW ME16 .... 6 C
ORP BR6 .... 56 A
ORP BR6 .... 76 C
OXTED RH8 .... 118 C
RSEV TN14 .... 102 A
STMC/STPC BR5 .... 56 C
STPH/PW TN12 .... 173 J7
STPH/PW TN12 .... 198 A
STRD ME2 .... 85 K1
SWLY BR8 .... 58 B
Station Approach Rd TIL RM18 .... 27 H
Station Ct BGR/WK TN15 .... 105 F
Station Hl RTON TN11 .... 167 H
Station Rd BGR/WK TN15 .... 105 F
BH/WHM TN16 .... 121 H
CRBK TN17 .... 212 B
DART DA1 .... 22 C
DIT/AY ME20 .... 109 G
DIT/AY ME20 .... 109 K
EDEN TN8 .... 142 B
EDEN TN8 .... 164 C
EYN DA4 .... 42 A
EYN DA4 .... 59 G8
GRH DA9 .... 25 F
GVW DA11 .... 26 C
HART DA3 .... 43 K
HDCN TN27 .... 200 B
HDCN TN27 .... 203 J
HOO/HM ME3 .... 31 F
MAID/BEAR ME14 .... 6 C2
MAID/SHEP ME15 .... 132 A
MEO DA13 .... 44 A
MEO DA13 .... 63 H
ORP BR6 .... 56 A
RHAM ME8 .... 70 D
RMAID ME17 .... 137 H
RRTW TN3 .... 205 F
RSEV TN14 .... 77 G
RSEV TN14 .... 78 D
RSEV TN14 .... 101 K
RSIT ME9 .... 72 A
RSIT ME9 .... 95 K
RYE TN31 .... 244 E
SCUP DA14 .... 38 B
SEV TN13 .... 101 G
STMC/STPC BR5 .... 56 D1
STPH/PW TN12 .... 173 H
STPH/PW TN12 .... 198 B
STRD ME2 .... 2 B
STRD ME2 .... 66 B
SWLY BR8 .... 58 B1
TENT TN30 .... 230 A
WBY/YAL ME18 .... 152 A

Station Rd East *OXTED* RH8 ... **118** C8
Station Rd West *OXTED* RH8 ... **118** C8
Station St *SIT* ME10 ... **94** A2
Steadman Cl *HOO/HM* ME3 ... **48** B1
Stede Hl *RMAID* ME17 ... **137** K6
Stedman Cl *BXLY* DA5 ... **40** B1
Steele Av *GRH* DA9 ... **25** F4
Steele's La *MEO* DA13 ... **63** G8
Steele St *STRD* ME2 ... **49** F6
Steellands Ri *WADH* TN5 ... **232** C5
Steep Cl *ORP* BR6 ... **76** A2
Steeple Heights Dr *BH/WHM* TN16 .. **97** H4
Steerforth Cl *ROCH* ME1 ... **2** C6 3
Steers Pl *RTON* TN11 ... **150** A4
Stella Cl *STPH/PW* TN12 ... **196** D1 4
Stephen Cl *ORP* BR6 ... **56** A7
Stephen's Rd *STH/RUST* TN4 ... **10** C1
Stepneyford La *CRBK* TN17 ... **228** A5
Steps Hill Rd *RSIT* ME9 ... **91** G8
Step Style *SIT* ME10 ... **94** C4 2
Sterling Av *MAIDW* ME16 ... **132** C1
Sterling Rd *SIT* ME10 ... **93** J5
Sterndale Rd *DART* DA1 ... **23** J6 2
Stevens Cl *BXLY* DA5 ... **40** A2
HDCN TN27 ... **183** F3
RDART DA2 ... **42** D3
SNOD ME6 ... **85** K6 7
Stevenson Cl *MAID/SHEP* ME15 ... **6** C4 1
Stevenson Wy *DIT/AY* ME20 ... **108** D2
Stevens Rd *DIT/AY* ME20 ... **86** E8
Stewart Rd *STH/RUST* TN4 ... **190** C7
Stickens La *E/WMAL* ME19 ... **108** C8
Stickfast La *RMAID* ME17 ... **180** B2
RSIT ME9 ... **73** F5
Stilebridge La *RMAID* ME17 ... **177** G1
STPH/PW TN12 ... **176** E3
Still La *STH/RUST* TN4 ... **189** K4 2
Stirling Cl *RHAM* ME8 ... **90** B2
ROCH ME1 ... **2** A6
Stirling Dr *ORP* BR6 ... **76** C1
Stirling Rd *E/WMAL* ME19 ... **129** H3
Stisted Wy *HDCN* TN27 ... **183** F3
Stockbury Dr *MAIDW* ME16 ... **110** D7
Stockenbury *STPH/PW* TN12 ... **151** H8
Stockers Brow *RSIT* ME9 ... **94** B7
Stockers Hl *RSIT* ME9 ... **94** B7
Stockett La *RMAID* ME17 ... **154** C3
Stock Hl *BH/WHM* TN16 ... **97** H3
Stockland Green Rd *RRTW* TN3 ... **189** G6
Stock La *RDART* DA2 ... **41** F2
Stocks Green Rd *RTON* TN11 ... **169** G1
Stocks Rd *TENT* TN30 ... **247** K3
Stockton Cl *MAID/BEAR* ME14 ... **111** H6
Stoke Rd *HOO/HM* ME3 ... **33** J7
HOO/HM ME3 ... **35** F1
Stoneacre Cl *RHAM* ME8 ... **90** A1
Stoneacre La *MAID/SHEP* ME15 ... **134** D8
Stonebridge Green Rd
HDCN TN27 ... **183** G2
Stonebridge Rd *GVW* DA11 ... **26** B4
Stone Court La *RTWE/PEM* TN2 ... **192** A6
Stonecroft *MEO* DA13 ... **83** H6 2
Stonecross Lea *WALD* ME5 ... **68** C5
Stonegate Cl *STMC/STPC* BR5 ... **38** D8 2
Stone Hill Rd *HDCN* TN27 ... **183** F4
Stonehorse La *HOO/HM* ME3 ... **49** F3
Stonehouse La *ORP* BR6 ... **76** E4
PUR RM19 ... **13** J5
Stonehouse Rd *ORP* BR6 ... **76** E4
Stoneings La *RSEV* TN14 ... **99** F5
Stoneleigh Rd *OXTED* RH8 ... **141** J1
Stone Pit La *HAWK* TN18 ... **244** B1
Stone Place Rd *GRH* DA9 ... **24** D4
Stones Cross Rd *SWLY* BR8 ... **57** K2
Stonestile Rd *HDCN* TN27 ... **179** J7
Stone St *CRBK* TN17 ... **225** K1
GVE DA12 ... **27** J5
RTW TN1 ... **11** D3
Stone Street Rd *BGR/WK* TN15 ... **125** G3
Stoneswood Rd *OXTED* RH8 ... **141** F1
Stonewall Park Rd *RRTW* TN3 ... **205** J3
Stonewood *RDART* DA2 ... **43** H1
Stoney Bank *GILL* ME7 ... **69** G5
Stony Cnr *HART* DA3 ... **63** F1
Stony La *ROCH* ME1 ... **87** G1
Stopford Rd *GILL* ME7 ... **5** D4
Stornaway Strd *GVE* DA12 ... **46** C2
Stour Cl *STRD* ME2 ... **48** E7
TONN TN10 ... **170** B1
Stour Rd *DART* DA1 ... **22** D2
Stour Valley Wk *RMAID* ME17 ... **160** D2
Stowe Rd *ORP* BR6 ... **56** C8
Strand Approach Rd *GILL* ME7 ... **5** E1
Strand Cl *MEO* DA13 ... **63** H4
Stratford Av *RHAM* ME8 ... **70** A6
Stratford La *RHAM* ME8 ... **70** C6 3
Stratford Rd *E/WMAL* ME19 ... **107** J6
Stratford St *RTW* TN1 ... **11** E2
Stratton Ter *BH/WHM* TN16 ... **120** C6 3
Strawberry Cl *RRTW* TN3 ... **206** D6
Strawberry Flds *RYE* TN31 ... **244** D7
SWLY BR8 ... **40** B7 3
Strawberry V *TON* TN9 ... **170** C5 1
Straw Mill Hl *MAID/SHEP* ME15 ... **6** B6
Stream La *HAWK* TN18 ... **235** F7
Stream Pit La *HAWK* TN18 ... **243** J1
Streamside *DIT/AY* ME20 ... **109** F5
Stream Side *TONN* TN10 ... **148** D7
The Stream *DIT/AY* ME20 ... **109** F5
Streatfield *EDEN* TN8 ... **164** D5
Street End Rd *WALD* ME5 ... **68** C6
Streetfield *RMAID* ME17 ... **158** D7
Streetfield Rd *RHAM* ME8 ... **70** C5 4
The Street *BGR/WK* TN15 ... **81** K1
BGR/WK TN15 ... **127** F7
CRBK TN17 ... **199** G8
CRBK TN17 ... **215** H6
CRBK TN17 ... **227** F8
E/WMAL ME19 ... **106** C1
E/WMAL ME19 ... **107** H2
EYN DA4 ... **60** A1
GILL ME7 ... **89** J5
GVE DA12 ... **47** H3
GVE DA12 ... **64** D1
HDCN TN27 ... **183** K7
HDCN TN27 ... **183** F3
HOO/HM ME3 ... **33** F3
MAID/BEAR ME14 ... **111** J3
MAID/BEAR ME14 ... **112** C5
MAID/BEAR ME14 ... **134** E2
MEO DA13 ... **63** H5
RMAID ME17 ... **158** D7
RSIT ME9 ... **71** H2
RSIT ME9 ... **72** A3
RSIT ME9 ... **73** K2
RSIT ME9 ... **91** G2
RSIT ME9 ... **93** F4
RSIT ME9 ... **95** H8
RSIT ME9 ... **95** F3
RSIT ME9 ... **115** K7
RSIT ME9 ... **115** K1
STRD ME2 ... **85** H1
TENT TN30 ... **247** J4
WBY/YAL ME18 ... **129** F6
WBY/YAL ME18 ... **130** E7
Strettitt Gdns *STPH/PW* TN12 ... **173** H1
Strickland Av *DART* DA1 ... **23** J3
Strickland Wy *ORP* BR6 ... **56** A8 2
Strover St *GILL* ME7 ... **4** C1
Strumer Ct *WBY/YAL* ME18 ... **129** J4
Struttons Av *GVW* DA11 ... **27** G8
Stuart Cl *MAID/BEAR* ME14 ... **7** E1
RTWE/PEM TN2 ... **206** E6
SWLY BR8 ... **40** C5
Stuart Rd *GILL* ME7 ... **5** D5
GVW DA11 ... **27** H5
Stubbs Hl *ORP* BR6 ... **76** D8
Studland Cl *BFN/LL* DA15 ... **38** A1 2
Studley Ct *SCUP* DA14 ... **38** C3
Studley Crs *HART* DA3 ... **44** D7
Sturdee Av *GILL* ME7 ... **5** E4
Sturla Rd *CHAT* ME4 ... **4** A6
Sturry Wy *RHAM* ME8 ... **69** K4
Styants Bottom Rd *BGR/WK* TN15 .. **125** K1
Style Cl *RHAM* ME8 ... **90** B2
Styles Cl *EDEN* TN8 ... **165** H1
Suffolk Av *RHAM* ME8 ... **70** C5
Suffolk Rd *DART* DA1 ... **23** H5
GVE DA12 ... **28** A5
MAID/SHEP ME15 ... **133** K6
SCUP DA14 ... **38** D4
Suffolk Wy *BGR/WK* TN15 ... **9** E4
Sullivan Cl *DART* DA1 ... **22** E5
Sullivan Rd *TONN* TN10 ... **170** E1
Sultan Rd *WALD* ME5 ... **88** D4
Summer Cl *TENT* TN30 ... **230** C5
Summerhill *HDCN* TN27 ... **179** J8
Summerhill Av *STH/RUST* TN4 ... **189** K5 2
Summerhill Rd *DART* DA1 ... **23** G6
STPH/PW TN12 ... **177** H6
Summerhouse Dr *RDART* DA2 ... **40** A3
Summervale Rd *STH/RUST* TN4 ... **206** C5
Sunburst Cl *STPH/PW* TN12 ... **196** D1 5
Sun Ct *ERITH* DA8 ... **22** C1
Sunderland Cl *ROCH* ME1 ... **2** A5
Sunderland Dr *RHAM* ME8 ... **70** D6
Sundridge Cl *DART* DA1 ... **23** K5
Sundridge Dr *WALD* ME5 ... **88** B2
Sundridge Hl *RSEV* TN14 ... **99** J5
STRD ME2 ... **66** B4
Sundridge La *RSEV* TN14 ... **99** H4
Sundridge Rd *RSEV* TN14 ... **100** C7
Sun Hl *HART* DA3 ... **61** F6
Sun La *GVE* DA12 ... **27** K8
Sunningdale Cl *RHAM* ME8 ... **70** A8 4
Sunningdale Dr *RHAM* ME8 ... **70** A8
Sunninghill *GVW* DA11 ... **27** F8 2
Sunningvale Av *BH/WHM* TN16 ... **97** G4
Sunningvale Cl *BH/WHM* TN16 ... **97** H3
Sunny Bank *SIT* ME10 ... **94** C1
Sunnyfields Cl *RHAM* ME8 ... **70** B6
Sunnymead Av *GILL* ME7 ... **5** E3
Sunnyside Rd *STH/RUST* TN4 ... **206** B2
Sun Rd *SWCM* DA10 ... **26** A5
Superior Dr *ORP* BR6 ... **76** A2 4
Surrenden Rd *STPH/PW* TN12 ... **198** A3
Surrey Cl *RTWE/PEM* TN2 ... **206** E6
Surrey Rd *MAID/SHEP* ME15 ... **133** K6
Susan's Hl *RASHW* TN26 ... **231** K4
Sussex Border Pth *EDEN* TN8 ... **184** C6
HAWK TN18 ... **235** G8
RRTW TN3 ... **204** A2
TENT TN30 ... **247** J7
WADH TN5 ... **232** E2
Sussex Cl *RTWE/PEM* TN2 ... **11** E6
Sussex Dr *WALD* ME5 ... **88** B2
Sussex Ms *RTWE/PEM* TN2 ... **10** C5 9
Sussex Rd *DART* DA1 ... **23** K6
MAID/SHEP ME15 ... **133** K5
SCUP DA14 ... **38** C3
STMC/STPC BR5 ... **56** D3
TON TN9 ... **170** A6
Sutherland Av *BH/WHM* TN16 ... **97** H4
STMC/STPC BR5 ... **56** A3
Sutherland Cl *GVE* DA12 ... **28** E8 4
Sutherland Rd *RTW* TN1 ... **11** D5
Sutton Baron Rd *RSIT* ME9 ... **92** E6
Sutton Cl *RHAM* ME8 ... **70** D6
Sutton Ct *STPH/PW* TN12 ... **196** C1
Sutton Forge *STPH/PW* TN12 ... **196** D1
Sutton Rd *MAID/SHEP* ME15 ... **133** H6
RMAID ME17 ... **156** E2
Sutton St *MAID/BEAR* ME14 ... **135** F3
Swadelands Cl *RMAID* ME17 ... **160** C1
Swaffield Rd *SEV* TN13 ... **9** E1
Swain Cl *STRD* ME2 ... **48** E6
Swain Rd *RHAM* ME8 ... **69** J8
TENT TN30 ... **230** B3
Swaisland Rd *DART* DA1 ... **22** E4
Swaislands Dr *DART* DA1 ... **22** C4
Swaledale Rd *RDART* DA2 ... **24** B7
Swale Rd *DART* DA1 ... **22** D2
STRD ME2 ... **48** B7
Swallow Cl *GRH* DA9 ... **24** E4
Swallow Dr *RTWE/PEM* TN2 ... **191** F8
Swallow Ri *WALD* ME5 ... **88** B1
Swallow Rd *DIT/AY* ME20 ... **108** D4
Swallowtail Cl *STMC/STPC* BR5 ... **56** E1 9
Swan Cl *SIT* ME10 ... **94** C2
STMC/STPC BR5 ... **38** B8
Swan Cottages *TENT* TN30 ... **247** J3
Swanland Dr *TON* TN9 ... **169** K7
Swan La *CRBK* TN17 ... **212** E3
DART DA1 ... **22** C6
EDEN TN8 ... **164** C2
Swanley La *SWLY* BR8 ... **40** C8
Swanley Village Rd *SWLY* BR8 ... **40** E6
Swanmead Wy *TON* TN9 ... **170** D4
Swan Rdg *EDEN* TN8 ... **164** D2
Swanscombe St *SWCM* DA10 ... **26** A5
Swanstree Av *SIT* ME10 ... **94** C4
Swan St *E/WMAL* ME19 ... **108** A6
TENT TN30 ... **247** G3
Swanton Rd *WBY/YAL* ME18 ... **128** B7
Swanzy Rd *RSEV* TN14 ... **102** A7
Sward Rd *STMC/STPC* BR5 ... **56** B3
Swattenden La *CRBK* TN17 ... **225** H4
Swaynesland Rd *OXTED* RH8 ... **141** K5
Sweeps Hill Cl *RTWE/PEM* TN2 ... **191** K7 5
Sweeps La *STMC/STPC* BR5 ... **56** E2
Sweetings La *RRTW* TN3 ... **221** F5
Sweets La *E/WMAL* ME19 ... **130** E2
Sweyne Rd *SWCM* DA10 ... **25** K5
Swievelands Rd *BH/WHM* TN16 ... **97** F6
Swift Cl *DIT/AY* ME20 ... **108** E4
Swift Crs *WALD* ME5 ... **68** C8
Swifts Vw *CRBK* TN17 ... **214** E8
Swiller's La *GVE* DA12 ... **47** H3
Swinburne Gdns *TIL* RM18 ... **27** J1
Swingate Av *HOO/HM* ME3 ... **31** G1
Swingate Cl *WALD* ME5 ... **88** C4
Swinton Av *HOO/HM* ME3 ... **50** A1
Sycamore Cl *GVE* DA12 ... **28** A6 2
Sycamore Crs *MAIDW* ME16 ... **132** C1
Sycamore Dr *DIT/AY* ME20 ... **109** J5
SWLY BR8 ... **40** B8
Sycamore Gdns *STPH/PW* TN12 .. **193** H1 3
Sycamore Rd *DART* DA1 ... **23** G6
STRD ME2 ... **66** D1
Sychem La *RTON* TN11 ... **192** C1
Sychem Pl *STPH/PW* TN12 ... **172** C7
Sydney Av *SIT* ME10 ... **93** H2
Sydney Rd *CHAT* ME4 ... **4** A5
TIL RM18 ... **27** H1
Sylewood Cl *ROCH* ME1 ... **67** G6 4
Sylvan Cl *OXTED* RH8 ... **119** F8
Sylvan Gld *WALD* ME5 ... **88** B6
Sylvan Rd *RHAM* ME8 ... **69** K6
Sylvestre Cl *STRD* ME2 ... **85** K2 5
Symmonds Dr *SIT* ME10 ... **94** B1
Symonds Cl *BGR/WK* TN15 ... **80** D1
Symonds La *WBY/YAL* ME18 ... **152** C7
Symonds Rd *HOO/HM* ME3 ... **31** F3
Symons Av *CHAT* ME4 ... **3** F6

T

Tadburn Gn *WALD* ME5 ... **88** C2
Taddington Wood La *WALD* ME5 ... **87** K4
The Tail Race *MAID/SHEP* ME15 ... **6** B5
Tainter Rd *RTON* TN11 ... **149** K5
Talbot Pk *RTWE/PEM* TN2 ... **11** F2
Talbot Rd *HAWK* TN18 ... **235** F6

MAIDW ME16 110 C8
Tallents Cl *EYN* DA4 42 A5
Tall Trees Cl *RMAID* ME17 158 B4
Tally Rd *OXTED* RH8 141 J2
Talus Cl *PUR* RM19 13 H4
Tamar Dr *STRD* ME2 48 E8
Tamarind Cl *GILL* ME7 89 H2
Tamar Rd *TONN* TN10 170 B1
Tamesis Strd *GVE* DA12 46 B3
Tangier La *RRTW* TN3 207 G8
Tanglewood Cl *RHAM* ME8 69 K8
Tangmere Cl *GILL* ME7 5 F3
Tanhouse Rd *OXTED* RH8 140 B3
Tanker Hl *RHAM* ME8 70 A8
Tank Hill Rd *PUR* RM19 12 E4
Tank La *PUR* RM19 12 E4
Tanners Md *EDEN* TN8 164 C5
Tannery Rd *TON* TN9 170 C5
Tanyard *HAWK* TN18 243 J1
Tanyard Hl *GVE* DA12 47 H4
Tanyard La *STH/RUST* TN4 189 K5
The Tanyard *CRBK* TN17 225 K2 4
Tarling Cl *SCUP* DA14 38 C1
Tarragon Rd *MAIDW* ME16 132 B3
Tasker Cl *MAID/SHEP* ME15 134 D3
Tassell Cl *E/WMAL* ME19 108 E5
Taswell Rd *RHAM* ME8 70 D5
Tates *HAWK* TN18 235 G5
Tates Orch *HART* DA3 62 A3
Tatler Cl *WALD* ME5 88 E4
Tatsfield La *BH/WHM* TN16 97 K8
Tattlebury La *CRBK* TN17 212 E6
Tattlebury Rd *HDCN* TN27 179 K7
Taunton Cl *BXLYHN* DA7 22 A2
MAID/SHEP ME15 134 B8 10
Taunton Rd *GVW* DA11 26 B4
Taunton V *GVE* DA12 46 A1
Taveners Rd *RHAM* ME8 70 A7
Tavern Cl *BGR/WK* TN15 105 F7 2
Tavistock Cl *RHAM* ME8 70 B7 1
SIT ME10 93 J2
WALD ME5 88 A5
Tay Cl *WALD* ME5 88 C1
Taylor Cl *ORP* BR6 56 A8
RMAID ME17 137 H8
Taylor Rd *SNOD* ME6 85 J7
Taylor Rw *RDART* DA2 41 F1
Taylors Cl *SCUP* DA14 38 A2
Taylors La *E/WMAL* ME19 83 G8
HOO/HM ME3 48 B3
HOO/HM ME3 48 A1
STRD ME2 2 B1
Taylor St *STH/RUST* TN4 189 K6
Tea Garden La *RRTW* TN3 206 A5
Teal Av *STMC/STPC* BR5 56 E1
Teal Cl *HOO/HM* ME3 37 G1 3
Teapot La *DIT/AY* ME20 109 J4 2
Teasaucer Hl *MAID/SHEP* ME15 133 F6
Teasel Cl *MAID/BEAR* ME14 134 B2
Teasel Rd *WALD* ME5 88 A2
Tebbs Wy *BGR/WK* TN15 126 C3
Tedder Av *WALD* ME5 68 B7
Tedder Rd *STH/RUST* TN4 190 B7
Teesdale Rd *RDART* DA2 24 B7
Telegraph Hl *HOO/HM* ME3 48 B3
Telston La *RSEV* TN14 101 H4
SEV TN13 101 G4
Tempest Rd *E/WMAL* ME19 129 H3
Templar Dr *GVW* DA11 45 H3
Temple Gdns *SIT* ME10 94 C3 2
Temple Hl *DART* DA1 23 J4
Temple Hill Sq *DART* DA1 23 J4
Temple Wy *E/WMAL* ME19 108 D6
Ten Acre Wy *RHAM* ME8 70 E5 5
Tenchley's La *OXTED* RH8 141 H2
Tennyson Av *HOO/HM* ME3 31 G7
Tennyson Rd *DART* DA1 23 K4
GILL ME7 4 C5
Tennyson Wk *GVW* DA11 44 E1
TIL RM18 27 J1
Tensing Av *GVW* DA11 45 F1 2
Tenterden Rd *CRBK* TN17 238 D2
HDCN TN27 217 K6
WALD ME5 88 C1 2
Terence Cl *CHAT* ME4 4 A6 2
GVE DA12 28 C8 2
Terminus Rd *MAIDW* ME16 132 A4
Tern Crs *STRD* ME2 48 B8
Terrace Rd *MAIDW* ME16 6 B3
SIT ME10 94 C3
The Terraces *RDART* DA2 24 B6
Terrace St *GVE* DA12 27 J5
The Terrace *GVE* DA12 27 J5
ROCH ME1 2 C3 6
SEV TN13 123 F1
Terry's Lodge Rd *BGR/WK* TN15 104 C1
Terry Wk *DIT/AY* ME20 108 C4 3
Testers Cl *OXTED* RH8 141 F2
Teston La *MAID/SHEP* ME15 131 G7
Teston Rd *E/WMAL* ME19 106 D6
E/WMAL ME19 129 K1
Teynham Gn *RHAM* ME8 69 H2
Thackeray Rd *DIT/AY* ME20 108 D3
Thames Av *HOO/HM* ME3 33 F2
RHAM ME8 70 B6
Thames Ga *DART* DA1 23 K4
Thames Rd *DART* DA1 22 D2
TONN TN10 170 C1
Thames Vw *HOO/HM* ME3 31 H7
Thames Wy *GVW* DA11 26 E7
Thamley *PUR* RM19 12 E4
Thatch Barn Rd *HDCN* TN27 180 B8
Thatcher Rd *STPH/PW* TN12 198 A2
Thatchers La *HOO/HM* ME3 31 G1
The Thatchers *MAIDW* ME16 132 B1 7
Thelma Cl *GVE* DA12 46 C3
Theobalds *HAWK* TN18 235 F4
Theodore Cl *RTWE/PEM* TN2 190 E7
Theodore Pl *GILL* ME7 4 C3 2
Third Av *CHAT* ME4 68 D5
GILL ME7 5 E5
Third St *RRTW* TN3 205 J3
Thirlemere Cl *MAIDW* ME16 110 D6 2
Thirlmere Cl *GILL* ME7 69 H1
STRD ME2 49 H5 2
Thirlmere Rd *STH/RUST* TN4 206 C1
Thirza Rd *DART* DA1 23 J5
Thistlebank *WALD* ME5 88 B3
Thistledown *MAID/BEAR* ME14 134 B2 5
Thistledown Cl *GILL* ME7 89 H2 1
Thistle Rd *GVE* DA12 28 B6
Thomas Dr *GVE* DA12 28 A8
Thomas Rd *SIT* ME10 94 C2
Thomas St *ROCH* ME1 2 C5
STH/RUST TN4 10 C2
Thompson Cl *RHAM* ME8 70 D6 4
Thomson Cl *SNOD* ME6 85 K5 2
Thong La *BGR/WK* TN15 126 E1
GVE DA12 28 D8
Thorn Cl *WALD* ME5 87 J5
Thorndale Cl *WALD* ME5 87 J1
Thornden La *CRBK* TN17 238 E6
Thorndike Cl *CHAT* ME4 68 A6 1
Thorndon Cl *STMC/STPC* BR5 38 A7
Thorndon Rd *STMC/STPC* BR5 38 A7
The Thorn Est *HDCN* TN27 183 H8
Thornfield Gdns *RTWE/PEM* TN2 208 A1
Thornham Rd *RHAM* ME8 69 K3
Thornhill Pl *MAID/BEAR* ME14 7 D1
Thorn Rd *STPH/PW* TN12 197 F3
Thorn's Meadow *BH/WHM* TN16 121 J2
Thorold Rd *CHAT* ME4 4 B5
Thorpe Av *TONN* TN10 170 C1
Thorpe Wk *RHAM* ME8 89 K3
Thrale Wy *RHAM* ME8 90 B2
Three Elm La *TONN* TN10 149 H8
Three Gates Rd *HART* DA3 61 F4
Three Leg Cross Rd *WADH* TN5 232 B3
Threshers Dr *MAID/BEAR* ME14 133 K1
The Thrift *RDART* DA2 43 H1
Thrush Cl *WALD* ME5 68 C7
Thursland Rd *SCUP* DA14 39 F3
Thurston Dr *STRD* ME2 48 C7
Thyssel La *RYE* TN31 244 E8
Tibbs Court La *STPH/PW* TN12 193 H7
Ticehurst Cl *STMC/STPC* BR5 38 B5 2
Tichborne Cl *MAIDW* ME16 110 C8
The Tideway *ROCH* ME1 67 H6
Tilbury Cl *STMC/STPC* BR5 38 C7
Tilbury Gdns *TIL* RM18 27 H3
Tilbury Rd *RHAM* ME8 70 D4
Tilden Cl *RASHW* TN26 219 J7
Tilden Gill Rd *TENT* TN30 230 C7
Tilden La *STPH/PW* TN12 176 C6
Tilden Rd *HDCN* TN27 180 C4
Tilebarn Cnr *TONN* TN10 170 E2
Tile Flds *RMAID* ME17 136 B4
Tile Kiln La *BXLY* DA5 22 A8
Tile Lodge Rd *HDCN* TN27 161 K7
Tilghman Wy *SNOD* ME6 86 A5
Till Av *EYN* DA4 59 J4
Tillingbourne Gn
STMC/STPC BR5 56 B1 3
Tilmans Md *EYN* DA4 59 J4
Tilsden La *CRBK* TN17 226 A3
Tilton Rd *BGR/WK* TN15 105 F7
Timber Bank *MEO* DA13 83 G6
Timberbank *WALD* ME5 68 B8 1
Timbertop Rd *BH/WHM* TN16 97 G5
Timber Tops *WALD* ME5 88 E6
Tinker Pot La *BGR/WK* TN15 80 D8
Tinkerpot Ri *BGR/WK* TN15 103 G1
Tinkers La *WADH* TN5 232 B3
Tintagel Gdns *STRD* ME2 48 E7 2
Tintagel Rd *STMC/STPC* BR5 56 D6
Tintern Rd *MAIDW* ME16 110 C7
Titchfield Rd *MAID/SHEP* ME15 134 B8
Titsey Hl *OXTED* RH8 119 F3
WARL CR6 118 D3
Titsey Rd *OXTED* RH8 119 F6
Tobruk Wy *WALD* ME5 68 A8
Toby Gdns *RTON* TN11 150 A6 3
Toddington Crs *WALD* ME5 87 J5
Tolgate La *STRD* ME2 2 B1 3
Tolgate Wy *MAID/BEAR* ME14 110 E3
Tolhurst Rd *STPH/PW* TN12 172 C7
Toll *GRH* DA9 24 B3
Tollgate Ms *BGR/WK* TN15 105 G7
Tollgate Pl *HDCN* TN27 200 C1
Tollgate Rd *RDART* DA2 24 C6
Tolsey Md *BGR/WK* TN15 105 G6
Tom Joyce Cl *SNOD* ME6 85 J7
Tomlin Cl *SNOD* ME6 85 K6
STPH/PW TN12 198 A2
Tonbridge By-pass *RSEV* TN14 146 C4
RTON TN11 146 E6
Tonbridge Rd *BGR/WK* TN15 126 C4
MAIDW ME16 131 K4
RTON TN11 147 H8
RTWE/PEM TN2 191 H7
SEV TN13 9 E6
WBY/YAL ME18 129 G6
Tonge Rd *SIT* ME10 94 C2
Tong La *STPH/PW* TN12 210 E3
Tong Rd *STPH/PW* TN12 210 E1
Tongswood Dr *HAWK* TN18 235 J5
Tooley St *GVW* DA11 26 E6
Top Dartford Rd *SWLY* BR8 40 D4
Toplands Av *SOCK/AV* RM15 13 F1
Torbay Rd *STPH/PW* TN12 173 K1
Toronto Rd *GILL* ME7 5 E4
TIL RM18 27 H1
Torrens Wk *GVE* DA12 46 B3
Torrington Cl *WBY/YAL* ME18 129 F6
Tovil Gn *MAID/SHEP* ME15 6 B5
Tovil Hl *MAID/SHEP* ME15 6 B6
Tovil Rd *MAID/SHEP* ME15 6 C5
Tower Cl *GVE* DA12 46 B3
ORP BR6 56 A6
Tower Cft *EYN* DA4 59 H6
Tower Gdns *MAID/BEAR* ME14 134 D3
Tower Hl *E/WMAL* ME19 107 F7
Tower La *MAID/BEAR* ME14 134 C2
Tower Rd *DART* DA1 23 F6
ORP BR6 56 A6
Towers Wd *EYN* DA4 42 C6
Tower Vw *E/WMAL* ME19 129 K2
Town Acres *TON* TN9 170 C2
Townfield Cnr *GVE* DA12 27 K7
Town Hl *E/WMAL* ME19 108 A5
RRTW TN3 221 J2
Town Hill Cl *E/WMAL* ME19 108 A5
Townland Cl *HDCN* TN27 217 K5
Town Rd *HOO/HM* ME3 31 F8
Townsend Rd *SNOD* ME6 85 H5
Townshead Cl *SCUP* DA14 38 C4
Toy's Hl *BH/WHM* TN16 143 J2
EDEN TN8 143 J7
The Tracies *RSIT* ME9 72 B8
Tradescant Dr *MEO* DA13 63 J3
Trafalgar Rd *DART* DA1 23 H8
GVW DA11 27 H6
ROCH ME1 86 B2
Trafalgar St *GILL* ME7 4 C3
Tramways *CHAT* ME4 4 C6
Transfesa Rd *STPH/PW* TN12 173 J7
Trapfield Cl *MAID/BEAR* ME14 134 E2
Trapfield La *MAID/BEAR* ME14 134 E2
Trapham Rd *MAIDW* ME16 6 A2
Travers Gdns *RSIT* ME9 115 K1
Travertine Rd *WALD* ME5 88 C5
Trebble Rd *SWCM* DA10 25 K5
Trebilco Cl *RTWE/PEM* TN2 190 D7
Tredegar Rd *RDART* DA2 40 D1
Treebourne Rd *BH/WHM* TN16 97 G4
Tree La *BGR/WK* TN15 126 E6
Treetops *BGR/WK* TN15 102 E4
GVE DA12 45 J3
TON TN9 170 B7
Trelawn Crs *WALD* ME5 88 C4
Trellyn Cl *MAIDW* ME16 131 K4
Trench Rd *TONN* TN10 148 B8
Trentham Dr *STMC/STPC* BR5 56 B1
Trenton Cl *MAIDW* ME16 110 B7
Trent Rd *WALD* ME5 88 C1
Trevale Rd *ROCH* ME1 67 G5
Trevelyan Cl *DART* DA1 23 J3
Trevereux Hl *OXTED* RH8 142 A3
Trevino Dr *WALD* ME5 88 A4
Trevithick Dr *DART* DA1 23 J3
Trevor Dr *MAIDW* ME16 132 B1
Trewin Cl *DIT/AY* ME20 109 H4
Trident Cl *STRD* ME2 3 E1
Trinity Cl *RTWE/PEM* TN2 11 F3
Trinity Gdns *DART* DA1 23 G5
Trinity Rd *GILL* ME7 4 C2
GVE DA12 27 K6
Tristan Gdns *STH/RUST* TN4 206 C2
Trivett Cl *GRH* DA9 25 F4
Trolling Down Hl *RDART* DA2 24 A8
Troodos Hl *MAID/BEAR* ME14 111 F6
Trosley Av *GVW* DA11 27 J8
Trottiscliffe Rd *E/WMAL* ME19 106 E3
Trotts La *BH/WHM* TN16 120 C6
Trotwood Cl *WALD* ME5 88 B6
Troy La *EDEN* TN8 163 K2
Troys Md *RMAID* ME17 136 B4
Trubridge Rd *HOO/HM* ME3 50 E1
Truro Cl *RHAM* ME8 70 A3
Truro Rd *GVE* DA12 46 A1
Truro Wk *TONN* TN10 170 D1
Trycewell La *BGR/WK* TN15 104 D8
Tubbenden La South *ORP* BR6 75 J1
Tubs Hl *SEV* TN13 8 C3
Tudeley La *RTON* TN11 171 H6

TON TN9 170 D7
Tudeley Rd TON TN9 170 E7
Tudor Av MAID/BEAR ME14 7 E1
Tudor Cl DART DA1 22 E5
GVW DA11 27 F7
Tudor Ct RTWE/PEM TN2 10 A6 3
SWLY BR8 57 K4
Tudor Crs RSEV TN14 102 A4
Tudor Dr RSEV TN14 102 A3
Tudor Gv HOO/HM ME3 50 A2
RHAM ME8 70 B6
Tufa Cl WALD ME5 88 C5
Tufnail Rd DART DA1 23 J5
Tufton Rd RHAM ME8 70 C5
Tufton St MAID/BEAR ME14 7 D3
Tulip Tree Cl TON TN9 170 A6
Tumblefield Rd BGR/WK TN15 82 A6
Tumblers Hl RMAID ME17 157 H7
Tunbury Av WALD ME5 88 A3
Tunbury Av South WALD ME5 88 A5
Tunnel Rd RTW TN1 11 D2
Tunstall Rd RSIT ME9 93 H6
Tupman Cl ROCH ME1 2 B4
Turgis Cl RMAID ME17 157 G2
Turnbull Cl RDART DA2 24 D6
Turnden Rd CRBK TN17 225 G3
Turner Av CRBK TN17 225 K3
Turner Ct DART DA1 23 F4
Turner Rd BH/WHM TN16 74 B7
RDART DA2 43 G1
TONN TN10 170 E1
Turners Av TENT TN30 230 B6
Turners Gdns SEV TN13 124 A7
Turners Green La WADH TN5 220 B8
Turners Green Rd WADH TN5 220 B7
Turner's Oak Shaw HART DA3 61 K6
Turner St HOO/HM ME3 31 G1
Turnpike Dr ORP BR6 76 D4
Turnstone HART DA3 44 B8
Turnstone Rd WALD ME5 88 D4
The Turnstones GVE DA12 28 A8
Tuscan Dr WALD ME5 88 D5
Tutsham Wy STPH/PW TN12 173 H8
Tuxford Rd STH/RUST TN4 206 A1
Tweed Rd TONN TN10 170 C1
Twisden Rd E/WMAL ME19 108 D6
Twisleton Ct DART DA1 23 G5
Twitton La RSEV TN14 101 G3
Twitton Mdw RSEV TN14 101 G3
Two Gates Hl HOO/HM ME3 48 E1
Twydall Gn RHAM ME8 69 J3
Twydall La RHAM ME8 69 J4
Twyford Cl RHAM ME8 70 D4 2
Twyford Rd RTON TN11 150 A5
Tydeman Rd MAID/SHEP ME15 134 B4
Tye La ORP BR6 75 H1
Tyland La MAID/BEAR ME14 111 F3
Tyler Cl E/WMAL ME19 108 D6
Tyler Dr RHAM ME8 90 B2
Tylers Green Rd SWLY BR8 57 K3
Tyne Cl WALD ME5 88 C1
Tynedale Cl RDART DA2 24 C7 2
Tyne Rd TONN TN10 170 B1
Typhoon Rd E/WMAL ME19 129 H3

U

Uckfield La EDEN TN8 185 J1
Ufton Cl MAID/SHEP ME15 134 A5
Ufton La SIT ME10 93 K3
Ulcombe Hl RMAID ME17 158 D5
Ulcombe Rd HDCN TN27 180 A8
RMAID ME17 157 G3
Underdown Av CHAT ME4 68 A5 1
Underlyn La STPH/PW TN12 176 C6
Underriver House Rd RTON TN11 147 G3
Underwood Cl MAID/SHEP ME15 6 C5 3
Unicorn Wk GRH DA9 24 E4 2
Unicumes La MAIDW ME16 132 C4
Union St CHAT ME4 4 A4 6
MAID/BEAR ME14 7 D2
ROCH ME1 2 C3 7
Unity St SIT ME10 93 K3
University Wy DART DA1 23 G2
Unwin Cl DIT/AY ME20 110 A3 1
Upbury Wy CHAT ME4 4 A4
Upchat Rd HOO/HM ME3 49 K2
Updale Rd SCUP DA14 38 A2
Uplands Cl STRD ME2 48 C8 4
Uplands Rd ORP BR6 56 C5
Uplands Wy SEV TN13 8 B2
Upnor Rd STRD ME2 49 J6
Upper Austin Lodge Rd EYN DA4 79 G1
Upper Av MEO DA13 45 F6
Upper Barn Hl MAID/SHEP ME15 153 J3
Upper Britton Pl GILL ME7 4 B3 1
Upper Bush Rd STRD ME2 65 J4
Upper Cumberland Wk RTW TN1 11 D6
Upper Dr BH/WHM TN16 97 G5
Upper Dunstan Rd STH/RUST TN4 11 D1
Upper Fant Rd MAIDW ME16 132 C4
Upper Field Rd SIT ME10 94 C1
Upper Green Rd RTON TN11 148 C1
Upper Grosvenor Rd
STH/RUST TN4 11 D2
Upper Haysden La STH/RUST TN4 169 H8
Upper Hunton Hl
MAID/SHEP ME15 154 A3
Upper Luton Rd WALD ME5 4 B5
Upper Ml WBY/YAL ME18 130 B6
Upper Nellington RRTW TN3 206 A2
Upper Profit RRTW TN3 205 K3
Upper Rd MAID/SHEP ME15 7 E5
Upper Spring La BGR/WK TN15 126 B1
Upper Stephens RRTW TN3 205 K3
Upper Stone St MAID/SHEP ME15 7 D4
Upper St RMAID ME17 136 C3
RMAID ME17 157 H1
Upperton Rd SCUP DA14 38 A3
Upton Quarry RRTW TN3 205 J3 4
Uptons HDCN TN27 180 A8
Uridge Crs TONN TN10 170 C2 1
Uridge Rd TONN TN10 170 C2
Urquhart Cl WALD ME5 88 B1 2
Usborne Cl STPH/PW TN12 198 A3
Uvedale Rd OXTED RH8 118 D8

V

Vale Av RTW TN1 10 C4 5
STH/RUST TN4 189 K5
Vale Dr WALD ME5 87 J1
Valenciennes Rd SIT ME10 93 K3
Valentine Cl GILL ME7 69 H5
Valentine Dr HOO/HM ME3 33 F3
Valentine Rd MAID/SHEP ME15 134 A7 3
Valerian Cl WALD ME5 87 K2
Vale Ri TON TN9 170 D5
Vale Rd DART DA1 22 E7
GVW DA11 26 E6
HAWK TN18 235 F3
MAID/SHEP ME15 154 E2
RTW TN1 10 C4
STH/RUST TN4 189 K5
TON TN9 170 B5 5
TON TN9 170 D5
Valetta Wy ROCH ME1 2 B4
Valiant Rd WALD ME5 88 D4
The Vallance RSIT ME9 95 H8
Valley Cl DART DA1 22 C5
Valley Dr GVE DA12 46 A2
MAID/SHEP ME15 133 F8
RTON TN11 150 B4
SEV TN13 9 D4
Valley Forge Cl TONN TN10 171 F2
Valley Gdns GRH DA9 25 G5
Valley La BGR/WK TN15 82 D4
MEO DA13 83 H4
Valley Ri WALD ME5 88 A4
Valley Rd DART DA1 22 C5
GILL ME7 5 E4
HART DA3 61 G5
STH/RUST TN4 206 C2
STMC/STPC BR5 38 C6
The Valley RMAID ME17 154 D3
Valley Vw BH/WHM TN16 97 G5
GRH DA9 25 G5
STH/RUST TN4 190 A4
Valley View Rd ROCH ME1 67 G5
Vancouver Dr RHAM ME8 69 K5
Vanessa Wk GVE DA12 46 C3
Vanessa Wy BXLY DA5 40 A1
Vange Cottage Ms ROCH ME1 2 B4 5
Vanguard Wy EDEN TN8 142 A5
LING RH7 184 A6
OXTED RH8 118 D4
Vanity La RMAID ME17 154 D6
Vanquisher Wk GVE DA12 46 C1
Varnes St DIT/AY ME20 86 E8
Vaughan Av TONN TN10 148 E8
Vauxhall Cl GVW DA11 27 G6
Vauxhall Crs SNOD ME6 85 K8
Vauxhall Gdns TON TN9 170 C7
Vauxhall La RTON TN11 170 D8
STH/RUST TN4 189 K3
Vauxhall Pl DART DA1 23 H6
Veles Rd SNOD ME6 85 J6
Venners Cl BXLYHN DA7 22 B1
Ventnor Cl WALD ME5 68 D6
Vermont Rd STH/RUST TN4 206 B2 2
Vernon Cl BGR/WK TN15 80 E4
STMC/STPC BR5 38 C8
Vernon Rd RTW TN1 11 E1
SWCM DA10 26 A5
Verona Gdns GVE DA12 46 B2
Veryan Cl STMC/STPC BR5 56 D1
Vesper Ct HDCN TN27 202 A5
Vestry Rd RSEV TN14 102 A6
Vexil Cl PUR RM19 13 H4
Via Romana GVE DA12 28 E7
Vicarage Cl DIT/AY ME20 109 K3
HOO/HM ME3 34 D3
STRD ME2 85 K1
Vicarage Dr GVW DA11 26 D5 1
Vicarage Hl BH/WHM TN16 120 D5
Vicarage La GVE DA12 28 D8
HOO/HM ME3 51 F2
MAID/SHEP ME15 132 B7
RSIT ME9 72 B3
Vicarage Rd GILL ME7 4 C3
SIT ME10 73 J7
STH/RUST TN4 189 K4
STRD ME2 2 B1
STRD ME2 85 H1
WBY/YAL ME18 152 E5
Vicary Wy MAIDW ME16 6 A2
Victoria Cl RMAID ME17 159 J7
WALD ME5 87 J4 1
Victoria Dr EYN DA4 42 C7
WBY/YAL ME18 129 H4
Victoria Gdns BH/WHM TN16 97 G2
Victoria Hill Rd SWLY BR8 40 C6
Victoria Rd BFN/LL DA15 38 A1
CHAT ME4 4 B6
DART DA1 23 G4
EDEN TN8 164 C6
GVW DA11 27 G7
RTON TN11 150 B8
RTW TN1 11 D3 9
SIT ME10 93 J2
STH/RUST TN4 189 J5
WALD ME5 87 K4
Victoria St DIT/AY ME20 86 E8
GILL ME7 5 D2
MAIDW ME16 6 B3
ROCH ME1 2 C3
STRD ME2 2 B1
Victoria Ter ROCH ME1 2 A6
Victory Wy GRH DA9 24 B3
Vidgeon Av HOO/HM ME3 32 E8
View Cl BH/WHM TN16 97 G3
Viewlands Av BH/WHM TN16 98 E7
View Rd HOO/HM ME3 31 G7
Vigilant Wy GVE DA12 46 C3
Vigo Rd BGR/WK TN15 82 E7
Viking Rd GVW DA11 44 D1
Viking Wy BGR/WK TN15 80 D1
Villa Cl GVE DA12 28 E8
Village Green Av BH/WHM TN16 97 J4
Village Green Rd DART DA1 22 D3
Village Green Wy BH/WHM TN16 97 J4
Villa Rd HOO/HM ME3 48 A3
Vincent Rd DIT/AY ME20 87 H7
SIT ME10 94 D3
Vincent Sq BH/WHM TN16 74 B8
Vine Av SEV TN13 9 D3
Vine Court Rd SEV TN13 9 E3
The Vineries GILL ME7 5 E3
Vine Rd ORP BR6 76 A2
Viners Cl SIT ME10 93 K5
Vines La ROCH ME1 2 C3
RTON TN11 147 G5
The Vine SEV TN13 9 E3
Vine Wk STPH/PW TN12 198 A3
Vineyard Crs RHAM ME8 70 E5 6
Viney's Gdns TENT TN30 230 C5
Vinson Cl ORP BR6 56 B5
Vinters Rd MAID/BEAR ME14 7 E3
Vintners Wy MAID/BEAR ME14 134 A2 4
Violet Cl WALD ME5 88 B6
Virginia Rd GILL ME7 4 C1 6
Vixen Cl WALD ME5 68 D8
Volante Dr SIT ME10 73 K7
Volante Wy GVE DA12 46 B2
Vulcan Cl WALD ME5 68 C7

W

Wade Av STMC/STPC BR5 56 E4
Wadham Pl SIT ME10 94 C4
Wadlands Rd HOO/HM ME3 31 G1
Waghorn Rd SNOD ME6 85 K6 9
Waghorn St CHAT ME4 4 B6 2
Wagoners Cl MAID/BEAR ME14 134 A2 5
Wagon La STPH/PW TN12 174 A5
Wagtail Wy STMC/STPC BR5 56 E1
Waid Cl DART DA1 23 J5
Wainscott Rd STRD ME2 49 J4
Wainscott Wk STRD ME2 49 J3
Wakefield Rd GRH DA9 25 H4
Wakehurst Cl RMAID ME17 154 B3 1
Wakeley Rd RHAM ME8 70 D5
Wakely Cl BH/WHM TN16 97 G5
Wake Rd ROCH ME1 67 H6
Waldeck Rd DART DA1 23 J6
Waldenhurst Rd STMC/STPC BR5 56 E4
Waldens Cl STMC/STPC BR5 56 E4
Waldens Rd STMC/STPC BR5 57 F3
The Waldens RMAID ME17 158 C4
Walderslade Rd CHAT ME4 68 A7
WALD ME5 68 A8 1
WALD ME5 88 A3
Walderslade Woods WALD ME5 87 J4
Waldron Dr MAID/SHEP ME15 133 F8
The Waldrons OXTED RH8 140 D2
Walker Cl DART DA1 22 C2
Walkhurst Rd CRBK TN17 227 G7
Walkley Rd DART DA1 22 E4
Wallace Cl RTWE/PEM TN2 207 F6

Wallace Gdns *SWCM* DA10 **25** K5 3
Wallace Rd *ROCH* ME1 **67** K6
Wallbridge La *RHAM* ME8 **71** G3
Wall Cl *HOO/HM* ME3 **32** E7
Waller Hl *CRBK* TN17 **215** J1
Wallers *RRTW* TN3 **188** E7
Wallhouse Rd *ERITH* DA8 **12** A7
Wallis Av *MAID/SHEP* ME15 **156** A1
Wallis Cl *RDART* DA2 **40** D1
The Wall *SIT* ME10 **93** K1
Walmer Gdns *SIT* ME10 **93** J1
Walmers Av *HOO/HM* ME3 **47** K2
Walnut Cl *STPH/PW* TN12 **173** J8
WALD ME5 **68** C6
Walnut Hill Rd *MEO* DA13 **45** F8
Walnuts Rd *ORP* BR6 **56** B5
Walnut Tree Av *DART* DA1 **23** H8
MAID/SHEP ME15 **155** G1
Walnut Tree Ct *DIT/AY* ME20 **109** F5
Walnut Tree Dr *SIT* ME10 **93** J2 1
Walnut Tree La *MAID/SHEP* ME15 **155** G1
Walnut Tree Wy *MEO* DA13 **63** H3
Walnut Wy *RTWE/PEM* TN2 **190** D6
SWLY BR8 **40** A7
Walpole Cl *E/WMAL* ME19 **108** D6 4
Walsham Rd *WALD* ME5 **88** A5
Walsingham Cl *RHAM* ME8 **90** A3
Walsingham Rd *STMC/STPC* BR5 **38** C6
Walter Burke Av *ROCH* ME1 **86** B1 1
Walter's Farm Rd *TON* TN9 **170** C5
Walters Green Rd *RTON* TN11 **187** G8
Walters Rd *HOO/HM* ME3 **33** F8
Waltham Cl *DART* DA1 **22** D5
STMC/STPC BR5 **56** E5
Waltham Rd *RHAM* ME8 **69** J3
Walton Rd *SCUP* DA14 **38** C1
TONN TN10 **149** F8
Wanden La *HDCN* TN27 **182** B5
Wansbury Wy *SWLY* BR8 **58** D2
Warblers Cl *STRD* ME2 **2** A1
Warden Cl *MAIDW* ME16 **132** C2
Warden Mill Cl *WBY/YAL* ME18 **130** B7
Warden Rd *ROCH* ME1 **2** C5
Wardsbrook Rd *WADH* TN5 **232** B7
Wardwell La *RSIT* ME9 **72** B4
Ware St *MAID/BEAR* ME14 **134** C1
Warham Rd *RSEV* TN14 **101** K3
Waring Cl *ORP* BR6 **76** A2
Waring Dr *ORP* BR6 **76** A2
Waring Rd *SCUP* DA14 **38** D4
Warland Rd *BGR/WK* TN15 **80** E4
Warlingham Cl *RHAM* ME8 **70** D5 2
Warmlake Rd *RMAID* ME17 **156** D5
Warner St *CHAT* ME4 **3** F5 4
Warnford Gdns
MAID/SHEP ME15 **133** G6 2
Warnford Rd *ORP* BR6 **76** A1
Warren Av *ORP* BR6 **76** A1
Warren Cl *SIT* ME10 **94** C4 3
Warren Ct *BGR/WK* TN15 **9** E4
Warren Dr *ORP* BR6 **76** C1
Warren Gdns *ORP* BR6 **76** B1
Warren La *OXTED* RH8 **140** E5
RSIT ME9 **91** F3
Warren Rd *DART* DA1 **41** H1
MEO DA13 **44** C3
MEO DA13 **65** F3
ORP BR6 **76** A1
SCUP DA14 **38** D1
WALD ME5 **87** J6
The Warrens *HART* DA3 **62** A3
Warren St *RMAID* ME17 **139** K8
The Warren *GVE* DA12 **46** A2
RTON TN11 **187** J2
WADH TN5 **232** C5
Warren Vw *GVE* DA12 **47** H4
Warren Wood Rd *ROCH* ME1 **67** J7
Warrington Rd *STPH/PW* TN12 **173** H8
Warrior Av *GVE* DA12 **45** K2
Warwick Cl *ORP* BR6 **56** B7
Warwick Crs *ROCH* ME1 **66** E4
SIT ME10 **93** H1
Warwick Gdns *MEO* DA13 **63** H6
Warwick Pk *RTWE/PEM* TN2 **11** D6
Warwick Pl *GVW* DA11 **26** C4
MAIDW ME16 **6** B3
Warwick Rd *RTW* TN1 **10** C5
SCUP DA14 **38** C3
Washneys Rd *ORP* BR6 **76** B8
Washpond La *WARL* CR6 **96** A5
Wassall La *CRBK* TN17 **238** C7
Watchmans Ter *WALD* ME5 **4** C6 4
Watercress Dr *RSEV* TN14 **102** A7
Watercroft Rd *RSEV* TN14 **77** G5
Waterdales *GVW* DA11 **26** E7
Waterditch La *RMAID* ME17 **139** K8
Waterdown Rd *STH/RUST* TN4 **206** C5
Waterfield *RTWE/PEM* TN2 **207** F7
Wateringbury Cl *STMC/STPC* BR5 **38** C8
Wateringbury Rd *E/WMAL* ME19 **130** D3
Waterlakes *EDEN* TN8 **164** C6
Water La *E/WMAL* ME19 **108** A6
EDEN TN8 **163** H7
HAWK TN18 **225** G7
HDCN TN27 **199** J2
HDCN TN27 **201** J4
MAID/BEAR ME14 **135** G1
MAID/SHEP ME15 **153** H8
OXTED RH8 **118** E5
PUR RM19 **12** E4
RMAID ME17 **158** D3
RSEV TN14 **78** C7
SCUP DA14 **39** G1
Waterloo Pl *TON* TN9 **170** B6 5
Waterloo Rd *CRBK* TN17 **225** K1
GILL ME7 **4** C4
SIT ME10 **93** J1
TON TN9 **170** B6
Waterloo St *GVE* DA12 **27** K6 5
MAID/SHEP ME15 **7** D4
Waterlow Rd *MAID/BEAR* ME14 **7** D1
MEO DA13 **83** H7
Waterman's La *STPH/PW* TN12 **193** K3
Watermeadow Cl *GILL* ME7 **69** G8
Watermill Cl *MAIDW* ME16 **132** B1 8
STRD ME2 **49** H6 3
Water Mill Wy *EYN* DA4 **42** A7
Watermint Cl *STMC/STPC* BR5 **56** E1 10
Waters Edge *MAID/SHEP* ME15 **6** C5
Waterside *DART* DA1 **22** B4
MAID/BEAR ME14 **6** C2
Waterside La *GILL* ME7 **5** F1
Waterside Ms *WBY/YAL* ME18 **130** B8
Water Slippe *RTON* TN11 **149** K5
Waters Pl *GILL* ME7 **69** H8
Waterton Av *GVE* DA12 **28** B6
Watery La *BGR/WK* TN15 **103** H7
SCUP DA14 **38** C4
Watkins Cl *STPH/PW* TN12 **198** A1
Watling Av *WALD* ME5 **5** D6
Watling Pl *SIT* ME10 **94** B3
Watling St *DART* DA1 **24** A6
GVE DA12 **46** D6
GVW DA11 **45** J3
MEO DA13 **44** C1
STRD ME2 **2** A1
WALD ME5 **5** D6
Watson Av *WALD* ME5 **87** J1
Watson's Hl *SIT* ME10 **93** K1
Watts' Av *ROCH* ME1 **2** C4
Watts Cl *SNOD* ME6 **86** A6
Watts Crs *PUR* RM19 **13** G4
Watt's Cross Rd *RTON* TN11 **169** F1
Watts' St *CHAT* ME4 **3** E5
Wat Tyler Wy *MAID/SHEP* ME15 **7** D4
Waveney Rd *TONN* TN10 **170** B1
Waverley Cl *RMAID* ME17 **154** C4
WALD ME5 **88** E4
Waverley Dr *RTWE/PEM* TN2 **191** F8
Wayfield Rd *WALD* ME5 **68** A7
Waylands *SWLY* BR8 **58** C1
Waylands Cl *RSEV* TN14 **100** A2
Wayne Cl *ORP* BR6 **56** A7
Wayside *TENT* TN30 **230** B4 1
Wayside Av *TENT* TN30 **230** B3
Wayside Dr *EDEN* TN8 **164** D3
Wayville Rd *DART* DA1 **24** A6
Weald Cl *MAID/SHEP* ME15 **133** J8
MEO DA13 **45** F5
RSEV TN14 **145** K4
Weald Ct *RTON* TN11 **147** H8
SIT ME10 **93** J4
Wealden Av *TENT* TN30 **230** B4
Wealden Cl *RTON* TN11 **169** J1
Wealden Wy *DIT/AY* ME20 **109** J6
Weald Rd *SEV* TN13 **123** K7
Weald Vw *STPH/PW* TN12 **194** B5
WADH TN5 **220** B8
Weald View Rd *TON* TN9 **170** B7
Wealdway *BGR/WK* TN15 **105** K8
MEO DA13 **45** J6
RRTW TN3 **188** B8
STPH/PW TN12 **151** F4
WBY/YAL ME18 **127** K4
WBY/YAL ME18 **150** D1
Weardale Av *RDART* DA2 **24** B8
Weare Rd *STH/RUST* TN4 **190** C6
Weatherly Cl *ROCH* ME1 **2** C4 7
Weavering Cl *STRD* ME2 **49** G4
Weavering St *MAID/BEAR* ME14 **134** A2
Weavers Cl *GVW* DA11 **27** H7 1
STPH/PW TN12 **198** B2
Weavers La *RSEV* TN14 **102** A8
The Weavers *HDCN* TN27 **217** K5
MAIDW ME16 **132** B2
Webb Cl *HOO/HM* ME3 **32** E8
Webster Rd *RHAM* ME8 **70** C5
Wedgewood Cl *MAIDW* ME16 **132** B1 9
Wedgewood Dr *WALD* ME5 **68** B7
Wedgwoods *BH/WHM* TN16 **97** G8 1
Weeds Wood Rd *WALD* ME5 **88** A2
Weeks La *HDCN* TN27 **217** K1
Week St *MAID/BEAR* ME14 **6** C2
Weird Wd *HART* DA3 **44** D8
Welbeck Av *STH/RUST* TN4 **190** C6
Weld Cl *STPH/PW* TN12 **198** B2
Welland Rd *TONN* TN10 **170** B2
Well Cl *RTON* TN11 **168** D5
Wellcome Av *DART* DA1 **23** H3
Weller Av *ROCH* ME1 **3** D6
Weller Rd *STH/RUST* TN4 **206** B
Wellers Cl *BH/WHM* TN16 **120** C
Well Fld *HART* DA3 **62** A
Well Hl *ORP* BR6 **77** J
Well Hill La *ORP* BR6 **77** J
Wellington Cottages *HAWK* TN18 **234** E
Wellingtonia Wy *EDEN* TN8 **164** C
Wellington Pl *MAID/BEAR* ME14 **6** C
Wellington Rd *DART* DA1 **23** F
GILL ME7 **4** C
SIT ME10 **93** G
STMC/STPC BR5 **56** C
TIL RM18 **27** H
Wellington St *GVE* DA12 **27** K
Wellington Wy *E/WMAL* ME19 **129** H
Wellmeade Dr *SEV* TN13 **9** D
Well Penn Rd *HOO/HM* ME3 **31** G
Well Rd *MAID/BEAR* ME14 **7** D
RSEV TN14 **102** A
Wells Cl *RTW* TN1 **10** C4
TENT TN30 **230** A
TON TN9 **170** D
Wells Rd *STRD* ME2 **66** C
Well St *E/WMAL* ME19 **108** C
MAID/SHEP ME15 **154** E
Well Winch Rd *SIT* ME10 **93** J
Welton Cl *TON* TN9 **169** K
Wemmick Cl *ROCH* ME1 **67** J7
Wendover Cl *STRD* ME2 **86** A1
Wendover Wy *ORP* BR6 **56** B3
Wents Wd *MAID/BEAR* ME14 **134** B
Wentworth Cl *GVW* DA11 **45** H3
ORP BR6 **75** K1
Wentworth Dr *DART* DA1 **22** D
HOO/HM ME3 **31** G
RHAM ME8 **70** B7
SIT ME10 **93** H1
Wesley Cl *MAIDW* ME16 **131** K
STMC/STPC BR5 **38** D
Wessex Dr *ERITH* DA8 **22** B
Westbourne St *SIT* ME10 **93** K
Westbrook Dr *STMC/STPC* BR5 **56** E
Westbrooke Cl *CHAT* ME4 **4** A6
Westbury Ter *BH/WHM* TN16 **120** C
Westcott Av *GVW* DA11 **45** H
Westcourt St *GILL* ME7 **3** F
West Crescent Rd *GVE* DA12 **27** J
West Cross *TENT* TN30 **229** K
West Cross Gdns *TENT* TN30 **229** K
West Dr *RMAID* ME17 **157** K
WALD ME5 **87** J
Wested La *SWLY* BR8 **58** D
West End *BGR/WK* TN15 **102** D
BH/WHM TN16 **121** H
Westergate Rd *STRD* ME2 **48** E6
Westerham Cl *RHAM* ME8 **69** J
Westerham Hl *BH/WHM* TN16 **120** B
Westerham Rd *BH/WHM* TN16 **121** G
HAYES BR2 **74** C
OXTED RH8 **118** E
RSEV TN14 **122** C
SEV TN13 **122** E
SIT ME10 **93** H
Westerhill Rd *RMAID* ME17 **154** C
Western Av *HAWK* TN18 **235** F
Western Cross Cl *GRH* DA9 **25** H
Western Rd *BGR/WK* TN15 **105** F
HAWK TN18 **235** F
MAIDW ME16 **132** C
RTW TN1 **11** E
STH/RUST TN4 **189** K
WADH TN5 **220** B
Westfield *SEV* TN13 **9** E
Westfield Cl *GVE* DA12 **45** K
Westfields *HDCN* TN27 **183** K
Westfield Sole Rd
MAID/BEAR ME14 **88** E
Westfield Ter *CRBK* TN17 **225** F
Westgate Rd *DART* DA1 **23** G
Westharold *SWLY* BR8 **40** A8
West Heath Cl *DART* DA1 **22** C5
West Heath La *SEV* TN13 **123** K
West Heath Rd *DART* DA1 **22** C
West Hl *DART* DA1 **23** G
ORP BR6 **74** E
OXTED RH8 **140** B
West Hill Bank *OXTED* RH8 **140** B
Westhill Cl *GVE* DA12 **27** J
West Hill Dr *DART* DA1 **23** F
West Hill Ri *DART* DA1 **23** G
West Kent Av *GVW* DA11 **26** D
Westlands Av *SIT* ME10 **93** G
Westlands Wy *OXTED* RH8 **118** B
West La *HOO/HM* ME3 **21** F
SIT ME10 **94** B
Westmarsh Cl *MAID/SHEP* ME15 **134** B
Westmead *DIT/AY* ME20 **109** G2
West Mill Rd *DIT/AY* ME20 **109** G
Westmoreland Dr *RSIT* ME9 **72** A
Westmore Rd *BH/WHM* TN16 **97** G
Westmorland Cl
MAID/SHEP ME15 **134** A
Westmorland Gn
MAID/SHEP ME15 **134** A

Westmorland Rd
MAID/SHEP ME15 134 A7
West Motney Wy *RHAM* ME8 70 C3
Westmount Av *CHAT* ME4 3 F5
Weston Av *WTHK* RM20 13 K4
Weston Rd *STRD* ME2 2 A1
West Park Av *STH/RUST* TN4 190 A5
West Park Rd *MAID/SHEP* ME15 7 E5
Westree Rd *MAIDW* ME16 6 B4
West Rdg *SIT* ME10 93 J4
Westrise *TON* TN9 170 A7
West Rd *CRBK* TN17 212 D6
GILL ME7 4 A1
West Shaw *HART* DA3 43 J7
West St *BGR/WK* TN15 105 F3
E/WMAL ME19 107 K6
GILL ME7 5 D2
GVW DA11 27 H5
MAID/SHEP ME15 153 J6
RMAID ME17 137 G8
RMAID ME17 138 E6
SIT ME10 93 K2
STRD ME2 49 G5
West View Rd *DART* DA1 23 J5
SWLY BR8 58 A3 1
West Wk *MAIDW* ME16 132 B3
Westway *RMAID* ME17 154 C3
RTWE/PEM TN2 191 K7
Westways *BH/WHM* TN16 120 C5
EDEN TN8 164 C4
Westwell Cl *STMC/STPC* BR5 56 E5
Westwell Ct *TENT* TN30 229 K7
Westwood Rd *MAID/SHEP* ME15 133 G7
MEO DA13 43 K3
West Wood Rd *RSIT* ME9 90 E7
Westwood Rd *STH/RUST* TN4 206 A1
STPH/PW TN12 151 G8
Wetheral Dr *WALD* ME5 88 C2
Weybridge Cl *WALD* ME5 88 D2
Wey Cl *WALD* ME5 88 D1
Weyhill Cl *MAID/BEAR* ME14 7 F1
Wharfedale Rd *RDART* DA2 24 B7 3
Wharf La *HOO/HM* ME3 15 G8
Wharf Rd *GILL* ME7 4 C1 7
GVE DA12 28 B5
MAID/SHEP ME15 6 B5
Whatman Cl *MAID/BEAR* ME14 7 F1 5
Wheatcroft Cl *SIT* ME10 94 C2
Wheatcroft Gv *RHAM* ME8 70 C7
Wheatear Wy *WALD* ME5 68 C7 4
Wheatfield *E/WMAL* ME19 108 C5
Wheatfield Cl *CRBK* TN17 225 J1
Wheatfield Dr *CRBK* TN17 225 J1
Wheatfield Lea *CRBK* TN17 225 J1
Wheatfields *MAID/BEAR* ME14 133 K2 4
WALD ME5 88 E4
Wheatfield Wy *CRBK* TN17 225 J1
Wheatley Cl *GRH* DA9 25 F4 4
Wheatsheaf Cl *MAID/SHEP* ME15 133 H6
Wheatsheaf Hl *RSEV* TN14 77 G4
RSEV TN14 144 B2
Wheatsheaf Wy *TONN* TN10 148 D8
Wheeler Av *OXTED* RH8 118 B8
Wheeler's La *RMAID* ME17 154 D6
The Wheelers *RHAM* ME8 69 J8
Wheeler St *HDCN* TN27 200 B1
MAID/BEAR ME14 7 D2 5
Whetsted Rd *STPH/PW* TN12 172 E6
Whiffen's Av *CHAT* ME4 3 F3
Whiffen's Avenue W *CHAT* ME4 3 F3 2
Whimbrel Gn *DIT/AY* ME20 108 D4
The Whimbrels *CHAT* ME4 50 C5 2
Whinfell Wy *GVE* DA12 46 C2
Whippendell Cl *STMC/STPC* BR5 38 C6
Whippendell Wy *STMC/STPC* BR5 38 C6
Whistler Rd *TONN* TN10 148 D7
Whitby Cl *BH/WHM* TN16 97 F6
GRH DA9 25 F4
Whitchurch Cl *MAIDW* ME16 6 B3
Whitcombe Cl *WALD* ME5 88 D4
White Av *GVW* DA11 45 G1
Whitebeam Dr *RMAID* ME17 154 B3
White Bear Pas *STH/RUST* TN4 10 C5 10
Whitebine Gdns *STPH/PW* TN12 151 J8
Whitebread La *RYE* TN31 245 G6
White Cottage Rd *TONN* TN10 148 C8
Whitecroft *SWLY* BR8 40 B7 4
Whitefield Cl *STMC/STPC* BR5 38 D8 3
Whitefield Rd *STH/RUST* TN4 10 C1
White Friars *SEV* TN13 8 C6
Whitegate Cl *STH/RUST* TN4 189 K6
Whitegates Av *BGR/WK* TN15 80 D2 5
Whitehall Dr *RMAID* ME17 158 B3
Whitehall La *ERITH* DA8 22 C1
Whitehall Rd *MAID/BEAR* ME14 113 J8
SIT ME10 93 K4
White Hart Cl *SEV* TN13 124 A7
White Hart Rd *ORP* BR6 56 B4
White Hart Wd *SEV* TN13 124 A8
Whitehead Cl *RDART* DA2 41 F1
Whiteheads La *MAID/BEAR* ME14 134 D2
Whitehill *BGR/WK* TN15 105 H3
Whitehill La *GVE* DA12 46 A1
Whitehill Pde *GVE* DA12 45 K1
White Hill Rd *MAID/BEAR* ME14 90 A5
Whitehill Rd *DART* DA1 22 D4
GVE DA12 27 K8
HART DA3 43 J7
MEO DA13 43 J5
MEO DA13 63 J7
Whitehorse Hl *WALD* ME5 4 B5 6
White Horse La *MAID/SHEP* ME15 134 C7
White Horse Rd *MEO* DA13 84 A5
Whitehouse Cl *HOO/HM* ME3 51 F2 1
Whitehouse Crs *ROCH* ME1 87 F6
White House Rd *RSEV* TN14 145 H1
Whitelake Rd *TONN* TN10 170 C1
White La *BH/WHM* TN16 119 F2
Whiteleaves Ri *STRD* ME2 66 A4
White Lodge Cl *SEV* TN13 9 D2
White Oak Cl *TON* TN9 170 B7 2
White Post Hl *EYN* DA4 59 K4
White Post La *MEO* DA13 63 J1
Whitepost La *MEO* DA13 83 G4
White Rd *CHAT* ME4 68 B5
White Rock Ct *MAIDW* ME16 6 B4 3
White Rock Pl *MAIDW* ME16 6 B4
Whites Cl *GRH* DA9 25 H5
White's La *HAWK* TN18 235 H4
Whitewall Rd *STRD* ME2 49 J6
Whitewall Wy *STRD* ME2 3 D1
Whitewebbs Wy *STMC/STPC* BR5 38 A6
Whitewood Cottages
BH/WHM TN16 97 G7
Whitmore St *MAIDW* ME16 132 C4
Whitney Wk *SCUP* DA14 39 F4
Whybourne Crest *RTWE/PEM* TN2 11 F6
Whyman Av *CHAT* ME4 68 B5
Wichling Cl *STMC/STPC* BR5 56 E5 3
Wickenden Rd *SEV* TN13 9 E1
Wickham Cl *RSIT* ME9 72 A8
Wickham Gdns *STH/RUST* TN4 206 C1
Wickham St *ROCH* ME1 3 D5
Wickhams Wy *HART* DA3 62 A2 1
Wickhurst Rd *RSEV* TN14 145 H3
Wicksteed Cl *BXLY* DA5 40 A1
Widbury Cl *RRTW* TN3 205 J3 5
Widgeon Rd *STRD* ME2 48 C8
Wierton Hl *RMAID* ME17 155 K7
Wierton La *RMAID* ME17 156 A4
Wierton Rd *RMAID* ME17 156 A5
Wigmore Rd *RHAM* ME8 89 J1
Wihtred Rd *RSIT* ME9 94 E4
Wilberforce Rd *RMAID* ME17 154 D3
Wilberforce Wy *GVE* DA12 46 A3
Wilde Cl *TIL* RM18 27 J1
Wildernesse Av *BGR/WK* TN15 124 D1
Wildernesse Mt *SEV* TN13 9 F1
Wilderness Gdns *RYE* TN31 244 D7
Wilderness Rd *OXTED* RH8 140 C1
Wildfell Cl *MAID/BEAR* ME14 88 D6
Wildman Cl *RHAM* ME8 90 A3
Wildwood Cl *RMAID* ME17 158 C4
Wildwood Gld *GILL* ME7 89 H1
Wilfred St *GVE* DA12 27 J5 14
Wilks Av *DART* DA1 23 J8
Wilks Cl *RHAM* ME8 70 E4
Will Adams Wy *GILL* ME7 69 G5
RHAM ME8 5 F5
Willesley Gdns *CRBK* TN17 214 E8 2
William Judge Cl *TENT* TN30 230 D7
William Luck Cl *STPH/PW* TN12 151 G8 2
William Rd *STRD* ME2 66 B4 1
William St *GVE* DA12 27 J6
RHAM ME8 70 D4
SIT ME10 93 K3
STH/RUST TN4 10 C2
Willington Gn *MAID/SHEP* ME15 134 A7
Willington St *MAID/SHEP* ME15 134 A7
Willow Av *HOO/HM* ME3 51 F3 16
SWLY BR8 58 C1
Willowbank Dr *HOO/HM* ME3 33 F2
Willowby Gdns *RHAM* ME8 90 B2
Willow Cl *STMC/STPC* BR5 56 C3
Willow Crs *STPH/PW* TN12 172 C7
STPH/PW TN12 198 B1
Willow La *STPH/PW* TN12 174 C6
Willow Lea *TONN* TN10 148 C7
Willowmead *DIT/AY* ME20 108 C4
Willow Pk *RSEV* TN14 101 H4
Willow Ri *MAID/SHEP* ME15 134 B5
Willow Rd *DART* DA1 23 F7
DIT/AY ME20 108 D3
STRD ME2 48 D8
Willowside *SNOD* ME6 85 K5
The Willows *RHAM* ME8 70 B4
RSIT ME9 72 A8
Willow Tree Rd *RTWE/PEM* TN2 10 A6
Willow Wk *MEO* DA13 83 G3
RTWE/PEM TN2 190 E6
Willow Wy *MAID/SHEP* ME15 7 E4
Willow Wents *WBY/YAL* ME18 128 E5
Willow Wood Rd *MEO* DA13 83 G4
Wilman Rd *STH/RUST* TN4 190 A7
Wilmar Wy *BGR/WK* TN15 102 D7
Wilmington Av *ORP* BR6 56 D6
Wilmington Court Rd *RDART* DA2 40 D1
Wilmington Wy *RHAM* ME8 69 J4
Wilmot Rd *DART* DA1 22 E4
Wilson Av *ROCH* ME1 67 J5
Wilson Cl *MAID/SHEP* ME15 134 A7
RTON TN11 169 J1
Wilson La *EYN* DA4 42 E7
Wilson Rd *TONN* TN10 170 E1
Wilsons La *MAID/SHEP* ME15 154 A2
Wilsons Wy *MEO* DA13 83 G3
Wilton Dr *DIT/AY* ME20 109 F6
Wiltshire Cl *RDART* DA2 24 C6
WALD ME5 68 D6
Wiltshire Rd *ORP* BR6 56 B4
Wiltshire Wy *MAID/SHEP* ME15 134 A7 4
RTWE/PEM TN2 190 D7
Wimborne Av *STMC/STPC* BR5 38 A8
Wimbourne Dr *RHAM* ME8 70 A8
Winch Cl *CRBK* TN17 225 K3
Winchelsea Rd *WALD* ME5 88 C1
Winchester Av *WALD* ME5 88 A2
Winchester Crs *GVE* DA12 46 A1
Winchester Rd *HAWK* TN18 235 G4
ORP BR6 56 D8
TONN TN10 170 D2
Winchester Wy *RHAM* ME8 70 D5
Winch's Garth *STPH/PW* TN12 198 B1 1
Wincliff Rd *TON* TN9 170 B6
Windermere Cl *DART* DA1 22 E7
Windermere Dr *RHAM* ME8 70 A7
Windermere Gv *SIT* ME10 93 J3
Windhover Wy *GVE* DA12 46 B2
Windmill Cl *STRD* ME2 49 G5
Windmill Ct *RMAID* ME17 155 H3 1
Windmill Hts *MAID/BEAR* ME14 134 D2
Windmill Hl *BGR/WK* TN15 106 A7
RMAID ME17 159 F6
STPH/PW TN12 193 K5
Windmill La *BGR/WK* TN15 106 A6
WADH TN5 220 E6
Windmill La East *E/WMAL* ME19 107 K8
Windmill La West *E/WMAL* ME19 107 J8
Windmill Pk *BGR/WK* TN15 105 K7
Windmill Rd *GILL* ME7 4 C5
SEV TN13 145 K1
SIT ME10 73 J8
Windmill St *GVE* DA12 27 J6
RTWE/PEM TN2 11 E4 8
STRD ME2 49 G5
Windsor Av *CHAT* ME4 3 F6
Windsor Cl *MAID/BEAR* ME14 7 E1
Windsor Dr *DART* DA1 22 D5
ORP BR6 76 B2
SIT ME10 93 J4
Windsor Rd *GILL* ME7 5 D3
GVE DA12 45 J2
Windward Rd *ROCH* ME1 67 H5
Windyridge *GILL* ME7 69 F5
Winfield La *BGR/WK* TN15 126 E4
Winford Ms *ROCH* ME1 2 A6
Wingate Rd *SCUP* DA14 38 D3
Wingfield Rd *GVW* DA11 27 J6
Wingham Cl *MAID/SHEP* ME15 134 B7
RHAM ME8 69 K3
Wingrove Dr *MAID/BEAR* ME14 134 A1
STRD ME2 2 C1
Winifred Rd *DART* DA1 22 E4
MAID/SHEP ME15 134 B3
Winnipeg Dr *ORP* BR6 76 A2
Winser Rd *CRBK* TN17 238 E5
Winston Cl *GRH* DA9 24 E5
Winston Dr *STRD* ME2 49 J4
Winstone Scott Av *RRTW* TN3 205 H2 1
Winston Rd *STRD* ME2 66 C1
Winterfield La *E/WMAL* ME19 108 C6
Wireless Rd *BH/WHM* TN16 97 H2
The Wirrals *WALD* ME5 88 B2
Wiseacre *RRTW* TN3 221 J3
Wise's La *BGR/WK* TN15 81 K5 2
RSIT ME9 93 F3
Wisley Rd *STMC/STPC* BR5 38 B5
Wisteria Gdns *SWLY* BR8 40 A7
Witches La *SEV* TN13 123 F2
Witham Wy *STRD* ME2 48 E7
Withens Cl *STMC/STPC* BR5 56 D1 7
Withyham Rd *RRTW* TN3 204 D8
Wittersham Cl *WALD* ME5 88 C1
Wittersham Rd *CRBK* TN17 246 C2
TENT TN30 247 G1
Wivenhoe Cl *RHAM* ME8 70 D4
Wodehouse Cl *DIT/AY* ME20 108 D2 3
Wodehouse Rd *DART* DA1 23 K3
Wolfe Rd *MAIDW* ME16 132 B4
Wolf's Hl *OXTED* RH8 140 E2
Wolf's Rd *OXTED* RH8 141 F1
Wolfs Wd *OXTED* RH8 140 E3
Wollaston Cl *RHAM* ME8 90 A3
Wolseley Rd *STH/RUST* TN4 190 C7
Wolsey Ms *ORP* BR6 76 A1
Wolsley Cl *DART* DA1 22 B4
Wombwell Gdns *GVW* DA11 26 E8
Wood Av *PUR* RM19 13 G4
Woodberry Dr *SIT* ME10 94 C3
Woodberry Gv *BXLY* DA5 40 A1
Woodbridge Dr *MAID/SHEP* ME15 6 B6
Woodbury Cl *BH/WHM* TN16 97 K5
Woodbury La *TENT* TN30 230 A7
Woodbury Park Gdns
STH/RUST TN4 11 D2

Woodbury Park Rd STH/RUST TN4 .. 10 C2
Woodbury Rd HAWK TN18 235 G3
WALD ME5 87 K5
Woodchurch Cl WALD ME5 88 C1 3
Woodchurch Crs RHAM ME8 69 K4
Woodchurch Rd TENT TN30 230 C6
Wood Cl BXLY DA5 40 B1
DIT/AY ME20 109 J6
Woodcock La CRBK TN17 237 F3
RMAID ME17 159 J8
Woodcocks HDCN TN27 200 B1 4
Woodcourt Cl SIT ME10 93 K4
Woodcut MAID/BEAR ME14 111 G6
Wood Dr SEV TN13 8 B5
Wood End SWLY BR8 57 K1 1
Woodfall Dr DART DA1 22 C3
Woodfield Av GVW DA11 27 J8
RTON TN11 169 J1
Woodfield Rd TON TN9 170 B6
Woodfields SEV TN13 123 F2
Woodfield Wy HOO/HM ME3 49 J2
Woodford Rd MAIDW ME16 132 B4
Woodgate La RSIT ME9 92 B4
Woodgate Rd E/WMAL ME19 107 F2
Woodgate Wy TON TN9 170 D7
Woodgers Gv SWLY BR8 40 C7 1
Woodhill Pk RTWE/PEM TN2 191 J8
Woodhurst WALD ME5 87 J2
Woodhurst Cl STRD ME2 66 A4
Woodhurst La OXTED RH8 140 C2
Woodhurst Pk OXTED RH8 140 C1
Woodland Av HART DA3 62 A2
Woodland Cl E/WMAL ME19 107 J6
HART DA3 44 D8
STH/RUST TN4 190 B7
Woodland Ct OXTED RH8 118 B7
Woodland Dr EDEN TN8 164 D3
Woodland Ri BGR/WK TN15 124 D1
OXTED RH8 140 C1
Woodland Rd STH/RUST TN4 190 C7
Woodlands RMAID ME17 154 B3
RTWE/PEM TN2 192 B7
STPH/PW TN12 173 H7
WALD ME5 88 B4
Woodlands Av SNOD ME6 85 J6 2
Woodlands Cl
MAID/BEAR ME14 111 H7 1
SWLY BR8 40 C7 2
WBY/YAL ME18 130 E6
Woodlands La GVE DA12 47 G5
Woodlands Pk BXLY DA5 39 K2
Woodlands Ri SWLY BR8 40 C7 3
Woodlands Rd DIT/AY ME20 109 G5
GILL ME7 5 F6
ORP BR6 76 B2
SIT ME10 94 C3 3
TON TN9 170 A8
The Woodlands ORP BR6 76 C2
Woodland Vw TENT TN30 247 K2
Woodland Wy GRH DA9 25 F4
MAID/BEAR ME14 111 H7
STH/RUST TN4 189 H3
Wood La CRBK TN17 228 A3
RDART DA2 42 E1
Woodlark Rd CHAT ME4 50 B5
Woodlea DIT/AY ME20 108 C4
HART DA3 44 D8
Woodleas MAIDW ME16 131 K4
Woodley Rd ORP BR6 56 D6
Woodmount SWLY BR8 58 A4
Woodpecker Gld RHAM ME8 69 K8
Woodpecker Rd DIT/AY ME20 108 D5
Wood Rd BH/WHM TN16 97 G5
Woodruff Cl RHAM ME8 71 G2
Woodrush Pl CHAT ME4 50 C5
Woodsgate Wy
RTWE/PEM TN2 191 H8 2
Woodside MEO DA13 83 G6
ORP BR6 76 B1
RHAM ME8 69 J8
Woodside Cl BXLYHN DA7 22 A3
RTWE/PEM TN2 192 A8
Woodside Dr RDART DA2 40 B2
Woodside Gdns SIT ME10 93 J4
Woodside Rd BXLYHN DA7 22 A3
MAID/SHEP ME15 133 J7
RSEV TN14 121 K3
RTWE/PEM TN2 192 A8
SEV TN13 8 C2
STH/RUST TN4 206 C2
TON TN9 170 B7
Woodstock Rd SIT ME10 93 K5
STRD ME2 2 A1
Wood St GILL ME7 4 A2
RSIT ME9 95 G6
RTW TN1 11 D3
STRD ME2 66 A4
SWLY BR8 41 F6
Wood View Cl BGR/WK TN15 80 D3 3
Woodview Crs RTON TN11 169 J1
Woodview Ri STRD ME2 48 E5
Woodview Rd SWLY BR8 39 K7
Woodville Pl GVE DA12 27 J6 3
Woodville Rd MAID/SHEP ME15 7 D5
Woodward Ter GRH DA9 24 D5
Woolaston Cl MAID/SHEP ME15 6 C6 2
Wooldeys Rd RHAM ME8 70 C4
Woolett Rd SIT ME10 93 G1
Woollett Cl DART DA1 22 D3
Woollett St MAID/BEAR ME14 7 D2 6
Woolley Cl STH/RUST TN4 189 K5 3
Woolley Rd MAID/SHEP ME15 134 B6
STH/RUST TN4 189 K5
Woolwich Cl WALD ME5 68 B7
Wopsle Cl ROCH ME1 67 J7
Worcester Av E/WMAL ME19 129 J4
Worcester Cl GRH DA9 25 G4
MEO DA13 45 G5
STRD ME2 48 D6
Worcester Dr SIT ME10 73 J8
Worcester Rd MAID/SHEP ME15 133 K7
Wordsworth Cl TIL RM18 27 K1 3
WALD ME5 68 D7
Wordsworth Rd
MAID/BEAR ME14 111 H7
Wordsworth Wy DART DA1 23 K3
DIT/AY ME20 108 E2
Workhouse La MAID/SHEP ME15 154 C2
Workhouse Rd E/WMAL ME19 107 G1
RMAID ME17 157 J6
Worlds End La ORP BR6 76 B3
Wormdale Hl RSIT ME9 92 A3
Wormdale Rd RSIT ME9 91 K2
Worships Hl SEV TN13 8 A2
Wotton Cl MAID/SHEP ME15 156 A1 7
Wotton Gn STMC/STPC BR5 56 E1
Wouldham Rd ROCH ME1 66 B8
Wrangleden Cl
MAID/SHEP ME15 156 A1 8
Wrangleden Rd MAID/SHEP ME15 .. 155 K1
Wrangling La MEO DA13 84 D1
Wren Cl DIT/AY ME20 108 D5
STMC/STPC BR5 38 E8
Wren Rd SCUP DA14 38 D1
Wrens Ct RSIT ME9 93 F6
Wrens Cft GVW DA11 45 F2 6
Wrens Rd RSIT ME9 92 E8
Wren Wy WALD ME5 68 C8 3
Wright Cl RHAM ME8 69 K4
Wrights Cl TENT TN30 230 A6 2
Wrotham Hill Rd BGR/WK TN15 82 A8
Wrotham Rd BGR/WK TN15 105 F7
GVW DA11 45 H2
MEO DA13 45 G7
Wrotham Water La
E/WMAL ME19 105 K2
Wrotham Water Rd
E/WMAL ME19 105 K2
Wulfred Wy BGR/WK TN15 103 F5
Wyatt Cl BGR/WK TN15 105 F7
Wyatt Pl STRD ME2 2 A1
Wyatt Rd DART DA1 22 C2
Wyatt St MAID/BEAR ME14 7 D3
Wybourne Ri RTWE/PEM TN2 11 D6
Wybournes La HOO/HM ME3 32 D3
Wycliffe Rw GVW DA11 27 G7
Wye Cl ORP BR6 56 A4
Wye Rd BGR/WK TN15 105 G6
GVE DA12 28 A8
TONN TN10 170 C1
Wykeham Cl GVE DA12 46 B4
Wykeham Gv RMAID ME17 135 J7
Wykeham Rd SIT ME10 94 C2
Wykeham St STRD ME2 49 G6
Wyke Manor Rd
MAID/BEAR ME14 7 D3 7
Wyles Rd CHAT ME4 3 E6
Wyles St GILL ME7 4 C1
Wylie Rd HOO/HM ME3 33 F8
Wyndham Av RTON TN11 168 D5
Wyndham Cl RTON TN11 168 D5
Wyndham Rd CHAT ME4 3 E6
Wynford Gv STMC/STPC BR5 38 C8
Wynnstow Pk OXTED RH8 140 D2
The Wytchlings RMAID ME17 158 B4
Wytherling Cl MAID/BEAR ME14 .. 134 B1 5
Wyvern Cl DART DA1 23 F6
ORP BR6 56 C7
SNOD ME6 85 K7
Wyvill Cl RHAM ME8 90 B1

Y

Yalding Cl STMC/STPC BR5 56 E1 11
STRD ME2 49 G5
Yalding Hl WBY/YAL ME18 152 E3
Yantlet Dr STRD ME2 48 B7
Yardley Cl TON TN9 170 D3
Yardley Park Rd TON TN9 170 C3
Yarrow Ct MAID/BEAR ME14 134 B1 6
Yarrow Rd WALD ME5 87 K2
Yaugher La RSIT ME9 90 E3
Yelsted La MAID/BEAR ME14 88 E7
RSIT ME9 90 D5
Yelsted Rd RSIT ME9 90 D7
Yeoman Dr GILL ME7 69 G5
Yeoman Gdns STPH/PW TN12 173 G8
Yeoman La MAID/BEAR ME14 134 D3
Yeoman's Mdw SEV TN13 8 C5
Yeoman Wy MAID/SHEP ME15 134 D4
Yew Rd HOO/HM ME3 51 F3 17
The Yews GVE DA12 28 A8
Yew Tree Cl DIT/AY ME20 109 J5
HART DA3 44 E8
SEV TN13 123 F2
WALD ME5 88 E5
Yew Tree Green Rd
STPH/PW TN12 194 E5
Yew Tree Rd STH/RUST TN4 190 A6
Yopps Gn BGR/WK TN15 126 E5
York Av GILL ME7 4 B4
WALD ME5 87 K3
York Hl WALD ME5 4 C6 5
York Pde TONN TN10 148 C8
York Rd BH/WHM TN16 97 F6
DART DA1 23 J6
GVE DA12 45 K1
GVW DA11 26 E6
MAID/SHEP ME15 7 F6
ROCH ME1 2 C5
RTW TN1 10 C3
TONN TN10 170 D1

Z

Zambra Wy BGR/WK TN15 102 D7
Zelah Rd STMC/STPC BR5 56 C4
Zetland Av GILL ME7 5 E6
Zillah Gdns RHAM ME8 69 J8
Zion Pl GVE DA12 27 J6 4

Index - featured places

Abbey Court Special School
STRD ME2 48 D6
A B C Cinema
GVE DA12 27 J5
A B C Cinema
RTW TN1 10 C4
Acorn Business Centre
MAIDW ME16 132 C4
Acorn Industrial Park
DART DA1 22 D4
Airport Industrial Estate
BH/WHM TN16 97 H2
Alan Carter Gallery
OXTED RH8 118 C8
Albany Clinic
BFN/LL DA15 38 B2
Alexandra Hospital
WALD ME5 88 A6
Allhallows & Stoke CP School
HOO/HM ME3 35 F1
Allington CP School
MAIDW ME16 110 B7
All Saints C of E Primary School
CHAT ME4 4 A5
All Saints C of E Primary School
MAID/SHEP ME15 7 D4
Alwin Gallery
STH/RUST TN4 10 C5
Amherst County Junior School
SEV TN13 123 F2
Anchorians All Weather
Sports Club
RHAM ME8 70 C5
Angel Indoor Bowling
TON TN9 170 C5
Angley School
CRBK TN17 225 H1
Anthony Roper County
Primary School
EYN DA4 59 H6
Archbishops Palace
MAIDW ME16 6 C3

Arden Business Centre
STRD ME2 .... **3** E1
Arden Business Park
STRD ME2 .... **3** D1
Arden Junior School
GILL ME7 .... **5** D1
The Artisan Gallery
GRH DA9 .... **24** E6
Ascot Hever Golf Club
EDEN TN8 .... **165** K5
Ashford Borough Council
TENT TN30 .... **230** B6
The Ashworth Practice
ORP BR6 .... **56** C4
Assembly Hall Theatre
RTWE/PEM TN2 .... **11** D4
Astor of Hever School
MAIDW ME16 .... **132** C3
The Atman Clinic
STH/RUST TN4 .... **10** C1
Aveley Primary School
SOCK/AV RM15 .... **13** J1
Avenue Theatre
SIT ME10 .... **94** A3
Avicenna Medical Centre
E/WMAL ME19 .... **108** C4
Axton Chase School
HART DA3 .... **44** A8
Aylesford CP School
DIT/AY ME20 .... **109** H5
Aylesford St Marks
C of E Primary School
DIT/AY ME20 .... **86** E8
Aylesford St Peters
C of E Primary School
DIT/AY ME20 .... **110** A3
Aylesford Secondary School
DIT/AY ME20 .... **109** H5
Bad Apple Theatre Co
RTW TN1 .... **11** E3
Balfour CP Infant School
CHAT ME4 .... **67** K5
Balfour Junior School
CHAT ME4 .... **3** E6
Ballard Business Park
STRD ME2 .... **66** E1
Ballater Surgery
ORP BR6 .... **56** A4
Balmoral Clinic
GILL ME7 .... **4** C3
The Bank Street Gallery
BGR/WK TN15 .... **9** E4
Bapchild & Tonge
C of E Primary School
SIT ME10 .... **94** E3
Barming CP School
MAIDW ME16 .... **131** K4
Barnes Cray Primary School
DART DA1 .... **22** D3
Barnsole CP Infant School
GILL ME7 .... **5** E4
Barnsole Junior School
GILL ME7 .... **5** E4
Barrow Grove CP School
SIT ME10 .... **93** J2
The Barry Clinic
STH/RUST TN4 .... **10** C1
Beacon Hill Industrial Estate
PUR RM19 .... **13** F4
Bean Primary School
RDART DA2 .... **43** H2
Bearsted Golf Club
MAID/BEAR ME14 .... **134** D1
Bearsted Green Business Centre
MAID/BEAR ME14 .... **134** E1
Bedensfield Clinic
SCUP DA14 .... **39** F3
Bedgebury Junior School
CRBK TN17 .... **223** J5
Beechcroft Farm
Industrial Estate
BGR/WK TN15 .... **61** J7
Beechings Industrial Centre
RHAM ME8 .... **69** H2
Bell Shopping Centre
SIT ME10 .... **94** A2
Bell Wood CP Infant School
MAID/SHEP ME15 .... **156** A1
Bellwood CP Junior School
MAID/SHEP ME15 .... **156** A1
Benenden C of E Primary School
CRBK TN17 .... **227** F8
Benenden Girls School
CRBK TN17 .... **227** F6
Benenden Hospital
CRBK TN17 .... **228** A3
Benenden School
CRBK TN17 .... **226** E6
Bennett Memorial
Diocesan School
STH/RUST TN4 .... **10** A1
Bentley Street Industrial Estate
GVE DA12 .... **27** K5
Bethany School
CRBK TN17 .... **213** G1
Bexley Hospital
BXLY DA5 .... **22** B8
Bidborough Primary School
STH/RUST TN4 .... **189** H3
Biddenden Club House
HDCN TN27 .... **217** K5
Biggin Hill Business Park
BH/WHM TN16 .... **97** H2
Biggin Hill Junior School
BH/WHM TN16 .... **97** J3
Birchwood County
Primary School
SWLY BR8 .... **40** A6
Birkbeck Primary School
SCUP DA14 .... **38** C1
Bishops Down CP School
STH/RUST TN4 .... **10** A2
Blacklands County Junior School
E/WMAL ME19 .... **108** D7
Black Lion Leisure Centre
GILL ME7 .... **4** B2
Blackthorn Medical Centre
MAIDW ME16 .... **132** A3
Blenheim Junior & Infant School
ORP BR6 .... **56** D6
Bligh Way CP School
STRD ME2 .... **48** B7
Blubery House Cranbrook School
CRBK TN17 .... **225** K1
Bobbing CP School
RSIT ME9 .... **73** G7
Bodiam Castle (NT)
RBTBR TN32 .... **243** G6
Bodiam Manor School
RBTBR TN32 .... **243** F6
Bodiam Primary School
RBTBR TN32 .... **243** F6
Borden C of E Primary School
RSIT ME9 .... **92** E3
Borden Grammar School
SIT ME10 .... **94** A3
Borough Green Medical Centre
BGR/WK TN15 .... **105** F7
Borough Green Primary School
BGR/WK TN15 .... **105** G7
Borstal Manor County
Junior School
ROCH ME1 .... **66** E4
Borstal Village Surgery
ROCH ME1 .... **66** E4
Bough Beech Sailing Club
EDEN TN8 .... **166** D2
Boughton Monchelsea
County Primary School
RMAID ME17 .... **155** H4
Bower Grove School
MAIDW ME16 .... **132** B4
The Bower Mount Clinic
MAIDW ME16 .... **6** A3
Bowes Industrial Centre
MEO DA13 .... **63** G8
Bowls Centre
MAID/BEAR ME14 .... **7** D3
Boxmend Industrial Estate
RMAID ME17 .... **156** B3
Boyd Business Centre
STRD ME2 .... **3** D1
Bradbourne School
RSEV TN14 .... **101** J8
Bradfields School
WALD ME5 .... **68** B8
Braeside Surgery
EYN DA4 .... **59** K4
Branbridges Industrial Estate
STPH/PW TN12 .... **173** J1
Brasted Surgery
BH/WHM TN16 .... **121** J4
Brattle Farm Museum
STPH/PW TN12 .... **197** K5
Bredgar C of E Primary School
RSIT ME9 .... **116** A1
Bredhurst C of E School
GILL ME7 .... **89** J5
Brenchley & Matfield
C of E Primary School
STPH/PW TN12 .... **193** J6
Brent CP School
RDART DA2 .... **24** B6
Bridge Industrial Centre
MAIDW ME16 .... **6** B5
Brittania Business Park
DIT/AY ME20 .... **109** J6
Broadwater CP School
RTWE/PEM TN2 .... **206** E6
Broadway Shopping Centre
MAIDW ME16 .... **6** C3
Bromley Hospitals N H S Trust
ORP BR6 .... **56** A8
Bromley Museum
ORP BR6 .... **56** C4
Brompton Medical Centre
GILL ME7 .... **4** A2
Brompton Westbrook CP School
GILL ME7 .... **4** A3
Brookfield County Infant School
DIT/AY ME20 .... **108** E4
Brookfield CP Junior School
DIT/AY ME20 .... **108** D4
Brookhurst Surgery
ORP BR6 .... **56** B6
The Brook Theatre Arts &
Entertainment Ltd
CHAT ME4 .... **3** F3
Broomhill Bank School
RRTW TN3 .... **189** G8
Brunswick House Clinic
MAIDW ME16 .... **6** B2
Brunswick House CP School
MAIDW ME16 .... **6** B2
Bryony School
RHAM ME8 .... **69** K7
Bryony School
RHAM ME8 .... **90** C1
Burnham Trading Estate
DART DA1 .... **23** G3
Burrswood Medical Centre
RRTW TN3 .... **204** D6
Burwood School
ORP BR6 .... **56** E6
Business Centre
WBY/YAL ME18 .... **131** F6
The Butts County Infants School
SIT ME10 .... **73** K8
Byron CP School
GILL ME7 .... **5** D5
Byron House Surgery
GILL ME7 .... **4** C5
Cage Green County
Primary School
TONN TN10 .... **170** D1
Canal Industrial Park
GVE DA12 .... **28** A5
Cannock House School
ORP BR6 .... **77** G1
Canterbury Road CP School
SIT ME10 .... **94** C3
Capel CP School
RTON TN11 .... **172** B7
Cascades Leisure Centre
GVE DA12 .... **46** D2
Castle View Business Centre
ROCH ME1 .... **3** D2
Cecil Road County Primary School
GVW DA11 .... **27** G7
The Cedans School
ROCH ME1 .... **2** C4
Central Business Park
STRD ME2 .... **3** E1
Central Theatre
CHAT ME4 .... **3** F4
Chalklin Business Park
RTWE/PEM TN2 .... **190** E6
Chantry Medical Practice
SEV TN13 .... **9** D4
Chapter School
STRD ME2 .... **48** C7
Charles Darwin School
BH/WHM TN16 .... **97** K2
Chart Hills Golf Club
HDCN TN27 .... **200** E8

Chatham Grammar School for Boys *CHAT* ME4 ... 68 A5
Chatham Grammar School for Girls *WALD* ME5 ... 4 C6
Chatham South School *CHAT* ME4 ... 68 A6
Chaucer Business Park *BGR/WK* TN15 ... 103 H6
Chelsfield Park Hospital *ORP* BR6 ... 77 G1
Chelsfield Primary School *ORP* BR6 ... 77 F1
Chequers Shopping Centre *MAID/BEAR* ME14 ... 7 D3
Chevening Primary School *RSEV* TN14 ... 122 D1
Chiddingstone C of E School *EDEN* TN8 ... 166 E7
Child Health Centre *STRD* ME2 ... 48 D8
Chinese Medical Centre *DART* DA1 ... 23 H5
Church House Surgery *TON* TN9 ... 170 C4
Churchill Business Park *BH/WHM* TN16 ... 120 D5
Churchill Clinic *WALD* ME5 ... 68 B7
Churchill Gallery *BH/WHM* TN16 ... 120 C6
Churchill School *BH/WHM* TN16 ... 120 C4
Cinema *MAID/SHEP* ME15 ... 7 D3
Civic Centre *DART* DA1 ... 23 H5
Civic Centre *GVW* DA11 ... 27 J6
Clanricarde Medical Centre *RTW* TN1 ... 10 C4
Claremont CP School *RTWE/PEM* TN2 ... 11 D5
Clearways Industrial Estate *BGR/WK* TN15 ... 80 D3
Cleeve Park School *SCUP* DA14 ... 38 D1
Cliffe Woods County Primary School *HOO/HM* ME3 ... 31 H6
Cliffe Woods Surgery *HOO/HM* ME3 ... 31 G6
The Clinic *GVE* DA12 ... 45 K1
Clock House Gallery *TON* TN9 ... 170 C3
The Club House *MAID/BEAR* ME14 ... 7 E2
Cobham CP School *GVE* DA12 ... 64 D1
Cobtree Medical Centre *RMAID* ME17 ... 157 F6
Colebrook Industrial Estate *RTWE/PEM* TN2 ... 190 E5
Colebrook Industrial Estate *RTWE/PEM* TN2 ... 191 F5
College *SIT* ME10 ... 93 H3
The College Practice *MAID/SHEP* ME15 ... 6 C4
Colliers Green Primary School *CRBK* TN17 ... 214 A4
Collingwood Industrial Estate *RMAID* ME17 ... 157 G4
Combe Bank School *RSEV* TN14 ... 122 A2
Compass Centre *CHAT* ME4 ... 50 C6
The Computer Surgery *MAIDW* ME16 ... 110 C7
Connections Business Park *RSEV* TN14 ... 101 K7
Conquest Industrial Estate *STRD* ME2 ... 66 E1
Copperfields Shopping Centre *DART* DA1 ... 23 H5
Corinthian Sports Club *HART* DA3 ... 61 J3
Cornwallis School *MAID/SHEP* ME15 ... 155 F3
Cottage Industrial Estate *DIT/AY* ME20 ... 110 B4
Council Offices *CRBK* TN17 ... 225 J1
Council Offices *SEV* TN13 ... 9 D4
County Hall *MAID/BEAR* ME14 ... 7 D2
County Primary Infant School *RHAM* ME8 ... 70 B6
Court View Surgery *STRD* ME2 ... 48 E7
Coxheath CP School *RMAID* ME17 ... 154 C3
Cranbrook Clinic *CRBK* TN17 ... 225 K1
Cranbrook Golf Club *CRBK* TN17 ... 227 F2
Cranbrook Primary School *CRBK* TN17 ... 214 E8
Cranbrook Rugby Football Club *CRBK* TN17 ... 214 E8
Cranbrook School *CRBK* TN17 ... 225 K1
The Crane Surgery *CRBK* TN17 ... 225 K1
Crayfield Industrial Park *STMC/STPC* BR5 ... 38 D7
Crayfields Business Park *STMC/STPC* BR5 ... 56 D2
Crayford Industrial Estate *DART* DA1 ... 22 C4
Crayford Leisure Centre & Greyhound Stadium *DART* DA1 ... 22 B5
Crayford Medical Centre *DART* DA1 ... 22 C4
Crayside Industrial Estate *DART* DA1 ... 22 D2
Crayside Industrial Estate *DART* DA1 ... 22 E2
Crescent Surgery *STMC/STPC* BR5 ... 56 C2
Crest Industrial Estate *STPH/PW* TN12 ... 176 C8
Crockenhill CP School *SWLY* BR8 ... 57 K3
Crockham Hill C of E Primary School *EDEN* TN8 ... 142 C4
Crosshall Surgery *STMC/STPC* BR5 ... 56 D1
Crowden House Cranbrook School *CRBK* TN17 ... 226 A1
Crown & County Courts *MAIDW* ME16 ... 6 C4
Crown Court Clinic *ROCH* ME1 ... 3 D3
Cudham School *BH/WHM* TN16 ... 98 A3
Culverstone Gm Primary School *MEO* DA13 ... 83 F3
Cuxton County Infant School *STRD* ME2 ... 66 A4
Cuxton CP Junior School *STRD* ME2 ... 66 A4
Cuxton Industrial Estate *STRD* ME2 ... 66 B4
Cygnet Leisure Centre *GVW* DA11 ... 27 F8
Dajen Business Park *CHAT* ME4 ... 68 D5
Dale Hill Hotel & Golf Club *WADH* TN5 ... 232 D5
Danecourt School *RHAM* ME8 ... 69 H4
Darenth CP School *RDART* DA2 ... 42 E4
Dartford Borough Council *DART* DA1 ... 23 G7
Dartford County Court *DART* DA1 ... 23 H5
Dartford FC *EYN* DA4 ... 41 K6
Dartford FC *RDART* DA2 ... 24 A7
Dartford Golf Club *DART* DA1 ... 22 E8
Dartford Grammar School *DART* DA1 ... 23 F5
Dartford Grammar School for Girls *DART* DA1 ... 23 F6
Dartford Hospital School *HART* DA3 ... 44 B8
Dartford Magistrates Court *DART* DA1 ... 23 G5
Dartford Natural Health Centre *DART* DA1 ... 23 H6
Dartford West Boys School *DART* DA1 ... 23 G6
Dartford West Health Centre *DART* DA1 ... 23 F5
Dartford West High School for Girls *DART* DA1 ... 23 F6
Deacon Industrial Estate *DIT/AY* ME20 ... 110 A4
Deacon Trading Centre *STRD* ME2 ... 2 A2
Delce Junior School *ROCH* ME1 ... 2 C6
Detling C of E Primary School *MAID/BEAR* ME14 ... 112 C5
Ditton C of E Junior School *DIT/AY* ME20 ... 109 G5
Ditton Infant School *DIT/AY* ME20 ... 109 G5
Dolphin Yard Sailing Barge Museum *SIT* ME10 ... 94 B1
Dorton College of Further Education *BGR/WK* TN15 ... 124 C1
Douglas Moat Practice *STH/RUST* TN4 ... 10 C5
Dover Road Primary School *GVW* DA11 ... 27 F7
Downe Primary School *ORP* BR6 ... 75 F6
Down Ho *ORP* BR6 ... 75 F7
Downsview Junior School *SWLY* BR8 ... 40 D8
Downs Way School *OXTED* RH8 ... 118 C6
Dr Ali Surgery *CHAT* ME4 ... 3 F4
Dulwich College Preparatory School *CRBK* TN17 ... 226 C2
Dunton Green County Primary School *SEV* TN13 ... 101 G7
East Borough CP School *MAID/BEAR* ME14 ... 7 E2
East Farleigh CP School *MAID/SHEP* ME15 ... 132 A8
East Peckham Primary School *STPH/PW* TN12 ... 151 H7
Edenbridge CP School *EDEN* TN8 ... 164 C5
Edenbridge & District War Memorial Hospital *EDEN* TN8 ... 164 C7
Edenbridge Golf & Country Club *EDEN* TN8 ... 164 A4
Edenbridge Leisure Centre *EDEN* TN8 ... 164 B4
The Edenbridge Medical Centre *EDEN* TN8 ... 164 C5
Eden Valley School *EDEN* TN8 ... 164 C4
Education Centre *MAID/BEAR* ME14 ... 6 C2
Egerton CP School *HDCN* TN27 ... 183 F3
Elaine CP School *STRD* ME2 ... 48 D7
Elm House Gallery *EDEN* TN8 ... 165 H1
The Elms Medical Centre *HOO/HM* ME3 ... 50 E1
The Elms Medical Practice *HOO/HM* ME3 ... 19 G5
English Martyrs Catholic Primary School *STRD* ME2 ... 49 G6
Essex County Council *TIL* RM18 ... 27 H1
Eurolink Industrial Centre *SIT* ME10 ... 94 B1
Eurolink Industrial Centre *SIT* ME10 ... 94 B2
Eurolink Industrial Centre *SIT* ME10 ... 94 C2

Eurolink Industrial Estate
SIT ME10 .... 94 C1
Eye Hospital
MAID/BEAR ME14 .... 7 D3
Eynsford Castle
EYN DA4 .... 59 H6
Eynsford Cricket Club
EYN DA4 .... 59 H6
Fairfax Gallery
RTW TN1 .... 10 C5
Fairfield Pool & Leisure Centre
DART DA1 .... 23 H6
Fairview Industrial Estate
OXTED RH8 .... 140 E4
Fairview Schools
RHAM ME8 .... 89 K1
The Family Medical Centre
WALD ME5 .... 88 D4
Farnborough Primary School
ORP BR6 .... 75 J1
Fawkham Manor Hospital
HART DA3 .... 61 H5
Fawkham Primary School
HART DA3 .... 61 F5
Featherby CP School
RHAM ME8 .... 69 H3
Featherby Junior School
RHAM ME8 .... 69 H3
Fleetdown Infants School
RDART DA2 .... 24 B7
Fleetdown Junior School
RDART DA2 .... 24 B8
Fleetway Sports Club
GVE DA12 .... 27 K7
Fondu Sports Club
PUR RM19 .... 13 G4
Fordcombe C of E Primary School
RRTW TN3 .... 204 E1
Forge Lane CP School
GILL ME7 .... 5 E2
Fort Luton Museum
CHAT ME4 .... 68 B5
Fort Pitt Grammar School
ROCH ME1 .... 3 E4
Fossebank New School
RTON TN11 .... 147 J7
Four Elms CP School
EDEN TN8 .... 165 H1
Friends of Orpington Hospital
ORP BR6 .... 75 K2
Frittenden Primary School
CRBK TN17 .... 199 G8
Fulston Manor School
SIT ME10 .... 94 A4
Furness School
SWLY BR8 .... 40 C4
Furness Swanley Football Club
SWLY BR8 .... 58 A1
Gads Hill House School
STRD ME2 .... 48 B4
The Gallery
CRBK TN17 .... 225 K1
The Gallery
MAID/SHEP ME15 .... 7 D3
The Gallery
ORP BR6 .... 56 B4
The Gallery
STH/RUST TN4 .... 190 A4
Galley Hill Industrial Estate
SWCM DA10 .... 25 K4
Gaza Trading Estate
RTON TN11 .... 146 B7
Geoffrey Whitworth Theatre
DART DA1 .... 22 C3
The Gillingham College
GILL ME7 .... 5 F4
Gillingham Football Club
GILL ME7 .... 5 E3
Gillingham Golf Club Ltd
GILL ME7 .... 5 E6
Gillingham Medical Centre
GILL ME7 .... 5 F4
The Glade Business Centre
WTHK RM20 .... 13 K5
Glencoe CP Junior School
CHAT ME4 .... 4 A6
Godden Green Clinic
BGR/WK TN15 .... 125 F4
Goldsmiths College Sports Ground
SCUP DA14 .... 39 G1
Golf Centre
STMC/STPC BR5 .... 38 E6
Gordon CP Junior School
STRD ME2 .... 49 F6
Gore Court Cricket Club
SIT ME10 .... 93 G1
Goudhurst & Kilndown C of E Primary School
CRBK TN17 .... 212 E6
Graham Gallery
STH/RUST TN4 .... 10 C4
Grange Park College
E/WMAL ME19 .... 108 A4
The Granville School
SEV TN13 .... 8 C2
Gravesend County Court
GVE DA12 .... 27 J5
Gravesend Cricket Club
GVW DA11 .... 27 H6
Gravesend Grammar School for Boys
GVE DA12 .... 28 A6
Gravesend Grammar School for Girls
GVW DA11 .... 27 H7
Gravesend Museum
GVW DA11 .... 27 J5
Gravesend & Northfleet Football Club Ltd
GVW DA11 .... 26 D5
Gravesend & North Kent Hospital
GVW DA11 .... 27 H5
Gravesend Rowing Club
GVE DA12 .... 27 K5
Gravesend Yacht Club
GVE DA12 .... 28 A5
Gravesham Borough Council
GVW DA11 .... 26 D7
Gravesham Borough Council
GVW DA11 .... 27 J6
Grays Farm Primary School
STMC/STPC BR5 .... 38 C6
Great Comp Garden
BGR/WK TN15 .... 106 A8
Great Hollenden Business Centre
RTON TN11 .... 147 G4
Greenacres Dental Health Centre
DIT/AY ME20 .... 109 J5
Greenhithe Health Clinic
GRH DA9 .... 25 G4
Green Street Primary School
ORP BR6 .... 76 A2
Greenvale Infant School
CHAT ME4 .... 4 A6
Grosvenor Medical Centre
RTW TN1 .... 10 C3
Grove Dairy Farm Business Centre
RSIT ME9 .... 73 F8
Grovehurst Surgery
SIT ME10 .... 73 K5
Grove Park CP School
SIT ME10 .... 73 G8
Guardian Industrial Estate
STPH/PW TN12 .... 176 C7
Guelder Rose Medical Centre
STPH/PW TN12 .... 198 B2
The Guildhall Museum
ROCH ME1 .... 2 B2
Guru Nanak Sports Club
GVE DA12 .... 27 K6
Hadlow College
RTON TN11 .... 149 K6
Hadlow CP School
RTON TN11 .... 150 A6
Halling County Primary School
STRD ME2 .... 86 A3
Halstead Place School
RSEV TN14 .... 77 F7
Halstead Primary School
RSEV TN14 .... 77 G7
Harenc School
SCUP DA14 .... 38 D3
Harrietsham Primary School
RMAID ME17 .... 137 J8
Hartley CP School
HART DA3 .... 61 K3
Haslemere Industrial Estate
MAID/SHEP ME15 .... 156 B1
Haslemere Trading Estate
MAID/SHEP ME15 .... 156 B1
Hawkhurst C of E Primary School
HAWK TN18 .... 235 F6
Hawkhurst Squash Club
HAWK TN18 .... 234 E4
Hawkwell Business Centre
RTWE/PEM TN2 .... 192 B4
Hayesbrook School
TON TN9 .... 170 A6
Hazelwood School
OXTED RH8 .... 140 E2
Hazlitt Theatre
MAID/BEAR ME14 .... 7 D3
Headcorn CP School
HDCN TN27 .... 180 A8
The Headcorn Gallery
HDCN TN27 .... 200 A1
Heath Farm School
HDCN TN27 .... 161 K7
Heathfield College
HAYES BR2 .... 74 B2
Helen Alison School
MEO DA13 .... 63 H4
Hempstead Infant School
GILL ME7 .... 89 H1
Hempstead Junior School
GILL ME7 .... 89 H2
Henley Business Park
STRD ME2 .... 3 D1
Herton Court School
SCUP DA14 .... 38 D2
Hever C of E Primary School
EDEN TN8 .... 165 K8
Hever Golf Club
EDEN TN8 .... 165 K5
Hever Golf Clubhouse
EDEN TN8 .... 165 K5
Hextable Comprehensive School
SWLY BR8 .... 40 C6
Hextable CP School
SWLY BR8 .... 40 C4
Higham CP School
HOO/HM ME3 .... 48 B1
High Elms Golf Course
ORP BR6 .... 75 H3
High Firs CP School
SWLY BR8 .... 58 C1
High Halden C of E Primary School
RASHW TN26 .... 219 K7
High Halstow Primary School
HOO/HM ME3 .... 32 E3
Highsted School for Girls
SIT ME10 .... 94 A4
The Highways Primary School
ORP BR6 .... 76 D1
Hildenborough Primary School
RTON TN11 .... 147 G8
Hilden Oaks School
TONN TN10 .... 170 B2
Hill School
BH/WHM TN16 .... 120 B2
Hills Surgery
RHAM ME8 .... 70 A8
Hilltop Primary School
STRD ME2 .... 49 H5
Hillyfields Junior School
GILL ME7 .... 5 D2
Historical Society Museum
CHAT ME4 .... 3 F3
Historic Vehicles Collection
CRBK TN17 .... 238 C3
Hollingbourne County Primary School
RMAID ME17 .... 136 B4
Holmesdale Community School
SNOD ME6 .... 85 K7
Holmewood House School
RRTW TN3 .... 205 K4
Holy Family Catholic Primary School
RMAID ME17 .... 156 A2
Holy Innocents RC Primary School
ORP BR6 .... 56 A7
Holy Trinity C of E Primary School
DART DA1 .... 23 F4
Holy Trinity C of E School
GVE DA12 .... 27 K6
Homefarm Estate
DIT/AY ME20 .... 109 K5
Homeopathic Hospital
RTW TN1 .... 10 C4
Homewood School
TENT TN30 .... 230 B5
Honeycrest Industrial Park
STPH/PW TN12 .... 198 A1
Hoo St Werburgh C P School
HOO/HM ME3 .... 50 E1

Horsmonden CP School
STPH/PW TN12 .... **194** E8
Horsted CP Junior & Infants School
WALD ME5 .... **87** J1
Horsted Retail Park
WALD ME5 .... **67** J8
Horton Kirby C of E Primary School
EYN DA4 .... **42** B8
Horton Kirby & South Darenth Parish Council
EYN DA4 .... **42** B7
Horton Kirby Trading Estate
EYN DA4 .... **42** B7
Hospital
HAWK TN18 .... **234** D4
Hospital Barn Farm
MAID/SHEP ME15 .... **153** K2
Howard School
RHAM ME8 .... **70** A6
Hugh Christie School
TONN TN10 .... **148** D8
The Hundred of Hoo School
HOO/HM ME3 .... **50** D1
Hunton CP School
MAID/SHEP ME15 .... **153** H7
Hylands Clinic
MAID/BEAR ME14 .... **7** D3
Ide Hill School
RSEV TN14 .... **144** A2
Ifield School
GVE DA12 .... **45** K3
Ightham County Primary School
BGR/WK TN15 .... **104** B8
Imperial Retail Park
GVW DA11 .... **27** H5
The Industrial Estate
EDEN TN8 .... **164** B3
Invicta Grammar School
MAID/BEAR ME14 .... **7** F3
Invicta Sports Club
DART DA1 .... **23** G4
Istead Rise CP School
MEO DA13 .... **45** F6
Ivy Bower Surgery
GRH DA9 .... **25** G4
Iwade CP School
RSIT ME9 .... **73** J2
Jarvis Great Danes Hotel & Country Club
RMAID ME17 .... **135** K5
John Goodhew Medical Centre
SIT ME10 .... **73** K5
John Mayne C of E Primary School
HDCN TN27 .... **217** J5
Joyce Green Hospital
DART DA1 .... **23** J1
Joydens Wood CP School
BXLY DA5 .... **40** B2
The Judd School
TON TN9 .... **170** A6
Kemsing CP School
BGR/WK TN15 .... **102** E4
Kemsing Parish Council
BGR/WK TN15 .... **102** E4
Kenden Business Park
STRD ME2 .... **49** J6
Kent College for Girls
RTWE/PEM TN2 .... **191** K3
Kent County Council
DART DA1 .... **23** G5
Kent County Council
GVW DA11 .... **27** H5
Kent County Council
GVW DA11 .... **45** F1
Kent County Council
MAIDW ME16 .... **110** D5
Kent County Council
MEO DA13 .... **83** H6
Kent County Council
RDART DA2 .... **41** F2
Kent Kraft Industrial Estate
GVW DA11 .... **26** A3
Kents Potters Gallery
MAID/BEAR ME14 .... **7** D2
Kent & Sussex Hospital
STH/RUST TN4 .... **10** C3
The Kent Youth Theatre
WALD ME5 .... **88** E5
Kestner Industrial Estate
GRH DA9 .... **25** F3
Keston C of E Primary School
HAYES BR2 .... **74** C1
Kevington CP School
STMC/STPC BR5 .... **56** E2
Kincade Gallery
GRH DA9 .... **24** E6
Kingfisher CP School
WALD ME5 .... **68** C7
Kingsdown Industrial Estate
DIT/AY ME20 .... **109** F6
The Kings Family Practice
CHAT ME4 .... **4** B5
The Kings Family Practice
CHAT ME4 .... **50** C4
Kings Farm Infant School
GVE DA12 .... **45** K3
Kings Farm Junior School
GVE DA12 .... **45** K2
Kings Hill Golf Club
E/WMAL ME19 .... **129** J4
Kings Hill Primary School
E/WMAL ME19 .... **107** J8
Kings Hill Primary School
E/WMAL ME19 .... **129** J3
Kings Preparatory School
ROCH ME1 .... **2** C3
Kings Road Clinic
WALD ME5 .... **68** E5
Kings School Rochester
ROCH ME1 .... **2** B2
Kingstanding Business Park
RTON TN11 .... **191** F4
King Street Surgery
MAID/SHEP ME15 .... **7** D3
Kingswood CP School
RMAID ME17 .... **158** C4
Kingswood Surgery
RMAID ME17 .... **158** B4
Kingswood Surgery
RTWE/PEM TN2 .... **11** E4
Kit's Coty House
DIT/AY ME20 .... **87** H8
Knights Park Industrial Estate
STRD ME2 .... **2** A2
Knockholt School
RSEV TN14 .... **99** H4
Laddingford Farm Industrial Estate
WBY/YAL ME18 .... **174** B2
Lady Boswell C of E School
BGR/WK TN15 .... **9** E4
Lamberhurst C of E School
RRTW TN3 .... **210** E8
Lamberhurst Golf Club
RRTW TN3 .... **210** E8
Lamberhurst Surgery
RRTW TN3 .... **221** J1
Langafel C of E Primary School
HART DA3 .... **44** B8
Langton Green CP School
RRTW TN3 .... **205** H2
Lansdowne County Primary School
TIL RM18 .... **27** G1
Lansdowne CP School
SIT ME10 .... **94** D3
Lansdowne Road Clinic
RTW TN1 .... **11** D3
Larkfield Leisure Centre
DIT/AY ME20 .... **108** E3
Larkfield Trading Estate
DIT/AY ME20 .... **109** F1
Lawn CP School
GVW DA11 .... **26** D5
Leeds & Broomfield C of E School
RMAID ME17 .... **135** J7
Leeds Castle
RMAID ME17 .... **136** A7
Leesons Infant School
STMC/STPC BR5 .... **38** B8
Leigh City Technology College
DART DA1 .... **23** K7
Leigh Green Industrial Estate
TENT TN30 .... **230** E8
Leigh Primary School
RTON TN11 .... **168** D5
Leisure Centre
MAID/SHEP ME15 .... **7** F5
Leybourne Business Centre
E/WMAL ME19 .... **108** C4
Leybourne C of E Primary School
E/WMAL ME19 .... **108** C4
Limpsfield Chart Golf Club
OXTED RH8 .... **119** G8
Limpsfield C of E School
OXTED RH8 .... **119** F8
Limpsfield Grange School
OXTED RH8 .... **118** E6
Limpsfield Lawn Tennis Club
OXTED RH8 .... **118** E7
Liongate Clinic
STH/RUST TN4 .... **10** C2
Littlebrook Business Centre
DART DA1 .... **24** B2
Livingstone Hospital
DART DA1 .... **23** J6
Loaland Business Centre
STRD ME2 .... **49** J6
London Beach Golf Club
TENT TN30 .... **230** A2
London Road Trading Estate
SIT ME10 .... **93** J2
Long Mead CP Junior & Infant School
RTON TN11 .... **170** B1
Loose Junior School
MAID/SHEP ME15 .... **133** G8
Lordswood Health Centre
WALD ME5 .... **88** D5
Lordswood Industrial Estate
WALD ME5 .... **88** D5
Lordswood Leisure Centre
WALD ME5 .... **88** D3
Lower Halston CP School
RSIT ME9 .... **72** A4
Lowfield Medical Centre
DART DA1 .... **23** H6
Lullingstone Castle
EYN DA4 .... **78** E1
Lunsford CP School
DIT/AY ME20 .... **108** E4
Luton CP Junior School
CHAT ME4 .... **4** C6
Luton Infant School
CHAT ME4 .... **4** C6
Luton Medical Centre
WALD ME5 .... **68** D5
Lynsted CP School
RSIT ME9 .... **95** H7
Madginford Park CP Junior School
MAID/SHEP ME15 .... **134** C4
Madginford Park Infant School
MAID/SHEP ME15 .... **134** B4
Maidstone Borough Council
MAIDW ME16 .... **6** B4
Maidstone Grammar School
MAID/SHEP ME15 .... **7** E5
Maidstone Grammar School for Girls
MAIDW ME16 .... **6** B1
Maidstone Hospital
MAIDW ME16 .... **132** A2
Maidstone Industrial Centre
MAIDW ME16 .... **6** C2
Maidstone Lawn Tennis Club
MAIDW ME16 .... **132** C1
The Malling School
E/WMAL ME19 .... **108** D7
Manor Gallery
GVE DA12 .... **27** J6
Manzoori Clinic
SWLY BR8 .... **40** C5
The Maplesden Noakes School
MAIDW ME16 .... **6** B2
Marden CP School
STPH/PW TN12 .... **196** B1
Marden Medical Centre
STPH/PW TN12 .... **176** C8
Mardyke Surgery
PUR RM19 .... **12** E4
Marlborough House School
HAWK TN18 .... **234** E4
Marlowe Park Medical Centre
STRD ME2 .... **66** C1
Marshlands Medical Practice
HOO/HM ME3 .... **48** B3
Mascalls Secondary School
STPH/PW TN12 .... **193** J2
Matrix Business Centre
DART DA1 .... **23** H4
Maundene CP School
WALD ME5 .... **88** B1
May Avenue Industrial Estate
GVW DA11 .... **27** G7
Mayplace Primary School
BXLYHN DA7 .... **22** A3

Maypole Community School BXLY DA5 ... 22 B8
Meadows Memorial School STH/RUST TN4 ... 189 K4
The Mead School RTWE/PEM TN2 ... 10 C6
The Medical Centre STRD ME2 ... 49 G6
The Medical Practice MAID/SHEP ME15 ... 133 K7
Medway Community College CHAT ME4 ... 68 B5
Medway Hospital GILL ME7 ... 4 B5
Medway Little Theatre ROCH ME1 ... 3 D3
Medway Rugby Football Club ROCH ME1 ... 2 B6
Medway Towns Rowing Club ROCH ME1 ... 2 A5
Medway Trading Estate MAIDW ME16 ... 6 C4
Medway Yacht Club HOO/HM ME3 ... 50 C3
Meopham CP School MEO DA13 ... 63 H4
Meopham Medical Centre MEO DA13 ... 63 H6
Meopham Parish Council MEO DA13 ... 63 G7
Meopham School MEO DA13 ... 63 H6
Meredale CP Infant School RHAM ME8 ... 70 D5
Mereworth CP School WBY/YAL ME18 ... 129 F6
Middlesex Hospital Sports Ground CHST BR7 ... 38 A3
Midfield Primary School CHST BR7 ... 38 B5
Mid Kent Business Park SNOD ME6 ... 86 A6
Mid Kent College of Higher & Further Education MAIDW ME16 ... 132 B3
Mid Kent College of Higher & Further Education ROCH ME1 ... 3 D5
Mid Kent College of Higher & Further Education ROCH ME1 ... 67 J8
Mid Kent School MAID/BEAR ME14 ... 7 D2
Mid Kent Shopping Centre MAIDW ME16 ... 110 C7
Mierscourt Primary School RHAM ME8 ... 70 C7
Milehams Industrial Estate PUR RM19 ... 12 E3
Milestone School HART DA3 ... 62 A5
Millside Industrial Estate DART DA1 ... 23 G3
Milstead & Frinsted C of E Primary School RSIT ME9 ... 116 E5
Milton Road Business Park GVE DA12 ... 27 K6
Minterne CP School SIT ME10 ... 93 J4
Mole Hill Copse CP School MAID/SHEP ME15 ... 133 K7
Moor House School OXTED RH8 ... 140 D3
More Park R C Primary School E/WMAL ME19 ... 108 B6
Moreton Industrial Estate SWLY BR8 ... 58 E1
Morley Business Centre TON TN9 ... 170 D5
Mote Cricket Club MAID/SHEP ME15 ... 7 E4
Mote Medical Practice MAID/SHEP ME15 ... 133 H7
Mote Park Sailing Club MAID/SHEP ME15 ... 134 A3
Motorway Industrial Estate DIT/AY ME20 ... 110 C4
Murray Business Centre STMC/STPC BR5 ... 38 C8
Murston County Primary Infant School SIT ME10 ... 94 C1
Murston CP Junior School SIT ME10 ... 94 C1
Museum & Art Gallery MAID/BEAR ME14 ... 6 C2
The Museum CRBK TN17 ... 225 K1
Music School MAID/SHEP ME15 ... 6 C4
Napier Road Junior School GILL ME7 ... 5 D4
Napier Road Secondary School GILL ME7 ... 5 D4
Neptune Industrial Estate STRD ME2 ... 3 E1
Nevill Golf Club RTWE/PEM TN2 ... 207 J7
New Ash Green County Primary School HART DA3 ... 62 A6
New Beacon School SEV TN13 ... 8 B6
New Grove Green Surgery MAID/BEAR ME14 ... 134 B1
New Hythe Business Park DIT/AY ME20 ... 109 G1
Newington C of E Primary School RSIT ME9 ... 72 A7
Newington Industrial Estate RSIT ME9 ... 71 J8
New Road CP School CHAT ME4 ... 4 A5
New Road Surgery CHAT ME4 ... 3 F4
New Surgery BH/WHM TN16 ... 97 G8
New Swan Valley Community School SWCM DA10 ... 26 A6
Nizels Hotel Golf & Leisure Club RTON TN11 ... 146 C5
The Noble Clinic STPH/PW TN12 ... 193 K6
North Borough CP Junior School MAID/BEAR ME14 ... 111 F7
Northcourt County Primary School GVE DA12 ... 28 B7
North Cray Primary School SCUP DA14 ... 39 F4
North Downs Business Park RSEV TN14 ... 100 E3
North Farm Industrial Estate RTWE/PEM TN2 ... 190 E5
Northfleet Boys School GVW DA11 ... 26 E7
Northfleet Industrial Estate GVW DA11 ... 26 B3
Northfleet School for Girls GVW DA11 ... 26 E8
North Kent Magistrates Court CHAT ME4 ... 3 F3
North West Kent College GVE DA12 ... 28 C7
North West Kent College of Technology DART DA1 ... 23 G6
Nugent Industrial Park STMC/STPC BR5 ... 56 D1
Oakfield CP Junior School DART DA1 ... 23 G8
Oakland Primary School BH/WHM TN16 ... 97 G3
Oaklands CP Junior & Infant School WALD ME5 ... 88 A2
Oaklands Junior School BH/WHM TN16 ... 97 G3
Oaks County Infant School SIT ME10 ... 93 J4
Oak Trees CP School MAID/SHEP ME15 ... 133 J7
Oakwood Hospital MAIDW ME16 ... 132 A3
Oakwood Park Grammar School MAIDW ME16 ... 132 C3
Oasthouse Theatre RHAM ME8 ... 70 C6
Offham CP School E/WMAL ME19 ... 107 F6
Offham Cricket Club E/WMAL ME19 ... 107 F7
Oldborough Manor Community School MAID/SHEP ME15 ... 133 H7
The Old Guild Theatre GVW DA11 ... 26 E7
Old Judd Rugby Club TON TN9 ... 170 B4
Orchard Business Centre MAIDW ME16 ... 110 C6
Orchard Business Centre RTWE/PEM TN2 ... 190 D6
Orchard Business Centre TON TN9 ... 170 D6
Orchard Industrial Estate MAID/SHEP ME15 ... 156 B3
Orchard Medical Centre RMAID ME17 ... 154 C4
Orchard Place Business Centre E/WMAL ME19 ... 106 C8
The Orchard Theatre DART DA1 ... 23 H5
Orpington College of Further Education ORP BR6 ... 56 B5
Orpington Mental Health Centre ORP BR6 ... 56 A7
Orpington Retail Park STMC/STPC BR5 ... 56 D1
Orpington Sports Centre ORP BR6 ... 56 B5
Orpington Superbowl ORP BR6 ... 56 B5
Otford County Primary School RSEV TN14 ... 101 J3
Otford Medical Practice RSEV TN14 ... 101 K2
Our Lady of Hartley RC School HART DA3 ... 62 A2
Our Ladys RC Primary School DART DA1 ... 23 F5
Oxleas N H S Trust BXLY DA5 ... 22 B8
Oxleas NHS Trust ORP BR6 ... 56 C4
Oxted County School OXTED RH8 ... 118 D7
Oxted Gallery OXTED RH8 ... 118 C8
Oxted Health Centre OXTED RH8 ... 118 D8
Oxted & Limpsfield Hospital OXTED RH8 ... 118 B6
Paddock Wood Business Centre STPH/PW TN12 ... 173 J7
Paddock Wood CP School STPH/PW TN12 ... 173 J8
Paddock Wood Town Council STPH/PW TN12 ... 173 H8
Painters Ash Primary School GVW DA11 ... 44 E1
Palace Industrial Estate MAID/SHEP ME15 ... 156 B2
Palace Wood County Junior School MAIDW ME16 ... 110 C8
Parker Industrial Centre RDART DA2 ... 24 B6
Park Road Industrial Estate SWLY BR8 ... 40 C8
Park Way CP School MAID/SHEP ME15 ... 7 E6
Parkwood Hall School SWLY BR8 ... 40 E8
Parkwood Industrial Estate MAID/SHEP ME15 ... 156 C2
Parkwood Infant School RHAM ME8 ... 90 B1
Parkwood Junior School RHAM ME8 ... 90 A1
Parrock Street Surgery GVE DA12 ... 27 J5
Pedham Place Industrial Estate SWLY BR8 ... 58 D2
Pegasus Gallery SEV TN13 ... 9 D4
Pembury Hospital RTWE/PEM TN2 ... 191 G7
Pembury Primary School RTWE/PEM TN2 ... 191 K6
Penhurst Place RTON TN11 ... 187 K2
Penshurst C of E Primary School RTON TN11 ... 187 J2

Perry Hall School *ORP* BR6 56 A3
Phoenix Industrial Estate *STRD* ME2 3 D1
Phoenix Surgery *ROCH* ME1 87 F6
Platt C of E Primary School *BGR/WK* TN15 105 J7
Platt Industrial Estate *BGR/WK* TN15 105 J6
Plaxtol CP School *BGR/WK* TN15 126 E7
Pluckley C of E Primary School *HDCN* TN27 183 J7
Police Station and Magistrates Court *RTW* TN1 11 D3
Postley Industrial Centre *MAID/SHEP* ME15 7 D5
Poultwood Golf Club *RTON* TN11 149 F5
Poverest Primary School *STMC/STPC* BR5 56 B2
Pratts Bottom Primary School *ORP* BR6 76 D6
Premier Business Park *CHAT* ME4 68 C5
Preston Hall Hospital *DIT/AY* ME20 109 K5
Princes Park Medical Centre *WALD* ME5 68 C8
Princess Christian's Hospital *RTON* TN11 147 J4
Priory School *STMC/STPC* BR5 56 D5
Prison *MAID/BEAR* ME14 6 C2
Purfleet Primary School *PUR* RM19 12 E4
Quarry Wood Industrial Estate *DIT/AY* ME20 109 J7
Queenborough Yacht Club *QBOR* ME11 55 K1
Queen Marys Hospital *SCUP* DA14 38 B3
Queen Victoria Cottage Hospital *RTON* TN11 170 C8
Railway Street Industrial Estate *GILL* ME7 5 D2
Rainham Mark Grammar School *RHAM* ME8 70 A4
Rainham School for Girls *RHAM* ME8 69 K6
Ravensquay Business Centre *STMC/STPC* BR5 56 C2
Raynehurst CP School *GVE* DA12 46 C1
Rectory Business Centre *SCUP* DA14 38 C2
Rectory Paddock School *STMC/STPC* BR5 38 D7
Regional Sports Centre *TIL* RM18 27 J1
Regis Manor County Primary School *SIT* ME10 73 K7
Reynolds Health Centre *DART* DA1 23 G5
Richmond County Infants School *GILL* ME7 4 C2
Ridge View School *TONN* TN10 170 D1
Riding School *E/WMAL* ME19 131 F2
Riverhead County Infant School *SEV* TN13 8 B1
Riverside Business Centre *TON* TN9 170 B5
Riverside Industrial Estate *DART* DA1 23 H4
Riverside Medical Practice *STRD* ME2 86 A2
Riverside Retail Park *RSEV* TN14 102 A6
Riverview Clinic *GVE* DA12 46 C3
Riverview Park Surgery *GVE* DA12 46 B2
Riverview Primary School *GVE* DA12 46 B2
The Robert Napier School *GILL* ME7 5 E5
Rochester Airport Industrial Estate *ROCH* ME1 67 H8
Rochester Airport Industrial Estate *WALD* ME5 87 H1
Rochester Grammar School for Girls *ROCH* ME1 2 C6
Rochester Health Centre *ROCH* ME1 3 D5
The Rochester Mathematical School *ROCH* ME1 67 G5
Rochester Museum *ROCH* ME1 2 C3
Rochester Tutors Independent College *ROCH* ME1 3 D4
Rodmersham CP School *RSIT* ME9 94 C7
Rodmersham Squash Club *RSIT* ME9 94 B8
Rolvenden Primary School *CRBK* TN17 238 C3
Roseacre Junior School *MAID/BEAR* ME14 134 C2
Rose Cottage Surgery *STPH/PW* TN12 198 B3
Rose Hill School *STH/RUST* TN4 10 A2
Rosherville C of E School *GVW* DA11 27 F5
Rowhill School *RDART* DA2 41 F2
Royal Park Primary School *SCUP* DA14 39 F1
Royal Victoria Place Shopping Centre *RTW* TN1 11 D3
Rusthall Medical Centre *STH/RUST* TN4 206 A2
Ruxley Corner Industrial Estate *SCUP* DA14 38 E4
Ryarsh CP School *E/WMAL* ME19 107 J2
Sackville School *RTON* TN11 147 G8
Sacred Heart School *RTWE/PEM* TN2 207 K2
St Albans CP School *DART* DA1 23 J5
St Andrews Medical Centre *STH/RUST* TN4 190 A5
St Andrews School *ROCH* ME1 2 C3
St Anselms RC Primary School *DART* DA1 23 K4
St Augustine RC Primary School *RHAM* ME8 90 A3
St Augustine School *STH/RUST* TN4 190 A7
St Barnabas C of E Primary School *RTW* TN1 11 D2
St Bartholomews Hospital *ROCH* ME1 3 E4
St Bartholomews Hospital *SWLY* BR8 40 C8
St Bartholomews RC Primary School *SWLY* BR8 40 B8
St Benedicts School *WALD* ME5 88 D4
St Botolphs C of E Primary School *GVW* DA11 26 E6
St Francis RC Primary School *MAID/BEAR* ME14 7 D2
St Georges C of E County Primary School *BGR/WK* TN15 105 F3
St Georges C of E School *GVW* DA11 27 H8
St Georges School *RTWE/PEM* TN2 208 B1
St Gregorys RC School *STH/RUST* TN4 190 A7
St Helens C of E Primary School *HOO/HM* ME3 31 G1
St Hilarys School *SEV* TN13 9 D1
St James C of E Primary School *HOO/HM* ME3 21 G8
St James CP School *E/WMAL* ME19 108 D6
St James's Junior & Infant School *RTWE/PEM* TN2 11 E
St John Fisher Catholic School *CHAT* ME4 3 F
St John Fisher RC Secondary School *ROCH* ME1 3 E
St Johns C of E Infant School *CHAT* ME4 3 E
St Johns C of E Primary School *MAID/BEAR* ME14 133 K
St Johns Hill Surgery *SEV* TN13 9 E
St Johns Infant School *STH/RUST* TN4 10 C
St Johns Primary School *STH/RUST* TN4 190 B
St Johns RC Comprehensive School *GVE* DA12 28 A
St Johns RC Primary School *GVE* DA12 28 A
St Joseph RC School *DART* DA1 22 B
St Josephs Preparatory School *GVE* DA12 27 K
St Josephs RC School *GVW* DA11 26 E
St Katherines CP School *SNOD* ME6 85 J
St Lukes School *STH/RUST* TN4 190 C
St Margaret Clitherow RC Primary School *RTON* TN11 148 A
St Margarets at Troy Town C E Primary School *ROCH* ME1 2 C
St Margarets C of E Junior School *RHAM* ME8 70 B
St Margarets Old School *BGR/WK* TN15 147 F
St Marks C of E Primary School *STH/RUST* TN4 206 C
St Marys Abbey *E/WMAL* ME19 108 A
St Mary & St. Josephs RC School *SCUP* DA14 38 A
St Marys C of E Primary School *SWLY* BR8 58 B
St Marys CP School *STRD* ME2 49 G
St Marys Infant School *GILL* ME7 5 D
St Marys Island Church of England Aided Primary School *CHAT* ME4 50 C
St Marys Middle School *OXTED* RH8 118 C
St Marys RC County Primary School *TIL* RM18 27 G
St Matthews C of E Infant School *ROCH* ME1 2 A
St Michaels C of E Primary Junior School *MAIDW* ME16 6 B
St Michaels C of E Primary School *TENT* TN30 230 B
St Michaels RC Primary School *CHAT* ME4 3 F
St Nicholas School *STRD* ME2 2 A
St Olaves Grammar School *ORP* BR6 56 C
St Paulinus C of E Primary School *DART* DA1 22 B
St Pauls C of E Infant School *RRTW* TN3 206 A
St Pauls C of E Junior School *STH/RUST* TN4 206 A
St Pauls C of E School *SWLY* BR8 40 E
St Pauls County Infant School *MAID/BEAR* ME14 111 G
St Pauls Cray C of E Primary School *STMC/STPC* BR5 38 D
St Pauls Cray Health Clinic *STMC/STPC* BR5 38 B
St Peter Chanel RC School *SCUP* DA14 38 D
St Peters County Infant School *ROCH* ME1 2 C

St Peters Primary School
RTWE/PEM TN2 ... 11 E4
St Peters RC Primary School
SIT ME10 ... 93 J3
St Philomenas RC Primary School
STMC/STPC BR5 ... 56 D4
St Saviours Surgery
MAID/SHEP ME15 ... 133 K8
St Simon Stock RC Comprehensive School
MAIDW ME16 ... 132 C2
St Stephens C of E Infant School
MAID/SHEP ME15 ... 6 B5
St Stephens CP School
TON TN9 ... 170 D6
St Thomas C of E Primary School
RRTW TN3 ... 205 F8
St Thomas More RC Primary School
WALD ME5 ... 88 B2
St Thomas of Canterbury Primary School
RHAM ME8 ... 69 J4
St Thomas School
SIT ME10 ... 94 D4
St Werburgh CP Junior School
HOO/HM ME3 ... 50 D1
St Werburgh Medical Centre
HOO/HM ME3 ... 33 F8
St Werburgh Medical Practice
HOO/HM ME3 ... 37 G1
St William of Perth RC Primary School
ROCH ME1 ... 2 B6
Sandhurst CP School
HAWK TN18 ... 243 K1
Sandling CP School
MAID/BEAR ME14 ... 111 H6
Sandown Court School
RTWE/PEM TN2 ... 190 E8
School House Aveley School
SOCK/AV RM15 ... 13 J1
School of Health
RDART DA2 ... 24 A5
Seal St Lawrence Primary School
BGR/WK TN15 ... 125 J3
Sedleys C of E Primary School
MEO DA13 ... 44 B3
Senacre Technology School
MAID/SHEP ME15 ... 133 K8
Senacre Wood CP School
MAID/SHEP ME15 ... 134 B7
Sessions House
MAID/BEAR ME14 ... 7 D2
Sevenoaks Business Centre
RSEV TN14 ... 101 K7
Sevenoaks CP School
SEV TN13 ... 9 D1
Sevenoaks Hospital
SEV TN13 ... 102 A8
Sevenoaks School
BGR/WK TN15 ... 9 E5
Sevenoaks Swimming Centre
BGR/WK TN15 ... 9 E4
Sevenoaks Town Council
SEV TN13 ... 9 D1
Sevenoaks Way Industrial Estate
STMC/STPC BR5 ... 38 D8
Shamel Business Centre
STRD ME2 ... 2 C1
Shawcroft School
STMC/STPC BR5 ... 57 F2
Shears Green CP School
GVW DA11 ... 45 G1
Shears Green Infant School
GVW DA11 ... 45 G1
Sheldon Business Centre
STRD ME2 ... 49 J6
Shenstone School
DART DA1 ... 22 A4
Shepway County Primary Junior Mixed School
MAID/SHEP ME15 ... 134 A6
Shepway CP Infants School
MAID/SHEP ME15 ... 134 A6
Sheridale Business Centre
STRD ME2 ... 2 A2
Sherwin Knight County Junior & Infant School
STRD ME2 ... 66 D1
Sherwood Park Infant School
RTWE/PEM TN2 ... 11 F1
Sherwood Park Primary School
RTWE/PEM TN2 ... 11 F1
Shipbourne CP School
RTON TN11 ... 148 C1
Shopping Arcades
MAID/BEAR ME14 ... 6 C3
Shoreham County Primary School
RSEV TN14 ... 78 C6
Shorne C of E Primary School
GVE DA12 ... 47 H3
Sidcup Health Centre
SCUP DA14 ... 38 B1
Sidcup Hill Primary School
SCUP DA14 ... 38 C3
Sidcup Sports Club
SCUP DA14 ... 38 A2
Sikh Temple
DART DA1 ... 23 G6
Sikh Temple
GILL ME7 ... 5 D3
Sikh Temple
GVE DA12 ... 27 J7
Singlewell CP School
GVE DA12 ... 46 A4
Siri Guru Ravidass Temple
STRD ME2 ... 49 G6
Sissinghurst Primary School
CRBK TN17 ... 215 H6
Sittingbourne Industrial Park
SIT ME10 ... 93 H1
Sittingbourne Industrial Park
SIT ME10 ... 94 A1
Sittingbourne Memorial Hospital
SIT ME10 ... 94 A3
Sittingbourne & Milton Regis Golf Club
RSIT ME9 ... 92 A3
Sittingbourne Sports Centre
SIT ME10 ... 94 B3
The Skinners School
STH/RUST TN4 ... 10 C1
Skinner Street CP School
GILL ME7 ... 4 C2
Ski Slope
STMC/STPC BR5 ... 38 E6
Slade CP School
TON TN9 ... 170 B4
Smarden CP School
HDCN TN27 ... 202 A5
Snodland Clinic
SNOD ME6 ... 85 K6
Snodland CP School
SNOD ME6 ... 85 J6
Solefield School House
SEV TN13 ... 9 D6
Solefields School
SEV TN13 ... 9 E6
Solomons Temple
RSIT ME9 ... 139 K1
The Somerfield Hospital
MAIDW ME16 ... 6 A2
South Avenue County Infant School
SIT ME10 ... 94 B3
South Aylesford Retail Park
DIT/AY ME20 ... 109 J6
South Borough CP School
MAID/SHEP ME15 ... 7 D5
Southfields School
GVE DA12 ... 45 K3
Spa Industrial Park
RTWE/PEM TN2 ... 190 E6
Spectrum Business Centre
STRD ME2 ... 49 J6
Speldhurst Primary School
RRTW TN3 ... 188 E7
Spinnens Acre County Junior School
WALD ME5 ... 88 E5
Spotlites Theatre Company Ltd
CHAT ME4 ... 4 A5
Springfield Industrial Estate
HAWK TN18 ... 235 F3
Stag Theatre
SEV TN13 ... 9 D4
Stansted C of E Primary School
BGR/WK TN15 ... 82 A5
Staplehurst CP School
STPH/PW TN12 ... 198 A3
Stocks Green CP School
RTON TN11 ... 169 J1
Stonecross Surgery
WALD ME5 ... 68 D5
Strood Swimming Pool
STRD ME2 ... 48 E7
Strood Yacht Club
STRD ME2 ... 2 A2
Sundridge Primary School
RSEV TN14 ... 122 A4
Surex Swimming Pools
BH/WHM TN16 ... 97 H2
Sussex Road CP School
TON TN9 ... 170 A6
Sutton at Hone C of E Primary School
EYN DA4 ... 41 K5
Sutton at Hone & Hawley Parish Council
EYN DA4 ... 42 A4
Sutton Valence CP School
RMAID ME17 ... 157 F7
Sutton Valence School
RMAID ME17 ... 157 G7
Swan Business Park
DART DA1 ... 23 G3
Swanley School
SWLY BR8 ... 40 A8
Swanley Town Council
SWLY BR8 ... 40 B8
Swanley White Oak County Primary School
SWLY BR8 ... 40 B7
Swanscombe Business Centre
SWCM DA10 ... 25 K4
Sweyne CP Junior School
SWCM DA10 ... 26 A6
Swingate County Infant School
WALD ME5 ... 88 D5
Tandridge Golf Club
OXTED RH8 ... 140 A2
Target Business Centre
MAID/SHEP ME15 ... 156 B2
Tatsfield Primary School
BH/WHM TN16 ... 97 H8
Teardrop Industrial Park
SWLY BR8 ... 59 F2
Temple Hill County Infant & Primary School
DART DA1 ... 23 K4
Temple School
STRD ME2 ... 49 G5
Tennis Club
GILL ME7 ... 5 E5
Tenterden C of E Junior School
TENT TN30 ... 230 A7
Tenterden County Primary School
TENT TN30 ... 230 B7
Tenterden Golf Club
TENT TN30 ... 230 D5
Tenterden Leisure Centre
TENT TN30 ... 230 B7
Teynham Medical Centre
RSIT ME9 ... 95 K4
Teynham Parochial C of E (Controlled) Primary School
RSIT ME9 ... 95 K4
Thames Gateway NHS Trust
RDART DA2 ... 24 B6
Thameslink Healthcare Services N H S Trust
RDART DA2 ... 24 B5
Thames View CP School
RHAM ME8 ... 70 A4
Thamesview School
GVE DA12 ... 46 C1
The Thomas Aveling School
ROCH ME1 ... 67 H6
Thornhills Medical Centre
DIT/AY ME20 ... 108 E5
Thurrock Business Centre
WTHK RM20 ... 13 K6
Thurrock Council
PUR RM19 ... 12 D4
Ticehurst C of E Primary School
WADH TN5 ... 232 B6
Tilbury Fort
TIL RM18 ... 27 K3
Tilbury Surgery
TIL RM18 ... 27 H1
Tonbridge Football Club
RTON TN11 ... 170 B1
Tonbridge Grammar School for Girls
TON TN9 ... 170 C7
Tonbridge Hillview School
TON TN9 ... 170 D6
Tonbridge Market
TON TN9 ... 170 B4

Tonbridge Oast Theatre *RTON* TN11 .... **169** K2
Tonbridge School *TONN* TN10 .... **170** B3
Tonbridge Town Sailing Club *RTON* TN11 .... **169** G6
Tovil Green Business Park *MAID/SHEP* ME15 .... **6** B6
Tower Industrial Estate *BGR/WK* TN15 .... **104** D1
Town Hall *DART* DA1 .... **22** C4
Town Hall *MAID/BEAR* ME14 .... **6** C3
Town Hall *RTW* TN1 .... **10** C3
Town Hall *TENT* TN30 .... **230** A7
Town Medical Centre *SEV* TN13 .... **9** D4
Toy & Model Museum *RRTW* TN3 .... **211** F7
Trenchwood Medical Centre *TONN* TN10 .... **170** C1
Trinity Theatre & Arts Association *RTW* TN1 .... **10** C4
Trottiscliffe C of E Primary School *E/WMAL* ME19 .... **106** C1
Tudor Hotel Golf & Country Club *MAID/BEAR* ME14 .... **135** F3
Tunbridge Wells Borderers Sports Club *RTWE/PEM* TN2 .... **207** F6
Tunbridge Wells Centre *RTW* TN1 .... **10** C3
Tunbridge Wells Golf Club *STH/RUST* TN4 .... **10** A4
Tunbridge Wells Grammar School for Boys *STH/RUST* TN4 .... **190** A6
Tunbridge Wells Grammar School for Girls *STH/RUST* TN4 .... **10** B1
Tunbridge Wells Hockey Club *RTW* TN1 .... **11** D6
Tunbridge Wells Independent Hospital *RRTW* TN3 .... **204** E3
Tunbridge Wells Museum & Art Gallery *STH/RUST* TN4 .... **10** C3
Tunbridge Wells Nuffield Hospital *RTWE/PEM* TN2 .... **11** F4
Tunbridge Wells Sports Centre *STH/RUST* TN4 .... **190** A7
Tunbury Avenue Surgery *WALD* ME5 .... **88** A4
Tunbury CP School *WALD* ME5 .... **88** A5
Tunnel Industrial Estate *WTHK* RM20 .... **13** K4
Tunnel Industrial Estate *WTHK* RM20 .... **13** K6
Tunstall C of E Primary School *RSIT* ME9 .... **93** H6
Twenty Twenty Industrial Estate *MAIDW* ME16 .... **110** C6
Twydall Health & Welfare Clinic *RHAM* ME8 .... **69** J3
Twydall Infant School *RHAM* ME8 .... **69** J4
Twydall Junior School *RHAM* ME8 .... **69** J4
Tyrwitt Drake Museum of Carriages *MAID/SHEP* ME15 .... **7** D4
U C I Cinema *WTHK* RM20 .... **13** K4
Ulcombe C of E Primary School *RMAID* ME17 .... **158** D8
Underhill School *RMAID* ME17 .... **156** E7
Underling Industrial Estate *STPH/PW* TN12 .... **177** F4
Union Mill *CRBK* TN17 .... **225** K2
University of Greenwich *CHAT* ME4 .... **50** C6
University of Greenwich *DART* DA1 .... **23** F8
University of Greenwich *DART* DA1 .... **23** J8
University of Greenwich *E/WMAL* ME19 .... **129** J3
Upbury Manor School *GILL* ME7 .... **4** B4
Upchurch Primary School *RSIT* ME9 .... **71** H3
Upnor Castle *STRD* ME2 .... **50** A4
Valence School *BH/WHM* TN16 .... **121** F5
Valley Park Community School *MAID/BEAR* ME14 .... **7** F3
Vestry Industrial Estate *RSEV* TN14 .... **101** K6
Vigo CP School *MEO* DA13 .... **83** H6
Vigo Rugby Club *MEO* DA13 .... **83** K5
The Vine Medical Centre *MAIDW* ME16 .... **132** C3
Wainscott CP School *STRD* ME2 .... **49** J4
Wakeley CP School *RHAM* ME8 .... **70** D5
Walderslade CP School *WALD* ME5 .... **88** B3
Walderslade Medical Centre *WALD* ME5 .... **68** B8
Walnuts Leisure Centre *ORP* BR6 .... **56** B5
Warders Medical Centre *TON* TN9 .... **170** C4
Warren Road Primary School *ORP* BR6 .... **56** A8
Warren Wood CP School *ROCH* ME1 .... **67** H6
Warsop Trading Estate *EDEN* TN8 .... **164** D6
Watermill Museum *LING* RH7 .... **163** G6
Wayfield CP School *WALD* ME5 .... **68** B7
Weald CP School *RSEV* TN14 .... **145** K4
Weald Gallery *RSEV* TN14 .... **121** K5
Weald of Kent Golf Club *HDCN* TN27 .... **179** J5
Weald of Kent School for Girls *TON* TN9 .... **170** D7
Weald Sports Centre *CRBK* TN17 .... **214** D8
Wentworth County Infant School *DART* DA1 .... **22** C6
Wentworth CP Junior School *DART* DA1 .... **22** D6
West Borough County Primary School *MAIDW* ME16 .... **132** B3
West Borough Secondary School *MAIDW* ME16 .... **132** B3
West Borough Sports Centre *MAIDW* ME16 .... **132** C3
Westcourt County Primary School *GVE* DA12 .... **28** B8
Westgate CP School *DART* DA1 .... **23** G6
West Heath School *SEV* TN13 .... **123** K8
West Hill County Primary School *DART* DA1 .... **22** E5
West Hill Hospital *DART* DA1 .... **23** G5
West Kent College *TON* TN9 .... **170** B6
West Kent College of Further Education *STH/RUST* TN4 .... **190** A7
West Kent College of Further Education *TON* TN9 .... **170** A6
West Kingsdown Industrial Estate *BGR/WK* TN15 .... **80** D
West Kingsdown Medical Centre *BGR/WK* TN15 .... **80** E
Westlands Secondary School *SIT* ME10 .... **93** C
West Lane Trading Estate *SIT* ME10 .... **94** B
West Lodge School *BFN/LL* DA15 .... **38** B
West Malling C of E Primary School *E/WMAL* ME19 .... **107** K
West Malling Golf Club *E/WMAL* ME19 .... **106** E
West Malling Group Practice *E/WMAL* ME19 .... **107** K
West Malling Industrial Park *E/WMAL* ME19 .... **107** G
West View Hospital *TENT* TN30 .... **229** J
Wheelbarrow Park Estate *STPH/PW* TN12 .... **176** B
Whitehill House Surgery *DART* DA1 .... **22** D
Whitehill Junior School *GVE* DA12 .... **45** K
The White House Gallery *BH/WHM* TN16 .... **120** D
Wildernesse Golf Club *BGR/WK* TN15 .... **124** E
Wildernesse School *BGR/WK* TN15 .... **102** C
Wilderness Sports Centre *BGR/WK* TN15 .... **102** C
Wilmington Grange Grammar School for Girls *RDART* DA2 .... **22** E
Wilmington High School *RDART* DA2 .... **40** E
Wilmington Parish Council *DART* DA1 .... **23** C
Wilmington Primary School *RDART* DA2 .... **40** E
Windmill Business Centre *MEO* DA13 .... **63** C
Winterton Surgery *BH/WHM* TN16 .... **120** D
Wish Valley Surgery *HAWK* TN18 .... **235** F
Wittersham Primary School *TENT* TN30 .... **247**
Wolfs Wood Primary School *OXTED* RH8 .... **140** E
Woodfalls Business Centre *WBY/YAL* ME18 .... **152** E
Woodlands CP Junior School *TONN* TN10 .... **148** E
Woodlands CP School *GILL* ME7 .... **5** F
Woodlands Health Centre *STPH/PW* TN12 .... **173** H
Wren Industrial Estate *MAID/SHEP* ME15 .... **156** E
Wrotham Parish Council *BGR/WK* TN15 .... **81** K
Wrotham Road CP School *GVW* DA11 .... **27**
Wrotham Road Health Clinic *GVW* DA11 .... **27**
Wrotham Secondary School *BGR/WK* TN15 .... **105** C
Yalding C of E Primary School *WBY/YAL* ME18 .... **152** E
Yardley Court Preparatory School *RTON* TN11 .... **171** F
Yew Tree Industrial Estate *DIT/AY* ME20 .... **109** H
York Road CP School *DART* DA1 .... **23** J
Zobel College *SEV* TN13 .... **9** D

age 11

04

Calverley Park Crs
Camden Hl
Camden Pk
Catherine Pl
Guildford Rd
Meadow Hill Rd
Mount Pleasant Av

age 27

66

Cremorne Rd

17

Weavers Cl

5

Bank St
Bath St
Berkley Rd
Bernard St
Brewhouse Yd
Chase Sq
Garrick St
Horn Yd
Jury St
Manor Rd
New Swan Yd
Parrock St
Railway Pl
Wilfred St

age 51

3

Aster Rd
Bay Cl
Beech Rd
Berry Rd
Cherry Rd
Clover Rd
Cypress Av
Damson Dr
Elder Cl
Elm Rd
Larch Crs
Maple Rd
Marine Dr
Oak Cl
Oak Rd
Willow Av
Yew Rd

age 56

13

Cotswold Ri
Marlborough Cl

33

Coleridge Wy
Wendover Wy

34

Aynscombe Angle
Deakins Ter
Devonshire Rd
Lamorna Cl

35

Mortimer Rd

2

Cross Rd
Sidmouth Rd

32

Burwash Cl
Copper Beech Cl
Roberts Cl

38

Ampleforth Cl

age 67

18

Lankester Parker Rd

age 68

A1

Military Rd
Whiffen's Avenue W

A2

Cambridge Ter
James St
Rhode St
Sir John Hawkins Wy

A4

Athelstan Rd
Freeman Gdns
Hillcrest Rd
Kingswood Av
Parham Rd
Pretoria Rd

33

Chalk Pit Hl
Hope St
Melbourne Rd

37

Flamingo Cl
Goose Cl

C4

Chamberlain Rd
Waghorn St

C7

Kinross Cl
Penfold Cl
Snowdon Cl
Wheatear Wy

D1

Lawrence St
Theodore Pl

D5

1 Durrell Gdns

D7

1 Hampshire Cl

D8

1 Allen Cl
2 Judkins Cl
3 Manchester Cl
4 Ryegrass Cl

E1

1 Avondale Rd
2 Balmoral Rd
3 Buckingham Rd
4 Connaught Rd
5 Edinburgh Rd
6 Glanville Rd
7 Osborne Rd

E2

1 Marathon Paddock

Page 70

D6

1 Gloucester Cl
2 Longford Cl
3 Middlefields
4 Thompson Cl

E5

1 Banky Fields Cl
2 Bedson Wk
3 Bythorne Ct
4 Harwood Rd
5 Ten Acre Wy
6 Vineyard Crs

E6

1 Bramley Cl

Page 88

B1

1 Greenacre Cl
2 Urquhart Cl

B6

1 Bellgrove Ct
2 Spenlow Dr
3 Trotwood Cl

C2

1 Chegwell Dr
2 Greenwich Cl
3 Richmond Cl

C4

1 Hornbeam Av
2 Moonstone Dr

Page 132

E2

1 Birnam Sq
2 Goudhurst Cl
3 Kingsdown Cl

E3

1 Hever Gdns
2 Rycault Cl
3 White Rock Ct

Page 133

G1

1 Camden St
2 Cromwell Rd
3 Lucerne St
4 Princes St
5 Wheeler St
6 Woollett St

G6

1 Corrance Gn
2 Warnford Gdns

Page 134

B3

1 Laxton Cl

B8

1 Betsham Rd
2 Cheltenham Cl
3 Chiddingstone Cl
4 Chislehurst Cl
5 Doncaster Cl
6 Epsom Cl
7 Fontwell Cl
8 Goodwood Cl
9 Groombridge Sq
10 Taunton Cl

Page 206

E5

2 The Goodwins
3 School Ri

Page 207

F2

1 Belgrave Rd
2 Clarence Rw
3 Culverden St
4 Dudley Rd
5 Grosvenor Wk
6 Hanover Rd
7 Lime Hill Rd
8 Mount Ephraim Rd
9 Rock Villa Rd

F4

1 Berkeley Rd
2 Castle St
3 Cumberland Yd
4 Grove Av
5 Little Mount Sion
6 Market St
7 The Pantiles
8 South Gv
9 Sussex Ms
10 White Bear Pas

G1

1 Hill St
2 Mercer St
3 Norman Rd
4 St Barnabas' Cl
5 St Stephons Ct

G2

1 Calverley Rd
2 The Ferns
3 Garden Rd
4 Garden St
5 Lansdowne Sq
6 Monson Rd
7 Monson Wy
8 Newton Rd
9 Victoria Rd

G5

1 Beau Nash Wy

H3

1 Bucklers Cl
2 Calverley Ct
3 Cambridge St
4 Oakfield Court Rd
5 Park St
6 Prince's St
7 St Peter's St
8 Windmill St

Notes